Foreword

SINCE THE END of the cold war, increasing numbers of persons in countries around the world have been forced from their homes by armed conflict, internal strife, and systematic violations of human rights. Unlike refugees, who cross a border and have recourse to an established system of international protection and assistance, those who are displaced internally fall within the domestic jurisdiction and therefore under the sovereignty of the state. They are nearly always destitute and acutely in need of international protection. However, they are without legal or institutional bases for receiving protection and assistance from the international community. For this very reason, internal displacement poses a challenge to the international community to develop norms, institutions, and operating strategies for prevention, addressing its consequences, and finding durable solutions.

The international community's recognition of the magnitude of the crisis and the urgent need for action led the secretary-general of the United Nations, at the request of the Commission on Human Rights, to appoint a representative on internally displaced persons. In 1992 the assignment was given to Francis M. Deng, senior fellow in the Foreign Policy Studies Program of the Brookings Institution and a former Sudanese diplomat. His mandate as representative has largely focused on developing legal and institutional frameworks for providing international protection and assistance to the internally displaced and engaging governments and other actors in dialogues in an effort to improve their conditions. The idea for this study emerged from discussions between former Secretary-General Boutros Boutros-Ghali and Deng. The secretary-general asked Deng, apart from the normal requirements of his mandate, to conduct an in-depth examination of the problem and develop a comprehensive global strategy for providing effective protection, assistance, and reintegration support to the internally displaced.

In response to this request, the Brookings Institution undertook a collaborative project with the Refugee Policy Group (RPG), an independent center for policy research and analysis concerning refugee and related humanitarian emergency issues. Roberta Cohen, senior adviser to RPG and guest scholar at the Brookings Institution, joined the project as associate and then co-director.

Two studies have emerged from the project: the volume entitled *Masses in Flight: The Global Crisis of Internal Displacement*, which is an in-depth examination of the overall problem of internal displacement written by Cohen and Deng (Brookings, 1998); and this volume of case studies, prepared by leading experts with professional or academic expertise in the issues and countries they discuss. The authors of the case studies come from diverse backgrounds. Some have direct experience with international organizations working to protect and assist displaced populations. Others have led distinguished academic careers. The editors are most grateful for the research and analysis they have provided, which also contributed substantially to the development of a comprehensive strategy for addressing internal displacement in *Masses in Flight*.

The editors come to their subject from different but complementary backgrounds. Deng, who directs the Africa Project at the Brookings Institution, has had a distinguished diplomatic career. Before leaving the Sudanese diplomatic service in 1983, he served as ambassador to Canada, the Scandinavian countries, and the United States and as minister of state for foreign affairs. He is currently acting chairman of the Africa Leadership Forum because the founding chair, General Olusegun Obasanjo, former head of state of Nigeria, remains a political prisoner in his country. Roberta Cohen has held senior positions on human rights in nongovernmental organizations (NGOs) and in the U.S. government, where she served as deputy assistant secretary of state and senior adviser to the U.S. delegation to the United Nations. She has also served as consultant to international organizations and NGOs on humanitarian and refugee issues and played a major role in bringing the subject of internal displacement onto the agenda of the Commission on Human Rights.

The editors wish to express appreciation to a number of individuals for their direct contribution to the preparation of this volume. In particular, they are grateful to Terrence Lyons, who assisted in selecting the case studies and whose reading of early versions of the papers proved constructive to the editorial process. They also acknowledge with appreciation Jennifer McLean's role in coordinating the overall effort, compiling the work of the case study authors, and coauthoring the case study on Tajikistan. Janet Mowery edited the manuscript, Kurt Lindblom provided editorial support, and Susan Fels prepared the index.

Because of the unusual nature, diversity, and remoteness of the sources in the research conducted outside Brookings, the manuscript has not been subjected to normal verification procedures established for research publications of the Brookings Institution. Nonetheless, the authors and editors have made a concerted effort to provide citations where they are needed and to ensure that the citations are as accurate and complete as possible.

Finally, Brookings gratefully acknowledges the financial support of the project's funders, who not only made the overall study, including the case studies, possible but also supported the authors' concurrent efforts to strengthen international and regional arrangements for the internally displaced. Since the project's inception, it has received generous support from the Office of the UN Secretary-General, the Ford Foundation, the McKnight Foundation, the Rockefeller Brothers Fund, and the governments of Austria, the Netherlands, Norway, and Sweden.

The views expressed in the case studies are those of the authors alone and should not be ascribed to the people or organizations whose assistance is acknowledged above, to the editors of this volume, or to the trustees, officers, and other staff members of the Brookings Institution.

Michael H. Armacost
President

June 1998
Washington, D.C.

Contents

xi

Tables

Figures

Acronyms

AAA	Armenian Assembly of America
AFL	Armed Forces of Liberia
AICF	Aide Internationale Contre la Faim (International Action against Hunger)
ANM	Armenian National Movement
APF	Azerbaijan Popular Front
CBIHA	Coordination Bureau for International Humanitarian Aid, Georgia
CERD	Committee on the Elimination of Racial Discrimination (UN)
CINEP	Centro de Investigación y Educación Popular
CIS	Commonwealth of Independent States
CODHES	Consultoría de Derechos Humanos y Desplazamiento (Consultation for Human Rights and Displacement), Colombia
CPDIA	Consulta Permanente para el Desplazamiento Interno en las Américas (Permanent Consultation on Internal Displacement in the Americas), Costa Rica
CRS	Catholic Relief Services
CSCE	Conference on Security and Cooperation in Europe (replaced by OSCE)
DAS	Departamento Administrativo de Seguridad (Department of Administrative Security), Colombia
DHA	Department of Humanitarian Affairs (UN, replaced by OCHA)
DPA	Department of Political Affairs (UN)
DPKO	Department of Peace-Keeping Operations (UN)
EC	European Community (replaced by EU)
ECHO	European Community Humanitarian Office
ECOMOG	Economic Community Monitoring Group (ECOWAS)

ECOSOC	Economic and Social Council (UN)
ECOWAS	Economic Community of West African States
ELN	National Liberation Army, Colombia
EPDP	Eelam People's Democratic Party, Sri Lanka
EPL	People's Liberation Army, Colombia
EU	European Union
FARC	Revolutionary Armed Forces of Colombia
FONCODES	Fondo Nacional de Compensación y Desarrollo Social (National Fund for Compensation and Social Development), Peru
Frodebu	Front for Democracy in Burundi
GAD	Grupo de Apoyo a Desplazados (Support Group for the Displaced), Colombia
IASC	Inter-Agency Standing Committee (UN)
ICRC	International Committee of the Red Cross
IDPs	internally displaced persons
IFOR	Implementation Force, former Yugoslavia
IFRC	International Federation of Red Cross and Red Crescent Societies
IGAD	Inter-Governmental Authority on Development, Djibouti
IGNU	Interim Government of National Unity, Liberia
IMF	International Monetary Fund
INADE	Instituto Nacional de Desarrollo (National Institute for Development), Peru
INCORA	Institute of Agrarian Reform, Colombia
INPFL	Independent National Patriotic Front of Liberia
INURBE	National Institute for Social Housing and Urban Reform, Colombia
IOC	Integrated Operations Centre, Rwanda (UN)
IOCC	International Orthodox Christian Charities
IOM	International Organization for Migration
IPKF	Indian Peace-Keeping Forces, Sri Lanka
IRC	International Rescue Committee
IRIN	Integrated Regional Information Network, Rwanda (UN)
JVP	Janatha Vimukthi Peramuna, Sri Lanka
LDF	Lofa Defense Force, Liberia
LNTG	Liberian National Transitional Government
LPC	Liberia Peace Council
LRA	Lord's Resistance Army, Uganda
LTTE	Liberation Tigers of Tamil Eelam, Sri Lanka
MRR&SW	Ministry of Reconstruction, Rehabilitation, and Social Welfare, Sri Lanka
MRTA	Tupac Amaru Revolutionary Movement, Peru
MSF	Médecins sans Frontières
NATO	North Atlantic Treaty Organization
NGO	nongovernmental organization

NIF	National Islamic Front, the Sudan
NPA	Norwegian People's Aid
NPFL	National Patriotic Front of Liberia
NRC	Norwegian Refugee Council
NSRCC	National Salvation Revolutionary Command Council, the Sudan
OAU	Organization of African Unity
OCHA	Office for the Coordination of Humanitarian Affairs (UN)
OFDA	Office of Foreign Disaster Assistance (USAID)
OLF	Oromo Liberation Front, Ethiopia
OLS	Operation Lifeline Sudan (UN)
ORC	open relief center, Sri Lanka
OSCE	Organization for Security and Cooperation in Europe
PA	People's Alliance, Sri Lanka
Palipehutu	Party for the Liberation of the Hutu People, Burundi
PAR	Proyecto de Apoyo para el Repoblamiento (Support Project for Returnees), Peru
PLOTE	People's Liberation Organization of Tamil Eelam, Sri Lanka
PRONAA	Programa Nacional de Apoyo Alimentario (National Program for Food Support), Peru
QIPs	quick-impact projects
RBF	Russian Border Forces
RI	Relief International
ROSG	Rwanda Operations Support Group
RPA	Rwandese Patriotic Army
RPF	Rwanda Patriotic Front
RRC	Relief and Rehabilitation Commission, the Sudan
SEDs	small enterprise development projects
SFOR	Stabilization Force, former Yugoslavia
SLFP	Sri Lanka Freedom Party
SPLA	Sudan People's Liberation Army
SPLM	Sudan People's Liberation Movement
SRRA	Sudanese Relief and Rehabilitation Association
SRSG	special representative of the secretary-general
SSIA	South Sudan Independence Army
SSIM	South Sudan Independence Movement
TELO	Tamil Eelam Liberation Organization, Sri Lanka
ULIMO	United Liberation Movement for Democracy, Liberia
UMCOR	United Methodist Committee on Relief
UNAMIR	United Nations Assistance Mission for Rwanda
UNDP	United Nations Development Programme
UNDRO	United Nations Disaster Relief Office (replaced by OCHA)
UNESCO	United Nations Educational, Scientific, and Cultural Organization
UNHCR	United Nations High Commissioner for Refugees
UNICEF	United Nations Children's Fund

UNMOT	United Nations Mission of Observers in Tajikistan
UNOMIG	United Nations Observer Mission in Georgia
UNOMIL	United Nations Observer Mission in Liberia
UNP	United National Party, Sri Lanka
UNPA	United Nations Protected Area, former Yugoslavia
UNPF-HQ	United Nations Peace Forces-Headquarters, former Yugoslavia
UNPREDEP	United Nations Preventive Deployment Force, former Yugoslavia
UNPROFOR	United Nations Protection Force, former Yugoslavia
UNREO	United Nations Rwanda Emergency Office
UNSCOL	United Nations Special Coordinating Office for Liberia
Uprona	Union for National Progress, Burundi
USAID	U.S. Agency for International Development
USCR	U.S. Committee for Refugees
USDA	U.S. Department of Agriculture
UTO	United Tajik Opposition
WFP	World Food Programme
WHO	World Health Organization

CHAPTER ONE

Introduction

Roberta Cohen and Francis M. Deng

THE COERCED DISPLACEMENT of persons within the borders of their own countries by armed conflicts, internal strife, and systematic violations of human rights has become a pervasive feature of the post–cold war era. Large numbers of persons are regularly turned into "refugees" within their national borders, dispossessed by their own governments and other controlling authorities, and forced into a life of destitution and indignity. Their plight not only poses a humanitarian challenge but also threatens the security and stability of countries, regions, and through a chain effect, the international system of which they are an integral part. As portions of a country, or an entire country, fall into disarray, neighboring countries are forced to bear the brunt of refugee flows and cope with the resulting substantial political and economic disruptions. Violence and instability may spread through entire regions. Regional and international responses are required as much by a collective interest in regional stability and global peace and security as by humanitarian and human rights concerns.

When internally displaced persons (IDPs) were first counted in 1982, 1.2 million were found in eleven countries. By 1997 the number had soared to more than 20 million in at least thirty-five countries.[1] Although some regions are more affected than others, the crisis is global in dimension and magnitude. And while the international community has a well-established legal and institutional system of protection and assistance for

1

refugees who cross into other countries, no such system is in place for those trapped within the borders of their countries and who therefore fall under state sovereignty.

The tragedy of internal displacement goes beyond statistics and the plight of those directly affected; it reflects a breakdown within a society, in which both fundamental human rights and freedoms and economic and social development are gravely compromised. In countries where there is massive displacement and many are in dire need of elemental protection and assistance, the impact extends well beyond those counted as displaced. Both the communities left behind by the displaced and the areas where the displaced find refuge are severely disrupted, with long-term political and economic consequences.[2] In some cases, the degree of displacement may be so high that one can speak of whole societies becoming displaced.

All of the countries discussed in this volume have experienced substantial internal displacement, numbering in the millions in some. In many, crises of displacement have caused serious problems in neighboring states, and some have threatened entire regions.

The ten case studies explain the historical factors leading to internal displacement, describe the circumstances and manifestations of displacement, discuss the national, regional, and international efforts to deal with the problem, and make recommendations for further action. The case studies were chosen for reasons of geographic distribution and for the different circumstances of displacement each represents. Other factors in the choice were access to the countries concerned and the varied responses of governments and the international community. They were initially written to support a broader study on internal displacement undertaken by the editors, *Masses in Flight: The Global Crisis of Internal Displacement* (Brookings, 1998).

The cases are presented by region. Africa is the subject of four case studies because it is the continent with the largest number of internally displaced persons (more than 9 million) and where civil conflict combined with poverty and the desperate need for outside assistance are more widespread than anywhere else. In Rwanda and Burundi, genocide and genocidal acts feature prominently in the massive uprooting of the population; in Liberia, displacement is related to the collapse of the state; and in the Sudan, the continent's longest-running civil war has produced more internally displaced persons than any other country in the world, approximately 4 million. Two case studies are included for each of the other major continents. In Europe, with close to 5 million internally displaced persons, the former Yugoslavia has been the site of a huge international relief effort, arguably more visible than any other comparable effort. The Caucasus region of the former Soviet Union, comprising Chechnya, Azerbaijan, Armenia, and Georgia, is an ethnically complex and strategically important area where the outcome of conflict and displacement will have serious long-term implications for the region's stability. For Asia, which also has close to 5 million internally displaced persons, the study on Sri Lanka shows a government basically willing to assist its displaced populations, all the while engaged in combat with the minority population composing the displaced. The study on Tajikistan spotlights government cooperation with the United Nations as a significant factor in bringing substantial amelioration. For Latin America, where since 1990 the total number of internally displaced persons has declined to between 1 and 2 million, the case study on Colombia illustrates a unique instance in which criminal violence and a near collapse of governmental authority have combined to uproot hundreds of thousands. The Peru case study highlights how marginalized indigenous populations are the most affected by the insurgency and how suspicions between the government and nongovernmental groups undermine solutions.

In most of the countries discussed here—as in the great majority of cases of internal displacement worldwide—the predominant cause of displacement was conflict among different ethnic groups or between governments and minorities of a different race, language, culture, or religion. Why communities that in many instances had lived together peacefully for decades or even centuries should become embroiled in combat and violence is one of the questions that arise repeatedly. Sometimes, communal rivalries were first exacerbated by the policies of a colonial power that favored one community over another, and subsequently by political elites that sought to gain, perpetuate, or strengthen their hold on power by excluding other groups or by inciting against a particular group demonized as "the enemy" or "the other." Divisive colonial policies and/or a competition for political power, in which ethnicity is used as a weapon, have been major factors in the civil strife that has sundered Rwanda, Burundi, the Sudan, Sri Lanka, the Caucasus region of the former Soviet Union, and the former Yugoslavia.

But competition for scarce economic resources has also contributed significantly to the civil strife that has brought about large-scale internal displacement in many countries. High population density and consequent heavy pressure on the land seriously exacerbated tensions between Hutus and Tutsis in Rwanda and Burundi, and between Sinhalese and Tamils in Sri Lanka. In Liberia, tension between the Americo-Liberian coastal elite, long the possessors of a monopoly on political and economic power, and the exploited indigenous peoples of the interior set the stage for the violence that led to the collapse of governance. In Colombia, conflict over land has been one of the main causes of the generalized violence that has led to large-scale internal displacement over the past decade. In Central America and Peru, the divide between minority European-origin elites wielding political and economic power and impoverished Indian majorities has been the predominant underlying factor in civil strife leading to internal displacement. In the Sudan, disparity in state-controlled economic resources and development opportunities between North and South in particular and between the center and the periphery in general has been a major factor in the civil war. The study on Tajikistan finds competition for control of resources and political power following accession to independence to have been the primary cause of the fighting that at one time or another has uprooted some 10 percent of that country's population.

Outside influence has also played a role. Cold war policies of the United States and the former Soviet Union contributed heavily to the crises of governance in Africa, Asia, and Latin America that led to large-scale internal displacement. In Liberia, U.S. military and economic aid, provided on grounds of Liberia's importance as a cold war asset, helped Samuel Doe's government keep its hold on power despite egregious human rights abuses and widespread unpopularity, and American assistance not only continued but actually increased when Doe's abuses intensified after fraudulent elections in 1986. When at the end of the decade the United States finally distanced itself from Doe, the weaponry that Washington had supplied fueled the generalized violence that accompanied and followed his fall. Although not dealt with in this volume, Soviet arms similarly contributed to maintaining Mengistu Haile Mariam in power in Ethiopia and made possible his government's failed attempt to hold on to Eritrea and defeat a Tigrean insurgency, costing tens of thousands of lives and causing massive displacement. Cold war policies and rivalries also played a dominant role in other conflicts that uprooted millions and killed hundreds of thousands during the 1980s, most notably in civil wars in Angola and Mozambique, in Central America, and in the conflicts in Afghanistan and Cambodia.

The salient fact about war in the post–cold war era is that, apart from Iraq's invasion of Kuwait, it has taken place almost exclusively *within* the borders of states. In all the cases studied in this volume, it was strife within state borders, or between states newly emerged from the collapse of a larger state entity—the former Yugoslavia and the former Soviet Union—that was the immediate cause of large-scale internal displacement.

Wars within states often reflect a crisis of national identity in a society. This occurs when a state becomes monopolized by and identified with the dominant group or groups to the exclusion or marginalization of other groups, which are thereby denied the protection and assistance that a state owes its citizens. The vacuum of responsibility created by this crisis calls for the involvement of the international community to provide alternative protection and assistance.

Sovereignty and the related principles of territorial integrity and non-interference in the internal affairs of states present a serious challenge to the ability of international and regional organizations to intercede in crises of civil strife that cause internal displacement. The case of the Sudan illustrates the devastating effect that governmental obstruction of international relief efforts can have. Resistance by the Sudan's government, rationalized and defended on grounds of state sovereignty, caused hundreds of thousands to die of starvation in the late 1980s and severely limited in later years the international community's efforts to assist millions of internally displaced persons within that country's borders. Operation Lifeline Sudan, established with the agreement of the Sudanese government in 1989, opened relief corridors through which assistance could be channeled to populations at risk in southern Sudan and in government-held territory. However, a change of government in Khartoum brought policy reversals that substantially reduced the program's scope and reach. As case study author Hiram Ruiz points out, "As a result of Sudanese government policies and actions, most displaced Sudanese, particularly those in government-controlled areas, have been left to fend for themselves."

Burundi is another complex example of a country acutely divided by politicized ethnic conflict where the government's role is problematic. Since the country became independent in 1962, strife between majority

Hutu and minority Tutsi has resulted in hundreds of thousands of deaths in both groups and the uprooting of even larger numbers. The case study points out that the "internally displaced Tutsi living in designated camps receive protection from the Burundi military," which is Tutsi-dominated, whereas displaced Hutu "receive little or no security from government security forces and regard the military as a predator." The government does not, however, actively seek to obstruct international assistance efforts to the displaced. The most serious obstacle has been its inability to prevent widespread violence throughout its territory, some of which has been directed against international relief personnel.

Tajikistan and Sri Lanka are examples of states that have welcomed and facilitated international assistance to their internally displaced populations. In Sri Lanka, the majority Sinhalese government over the years has made extensive and sincere efforts to ease the plight of displaced Tamils, setting up camps to provide food and running programs to assist them. Even in these two countries, however, humanitarian and human rights organizations have encountered serious instances of noncooperation. The authors of the case study found that, as military objectives have gained priority in Sri Lanka, many basic needs of the displaced are not being adequately met.

These case studies illustrate the considerable difficulties humanitarian agencies encounter in operating in a framework of state sovereignty and the suspicions that their efforts to assist all sides to a conflict can arouse even on the part of governments that welcome international assistance.

Two steps advocated in the editors' companion volume, *Masses in Flight*, could in some measure mitigate the international legal vacuum that prevails in instances of internal displacement. One is the promotion of the concept of sovereignty as responsibility. Under this concept, a state can claim the prerogatives of sovereignty only so long as it carries out its internationally recognized responsibilities to provide protection and life-supporting assistance to its citizens. Failure to do so would cause it to forfeit traditional rights of sovereignty and legitimize the involvement of the international community.

The second is the Guiding Principles on Internal Displacement, developed by a team of international lawyers under the direction of the representative of the secretary-general on internally displaced persons. The principles bring together in one document the various legal norms applicable to the internally displaced and offer a remedy for the significant gaps that have been identified. Although the principles do not have legal force, they set standards that should put both governments and rebel groups on notice that their conduct is open to scrutiny and will be measured against specific standards. They reflect the needs of the displaced, their corresponding rights, and the duties and obligations of states. They should provide the international community with standards for legitimate action and facilitate conformity and preventive predisposition on the part of governments.

A related issue is the extent to which the international community should be considered to have an obligation to come to the aid of endangered populations. Over the past decade, enormous progress has been made in meeting the challenges posed by humanitarian emergencies. An array of UN, intergovernmental, and nongovernmental agencies now field a multitude of programs to meet emergency needs. The case studies show that the international community has demonstrated both the will and the ability to deliver food, medicine, and other basic supplies in large quantities to endangered populations even in remote areas. To be sure, international assistance has not always been as timely or adequate as circumstances might require, such as in Liberia and the Sudan at different points. In other countries, such as Colombia and Peru, the international community has largely avoided involvement.

Nonetheless, the obligation to assist populations in immediate danger of starvation now appears to be almost unreservedly recognized. Paradoxically, serious questions arise over the extent to which the international community is committed to preventing atrocities such as genocide and other crimes against humanity that are perpetrated against unprotected populations and that lead to mass displacement. In Rwanda, the occurrence of genocide was indisputable, and in both Burundi and the former Yugoslavia instances of genocide were evident. The Genocide Convention of 1948 establishes a commitment on the part of the international community to prevent genocide but sets up no mechanism to ensure that the commitment is fulfilled. Despite warning signs in the former Yugoslavia, in Rwanda, and in Burundi, the international community failed to act until after genocide or genocide-like actions had taken place, and even then international intervention was inadequate to prevent further serious abuses. Peacekeeping forces sent to both Rwanda and the former Yugoslavia helped to safeguard the delivery of humanitarian assistance, but these forces either did not consider it part of their mandates or did not have sufficient backup and capacity to protect the displaced and other affected populations from persecution and attack. In Liberia, a regional force was dispatched to the scene, but there was little oversight of its protection role or effort on the part of the international community itself to provide protection.

A number of the case studies point out the discrepancy between the international protection that is provided more or less automatically to refugees and the absence of a comparable framework for the internally displaced. The 1951 Convention Relating to the Status of Refugees and its 1967 protocol give the United Nations High Commissioner for Refugees (UNHCR) an international legal basis for stepping in to ensure the protection of refugees. Most governments comply more or less readily with their obligations under these agreements, although state actions have caused a steady erosion of refugee protection in recent years, and UNHCR has been impeded at times from carrying out its mandate to protect refugees where state authority has collapsed or rebel forces prevail. Nonetheless, the existing normative and political framework makes it possible for UNHCR to intercede. But neither UNHCR nor any other international humanitarian agency has a similar legal basis for intervening to protect internally displaced populations. The International Committee of the Red Cross (ICRC) is mandated to protect civilians in war zones, but by no means are all internally displaced persons to be found in war zones, and even when they are, the ICRC can operate only with the consent of the governments or rebel forces, which may refuse entry.

How then are internally displaced populations to be assisted and protected? Since there is no international humanitarian agency specifically assigned to provide protection and assistance to the internally displaced, two alternative methods have evolved for dealing with the resulting gap: the various United Nations humanitarian agencies operating each according to its mandate, with their efforts in principle coordinated at the headquarters level by the UN's emergency relief coordinator and in the field by resident representatives/coordinators; or a lead agency assigned to deal with the emergency and charged with overall responsibility for the displaced and other affected populations.

The lead agency method was practiced in the former Yugoslavia and in Tajikistan, where UNHCR was the lead agency in both cases. In the former Yugoslavia, UNHCR was designated by the UN secretary-general to assume the lead agency role, with responsibility not only for refugees—its traditional mandate—but also for internally displaced persons and other war victims. In Tajikistan, UNHCR agreed, in the absence of a resident or humanitarian coordinator, to play the lead role in assisting and protecting both refugees and internally displaced persons returning to their homes, until it turned these responsibilities over to the ICRC, the Organization for Security and Cooperation in Europe (OSCE), and others in 1996.

Thomas Weiss and Amir Pasic, the authors of the case study on the former Yugoslavia, find that UNHCR "responded quickly and well" in providing humanitarian assistance and "managed to orchestrate triage of the most acute needs, whose relative satisfaction was remarkable given the politically hostile terrain." In the area of protection, however, they point out that UNHCR's efforts were often inadequate. In Tajikistan, Jennifer McLean and Thomas Greene find the agency to have done a commendable job in the areas of relief and initial reintegration support and to have had some noteworthy successes in protection as well. They say that the "marked decrease in violence against returnees between 1993 and 1996 was due in large part" to UNHCR's "active international presence."

The coordinated agency operation method, practiced in most of the other countries discussed in this volume, has reaped less favorable reviews. Larry Minear and Randolph Kent, the authors of the Rwanda case study, say coordination was sorely deficient in the international response to the crisis that erupted in Rwanda in 1994. They note that the existence of both a resident and a humanitarian coordinator caused serious problems, as did the lack of clear lines of authority between them and with the special representative of the secretary-general on Rwanda. They point to problems resulting from artificial distinctions made between internally displaced persons and refugees and between relief, recovery, and development assistance. And they point out that major UN agencies resisted overall direction: "UNHCR felt that its mandate would not allow it to commit its resources fully to . . . IDP programs. WFP [the World Food Programme] was engaged in a wide range of activities, including but not limited to IDPs. . . . UNICEF, too, though heavily involved in the IDP camps, had nationwide commitments and priorities well beyond IDPs" and was "reluctant to get involved in IDP solutions that might have negative human rights consequences." Deficient coordination by international humanitarian agencies in Burundi and in Liberia also left substantial gaps in protection, assistance, and rehabilitation programs. The Burundi case study in fact concludes that "the time has come to designate a new or existing UN agency to address the needs of internally displaced populations."

UNHCR's difficulty in protecting displaced populations in the former Yugoslavia and its relative success in Tajikistan illustrate the problems involved in providing protection in complex emergencies. Protection for abused populations within the borders of their own states is a problem for which the United Nations and its various humanitarian agencies have yet to find satisfactory solutions, whether operating independently under an umbrella of coordination or according to the lead agency method. In Yugoslavia, UNHCR by itself was powerless to enforce protection, and neither the UN nor the major powers were prepared to do so until the allied intervention in 1995. In Tajikistan, UNHCR by and large enjoyed the confidence and support of the government and was able to protect returning displaced persons in a number of situations. In Sri Lanka, government cooperation was also noteworthy, as demonstrated by UNHCR's setting up of open relief centers where it could provide a relatively safe environment.

In their field operations, humanitarian agencies have employed a range of solutions to enhance protection, from the introduction of better lighting and more secure placement of essential services in camps to the evacuation of persons at risk, in particular women and children, and the establishment of corridors of relief and protected areas. Greater attention is needed to protection, and in this volume, several authors call for more international programs to improve the physical safety of uprooted populations. At the same time, humanitarian organizations by themselves cannot be expected to provide the kind of enhanced protection needed by displaced populations when armed forces—whether insurgent or governmental—are intent upon doing harm to a particular population. Repeatedly in Rwanda, Burundi, Liberia, the Sudan, the former Yugoslavia, the Caucasus, and even Tajikistan and Sri Lanka, UN humanitarian agencies were prevented from delivering assistance to distant or beleaguered populations or were unable to protect endangered groups from attack.

In such cases, international force may be needed, as employed in Iraq in 1991, Somalia in 1992, and the former Yugoslavia in 1995. But its effectiveness is likely to be limited unless accompanied by measures to address the underlying causes that throw societies into crisis. As virtually all the case studies suggest, it is only through a broader commitment to finding solutions to conflict that internal displacement can ultimately be resolved.

Humanitarian assistance is most effective when it is part of a larger strategy that seeks to facilitate progress toward political solutions. Otherwise it can become, as Weiss and Pasic point out in the case study on Yugoslavia, "a substitute for a clear strategy to end violence." On the other hand, if humanitarian assistance is subordinated to political objectives, it can put displaced persons at risk. As Colin Scott notes, in Liberia the denial of assistance, on political grounds, to civilians in areas controlled by certain factions conflicted with humanitarian principles. Clearly, a balance needs to be struck between political and humanitarian goals so that assistance, while meeting humanitarian criteria, does not impede progress toward political solutions. Thomas Greene warns that in the Caucasus, "Unless aid is made conditional, the countries of the area will continue to avoid resolution of their disputes, ensuring continued displacement and instability." By insisting on progress toward resolution of conflicts, and directing assistance to this goal, the international community can help bring about political settlements that will prevent future displacement.

Several contributors to this volume call for a greater role for the international community in mediating internal disputes. They point out that too little attention is given to prevention or to expending the political capital needed to resolve the internal conflicts that cause displacement. In the case study on Colombia, Liliana Obregón and Maria Stavropoulou call for an external mediator between the government and guerrilla groups in light of the growing violence in that country, a displaced population that is reaching nearly a million, and the spilling over of displaced persons into neighboring states. In Sri Lanka, H. L. Seneviratne and Maria Stavropoulou also call for external assistance in mediating peace, although the government has been resistant; and in the Sudan, Ruiz recommends renewed mediation efforts by neighboring states belonging to the Inter-Governmental Authority on Development (IGAD). In Burundi, the U.S. Committee for Refugees proposes international mediation as well.

Because displacement is an indicator of profound problems within a society, settlements must address the fundamental causes of the conflicts, a point repeatedly emphasized by the authors of these case studies. They must include measures to strengthen democratic institutions and to protect human rights, in particular the rights of minorities and other ethnic and indigenous communities, whose disadvantaged status is at the root of many conflicts. Settlements must include safeguards for NGOs, whose members are often under attack yet whose work with the displaced is vital in view of the limited response of governments and the entrenched distrust sometimes found between the state and displaced populations. Settlements must also address the economic disparities that are at the heart of and exacerbate many conflicts. In particular, access to land, property, and a means of survival are critical, especially in facilitating returns and reintegration.

Regional approaches are also suggested, especially where the resolution of conflict in one country can directly influence the settlement of conflict in another and where internal and external displacement are interrelated and constitute two sides of one problem. Such is the case in the north Caucasus and the Great Lakes region of Africa. Indeed, Minear and Kent strongly criticize international agencies for dealing with displacement and refugee issues in Rwanda and Burundi as if they were self-contained problems without relationship to one another.

The difficult and complex issues that internal displacement raises do not lend themselves to easy answers or simple solutions from outside. Nonetheless, all the case studies demonstrate the need for greater international attention. In the aftermath of World War II, the international community responded effectively to the plight of millions of Europeans who were forced to flee their countries as refugees. The magnitude of today's crisis and the challenge it poses to the international community is hardly less acute or pressing than the post–World War II refugee crisis. A normative and institutional framework unique to this problem is needed to increase protection and assistance for populations forcibly displaced within their own borders.

The development of guiding principles for the internally displaced is an important first step toward holding governments and insurgent groups accountable for their actions with regard to displaced populations. As earlier noted, the Guiding Principles on Internal Displacement contain norms that apply to actual situations of displacement and to the post-conflict period and also include protections *against* forcible displacement. They could help create the moral and political climate needed for enhanced international attention and guide the action of international humanitarian and development agencies in dealing with crises of internal displacement. The appropriate organs of the United Nations can give

authority to these principles through acknowledgment and commenda-
tion for observance.

As to institutional arrangements, the case studies largely demonstrate
that the needs of the internally displaced are more effectively addressed
when one international agency is assigned responsibility for them in a
particular emergency. Yet the creation of a new agency to deal exclusively
with problems of internal displacement faces obstacles of political will,
lack of resources, and operational complexities. Moreover, assigning responsibility for the internally displaced to an existing agency, like
UNHCR, is also problematic. UNHCR has been enlarging its role with
regard to the internally displaced and has performed well in notable
instances, but proposals for expanding its mandate beyond refugees have
met with resistance both from within and outside the agency.

The best alternative is to make the collaborative approach more effective through improved use of existing mandates and capacities. Past
efforts in this direction have been obstructed by notorious problems of
coordination, which have left the internally displaced without adequate
protection and assistance. A more targeted approach therefore needs to
be considered, namely the assignment of principal responsibility for the
internally displaced, within the existing collaborative approach, to one
operational agency in each serious emergency. An effective interagency
coordinating mechanism could then be used to promote support for this
principal agency. And the different agencies would be encouraged to
carve out specific areas of expertise in situations of internal displacement
so that an effective division of labor could be established.

What is essential is that there be predictable responses in situations
of internal displacement and that attention be paid not only to material
assistance needs but also to the protection of the physical security and
human rights of the displaced. Too much of the debate surrounding
internal displacement has concentrated on the delivery of emergency
relief. To be effective, strategies to address mass displacement need to
be broader and more comprehensive. They need to integrate protection
with assistance, focus on prevention, and be accompanied by political
initiatives that seek to resolve conflicts; and they need to include plans
for reintegration and development. In the process, they must engage local
actors, national institutions, and nongovernmental organizations. At the
same time, regional and intergovernmental bodies need to strengthen
their own response systems in the areas of prevention, protection, and

development to supplement local capacities, prevent the conditions that produce displacement, and promote political solutions.

The country profiles that follow afford the reader an opportunity to judge the seriousness of crises of internal displacement in context. Yet there are at least twenty more countries worldwide similarly affected. The political and economic dislocations can be felt both within the affected countries and across their borders, at their most benign burdening neighboring states with refugee flows and at their worst spreading violence and instability through entire regions. The strengthening of national, regional, and international capacities in response must therefore become one of the international community's highest priorities. Timely prevention is as much a matter of international political and strategic interest as it is of humanitarian concern.

Notes

1. These estimates are provided by the U.S. Committee for Refugees (Washington, D.C.) and are cited in Roberta Cohen and Francis M. Deng, *Masses in Flight: The Global Crisis of Internal Displacement* (Brookings, 1998).

2. See Steven Holtzman, "Conflict-Induced Displacement through a Development Lens," paper prepared for the Brookings Institution in May 1997, discussed in Cohen and Deng, *Masses in Flight*.

CHAPTER TWO

Burundi: A Patchwork of Displacement

U.S. Committee for Refugees

IN 1996 VIOLENCE in the central African nation of Burundi escalated dramatically. Between 15,000 and 40,000 Burundians were killed, according to various estimates. A coup brought new leaders to power, the civil war spread to previously calm areas of the country, and neighboring nations imposed an economic embargo in an effort to restore peace and democracy. Burundi's military forcibly relocated approximately 100,000 persons into special camps, and refugees fled the country in growing numbers in the final months of the year. The number of internally displaced persons fluctuated dramatically and repeatedly during 1996, as large numbers suddenly fled and rapidly returned home when local conditions permitted. At year's end there were 400,000 displaced persons, 100,000 more than when the year began.

The nature of displacement in Burundi has become increasingly complex, and international relief agencies are faced with a moral dilemma. In early 1996 the government began a policy of regrouping civilians into camps on the premise that the state could no longer ensure security in conflict zones. While the Burundian authorities are entitled to regroup

This article is based largely on the on-site visits and analysis of USCR policy analysts Jeff Drumtra and Hiram A. Ruiz and consultant Cathy Watson.

Republic of Burundi

RWANDA

Kagera River

Murore
•

KIRUNDO

MUYINGA

CIBITOKE
• Cibitoke

Ruzizi River

• Ibuye
• Ngozi

NGOZI

Muyinga
•

Muramba
•

Mugera
•

Bubanza
•

KAYANZA

KARUZI

• Kigamba

CANKUZO

ZAIRE

BUBANZA
Muzinda
•

Muramvya
•

•Kayongozi

⊕Bujumbura

MURAMVYA

Ruvuvu River

RUYIGI

BUJUMBURA

Gitega
•

•Ruyigi

GITEGA

Matana •

TANZANIA

BURURI

RUTANA

•Bururi

Rumonge
•

Lake Tanganyika

Malagarasi River

Bukemba
•

MAKAMBA

• Nyanza-Lac

| 0 | | 30 mi. |
| 0 | | 30 km. |

16

populations temporarily for their own protection under the Geneva Conventions, reports suggest that the recent *regroupements* solely target Hutu. Any policy of ethnic segregation risks exacerbating the conflict. Poor conditions in the camps have placed international aid organizations in the position of participating in the government's military strategy. As many as 500,000 civilians may soon be affected.[1]

A Wide Array of Displacement Issues

Any survey of the world's internally displaced populations is virtually obliged to include Burundi as a classic, tragic case study. The Burundi crisis involves a striking number of displacement issues that are echoed in other emergencies in different parts of the world.

Burundi's displaced population, for example, is large yet difficult to count—a problem that hinders proper assessment of humanitarian needs and complicates the targeting of relief. The factors forcing Burundians to flee their homes are varied: some segments of the population are displaced as a by-product of civil war, others as a deliberate result of "ethnic cleansing," still others as a result of historic fears so ingrained that many Burundians flee reflexively at the first rumor of impending danger in their area.

Security and protection issues are major factors in Burundi's displacement. Some uprooted Burundians have gravitated to areas where they can receive protection from the national army, while others fear the army and have deliberately fled from it. Thousands of displaced Burundian families have moved to clearly delineated camps, while tens of thousands of others survive on their own, outside of camps—thereby raising questions about the relative advantages and disadvantages of camps.

Food relief and other forms of humanitarian assistance are contentious issues in Burundi. Thousands of uprooted Burundians no longer have access to land for farming, while thousands of other displaced Burundians are still able to engage in agriculture. Thousands of displaced Burundians who need relief assistance do not receive it regularly, while large numbers of uprooted Burundians who probably need little or no relief have attracted significant amounts of it.

Humanitarian assistance to internally displaced Burundians has become highly politicized, subjecting relief workers to extraordinary dangers and to accusations that they lack neutrality merely because they are going about their daily job of distributing relief and assessing needs.

Although the need for humanitarian assistance is great, some relief agencies have begun to question whether, in some areas of Burundi, the existence of relief programs might inadvertently prolong conflict. Some sectors of Burundian society appear to profit politically and economically from the country's massive displacement and the relief deliveries that flow to people in need.

Yet another issue in Burundi, as well as in some other emergencies around the world, is whether the displacement of many families might be permanent, not just a temporary dislocation, after so many years of strife. Burundi's conflict has produced ethnic segregation in many areas. It is possible that large numbers of displaced persons may never feel safe enough to return home. If that proves to be the case, Burundi will face complicated questions about land tenure, resettlement, and social reconciliation long after the overt conflict subsides.

It is doubtful that any country on earth faces the diverse array of population displacement issues found in Burundi. It was among the countries of primary concern to the representative of the UN secretary-general on internally displaced persons, Francis Deng. After his mission to the country from August 30 to September 4, 1994, Deng reported: "Displacement has become a way of life for many of the people of Burundi."[2] Victims in Burundi's conflict desperately need to benefit from lessons learned in other displacement emergencies elsewhere in the world. Failing that, perhaps the world can learn appropriate lessons from the wide range of issues confronting the uprooted people of Burundi.

Overview of Burundi's Turmoil

Burundi has provoked powerful descriptions of despair from many outsiders who have taken the time to observe the chain of tragic events there. A 1994 report by an international human rights organization characterized Burundi as "a sick society."[3] A 1995 report by the U.S. Committee for Refugees stated that in the previous three decades of documenting emergencies worldwide, "rarely has the U.S. Committee for Refugees encountered a political and societal emergency as complex as in present-day Burundi." By late 1995 an official report by a UN human rights investigator documented "an increasingly marked genocidal trend" in Burundi.[4] By mid-1996 the U.S. Department of State asserted that much of the violence in Burundi "constituted genocide."[5]

Burundi has a long history of deadly political and ethnic violence. More than 80 percent of Burundi's estimated 5.5 million people are ethnic Hutu. Ethnic Tutsi constitute most of the remaining population. Despite their minority numbers, Tutsi historically have maintained political and military power. Struggles over political power led to eruptions of violence and large population displacements in 1965, 1969, 1972, 1988, 1991, 1993, and 1994–96. Since 1993 regular violence has pushed Burundi toward full-scale civil war. The most conservative estimates suggest that more than thirty years of strife and on-again, off-again violence have killed at least 130,000 Burundians. Other estimates suggest a thirty-year death toll as high as 320,000. Massacres claimed as many as 2,500 lives per month during early 1996, according to a controversial estimate by the then U.S. ambassador to Burundi.

For many Burundians, displacement from their homes has become a way of life. At critical moments of danger since the 1960s, hundreds of thousands of Burundians have repeatedly fled their farms and villages. In late 1993, a violent upheaval killed some 50,000 persons and pushed one quarter of Burundi's terrified population from their homes. By mid-1996 ongoing violence was keeping an estimated 700,000 persons uprooted, including nearly 300,000 who were refugees in the neighboring countries of Zaire and Tanzania, and approximately 400,000 internally displaced in Burundi.[6] Violence and population displacement were particularly severe in the northern half of the country.

One reflection of the deep schism in Burundian society is that different terms have been coined to describe the country's uprooted population. Ethnic Tutsi who have fled to camps or private homes in villages are called "displaced," while ethnic Hutu who have fled from their homes to remote areas of the hilly countryside are called "dispersed." To some extent, the different labels reflect the different humanitarian needs of the two uprooted populations and the different challenges facing relief groups trying to provide assistance. However, political extremists in Burundi have used the terms "displaced" and "dispersed" to categorize uprooted people according to their ethnicity and to create artificial competition between the two groups over limited supplies of humanitarian assistance. In order to avoid lending credence to the unfortunate politicization of an important concept such as "displaced persons," this chapter generally uses the word "displaced" to refer to all uprooted people within Burundi, regardless of ethnic identity.

The distrust pervading Burundian society runs so deep that simple acts of survival—such as living in a settlement for displaced persons—can be interpreted as acts of provocation. On the one hand, many Hutu claim that uprooted Tutsi have congregated safely in displaced persons camps as part of a broad strategy to evacuate Tutsi residents from rural areas so that the Tutsi-dominated military can massacre rural Hutu more efficiently. Many Tutsi extremists and military leaders, on the other hand, appear to regard Hutu civilians' attempts to escape toward safer areas as proof that they are rebel sympathizers.

Although many internally displaced Burundians have encountered problems related to poor nutrition, inadequate shelter, and poor or non-existent health care, their greatest need appears to be physical security. Much of the Hutu population feels threatened by the Tutsi-dominated military and roving gangs of Tutsi youths, and members of both ethnic groups have been victimized by Hutu rebels who have grown militarily stronger since 1995. The country's general insecurity has forced international relief groups to curtail delivery of humanitarian assistance and, in some cases, to terminate entire aid programs. These developments hinder the international community's ability to monitor humanitarian and human rights conditions in Burundi's rural areas, which has the effect of worsening the isolation in which victims of the conflict suffer.

Decades of tension have produced a Burundian society riven by ethnic mistrust, ethnic segregation, and political paralysis, particularly at society's highest levels. The violence is driven by all these factors: ethnic animosity has stimulated what some foreign observers define as acts of genocide; pervasive fear has engendered a kill-or-be-killed mentality; a culture of official impunity has allowed acts of violence to persist unconstrained by justice or accountability; political ideology has prompted some combatants to fight for the restoration of democracy; and political opportunism has convinced some Burundians that sustained chaos enables them to retain political power and economic privilege.

Many observers inside and outside Burundi have expressed concern that the level of conflict will worsen, resulting in even greater death and population displacement. Previous episodes of violence have demonstrated that Burundi can explode suddenly and is capable of producing a million or more new refugees and internally displaced persons in the span of a few days. In a mid-1996 report, UN Secretary-General Boutros Boutros-Ghali stated that if current trends continue, "human suffering is likely to escalate to unprecedented levels in Burundi."[7]

Causes of Internal Displacement

Politically inspired ethnic conflict is not a new phenomenon in Burundi, and therefore massive displacement of the nation's population is, sadly, not a new occurrence in the country's history. Since the mid-1960s, in fact, displacement has become endemic, produced by Burundian society's tangled web of mistrust, resentment, privilege, retaliation, and injustice. Time after time over the years, the country's political power struggles and ethnically biased social policies have triggered violence, resulting in staggering death tolls and traumatized civilians fleeing their homes.

The instability created by these upheavals has produced a prevailing mindset among many Burundians, perceptively described in a 1995 report by Paulo Sergio Pinheiro, the UN special rapporteur for human rights in Burundi:

> Burundians are currently living in an atmosphere of mistrust, hatred, and exclusion, withdrawn into themselves and often hostile to anything unfamiliar. Since the loss of loved ones recurs generation after generation . . . the accumulated grief has been transmitted to their descendants for decades. Because of these sad memories or a desire for revenge, Burundi society has become paralyzed and Burundi culture stifled, with no solution in sight. This state of mind could well have psychotic consequences, which are very difficult to cope with at the national level and . . . create a context conducive to the development of extremist and totalitarian ideologies among the population.[8]

In Burundi perhaps more than in most other countries, outsiders cannot fully understand the causes of the current situation without examining the country's past.

Pre-Independence Burundi

Unlike most African states, Burundi was not an artificial creation of colonial rule. Before colonization, Burundi had been a strong, organized kingdom for centuries. Society consisted of four groups: the *Ganwa*, politicians and rulers of royal blood (today regarded as a Tutsi subgroup); the *Tutsi*, mainly cattle keepers; the *Hutu*, mainly cultivators; and the *Twa*, potters, entertainers, and hunters. All groups spoke the Kirundi language and shared the same culture. The Mwami, or king, played a unifying role as the primary focus for popular loyalties.

Society was a hierarchical web of patron-client ties, with the princely Ganwa enjoying the highest status and the Twa the lowest. How Tutsi and Hutu related is less clear; the history of such matters is fiercely politicized in modern-day Burundi. Overall, however, Tutsi were of higher status than Hutu. There were more Tutsi chiefs, and Tutsi were traditionally the landowners. The societal hierarchy, however, was somewhat fluid, and "ethnicity" was determined more by occupation than by heritage. A rich Hutu could come to be regarded as a Tutsi. An impoverished individual could be ethnically Tutsi but socially Hutu, beholden to a patron. Tutsi and Hutu regularly intermarried.

Sixty-three years of colonial rule greatly affected relationships among the four groups. Burundi was absorbed by German East Africa in 1899, and Belgium took control in 1916. The Europeans, laden with their own racial and class prejudices, increased the potential for conflict in Burundi society. European colonists tended to identify with the Tutsi, who were often tall and fine-featured. Tutsi received preference in the colonial-run school system. The Europeans ousted traditional Hutu chiefs and ruled the country through the pool of better-educated Tutsi and Ganwa. Ethnic tensions were exacerbated by the colonists' draconian system of forced labor, the bulk of which fell on Hutu shoulders, with Tutsi installed as overseers.

A 1934 census by Belgian rulers blurred social and ethnic lines. Persons who owned more than ten cows were arbitrarily classified as Tutsi. As a result, relatively wealthy Hutu suddenly "became" Tutsi, and some poorer Tutsi "became" Hutu. Already identified with relative deprivation, "Hutuness" became even more strongly associated with poverty and powerlessness. The census classified 84 percent of the population as Hutu, 14 percent as Tutsi, and 1 percent as Twa. These suspect percentages are still applied to Burundi today. In 1948, Belgian administrators began to move Burundi toward a modest degree of self-rule. Two main political parties came to the fore, one of which exists to this day, the Union for National Progress, known by its French acronym, Uprona.

A perverse pattern that was repeated years later became evident in 1959: tensions between Hutu and Tutsi in neighboring Rwanda affected ethnic tensions in Burundi. In that year, tens of thousands of Rwandan Tutsi refugees fled into Burundi. Rwanda's ethnic strife prompted Burundi's Tutsi leaders to view their own country's majority Hutu population with more fear and disdain, and Tutsi elite began to implement policies designed to block Hutu participation in politics and other facets of Burundian society.

Uprona swept Burundi's pre-independence legislative elections in 1961 and sought balanced Tutsi and Hutu representation at the highest levels of the new political structure. Two weeks after the election, however, Uprona's moderate leader who was designated to be prime minister, Louis Rwagasore, was assassinated by agents of a weak but outspoken pro-Hutu political party. The murder deprived Burundi of its one undisputed leader who seemed to be above acting on the basis of ethnicity.

The assassination, coupled with a Hutu revolution taking place in neighboring Rwanda, exerted a divisive influence on Burundian society as the country headed into independence. Tutsi militants attacked Hutu politicians and trade unionists near Bujumbura, the capital, killing four and setting Hutu houses ablaze. A subsequent government, led by a Hutu prime minister, jailed the attackers. The next government, headed by Tutsi, released them.

Turmoil and Displacement from 1962 to 1973

Following national independence in 1962, sporadic attacks by youth wings continued, and maneuvering for political control sparked significant violence and refugee outflows in 1965 and 1969.

Burundi's King Mwambutsa used his prestige to arbitrate leadership disputes in the first years of independence. He balanced ethnicities in five governments between 1963 and 1965, two of which had Hutu prime ministers. Ethnic violence in nearby Rwanda, however, continued to aggravate ethnic tensions in Burundi. Thousands of Rwandan Tutsi refugees spilled into Burundi and used it as a base for armed incursions into Rwanda. In 1965 a Rwandan refugee assassinated Burundi's prime minister, a Hutu. The assassin was not punished.

Four months after the prime minister's assassination, national elections gave Hutu politicians majority seats in parliament, but the king refused to accept a Hutu as prime minister, appointing a Tutsi instead. A subsequent coup attempt by Hutu army officers resulted in the deaths of some 500 Tutsi. Tutsi responded by slaying 2,500 to 5,000 Hutu, including several politically prominent officials. It is believed that several hundred Hutu fled the country.

Burundi's monarchy was deposed in 1966, thereby eliminating a stabilizing element in the political system. Power increasingly shifted to the military and to Tutsi from southern Burundi. Uprona was declared the country's sole political party. Hutu were purged from the army. In 1969 the discovery of a Hutu coup plot provoked more purges and the execution of sixty to a hundred Hutu intellectuals. A second wave of refugees fled, though no estimate of their numbers is available.

Massive violence in 1972 permanently changed Burundi. The full story of how the 1972 massacres began may never be fully known, but by the time they subsided in 1973, an estimated 80,000 to 150,000 persons were dead, some 300,000 had fled the country, and uncounted numbers were internally displaced.[9] The overwhelming majority of the dead were Hutu, as were virtually all of the refugees.

The violence was triggered when Burundian Hutu militants, based in refugee communities in Tanzania, attacked and killed an estimated 2,000 Tutsi in southern Burundi. The attack terrified Burundi's Tutsi elite, who assumed—or pretended—it was the beginning of the mass Hutu uprising they had always feared. Although Burundi's Tutsi-dominated military quashed the rebellion within days, soldiers and Tutsi gangs associated with Uprona continued to massacre Hutu civilians for months. Burundi's government-run radio exhorted Tutsi to attack their Hutu neighbors.[10]

Educated Hutu were specially targeted for death: secondary school and university students, teachers, nurses, doctors, priests, pastors, drivers, headmasters, businessmen, shopkeepers, civil servants, bank clerks, professors, and others. Although thousands of Hutu peasants also died, the virtual extermination of the Hutu elite deprived the Hutu population of an entire generation of leaders and intellectuals.

Many Tutsi defended the bloody repression as legitimate self-defense against an ethnic group that outnumbered the Tutsi population six to one—a siege mentality that persists among some segments of the Tutsi population to this day. The great majority of Burundi's Hutu population, however, appeared to have no link to the Hutu militants who initiated the violence. Most Hutu stayed at home as government officials instructed, making many of them easy targets for death.

Although the killing was largely one-sided, members of both ethnic groups view the tragedy of 1972 as proof that their own group is vulnerable to extermination. The bloody events of 1972 instilled a kill-or-be-killed mentality in times of extreme crisis.

Violence and Displacement from 1974 to 1992

In the aftermath of the 1972 slaughter, significant violence and population displacement did not recur in Burundi until 1988 and 1991.

The country's military-dominated government conducted no investigation into the 1972 massacres. With the alleged "Hutu menace" eliminated for the time being, Tutsi leaders turned their attention to infighting within their own ranks. In 1976, Colonel Jean Baptiste Bagaza, a Tutsi, seized power in a bloodless coup. Although no major massacres occurred during his eleven-year rule, Bagaza refused to acknowledge openly the country's ethnic tensions and gradually concentrated power in the hands of a closed inner circle of Tutsi colleagues from his home area of southern Burundi.

A month after taking power, Bagaza's government invited back the Hutu refugees of 1972–73. Two years later, land reforms beneficial to Hutu became law. Bagaza also promoted a "villagization" program designed to move rural peasants into villages. It is indicative of the climate of fear that many Hutu thought they were being made to live in groups so that they could be more easily killed.

Bagaza's deteriorating human rights record and his narrow base of support at home and abroad prompted a coup in 1987 by his associate Major Pierra Buyoya. In the first year of Buyoya's rule, sixteen of the twenty top government officials were Tutsi, as were eleven of the fifteen provincial governors. Buyoya moved to increase Hutu representation, however, after an outbreak of ethnic violence in 1988.

The violence of 1988 flared in the extreme northern provinces of Kirundo and Ngozi, where education discrimination against Hutu was particularly severe and a Hutu rebel group, known as the Palipehutu (Party for the Liberation of the Hutu People), was particularly strong. Ethnic tensions had been mounting over the expulsion of Hutu students following school strikes. Bands of Hutu led by Palipehutu activists killed several thousand Tutsi. The army retaliated by killing thousands of Hutu civilians, regardless of whether they had participated in the attacks against Tutsi. Between 5,000 and 20,000 persons perished in a span of less than ten days before the violence subsided. A government investigation subsequently acknowledged that Burundian soldiers participated in the violence, but justified their actions. More than 60,000 refugees, mostly Hutu, fled to Rwanda.

The 1988 explosion stunned Burundi. The massacres demonstrated to the Hutu population that the army was still prepared to use maximum force against them. The outbreak reminded Tutsi that they remained physically vulnerable until soldiers could reach the scene. The killings spurred Buyoya to begin reforms. Under pressure from donor countries and with the support of Tutsi moderates, Buyoya created the Commission of National Unity, half Tutsi and half Hutu, to explore the ethnic question. Buyoya shuffled his cabinet, removing Tutsi hard-liners and increasing the number of Hutu from six to twelve, thereby giving Hutu a majority of the twenty-three posts. A Hutu was appointed prime minister for the first time since 1965. An amnesty was declared for the 60,000 refugees who had fled to Rwanda. All but 1,000 of the refugees returned within six months.

A national referendum in early 1991 adopted the Unity Charter, which officially repudiated ethnic discrimination. A year later, the country adopted a new constitution that ended twenty-six years of one-party rule by Uprona and allowed for a pluralist system. Tutsi hard-liners resisted the reforms and mounted failed coup attempts against Buyoya in 1989 and 1992.

Tensions persisted despite the reforms. The military remained almost exclusively Tutsi. Hutu continued to regard the army as the ultimate killer; Tutsi continued to view it as the ultimate protector. The judiciary remained highly politicized and almost entirely Tutsi. The Commission of National Unity seemed to conclude that Hutu were primarily to blame for the country's tragedies and implied incorrectly that Tutsi and Hutu suffered equally in the 1972 massacres. The Buyoya reforms increased the Hutu population's hunger for greater change and created friction between the Hutu majority and local Tutsi government officials.

Palipehutu militants, concerned that the reforms might undermine their support in the Hutu community, launched a series of terrorist attacks against police and military posts near Bujumbura in late 1991. Reprisals by the military left an estimated 1,000 people dead, and forced 40,000 Hutu to flee the country to Zaire and Rwanda. Additional attacks into Burundi from Hutu refugee camps in Rwanda occurred in 1992. The army response this time, however, was more restrained, prompting donors like the U.S. Agency for International Development (USAID) to conclude overoptimistically that the military was getting better at controlling its response. Most of the 40,000 refugees who fled in 1991 returned to Burundi by 1993.

Violence and Displacement from 1993 to 1996

There was cause for great hope in Burundi in 1993 when the country held its first democratic presidential election in an atmosphere of calm and openness. Within months, however, the country's first Hutu president was assassinated, approximately 50,000 persons of both ethnic groups died in widespread violence, and approximately 1.5 million persons—a quarter of the entire population—became refugees or were internally displaced. An increasingly bloody low-intensity conflict, verging on full-scale civil war, has endured since 1993 and continues at this writing in 1998.

The year leading up to Burundi's mid-1993 national elections was generally calm, although human rights abuses did occur, and the presidential campaign became increasingly "ethnicized" toward its conclusion. Government media openly supported the Uprona party and the incumbent president, Buyoya. The Front for Democracy in Burundi, known by its acronym as Frodebu, emerged as the strongest opposition party.

The presidential election that took place on June 1, 1993, was observed by scores of foreign observers and about 1,000 local monitors. Ninety-seven percent of the electorate went to the polls and elected the Frodebu candidate Melchior Ndadaye, a Hutu, who received nearly two thirds of the popular vote. The National Democratic Institute, an American organization that observed the polling, described the election as "an historic model" for other countries in the region.[11] A round of legislative elections four weeks later awarded the Frodebu party 71 percent of the popular vote and overwhelming control of the National Assembly.

Many Tutsi reacted with bitterness and fear, complaining that the Hutu population had voted as an ethnic block for the predominantly Hutu Frodebu party. The defeated Uprona party had offered slates of candidates who were more ethnically mixed. The day after the presidential election, the victorious Ndadaye, the defeated Buyoya, and the army chief of staff went on national radio to assure listeners that the election was a victory for all Burundians. Buyoya said he accepted the election results and urged the people to do the same. Tutsi university students, however, conducted a series of demonstrations in Bujumbura to denounce the election as little more than an ethnic census.

A weak coup attempt by a handful of military officers immediately after the legislative election was easily suppressed and widely condemned by Burundians of both ethnic groups. President Ndadaye sought to reassure the Tutsi population by appointing a moderate Tutsi as prime minister and installing Tutsi in nine of twenty-three cabinet positions. He also promised the army that no officer would be fired.

The new president's confidence-building measures, however, did not assuage the concerns of extremists. Extremist Tutsi were convinced that

Ndadaye's plan to form a presidential guard composed of Hutu was the first step in eroding the authority of the Tutsi-dominated military. Tutsi civil servants at lower echelons of the government found their jobs being handed to Frodebu supporters. Tensions over land tenure increased as Burundian Hutu refugees began repatriating in large numbers before and after the election and pressed to reclaim their property. Many hardline Hutu, meanwhile, regarded Ndadaye's policies as too moderate.

Despite the disagreements surrounding the policies of the new government, most Burundians were stunned by the events of October 21, 1993, when sections of the Tutsi-dominated military assassinated the newly elected president and several other high government officials. The military coup sparked massive violence in most regions of the country, as civilian Tutsi and Hutu attacked each other, and sections of the military attacked Hutu. Only the two southernmost provinces of Bururi and Makamba escaped violence. Weeks of massacres left 30,000 to 100,000 persons dead—the most accurate estimate is probably about 50,000. For the first time in the long history of Burundian bloodlettings, the Tutsi community suffered losses on a massive scale, possibly rivaling the death toll among Hutu. An estimated 600,000 refugees, primarily Hutu, fled to Rwanda, Tanzania, and Zaire. Some 500,000 to 700,000 persons of both ethnic groups became internally displaced in Burundi.

An International Commission of Inquiry subsequently concluded that officials of both ethnic groups were complicit in the violence. "In places where large numbers of Tutsi were killed, some [local Hutu administrators] incited and participated in these summary executions," the investigation stated in its final report. In about half of the communes, large numbers of Tutsi were killed. (Burundi is organized administratively into provinces, each composed of smaller communes.) "Likewise . . . some Tutsi civil servants used their status and influence to facilitate the massacre of Hutu."[12]

Although some local Frodebu officials responded to the coup by inciting massacres, others worked to prevent killings or had to flee from soldiers to save their own lives. Large-scale killings of Tutsi ceased after three days in most affected areas. As in Burundi's previous upheavals, however, bloody reprisals against the Hutu population by the military and by Tutsi gangs continued for several weeks.

The military coup attempt that originally sparked the violence unfolded in bizarre fashion. Two days after seizing power, the coup leaders bowed to international pressure and returned official control to the remnants of the democratically elected civilian government, many of whose top members were still in hiding. Some observers have characterized the events of October 1993 as "the most successful failed coup in history." It left in place a weak shell of a government whose top civilian officials lived in daily fear of assassination by the army. Others have labeled the situation a "creeping coup": from 1994 to 1996, extremist Tutsi politicians gradually exploited the country's power vacuum to diminish the president's legal power, override the constitution and the national assembly, and shift political power to small, extremist Tutsi parties that had received no significant support in the 1993 election.[13]

In January 1994, following the death of President Ndadaye, a new president was appointed after two months of intense negotiations. The new president, Cyprien Ntaryamira, a Hutu member of Frodebu, was killed three months later in the same plane crash that killed Rwandan president Juvenal Habyarimana. President Ntaryamira's death, and a genocide under way against Tutsi in neighboring Rwanda during mid-1994, raised tensions in Burundi, but major violence was averted.

Another Hutu member of Frodebu, Sylvestre Ntibantunganya, replaced Ntaryamira as interim president and eventually was appointed, after tense negotiations, to remain president until the completion of the five-year presidential term. Continuing insecurity in the country, which kept hundreds of thousands of Burundians displaced from their homes, made an election then impossible. Although the presidency remained in Frodebu hands, Tutsi-dominated opposition parties managed in 1994 to negotiate significantly greater power for themselves disproportionate to their size.

Security conditions deteriorated during the period from 1994 to 1996. Displaced Burundians were both victims and perpetrators of violence in the countryside. Hutu militants began staging ambushes against soldiers and displaced Tutsi living in camps. Hutu rebels demonstrated improved military capabilities and organized themselves into a coalition, the Front for the Defense of Democracy. The rebels mounted cross-border terrorist attacks from Zaire, disrupted the electrical supply to Bujumbura, and in early 1996 infiltrated areas of Burundi that had previously been beyond their reach.

The army responded by killing Hutu indiscriminately and raiding predominantly Hutu sections of the Bujumbura area, ostensibly to search for arms. Hutu gangs retaliated by attacking Tutsi civilians in the suburbs. Hundreds, perhaps thousands, died in these raids and counterraids, and tens of thousands were forced from their homes. An estimated 60,000 Hutu fled the Bujumbura suburb of Kamenge in mid-1995 as an urban war raged there among armed Hutu, armed Tutsi civilians, and the military. By late 1995 only one neighborhood of Bujumbura remained ethnically mixed. Many Hutu residents near Bujumbura initially fled to the hills surrounding the capital. Even the hills proved to be unsafe from attacks, however, and much of the uprooted population was forced to flee deeper into the countryside. At least 100,000 additional persons became displaced in early 1996, particularly in the central provinces of Gitega and Karuzi, as the rebels became more aggressive.

Entire areas were "cleansed" of Hutu inhabitants, and Burundian society became increasingly segregated. There was a "growing ethnic bias of Burundi's institutional and political system at the national level," stated a late-1995 report by Pinheiro, the UN special rapporteur for human rights in Burundi. "There is no future . . . for Hutu intellectuals in the country," he concluded.[14] Frodebu officials, as well as a few prominent Tutsi linked to opposition political parties, were victims of regular political assassinations. Conflict permeated the lives of urban and rural Burundians. Each month brought new political standoffs and a higher death toll.

Outsiders can gain a clearer sense of the relentless violence in Burundi—and the corrosive fear it engenders among average people—from the following partial chronology of some of the major incidents that occurred during a few months in 1995.

In early March, twenty-three persons died in several attacks involving armed gangs and displaced persons in northeast Burundi. On March 3, three died and forty-five were injured by a grenade at a secondary school in the northeast. On March 5, twenty-one Hutu were reported to have been killed by displaced Tutsi in the northwest, in Cibitoke province. Between March 11 and 20, a government minister was assassinated in broad daylight in Bujumbura, and eight other persons were killed in the capital. On March 24, between 150 and 200 persons were killed, mostly Hutu, by Tutsi militia in Bujumbura. In late March, twelve people died when a camp for Rwandan refugees was attacked in northern Burundi. On March 29, a massacre killed approximately 260 persons in northeast Burundi, in Muyinga province. In another March 29 incident, a grenade killed three students at a secondary school. Throughout March, twenty-four armed combatants were killed in several clashes near Bujumbura. On April 23, twenty-nine civilians were killed in a clash between the military and armed gangs in northwest Burundi. On May 4, eighteen persons were reported to have been killed in a Hutu militia attack near the country's largest displaced persons camp in the north. Between June 2 and 7, some 20,000 Hutu fled an army sweep in Bujumbura. Between June 3 and 5, thirty persons died in attacks in three widely scattered provinces. On June 17, more than fifty persons were killed by Tutsi gangs and soldiers in a Bujumbura suburb. In late June, more than 100 persons, mostly women and children, were killed by the military near Bujumbura. On June 23, twelve persons were killed by armed gangs in Bujumbura. On June 28, fifteen small children were killed in an attack on a primary school in northern Burundi's Kayanza province.

Continuing the chronology, on July 2, twenty-five people were killed in clashes between armed gangs and the local population in the north, in Kayanza province. In early July, 117 persons were killed during a military sweep near Bujumbura. On July 11, at least 100 were killed in several clashes in the north, in Ngozi province. On July 22, about fifteen persons died during a military sweep outside Bujumbura. On August 6, forty-seven persons living in a camp for displaced persons were killed in an armed attack in the northwest province of Cibitoke. On September 18, approximately 100 persons were massacred north of Bujumbura, allegedly by soldiers, and seven soldiers were killed.

The frequency of incidents and the pace of killings only accelerated in the first half of 1996. A UN report in May 1996 described "a marked deterioration in the security situation in Burundi since early March [1996]." [15]

No reliable estimates exist for the total number of deaths during 1994–96, but foreign observers on the ground reported that the violence worsened year by year. Various relief workers and UN personnel estimated that an average of 400–500 persons were killed per month during 1994 (about 5,000 deaths during the year); as many as 800 were killed per month in 1995 (about 10,000 during the year); and perhaps 1,200 were killed per month in the first half of 1996 (about 15,000 deaths if sustained over a full year). The U.S. ambassador to Burundi in early 1996, Robert Krueger, publicly estimated that the spiral of violence had pushed the number of deaths as high as 2,500 per month in early 1996—a rate of 30,000 deaths per year, if accurate.

It is likely that each incident in the above 1995 chronology—as well as scores of unreported security incidents—provoked many survivors to flee, sometimes for days, sometimes indefinitely. The sudden displacement of a few hundred persons in isolated communities rarely gets reported, but these relatively small displacements occurring almost daily have uprooted hundreds of thousands of Burundians since 1994.

Summary: Causes of Internal Displacement

Even this cursory review of Burundi's history sheds light on the causes of the country's internal displacement in previous years, as well as currently. A history of massacres has taught the people of Burundi, regardless of their ethnicity, that their personal survival hinges on their ability to flee and seek a safer place temporarily. For many peasant Burundians, the lesson of the past is that violence can erupt suddenly and can rapidly become all-encompassing. It is a lesson handed down from generation to generation. Some of the underlying causes of internal displacement in Burundi follow:

- First, a pervasive psychology of "flee or be killed" has become the lasting legacy of the 1972 slaughter and the 1993 upheaval. The 1994 genocide in neighboring Rwanda has reinforced the psychology of flight in Burundi.
- Second, the smaller massacres that have occurred almost daily since 1994 serve to validate the historical lessons of fear and mistrust. Fear is so ingrained that large numbers of Burundians have learned to flee their homes not only in reaction to danger but also in anticipation of it.
- Third, much of Burundi's displacement since 1993 has been caused by "ethnic cleansing." Displacement is no longer merely an accidental by-product of violence; it has become a deliberate goal of the violence.
- Fourth, both ethnic groups in Burundi regard themselves as vulnerable. The sense of vulnerability has become an important part of their self-identity. Hutu are demographically dominant but see themselves as vulnerable to the political and military power of Tutsi. Tutsi are politically and militarily powerful but view themselves as vulnerable to the demographic dominance of Hutu. Members of both ethnic groups regard themselves as victims, despite the fact that many massacres in Burundian history have been largely one-sided.
- Fifth, a pattern is evident in the many violent eruptions over the decades: regardless of how the violence begins, there is almost

always massive retaliation against Hutu by the Tutsi-dominated military. As a result, many Hutu instinctively flee at the mere sight of soldiers or at the distant sound of their vehicles. The country's forces of order, unfortunately, create new disorder and displacement—deliberately in some cases, inadvertently in others.

- Sixth, population displacement in Burundi often exacerbates rather than alleviates the conflict. Uprooted Burundians of one ethnic group are often regarded as dangerous by members of the other ethnic group. The military suspects that many internally displaced Hutu are rebels. Many Hutu suspect that camps of displaced Tutsi are bases for militia activity. There is some truth to these mutual suspicions. The result is that displacement at times begets more violence, causing still more people to flee. In short— at least in Burundi—displacement causes more displacement.

These are only partial explanations of the population displacement in Burundi, of course. This review of Burundi's history indicates that some actors create violence and displacement as a way to achieve political control by force that they are unable to achieve or maintain through nonviolent legal means. Some elements in Burundi create violence and displacement for the economic rewards it brings them through banditry, confiscation of property, and skimming of relief aid. Still other Burundians commit violence and force displacement based on pure fear or hate, reinforced by decades of grievances, real or imagined.

Burundi's History of Internal Displacement

Some Burundians temporarily fled to safe areas within Burundi during the upheavals of the 1960s, 1970s, and 1980s, yet no estimates are available today of the size of those internally displaced populations. Even the massive violence of 1972 that led some 300,000 Burundian Hutu to flee the country entirely left no hint about the number of people who became internally displaced instead of refugees in another country.

The paucity of data—even the lack of wild guesses—indicates the extent to which the international community routinely ignored the existence of internally displaced persons and their needs in Burundi and many other countries until recently. The 1988 bloodshed in Burundi, which created about 60,000 refugees, produced "tens of thousands" of internally displaced persons, according to a report at the time by the

U.S. Committee for Refugees. The agency was unable to offer a more specific estimate, however. It was not until the violence of 1993 that Burundi's phenomenon of internal displacement gained widespread attention.

In retrospect, the huge population displacement that occurred in 1972 profoundly changed Burundi. Central Bujumbura and other business zones became Tutsi preserves. Hutu widows, their houses seized by Tutsi, moved to the city outskirts. Many Tutsi moved to urban areas from the interior where they felt unsafe among Hutu neighbors. Others moved to Bujumbura to fill the many jobs left vacant by Hutu who had died or fled. The flat, fertile, palm oil–producing strip of land along Lake Tanganyika, south of Bujumbura, previously had been home to few Tutsi. Most had preferred to live in the cool hills where their cattle could thrive; those living along the lake before 1972 had been mainly government officials. With the death and flight of so many Hutu, Tutsi rushed to occupy the lucrative palm plots and also took the shops of Hutu. Much of the 1972 population displacement became permanent, and the nation's economy suffered.

Demographics of Burundi's Internally Displaced Population

The precise number of persons internally displaced by the violence of 1993–96 is difficult to determine. Security concerns at times have limited the access of international relief agencies and hampered their ability to make sophisticated estimates. Many displaced Hutu have dispersed into the hills and swamps to hide and do not reside in designated camps because they consider camps vulnerable to attack. Local leaders of both ethnic groups routinely inflate the number of uprooted families in an effort to attract more aid and gain more sympathy for their political cause. "In some camps," noted one relief worker, "those in charge are so hostile that it becomes dangerous even to ask about numbers or need. They will bluntly say that it's none of your business." [16]

It is believed that some 500,000 to 700,000 persons were internally displaced in late 1993 by the violence that erupted in October of that year. Violence persisted at lower levels in 1994, creating more displacement even as some uprooted Burundians cautiously returned home. Uncertainty about the actual number of internally displaced people in Burundi remained a prime issue of discussion among relief officials and Burundian authorities throughout 1994–95 and made disputes over the number of beneficiaries who should receive food aid all the more complicated. Relief workers estimated that a quarter-million displaced persons were located in the four northern provinces of Kirundo, Ngozi, Kayanza, and Muyinga; the four western provinces of Bujumbura, Muramvya, Bubanza, and Cibitoke contained an estimated 150,000; and the four central provinces of Gitega, Ruyigi, Karuzi, and Rutana contained an estimated 60,000 displaced.[17]

By mid-1996, a report by UN Secretary-General Boutros-Ghali offered "a conservative guess" that at least 300,000 Burundians remained internally displaced.[18] The U.S. Committee for Refugees also estimated that 300,000 were displaced in early 1996, noting that "tens of thousands, possibly hundreds of thousands, became newly displaced during 1995, but many were able to return home shortly afterwards." Amnesty International put the total of internally displaced Tutsi residing in camps in late 1995 at 200,000 in addition to the more than 200,000 Hutu estimated to be internally dispersed around the country "moving from place to place to evade attacks."[19]

A Burundian government official asserted that up to 68 percent of displaced persons living in camps were widows and their children. Although exact estimates are unavailable, the 1994 report by the representative of the secretary-general on internally displaced persons, Francis Deng, noted that among those he visited, "many were women and children, or rather widows and orphans."[20]

Divided Displacement in a Divided Society

Since early 1996, displaced Tutsi have been living in approximately 100 military-protected camps, mostly in northern and central Burundi. Most camps are crowded and have only basic services. Although some uprooted Hutu also live in camps, larger numbers of Hutu have dispersed to marshes, valleys, and woods in a deliberate effort to avoid contact with the Burundian military, whom they fear. Many uprooted Hutu live in the homes of friends and relatives or have built temporary shelters.

Most internally displaced Burundians of both ethnic groups remain near their areas of origin, often only a few hours' walk from their homes. Perhaps 90 percent live within their province of origin, according to a study by the World Food Programme (WFP), and 70 percent live in their home commune. Their proximity to home enables some uprooted Hutu to do small amounts of farming, sometimes on their own land. Few displaced Hutu feel safe enough to spend nights at home, however, pre-ferring instead to seek shelter in the woods.

"The massive use of political violence permits the reorganization of Burundian geography by the creation of islets of homogenous groups . . . for political and military reasons," a Médecins sans Frontières report observed in late 1995.[21] A confidential report by a human rights group in late 1995 concluded that "in the aftermath of the genocide in Rwanda, Burundi's Tutsi minority has come to see safety in a form of *apartheid*. 'Ethnic cleansing' in Burundi has resulted in the balkanization of the country: Tutsi reside in urban areas, primarily the capital, and [in] the camps for internally displaced; Hutu are grouped together in the provinces."

For Tutsi living in camps or confined to towns or administrative centers and unable to travel easily, their predicament is akin to being prisoners in their own country. For uprooted Hutu, their physical displacement is the most visible manifestation of the social, educational, and economic "displacement" they have suffered. Many Hutu who have not been "cleansed" from their homes have nonetheless been "cleansed" from schools, from the military, and from a range of occupations over the years.

Security Concerns of Internally Displaced Burundians

Internally displaced Burundians of both ethnic groups encounter pro-tection concerns, but of significantly different magnitude. Most displaced Tutsi are congregated in large groups under military protection. Al-though some have been victimized by banditry, frontal attacks by Hutu rebels have been infrequent. Some displaced Tutsi have suggested to foreign visitors that soldiers supposedly protecting the camps are forcing some occupants to remain in the camps against their will, infringing on their freedom of movement. According to the 1994 report by Francis Deng, "Many of the displaced Tutsi . . . mentioned that they could not return home because they were afraid of their Hutu neighbors. On the other hand, the point was often made that the Tutsi were being kept in the camps as much by their own quest for protection as for reasons of political manipulation by the Tutsi elites and on occasion the military." The report suggested that some Tutsi displaced persons might be in the camps involuntarily, "to give the Tutsi [leaders] an alibi and a leverage in the political negotiations."[22] Other UN officials in Burundi expressed similar opinions. There was no way to ascertain, however, how many occupants would depart the camps if allowed. Burundian government officials publicly denied the charges. They insisted that displaced persons could return home when they wished and that the government had been formulating a "reinstallation" program.

Most displaced Hutu, in contrast, live in smaller groupings in more remote areas without armed protection. They have reason to fear both the military and Hutu rebels, who often kill indiscriminately. With the breakdown in government administration, uprooted Hutu dispersed in the countryside are vulnerable to banditry as well. The military assumes that Hutu civilians give assistance to Hutu rebels in the current conflict. This makes all Hutu civilians potential targets in the military's thinking. Many Hutu, meanwhile, regard the heavily guarded camps for displaced Tutsi as bases for Tutsi civilian militia, or as safe zones intended to keep Tutsi out of the line of fire while soldiers slaughter the rural Hutu population.

These attitudes of suspicion toward Burundi's uprooted populations have been reinforced by the fact that these accusations contain kernels of truth—some displaced Hutu have taken up arms and committed abuses, some Hutu are sympathetic to the rebels, and some displaced Tutsi have mounted attacks from their camps.

In mid-1996 the international community was poorly positioned to improve security for internally displaced Burundians, as suggested by UN Secretary-General Boutros-Ghali's statement that "the UN has limited capacity to observe what is happening on the ground."[23] A proposal in early 1996 by Burundi's President Ntibantunganya would transfer law enforcement responsibilities from the army to a national police force and gendarmerie. Its purpose would be to improve protection of displaced populations by eliminating the heavy-handed tactics of the army. Others doubt that the proposal would produce better protection.

Security Concerns of Humanitarian Aid Operations

"The deteriorating security situation is severely restricting the ability of international aid groups to deliver assistance to the needy displaced and dispersed [populations] in Burundi," a report by Médecins sans Frontières declared in late 1995. The agency noted that escalating violence against relief workers included attacks on clearly marked relief vehicles, hijackings of relief vehicles, ambushes, robberies, and threats made against specific relief workers.

Eleven foreign employees of international agencies were killed in a seventeen-month period through the end of 1995. During ten months of 1995, some twenty-seven threats and acts of aggression—including murder, kidnapping, and armed robbery—occurred against humanitarian agencies working in Burundi, according to the MSF report.[24] Three Italian priests were murdered in September 1995. In an ambush on a Red Cross convoy in November 1995, one worker was killed and six were wounded. In December 1995, grenade attacks on the offices of international relief agencies in Gitega, in central Burundi, forced relief agencies to withdraw foreign staff from that area. Three agencies temporarily evacuated all foreign personnel. In the northern province of Ngozi, grenade attacks against the offices and homes of international agencies forced the evacuation of seventy-eight foreign staff working there in December 1995. Most humanitarian operations were temporarily suspended nationwide in late 1995 and early 1996 because of threats against relief groups.

The temporary aid suspension did not alleviate the insecurity. Ten attacks against foreigners occurred during a single week in April 1996. In June 1996, three expatriate relief workers of the International Committee of the Red Cross (ICRC) were ambushed and killed north of Bujumbura, prompting a withdrawal of all ICRC foreign staff.

"Staff of relief agencies are advised to exercise extreme caution and to undertake only the most essential travel" throughout the country, the United Nations warned in mid-1996.[25] The UN secretary-general and the UN Department of Humanitarian Affairs (DHA) assessed the feasibility of deploying special UN guards in Burundi to protect humanitarian operations. Many relief workers in Burundi opposed the plan and warned that armed guards would inadvertently attract attacks and place relief workers in greater danger. The UN team concluded that "in the current context of violence and instability, United Nations guards would not be able to guarantee the security of humanitarian personnel in Burundi; indeed, in the present environment, the guards could themselves become potential targets for extremist groups, thus intensifying the security problems already faced by the international humanitarian effort."[26]

Some relief agencies charged that the military and Tutsi militia were perpetrating the attacks to punish aid groups for a perceived bias in favor of the Hutu population. The country's radicalized climate appeared to lead many extremists on both sides to reject the notion of impartial aid.

"Serious consequences can befall organizations whose neutrality is mis-interpreted by groups within Burundi," USAID observed.[27] Widespread rumors among Tutsi alleged that relief agencies were supplying arms and funds to Hutu militias.

The violence against relief workers has seriously disrupted the delivery of humanitarian assistance. Hard-hit areas of northwest Burundi became virtually inaccessible, preventing relief programs or even accurate needs assessments. By mid-1996, many relief groups had withdrawn their per-sonnel from the countryside to Bujumbura, and some had shut down all operations. The international community was losing its ability to monitor the violence and population displacement in much of the country.

Food, Health, and Other Needs

Burundi is an agricultural nation. Perhaps 95 percent of the Burundian population normally engages in at least a small amount of farming, and massive population displacements have severely disrupted the country's agricultural production for long periods. The violence and displacement in October 1993 caused at least a 20 percent drop in crop production, according to one study.[28] In Burundi's subsistence economy, crop losses of that magnitude can translate rapidly into food shortages. The UN reported in 1994 that food shortages were most severe in Burundi's prov-inces most afflicted with insecurity and looting. Cattle rustling and theft of seeds and foodstuffs were reported, as refugees, returnees, the dis-placed, and the local population competed for limited available food supplies.

UN and private relief experts wrestled to ascertain Burundi's real food needs throughout the 1994–96 period. It has been a controversial and contentious topic. In mid-1994, WFP temporarily provided food to some 600,000 beneficiaries, the vast majority of whom were presumed to be displaced. WFP experienced a major, regionwide shortage of food aid in 1995. Representatives of WFP, donor governments, and some private relief groups believed that many food beneficiaries in Burundi did not need assistance, and that Burundi's food emergency no longer existed. In his November 1994 report on Burundi, Francis Deng concluded that "food availability did not seem to be a serious problem." He added that "what seemed to be lacking most in the camps of the displaced was basic organization," in contrast to the situation in camps for refugees, which were organized and supervised by UNHCR.[29]

By early 1995 the number of food beneficiaries had been cut to about 500,000, mostly internally displaced. By May 1995, WFP was assisting only about 217,000 persons, including 116,000 displaced Tutsi and 111,000 uprooted Hutu. It is unlikely that all displaced Burundians received food aid, however, and perhaps not all WFP beneficiaries were actually displaced.

In April 1995, President Ntibantunganya issued an appeal for food aid that listed 458,000 internally displaced persons, including 296,000 displaced Tutsi living in camps and 162,000 Hutu dispersed in the countryside. The government's numbers were not viewed as reliable, however, and WFP continued to pare its beneficiary rolls. In mid-1995, in response to new upheavals, WFP slightly increased its assistance rolls to about 340,000 persons who were believed to be uprooted.

A food needs assessment team traveled to Burundi in May and June 1995, representing WFP, USAID, the European Union, and Burundian officials. It concluded that "the majority of the affected population in camps have access to land and, in some provinces, 85 percent of the displaced are farming. Harvest forecasts . . . are excellent, significantly reducing the requirement for emergency assistance. Most camps have well-stocked local markets on site, and additional markets within one kilometer of the camps."[30] The assessment team recorded malnutrition levels of about 2 percent among infants, less than half the infant malnutrition rate measured before the 1993 crisis.

By the end of 1995, WFP was assisting about 120,000 persons, mostly in camps for the displaced. The agency planned to feed only 80,000 of the most vulnerable persons in 1996. The steady reductions throughout 1995 were intended to limit the number of fraudulent beneficiaries, bolster Burundi's farming sector, discourage dependency, and encourage displaced persons to return to safe home areas.

Burundi's volatile security situation continued to alter assessments, however. In November 1995, USAID predicted that food aid needs would increase, particularly in the northwest. "Large areas are void of inhabitants," USAID reported. "Few people are working in the fields at a time when the cotton and cassava are ready to harvest."[31] UN officials agreed that food need assessments could only be considered temporary because of Burundi's spiraling violence and warned that increasingly organized rebel Hutu groups would probably widen the conflict and exacerbate the displacement crisis. Relief workers had stockpiled relief food and made other contingency plans, UN Secretary-General Boutros-Ghali announced in mid-1996.

The unpredictable pattern of violence was only one factor complicating food evaluations, however. Relief officials often disagreed over the needs of displaced Tutsi and Hutu populations. Some Burundian officials and international aid workers argued that displaced Tutsi living in camps needed greater food aid because access to farm land and markets was made difficult by dangerous roads, whereas Hutu displaced throughout the countryside could often farm and support themselves. Other relief and human rights workers analyzed needs differently. They pointed out that the crops of many displaced Hutu had been stolen or burned by Hutu rebels and that some displaced farmers had been chased away again before they could harvest on borrowed land.

Another major factor complicating food relief in Burundi is the extent to which food aid has been politicized in the country's ethnically polarized environment. "It is important to note that international humanitarian aid issues are being exploited by political parties for political ends," Francis Deng reported in late 1994. "Reductions in food aid to displaced persons, or reluctance on the part of international agencies to become involved with assistance to them, is seen through ethnic lenses and criticized. International agencies find themselves struggling to avoid becoming pawns in the political game. . . . They risk allowing the situation to distort their assessment of humanitarian needs." [32]

Some relief officials charged that many internally displaced Hutu were being given assistance because displaced Tutsi were receiving it—an artificial and expensive equilibrium. In other areas, according to critics, the Tutsi displaced were given free food because it was politically difficult to deny them aid while providing it to Hutu refugees from Rwanda living nearby in northern Burundi. Relief officials widely blamed displaced Tutsi in the north for attacking the camps of Rwandan refugees to steal large quantities of food aid intended for the refugees.

The reality was that food distributions in Burundi were linked to numerous criteria besides objective nutritional needs. Food handouts were calibrated to try to exhibit the ethnic neutrality of relief agencies, to dampen violence aggravated by hungry stomachs, and to maintain working relationships with Burundi's military and political leaders who had a vested political and economic interest in food distributions to their constituencies. It was general knowledge in Bujumbura that the military profited from the inflated food distribution lists.

"Government officials say that food aid to the displaced and dispersed is needed to promote peace and stability," a UN official in Burundi said.

"That is a thinly veiled threat that if the displaced do not receive free food, the country will plunge into chaos. In speeches on the radio, Tutsi government officials have claimed that the international community is starving the displaced."

The ongoing politicization of humanitarian aid, as a result of ethnic divisions and endemic violence, rendered accurate assessment of food needs for the internally displaced impossible. Francis Deng noted that "some of the most serious problems the displaced and dispersed populations generally face are in the health domain, largely because of the disruption of health services" as a result of the conflict.[33]

The gradual curtailment of rural health assistance programs during early 1996 because of insecurity hampered already difficult efforts to monitor the health needs of uprooted Burundians. In 1994 the country's health system operated at 50 percent of normal capacity as a result of the destruction of rural health clinics and the loss of medical stocks and local medical personnel who had to flee. Displaced Hutu are believed to have suffered "great loss of life" because health care was unavailable to them in the months after the October 1993 violence, one UN study suggested. The country's ongoing conflict since 1994 likely has reduced medical capacity still further. In 1995 medical facilities in Bujumbura were overcrowded and ill-equipped to treat serious injuries suffered in the violence.

Nutritional surveys in 1995 found no seriously widespread nutritional problems, though experts warned that the situation could change rapidly in 1996 as the conflict intensified and food aid distributions remained at reduced levels. Malaria, diarrhea, dysentery, and respiratory infections were reported among children, though not at epidemic levels. Health workers warned that rates of HIV infection and other sexually transmitted diseases—already prevalent among urban Burundians—might increase dramatically in rural areas, especially if health services remained inadequate or unavailable.

Some 14,000 unaccompanied children had been identified by early 1995. More than 11,000 were placed with extended families or in foster care by the end of 1995.

Burundian officials have proposed a new housing program for the displaced population. They argue that uprooted families need access to land in order to become self-sufficient, and they need more adequate housing as the conflict rages on with no end in sight. Many camps containing uprooted Tutsi are particularly crowded, filled with makeshift shacks that often lack even plastic sheeting. Critics of the government housing plan contend, however, that the establishment of new displacement sites with improved housing and farm land might have the effect of creating a permanent separation of Hutu and Tutsi populations.

One foreign relief worker in Burundi countered that "international aid can play an important role in helping stabilize the situation in Burundi. Donor governments are being too 'technical' in their assessment of needs. They need to be sensitive to the fact that the situation is more complex than just weighing up facts and figures." Francis Deng cautioned that "while it is often true that the Tutsi displaced may be less needy in terms of food and security . . . it cannot be excluded that in certain cases, there will be serious and real problems." In his recommendations to the UN secretary-general, Deng stated that "since reductions in emergency aid can have serious political repercussions, they have to be avoided." [34]

International Response

The international response to Burundi's political and humanitarian crisis has been dogged, if not always consistent and coordinated. The World Health Organization and UNICEF appealed to international donors for a combined $6.3 million to support health care and nutrition monitoring programs in Burundi during 1996. UNICEF requested $2.1 million for water and sanitation projects. In total, UN humanitarian agencies appealed for $50.9 million to fund food assistance, emergency relief, health care and nutrition, water and sanitation, agriculture, education, human rights, and other programs during 1996. Overall levels of international aid to Burundi by 1996 were half of the levels attained in 1992, the year before violence erupted and made most long-term development programs impractical. Major donors in 1995–96 included the United States, the European Union, France, Belgium, and China.

Nine UN agencies involved in relief, development, and human rights were operating in Burundi in 1995–96, along with at least a dozen private U.S.-based relief organizations and a number of private European relief agencies. UN agencies provided food deliveries to displaced populations, monitored nutrition levels, developed water supply systems, distributed agricultural tools, rehabilitated health structures, and supported the national health system, the control of epidemics, and AIDS prevention. UN organizations conducted programs in basic education, peace education, support to disadvantaged children, replenishment of herds, and human rights monitoring and provided direct financial support to government ministries engaged in managing humanitarian programs. Food-for-work programs and income generation projects were planned for 1996.

Private relief agencies provided an equally wide range of support for displaced Burundians and the general population: food deliveries, water systems, medical services, school reconstruction, civic education, and transmission of objective news on radio. One of the largest agencies, ICRC, distributed food, water, seeds, and agricultural tools, constructed latrines, and helped trace lost family members. The U.S.-based Catholic Relief Services distributed food, pots, blankets, and soap to internally displaced populations and conducted reconciliation workshops. Médecins sans Frontières provided medical personnel for surgeries, maternity care, and internal medicine and operated several hospitals and mobile health clinics.

UN and private relief agencies tried to expand development programs in returnee areas; they constructed shelters and installed water systems, among other things, to encourage displaced persons to return home. In anticipation of worsening humanitarian conditions, the relief community in Burundi stockpiled cars, emergency response personnel, and satellite communications equipment.

Despite the extensive planning and programming, relief workers themselves pointed out several gaps in coverage in mid-1996. Widespread insecurity was forcing the curtailment of established programs in virtually all sectors. Greater financial assistance from donors was urgently needed to fund air deliveries of food to rural areas that had suddenly become inaccessible by road because of the violence. Poor communication existed between the relief community and Burundian authorities, creating coordination problems and a lack of strategic planning.

The world's political response to Burundi was a picture of frantic activity and not a significant success as of mid-1996. Several prominent world statesmen, including former U.S. president Jimmy Carter and former Tanzanian president Julius Nyerere, attempted to mediate conflicts in the region, with little to show for their efforts. Nyerere in particular focused his efforts on Burundi, with widespread moral support from the diplomatic community. UN Secretary-General Boutros-Ghali urged the UN Security Council to approve the establishment of a contingency intervention force in case the conflict in Burundi deteriorated further. The Security Council refused.

The United States quietly declared in mid-1996 that "much, but not all, of the ethnic violence in Burundi since 1993 constituted genocide," but American officials indicated that their interpretation of the 1948 Convention on the Prevention of Genocide did not oblige the United States to take decisive action against genocide.[35] An impressive flow of high-level American officials visited Burundi in late 1995 and early 1996, and U.S. President Bill Clinton demonstrated his concern by appointing a special presidential envoy to Burundi in mid-1996. The UN secretary-general also had a special UN envoy assigned to Burundi, based full-time in Bujumbura. Although thirty-five UN human rights monitors were authorized to begin operation in Burundi, only four had arrived by mid-1996. The Organization of African Unity (OAU) increased the number of its military observers to sixty, but the OAU program remained ineffective in curbing most human rights excesses by the Burundian military. An International Commission of Inquiry investigating the 1993 coup and massacres was short of money and staff, causing delays in its final report.

Delays in the international community's response were only part of the problem. Proposed solutions to stop the violence, put forth at the international level, were often blocked by a lack of political will at the local level. As long as the Burundian military and Tutsi politicians remain opposed to a multinational force, the UN Security Council is unlikely to approve one. However, it remains unclear what a peacekeeping force could accomplish in a context where there is no clear front line and no peace talks between parties to the conflict. In addition, Francis Deng noted in his November 1994 mission that "questions were raised . . . about the deployment of an extensive monitoring mission at this time. Some felt that large numbers of international 'witnesses' would be received with hostility and could jeopardize the presence of international agencies in the country."[36]

Disparities in Treatment

Three distinct population groups are uprooted in Burundi, and it is inevitable that there have been disparities in the assistance and protection they have received. The three uprooted populations are internally displaced Tutsi, internally displaced Hutu, and Rwandan Hutu refugees living in camps in northern Burundi. In some cases, the disparities in their treatment are justified by their different needs. In some cases, the disparities appear to be unfair but excusable, the result of logistical constraints. In other cases, particularly in the area of protection, the inequalities are clearly wrong. The overall differences in the treatment of the groups—whether fair or not—have aggravated tensions and contributed to violence.

As discussed throughout this case study, internally displaced Tutsi living in designated camps receive protection from the Burundi military. Internally displaced Hutu receive little or no security from government security forces and regard the military as a predator seeking to kill them rather than as a protector seeking to save them. This disparity stands as a shameful indictment of the Burundian military and its failure to serve the interests of a large portion of the citizenry it supposedly exists to defend.

There is a real or imagined disparity in humanitarian aid to displaced Tutsi and Hutu, as discussed in the food needs section of this chapter. Uprooted Tutsi live in camps that are more accessible to assistance, though assistance to them is often minimal. Displaced Hutu who are dispersed throughout the countryside are much more difficult to reach with aid. Aid agencies providing assistance to displaced Hutu have been targeted for violence by Tutsi groups that perceive an aid disparity in favor of the Hutu population. Food distribution data suggest that during 1994 and part of 1995 international assistance agencies in fact maintained roughly equal food distributions to the two ethnic groups, contrary to some local perceptions.

Real or perceived disparities also exist in the treatment of Rwandan Hutu refugees and internally displaced Burundian Tutsi. Some 160,000 Rwandan Hutu refugees fled to Burundi in 1994, where they settled into several camps under the care and protection of UNHCR. The lack of a UN organization similarly mandated to serve the needs of displaced Burundian Tutsi created an immediate disparity.

The presence of the Rwandan refugees exacerbated local tensions. Many Burundian Tutsi resented the international aid going to Rwandan Hutu refugees, whom they associated with the 1994 massacre of Tutsi in Rwanda. When WFP began to reduce aid to uprooted Burundians, displaced Tutsi and Tutsi government officials reacted angrily, often violently. Warehouses where food for the refugees was stored were attacked and robbed, and trucks transporting food to the refugee camps were ambushed. Animosity toward the refugees mounted, even though relief workers at times in 1994 willingly diverted refugee relief supplies to meet the dire needs of internally displaced Burundians. "One cannot ignore the important role food aid has played in maintaining a fragile security in the provinces where there are internally displaced [Tutsi] and [Hutu] refugees," a USAID report warned. "The withdrawal of aid to the internally displaced while refugees continue to receive . . . rations, will inflame ethnic tensions."[37]

The warning by USAID was accurate. In June 1994 it was reported that some 100 Rwandan Hutu refugees were killed while Burundian soldiers stood by. In July 1994, forty-one Rwandan refugees were murdered in a chapel. In October 1994, fifty-four Rwandan Hutu refugees—including women and children—were machine-gunned by assailants. Armed assailants killed twelve Rwandan Hutu refugees and wounded twenty-two others in one camp in March 1995. Some 40,000 Rwandan refugees fled the camps. In May 1995 armed men hijacked eighteen WFP trucks transporting food to the refugee camps; Burundian soldiers present at the scene did not intervene to stop the hijacking. Most food on the trucks was allegedly diverted to camps for internally displaced Tutsi. In June 1995 as many as 10,000 refugees again fled the camps in response to threats from Burundian Tutsi.

In early 1996 thousands of refugees left Burundi and returned to Rwanda under coercion by Burundian authorities. UNHCR lodged formal protests with Burundian officials over numerous instances of *refoulement*. Significant numbers of Rwandan refugees in Burundi fled to Tanzania. By mid-1996 about 80,000 Rwandan refugees officially remained in Burundi.

Prospects for Return Home of Internally Displaced

Often lost amid the gloom surrounding events in Burundi is the fact that many tens of thousands of internally displaced Burundians returned to their homes during the 1994–96 period. Some were forced to flee yet again, and those who remain at home often live in dangerous circumstances. But Burundi is a densely populated country, and rural Burundians in particular feel a strong pull to the land of their families.

History offers contradictory lessons about whether currently displaced Burundians can be expected to return home. When some 60,000 Burundian Hutu fled to neighboring countries because of violence in 1988, many observers expected them to remain in asylum for a year or so before risking a return home. Within six months, however, 98 percent of them had gone home, leaving only 1,000 in exile. In 1993 thousands of Hutu refugees returned immediately before and after the election of President Ndadaye—so many and so quickly that their return inadvertently contributed to instability. There is historical precedent, then, for a quick return of displaced Burundians.

History also suggests, however, that many uprooted Hutu and Tutsi will not return to their original homes. As discussed in an earlier section of this chapter, much of the population displacement created by the 1972 massacres became locked in place, profoundly changing settlement patterns in Burundi. Many Hutu residents of Bujumbura left the city permanently. Many Tutsi moved into the capital permanently. Similarly, the displacement of 1993–96 seems to have produced more "urbanization" of the Tutsi population, drawing uprooted Tutsi off their farms and into towns and administrative centers.

The opportunity for large-scale return appears grim in mid-1996, as violence worsens. If and when the conflict subsides, however, there are four reasons to expect most uprooted Burundians to find their way back home rapidly. First, each family's emotional tie to its ancestral land presumably remains as strong now as previously. Second, life for most displaced Hutu and Tutsi is unpleasant. Tutsi live trapped in small enclaves, while many Hutu live with minimal services. Third, many displaced Hutu already live within easy walking distance of their own land. Fourth, in a densely settled country such as Burundi, permanently vacated land is scarce. Families trying to settle in a new area have limited options.

Conversely, there are reasons why many uprooted Burundians may never return home, or at least no time soon. First, uprooted Tutsi might conclude that their rural home can never again ensure their safety. More Tutsi perished in the 1993 killings than in any previous massacre in Burundi, and Tutsi families might be convinced that peace is merely a calm before the next inevitable storm of violence. Second, even if widespread violence can be avoided in the future, individual acts of revenge are likely. Third, Tutsi political and military leaders might continue to have political or economic reasons to discourage displaced Tutsi from leaving camps. Fourth, the military as currently constituted will complicate any return home. The presence of the army in returnee areas might attract Tutsi returnees, but it would likely deter the return of many Hutu. The army is seen as a protector by Tutsi, and as a predator by Hutu. Fifth, many educated Hutu well remember that Hutu elite historically are the first targets of the army. Tutsi already widely suspect that educated Hutu, being influential members of their own communities, support the Hutu rebels and militias. Sixth, the Burundian judiciary remains under Tutsi control, and thousands of Hutu remain in jail. Some have been executed extrajudicially, and others have disappeared in custody, according to Amnesty International. Special local commissions established to investigate the 1993 massacres largely exonerated Tutsi suspects and detained only Hutu individuals. Seventh, government plans to give uprooted families houses and new land may, if implemented, persuade displaced persons to settle permanently where they are. Eighth, the home regions of many Hutu were "ethnically cleansed" not only geographically but also occupationally and educationally. Even if their geographic cleansing ends, many educated Hutu may have no compelling reason to return to their former homes.

Recommendations for Burundi

The causes of Burundi's violence run deep into the politics and psychology of the country and its people. Even in periods of relative peace, the reality of having military and political power concentrated in the hands of Burundi's demographic minority plants the seeds for the next eruption of violence and displacement. The stratified power relationships in Burundi must change if the country is to find a path that is different from its historical path of conflict. Endemic population displacement is a serious problem in Burundi, but it cannot be resolved permanently unless Burundi society changes the way it governs itself, the way it maintains order, and the way it provides or blocks opportunity for its individual members.

The government and military of Burundi should negotiate directly with rebel leaders. Many rebels are motivated primarily by ethnic hate or have been influenced by the extremist ideology of Rwandan Hutu leaders who live in exile. It is possible, however, that some rebels and their more moderate supporters are motivated by democratic principles and valid grievances about the virtual annulment of Burundi's democratic 1993 election. Agreements reached by fair negotiation should be adhered to by the military, as well as by rebel militia.

Negotiations should seek a cease-fire in the current civil war and scrupulous recognition of the neutrality of international relief agencies. Medium-term negotiations should seek reforms in the local judicial investigations of the 1993 massacres, agreement to accept and protect international human rights observers in all communes, and moderation of extreme views in the mass media; negotiations should also determine how to bring to justice military officers responsible for the 1993 coup attempt. Ultimately, negotiators should seek at least a partial restoration of the democratic reforms forfeited since 1993, greater ethnic integration at all levels of the military, and fundamental reforms in Burundi's one-sided judicial system. Democratic reforms should include clear and effective mechanisms for protection of minorities within the principle of broadly representative government.

Outside the framework of negotiations, the current government of Burundi should exert control over small, extremist Tutsi political groups and youth groups. The government should pursue its plan to shift responsibility for internal law and order from the military to a multiethnic *gendarmerie* or a new, multiethnic national police force. Police or *gendarmes* should receive specialized training in human rights and the rule of law, and explicit duties and training regarding protection of all civilians, including minorities. The government and military should disarm Tutsi militia unilaterally and prosecute individuals complicit in attacks against Burundian civilians and international relief workers. Authorities should pledge to adhere to findings and recommendations from the International Commission of Inquiry investigation into the 1993 violence.

Officials should enforce policies of ethnic integration and tolerance in higher education and other sectors. The Uprona and Frodebu political parties should reinvigorate their previous efforts to be broadly multiethnic. Authorities should clarify laws relating to land tenure and property rights to implement fair and speedy adjudication procedures. The government should strengthen the property and inheritance rights of women so that displaced widows and single mothers have homes to which they can return with legal assurances.

Burundi's Hutu rebels should publicly renounce the racist, extremist ideology of the Rwandan Hutu regime exiled in Zaire, with whom the Burundi rebels have ties. Rebel leaders should punish rebel atrocities committed against civilians and international relief workers. The rebels should moderate their own radio broadcasts into Burundi to convey a message of ethnic reconciliation and democratic power-sharing.

All these recommendations are geared toward creating a climate of security, accountability, and mutual respect. Doing so will not be an easy task, and agreements will be subject to sabotage from extremists on all sides. Even moderates in both ethnic groups feel victimized, mistrustful, and physically vulnerable. The international community will have to remain deeply involved in breaking the cycle of violence and nudging along the process of accountability and reform.

Recommendations to the International Community

The international community should facilitate and provide proper mediation to negotiations. Western governments should be prepared to meet publicly with Hutu rebel leaders who have renounced extremist ethnic views and should insist that such leaders be included in negotiations. A standby military contingency force long advocated by former UN Secretary-General Boutros-Ghali should be prepared. Major nations should support the findings and recommendations of the International Commission of Inquiry's investigation into the events of 1993. Legal assistance should be provided to Burundi to help revise the constitution in ways that would ensure minority protections within an open democratic system.

The UN and OAU should provide a large and fully funded human rights monitoring program in Burundi. The OAU should invigorate its sixty-person military observer program there. The international community should offer training in Burundi to new personnel in a reformed judicial process, training to a new or expanded Burundian police force, and media training on standards and responsibility. Education assistance and exchange programs should be contingent on reforms in Burundi's education system.

International humanitarian assistance cannot solve Burundi's political and social problems, but assistance programs must remain one ingredient. Donor countries should place priority on funding programs that improve the physical security of uprooted Burundians and the general population. UNHCR should expand its mandate in Burundi to accept more responsibility for protecting internally displaced Burundians. Food distributions should remain tightly targeted so that populations are not kept uprooted unnecessarily. Aid programs such as shelter construction should carefully guard against validating and entrenching the "ethnic cleansing" that has occurred in Burundi.

Relief agencies unable to achieve proper security for their operations, or unable to properly monitor the final beneficiaries of their assistance, should be prepared to suspend operations in Burundi.

No easy solutions exist for Burundi's spiral of misery. The international community will have to demonstrate a serious and sustained commitment to peace and justice in Burundi in order to compel the fundamental changes that are needed.

Conclusions

This case study points out that Burundi faces a wide array of displacement issues that are pertinent worldwide. Although many are discussed throughout this chapter, several themes warrant final examination because they can lead to improved understanding of the dynamics surrounding internal displacement.

"Ethnic Cleansing": A Special Kind of Internal Displacement

In Burundi, Bosnia, Zaire, and elsewhere, "ethnic cleansing" rose to the level of standard policy. Although it seems obvious, it must be said explicitly: "ethnic cleansing" is a different kind of displacement. It is not accidental displacement as an inadvertent by-product of conflict. It is not meant to be a temporary displacement that allows the displaced to return home when the violence stops. It is displacement that is deliberate and highly targeted, meant to be permanent long after the violence ends. "Ethnic cleansing" is a policy of human eradication, and as such it imposes special trauma on the targeted population. "Ethnic cleansing" is millimeters away from genocide.

In most cases of internal displacement, one goal of conflict resolution is to enable displaced people to return home. But after an "ethnic cleansing," can targeted populations ever return? Would they want to? Those are important questions that carry important implications in our thinking about durable solutions and in our attempts to classify different types of internal displacement.

Burundi, unfortunately, may prove to be an instructive case study. Burundi's internally displaced populations are not all victims of "ethnic cleansing"—many are victims of generalized conflict. It remains to be seen whether those displaced by cleansing, in contrast to those displaced inadvertently, will become more radical politically and less able or willing to go home again.

The Internally Displaced without Camps

The experience in Burundi is evidence that it is a struggle for humanitarian relief agencies to assess and address the needs of internally displaced populations that are dispersed rather than living in identifiable camps. The task becomes even more difficult when relief workers must reach uprooted and dispersed populations while coping with armed conflict. The needs of uprooted persons living in camps are much easier to assess.

Conventional wisdom suggests that internally displaced persons who live on their own, outside of camps, usually have access to land and can engage in farming to make themselves self-sufficient. This is largely true in Burundi, but not uniformly so. Internally displaced persons who do not live in secure camps encounter special protection problems in a conflict such as Burundi's. Relief officials should be careful not to overestimate the ability of displaced people to farm amid insecurity. Those living in a noncamp environment are vulnerable to combatants and bandits and may lack seeds or tools. In Burundi, assessments of food needs vary tremendously, in part because the self-sufficiency of displaced Hutu dispersed in the countryside itself varies from month to month.

The Politics behind Ethnic Conflict and Displacement

Aid to internally displaced Burundians, especially food aid, is highly politicized. In Burundi, as elsewhere, politicians and combatants are increasingly adept at creating new displacement or prolonging existing displacement in order to score political points or attract aid that can be diverted from intended beneficiaries.

In Burundi and in other humanitarian emergencies, many political and military leaders are prepared to exploit their own followers, their own ethnic group, in order to achieve political goals. That is one reason why it is important for the world to look beyond the simplistic label "ethnic conflict" to see the political agendas that drive a specific conflict.

Population Displacement as a Cause of Conflict

An important lesson in Burundi, applicable elsewhere, is that internal displacement is not only a *result* of conflict; it can also be a *cause* of new layers of conflict. In Burundi the military and rebels regard internally displaced persons of the other ethnic group as combatants and conspirators, rather than as harmless bystanders shunted to the side of conflict. The act of fleeing to safety is regarded not as an innocent act of self-preservation but as a provocation that must be answered. Although the overwhelming majority of internally displaced Burundians are not participants in the violence, it must be acknowledged that some displaced Burundians *have* mounted armed attacks, and camps for internally displaced persons *have* been used as militia bases.

The experience of being uprooted can radicalize populations as well as traumatize them. Long after their physical displacement ends, a powerful political and social alienation may remain.

Gap in UN Accountability to Internally Displaced Persons

Currently no specific UN agency is mandated to assist and protect internally displaced persons in a way that is comparable to UNHCR's mandate to assist and protect refugees. This gap in the UN system caused some Burundians to doubt the neutrality of UNHCR and the United Nations and put UNHCR in a potentially dangerous position. Because UNHCR provided aid to Rwandan Hutu refugees in Burundi, internally displaced Burundian Tutsi expected similar attention to their needs. When they did not receive it, they attributed it to UN favoritism toward Hutu. Ad hoc efforts by UNHCR to steer relief to displaced Tutsi did not restore full trust.

The time has come to designate a new or existing UN agency to address the needs of internally displaced populations. Advocates of this proposal argue that it would result in a fairer, faster, and more effective humanitarian response. Judging by the Burundi experience, another argument in its favor is that it would bolster the UN's appearance of neutrality and could enhance the UN system's credibility on the ground.

Notes

1. Department of Humanitarian Affairs, "Burundi: Regroupement," memorandum, United Nations, February 27, 1997, para. 4.

2. Francis M. Deng, *Profiles in Displacement: Burundi*, Report of the Representative of the Secretary-General on Internally Displaced Persons, Commission on Human Rights, E/CN.4/1995/50/Add.2 (United Nations, November 28, 1994), para. 9 (hereafter Deng report).

3. Physicians for Human Rights, "Physicians Document Climate of Terror in Burundi; Urge Immediate International Attention," press release, August 10, 1994.

4. Commission on Human Rights, *Initial Report on the Human Rights Situation in Burundi*, Submitted by the Special Rapporteur, Mr. Paulo Sérgio Pinheiro, E/CN.4/1996/16 (United Nations, November 14, 1995), para. 118.

5. Department of State, *Country Reports on Human Rights Practices for 1996* (Burundi report), Washington, D.C., 1997.

6. See Hiram A. Ruiz, "Burundi's Uprooted People: Caught in the Spiral of Violence," U.S. Committee for Refugees, Washington, D.C., August 1995.

7. Security Council, *Report of the Secretary-General on the Situation in Burundi*, S/1996/335 (United Nations, May 3, 1996), para. 27.

8. Commission on Human Rights, E/CN.4/1996/16, para. 110.

9. For historical background see both René LeMarchand, *Rwanda and Burundi* (London: Praeger, 1970); and René LeMarchand and David Martin, *Selective Genocide in Burundi* (London: Minority Rights Group, 1974).

10. Human Rights Watch and others, "Commission internationale d'enquête sur les violations des droits de l'homme au Burundi depuis le 21 octobre 1993. Rapport final," July 1994, p. 7.

11. National Democratic Institute for International Affairs, "International Observer Delegation Post-Election Statement," Washington, D.C., June 1, 1993.

12. Human Rights Watch and others, "Commission internationale d'enquete," p. 177.

13. Filip Reyntjens, *Burundi: Breaking the Cycle of Violence*, (London: Minority Rights Group, 1995), p. 17.

14. Commission on Human Rights, E/CN.4/1996/16, paras. 16 and 87.

15. Security Council, S/1996/335, para. 43.

16. Interview, May 1995.

17. See Ruiz, "Burundi's Uprooted People."

18. Security Council, S/1996/335, para. 22.

19. Amnesty International, "Rwanda and Burundi, The Return Home: Myths and Realities," New York, February 20, 1996, pp. 30–31.

20. Deng report, para. 53.

21. Médecins sans Frontières, "Burundi: Breaking the Silence," New York, December 11, 1995, p. 2.

22. Deng report, para. 70.

23. Security Council, S/1996/335, para. 43.

24. Médecins sans Frontières, "Burundi: Breaking the Silence," pp. 9–13.

25. Security Council, S/1996/335, para. 23.

26. Security Council, *Report of the Secretary-General on the Situation in Burundi*, S/1996/116 (United Nations, February 15, 1996), para. 18.

27. United States Agency for International Development, Office of Foreign Disaster Assistance, "Burundi Situation Report #2 FY 1996," Washington, D.C., March 12, 1996, p. 2.

28. World Food Programme, "Special Alert No. 248, FAO/WFP Crop and Food Supply Assessment Mission to Burundi," United Nations, April 1994, p. 1.

29. Deng report, paras. 58–59.

30. United States Agency for International Development, Office of Foreign Disaster Assistance, "Burundi Situation Report #2 FY 1995," Washington, D.C., June 30, 1995, p. 4.

31. United States Agency for International Development, Office of Foreign Disaster Assistance, "Burundi Situation Report #1 FY 1996," Washington, D.C., November 29, 1995, p. 3.

32. Deng report, para. 114.

33. Ibid., para. 75.

34. Ibid., paras. 113–14.

35. For statement about genocide, see Department of State, *Country Reports on Human Rights Practices for 1996.*

36. Deng report, para. 110.

37. U.S. Agency for International Development, Office of Foreign Disaster Assistance, final report, "Burundi: A Humanitarian Overview," Washington, D.C., March 16, 1995, p. 9.

CHAPTER THREE

Rwanda's Internally Displaced: A Conundrum within a Conundrum

Larry Minear and Randolph C. Kent

THE HUMANITARIAN CHALLENGE of Rwanda's internally displaced population represented a conundrum within a conundrum. The problem of internal displacement was a conundrum in its own right, involving issues of morality and international politics on the one hand and operational and resource allocation matters on the other. Yet the IDP conundrum was part of a larger and even more intractable set of problems. These included government-sponsored genocide and its aftermath, the obligation and capacity of the international community to assist traumatized societies, and the inadequacy of humanitarian institutions and response mechanisms.

Regarding the genocide, the international community failed from the outset to identify what was taking place, responding to a fundamental crime against humanity as if it were simply a civil war between rival ethnic groups. Having ignored the early signs of the Rwandan government's plans and having moved slowly to provide assistance and protection during the early months of the genocide, the international community—especially members of the UN Security Council—shares responsibility for the slaughter of between 500,000 and 1 million people.

Yet the international community was hardly more successful in resolving the conundrum of the internally displaced. Distinctions made between internally displaced persons (IDPs) and refugees and among relief, recovery,

57

Republic of Rwanda

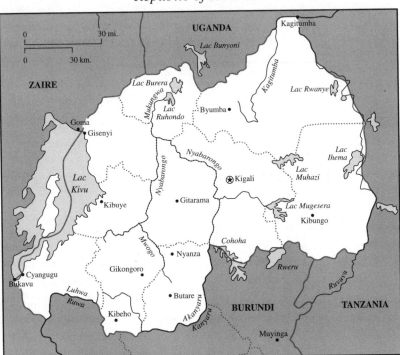

58

and development assistance hobbled efforts. Disproportionate attention and assistance to refugees at the expense of IDPs complicated the task of the new Rwandan authorities to reestablish a viable post-genocide polity and society. The focus on refugees concealed the extent to which their return would continue to be delayed until the situation of IDPs themselves was improved. Identification of individual Rwandans' responsibility for the crisis through equitable judicial proceedings, also a precondition for social and economic reconstruction, was not accorded appropriate priority. The regional nature of the humanitarian problem, including its connections with political and security factors, was also underestimated.

The fact that the massive humanitarian response to the major human cataclysm of the mid-1990s produced such unsatisfactory results raises troubling questions about the strategies pursued and the activities mounted. Its failure rightly leads to probing questions about the strategies of protection and assistance adopted and the institutional machinery activated. The implications range far beyond IDPs and far beyond Rwanda's borders. This chapter reviews these questions, concluding with specific recommendations for the future.[2]

The Genesis of the Crisis

The emergency that culminated in genocide had its antecedents in colonial and even precolonial times. Yet the immediate spark that led to the government-promoted holocaust was the shooting down on April 6, 1994, over Kigali of a plane carrying the presidents of Rwanda and Burundi. The perpetrators of the genocide were principally the Presidential Guard, the Rwandan military, and the paramilitary forces and militias known as "*interahamwe*." However, the morbid frenzy stirred by many local leaders and the threats made by the government's radio, Radio Mille Collines, against any Hutu who refused to participate in eliminating the Tutsi made the true number of "genocidaires" difficult to calculate.[3] Like the number of victims, the number of Hutu involved in carrying out the campaign, carefully planned in the months before April, is a matter of dispute.

The Historical Context

The backdrop to the genocide was formed by generations of fluctuating tensions between Hutu and Tutsi in Rwanda and elsewhere in the Great

Lakes region. Some historians have portrayed precolonial Rwanda as a bucolic accommodation among Hutu, Tutsi, and Twa, based upon a feudal structure dominated by cattle-owning Tutsi and supported by Hutu agricultural labor. "The truth," concludes one study, "is that the present can be explained only as a product of a long and conflict-ridden process, where many factors contribute to the total picture."[4]

The long history of Rwanda is one of a series of periodic Tutsi conquests interspersed with periods of Hutu absorption. Clan hierarchies rather than ethnicity, however, characterized Rwanda's social structure until the mid-nineteenth century, when the Tutsi king, Kigeri Rwabugiri (1860–95), assumed the throne. It was he who molded Rwanda into a Tutsi-dominated structure to consolidate his own power.

The fact that in both Rwanda and Burundi the Hutu represented the majority of the population did not deter German colonialists from perpetuating Tutsi domination when Germany established rule over the territory in 1899. On the contrary, Germany—as Belgium would do later from 1916 virtually to 1959—fostered Tutsi dominance as a means of maintaining control. From a political point of view, neither had any objection to strengthening the minority group's hold over the majority; from a racial point of view, both clearly felt more comfortable dealing with the European-featured Hamitic Tutsi than the predominantly Bantu Hutu.

In the decolonizing atmosphere of the late 1950s, the Tutsi grip on the country began to erode and Belgium shifted its support to the increasingly vociferous Hutu majority. Nineteen fifty-nine was a catalytic year in the modern history of Rwanda. It was the year of the *jacquerie*, or "peasants' revolt" of Hutu against Tutsi, and also the year that Belgium, for all intents and purposes, adopted a pro-Hutu policy. That year and those events were also marked by another catalytic moment—the massacre of hundreds of Tutsi and the flight of tens of thousands more across the border.

The years between 1959 and 1973 were punctuated by at least three distinct and bloody crises (in 1959–61, 1963–64, and 1973) during which approximately 600,000 Tutsi sought refuge in neighboring countries.[5] And although there was a discernible trend by the government of Rwanda to lay the foundation for some kind of accommodation between Tutsi (both within and outside the country) and the majority Hutu, government-perpetuated exclusion and demographic reality gave the minority Tutsi little cause for relief.[6]

The sense of Tutsi frustration and hopelessness was in no small part the result of the Rwandan government's lackluster efforts to deal with the issue of Tutsi roles and rights in Rwanda. This failure in turn explains to a significant extent the motivation that led eventually to the creation of the Rwanda Patriotic Front (RPF) and its military wing, the Rwandese Patriotic Army (RPA), as well as to the onset of civil war. Between 1990 and 1994, the RPF launched incursions into the country's northwestern and northeastern prefectures from Uganda in order to deal with what was called "the refugee crisis"—that is, the determination of the Rwandan refugees to return to their homes.

Supported by France, the army under President Juvenal Habyarimana brought the RPA invasion to a halt. However, the government lacked the capacity and resources to repel the invading force. The stalemate witnessed brave and exhausting efforts by regional leaders, the OAU, and the United Nations to bring both sides together in Arusha, Tanzania, to negotiate a settlement that would enable refugees to return and to participate in government on a mutually acceptable basis.

The Arusha Accords, agreed to initially in 1992 and reinforced by a series of cease-fire agreements and UN peacekeeping arrangements the following year, were finalized at a point when both sides had become trapped in an escalation of violence and shrill rhetoric. Nevertheless, there were formal agreements on a "broad-based transitional government," future elections, and a peacekeeping force that eventually would be called the United Nations Assistance Mission for Rwanda (UNAMIR). Yet below the surface of this diplomatic success, the day-to-day violence, and the exchange of hate messages between the government's Radio Mille Collines and the RPF's Radio Muhabura was a government solution to refugee demands. It involved annihilation of the problem and the people who embodied it.

Socioeconomic Context

The historical context that led from interaction between nomadic peoples and agriculturists in the fifteenth century to genocide in the twentieth cannot be divorced from central socioeconomic issues. Prominent among these were demographic, economic, and regional factors. The most densely populated of any African country, Rwanda suffered from a sharp downturn during the 1980s in world prices for coffee, its major export. "Combined with the effects of the civil war from October 1990, continued

Table 3-1. *Number of Rwandan and Burundian Refugees as of March 1995*

Country of Asylum	Burundi	Rwanda	Total
Burundi	0	243,000	243,000
Rwanda	6,000	0	6,000
Tanzania	78,000	589,000	667,000
Uganda	0	4,000	4,000
Zaire	132,000	1,149,000	1,281,000
Total	216,000	1,985,000	2,201,000

Source: UNHCR, Special Unit for Rwanda and Burundi, March 1995.

demographic pressure on available resources and decreasing agricultural yields," observes one analysis, "the economic crisis introduced yet another element of stress and instability into the Rwandese political and social fabric."[7]

Ironically, Rwanda received higher per capita inputs in official development assistance than other sub-Saharan African countries throughout recent decades. The fact that substantial aid flows did little to prevent the violence—and may have even exacerbated tensions by reinforcing the exclusionary politics of Rwanda's political elite—has also given the international community pause. In any event, a return to development assistance-as-usual, even if high levels of aid could be reestablished and sustained, seems out of the question.[8]

The fact that the conflict between the Habyarimana regime and the RPF in the beginning of the 1990s was sparked and fueled by Tutsi refugees in Uganda and that Hutu-Tutsi relations in Burundi were affected by events in Rwanda underscores the intensity of the regional dynamics at play. The accompanying table indicates the numbers of refugees from Rwanda and Burundi in various countries of the region a year after the beginning of the genocide in Rwanda.[9] The presence of refugees in each of the countries of the Great Lakes region from each of the other countries underscored the reality that in this part of the world, events do not respect national borders (see table 3-1).

The Anatomy of Displacement and Response

The effects of Rwanda's genocide and civil strife were staggering. Out of Rwanda's population of roughly 8 million at the beginning of the 1990s, some 2 million had become displaced within Rwanda's borders during the last eight months of 1994 and close to an additional 2 million had fled as new refugees to neighboring countries. The displaced included Tutsi, some of whom had remained in Rwanda during the genocide and others of whom were among the 600,000 "old caseload" refugees who entered with the victorious RPF. The displaced also included Hutu, who, as the military and political tide turned, feared reprisals from the new Tutsi regime and army.

The majority of the almost 2 million who had become refugees in neighboring countries between April and July 1994 fled in two distinct waves.[10] The first wave of approximately 300,000 crossed into Tanzania over a two-day period at the end of April 1994, as a substantial RPF force moved down from Uganda. The second wave of approximately 1.4 million fled during mid-July from what had been a temporary protection zone known as "Zone Turquoise" established a few weeks before by France in southwestern Rwanda.

The refugee population in and near camps could be classified in three groups. One was the leadership, including elements from the former Rwandan army (ex-FAR) and *interahamwe*, who were fundamentally responsible for the genocide and now engaged in political and military maneuvers to reassert their hold over Rwanda.[11] A second group comprised those who were coerced, brainwashed, or threatened into participating in the genocide. Members of a third group were innocent but were nevertheless swept up in the flood of humanity that crossed the borders in 1994. After 1994, many of this last group remained under the oppressive authority of "intimidators."[12] The makeup of the camps for internally displaced persons within Rwanda paralleled in most respects the refugee camps on the borders.

In light of the fact that a significant percentage of refugees were assumed to be guilty of crimes against humanity—or at least continued to bear arms—the prima facie refugee status accorded to all who had fled to Zaire and Tanzania was questionable. For the new post-genocide government of Rwanda, such a blanket determination was not only questionable but also highly objectionable.[13]

Major international organizations and the new authorities also had different assumptions about the composition of the IDP camps. The government assumed that a significant proportion of the IDPs, the overwhelming majority of whom were Hutu, were complicit in the genocide and "a dagger" at the government's throat. In contrast, the agencies viewed the internally displaced principally as people entitled to standard humanitarian and human rights attention and downplayed their roles in the genocide. According to international law, the right to international protection does not extend to persons suspected of complicity in crimes against humanity.[14]

By September 1994 the majority of IDPs had returned to their homes or settled elsewhere. Although accurate estimates of the number of remaining IDPs in late 1994 are not available, the internally displaced were generally members of one of four major groups. The first were those who decided to remain in the former Zone Turquoise in the southwestern part of the country after French forces withdrew in July. They were unable or unwilling to cross the border but did not feel able to return to their home communes. This group numbered approximately 350,000 in September 1994 and formed the populations that crowded into some twenty IDP camps around three southwestern prefectures.

A second group represented a large but difficult-to-quantify portion of "old caseload" refugees, principally from Uganda but also from Burundi and from areas in the Horn of Africa. A substantial number settled in north and southeastern Rwanda, the former bringing with them 400,000 to 600,000 head of cattle that wreaked devastation in the parklands.[15] The old caseload refugees posed a very complex problem. An embodiment of the discontent that led to the creation of the RPF and RPA and the new regime's loyal constituency, these returnees after so many years in exile had high expectations. Those among the 600,000 who lacked housing, employment, and land—or whose homes and lands had been occupied in the interim—represented a potentially explosive political and emotional issue.

The third group of IDPs was more amorphous and difficult to quantify. They were the impoverished and dispossessed in one of the poorest countries in the world. They included innumerable street children, those traumatized by the war, and the destitute, all of whom had been uprooted and received no assistance from a barely functioning social safety net.

Finally a fourth group were "*rescapés*," principally Tutsi who did not flee the genocide but chose to stay in the country even during the massacres. Ironically, these "survivors" were objects of suspicion by Tutsi who had felt compelled to flee. Some became objects of revenge by those who feared that the survivors would pinpoint the "*genocidaires*." Often the only recourse for the *rescapés* was to abandon their homes and seek shelter in different prefectures. They, too, became part of Rwanda's displaced population.

By and large, the IDPs in the camps were neither the government's natural constituency nor a priority item for attention or resource allocations. If there were any for whom the government had sympathy, it was those from the old caseload group, a sympathy not fully understood or appreciated by the international community at large. Conversely, the international community's preoccupation with the displaced from the former Zone Turquoise baffled the authorities.

Internally Displaced Persons and Refugees: An Intricate Interrelationship

The refugees who had fled to Tanzania and Zaire in the summer of 1994 triggered an immense international relief effort. The initial commitment to assist almost 2 million people generated resources of some US$1.1 billion between April and December 1994, excluding the costs of military contingents and direct contributions to NGOs. For the year beginning in January 1995, resources were provided at the level of about US$1 million per day.

The refugees commanded the media limelight and the lion's share of the resources, upstaging the difficult straits of the displaced within Rwanda's borders. The media focused intensely upon their plight, their exhaustion, and their losing battles with cholera. Little attention was paid to conditions in Rwanda or to those who had survived the genocide or, for that matter, to the interrelationship of the 1994 realities of Rwanda, refugee repatriation, and IDP return.

Of the officially reported $1.1 billion in aid available for the crisis in 1994, Rwanda itself received an estimated $372 million, or about one third. Of this sum, $50 million was allocated to Rwanda between January and April 1994—that is, before the genocide. The $372 million also included funds earmarked for IDP camps in Rwanda, funds that, to the distress of the Rwandan government, were not available for use elsewhere in the country.

Refugee-focused media attention and humanitarian activity isolated a single element of a complex problem that in reality linked together refugees, IDPs, and the state of Rwanda itself. Refugee repatriation was closely tied to the return of the IDPs to their home communes, the latter being a sort of vanguard for the former.[16] Yet the willingness of IDPs to return to their communes depended upon the extent to which they felt that security could be ensured and they could return to property that had not been confiscated and to a life reasonably free of persecution.

Such security depended in turn upon a functioning system of justice under which the innocent were protected and the guilty prosecuted. Also essential were central and local administrative systems and the delivery of services. Priorities included the restoration of damaged infrastructure, including roads, water and electricity systems, and housing, along with the provision of basic health and education.

Yet these components were not approached as integral elements of a common whole. No single international actor present in the Great Lakes region had the authority or, for that matter, the perspective to develop policy that transcended the borders of individual states. While the special representative of the secretary-general (SRSG) from his base in Rwanda undertook regional missions on the secretary-general's behalf to Kenya, Tanzania, and Zaire during late 1994 and early 1995, the resources of the UN system—including those of the peacekeepers, for which he was also responsible—had no overarching strategy or capacity to deal with the intersecting elements of the problem.[7]

Similarly, a regionwide meeting of governments, multilateral organizations, and UN agencies convened by the Organization for African Unity and UNHCR in Bujumbura in February 1995, represented a step in the right direction. Yet the meeting, which after much debate adopted a plan of action focusing on refugee return, did not address the broader issues that the crisis of the Great Lakes region required.

Misperceptions and Misunderstandings

To one extent or another, most humanitarian and peacekeeping operations experience problems in relating to the host authorities. These often stem in part from the government's misperceptions of the motives and intentions of the intervening actors, and vice versa. Problems reflect the highly charged nature of complex emergencies and also the reality that in attempting to bring stability to highly volatile situations, international actors may preempt, or appear to preempt, decisions by the resident political authorities.

When the new Rwandan government assumed power in July 1994, it was perhaps inevitable that the advice of the United Nations about a range of matters from economic policy and priorities to control over the Zone Turquoise would be viewed as co-opting Rwandan sovereignty. Yet the depth of misunderstanding that evolved was never anticipated or even recognized. The international community never fully comprehended the consequences of the genocide or the resentment harbored by the government and most Rwandans toward those whom the UN Security Council belatedly dispatched to preserve the peace. For their part, the Rwandan authorities showed scant regard for the dilemmas in which the peacekeepers and UN and other humanitarian organizations found themselves. The misunderstandings are crystallized in the issue of internal displacement.

DIFFERING PERCEPTIONS OF THE PROBLEM. There was a fundamental perceptual clash among major actors over IDPs and refugees. While the government regarded a considerable portion of the displaced as criminals responsible for the genocide, the humanitarian community took a position that reflected its mandated responsibilities for assistance and protection.

Determined to exact justice, the government did not find the humanitarian claims of IDPs and refugees and of those who articulated them compelling. The IDPs in particular were seen to be occupying vital agricultural land and faring far better than local people who were not receiving international aid. Furthermore, the administrations being established in the communes and prefectures where the IDP camps were located saw the international relief organizations and operations as challenges to their authority. There was persistent concern that IDP camps were the spearhead of the ex-FAR to regain control over Rwanda.

For their part, humanitarian organizations were on hand first and foremost to provide emergency assistance. Human rights issues were not of overriding concern, although, not having been present during the genocide, many were more concerned about what they saw as Tutsi violations of Hutu rights. Initially they were reluctant to reduce food rations and other services as a means to encourage IDPs and refugees to return to their home communes, viewing such actions as causes of additional hardship. Having worked diligently to assist the uprooted, many relief workers developed bonds with them. Over time, the approach of the agencies reflected a growing "clientism." Humanitarian organizations showed themselves reluctant at first to rethink their traditional aid strategies in light of the special circumstances related to the genocide.

The sharp clash of perceptions spelled trouble for both the government and such organizations. In the government's eyes, much of the population d by aid agencies as "relief beneficiaries" were *"genocidaires."* avowedly neutral and impartial humanitarian efforts to assist up-rooted people would be read by the authorities as highly political was not, of course, unprecedented. In this instance, however, the post-genocide landscape on which they worked frustrated agency efforts. Conversely, the ambivalent commitment of the authorities to equitable treatment of the uprooted Hutu populations received particularly close international scrutiny.

THE INTERNATIONAL MILITARY AND ITS MANDATE. The crisis in Rwanda represented a watershed in the number of national military contingents involved, in the permutations of multilateral and unilateral authorities under which they served, and in the types of humanitarian support functions they performed. Yet in a broad sense, the deployment of military assets showed the same imbalance—in timing, scale, and effects—as the humanitarian resources. Their net effect, not surprising although not planned, was likewise to complicate the challenges faced by the new Rwandan authorities.

When outside military forces were most needed—that is, during the onset of the genocide—the Security Council moved to reduce their ranks. The UN's peacekeeping presence, the principal international military presence within Rwanda during the early months of 1994, shrank from 2,500 on April 6 to 270 on April 21. Although on May 17 the Security Council authorized an increase to 5,500, only 1,257 soldiers were in place three months later. The response reflected a lack of understanding about what was actually taking place on the ground, the concern in national capitals about the safety of peacekeeping contingents, and the cumber-some international response machinery.

Despite limited ranks and lack of political support, UNAMIR troops in Kigali in the early weeks worked energetically to protect civilians and to support the work of the few aid groups on the scene. They sought to shelter vulnerable Tutsi in the Kigali stadium, patrol tense neighbor-hoods, and accompany or rescue beleaguered aid teams around the city. UN troops were later joined by French soldiers under Operation Tur-quoise and then by national contingents responding to requests from UNHCR for specific packages of services.[18]

During the Rwanda crisis, the presence and accomplishments of the panoply of international military personnel were far more evident during

Figure 3-1. *International Troops Responding to Rwanda Crisis, 1994*

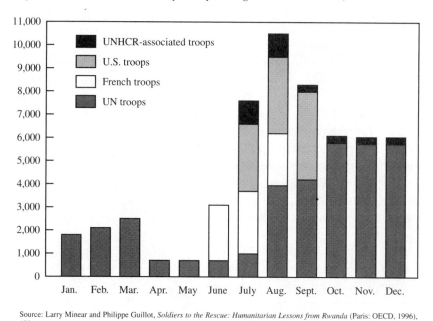

Source: Larry Minear and Philippe Guillot, *Soldiers to the Rescue: Humanitarian Lessons from Rwanda* (Paris: OECD, 1996), p. 130.

Note: Figures are approximations, based on available data. UNAMIR figures include observers and civilian police as well as troops.

the mass exodus to Zaire than during the dark days of the genocide. In retrospect, however, and despite media portrayals from Goma and Bukavu to the contrary, the troops did not contribute in a timely fashion what was most needed and what was most beyond the ability of other actors to provide: a climate of security in the refugee camps within which humanitarian activities could be carried out. However visible in Goma during the peak of the emergency from July through September, most troops had left the region by the time that disturbances in the refugee camps threatened refugees and aid operations alike. Assistance from the military, as from the aid groups, went disproportionately to refugees outside of Rwanda, to the detriment of IDPs within (see figure 3-1).[19]

In the aftermath of the RPF/RPA victory in Rwanda, UN peacekeeping forces by October had attained their requisite force strength. More than 5,500 troops and civilian support personnel were stationed in Rwanda with a mandate to monitor the security situation and assist in the repatriation and protection of refugees and returning IDPs.[20] By then, the logistical and security challenges that had deterred the commitment of military assets to Rwanda itself had been reduced.

Throughout most of the period from October 1994 through its December 1995 mission completion date, UNAMIR was in a difficult—many would say invidious—position. Its mandate was viewed by many in Rwanda as protecting the very people responsible for the genocide. UNAMIR, well aware of such perceptions, did all in its power to counter them. For example, it joined forces with the RPA to arrest intimidators in the Kibeho IDP camp.[21] UN peacekeepers also deployed their meager assets to support police training schools, infrastructure reconstruction, and even prison expansion programs. Yet such efforts could not overcome the prevailing contempt for an interventionist force perceived to be protecting the perpetrators of genocide.

THE HUMANITARIAN COMMUNITY AND ITS MANDATE. Humanitarian organizations affirm an obligation to provide assistance to those in need. In the case of Rwanda, however, the community of aid organizations faced a dilemma that affected nongovernmental, bilateral, and multilateral institutions alike: whether "they should feed the victims at the risk of giving the killers new strength."[22]

In late fall 1994, Médecins sans Frontières-France answered the question in the negative, terminating its programs rather than providing assistance. Other agencies weighed the options differently, reasoning that the presence of killers in the camps did not absolve them of their humanitarian obligations. By November 1994, however, some that had decided to stay the course announced that they would withdraw from the Goma camps until adequate humanitarian space for effective operations was reclaimed.[23]

The government of Rwanda clearly supported their decision to withdraw from Goma, for it saw humanitarian efforts there as inappropriate and contradictory under the circumstances. Its view of similar humanitarian efforts in the IDP camps was equally negative, if not even more so, for it maintained that the IDPs had no compelling reason to remain in camps. With the conflict ended and the killings stopped, the continued presence of IDPs in the camps was tantamount to a confession of complicity in genocide. The government's position that the innocent had nothing to fear in returning home ran counter to the fears IDPs expressed in the camps and to rumors of revenge killings heard from the communes.

Humanitarian organizations remained skeptical of the government's view of stability throughout the country and security at the local level. Humanitarian agencies saw their constituency consisting of frightened people with little hope about the future, few resources, and no means to provide for themselves.

Such contrasting perceptions were clearly paralleled in the refugee camps. The positions adopted by international relief workers there as well as within Rwanda created a deep and unbridgeable schism between a significant portion of the international community and the Rwandan government. International assistance—the major vehicle for outside intervention in the crisis—was perceived as making the government's assertion of its authority and performance of its tasks far more difficult.

THE COORDINATION MANDATE. A review of coordination arrangements among the major international actors calls into question whether senior UN officials at headquarters fully appreciated the disarray caused by their unwillingness to make basic institutional decisions about field structures. Fully eighteen months into the crisis, for example, no decisions had been made about the relationship between the special representative of the secretary-general and the UN humanitarian coordinator or about UNAMIR's relationship with the humanitarian community. The ability of agencies to adjust to the environment in the field, an environment itself highly subject to change, proved limited.

The relationship between UNAMIR and the humanitarian community suffered from a basic lack of understanding of each about the working methods and objectives of the other. The UN military, which had a reasonably clear organization and structure, was bemused by the seeming chaos among the UN agencies, let alone NGOs. As frustrations grew within UNAMIR over its difficulties in achieving productive working relationships with the RPA, some peacekeepers conveyed the view that these antagonisms would not be so great if the humanitarian community were assisting the Rwandan government effectively.

For its part, the humanitarian community was at times exasperated by UNAMIR's efforts to become involved in humanitarian activities, an area in which it had little expertise or comparative advantage. Many aid workers viewed the peacekeepers as underemployed, unreliable, and insensitive to the complexities of the situation facing post-genocide Rwanda. Certain UN agencies were also wary about the respective roles of the SRSG and the humanitarian coordinator. UNHCR for one was concerned that either might enter areas of its own specific mandate. Hence suspicions had to be surmounted even when the need for full cooperation was acknowledged.

A complicating factor was a divergence in priorities. Not all organizations were convinced that in post-genocide Rwanda IDPs should be the primary issue of concern. Many believed that primary attention should be given to restoring Rwandan society, promoting national reconciliation, and dealing with the endemic poverty that had predated the war. Differing perceptions about priorities also affected the development of common strategies for addressing IDP needs.

BILATERAL CROSSCURRENTS. The fundamental issue for many governments concerned the legitimacy of the new authorities, including their capacity to survive and carry out the requisite functions. Some governments were prepared to give them the benefit of the doubt and sought to provide assistance as quickly as possible to strengthen their hand. The Netherlands, for example, perhaps the most creative and effective donor in the circumstances, saw the need for disbursing funds quickly with few administrative requirements. Other governments moved with less dispatch, overlaying funds with heavy conditionality and delaying disbursement. The French lobbied other donors against providing substantial assistance for reconstruction, an approach widely viewed as playing out a bilateral political agenda in the region.[24]

Such crosscurrents in the disparity of views and interests among major donors had two important consequences for IDPs and the crisis as a whole. First, there was insufficient donor harmony to support the broad UN humanitarian objectives. Hence concerted pressure by donors to constrain the RPA's approach toward IDP camp closure and commune security could not be relied upon.

Second, there was little concerted action to address problems that were highly dependent upon resources and administrative efficiency. This was sadly evident in the results of the U.S.-driven Rwanda Operations Support Group (ROSG). Despite occasionally productive dialogue, the ROSG, comprising all major donor representatives at senior levels, failed to move on fundamental issues affecting Rwandan operations.[25] No specific proposals were adopted to ensure cross-border security or to stem the flow of arms into the Zairian refugee camps.

Despite pledges made during two 1995 Round Table exercises convened by the government and supported by the United Nations Development Programme (UNDP), neither the level of actual resources nor the speed of their delivery increased significantly. Here the ROSG could at least have pushed either to control the level of soaring Rwandan government expectations or to make good on well-intentioned donor commitments. The gap between the expressed concerns of donors for Rwanda and their actions exacerbated the sense of alienation and grievance felt by many Rwandan officials.

This gap also led to a peculiar donor dynamic that frustrated the Rwandan government as well as aid officials. In all too many instances, donors pledged resources to fund vitally needed programs and, when funds were delayed, then imposed conditions reflecting lack of confidence in the programs. To the embarrassment of several major donors, the urgency of translating pledges into disbursements was either lost on their capitals or a victim of cumbersome bureaucratic procedures.

The justice system was a case in point. Lack of resources, including some pledged by governments, greatly delayed the establishment of procedures for trying those suspected of participation in the genocide. The delays resulted in an increase in "rough justice," the rise of which in turn led donors to specify that funds would not be released if such "extrajudicial procedures" continued. Whether or not the rise of conditionality was a smoke screen for more sinister intentions, it reflected the profoundly disjointed approaches of bilateral donors.

Conventional Responses to Unparalleled Circumstances

Although misperceptions took their toll, the international humanitarian response was also marked by operating procedures and institutional conventions unsuited to the situation. Inadequate commitment, institutional incapacity, and lack of practical post-conflict recovery strategies were particularly problematic.

Inadequate Commitment

A persistent complaint of those who deal with internal displacement issues is that there is no single organization with clear-cut responsibility for IDPs. In Rwanda the UN humanitarian coordinator was given indirect responsibility for resolving the IDP problem but not the resources for doing so. The lack of resources would not necessarily have been crippling had the UN agencies been instructed to support him actively with personnel and material aid. Yet while credit must be given to individual agencies for assisting his initiatives, there was little institutional will or flexibility of mandate to provide the requisite human and material resources.

An instructive example of the strengths and weaknesses of the response was the Integrated Operations Centre (IOC), established in late November 1994 in the Ministry of Rehabilitation and Social Integration to provide an integrated approach for returning IDPs to their home communes. The IOC tackled four tasks.

First, it sought to deal with the political dimensions of IDP issues by adopting a community-wide strategy. A particular aid agency taking the lead could be singled out by the government for failure or by the humanitarian community for complicity in violating fundamental human rights; the IOC provided protective cover and a degree of security based upon common agreement and approaches.

Second, the IOC sought to engage the government in the planning process and in implementing agreed upon strategies. If the authorities remained unengaged, it was likely that the government would either act on its own—perhaps creating a rift between itself and the aid community—or leave the issue of the IDP camps to the agencies, opening them up to accusations of connivance with the perpetrators of the genocide or of incompetence.

The third challenge was to restore the balance between peacekeepers and the humanitarian community. Although given the contentiousness of closing the IDP camps the matter might have been left to UNAMIR, the humanitarian community felt obliged to become engaged in this issue, whatever the hazards. The agencies were concerned lest the political and peacekeeping roles of UNAMIR dictate the methods used to deal with the IDPs. They also believed that, with relative peace restored, the time was right to make clear that the peacekeepers were in Rwanda to support the work of humanitarian organizations.

Finally, the IOC was an instrument for addressing the practical dimensions of the IDP problem. In a world used to providing humanitarian assistance to millions, attention to an estimated 350,000 IDPs might seem a relatively simple exercise. In fact, the numbers were relatively large, and the complexity of the operation necessitated a fully integrated approach. At issue were not only humanitarian assistance in the camps and transport home but also preparations in the communes to receive returnees and publicity campaigns to encourage return.

Sensible in concept, the IOC encountered various difficulties, many from the agencies themselves. Although the International Organization for Migration (IOM) and a host of NGOs were fully on board, the UN organizations themselves were not. Despite considerable resources, UNHCR felt that its mandate would not allow it to commit its energies fully to IDP programs. The World Food Programme (WFP) was engaged in a wide range of activities, including but not limited to IDPs. Like UNHCR, it was concerned that the IOC solution fell between institutional stools: that is, it was neither multilateral nor governmental but a hybrid. UNICEF, too, though heavily involved in the IDP camps, had nationwide commitments and priorities well beyond IDPs. It was also reluctant to get involved in IDP solutions that might have negative human rights consequences.[26]

For its part, UNAMIR was fully engaged, although it temporarily withdrew support for the IOC in the midst of the Kibeho crisis of April 1995 (described below). The peacekeeping operation's mandated responsibilities for the IDPs made its involvement institutionally simpler and, far more than the individual agencies, it had personnel experienced in "operation-room" activities as well as spare computer and communications equipment fundamental to the IOC's information and operational functions.

From the UN side, the IOC thus fell short of its promise. Despite its efforts to facilitate cooperation, it encountered restrictions imposed by agency mandates and by lack of priority to IDP issues in agency headquarters and on the UN's Inter-Agency Standing Committee. Also problematic were uncertainties that stemmed from venturing into unconventional institutional arrangements. Rather than becoming an innovative and effective instrument for dealing with IDPs, the IOC mirrored the shortcomings of the agencies and the government in planning, although the humanitarian operations it orchestrated were highly effective in response to the Kibeho crisis.

Whatever the deficiencies of the IOC with respect to the agencies, its fundamental and almost fatal flaw resulted from its inability to bring the Ministry of Defense and the RPA into its orbit as active players. The only occasional participation of their representatives reflected a lukewarm institutional commitment. The assumption that the endorsement of its plans by the Ministry of Rehabilitation and Social Integration, which was ostensibly responsible for IDPs, and more particularly the minister himself, was sufficient ignored political realities within the government.

For all practical purposes, the Ministry of Defense and the RPA *were* the government in an otherwise enfeebled structure. They rapidly lost patience with the slow pace of returning IDPs to their communes and generally supported only those specific proposals they had endorsed in advance. The IOC's assumptions about the importance of the Ministry of Rehabilitation did not take into account the real intentions of the Defense Ministry in delaying camp closure in November 1996. The delays, it turned out, did not represent a basic change in approach but only a tactical concession to the international community, upon whose support and resources the post-genocide government depended.

Institutional Incapacity

While it does not necessarily hold that the problems of displacement in Rwanda and throughout the Great Lakes region would have been solved if the UN's institutional structures had been more coherent, those structures did little to facilitate international efforts.

Within Rwanda itself, there was lack of clarity about relationships among the SRSG, UNAMIR, and the UN humanitarian coordinator. Ostensibly, UNAMIR's force commander reported to the SRSG, but in effect UNAMIR's operational requirements and resources led at best to a very loose-knit UN command-and-control structure in the field. Similarly, although the UN humanitarian coordinator was also to report to the SRSG, his primary accountability was to the under-secretary-general for humanitarian affairs. In other words, the largely harmonious relations among these three entities did not translate into the operational coherence essential for moving IDPs from the camps.

Moreover, UN headquarters played too large a daily role in the affairs of UNAMIR and, for that matter, of the SRSG. The able and experienced UNAMIR force commander on crucial occasions was prevented from using his best judgment in responding to evolving challenges in the field by officials in New York who were less aware of local realities. For example, written instructions received from headquarters just before the Kibeho massacres forbade the force commander from using peacekeeping troops to intervene between IDPs and Rwandan army soldiers. Despite this order from New York, the force commander felt morally obliged to keep UNAMIR's Zambian battalion at Kibeho to maintain a presence that might lessen potential tensions.[27]

At the same time, the SRSG, an engaging individual with decades of diplomatic experience, needed greater control over the overall UN structure in Rwanda. He required authority to mobilize the UN peacekeepers and humanitarian organizations quickly and coherently to plan for moving IDPs. He also needed resources to implement recovery and stabilization activities quickly, which required having a trust fund in Rwanda rather than access to funds only through the tortuous administrative procedures of headquarters. Each of these would have contributed in a major way to the UN's overall response.[28]

The fact that the problems of refugees and IDPs were part of the same complex web of issues should also have spurred greater interest in a more permanent structure for dealing with the regional issues. UNAMIR's portfolio was limited to dealing with problems within territorial Rwanda, although on occasion in 1994 it did take a look at the evolving problems in the refugee camps outside. The humanitarian coordinator's brief likewise stopped at the border; UNHCR's priority tasks began there. The division of labor among UN organizations did not correspond to the regional dimensions of the problems at hand.

For various reasons, including sovereignty as well as institutional rigidity within the UN, more comprehensive approaches were not seriously attempted. Although UNHCR had its own special regional representative, it was not until November 1995—eight months after the initial proposal—that a regionwide information structure was established, the UN's Integrated Regional Information Network (IRIN). IRIN reported for the first time on all aspects of political, economic, humanitarian, and military events throughout the region that affected IDPs and refugees.[29] As a source of regionwide and systemwide information, IRIN was successful. Yet the international community needs to go beyond creating a center for information exchange and develop a more proactive and creative regional approach for interagency strategizing and implementation.

Lack of an Effective Strategy

The interlocking relationship among IDPs, refugees, and conditions in Rwanda required that the conditions at the local level be improved enough to attract people to return to their homes. But creating such conditions would have required the international community to understand and support post-genocide recovery. Though donors expressed sympathy for the government's burdens in rebuilding the nation, they were by and large unwilling to provide appropriate assistance in a timely manner.

Rwanda's needs did not fit into conventional aid systems or concepts. Rwanda was indeed in an emergency, but the principal victim of the emergency was the society itself. Blankets, nutritional feeding, plastic sheeting, and other emergency relief supplies were needed, of course, and for the most part were provided for a wide range of vulnerable groups, IDPs, and refugees. But also needed was a rapid but sensitive approach to societal stabilization. Such unconventional emergency relief required the international community to review its very conception of "survival needs."

It raised politically sensitive issues about the criteria of "relief" and challenged the procedures by which donors pledged and committed funds.

While massive funding poured into refugee camps across the borders, Rwanda itself became even more impoverished. Because the climate in Rwanda was so volatile and its government so heavy-handed, donors were unwilling to respond quickly to essential priorities there—the restoration of basic services, including electricity, water, and transportation, as well as social support such as health and education. As UNICEF and a variety of NGOs soon discovered, the needs of a traumatized society and of shattered families and orphaned children required special attention.

Equally conspicuous by their absence in the wake of the genocide were the essentials of law and order and security. The justice system had been destroyed. There was no police system; law and order was in the hands of an army that was essentially a guerrilla force that only recently had emerged from the bush. Local and central administration had been eviscerated as buildings were looted and files destroyed when the former regime retreated. A high proportion of civil servants were dead, internally displaced, or living in camps in Tanzania or Zaire. There were few facilities and personnel to register returning IDPs; where they did exist, staff usually lacked paper or pencils to perform even the simplest administrative tasks.

The situation was nothing less than an emergency, a society on the verge of collapse. While discussions ensued in political circles about the legitimacy of the new Rwandan regime, several key donors were equally perplexed on a more technical level about mechanisms for providing resources suitable for stabilizing the situation. Three problems loomed large.[30] The first was determining what types of support could actually be provided. Prisons, police forces, and military facilities—even salaries for civil servants and soldiers—were essential. Yet these items were regarded as too politically sensitive and in any event were not within the standard portfolios of aid groups on the scene at the time.[31]

Second, less politically sensitive needs, such as the justice system, were problematic. What was required? Courthouses? Legal texts, judges and magistrates, defense attorneys and prosecutors? More traditional adjudication systems? Funding for salaries, technical assistance, or training? The uncertainty stemmed in part from the government's own lack of clarity about its requirements. But there were more fundamental concerns not fully appreciated by outsiders. The government wanted "to put something in place" as a clear demonstration that there was a system, however basic, to which accusers and accused had recourse. Yet the urgency was lost amidst standard development discussions and broad-based projects. As a result, the most obvious change in the judicial system between late 1994 and late 1995 was an increase in the prison population and the explosive potential of the situation.

Third, the response mechanisms of even well-intentioned donors were too slow and cumbersome to provide an effective stabilization program. Such programs fell between donor stools, being neither traditional relief nor traditional development activities. There were no "funding pockets" that would readily meet such requirements. The absence of quick-disbursement resources was a source of obvious frustration to the government. Meanwhile, donors—some with ambivalent political agendas—faulted the government's maddeningly ineffective ministries for their inability to deal with the surge in local violence and the resettlement imperative.

Misperceptions and Conventional Responses Converge

The April 1995 massacre of several thousand IDPs in Kibeho camp by the RPA was, in a sense, the culmination of months of misperceptions and conventional responses.[32] Kibeho was one of the major camps among two dozen that in early 1995 were to be closed under Operation Retour. Devised by the IOC in December 1994, Operation Retour used a combination of "push" and "pull" methods to encourage IDPs to return home. The operation's implementation arrangements used UNAMIR and the RPA for security purposes, the transport capacities of UNHCR and IOM, and the humanitarian resources of the major UN agencies and

NGOs for the packages that returnees would take to their home communes. Over half of the camp populations had made the transition by mid-February 1995.

Despite that promising beginning, increased insecurity in the communes led to a reverse movement back to the camps. Operation Retour ground to a halt as those who returned, though modest in number, fueled the fears of the remaining camp occupants. Disregarding publicity campaigns and other inducements, approximately 190,000 people refused to move. A "new" Operation Retour was needed. From the end of February until the first week in April, the IOC worked on devising new plans and approaches.

Finally, on April 5, 1995, the IOC submitted a plan to the government for closing the camps. Elements included timetables for ending food distribution in the camps and beginning them in the communes, enhanced security measures in the communes, and cordoned-off camp sites for IDPs who insisted on remaining. Though harsher than the original Operation Retour, the plan still adequately protected the human rights of the occupants. Through the UN humanitarian coordinator, UN agencies insisted that this be the case or they would withdraw their support. The coordinator emphasized the point to the SRSG as the latter prepared to introduce the plan to the prime minister.

It was agreed that the plan would be launched by the minister of rehabilitation and social integration on April 18, with implementation to begin during the following two weeks. These plans were overtaken by events, however. By April 18, the RPA had already surrounded the main remaining IDP camps as a prelude to their imminent forced closure. Thus the operational plans made by the IOC and presented by the SRSG to the government could not be implemented.

The resulting violence at the Kibeho camp demonstrated that the gulf between governmental and international perceptions and responses was too wide to bridge. Rwanda's resentment over the ineffectiveness of the international response paralleled the outside world's frustrations with the government's seeming lack of flexibility and humanity. Where the former did not understand why resources for UNAMIR would not better be used to assist the government, the latter wondered how a supposedly broad-based regime offered only prison as an alternative to justice.[33]

The authorities increasingly felt that the international community offered only promises without results. Pledges to provide massive assistance to post-genocide Rwanda, including almost US$600 million pledged at the January 1995 Rwanda Round Table, had not fully materialized. International efforts to deal with the IDP problem seemed halting and ineffectual. Conversely, the international community saw itself, too, receiving only promises with no results. The government's frequent assurances that the essential "criteria of guilt" for the genocide would be elaborated remained unspecified after two years; trials based on those benchmarks had yet to begin. Its lackluster participation in the IOC planning process for IDPs, as promised, was viewed as another indicator of lack of serious intent.

Recommendations for the Future

The experience of the international community in providing assistance and protection to IDPs in Rwanda from 1994 to 1996 raises a number of key policy issues. The issues constitute something of a microcosm of the IDP challenge in other complex emergencies as well. We present these recommendations in the hope of improving humanitarian responses in general and in situations involving internal displacement. Few are new, but the recent experiences underscore the need once and for all to come to terms with the challenges identified.[34]

A Commitment to Address the Fundamental Issues

It is often observed that humanitarian action has become an alternative to political will rather than an embodiment of it. Indeed that appears to have been the case in Rwanda. Although large numbers of vulnerable groups required emergency relief, the central issue—and the central failing—of the international community's involvement in Rwanda was its unwillingness to confront the political issues that were the fundamental cause of the crisis.

The reluctance of the international community to become politically engaged was reflected in its unwillingness to support efforts to separate out those Rwandans in Zaire who should have been excluded from refugee status from those who were genuine refugees.[35] Its political timidity was also apparent in its willingness to tolerate, despite an arms embargo, the buildup of weapons along the Zairian-Rwandan border.[36] The failure of the major bilateral actors to agree on objectives that would have lent direction and support to UN efforts also demonstrated a lack of political will.

Although humanitarian resources are largely contingent on the good will of a small group of bilateral donors, humanitarian organizations need to be far more vocal than they were in this instance in demanding political action to resolve inherently political crises. Aid organizations need to be more willing to engage and challenge the governments on which they depend for resources. Although the humanitarian community cannot abandon those in need and still remain faithful to its mission and mandates, it must resist being used as a Potemkin village to protect the sensitivities of those who hold the key to real solutions.

In an effort to generate more effective advocacy among donor governments, the Inter-Agency Standing Committee (IASC) could play a far more potent role. It represents a forum for agreeing on common strategies and for conveying these to the political and peacekeeping elements of the UN system. NGOs, in addition to playing a more assertive role on the IASC, should use their sometimes greater access to the corridors of power to press for political solutions.

From a review of the recent past, it is apparent that in Rwanda and other major crises too much attention has been paid to "early warning systems" and too little to what might be called "early implementation systems." Before the cataclysmic events in Rwanda and before most such catastrophes, warnings were and are available about societies and social groups in distress. Even with such information, however, the international community has been slow to respond. Linked closely with the capacity to read the early warning signs, therefore, must be a capacity to mobilize advocacy efforts and to act with dispatch.

The Rwanda crisis, both the genocide and its consequences, such as the flood of the uprooted, also points to another indicator of international commitment: an in-depth understanding of the issues in a given emergency. The resources and responses first masked and later highlighted the profound lack of understanding of the nature of the problem. The fundamental issues must be better understood before they can be effectively addressed. The willingness to intervene is no substitute for a working understanding of the problems to be addressed.

Clear-Cut Policy and Institutional Responsibility for IDPs

The absence of an effective UN systemwide approach to IDPs was demonstrated in the response to the Rwanda crisis. In 1994 the responsibilities of the UN Rwanda Emergency Office (UNREO), the in-country coordination vehicle for humanitarian activities, were limited to Rwanda proper, while UNHCR had the lead responsibility for Rwandan refugees in neighboring countries. UNREO's responsibilities inside Rwanda stopped at the Rwandan border; refugees were a concern only once they had returned. Most of UNHCR's responsibilities also stopped at the border; IDPs within Rwanda were not its primary responsibility. Missing were clear-cut decisions of policy and institutional responsibility regarding IDPs that embodied integrated and multisectoral approaches and were supported by political authority.

Each of the major policy and institutional alternatives has advantages and disadvantages. An institution specifically designated to deal with IDPs would make unnecessary the tortuous process of identifying an entity to take responsibility with each new crisis. There would also be benefits from having a center of demonstrated experience and expertise at the ready. Some have suggested that the mandate of an existing institution such as UNHCR should be expanded to encompass responsibility for IDPs. There are strong arguments in support of this suggestion, including the similar operational needs of refugees and IDPs, UNHCR's established expertise in both assistance and protection, and the likely economies of scale to be realized by having a single institution serve both categories of uprooted populations.

On the other hand, the experience in Rwanda suggests the alternative of a "controlled ad-hocracy" such as is reflected in an Integrated Operations Centre. Such a structure could facilitate the development of common strategies, including the sharing of both responsibility and resources. It could also be adjusted to the particulars of a country-specific situation and lodge political, human rights, humanitarian, and peacekeeping components under a single operational umbrella. An existing agency deputized to deal with IDPs or an agency newly created solely for that purpose might simply add more bureaucracy to an already overly bureaucratic system. A single agency responsible for IDPs or an agency whose mandate is extended to include IDPs might also duplicate efforts, heighten competition for donor resources, and provoke more debates over definitions relating to the displaced. Any single humanitarian entity would probably also lack the authority and capacity to integrate essential political, human rights, humanitarian, and peacekeeping elements.

Whatever the preferred option, four points are essential to bear in mind. First, support from headquarters by UN political and humanitarian officials, including the Inter-Agency Standing Committee, is a prerequisite for effective policies and operations. Second, there must be in-country political support of humanitarian operations to assist and protect IDPs through a coherent UN field structure. Third, the institutional configuration chosen must be sufficiently flexible to meet field challenges affecting each IDP situation. Finally, the structure put in place must incorporate the range of expertise needed to assist IDPs effectively, from peacekeeping to human rights, from humanitarian concerns to those of politics. One lesson emerges clearly: UN operations in the field require greater coherence and attention to structure and more effective command-and-control arrangements than existed in Rwanda. In such a complex emergency, the SRSG should have overall responsibility for all aspects of the operation, with two deputies. One would be responsible for all aspects of humanitarian, recovery, and development assistance, the other for peacekeeping activities. All UN humanitarian and devel-opment organizations would report to the former, who would also be in charge of humanitarian and development issues in which the SRSG or the military were involved.[37]

The utility of this approach depends in part on the effectiveness of future SRSGs, which accordingly requires attention to the procedures by which they are selected. Success also depends upon the capacity of the SRSG office and its personnel. Agencies in the field generally do not resist overall coordination authority as long as priorities are agreed upon, headquarters concur, mandates are clear, and there is evident value to the arrangements. The value of a more structured UN system in the field is that the full weight of the system can be brought to bear on an issue such as IDPs without overtaxing any one component or making any single organization bear the political opprobrium of the authorities.

One factor that has inhibited development of a more coherent field structure has been the desire of individual agencies to preserve their independence. This is one reason for their reluctance to work across borders, as in the Great Lakes region. Even within agencies, "turf" concerns can result in unwillingness of representatives from the same agency in two adjoining countries to share information, let alone to co-operate in other operational ways. In the name of sovereignty, states have reinforced such rigidity by restricting attempts to work together across borders.

Yet if long- as well as short-term solutions to the IDP and refugee problems in the Great Lakes are to be found, greater attention must be paid to regional structures. The view of a geographical border as an operational dividing line proved to be as artificial and dysfunctional in Rwanda as the distinction attempted between IDPs and refugees. "The fact that the roles of the SRSG, the UNAMIR Force Commander and the Humanitarian Coordinator/Head of UNREO were limited to operations within Rwanda hampered coordination of policies inside Rwanda with those relating to refugees in neighbouring countries."[38] Regional information-sharing also requires a mechanism with the authority and capacity to monitor, analyze, and implement strategies and programs that will address refugee, IDP, peacekeeping, and even developmental issues from a regional perspective.

More Balanced Use of Resources

A pattern of resource allocation that favored refugees at the expense of IDPs was established in 1994. The halting and uneven international response to the genocide within the country from April 1994 onward contrasted sharply with the outpouring of assistance to those who fled the country. Contrasting international hyperactivity surrounding the cholera epidemic in Goma with earlier inactivity at the time of the genocide, MSF commented derisively, "The people who had sat stony-faced while innocents were massacred were suddenly deeply moved by the damage wrought by a bacterium."[39]

The subsequent pattern remained largely unchanged, despite considerable comment on the imbalance. "We have received more than $20 million in private donations and government funds to support relief work in the [refugee] camps," observed the president of CARE in February 1996, "and only $3 million to assist in Rwanda." The division of resources, he observed, was "inhumane, wrong-headed, and doomed to fail."[40]

In addition, the allocation of expenditures on assistance has worked to the detriment of protection. A consensus now exists that both the UN and the governments largely ignored the warning signs of the impending genocide that were evident at least as early as January 1994. The failure to take preventive action early in the year, followed by the failure to meet protection obligations once the genocide had begun, allowed the situation to become unmanageable. The world was then faced with unfulfillable protection needs and exorbitant assistance ones. "When ethnic massacres began in Rwanda in April 1994, the U.S. share of the cost of augmenting the U.N. force there would have been about $10 million," observes one analyst. "By July, with the U.N. force drawn down rather than supplemented, and with half a million Rwandans dead and two million refugees in neighboring countries, the U.S. finally felt compelled to commit nearly $500 million to the emergency relief effort."[41] What is true for U.S. investments was equally true for other governments.

Aid agencies such as UNICEF and CARE were often in the forefront of advocacy efforts on behalf of Rwanda's people. Yet they, no less than governments and the UN itself, have responsibilities to establish allocations that match the need. How humanitarian institutions frame the issues and their own roles has a direct bearing on the terms under which resources are provided and accepted. A more probing approach to the causes of human need by the media might also facilitate a more proportionate use of resources.[42]

Stabilizing Conflict-Affected Societies and Post-Conflict Recovery

The massive amount of resources expended for humanitarian operations in the Great Lakes region masks the narrow vision and inadequate mechanisms of international support for conflict-affected societies. We offer four specific recommendations:

- *The use of assessed contributions for humanitarian and development activities associated with UN peacekeeping operations.* Peacekeeping operations should be part of a more coherent approach to addressing the causes of conflict and stabilizing the affected society. Through the "framework" process established by the Department of Political Affairs, the Department of Peacekeeping Operations, and the Department of Humanitarian Affairs (now called the Office for the Coordination of Humanitarian Affairs—OCHA), the secretary-general should recommend to the Security Council that assessed contributions cover not only resources for peacekeepers but also resources for emergency and recovery activities.[43] OCHA should be responsible for working with the Bretton Woods institutions, UNDP, and other relevant agencies to indicate how such recovery programs might best be initiated and what the initial costs would be.

It may seem curious to recommend placing the funding mechanisms for emergency and recovery activities within the panoply of peacekeeping efforts. Those efforts, however, would not conflict with activities normally carried out by UN specialized agencies, which could themselves play prominent roles in supporting additional post-conflict activities under the overall aegis of the SRSG. The activities added to the UN peacekeeping mandates would be those that could promote post-conflict recovery and use the assets of the peacekeepers themselves in collaboration with UN agencies. To continue to make important aid activities depend on "voluntary" contributions while governments are "assessed" to raise funds for peacekeeping work seems contradictory and counterproductive.

- *More integrated and innovative UN programming.* A lesson from the experience in Rwanda is that if peacekeeping capacity had been used alongside the resources of the humanitarian and development agencies the potential to move more quickly into essential infrastructural and social rehabilitation would have been in place. Overall coordination would have been possible through the SRSG, with strong and equal roles for both the UN humanitarian coordinator and the UN force commander.

Whether the Rwandan government would have taken a different attitude if innovative UN structures and procedures had met its needs quickly and efficiently will remain a matter of speculation. But it is possible that the government's attitude toward the peacekeepers themselves might also have been more positive had they been an integral part of a comprehensive effort to restore the nation's ability to function.

- *More effective donor coordination of recovery strategies.* Despite the efforts of the Rwanda Operations Support Group, there was little coherence in the political objectives and strategies of donors.[44] They were slow to recognize that recovery assistance needed the delivery capacity of emergency relief and the substance of developmental activities. They set up arbitrary and unworkable distinctions between relief on the one hand and rehabilitation and development on the other. Conflicting political agendas and perceptions of the Rwandan government intruded into donor discussions.
- *More responsive aid.* The mechanisms of assistance should be reformed to ensure quicker and more appropriate assistance. In addition, SRSGs in future complex emergencies should have a trust fund available to enable them to respond quickly to immediate recovery requirements. Such funds could be drawn down quickly, unencumbered by the usual conditions and administrative requirements of donors.

Lessons from Rwanda

In the final analysis, most complex emergencies are about conundrums. In the case of the internally displaced, the reason is all too apparent. The plight of the displaced person—the more so of displaced populations as groups—poses multifaceted and multidimensional challenges. Simply gaining access to provide assistance is one example; the impediments confronted in offering protection are another. Both are frequently complicated by the absence of a perceived vested interest in the fate of those who have abandoned, for whatever reasons, the conventional relationship between themselves and the state.

Herein lies the source of the first conundrum: that the very issue of displacement rarely garners much priority from the authorities whose populations are displaced within their own borders. Where ethnic tensions are involved, IDPs are often a bigger source of political embarrassment than of humanitarian concern to the resident authorities. In Rwanda the state saw no abiding humanitarian interest in the situation, perceiving the IDPs, like the refugees who had fled the country, as linked inextricably to the genocide. Thus the connection between the conundrum of displacement and the overarching conundrum of genocide.

Issues related to displacement examined in this chapter—morality, policy, and resource allocations on the one hand and operational and practical matters on the other—were part and parcel of the reality and the residue of genocide. At issue was not the attempt of one party to best another in a political or military confrontation of wills, but rather of one ethnic group to eliminate another altogether. The fact that both parties were implicated in exclusive policies and politics over time and throughout the Great Lakes region complicated the challenge further still.

Both conundrums posed challenges to international political will; and the international community did not respond effectively to either one, in part because it failed to approach the former conundrum as firmly nested in the latter. To be sure, the world expressed horror at the events of April 1994, but ineffectually. Effective action would have required measures to separate those guilty of crimes against humanity from genuine IDPs and refugees, to respond more comprehensively to issues of regional security and stability, and to deal with the legitimate assistance and infrastructural needs of a society traumatized by conflict.

There is much to be distilled from the experience in Rwanda. Its lessons on displacement are many. Displacement promises to be a recurring problem as societies splinter and the state loses its claim on the loyalties of populations and its centrality in international relations. Although it is to be hoped that genocide will not recur in Rwanda or elsewhere, it, too, offers lessons too important to leave unexamined.

Notes

1. The unleashing of genocide within the context of the 1990–94 civil war led to confusion—some of it genuine, some of it intentionally obfuscatory—about what was actually taking place. The UN Human Rights Commission's special rapporteur on summary executions sounded an alarm by pointing out that massacres being perpetrated in Rwanda seemed tantamount to genocide: "The cases of intercommunal violence brought to the Special Rapporteur's attention indicate very clearly that the victims of the attacks, Tutsis in the overwhelming majority of cases, have been targeted solely because of their membership of a certain ethnic group, and for no other objective reason. Article II [of the Convention on the Prevention and Punishment of the Crime of Genocide], paragraphs (a) and (b), might therefore be considered to apply to these cases." See Report of the Special Rapporteur on Summary, Arbitrary and Extrajudicial Executions, E/CN.4/1994/7/Add. 1 (United Nations, Commission on Human Rights, August 11, 1993), para. 79. Human rights groups themselves early on identified the problem as "genocide" and urged the signatories to the Genocide Convention to intervene.

By contrast, the United Nations for a number of weeks studiously avoided using such terminology, although the UN secretary-general did inform the international community during the last week of April 1994 that a "genocide" had taken place. "Even in the face of convincing proof of the true nature of the massacres," reported Human Rights Watch, "a few Security Council members refused to acknowledge that they constituted genocide" and effectively prevented use of the term in Security Council resolutions. U.S. officials were specifically instructed to avoid the term. Describing what was happening as a civil war between traditional rivals offered a convenient rationale for avoiding obligations under the Genocide Convention.

2. Discussions of the Rwandan crisis and the international response have the benefit of a growing number of studies. The most comprehensive is *The International Response to Conflict and Genocide: Lessons from the Rwanda Experience*, 5 vols. Joint Evaluation of Emergency Assistance to Rwanda (Copenhagen, March 1996). Released after more than a year of work by some fifty-two consultants and researchers, the evaluation contains four separate studies and a synthesis report. Initially proposed by DANIDA (the Danish government's international aid agency), the evaluation was managed by a Steering Committee consisting of thirty-seven members drawn from governments, UN organizations, and nongovernmental organizations (NGOs) who guided the work and provided the $1.7 million necessary to carry it out. The finished product, which includes a useful

review of bibliographical resources, represents the most exhaustive review of any major humanitarian operation to date.

A number of other studies provide useful perspectives on the issues. One of the first to appear, featuring first-person accounts of Rwandans involved in the crisis, was African Rights, *Rwanda: Death, Despair and Defiance* (London: 1994; rev. 1995). A second study is a collection of essays by senior officials involved in Rwanda and other complex emergencies: Jim Whitman and David Pocock, eds., *After Rwanda: The Coordination of United Nations Humanitarian Assistance* (London: Macmillan, 1996). Of particular relevance are chapters by Major General R. A. Dallaire, "The Changing Role of UN Peacekeeping Forces: The Relationship between UN Peacekeepers and NGOs in Rwanda"; and Randolph Kent, "The Integrated Operations Centre in Rwanda: Coping with Complexity." A third volume, by Larry Minear and Philippe Guillot, *Soldiers to the Rescue: Humanitarian Lessons from Rwanda* (Paris: OECD, 1996), examines the role of international military forces in responding to the crisis. Various UN organizations and private aid agencies have also produced reviews of their own experiences. For example, see Department of Humanitarian Affairs, "Report on the Coordination of Humanitarian Activities in Rwanda," United Nations, 1995; and International Federation of Red Cross and Red Crescent Societies, "Under the Volcanoes: Special Focus on the Rwandan Refugee Crisis," in *World Disasters Report* (Geneva, 1994).

3. The moral complexities surrounding the genocide stem in part from the government's use of its official radio not only to urge the elimination of the Tutsi but also to threaten the lives of those Hutu who refused to take part in the slaughter. These threats were reinforced by *interahamwe*, who were not reluctant to act on the pronouncements of Radio Milles Collines, a privately owned and operated extremist broadcasting system established by members of the government and the wife of President Habyarimana. For examples of such broadcasts, see J. A. and C. Pott-Berry, eds., *Genocide in Rwanda: A Collective Memory* (London: CARE-UK, 1996). Such radio pronouncements should be put in the context of a Hutu majority, the vast majority of whom were minimally educated peasants, traditionally dominated by the Tutsi minority until the early 1960s. Also a reality was the perceived threat that a Tutsi army might take over the country.

4. *Historical Perspective: Some Explanatory Factors*, vol. 1 of *The International Response to Conflict and Genocide: Lessons from the Rwanda Experience*, Joint Evaluation of Emergency Assistance to Rwanda (Copenhagen, March 1996), p. 12.

5. The number of "old caseload" refugees returning to Rwanda generally used for planning purposes in 1994–95 was 600,000. The majority came from Uganda, where almost two generations of Rwandans lived both as official refugees and in some instances as "Ugandans." A much smaller percentage came from Burundi and an even smaller numbers from Tanzania, Kenya, and Zaire. The relationship between this planning figure and the numbers that fled Rwanda between 1959 and the early 1990s is very imprecise. The figure of 600,000 included those born in exile. The multidonor evaluation concludes that "this figure is contested by many [though is probably] the very best estimate available" (ibid., p. 30).

6. When the then-president Juvenal Habyarimana spoke about the possibility of refugees returning to Rwanda, he used the analogy of a "full glass" to suggest the negative consequences of any significant return. Similarly, there are many prominent persons within the Rwandan leadership today who question the need for a mass return of the Hutu who fled the country in 1994. There are also demographic and economic questions that the new government must face. The lack of adequate farmland for an economy based primarily on agriculture inevitably poses a disincentive to return. The ability of the country to support an additional 2 million people not only represents a serious economic issue but also raises questions of "ethnic balance."

7. *Historical Perspective: Some Explanatory Factors*, p. 11.

8. For discussion of such relationships, see Peter Uvin, *Development, Aid, and Conflict: Reflections from the Case of Rwanda* (Helsinki: UN University/WIDER, 1996).

9. Reprinted from *Historical Perspective: Some Explanatory Factors*, p. 55.

10. During April and May, 580,000 fled from Rwanda to Tanzania; in July, 1.2 million fled to Zaire. An additional 243,000 Rwandans who went to Burundi during April constitute the remainder of the 2 million persons referred to in the text.

11. Reliable sources state that among the refugee population were probably more than 40,000 persons belonging to the former military and political apparatus who had played an instrumental role in the planning or execution of the genocide and who, under the terms of UNHCR's mandate, would be undeserving of international protection. The government of Rwanda, however, estimated that the total number of guilty persons was around 170,000, or about 10 percent of the refugee population. This figure most likely included those in the first two groups referred to in the text.

12. Initially, many among the refugees were subjected to the authoritarian rule of what became known as the "intimidators," who either as former military or *interahamwe* officials ran some of the camps as virtual states within a state. The intimidators tried to control the exchange of information in the camps, perpetuated stories of terror and mass killings in Rwanda, and through their own brutality ensured camp compliance. This military influence was later reported to have been replaced by "more conventional civilian control." One analyst has asserted that "the camp populations have now become so indoctrinated that force is no longer needed to convince them of the terror that awaits across the borders. The 'bush-telegraph' tells them about the killings in the communes, about the prisons, about Kibeho. And this is what keeps them united in the camps and unwilling to return home."

13. The insensitivity of many well-intentioned humanitarian organizations was remarkable. At a mid-1995 reception for a visiting delegation to which senior Rwandan government officials were invited, one major multilateral organization displayed, amidst tables bulging with elegant canapés and drinks, copies of magazines featuring its work with Rwandan refugees in Zaire. Rwandans were also puzzled by the promotion by aid groups of conferences, workshops, and seminars

on reconciliation only months after the genocide had ended. While to aid agencies it seemed essential to move quickly to reconstruction, Rwandans believed that generous assistance to refugees and dispassionate discussions of reconciliation begged profound questions of justice.

14. Convention Relating to the Status of Refugees, Article 1F (1951).

15. The cattle brought through the northeastern parklands, or Akagera forest, had important symbolic as well as economic value. For many Rwandans—the very wealthy as well as the very poor—cattle represented bank accounts on the hoof. Cattle wealth is assumed to have provided a considerable portion of the resources used to build up the RPA, although the herds destroyed much of the parklands after the refugees returned. The situation became so politically sensitive that for almost two months the minister of rehabilitation and social integration operated out of the northwest in order to give higher priority to the problem. Human and livestock displacement and resettlement were thus intimately related.

16. In a January 1995 meeting between the UNHCR special representative for the Great Lakes and the UN humanitarian coordinator for Rwanda, the former noted the importance of successfully returning the IDPs to their home communes: "If the IDPs don't make it back safely, we'll find ourselves with at least an additional 150,000 in Zaire that we won't be able to handle."

17. The UN secretary-general also appointed separate representatives to deal with the region, including Ambassadors Aldo Romano Ajello and José Luis Jesus. These individuals, however, did not provide full-time presence in the region or have the mandate or capacity to deal with the regional nature of the problem.

18. For a more detailed account, see Minear-Guillot, *Soldiers to the Rescue*, chap. 4.

19. For an elaboration of these points, see Minear-Guillot, *Soldiers to the Rescue*.

20. The UNAMIR mandate, revised on May 17, 1994, provided for 6,000 uniformed troops, military observers, and civilian police. UNAMIR was charged with supporting and providing safe conditions for IDPs and other groups in Rwanda (both throughout the country and on the border) and with helping humanitarian organizations to provide aid. UNAMIR was to monitor border crossing points and could take action in self-defense against those who threatened protected sites and populations and the delivery and distribution of relief aid. Despite these wide-ranging duties, UNAMIR had Chapter VI rather than Chapter VII authority. A Chapter VII mandate would have permitted the use of deadly force to impose peace, empowering UN troops to tackle the broader challenge of restoring and maintaining law and order at the commune level. A Chapter VI mandate allowed deadly force to be used only in self-defense and in the protection of UN installations.

21. During the month of December, UNAMIR joined with the RPA in an ostensibly secret operation to root out the intimidators and perpetrators of genocide from the Kibeho camp. This joint operation was planned without the knowledge of the UN humanitarian coordinator, though UN aid agencies as well as NGOs were working in Kibeho. No incidents occurred, largely because word

had already spread throughout the camp about the upcoming operation and the apparently guilty had fled. Nevertheless, the fact that no provision was made for the safety of relief workers (let alone for innocent civilians) reflected poorly on UNAMIR's planning and did little to enhance its cooperation with civilian agencies. It was in part to prevent UNAMIR from taking such unilateral initiatives that the Integrated Operations Centre (described later) was created.

22. François Jean, ed., *Populations in Danger 1995* (London: Médecins sans Frontières, 1995), p. 45.

23. In November 1994, NGOs working in the camps in Zaire issued a joint statement condemning the continued intimidation by ex-FAR and *interahamwe* of the refugees and the international community's reluctance to address this challenge to recognized principles of refugee law and treatment. On the basis of this declaration, a number of NGOs withdrew their services.

24. The French government was identified with ongoing support for the ancient Hutu regime, which was francophone. Even after the transition from the Hutu to the Tutsi regime, the French were alleged to have continued supplying arms and military training to the discredited army.

25. On occasion, U.S. Assistant Secretary of State for African Affairs George Moose chaired meetings.

26. Given the constraints described in the text, it is nevertheless noteworthy that UNHCR provided a staff member for the IOC secretariat and, during the Kibeho crisis, major transport assistance. WFP, too, supplied a junior member of its staff to the IOC operation. UNICEF was highly supportive and provided a representative but was too overstretched to focus on the IDP issue. IOM and NGO involvement was considerable. UNAMIR, which detailed three people to the IOC, also provided telecommunications and computer equipment. Its threatened withdrawal from the IOC in the midst of the Kibeho crisis reflected the force commander's distress at not having received essential information from the IOC during the operation. As later became apparent, the information had been received but not transmitted within UNAMIR's own chain of command.

27. Conversations between the authors and UNAMIR Force Commander Major-General Guy Tousignant, most recently on October 18, 1996.

28. As early as September 1994 the SRSG proposed a Rwanda Emergency Normalisation Plan designed to address key infrastructure requirements. Such a plan would have gone a long way toward proving the international community's commitment to stabilizing the traumatized society of Rwanda. This type of plan would have been well suited for a quick-action trust fund to be established under the SRSG.

29. It is worth noting that one of IRIN's functions was to counteract the agencies' habit of failing to transmit information across borders on a regular basis to their colleagues. The conventional pattern of communications is from the field directly to headquarters; rarely does the field systematically transmit information to colleagues in neighboring countries. IRIN encouraged the agencies in the field to transmit information for circulation throughout all countries in the region as well as to the international community at large.

30. See Randolph C. Kent, "Rwanda: The Aid Impasse," *DHA News*, May–June 1995, pp. 27–29.

31. An example of the nature of the needs and the reluctance of the established aid agencies to take them on was provided by the challenge of improving the conditions in the country's prisons. In the absence of a UN organization with competence in that area, the humanitarian coordinator, in his personal capacity, was asked to assume the responsibility of special adviser to the SRSG on prisons.

32. The government's original figure of 300 and other figures ranging from 800 to 8,000 reflected the politics and the confusion surrounding the Kibeho incident. The most accurate figure probably came from an Australian military medical team that counted almost 4,000 corpses in areas into which it was allowed. (The team had covered only about half the area before being prevented from proceeding by the RPA.) Even after the worst two days of incidents, there were periodic shootings as the RPA reportedly continued its own "screening process." The final figures are not known, but somewhere between 4,000 and 8,000 deaths seems likely.

33. Originally it was thought that the government and donors had agreed that the shortage of Rwandan magistrates would be temporarily offset by magistrates from other francophone countries. It was assumed that a functioning justice system would relieve donors of the burdens of assisting the government to build prisons and, more important, would be a major step toward some form of accommodation, if not reconciliation, with Rwandans outside the country. After months of apparently successful discussions, the government rejected the idea of using foreign magistrates.

34. Ironically, the dysfunctional division of labor among the agencies regarding IDPs had been a recurring problem even before the crisis in Rwanda. In a 1994 report on displacement issues from a global perspective, the representative of the secretary-general on IDPs noted that "despite greater willingness on the part of UN agencies to develop more coherent collaborative arrangements, a vacuum of responsibility often exists in cases of internal displacement." Francis M. Deng, "Internally Displaced Persons: An Interim Report to the United Nations Secretary-General on Protection and Assistance," Refugee Policy Group and United Nations Department of Humanitarian Affairs, December 1994, p. 40. See also Roberta Cohen and Jacques Cuenod, *Improving Institutional Arrangements for the Internally Displaced* (Washington, D.C.: Brookings Institution–Refugee Policy Group Project on Internal Displacement, October 1995). See also Lance Clark, "Internal Refugees: The Hidden Half," in U.S. Committee for Refugees, *World Refugee Survey: 1988 in Review* (Washington, D.C., 1988), pp. 18–24.

35. Clauses in both the Geneva and OAU conventions on refugees allow individuals known to have carried arms or to have committed crimes against humanity to be denied refugee status.

36. The UN at the highest levels was officially informed about the introduction of arms into Zaire and was provided with documentary evidence by April 1995

that included pictures of arms caches. The evidence sparked little interest among senior UN officials.

37. Such an arrangement was tried for the first time in 1995 in Haiti, where the deputy SRSG served also as the UNDP resident representative and the DHA humanitarian coordinator. See Edwige Balutansky and others, *Haiti Held Hostage: International Responses to the Quest for Nationhood 1986–1996* (Providence, R.I.: Watson Institute, 1996), pp. 80–81, 107–8.

38. *Humanitarian Aid and Effects*, vol. 3 of *The International Response to Conflict and Genocide*, Joint Evaluation of Emergency Assistance to Rwanda (Copenhagen, March 1996), p. 159.

39. Rony Brauman, "Genocide in Rwanda: We Can't Say We Didn't Know," in Jean, *Populations in Danger*, p. 89.

40. Peter D. Bell, "Rwanda Aid Doesn't Add Up," *Christian Science Monitor*, February 2, 1996.

41. Kathleen Newland, "U.S. Refugee Policy: Dilemmas and Directions," Carnegie Endowment for International Peace, Washington, D.C., 1996, p. 40.

42. For a review of the role of the international media in influencing humanitarian activities and international policy in Rwanda and other major recent crises, see Larry Minear, Colin Scott, and Thomas G. Weiss, *The News Media, Civil War, and Humanitarian Action* (Boulder, Colo.: Lynne Rienner, 1996).

43. The "framework" arrangements established in 1994 among DPKO, DPA, and DHA principally concern sharing of information. However, by 1996 promising moves were under way to engage the capacities of each to assist in the preparation of peacekeeping proposals.

44. Despite two years of the donor-driven ROSG, few practical ideas emerged from the donors about how to support post-conflict recovery or societal stabilization.

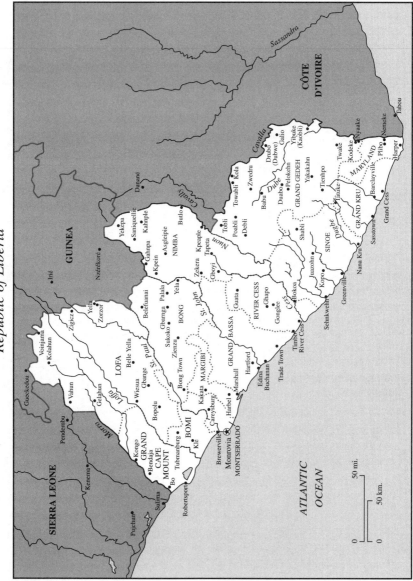

Republic of Liberia

CHAPTER FOUR

Liberia:
A Nation Displaced

Colin Scott

WHILE OFFICIAL ESTIMATES for internally displaced persons (IDPs) and refugees peak at 70 percent of the population, it is hard to see how a single Liberian family has not been displaced at some stage by Liberia's civil war. Starting with the 1989 incursion of Charles Taylor's National Patriotic Front of Liberia (NPFL), the crisis has run the length of the post–cold war period, bringing all political and economic normalcy to a halt. Yet it has only surfaced at isolated points on the agendas of Western capitals, and international action largely has been limited to a flawed regional security intervention accompanied by a frustrated humanitarian aid operation. Although the displacement has been widespread, a human manifestation of state collapse, Liberia has never received the sustained and concerted attention necessary to break the cycle of conflict and begin national recovery. It languishes, like Afghanistan and Somalia, in a category of "stateless societies," whose people remain beyond the reach of universally accepted standards for basic human rights.

This case study demonstrates:

(1) How the current displacement problem (IDPs and refugees) is a symptom of the collapse of Liberia as a state and therefore rooted in the complexities of the struggle for power, shrouded in ethnic

and regional politics. The maltreatment of the displaced is the latest episode in a history of neglect of indigenous populations by successive administrations since the founding of the state of Liberia.

(2) How the displaced thus far have been failed by the international response through a cluster of policy shortcomings, at both an international and an in-country level. These shortcomings include:

- the failure of external aid to offset the dynamics of conflict;
- the inadequate international security response to the growing crisis and outbreak of conflict;
- the troubled relationship between regional and multilateral security institutions once intervention had begun;
- the problems of managing tension between political-security and humanitarian objectives, particularly within the UN system, both internationally and within Liberia;
- the failure of aid coordination systems among and between UN agencies, the International Committee of the Red Cross, and nongovernmental organizations, both internationally and in Liberia; and
- the failure to address the special needs of IDPs, and, in particular, to respond to the vulnerability of women and children.

(3) How the displaced, IDPs and refugees, remain the core human capital for rebuilding Liberian society and are the future foundation of any nation-state. Their predicament reflects a crisis of national identity: finding common ground with allegiance to Liberia as a political and economic entity must replace the shifting ground of factional oppression. Full political, social, and economic recovery may take a generation of Liberian effort supported by long-term international commitment.

Although this study necessarily focuses on the role of external institutions in meeting the needs of the displaced, no findings can diminish the responsibility of the Liberian people to create the conditions necessary for the rehabilitation of their own country. As a minister of the Liberian National Transitional Government put it at an international forum in 1994, "Unless we address our problems, we will have a dead country and a dead people."[1] The resumption of all-out fighting in April 1996 only served to fuel the doubts about the feasibility of any external assistance and renewed speculation about the need for some kind of international trusteeship.

Clearly, the complex ethnic history of Liberia, which has received little external study, now has been thrown irreversibly into a new phase. The premise of this paper is that only Liberians themselves can address ethnic reconciliation. Though external actors should have some understanding of those issues, their main responsibility extends to assistance providing the context for national healing. This study therefore concentrates on extracting lessons from recent international actions, analyzing proximate causes of displacement, and assessing the condition of IDPs. The concluding section outlines the range of conditions necessary for a lasting transition from war to peace.

Historical and Political Background

This case study does not attempt to provide more than a summary of Liberia's 150-year history. For that the reader is referred to existing literature, which highlights the complex ethno-political and regional dynamics that have been at work throughout. Of particular salience is the evolution of relationships between coastal administrations and indigenous people in the interior of the country.[2] It is important to note that Liberia has struggled throughout its history to maintain statehood, experiencing repeated internal conflict, economic collapse, and self-interested external interventions. Not for the first time, Liberia has become a stage for regional ambition. The other key external dynamic has been the historical ambivalence of the United States toward Liberia, at times providing critical support, at others backing away from any commitment to an alliance or guarantee of statehood.

Of more immediate concern are the condition and prospects of the displaced as an indication of Liberia's viability as a nation: how far has recent history destroyed the potential of the different ethnic groups to coexist in a shared political-economic unit? Although normally understood as a Taylor-led NPFL struggle to remove Samuel Doe, the current civil war is perhaps better understood as a violent struggle for power that started with the military rebellion of 1980. The conflict has created a generation of "war children," mostly uneducated with little prospect of legitimate employment. As a consequence, Liberia has been thrown off a fragile (and arguably dysfunctional) path of development into a cycle of violence and failed peace initiatives. Breaking this cycle will require the establishment of political, economic, and social order in which the displaced have a real and durable stake.

A Chronology of Significant Milestones

The following chronology provides a guide to some of the more recent events that have direct bearing on the displaced of Liberia:

1821–22   Beginnings of settlement by freed American slaves.

1847   Liberia declares itself an independent republic.

1862   Recognition by the United States.

1919   Liberia becomes charter member of League of Nations.

1926   Firestone rubber plantation established.

1944–71   William Tubman administration.

1971–80   Tolbert administration.

1975   Liberia becomes one of the fifteen founding members of the Economic Community of West African States (ECOWAS).

1980   Samuel Doe leads military coup ending 150 years of domination by Americo-Liberians.

1980–90   Doe's regime (supported by the United States) marked by violence and suppression of repeated coup attempts.

1989   NPFL under the leadership of Charles Taylor commences rebellion in northern Liberia (December).

1990   NPFL reaches Monrovia but is repelled by ECOMOG (Economic Community Monitoring Group, ECOWAS) peacekeeping force (August). Doe killed. Interim Government of National Unity (IGNU) installed under Amos Sawyer.

1991   First peace talks fail. Yamoussoukro (Côte d'Ivoire) talks begin. United Liberation Movement for Democracy (ULIMO) begins operations against NPFL.

1992   NPFL launches new attack on Monrovia, repulsed by ECOMOG (October). UN secretary-general appoints special representative (November).

1993   New peace agreement signed at Cotonou, Benin (July). Disarmament fails amid increased factional fighting. UN Observer Mission in Liberia (UNOMIL) created and deployed.

1994   Sawyer resigns (March). IGNU replaced by Liberian National Transitional Government (LNTG). New peace process started in Akosombo, Ghana (September) under President Jerry Rawlings.

1995   Continuation of fighting. New peace accord signed at Abuja, Nigeria (August). LNTG II installed. Wider ECOMOG deployment halted by renewed fighting.

1996   Renewed factional fighting leads to all-out conflict in Monrovia (April). ECOMOG does not intervene. Foreign diplomatic and aid staff evacuated. Fresh peace accord signed in Abuja (August). New timetable for disarmament (November) and elections (May 1997) adopted.

The Phases of Conflict and International Response[3]

In order to structure information about the displaced across the constantly shifting circumstances of the crisis, the following phases, identified by prevailing security frameworks, are employed throughout this study: (1) Pre-1989: From Oligarchy to Tyranny; (2) 1989–90: Descent into Anarchy; (3) August 1990–92: Regional Intervention; (4) November 1992–96: Regional-UN Partnership.

The following section outlines these four phases of the conflict, each of which represents different needs and opportunities for intervention. For the displaced, a growing lack of humanitarian space within which agencies could operate highlights the shortcomings of a humanitarian-only response. The lack of an integrated security-humanitarian response throughout these phases is characteristic of the different attempts of external action and the source of their weakness.

PRE-1989: FROM OLIGARCHY TO TYRANNY. Founded by freed American slaves in the 1820s, Liberia declared itself an independent republic in 1847 at a time when much of Africa was being colonized by Europe. However, Liberia did not escape its own internal colonialization and for the next 130 years was dominated by a coastal Americo-Liberian elite that exploited the interior and indigenous population. Government was more of an extended family business than the microcosm of a U.S. democratic system that its institutions implied. This oligarchical arrangement only ended with Doe's overthrow of President Tolbert's government in 1980.

Throughout the 1960s, 1970s, and 1980s, Liberia was a major recipient of foreign aid, largely from the United States.[4] It is questionable how far this assistance addressed, or even intended to address, root causes of conflict such as poverty and inequality. Historically, the United States had always been the prime source of economic support for Liberia, dating back to the first settlement. Economic dependence grew steadily from the 1900s, when Washington approved a forty-year loan worth $1.7 million, and then a $5 million loan in the 1920s. But the United States maintained a diplomatic distance, careful not to create any form of alliance that would guarantee Liberian independence or territorial integrity. The establishment of the Firestone rubber plantation in 1926 was another U.S.-inspired economic landmark, matched in the post-war Tubman administration by an "Open Door" policy designed to open up the country's interior to foreign investors. As a result, mining and shipping income flourished, with exports in the 1960s growing by 18.4 percent annually.

Only with the arrival of the cold war did U.S. political interest in Liberia begin to catch up with economic investment. Liberia provided a key U.S. communications and logistical foothold in Africa. From 1946 to 1961 Liberia received $41 million in assistance, and $278 million between 1962 and 1980, making it the largest per capita recipient of aid in Africa. This trend was accelerated in the Doe years, when aid between 1981 and 1985 reached $402 million.

However, this aid was increasingly geopolitically driven, especially under the Reagan administration, when a stable base for CIA operations against Qaddafi's Libya became the major U.S. objective. Doe manipulated this opportunity to maximum advantage to increase his autocratic hold on power and subjugate his rivals. From 1980 to 1986, U.S. assistance totaled $434 million, of which $200 million was to support government debts and $66 million in military assistance. That aid continued to the consternation of critics in both Liberia and Washington, who were appalled by Doe's ever-worsening human rights violations. Little of the wealth created by a steady increase in GDP and development assistance trickled down to the general population, a trend characterized by the term "growth without development."

While U.S. aid had overt political and military agendas, other international development assistance did little to avert conflict. Liberia joined the International Monetary Fund and World Bank group in 1962, when it was already heavily in debt. A series of loan packages over the next three decades aimed at stabilizing the currency and bringing financial discipline to government did not succeed. No public accounts survive, but increasingly blatant corruption and embezzlement were reported by foreign observers. As Doe's regime foundered, foreign aid increasingly was diverted to pay off supporters and retain power. Exasperated by lack of cooperation, the World Bank closed down its operations in 1987, having seen little benefit from more than $250 million in loans to the government. According to a senior bank officials, the Bretton Woods institutions were pressured repeatedly by the United States, which had its own political agenda, to persevere with the strategy of financial stabilization.[5] Ultimately, one official noted, "Doe was just too frightened of his colleagues to comply" with any of the loan conditions (such as proper accounting) which would cut off his last line of support.[6]

Even in the final years of Doe's regime there were opportunities for the U.S. government to avert the all-out conflict that was to follow by easing him out of office. However, short-term policy objectives overrode longer-term considerations. International assistance was dominated by U.S. support to a crumbling regime, including arms that would be around to fuel the growing conflict. Doe's final miscalculation was that the United States, ultimately, would give in and not risk its "special relationship" and national interests in Liberia. As U.S. interest waned with the demise of cold war policies, and external assistance finally dried up, Doe lost control of his own political patronage system.

Charles Taylor, a former administrator in, and fugitive from, the Doe government, began his rebellion in the late 1980s through his National Patriotic Front of Liberia (NPFL). This homespun revolt was centered in the Gio and Mano ethnic regions of Nimba County, focus of previous anti-Doe uprisings and reprisals. Despite the ethnic roots of conflict, Taylor's rebellion was dependent on Libyan military support and the tacit support of officials in the Côte d'Ivoire and Burkina Faso governments. As regional interest grew, Western governments began accelerating their withdrawal.

DECEMBER 1989–AUGUST 1990: DESCENT INTO ANARCHY. As the NPFL rebellion spread, opportunities for conflict prevention, or conflict management, extended into the final days of a desperate regime. It is a matter of conjecture whether a U.S. military intervention would have "policed" the conflict in its early stages. Even as late as August 1990, when the NPFL forces looked set to overrun the capital, the presence of 2,000 marines off Monrovia gave hope of intervention to many Liberians. But U.S. and other international attention was focused on the growing crisis in the Gulf and fast-moving events in the collapse of the Soviet bloc. The European Community, equally preoccupied with events closer to its borders, was no more inclined to intervene. The conflict did not even make the agenda of the UN Security Council. The groundbreaking humanitarian intervention to protect Kurds in northern Iraq was still months away and dependent on much stronger geopolitical links. Sporadic attention from the international news media mirrored international indifference. With media resources committed to other theaters of war, coverage only emerged at heightened periods of fighting or atrocities.[7]

1990–92: REGIONAL INTERVENTION.[8] This phase was marked by a regional security intervention supported by sporadic diplomatic activity from the wider international community, which substituted a humanitarian response for more assertive action. As violence spread to Monrovia, and civilian massacres and widespread starvation were reported, exasperated representatives of the Economic Community of West African States (ECOWAS) took action. In August 1990, following a failed diplomatic approach that largely was rejected by Charles Taylor as onesided, ECOWAS set up a ceasefire monitoring group (ECOMOG). Its formal mandate was to keep the peace, restore law and order, and monitor the cease-fire. Although ECOWAS statements also cited humanitarian concerns, it was given no specific humanitarian tasks.[9] Overall, ECOWAS justifications stressed the threat to regional peace and security, including the attacks from Liberia on Sierra Leone and weapons flows from outside to insurgent forces.

Although ECOMOG was referred to as a peacekeeping force, the NPFL threat to resist it (as illegal and unwelcome) excluded any notion of consent, a key ingredient in conventional peacekeeping.[10] Its requisite neutrality was further jeopardized by the immediate onset of hostilities with NPFL troops. As one senior UN official put it, "Pushing Taylor out of Monrovia by force is hardly peace-keeping."[11] ECOMOG is therefore better understood (at least in its more aggressive phases) as peace-enforcing in the spirit of Chapter VII of the UN Charter, which helps explain some of its subsequent difficulties in accommodating humanitarian aid.

ECOWAS statements also presented the intervention as a legitimate regional initiative in its own right, not requiring Security Council approval.[12] Indeed the Security Council did not discuss Liberia until January 22, 1991, when it reaffirmed ECOWAS efforts. It backed ECOWAS again on May 7, 1992, endorsing the Yamoussoukro IV peace process. Only on November 19, 1992, in Resolution 788 did the Security Council invoke Chapter VII to back ECOWAS "peace-keeping forces."[13] Despite such sporadic attention, ECOWAS always had implicit UN support in the sense that, as one senior UN official put it, "the United Nations deferred to OAU, which in turn deferred to ECOWAS."

Following its arrival in Monrovia, ECOMOG was criticized by all sides to the conflict. It was accused of taking sides with the breakaway Independent National Patriotic Front of Liberia (INPFL) and Armed Forces of Liberia (AFL) factions and of failing to protect and feed Liberians. The INPFL criticized it for not attacking the NPFL, and the AFL blamed it for the capture of President Doe by INPFL. ECOMOG was also accused of widespread looting and systematically stockpiling goods for return to Nigeria. These criticisms persisted long after the November 1990 cease-fire.[14]

Although ECOMOG never had explicit humanitarian objectives, it did reduce hostilities and atrocities, and by establishing order in greater Monrovia it set up a safe haven for thousands of displaced Liberians. By securing the port and airport, it also assisted relief operations. In this phase ECOMOG functioned as a police force within its security zone and a defense force against the NPFL on the perimeter. "The re-establishment of peace in Monrovia was a practical pre-condition for the delivery of humanitarian aid," noted one senior UN humanitarian official.[15] "However, ECOMOG was in no way responsible," he confirmed, "for assessing, identifying, and providing humanitarian assistance." In this sense, "ECOMOG was a necessary element in the overall humanitarian strategy." During this period, there was sufficient separation between ECOMOG's security functions and the UN's humanitarian operations for the latter to accomplish their mission, at least within areas of government and ECOMOG control. Beyond the security zone, the NPFL-aligned "government in waiting" attempted to establish a parallel administration, although security was to be a far greater problem once UN or NGO humanitarian agencies left the safe haven of Monrovia.

During this phase there were arguably some missed opportunities for more constructive involvement by the UN on the diplomatic side. Despite criticism, the UN continued its policy of nonintervention established by Secretary-General Javier Perez de Cuellar. Following the ECOWAS meeting in Bamako in November 1990, which reaffirmed the standing of the Interim Government of National Unity (IGNU), prolonged peace negotiations failed to secure the previously agreed upon participation of the warring factions in government. Some observers felt a UN special representative at that stage might have worked to secure arrangements that did not leave the NPFL feeling left out. Others felt there was favoritism toward the IGNU in the UN political system (for example, allowing IGNU president Sawyer to address the General Assembly on the Liberian crisis) which implied recognition and further alienated the NPFL camp.

1992–96: REGIONAL-UN PARTNERSHIP. Following the renewal of fighting in October 1992 and criticism of its absence in all but the humanitarian mode, the UN attempted to increase its influence. However, the regional political and security context was becoming ever more complicated. This phase (still current at the time of writing) has been marked by successive peace accords, normally brokered by current ECOWAS "chairing" states and repeatedly broken by an increasing array of factional warlords. Major accords in Cotonou (July 1993), which established a UN Observer Mission in Liberia (UNOMIL), Akosombo (September 1994), Accra (December 1994), and Abuja (August 1995 and 1996), have merely punctuated episodes of oppression for the displaced.[16]

Following the NPFL offensive of October 1992 and increased military pressure, ECOMOG resumed a peace enforcement role. The implications for relief activities outside of Monrovia, already severely restricted by factional conflict, were decidedly negative. ECOMOG carried out air attacks on NPFL territory in late 1992 and 1993 in the name of security, hitting civilian, medical, and aid installations and drawing international criticism.[17] In a further effort to isolate the NPFL, ECOMOG imposed and enforced a ban on importing relief supplies from Côte d'Ivoire. Its association with anti-NPFL factions, the newly emerging United Liberation Movement for Democracy (ULIMO), and the AFL did nothing for its reputation as a guardian of human rights.

The Cotonou peace agreement of July 1993 set up a process to be followed in subsequent peace initiatives that attempted to include all parties to the power struggle. The agreement provided for the encampment of warring factions under the supervision of an expanded ECOMOG and a UN observer mission. This was a significant change in the security architecture, the creation of a "hybrid," with separation of armed peacekeeping and unarmed observer roles. The disarmament process was to coincide with the formation of a transitional government, which would include representatives from all factions and cover an interim period before elections in September 1994 and the installation of an elected regime.

The trend of events in the period since Cotonou has been negative, on both the political and the humanitarian fronts. An initial major problem was the lengthy delay in setting up UNOMIL and the expanded ECOMOG force necessary to give backup to the agreement. Once established, the "hybrid" military presence created role confusion about disarmament responsibility. Above all, the situation has been complicated by a proliferation of warring factions, including the emergence of another anti-NPFL force, the Liberia Peace Council (LPC), which was not a signatory to the agreement.

This further splintering along ethnic and linguistic lines has been the major political characteristic of the current phase, entangling the peace process and complicating humanitarian operations at every turn. The controlling agenda of the multiplying factions appears to rest as much on local power and material as on longer-term and wider political ambition. The presence of 400 UNOMIL staff (reduced to ninety by the end of 1994) and the persuasive powers of the international community whom they serve became outmatched by the obstacles. A longer-term pattern thus set in of constantly shifting alliances in a multifactional balancing of power.

Reviewing the situation in April 1994, the UN secretary-general's report reflected international frustration.[18] Despite some progress in the establishment of a transitional government, delays in the processes of filling cabinet posts, electoral prospects and, above all, disarmament raised doubts about the continuation of the UNOMIL mandate. Distressed by the slow implementation of peace arrangements, the secretary-general warned: "The patience of the international community is clearly running out. . . . The UN Security Council has implicitly warned the Liberian parties that progress must come, and soon, if UNOMIL is to continue playing any role in Liberia."[19]

With a further period of "no peace, no war" and no all-out assault on Monrovia from the NPFL, ECOMOG was able to resume more of a policing role. Although its task was complicated by the increase in factional fighting, ECOMOG tried to avoid involvement in these skirmishes. While the Cotonou agreement also had charged ECOMOG with supervising disarmament, it achieved little in this area, putting prior responsibility for disarmament on other parties instead.

However, ECOMOG was able to assist cross-line humanitarian operations by protecting convoys, a service not willingly rendered during 1992–93. Meanwhile, earlier tensions between ECOMOG and NGOs regarding cross-border operations eased, although ECOMOG continued to harbor doubts about NGO and UN agency neutrality. In addition, factional suspicion continued that aid agencies were being used as cover for spying and infiltration.

By February 1994, the UN secretary-general was able to report a good working relationship between ECOMOG and UNOMIL. However, ECOMOG's various identities as peacekeeper, peace-enforcer, and protector of Nigerian interests continued to create confusion. Despite measures in the Cotonou agreement to augment ECOMOG with East African troops, Nigerian forces predominated, still doing most of the "dirty work" in the outlying areas of Liberia.

During this period, ECOMOG was still unable to achieve the status of a neutral peacekeeping force. It functioned more as a regional police force, curbing the worst excesses, going on the offensive when necessary, but acting in a reactive rather than proactive fashion. Regional sensitivities persisted too, especially fear that the conflict would spread to neighboring Sierra Leone and Côte d'Ivoire. This political cocktail made for an ever-increasing intoxicant for violence and generated uncertainty and insecurity for aid operations.

Peace talks in Ghana between October and December 1994 represented a last-ditch effort to salvage the Cotonou framework. Despite signing the latest of multiple cease-fires, the talks broke up in early 1995 over disagreement on factional representation in the new Liberian National Transitional Government (LNTG, replacing IGNU). The first eight months of the year saw a return to fighting and failed peace initiatives catalogued in successive reports by the UN secretary-general to the Security Council. A new peace accord signed at Abuja in August created a second transitional government (LNTG II), and for the first time factional leaders became involved in government in Monrovia. Abuja also provided for ECOMOG and UNOMIL deployment into factional areas. However, a renewed attempt at ECOMOG deployment in December led to heavy fighting in the Tubmanburg area.

In the early months of 1996 tensions mounted inside Monrovia, leading to a standoff between yet another splinter group, ULIMO-J, and opposing factions. The April 1996 outbreak of all-out fighting in Monrovia marked a new high-water mark of violence, as ECOMOG for the first time stood aside to let the conflict engulf the center of town, including the UN and diplomatic enclave of Mamba Point. With the departure of virtually all international diplomatic and aid personnel, international

Table 4-1. *The Causes of Displacement in Liberia*

Underlying Causes	Proximate Causes
Structural factors	
A historically weak, externally created state	Collapsing state
	Shifting miltary balance of power
Internal security threatened by ethnic geography	Destabilizing population shifts
Political factors	
Centralization of power	Since Doe, military tyranny and repression
Long-term discrimination by political institutions against indigenous people	Rapid political transitions
	Violent leadership struggles
Exclusionary ideologies and intergroup interference	International indifference, regional politics
International and regional attitudes	
Economic and social factors	
Chronic economic weakness	Collapse of Liberian dollar
Concentration of wealth in coastal elites	Fortress Monrovia: the locus of wealth and focus of power struggle
Failure of development to redress inequities	
	Aid concentration in Monrovia
Competition for natural resources	Militarization of society
Cultural and perceptual factors	
Indigenous versus Americo-Liberian elites	Ethnic hatred
Ethnic competition	Monrovia elites versus interior rebels
	Normalization of violence

frustration reached new heights amid widespread skepticism about future commitment. Despite a revised Abuja accord in August 1996 and UN commitment to a revised timetable for disarmament and elections to follow in 1997, Liberia will require a fundamental revival in international donor interest.

The Causes of Displacement

Displacement in Liberia has been driven by the conflict, with all its devastating political, economic, and social consequences. As with any conflict, the debate surrounding the causation and prolongation of Liberia's power struggle is complex and controversial. Sources differ on the relative influence of colonial, regional, and ethnic politics. As a means of managing the universe of factors offered in various explanations, the table above has been adapted from a leading study on internal conflicts.[20] It distinguishes underlying or permissive causes from proximate or triggering factors. Although the categories overlap and interact, proximate causes date from the onset of the Doe military regime in 1980.

Clearly, more than a superficial analysis of such a mosaic of causal factors is beyond a case study of this length.[21] The contributions and omissions of the international community already have been described. However, certain factors with a particular bearing on the nature of displacement merit further discussion.

Coastal-Indigenous Tensions

Liberian history reveals a consistent inequality between coastal elites and indigenous populations, through a succession of exploitative arrangements. In his authoritative political history of Liberia, Amos Sawyer traces the emergence of such inequality through "institutional arrangements in which a Western-style, unitary form of government prescribed by a written constitution was imposed upon a settler-derived patrimonial authority structure and the various forms of patrimonial and clientelist arrangements of the indigenous societies."[22] The emergence of autocracy, Sawyer argues, was sealed by the increasing personalization of authority in the president throughout the twentieth century. The postwar administrations of Tubman and Tolbert perfected the sham of representative government; the state was run more as a family business.[23] Doe's rebellion replaced political autocracy with military tyranny built around his ethnic group (Krahn). This did nothing to reverse the fortunes of other indigenous groups and soon made their conditions worse.

Factionalization of Conflict

The factionalized nature of conflict along ethnic lines has had a marked effect on the patterns of displacement and the potential for reestablishing people's homes and livelihoods. Doe added to the brutal repression of his opponents by surrounding himself with appointees from his Krahn group, ensuring that future conflict (and revenge) would fall along ethnic lines. Rival power groups, at least initially, launched themselves from ethnic areas of support, starting a chain of violence and retribution that continues. In particular, the Gio-Mano groups were fertile grounds for Taylor's rebellion, having been the focus of reprisals following the failed coup attempt on Doe in 1985. Although not ethnically discrete, the main factions divide along the following ethnic lines:

- National Patriotic Front of Liberia (NPFL): led by Charles Taylor and largely composed of Mano and Gio from northern Nimba County near Côte d'Ivoire. It now controls Nimba, Bong, and parts of Grand Gedeh and Maryland.
- Armed Forces of Liberia (AFL): the residue of Doe's national army, mainly Krahn. Now led by Hezekiah Bowen and based in their former barracks in Monrovia.
- United Liberation Movement for Democracy (ULIMO): largely Mandingo and Krahn, this anti-NPFL force emerged in 1991–92, taking territory in Cape Mount and Bomi, but split in 1994 into two contesting factions.
  - ULIMO-K: led by Alhaji Kromah (Mandingo and Muslim), it controls parts of Lofa, Bomi, and Cape Mount Counties.
  - ULIMO-J: a Krahn force led by Roosevelt Johnson and confined to the former AFL barracks in Monrovia, with some presence in Bomi, Cape Mount, and Margibi Counties.
- Liberia Peace Council (LPC): led by George Boley, this Krahn force emerged in the southeast and has taken territory from the NPFL as it moved west.
- Lofa Defense Force (LDF): led by Francois Massaquoi, it was set up in 1994 to drive ULIMO-K out of Lofa.
- Central Revolutionary Council: an NPFL splinter group led by Tom Woewiyu, with territory in Nimba and Grand Bassa.

Despite their ethnic profile, political and material gain guide the actions of these groupings. The reemergence of conflict in 1996, for example saw ULIMO-K and NPFL, former adversaries, allied against ULIMO-J. The cult of leadership in each faction, enforced with ruthless violence, is ultimately stronger than ethnic ties. Territory constantly changes hands, complicating access to the displaced and preventing any resumption of normal livelihoods.

The Militarization of Civil Society

Although throughout its history Liberia has experienced episodic violent insurrection, violence has increased as the norm for the settlement of disputes since the early days of the Doe regime. Prolonged U.S. military assistance clearly provided Doe with the hardware to take oppression to a new level of violence. A series of well-documented human rights violations has been prepared by Human Rights Watch, a U.S.

organization. These reports catalogue the widespread involvement and targeting of civilian populations in factional and associated violence. Children, denied basic rights let alone those enshrined in international law (through the Convention on the Rights of the Child), have been schooled in the ways of the warlords.[24] Alienated from traditional rural livelihoods, with unreal expectations of the urban society to which they drifted, the uneducated youth have been an easy recruiting ground for lawless gangs posing as militia. Making a living through the barrel of a gun has become a norm, or, as one Liberian government minister put it, "An M-16 is worth more than an M.A."[25]

Regional Political Involvement

Regional involvement in Liberia predates the current crisis. However, alliances with other West African governments and support to the NPFL rebellion from within neighboring countries gave the current conflict immediate regional dimensions. The cross-border flow of refugees, along with fears of exported instability, heightened the involvement of neighboring countries and made the displaced within and without the country an explosive political issue. The Liberian crisis has dominated the ECO-WAS agenda, sidelining its main purpose of promoting economic cooperation across its membership. The Liberian crisis has had a particularly violent synergy with civil conflict in neighboring Sierra Leone, where causes and consequences of conflict have followed a similar, although less destructive, pattern.

The Length of Conflict

All of the above factors have been exacerbated by the duration of the conflict, which effectively dates back to the Doe power coup of 1980. In particular, the repeated failure of multiple peace agreements has thrown the country into a debilitating cycle of violence. The internally displaced despair of regaining their former lives, and refugees have lost confidence that conditions will allow them to return. Liberia appears to be following a pattern of chronic instability set by other sub-Saharan countries such as the Sudan, Angola, and Rwanda, where civil conflict establishes a self-generating equilibrium. In essence, the economic interests in sustaining the conflict, embodied in well-armed militia, currently outweigh any counterforces.

The Profile of Displacement

The human costs of displacement are apparent, but hard data have been difficult to collect, and official statistics do not tell the whole story. The lack of hard data is understandable. The last reliable census took place in 1974, a subsequent exercise in 1984 remaining unfinished. The baseline population figure most often used of 2.6 million at the outset of fighting is an extrapolation based on previous birth and mortality rates. Of this estimated population, at least 750,000 have fled as refugees to neighboring or distant countries, and an additional million have been displaced internally,[26] and an estimated 100,000–150,000 have died or been killed. These figures suggest that 700,000 members of the population have been unaffected by the crisis. Yet the UN reports that 1.8 million, virtually the entire remaining population, are dependent on aid. Violence has visited every one of Liberia's fifteen counties and territories. The official numbers therefore disguise the fact that every Liberian, from the wealthy merchant in Monrovia to the peasant farmer up-country, has had his way of life severely disrupted and, more often, destroyed.

Continued fighting has caused the numbers of displaced, where accessible to agencies, to fluctuate, making estimates only of temporary use. Outside Monrovia, lack of access has made the process of estimation even more inexact. More accurate figures will be more of a priority when communities start to settle and relief activities give way to rehabilitation. The cross-border flows have made the distinction between refugees and IDPs particularly artificial in the case of Liberia. For example, on the western borders with Sierra Leone, displaced from that country have become refugees inside Liberia and Liberians have moved in the opposite direction. Although every family may have been dislocated at some stage in the conflict, different levels of displacement are discernible. The following sections detail some of these variations.[27]

The Location

Across the four phases of the conflict, the patterns of displacement have become increasingly complicated and hard to trace. Before 1989, during phase 1, the actions of the Doe regime already were stirring social unrest, both in rural and urban areas. Ill-conceived agricultural programs, heightened corruption, and repression all contributed to the onset of social disintegration. Even the benefits of foreign ventures in Liberia, such as stable employment, were lost as order collapsed. Phase 2 created the overall pattern of mass displacement, externally and internally. As the NPFL rebellion drove people across international borders or toward the security of Monrovia, ECOMOG deployed outward to create a security zone, protecting the bulk of the internally displaced. In phase 3, the "greater Monrovia" security zone was further swollen with displaced people by continued fighting, especially after the October 1992 offensive. From that time, the security zone has been estimated to contain more than a million people, 30 percent more than before the war, over one half of whom are displaced. Since November 1992, the increasing factionalization of fighting throughout phase 4 has kept the displaced inside the security zone and made the picture in the interior changeable and unreliable.

The extrapolated figures on population losses are equally disturbing. In essence, Liberia has undergone three types of population change: areas like Lofa and Grand Gedeh have been effectively *deserted;* areas like Bong and Nimba have been heavily *depopulated;* and havens like Montserrado have been substantially *swollen.* The patterns of displacement have been driven by factional and ECOMOG activities; ethnic factors, both negative and positive, such as targeting by factions (negative) or maintaining links (positive); and levels of aid.

The Condition of the Displaced

The treatment of IDPs and the destruction of their communities has been chronicled by a series of UN and NGO sources.[28] The vulnerability of women and children to repeated violence and disregard of the most basic human needs has been a marked feature of these accounts. The International Committee of the Red Cross described this suffering as "the total breakdown of all moral standards and complete disregard for all the principles and values which are the very cornerstone of human society."[29] In addition, children have been co-opted or coerced into the armed factions, where they have been subjected to violence both as victims and as forced perpetrators.[30]

Despite these conditions, the displaced should not be mistaken as mere victims or passive recipients of aid. In late 1993 a joint UN agency mission looking at support for internally displaced women visited the crisis zone. As has been found in other emergencies, the mission found the conflict especially onerous on women, threatening their security and livelihoods, and destroying meager health and education services.[31] At the same time, the mission identified abundant local capacity to address many of the problems faced. In health matters, for example, they proposed "the future reconstruction of effective, broad-based public health systems . . . with a strong emphasis on training of local people."[32]

The Transformation of Livelihoods

Perhaps more telling than the estimated figures on displacement is the permanent transformation of people's livelihoods and markets. Although largely agricultural, Liberia showed signs of a society in transition before the onset of conflict. Economic forces throughout West Africa were causing migration to urban and coastal job zones, and in Liberia's free port, rubber, mineral, and associated industry were forcing changes to traditional societies as elsewhere in the region.

Moreover, because the majority of the population were vulnerable in many ways before actual displacement, rehabilitation of the displaced will require more than a simple return to the pre-war status quo. The food security situation was well analyzed by a World Food Programme report, which concluded: "Attaining food security in Liberia requires more than policies to restore Liberian society and the Liberian economy to the conditions prevailing before the war."[33] The report notes that before the war over 75 percent of the population gained their livelihood through agriculture, which accounted for 35 percent of GDP. This emanated from three major production systems: foreign commercial plantations, domestically owned commercial farms, and subsistence farms. However, although the commercial sector accounted for only 10 percent of employment, it produced 44 percent of output. Meanwhile, an estimated 160,000 families in the traditional subsistence sector were engaged in the production of staple food crops, mainly rice and cassava. Based on "slash and burn," and shifting cultivation without property rights, traditional farming occupied less than a quarter of the total commercial acreage. For the many displaced from the agricultural sector, return to such conditions may be neither desirable nor possible.

For women who had played an active role in pre-war subsistence agriculture, the transformation created by civil war was especially burdensome. An independent assessment found that "they were frequently daunted by the necessity to shoulder full responsibility for family survival

. . . and without other options for employment, many lost self-esteem as they came to depend entirely on relief supplies."[34]

The pre-war food marketing system also has been disrupted by the war. Previously, coastal-interior and urban-rural divisions were discernible. While the interior was self-sufficient in staples (mostly rice), there was little surplus to trade. Urban centers, mostly coastal, depended on imported rice financed by exports and food aid. This division has been heightened by the war. Within the ECOMOG security zone swollen by the displaced, food production has increased, but the population is still largely dependent on food aid. Outside the zone, insecurity has made agriculture too risky and food aid sporadic, forcing people to resort to hunting and gathering.

Additional disruption to the means of food production, including the destruction of assets and market structures, often as a military objective, will make the reconstruction of the agricultural sector more difficult. Moreover, subsistence farmers, who form a large proportion of the displaced and who have found other means to survive, may be less willing to resume a livelihood that is far from secure.

Displacement and the International Response

The neglect of the displaced in Liberia has resulted from a destructive synergy of internal and external forces. The collapse of the state, in which destructive ethnic allegiances replaced a weak national identity, has been met with an inadequate international response. A constant tension has persisted between political-security considerations and humanitarian agendas, a modern version of the age-old tension between order and justice. The following section summarizes by theme the shortcomings of the international response and then focuses in detail on the three institutional pillars of international response: regional organizations, the UN system, and NGOs.

The Shortcomings of Development

The lack of effective development assistance over three decades before 1989 is not just a judgment of hindsight. As early as 1970, the lack of widespread benefit despite considerable aid was already recognized as "growth without development." Throughout the 1980s, the preponderance of aid from the United States was aimed not at alleviating poverty but at furthering cold war objectives. Other international assistance failed to correct this imbalance. The international financial institutions, especially the World Bank, were clearly diffident about the prospects for their intervention well before Doe's 1980 coup.

Although the effectiveness of development assistance may not be the sole determinant of conflict, there is a growing body of opinion that it can address or neglect the structural conditions permitting conflict.[35] There is prima facie evidence that development assistance did little to address inequalities in Liberian society, and provided resources to those able to expropriate it, in such a way as to exacerbate inequalities. Doe was well able to manipulate international aid to support his subjugation of rival ethnic groups. Donors should have taken earlier measures to ensure that their aid, at the very least, "did no harm."

International Neglect of a Growing Crisis

As Doe's regime crumbled and the state seemed headed toward collapse (since at least the fraudulent election of 1986), the overall failure of the "international system" to respond was increasingly exposed. First, the inherent weakness of the "system," with its multiplicity of players and different agendas, was apparent (see figure 4-1). National agendas and priorities cut across multilateral peacekeeping and humanitarian initiatives. Even if the UN Security Council had been called in earlier in the crisis, say in early 1990, its ability to coordinate the different moving parts of the system still would have been limited. Second, most of the institutions within the system are crisis-oriented with short-term vision. The international system is not well geared to respond to the long-term decline and collapse of a failing state like Liberia. The displaced appear on the agenda as a humanitarian problem rather than a security problem; they present a logistical and institutional challenge for the relief community that requires a blend of compassion and order. Attempts to scare Western governments into perceiving the embryonic collapse of small West African states as a threat of wider global chaos have not succeeded.[36] The threat of longer-term scenarios does not necessarily trigger preventive action. Liberia epitomizes the weakness of a humanitarian-dominated international approach used as a palliative, a substitute for an appropriate security response.

Figure 4-1. *The International System at Work in the Liberian Crisis, 1989–94*

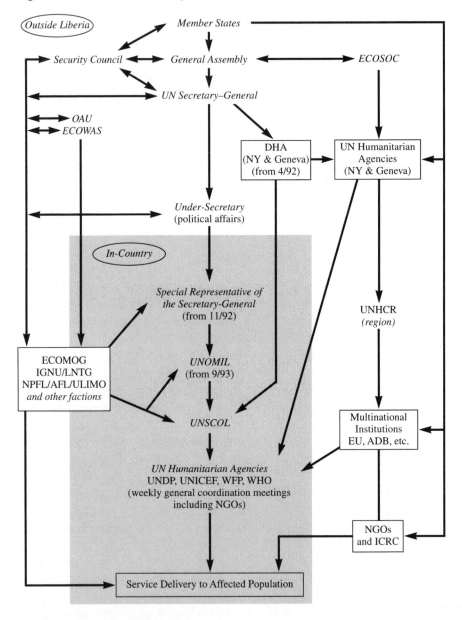

Source: Colin Scott, in collaboration with Larry Minear and Thomas G. Weiss, "Occasional Paper 20, Humanitarian Action and Security in Liberia, 1989–1994," Thomas J. Watson Jr. Institute for International Studies, Brown University, 1995, p. 52.
Note: Arrows represent lines of management, influence, and/or funding described by respondents.

The Problems of Regional Intervention

The intervention by ECOMOG has raised doubts about its legitimacy, accountability, and perceived impartiality. Accusations of human rights abuse, looting, and profiteering have tarnished its reputation as a guardian of the displaced. At root is a lack of clarity concerning its fundamental objective.

Observers offered a variety of explanations for ECOMOG's shifting role from peacekeeping to a more offensive stance. Clearly the shift was a reaction to the NPFL offensive, and in ECOMOG and the Interim Government's view, a matter of legitimate self-defense. Beyond the worsening military situation, some attributed to ECOMOG commanders an approach that was less humanitarian and more punitive. General Ishaya Bakut (1991–92) was seen as more willing to play the negotiating diplomatic role while his successors adopted a narrower military approach.

Others viewed the erosion of neutrality as inevitable in such a regional undertaking, a West African version of "mission creep." "Regional initiatives run the risk of being dominated by a single country or two," pointed out one senior UN official in July 1993.[37] He regarded ECOMOG as a subregional initiative, underscoring the desirability of a "broader, truly regional" approach that would enlist the political and military involvement of nations from southern and eastern Africa.

For other observers, the political agenda of Nigeria, the largest single contributor to ECOMOG, was fundamentally suspect. Regional domination, not peace, was at the heart of the intervention. Potential commercial interests in Liberia were also widely viewed as a strong incentive for ECOMOG to outlast the NPFL. Responding to criticisms of the restrictions on humanitarian operations during this period, one senior ECOWAS official noted the "need to balance between the interest of ensuring that relief gets to the needy wherever they may be and the imperatives of avoiding any activity which might compromise the security of peace enforcers." He explained, "Our experience in peace enforcement, which is the first of its kind ever undertaken by a regional organization, reveals that unlike peacekeeping, the peace enforcers have a right—indeed a duty—to guide and direct all relief agencies and the displaced population where to go and when to go. In such circumstances, freedom of action or movement is, by definition, restricted."[38] In any event, UN humanitarian operations in phase 4 lost such independence as they had established, becoming an integral part of a now more troubled regional political-security initiative.

The UN System: The Intersection of
Political and Humanitarian Issues

Many of the dilemmas of meeting the needs of the displaced fell, often by default, into the UN system where political, security, and humanitarian concerns intersect. The difficulties of humanitarian operations operating without political guidance were reversed with the arrival of a special representative of the secretary-general (SRSG). But problems of coordination and leadership were not fully resolved at any stage by arrangements between the UN Development Programme (UNDP), UN Department of Humanitarian Affairs (DHA), and the UN Special Coordinating Office for Liberia (UNSCOL). There was no agency specifically responsible for the welfare of the internally displaced. The renewed violence in 1996 rekindled fears that aid in a security vacuum might even inflame conflict.

PRE-1989: FROM OLIGARCHY TO TYRANNY—AID WITHOUT DEVELOPMENT. The failings of pre-war aid are covered in the previous section. Clearly, the UN development program was overshadowed by U.S. geopolitical concerns and unable to turn international aid away from a dangerous course.

1989–AUGUST 1990: DESCENT INTO ANARCHY—DIMINISHING AID. As reported, initial direct UN involvement in the crisis took a humanitarian rather than a political direction. An assessment mission led by the UN Disaster Relief Office (UNDRO) in February 1990, and a subsequent appeal, funded an UNDRO delegate and a UN Volunteer team. From March until May they distributed food and medicines alongside Catholic Relief Services (CRS) and Médecins sans Frontières (MSF)/Belgium teams in rebel and government-controlled areas. The initiative, however, was short-lived. Following a slaughter of Liberians sheltered in the United Nations compound in Monrovia on May 28, the UNDRO team was evacuated from Liberia along with the rest of the UN staff. From that point, the internally displaced were effectively without any international protection.

Responding in July 1990 to the worsening crisis, the UN secretary-general set up the in-country coordinating office, UNSCOL, under the UNDRO/UNDP representative to coordinate the work of United Nations humanitarian agencies. Based in Conakry, Guinea, and Freetown, Sierra Leone, UNSCOL's mandate also included being a close liaison for the exchange of information among the UN aid agencies in nearby countries, and preparation, once security improved, for their early return to Monrovia.[39] At this stage both the International Committee of the Red Cross (ICRC) and MSF/Belgium, feeling less constrained by security issues, were continuing relief work in Monrovia. MSF only left the country completely for ten days in August.

The UN's initial response was not without criticism, largely for doing too little, too late, too slowly. Some within and outside the UN system believed that the organization should have been more present and active within Liberia, even given the serious insecurity. But as in other emergencies, security rules (since revised) then required withdrawal of all UN personnel. A senior ECOMOG commentator, for example, felt the intervention force should have been accompanied by a humanitarian task force to deal with the desperate humanitarian needs apparent on landing. However, weeks passed after the ECOMOG intervention before the UN responded to calls for its return.

1990–1992: REGIONAL INTERVENTION—INDEPENDENT AID. In October 1990, Africa Watch, following up on warnings made since May, called on the United Nations to appoint a special representative to negotiate a peace and coordinate emergency assistance and demanded greater U.S. and Western European aid.[40] Only in late October did a UN security-relief assessment mission identify critical humanitarian needs and recommend a prompt return by UN agencies to work alongside ECOMOG. By the time of the UNSCOL assessment report at the end of November, the secretary-general had approved the UN's return, subject to security clearance, and a core team headed by the special coordinator had been set up in Monrovia. The secretary-general appealed for $13.8 million to mount "desperately needed relief operations." A joint UNICEF-Swederelief mission soon followed to detail and estimate the cost of further plans and coordination.[41] United Nations reports referred only to assistance for "greater Monrovia," though UN assistance had been approved for the rest of Liberia outside of ECOMOG control.

In assessing UN effectiveness in this phase of the crisis, three issues emerge: security, leadership, and geographic reach. Senior UN humanitarian officials felt that the organization, inhibited by "an excessively conservative view of security considerations," could and should have returned to Liberia earlier.[42] Although a massive UN presence would not have been feasible between June and November, a core of seasoned operational staff could have accomplished useful, if limited, work. Even a token presence might have conveyed international concern and perhaps also reduced atrocities, as it did in October 1992.

Leadership and geographical reach also emerged as key issues during this initial phase. By most accounts, UNSCOL, despite a succession of temporary heads, managed to provide a reasonable coordination for UN agencies and NGOs as well. "I thought the UN response was good," observed one NGO official. "The special coordinator seemed to strike an effective balance between humanitarian and political considerations, and was prepared to push things along apace."[43]

As for geographical reach, the United Nations established a troublesome pattern by failing to extend its initial involvement beyond ECOMOG lines into NPFL territory, where many thousands of IDPs could be found. Although UN assistance had been approved for Liberia as a whole, its operations from the outset were limited to the "greater Monrovia" security zone. Outside this zone there were considerable security risks, although external assistance was provided through NGOs such as MSF/Belgium, CRS, and Lutheran World Service, and through the ICRC.

At no time was an autonomous UN operation openly contemplated for the rebel-held areas. This had serious humanitarian and political consequences. It left many displaced outside the ECOMOG security zone bereft of UN assistance and confirmed the suspicions of the NPFL that UN humanitarian efforts, like their political counterparts, had an anti-insurgent bias. This perception was not sufficiently countered by political and humanitarian decisions made by the under secretary-general for political affairs at UN headquarters in New York. Even fellow UN officials believed that his nationality (Sierra Leonean) fueled suspicions of UN bias in favor of the interim government (IGNU) and the unwarranted delay of humanitarian operations in NPFL areas despite clear evidence of need.

In short, between the outbreak of the fighting in December 1989 and the start-up of major UN operations in late 1990, the groundwork was laid for many subsequent difficulties. Once established, UN humanitarian activities throughout 1991–92 were partially successful. However, with changes in the political and military situation beginning in November 1992, the fundamental issues of leadership, security, and geographical reach became increasingly intractable.

Without detailed terms of reference, UNSCOL established a structure and modus operandi in this period within the given political-security context. Its main task and accomplishment was to provide a framework for the implementation of humanitarian activities by operational United Nations agencies and associated relief agencies. UNSCOL did so using a consensual model, with weekly coordination meetings and many smaller planning meetings involving a mix of UN, NGO, and sometimes IGNU staff. "We were trying to get a broad understanding, with NGOs as essential partners," explained a senior UN official, "not one person's vision stamped on the community."[44]

One outcome of the UN's coordinating role in the early phase was a consolidated appeal for $135.5 million in July 1991 for a twelve-month relief and rehabilitation program. Building on the findings of a series of joint UN-NGO assessments of different needs such as food aid and health, the appeal report represented a general plan for humanitarian aid throughout Liberia.[45] Another contribution of UNSCOL was to negotiate arrangements within which humanitarian personnel were afforded access to civilian populations in government-controlled and, to a lesser extent, in rebel-held areas. The "good offices" of the UN coordinator benefited not only the UN agencies but also the associated NGOs.

There were also wider benefits. "I believe that much of the humanitarian assistance operation during 1991–92 was carried out in ways that facilitated peace among the warring factions," explained one UN official. "Just bringing together the technocrats in the health sector for meetings allows an exchange of views that considers the country as a whole."[46] That such cooperation across factional lines did not reinforce broader peace efforts, while regrettable, was hardly the responsibility of UNSCOL.

There were, however, two major UNSCOL shortcomings that persisted. First, its effectiveness varied according to the abilities of its coordinators. Rapid staff turnover (there were four UNSCOL heads in the first six months) and variations in assertiveness undercut sustained results, particularly in addressing difficult issues such as the respective duties of UNICEF and the World Health Organization (WHO) in the health sector. Stable leadership was established only when Ross Mountain took over the UNSCOL operation in June 1991, a position he held for two years.

Second, even after cross-line operations began in March 1991, UNSCOL did not succeed in ensuring that urgent human needs in NPFL territory were addressed. Although security was the main problem, two factors contributed to the failure. First, UNSCOL attempted to coordinate activities for the entire country from its base in Monrovia. Second, although UNSCOL managed in this phase to set up four UN operational centers in insurgent-controlled territory, it did not move quickly to mount operations and commit senior program managers there.

The damage that flowed from the decision to base humanitarian efforts in Monrovia was both logistical and political in nature. It was hard to reach greater Liberia from Monrovia, and NPFL suspicions of political bias in UN aid efforts were hard to refute. A UNSCOL report in July 1992 conceded the imbalance in coverage. "The UN system generally remained too focused on Monrovia," a UN aid official elaborated. "Our world-view was too much shaped by peering out through Monrovia spectacles, without sufficient appreciation for the perceptions and viewpoints in Gbargna," the NPFL headquarters.[47] A vivid illustration was provided by an NGO official who at one stage in 1992 reported that there were 120 UN vehicles in IGNU areas and only five in "greater Liberia."

The renewal of all-out conflict in October 1992 gave the UN's coordination role its most severe test. First, attacks on Monrovia led to demands for UN personnel to be withdrawn again to more secure locations. Second, having made the key decision to maintain some UN presence, the existing coordination mechanism had to deal with the influx of 200,000 new displaced persons into Monrovia. Third, NPFL military gains led to criticisms of UNSCOL by both IGNU and ECOMOG for working on the NPFL side of the line. Suspicions were not just about "feeding the enemy" but also about the withholding of information about the NPFL arms buildup, and even siding with the NPFL. Tensions between IGNU and the head of UNSCOL, Ross Mountain, exacerbated by other disagreements, subsequently led to an IGNU request for his removal. A vitriolic public campaign led by local press ultimately hastened his departure.

1992–96: REGIONAL-UN PARTNERSHIP—AID OVERSHADOWED AND FRUSTRATED. Until November 1992, UN involvement was primarily humanitarian. Subsequently, the nature of UN humanitarian coordination was radically changed, first by the addition of an in-country UN "political supremo," Trevor Gordon-Somers, as special representative of the secretary-general and second by the departure of the head of UNSCOL, Ross Mountain, in June 1993.

An early test of the new leadership was the dispute during 1993 over aid delivery to NPFL territory across the Côte d'Ivoire border. (This was called "cross-border" aid to distinguish it from "cross-line aid," which reached insurgent-held areas within Liberia from Monrovia.) Since 1990, some NGOs had used this route as the only practical way of gaining access to the area. But ECOMOG harbored suspicions that some NGOs were partial toward the NPFL and that aid deliveries were a cover for arms smuggling. Growing IGNU-ECOMOG pressure confronted the UN system with a stark dilemma.

Despite acknowledging that the cross-border route was the most effective, the UN did not challenge an initial ECOMOG prohibition in May 1993 on its use.[48] Moreover, in July 1993 the SRSG supported the ban by requesting the Ivorian government to enforce it. DHA was not consulted in advance about this decision. NGOs, unhappy about the perceived setback to their humanitarian activities, also criticized the SRSG for refusing to meet them to discuss his action.

The SRSG believed, however, that to push ahead with aid convoys without ECOMOG and UNOMIL monitoring units in place would jeopardize the entire Cotonou peace process, the top priority established by the Security Council mandate. He urged instead the use of cross-line routes that the NGOs found both logistically problematic and hindered by ECOMOG control. The resulting NGO protest, which enlisted international media, donor governments, and politicians, caused a breakdown in NGO relations with the UN, ECOMOG, and IGNU. Above all, the unity of the humanitarian effort that had been achieved between the UN and the NGOs was lost.

UN humanitarian activities thus experienced increasing pressure from both ECOMOG and the political side of the UN. "With the appointment of a special representative and the subsequent increase in the profile of the UN on political issues," commented one UN official in 1993, "the coordination of humanitarian assistance by UNSCOL became more difficult and remains so."[49] The tension was not confined to the field but extended to the secretariat of the United Nations in New York. The imbalance of power between the SRSG and UNSCOL was reinforced by the relationship between political and humanitarian departments at headquarters. At critical points, the under secretary-general for political affairs prevailed over the newly appointed under secretary-general for humanitarian affairs.

The nature and power of UNSCOL, already seriously eroded before the departure of Ross Mountain in mid-1993, were never restored. His replacement, Christian Lemaire, reverted to being the UNDP representative according to his brief. Some UNSCOL arrangements such as coordination meetings have continued, but without the impact of earlier efforts. Aid officials accepted the political reality that the SRSG had to be in overall control. But DHA and its channel of influence into the Liberian crisis through UNSCOL simply faded away, and with it, the unity of the humanitarian community, its main achievement.

During this phase, in which UN political activities eclipsed its humanitarian operations, a number of key issues confronted the United Nations and the humanitarian community as a whole. How far would failure on the political and security front jeopardize humanitarian operations? To what extent was humanitarian access compromised by the greater integration of aid activities into UN political goals and ECOMOG security structures? To what extent could, or should, humanitarian operations be insulated from political-security activities? Does solving such problems depend on renewed humanitarian leadership, or should NGOs and the ICRC spearhead neutral international aid independent of the UN?

The effort to implement a comprehensive peace agreement set out an expanded UN political operation that incorporated humanitarian activities. The Cotonou agreement included in UNOMIL's mandate "assistance, as appropriate, in the coordination of humanitarian assistance activities in the field in conjunction with the existing UN Humanitarian Relief operation." But the nature of what was "appropriate" was not made clear.

The secretary-general's report in April 1994 noted further civilian displacement and distress and continuing difficulties of access and logistics.[50] The report also expressed the hope that the new transitional government was "beginning to assume responsibility" for relief, resettlement, and rehabilitation activities throughout Liberia. Unfortunately neither UNOMIL nor the LNTGs have provided a clear framework for relief activities. In fact, humanitarian access has become even more complicated since Cotonou. Where once arrangements had to be made "only" with IGNU, the NPFL, and ECOMOG, by mid-1994 multiple Liberian factions and UNOMIL itself were insisting upon security clearances and other formalities.

The need to deal with an increase in interlocutors has called attention to the absence of UNSCOL and the lack of active leadership from UNDP, whose new country representative was not charged with coordinating the UN's humanitarian organizations. Consequently, individual UN agencies have become more involved in their own right in security matters, stepping, some UN staff reported, into a coordination vacuum. Along with efforts by the agencies to negotiate their own access have come serious discussions of the broader need for more clear-cut separation between the humanitarian and political elements of the UN system.

Ironically, such discussion of the need for greater autonomy for humanitarian activities has come at a time when the warring factions are no more likely to differentiate between humanitarian and political operations of the UN. Increased harassment by the factions even brought about a reunification of the aid community. In October 1994, the UN and NGO humanitarian agencies issued a statement suspending all aid in areas where factions operate because of continued insecurity and theft of supplies to support military operations.

To summarize, lethargic movement on the peace front has made for serious complications for UN humanitarian agencies. While they have lost many of the advantages of the independence they once enjoyed, there has been no dividend in the form of a better environment for rehabilitation work. Conversely, United Nations resources that could have helped consolidate and reinforce a serious peace are standing idle. World Food Programme plans to commit assistance to the rehabilitation of disarmed people, and similar projects by other UN agencies, remain frustrated.

For the international community, the inadequacies of a joint UN political-security and humanitarian mission raise a fundamental strategic issue: whether greater use of NGOs and the ICRC following a more independent role might have, or still could, offset these failings. A brief discussion of their achievements and shortcomings follows.

NGOs: UN Partners or Independent Actors?

Four main policy issues emerge from the activities of NGOs during the Liberian crisis: responsiveness, geographic coverage, coordination, and advocacy on humanitarian conditions. In response to the onset of the crisis, only a few external private organizations such as CRS, MSF/ Belgium, and the ICRC set up operations. Senior external NGO officials admitted that their agencies could have done more and earlier. However, operations became more perilous as the fighting intensified around Buchanan and Monrovia in the summer of 1990. Liberian NGOs, church missions, and a National Disaster Relief Commission were also active in this phase. The Christian network, through in-country operations with external support, remained a powerful humanitarian force throughout the crisis. The strength of these local organizations was widely praised and used by UN and NGO officials.

Many more external NGOs, along with the UN, used the ECOMOG shield of "law and order" to establish operations in late 1990. But in the early months of 1991, NGOs gravitated toward UNSCOL rather than IGNU. UNSCOL was perceived as the "nucleus of civilian reconstruction" and offered an easy point of entry into the local aid system. In the early months of the return to Monrovia, little NGO attention was paid to the possibilities of partnership with the embryonic government. NGOs kept their distance in part because of IGNU's lack of resources and credibility and so as not to prejudice relationships with the NPFL. Yet their major motivation was more immediate and practical. External NGOs were arriving in large numbers and intent on staking their respective claims for ready identification by home constituencies.

As for geographic coverage, NGOs were unsuccessful in becoming operational in NPFL territory, either in parallel with or as an alternative to Monrovia-based activities, with critical results for many displaced. Some believed that the suffering was more pronounced in the capital than in greater Liberia, although there were reports of widespread problems behind rebel lines. Some felt that scarce resources should be focused in a given area, though one conceded that such a consideration could equally have led it to become operational in NPFL-controlled areas. But above all, NGOs feared difficulties with security in dealing with the insurgents and resulting problems with access, logistics, and accountability. The hopes of most agencies that began in Monrovia on the assumption that an early peace settlement would soon be followed by uninhibited access to greater Liberia proved ill-founded.

The factor that tipped the balance for many NGOs was the UN's own geographic choice. Its decision to work out of Monrovia lent a certain legitimacy to NGOs based there and was seen as simplifying matters of logistics and security. An exception to the prevailing NGO thinking was that of MSF/Belgium, which in November 1990, when conditions were critical in Monrovia, urged that more NGOs work in Taylor-controlled areas. It set up parallel operations, one based in Monrovia and the other working across the border from Côte d'Ivoire. This example was followed by other NGOs as the military stalemate dragged on. Agencies such as the Lutheran World Service and CRS clearly did their best to meet needs in a transparently neutral manner.

By 1993 it was clear that conditions outside Monrovia were as bad as if not worse than in the capital, which then sheltered 1 million people. But all attempts at finding ways of servicing greater Liberia were ultimately frustrated by factional harassment, theft of vehicles, and looting of supplies, and resulted in periodic suspensions of aid to insecure areas, the latest in October 1994.

Coordination between NGOs and the UN worked reasonably well in the estimation of both parties, especially in phase 2, where relief objectives were largely complementary. Criticisms of NGO performance from UN sources included the lack of professionalism and experience among some field staff (conceded by some NGOs), and the need for greater flexibility in program operations in response to the changing political-security situation. Coordination became more complicated in phases 3 and 4 as UN-NGO tensions heightened. NGOs, no longer prepared to let UNSCOL talk for them, sought their own solutions.

In the area of advocacy, NGOs were actively involved in seeking to create and protect humanitarian space for their own activities, to mobilize international public opinion, and to challenge the policies and practices of the warring parties. Such efforts were widely recognized, although a certain tension emerged among the various advocacy initiatives, especially in phases 3 and 4.

NGO negotiations with the UN, IGNU, ECOMOG, and the NPFL to carve out space within which to function were clearly necessary. However, at certain points—for example, in the dispute over the cross-border aid through Côte d'Ivoire—their advocacy tested the limits of this role, creating mistrust and souring relations. IGNU commentators expressed concern about the "creeping control" of external NGOs over vital institutions and services of the country. This trend would only replace the "weak, dependent state with indirect control through foreign-based institutions."[51] This kind of "challenge to governance" necessitated greater use of local NGOs, they concluded. Such reaction against NGO assumption of governmental authority parallels national concerns in similar complex emergencies. In Liberia it created a backlash of resentment that the NGOs had to deal with later.

NGO efforts to challenge the belligerent parties also had mixed results. Some observers believed that the more outspoken agencies such as MSF/Belgium jeopardized their neutral status and put their operations at risk. But the alternate suggestion that politically charged activities such as human rights advocacy and conflict resolution be left to non-operational NGOs was not universally accepted throughout the NGO community. The most workable approach was some form of joint declaration either by NGOs alone or jointly with UN agencies (as in October

1994), although this was dependent on effective humanitarian leadership. The renewal of fighting in 1996, and the loss of a second generation of aid infrastructure, led the NGOs to reflect on growing criticism that they might be fueling the conflict.[52] Solidarity in demands on warring factions to respect their role and property was swiftly achieved, but it is questionable how long that can be maintained.

To summarize, in the early phases NGOs functioned more readily as implementing partners of UN programs or worked comfortably within the UN coordinating framework. As a result, their efforts suffered from some problems noted in the UN's own activities. Following November 1992, greater independence from the UN system brought its own problems of coordination, marginalization, and credibility without any guarantee of greater security or effectiveness. Both integration and independence carried heavy costs.

Conclusions

Access to the displaced of Liberia to assess and meet their needs can only take place as part of wider plan to restore security. That is the clear lesson of the years of conflict, which have afforded a diminishing "humanitarian space" in which to operate. How can Liberia reach peace on the political front and reconstruction on the social and economic track?

As a starting point, it should be assumed that IDPs and refugees form the core of potential civil society, and therefore form an essential part of peace and reconstruction; they are the human capital on which Liberia should be rebuilt. While the science of post-conflict reconstruction or rehabilitation is yet underdeveloped, the following are offered as components of a concerted response.

The Liberian People: National Identity and Ethnicity

Liberia is clearly rich ground for those studying the limits and destructive forces underlying nationalisms and ethnic fault lines. Although an examination of Liberian nationalism is beyond the scope of this case study, it is evident that if Liberia is to survive some notion of belonging to an identifiable nation-state must be revived in the popular consciousness. Whether it be a true marriage of polity and ethnicity, or a shotgun marriage built upon an "imagined" but viable community is a matter of contention.[53] The nation's predicament probably demands both a top-down and a grass-roots approach to reconstruction.

Although hard to quantify, much of Liberia's professional and skilled human capital fled with the onset of conflict. These "exiled elites" need to organize themselves into a far more powerful lobby to pressure the international community. A group such as the Friends of Liberia in Washington, D.C., needs to amass the resources and expertise that will give it a chance to compete for government attention alongside more powerful interests.

The internal power brokers in Liberia must be given a very clear message about their failures to maintain peace accords. It may be hard to distinguish the potential statesperson from the self-seeking warlord. They can only be judged on their acts, and those clearly derelict in their stated duties should be subject to international censure.

Civil society needs an opportunity to flourish, with ethnicity a basis for healthy pluralism rather than factional violence. History cannot be reversed, and Liberia will hardly return to its pre-war ethnic geography. Social recovery will not be a matter of rebuilding former ethnic divisions, although many displaced may choose to return to their home regions. Providing employment for a displaced population in conditions of reasonable security will have to take precedence over idealized social engineering.

Having undergone permanent transformation through a protracted civil war does not necessarily preclude the rebuilding of Liberia as a nation-state. Many developed countries, including Liberia's parent United States, look back on their civil wars as a defining moment in the creation of a nation. However, the multifactional involvement of civilians will make Liberian rehabilitation of a very different order.

Reconciliation more likely will be a matter of transformation of conflict into sustainable forms of coexistence rather than the outright resolution of differences. It is difficult to know what will work and who can achieve it. There may be much that Liberia can share and learn with other African nations that have undergone conflict and reconciliation, such as Uganda, Mozambique, and Ethiopia. Closer to home, parallel events in Sierra Leone may prove a useful comparison for Liberian society.

The International Community

International assistance, free from the pressures of cold war politics and the leadership problems of the Doe years, arguably has a better opportunity to intervene than on previous occasions. Two tasks should preoccupy international response: supporting peace through security and diplomatic measures, and supporting social and economic reconstruction measures. Regional institutions (such as ECOWAS and the OAU) and international institutions have a legitimizing role in the former, but the Liberian experience demonstrates that no such institution is alone powerful enough to take a leadership role. This can only be achieved by certain leading sovereign states, essentially the United States, members of the European Union, and Nigeria. But international institutions do have a critical role in promoting reconstruction, in particular assisting social and economic rehabilitation.

Assisting the displaced is one of a number of priorities for reconstruction activities. Such activities should include providing a sufficient level of internal security to enable economic activity to recover, to encourage refugees and IDPs to reestablish themselves, and to persuade the business community to invest; strengthening the government's capacity to carry out key activities; providing assistance to institutions of good governance, including the judiciary, and democratic rule; assisting in the demobilization and economic reintegration of ex-combatants; assisting the return of refugees and IDPs under the auspices of one coordinating agency that can address both protection and assistance issues; supporting the rejuvenation of household economies, especially by strengthening the subsistence-agricultural sector; assisting the recovery of communities through projects that rehabilitate the social and economic infrastructure; rehabilitating physical infrastructure of crucial importance for economic revival, such as major roads, bridges, marketplaces, and utilities; stabilizing the national currency and rehabilitating financial institutions; and giving priority to the basic needs of social groups (vulnerable women and children in particular) and geographic areas most affected by the conflict.[54] Conducting all these activities with a view to promoting national reconciliation would represent a cross-cutting theme.

Together, this list reads more like comprehensive state-building than a reconstruction of past institutions. Since all appear to be priorities, the timing and sequencing of such activities is problematic. The cost of such activities would be very taxing on an international community with no new international funds for reconstruction and increasing competition for overall development assistance funds. Improved coordination of donor funds by the UN system and the international financial institutions is crucial to bring maximum effect. At least two parallel time frames are anticipated. While political and security prerequisites for recovery demand short-term measures to build confidence and stability, the social and economic reconstruction will move along a much longer time-scale.

The Private Commercial Sector

The private sector is no stranger to Liberia. Since the development of an "Open Door" policy after World War II, Liberia has long experience with foreign investment, most of which was detrimental. The continuation of mining and logging activities throughout the conflict and renewed interest in the rubber industry are signs that Liberia has many potential advantages over competing sub-Saharan economies. The management of such investment to the benefit of a wide range of stakeholders (including militia and displaced people), particularly through employment, will be critical to economic normalization. The expertise of the international financial institutions, especially the World Bank and African Development Bank, should be applied vigorously to this task. On the regulatory side, there should be a requirement for some international monitoring and prohibition of the profiteering and arms trade that have grown on the Liberian conflict.[55]

A Synergy of Interventions

Concerted action by all parts of the international system will be required to address both security and development needs. As one Liberia-experienced UN official concluded, "Enough knowledge and experience exists for a team of officials drawn from the UN, its organizations and agencies, USAID, the European Union, the World Bank, the IMF and representatives of the relief community to . . . develop a credible collaborative response."[56] Synergies, to date not apparent in the international response, will be needed between (1) Western and African governments, especially the United States, the European Union, and Nigeria; (2) political-diplomatic, security, and development institutions, particularly within the UN system; (3) public and private sector interests; and (4) external international actors and democratic representatives of Liberian interests.

In short, a comprehensive reconstruction plan with international guarantees is required, building on the potential of displaced Liberians as one important pillar of reconstruction. Internally, the displaced will require the security of good governance, democratic rule, and judicial protection of individual political and economic rights. For better or worse, global economic trends will reshape a postwar Liberia. To give the displaced an opportunity in that new but uncertain order can only be an improvement on the crumbling disorder of the ancien regime and the anarchy that has overtaken it.

Epilogue: 1996–98

The second Ajuba peace accord was followed by a general election in July 1997, and in August, the installation of a government under President Charles Taylor. With the increasing return of the international aid community, 1998 presented Liberia with its best opportunity for peaceful recovery since the conflict began. Some assisted and spontaneous return of displaced people had already taken place by the end of 1997. However, the restoration of the homes and livelihoods of more than a million refugees and IDPs remains a critical precondition for social stability and sustainable peace. The UN consolidated appeal of January 1998 correctly focused on reintegration, and it is expected that the government's two-year priority national reconstruction program will have a similar theme. Nevertheless, effective international support to Liberia's recovery will depend upon a better performance in aid coordination by donors, the UN system, and NGOs than was witnessed in the first six years of the crisis.

Notes

1. Comments at "Humanitarian Action and Regional Security, 1989–94," international conference organized by the Humanitarianism and War Project, Thomas J. Watson Jr. Institute for International Studies, in Brussels, Belgium, November 1994.

2. See J. Gus Liebenow, *Liberia: The Quest for Democracy* (Bloomington: Indiana University Press, 1987); and Amos Sawyer, *The Emergence of Autocracy in Liberia: Tragedy and Challenge* (San Francisco: Institute for Contemporary Studies, 1992).

3. For structure and data this study draws heavily on Colin Scott, in collaboration with Larry Minear and Thomas G. Weiss, *Humanitarian Action and Security in Liberia 1989–94*, Occasional Paper 20 (Providence, R.I.: Thomas J. Watson Jr. Institute for International Studies, 1994). Permission to reproduce parts of that text granted by the publisher.

4. See R. Kramer, "Liberia: A Casualty of the Cold War's End," *CSIS Africa Notes*, July 1995.

5. Interviews with retired World Bank officials, June–July 1996. As late as 1986, USAID administrator Peter McPherson visited Liberia in an attempt to negotiate a rescue package for the Doe regime.

6. Interviews with retired World Bank officials.

7. See Larry Minear, Colin Scott, and Thomas G. Weiss, *The News Media, Civil War, and Humanitarian Action* (Boulder, Colo.: Lynne Rienner, 1996), pp. 47–50.

8. See Margaret A. Vogt, ed., *The Liberian Crisis and ECOMOG: A Bold Attempt at Regional Peace Keeping* (Lagos: Gabumo Publishing Company, 1992); and Clement Adibe, *Managing Arms in Peace Processes* (New York: UNIDIR, 1996).

9. ECOWAS communiqué, August 6–7, 1990. A subsequent ECOWAS statement in September was more explicit in stating a humanitarian objective: "stopping the senseless killing of innocent civilians." ECOWAS appears to have used the humanitarian imperative to strengthen its overall case for intervention.

10. Consent to a peacekeeping force by all warring factions was vital. See Boutros Boutros-Ghali, *An Agenda For Peace: Preventive Diplomacy, Peacemaking, and Peacekeeping*, Report of the Secretary-General (United Nations, 1992), para. 50; and Alan James, *Peacekeeping in International Politics* (Basingstoke, Hampshire, England: International Institute for Strategic Studies and MacMillan, 1990), pp. 1–16.

11. Quoted in Scott, Minear, and Weiss, *Humanitarian Action*, p. 9.

12. In line with article 52 of the UN Charter, which legitimizes regional initiatives consistent with the purposes and principles of the charter.

13. For details, see Security Council, *Report of the Secretary-General on Liberia*, S/25402 (United Nations, March 12, 1993).

14. See Africa Watch, "Waging War to Keep the Peace: The ECOMOG Intervention and Human Rights," *News from Africa Watch*, vol. 5, London, June 1993.

15. Quoted in Scott, Minear, and Weiss, *Humanitarian Action*, p. 10.

16. For details, see Jeremy Armon and Andy Carl, *Accord: The Liberian Peace Process, 1990–96* (London: Conciliation Resources, 1996), issue 1.

17. Africa Watch, "Waging War to Keep the Peace," p. 18.

18. Security Council, *Progress Report of the Secretary-General on UNOMIL*, S/1994/463 (United Nations, 1994).

19. Security Council Resolution 911 on "Extension of the Mandate of the U.N. Observer Mission in Liberia and Implementation of the Peace Agreement for Liberia" (United Nations, April 21, 1994).

20. Michael E. Brown, ed., *The International Dimensions of Internal Conflict* (MIT Press, 1996), table 17.1, p. 577.

21. For in-depth historical analysis, see Liebenow, *Liberia: The Quest for Democracy*; and Sawyer, *The Emergence of Autocracy in Liberia*.

22. Sawyer, *The Emergence of Autocracy in Liberia*, p. 263.

23. See "Family Connections and Government in Liberia under Tolbert, July 1976," figure 1, in Vogt, *The Liberian Crisis and ECOMOG*, p. 33.

24. General Assembly, *Convention on the Rights of the Child*, A/RES/44/25 (United Nations, December 5, 1989). See also Human Rights Watch/Africa, "Easy Prey: Child Soldiers in Liberia," New York, 1994.

25. Comment at "Humanitarian Action and Regional Security, 1989–94," international conference organized by the Humanitarianism and War Project.

26. An average figure derived from multiple UN, ICRC, and NGO sources.

27. Many of the data and much of the conceptualization in this section are taken from FAO, "Strategies for Food Security in Liberia: From Relief to Development," unpublished report prepared by Quentin Outram, University of Leeds, U.K., for the National Level Workshop to Review Strategies for Post-War Food Security, Monrovia, March 4, 1996.

28. See, for example, Security Council, *Report of the Secretary-General on Liberia*, S/25402 (United Nations, March 12, 1993); and Africa Watch, "Liberia: A Human Rights Disaster," New York, Human Rights Watch, 1990.

29. International Committee of the Red Cross, "Liberia: Appalling Plight of Civilian Population," Press Release no. 1787, October 5, 1994.

30. See Human Rights Watch/Africa, "Easy Prey."

31. UNDP, Gender in Development Program, "Support for Women in Internally Displaced Situations," Report of a Joint Mission of UNDP/UNICEF/UNIFEM/WHO/DHA, October 18–November 5, 1993.

32. Ibid., p. 6

33. FAO, "Strategies for Food Security in Liberia."

34. UNDP, "Support for Women in Internally Displaced Situations," p. 7.

35. See Peter Uvin, "Development, Aid and Conflict: Reflections from the Case of Rwanda," Research for Action 24, World Institute for Development Economics Research and United Nations University, Helsinki, 1996.

36. See Robert Kaplan, "The Coming Anarchy," *Atlantic Monthly* (February 1994), pp. 44–76.

37. Scott, Minear, and Weiss, *Humanitarian Action*, p. 11.

38. Ibid., p. 12.

39. UN Disaster Relief Office, Situation Report 90/1170, July 1990.

40. Africa Watch, "Liberia: A Human Rights Disaster."

41. UNICEF/Swederelief assessment report, December 14, 1990.

42. Scott, Minear, and Weiss, *Humanitarian Action*, p. 16.

43. Ibid.

44. Ibid., p. 17.

45. *Consolidated Appeal for Emergency Humanitarian Assistance for Liberia*, ST/SPQ/11 (United Nations, July 1991).

46. Scott, Minear, and Weiss, *Humanitarian Action*, p. 18.

47. Ibid.

48. See *Report of the Secretary-General on Liberia*, S/25402, para. 12; Letter from Commander of ECOMOG to UNSCOL, November 5, 1993.

49. Scott, Minear, and Weiss, *Humanitarian Action*, p. 20.

50. Security Council, S/1994/463.

51. Scott, Minear, and Weiss, *Humanitarian Action*, p. 25.

52. See John Prendergast and Colin Scott, "Aid with Integrity: Avoiding the Potential of Humanitarian Aid to Sustain Conflict," Office of Foreign Disaster Assistance Occasional Paper 2, Washington, D.C., March 1996.

53. The marriage of polity and ethnicity as the core of nationalism was suggested by Ernst Gellner in a lecture at the London School of Economics, February 1993. The concept of an imagined community is taken from Benedict Anderson, *Imagined Communities: Reflections on the Origin and Spread of Nationalism* (London: Verso, 1983).

54. Adapted from Nicole Ball, *Making Peace Work: The Role of the International Development Community* (Washington, D.C.: Overseas Development Council, 1996), p. 3.

55. For an analysis of the informal economy at work in the Liberian crisis, see Marc-Antoine de Montclos, "Liberia: Des Predateurs aux Ramasseurs de Miettes," in François Jean and Jean-Christophe Rufin, eds., *Economie des Guerres Civiles* (Paris: Hachette, 1996).

56. Hugh Cholmondley, "Conditions, Consequences and the Future of International Action in Liberia," unpublished mimeo, New York, May 1996.

Republic of the Sudan

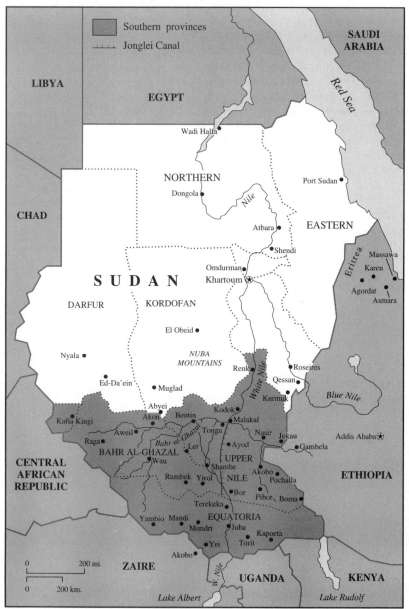

Southern provinces

⊥⊥⊥⊥ Jonglei Canal

SAUDI ARABIA

LIBYA

EGYPT

Red Sea

Wadi Halfa

NORTHERN

Port Sudan

Dongola

Nile

CHAD

Atbara

EASTERN

Shendi

Eritrea

Massawa

Karen

Omdurman

Khartoum

Agordat

Asmara

S U D A N

DARFUR

KORDOFAN

El Obeid

Nyala

NUBA MOUNTAINS

Renk

White Nile

Roseires

Qessan

Blue Nile

Ed-Da'ein

Muglad

Kurmuk

Abyei

Kodok

Kafia Kingi

Akon

Bentin

Malakal

Addis Ababa

Aweil

Bahr al-Ghazal

Tonga

Nasir

Jokau

Raga

Ler

Ayod

Gambela

BAHR AL-GHAZAL

Wau

UPPER

CENTRAL AFRICAN REPUBLIC

Rumbek

Yirol

Shambe

NILE

Akobo

Pochalla

ETHIOPIA

Bor

Pibor

Boma

Terekeka

Yambio

Mandi

EQUATORIA

Mundri

Juba

Kapoeta

Yei

Torit

Akobo

0   200 mi.

ZAIRE

0   200 km.

W. Nile

UGANDA

KENYA

Lake Albert

Lake Rudolf

138

CHAPTER FIVE

The Sudan:
Cradle of Displacement

Hiram A. Ruiz

DURING THE TWENTIETH CENTURY, few countries have suffered proportionately greater internal displacement of their populations than the
Sudan.[1] Civil war, primarily between northern and southern Sudanese
from 1955 through 1972 and from 1983 to the present, has left more than
1.5 million southern Sudanese dead and a majority of the remaining
southern Sudanese population uprooted. The massive level of often deliberate death and displacement has been one of the century's largest,
yet least-recognized, tragedies.

The conflict in the Sudan is multifaceted and has deep historical roots.
The conflict is depicted as regional: north (including east and west) versus
south. It is religious: overwhelmingly, northerners are Muslims, and
southerners are Christians or adherents to traditional African religions.[2]
It is racial, ethnic, and cultural, pitting northern "Arab" against southern
black African. It is about political and economic power: elite northerners
have dominated the Sudan politically and economically since independence and continue to covet the south's natural resources; southerners
seek their fair share of the political and economic pie (though some want

The author is grateful for the assistance of Millard Burr, author of several books and
articles on the Sudan, in the preparation of this chapter.

independence); and political conflicts exist among various groups in both the north and the south.[3] Also, even the geographic description of the conflict as north versus south is not fully accurate. People in some areas that are geographically in the north, such as the Nuba Mountains, Ingessina Hills, and Abyei, may be ethnically or culturally more "southern."

Since June 30, 1989, the principal "northern" element in the war has been the military of the Sudanese government, which is led by General Omar Hassan al-Bashir and dominated by members of the National Islamic Front (NIF), a Muslim fundamentalist party. NIF leader Hassan al-Turabi and his followers have managed to marginalize the traditional northern leadership. The NIF has declared the war with the southern forces a *jihad*, or holy war, and helped create a half-million-strong Islamicized People's Defense Force.

The southern opposition has been led primarily by the Sudan People's Liberation Movement (SPLM) and its military wing, the Sudan People's Liberation Army (SPLA), which advocate political power-sharing within a unified secular Sudan. John Garang, a Dinka (one of the largest ethnic groups in the south), heads both the SPLM and the SPLA. The SPLM and SPLA participate in the National Democratic Alliance, which represents a wide range of opponents to the NIF government. In 1991 a split in the SPLM and SPLA led to the formation of new southern splinter groups and to deadly interethnic fighting among southerners.

The conflict in the Sudan has been both pervasive and devastating: it is virtually impossible to find a southerner who has not lost a relative, and a majority of southerners have been displaced from their homes. The south as a whole has been ravaged by fighting, drought, disease, and starvation. Formal education has nearly ceased; health services have practically disappeared.[4]

Many of those uprooted fled to neighboring countries and beyond. According to the U.S. Committee for Refugees (USCR), a nongovernmental organization (NGO) that has reported on humanitarian conditions in the Sudan for many years, at the end of 1996 more than 430,000 southern Sudanese refugees were living in neighboring countries, including Uganda (200,000), Zaire (100,000), Ethiopia (70,000), Kenya (30,000), the Central African Republic (30,000), Egypt (1,500), and Eritrea (1,000).[5] Many other southern Sudanese have migrated to these and other countries at least in part for reasons related to the conflict but either have not applied for refugee status or have been denied it.

The vast majority of southern Sudanese forced from their homes are, however, internally displaced. Many fled to nearby towns, villages, or camps for internally displaced persons—in both government- and rebel-held areas—within the southern Sudan. A large number also fled to unwelcoming urban centers in northern Sudan, particularly the Khartoum area. At the end of 1996, USCR reported that as many as 4 million Sudanese, mostly southerners, were internally displaced throughout the Sudan.[6]

While man-made violence has killed and uprooted the majority of the victims, drought, which has struck the Sudan with unmerciful regularity since 1963, also has resulted in the deaths of countless Sudanese and the displacement of hundreds of thousands of others, not only in the south, but also in the west and north.[7]

In surveying the phenomenon of internal displacement worldwide, examining the case of the Sudan is particularly important. The Sudan has the world's largest internally displaced population, reason enough to scrutinize it. The Sudanese government's hostile response to its displaced citizens also makes the Sudanese example particularly relevant.

The Sudanese government has bombed camps for internally displaced persons, forcibly relocated displaced persons from Khartoum to camps where services are virtually nonexistent, and abducted displaced children and placed them in camps where human rights groups report that they are compelled to convert to Islam and undergo military-style training.[8] The government furthermore has tolerated the enslavement of displaced women and children, profiteered, and actively prevented international aid from reaching displaced people with urgent needs.[9]

The Sudanese government in Khartoum has been able to pursue these policies by insisting that the issue of internal displacement in the Sudan is a domestic concern and has donned the mantle of state sovereignty to keep the international community at bay.

A minority of displaced Sudanese have received limited assistance from the United Nations, through the initially groundbreaking but now highly compromised Operation Lifeline Sudan (OLS), or from international and local NGOs. However, as a result of Sudanese government policies and actions, most displaced Sudanese, particularly those in government-controlled areas, have been left to fend for themselves.

Although the government is widely criticized for its abuse of the civilian population, the SPLA has also been accused of stealing relief food in the field, exploiting camp populations for food, and recruiting men and boys from the camps into its ranks. SPLA units have also kidnapped several relief workers.[10] And clashes between southern groups have led to significant civilian death and suffering. Observers agree, however, that the level of abuse is much lower on the SPLA side. Some say that while widespread human rights abuse appears to be part of the government's policy in this conflict, that is not true for the SPLA.

Overview of Conflict and Displacement in the Sudan since 1983

For most of the years since its independence in 1956, the Sudan has been engulfed by a two-phased civil war. The violence has been the primary cause of death and destruction in the Sudan and shows no sign of abating as long as the underlying social conditions remain in place.

Although it is simplistic to say that the conflict in the Sudan is merely a war between north and south, there are fundamental differences in how northern and southern Sudanese perceive themselves and their country. Francis Deng, a noted Sudanese scholar and diplomat and the UN secretary-general's special representative on internally displaced persons, published an in-depth analysis of the subject of identity differences in the Sudan in which he noted, "It is now widely acknowledged that an acute crisis of national identity is at the core of the conflict." He wrote:

> The politically dominant and economically privileged northern Sudanese . . . see themselves as primarily Arab, deny the African in them, and seek to impose their self-perceived identity throughout the country. . . . In sharp contrast . . . southerners see themselves as unambiguously African, racially and culturally, with Western influences reflected in Christianity and secularism. . . . In this war of identities, the South has been joined by the non-Arab, though Muslim, communities of the North-South borders, notably the Nuba of Southern Kordofan and the Ingassana [sic] of Southern Blue Nile.[11]

Deng added that the answer to the question of whether the Sudan is Arab or African has "serious implications for the sharing of power, the distribution of resources, and opportunities for participation."[12]

Southerners' frustration with northern domination, suppression, and exploitation under shifting colonial rule as well as under Arab rule initiated the first period of civil war, from 1955 to 1972. That war ended with the signing of the 1972 Addis Ababa Agreement, which granted the south regional autonomy.[13]

Although some southerners were suspicious about the agreement and southern discontent continued, peace prevailed until 1983. According to Deng, the period between 1972 and 1983 was "the only time when the Sudanese from the North and the South came close to mutual acceptance and respect, not as one people or society, but as different racial, ethnic, and religious groups that could live together in a unified country."[14]

In 1983 the government broke up the south administratively, from one, Juba-based region into three separate regions. The government gave each region its own governing body but reduced the power they had held in the years following the Addis Ababa Agreement; as a result, the south was deprived of most of the autonomy it had gained from the agreement. The government also began debating the introduction of *Shari'a*, or Islamic, law, although it did not promulgate the law until September of that year. That led a group of southern officers to plan a mutiny.

The government learned of the plan and tried to preempt it by transferring the involved officers' forces from their bases in the south to sites in the north. The Aweil garrison moved north as ordered, but Bor-based battalion 105, under the leadership of John Garang, rejected the orders. It broke with Khartoum, and on May 16, 1983, left Bor for the Ethiopian border, where it was joined by elements from other battalions. This marked the birth of the SPLA and the start of the second civil war, which continues at the time of this writing.

In the early years of the second civil war, the SPLA was active primarily in rural areas. In the first half of 1985, however, the SPLA threatened government garrisons at Kapoeta and Torit in eastern Equatoria and occupied high ground overlooking the Juba airport. Despite these successes, it soon became clear that the rebels could not overrun Juba. Nevertheless, from that date on, no government garrison town in the south was safe from SPLA attacks.

Fighting associated with SPLA offensives in 1985 and 1986 resulted in the uprooting of about 50,000 people. The situation deteriorated in mid-1986 when famine hit Bahr al-Ghazal and Upper Nile and tens of thousands more became displaced. Nearly 100,000 displaced persons crowded into Malakal, the capital of Upper Nile province.

Beginning in 1985, as part of its campaign against the south, the government of Prime Minister Sadiq al-Mahdi supplied automatic weapons and military supplies to Arab raiders (*murahileen*) who were already responsible for a campaign of rape, rustling, and arson south of the Bahr al-Arab. The *murahileen* then used their enhanced firepower to depopulate hundreds of African villages in Bahr al-Ghazal.

In Upper Nile, the potentially oil-rich Bentiu Rural Council, with its population of 160,000, suffered extensive raiding by Arab groups from Kordofan. Thousands were killed and thousands more displaced by the Missiriya Arab *murahileen*. The catastrophe was so great that the region was generally depopulated by mid-1985.[15]

A February 1986 investigation by the Sudan Council of Churches found that "war and activities of armed gangs" had affected 187,000 people in Aweil and Gogrial districts of Bahr al-Ghazal. It predicted correctly that, henceforth, "war and activities of armed gangs from Southern Kordofan and Darfur would make relief work extremely difficult." Four months later, one quarter of Aweil Rural Council's 1 million people had been uprooted.[16] At year's end, the governor of Bahr al-Ghazal estimated that 100,000 people had already left for the north and that 300,000 others could be expected to follow.[17]

An SPLA attack on Kapoeta that began in September 1986 displaced tens of thousands more. More than 150,000 other southern Sudanese fled to refugee camps in Ethiopia.

Despite Large-Scale Displacement, Little Relief

Despite the growing problem of internal displacement, Sadiq al Mahdi's government appeared to make no effort to track the phenomenon.

The first overt indication that the SPLA hierarchy was concerned with the internally displaced was a mid-1986 report that the SPLA's nascent humanitarian arm, the Sudanese Relief and Rehabilitation Association (SRRA), was providing food aid to 20,000 internally displaced at Narus in the Equatoria region. Shortly afterward, the UN urged the funding of an emergency food airlift, Operation Rainbow, to supply the southern Sudan's major cities. The SPLA asked the UN to assist the displaced under SPLA control as well as those in government-controlled areas. The head of the Office of UN Emergency Operations in the Sudan supported that position. The Sudanese government declared him persona non grata, and Operation Rainbow never became an effective effort.[18]

Massive displacement continued in 1987. In the spring, widespread fighting in the populous Bor district prompted more than 90,000 of the district's 350,000 predominantly Dinka residents to flee to Juba. By mid-year, more than half of the district's population had fled either toward the north and Malakal or toward the south and Juba. Drought and a failed harvest in late 1987 led to even more displacement in the south.

Death and Displacement Reach New Heights in 1988

The evolution of the civil war into a countrywide conflict continued through 1988. SPLA tactics had evolved from localized ambushes in northern Upper Nile province to a full-blown capacity to threaten major district and provincial capitals. A successful SPLA offensive termed "Bright Star" gave the SPLA control over large areas of the southern Sudan, including the towns of Torit, Kapoeta, and Kajo Kaji.

The campaign also resulted in more civilian displacement, however. Southerners fleeing the fighting sought refuge in the government-held regional capitals—Juba, Malakal, Wau—or in towns that had been captured by the SPLA. Almost overnight, the number of internally displaced in Juba increased from 50,000 to 90,000. (By early 1990, the number of internally displaced southerners receiving regular food assistance in Juba had doubled to 185,000.) Their needs nearly overwhelmed the resources of almost a score of NGOs operating in the city.[19]

The fighting also prevented many southerners from being able to farm their land. Soon, man-made famine engulfed the south. In Aweil, nexus of an indescribable tragedy, the chairman of the town's relief committee pleaded for help and predicted that about 550,000 displaced would pass through Aweil. In one tragic episode, 10,000 displaced Dinka scrambled aboard a government train leaving Aweil. On the way, some 7,000 were dumped at Meiram, where children were kidnapped, adults were assaulted by militia, and thousands starved. After an arduous journey lasting more than three weeks, fewer than 2,000 Dinka reached Khartoum. Many died in the train station after arriving in the capital. As people continued to flee war and famine, NGOs warned that the fabric of community and village life was being torn apart in the southern Sudan.

Displaced persons from northern Bahr al-Ghazal also sought refuge and aid in the Abyei region, an area populated by the Ngok Dinka that is administratively in Kordofan, a northern province. According to Deng and Minear, the Ngok Dinka, who historically maintained relatively cordial relations with their northern neighbors, "played a bridging role in the North-South context." Nevertheless, they added, "Abyei became one of the areas where starvation was worst. People, especially children, died in masses within easy reach of government and international relief services simply because the government identified them as southerners and therefore part of the enemy camp."[20]

Yet as the humanitarian emergency mushroomed, the international food donor response, including that of the World Food Programme (WFP), the U.S. Agency for International Development (USAID), the U.S. Office of Foreign Disaster Assistance (OFDA), and the European Community, remained sporadic. Some NGOs operating in both the north and government-controlled areas of the south compiled data on the displaced population and warned the government's Relief and Rehabilitation Commission (RRC) that starvation was endemic throughout the south. Norwegian People's Aid (NPA), which had been active in SPLA territory since 1986, was most aware of the enormity of the problem in that area. Thanks to the NPA, the SRRA was able to provide food aid to 100,000 southern Sudanese in and near Kapoeta.

More than 250,000 southern Sudanese died as a result of man-made famine in 1988. Many of those deaths occurred in adequately secure, SPLA-held areas entirely accessible by cross-border operations from Kenya.[21] A large number of those who died could have been saved if the international community had been more willing to help civilians in a rebel-held zone—that is, outside the control of the recognized government. Its reluctance to do so because of the recognized government's objection highlights the degree to which, even today, the international community often accords state sovereignty more weight than human life.

Operation Lifeline Sudan I

To avoid a recurrence of the tragedy of 1988, the United Nations created Operation Lifeline Sudan (OLS). It was established at a time when the Sudanese government, still under Sadiq al-Mahdi, was engaged in an evolving peace process with the SPLA.

International frustration with the inadequate response to the Sudan's massive suffering triggered intensive diplomatic activities that resulted in a UN-sponsored conference on relief operations held in Khartoum in March 1989. By the time the conference was convened in Khartoum, a secure foundation had been laid to ensure its success. The U.S. government representative favored a large-scale program of aid to the displaced. The result of the conference was the decision to launch OLS I.

To facilitate access to as many civilians in the conflict areas as possible, including enormous numbers of internally displaced persons, the government, and later the SPLA, agreed to establish "corridors of tranquillity" through which OLS relief would pass safely. This agreement set the stage for what UN officials described as one of history's largest humanitarian interventions in an active civil war.[22]

OLS was a coordinated relief effort between UN agencies such as WFP, the United Nations Children's Fund (UNICEF), the United Nations Development Programme (UNDP), and other international organizations, including the International Committee of the Red Cross (ICRC) and international NGOs. OLS engendered optimism in the humanitarian community because both sides agreed to the vital and historic principle that OLS would have access to "war-affected people irrespective of who controls the territory in which they are located," and pledged to honor the safe corridors that would permit food aid to reach all those in need.[23] In a two-month period shortly after its inception, OLS I delivered more food to those in need in the southern Sudan—nearly 16,000 tons—than had been delivered from 1983 through 1988.[24]

During 1989, the international community channeled about $205 million directly to OLS I and mobilized as much as another $100 million for Sudanese relief in general. OLS I reportedly exceeded its 107,000-ton target of food aid (some observers question the accuracy of that figure) and also provided 3,760 tons of important nonfood materials, including agricultural hand tools, seeds, human and animal vaccines and medicines, and shelter materials. Food and livestock production rebounded, and nutrition showed measurable improvement.[25]

The National Islamic Front Comes to Power

On June 30, 1989, only four months after OLS became operational, a military coup deposed the elected civilian government of Sadiq al-Mahdi and brought al-Bashir and the NIF-backed National Salvation Revolutionary Command Council (NSRCC) to power.[26] The NIF took significant steps to consolidate its military and political position. It purged the military and other security forces of many of their more moderate officers, banned almost all trade, professional, and labor organizations, and purged women from many government posts. It "Islamicized" the judiciary and the universities.[27] Many observers have argued that the NIF's fundamentalist leaders are intent not only on maintaining northern Arab

Muslim control but also on eradicating southern culture and imposing Arab culture and Islam nationwide.[28]

Within a few months of coming to power, the NSRCC/NIF leaders made clear their more aggressive military intent. Within months, the NSRCC disbanded the RRC and appointed new, ultraconservative commissioners to head agencies dealing with the displaced. It then restricted the activities of NGOs and even forced some out of the north. RRC officials visiting Washington in December 1989 said that the government "would not allow any humanitarian program in the southern Sudan that does not support our [the government's] military objectives."

The government insisted that there be a renegotiation of OLS's terms of operation. In a working document prepared by the RRC, the government accepted the UN figure of 50,000 displaced at Torit and 50,000 at Kapoeta but would ascribe no internally displaced figure to problem areas in Upper Nile (Kongor, Bor, Pibor) and Bahr al-Ghazal (Akon, Yirol). OFDA reported that 71 percent of the 1.8 million displaced southerners in the conflict zone were in the SPLA sector, while only 29 percent were in government-held areas. Nevertheless, the government called for a major shift in allocation of relief supplies. It demanded that OLS channel 85 percent of the aid to government zones.

The government proposed to include in the allocation formula the million and a quarter displaced southerners who were then in and around Khartoum, which was not in the conflict area; it did so despite its past refusal to assist them and despite its refusal to guarantee that it would use the aid to assist them in the future. Sudanese government officials also wanted to clear every aid parcel that entered SPLA-held territory, claiming that relief agencies surreptitiously were shipping arms to the rebels.[29]

OLS officials went out of their way to accommodate the government's concerns at the substantial risk of losing SPLA cooperation. On March 18, 1990, the SPLA issued a statement making clear its disapproval of the results of the private negotiations between the Sudanese government and OLS and its unwillingness to have new terms of operation imposed upon it. It also reiterated its commitment to work out an agreement "on the basis of partnership between itself, the UN, and the government of Sudan."

Operation Lifeline Sudan II

An agreement acceptable to all parties was worked out, and OLS's second phase began in late March 1990. The UN appealed for 100,000 metric tons of food, roughly comparable to the target of the original OLS. Between April and December 1990, OLS was able to deliver much of that amount, though it encountered major logistical obstacles.[30]

The difficulties that OLS I had experienced in late 1989—such as relief trains not moving, barges remaining moored at the docks, and ICRC flights increasingly being curtailed—intensified in 1990. The government bombed OLS relief sites in the southern Sudan in September 1990. Some of the bombings occurred while UN and Red Cross planes and personnel were on site.

Each side in the war accused the UN of partiality toward the other. The government, alleging that OLS had violated Sudanese sovereignty by providing cover for military support for the insurgents, demanded tighter operational controls and accountability. The SPLA, which claimed to control more of the south than it had at the beginning of OLS I, sought a larger proportion of the available relief supplies while resisting calls for increased accountability.[31] At the beginning of 1991, the Sudanese government suspended indefinitely all OLS programs staged out of northern Sudan.[32]

At the July 1991 session of the UN Economic and Social Council in Geneva, Per Janvid, the UN secretary-general's special coordinator for emergency and relief operations in the Sudan, reviewed OLS II. He said that while "substantial quantities of food assistance were initially intended to have been transported by UN train and barge convoys through conflict areas . . . despite protracted negotiations neither train nor barge in the course of 1990 ever left on its humanitarian mission. Similarly, no road corridor through conflict zones had ever been opened during the year; hence, certain areas designated for relief food were never reached."[33]

Sudanese Refugees Forced to Return from Ethiopia

In February 1990, shortly before OLS II got off the ground, an Ethiopian rebel group, the Oromo Liberation Front (OLF), in coordination with the Sudanese military and other rebels at war with the government of Ethiopia, overran the Asosa camp for southern Sudanese refugees in Ethiopia. A majority of the refugees moved to other camps in Ethiopia, particularly to those at Itang, Fugnido, and Dimma. However, approximately 40,000 of the refugees, primarily Uduks, returned to the southern Sudan. A substantial number of others died en route.

A year later, in May 1991, the OLF overran the last functioning Sudanese refugee camp in Ethiopia. Within days, an additional 240,000 uprooted southerners surrounded the southern Sudanese town of Nasir— normally home to only 3,000 people. All told, 400,000 Sudanese were forced from Ethiopia. Once again, thousands died during the two-week trek back to Sudan. Others were killed by Sudan Air Force aerial bombardment.

Given the enormous difficulty of moving food to the isolated Nasir region by land, the UN and USAID frantically attempted to airlift food to Nasir, a district that had suffered two consecutive harvest failures and could barely feed its usual small population. Many wanted to return to their villages but were prevented from doing so by drought conditions in northern Upper Nile and by the start of a Sudanese government offensive. Consequently, in June 1991 there were still an estimated 200,000 former refugees—now internally displaced—at Jekou (near Nasir) and Akobo. Western aid agencies worked desperately to avert massive starvation.

The Conflict Enters the 1990s

The SPLA reached its greatest success in the southern Sudan in April 1991. At that time, it controlled much of the south, and many displaced persons returned to their villages. Although there was some drought-related movement in Bahr al-Ghazal, most of the 250,000 people at risk there managed to cope. Akon remained the area of greatest need within SPLA territory, partly because its isolated location made food aid delivery difficult.

Three international events in 1991 greatly affected the political framework in the Sudan, however. First, as the cold war dissolved, the super-powers' interest in the Sudan both shifted and diminished. The super-powers had viewed the Sudan as strategic because it borders Egypt, Ethiopia, and Libya. Since the late 1970s, the Soviet Union had supported Ethiopia, which in turn had ties with the SPLA rebels. Sudanese governments had leaned toward the West during the cold war period. Second, when the regime of Mengistu Haile Mariam fell, Ethiopia no longer provided the SPLA with military support or transit access. Left without the assistance of a regional power, the SPLA became more vulnerable to government attacks. Third, the Sudan's vocal backing of Iraq in the Persian Gulf War led to tensions with the United States and the

United Nations. The West's subsequent reduction of assistance to the Sudan caused severe cereal shortfalls and fuel shortages.[34]

In the immediate aftermath of the Gulf War, the U.S. government appeared to adopt a more receptive posture toward the SPLA. SPLA leader John Garang even traveled to Washington, D.C., in June 1991 and received promises of significant and qualitatively new U.S. relief and development support for the SRRA, the SPLM/SPLA's civilian relief arm.[35]

These U.S. promises evaporated when, in August 1991, differences that had been simmering for years within the SPLM/SPLA leadership led to a split in the SPLA and the creation of a southern splinter group (which itself later split into two groups).[36] The split came about as a result of a power struggle within the leadership, criticism of what dissidents described as Garang's authoritarianism, interethnic animosity, and the effects on the SPLA of the fall of Ethiopia's Mengistu and the loss of the support Mengistu had provided.

The mostly Dinka mainstream SPLM/SPLA faction, headed by Garang, continued to advocate a united, secular Sudan. The new "Nasir" faction, led by Riek Machar and Lam Akol, was largely non-Dinka and anti-Garang and purported to want independence or self-determination for the southern Sudan. In late 1991, Nasir faction forces (later known as SPLA-United) massacred Dinka civilians in Garang's home territory of Bor, sparking one of the most destructive periods of interethnic violence in the southern Sudan's history. Between 1991 and 1995, more southerners would die as a result of fighting between the two southern factions than at the hands of the Sudanese military.

Sudanese Military Launches New Offensive

By 1992, the NSRCC/NIF's third year in power, the government had received arms from Libya, Iraq, and China and was ready to win back the territory it had lost to the SPLA. A rearmed Sudanese military went on the attack and powered its way up the White Nile.

The splintered, weakened SPLA lacked firepower. It also lacked fuel and spares for its vehicles, so had to operate mainly on foot. Consequently, it was not able to meet the Sudanese military, with its tanks and artillery, in head-on battles. It therefore again resorted to guerrilla tactics. The SPLA sought to harass and wear down the military by ambushing its convoys. The government forces were able to take a number of towns, but these were mostly small, or not towns at all—islands in a vast territory controlled either by the SPLA or by nobody. The SPLA frequently ambushed military convoys sent to relieve those forces, sometimes delaying the convoys for weeks or months. Tens of thousands of southerners in Upper Nile and eastern Bahr al-Ghazal were forced to flee to the bush. In 1992 the UN Special Emergency Program for the Horn of Africa estimated that of a total Sudanese population of 26 million, some 7.6 million were victims of drought and war.

In 1993 the Sudanese military expanded its offensive in the south. Tens of thousands of Equatorians fled Kapoeta and Torit toward the frontiers with Uganda and Kenya. The government bombed SPLA towns and villages and was able to displace the SPLA from a number of areas. By June, the population of Juba, usually some 100,000, had swelled to as many as 250,000.[37] An estimated 450,000 displaced were located elsewhere in eastern Equatoria, and 220,000 others were located at the "Triple A camps" (Ame, Aswa, Atepi) and at Mundri, Yambio, and other locations.[38] The government offensive created an additional 50,000 internally displaced in the Kaya/Morobo area in August 1993, most of whom headed toward the Ugandan border. Eventually, nearly 400,000 southern Sudanese fled to Uganda and Kenya.

Attempts to Mediate Southern Split Fail

Efforts by church groups to patch up the quarrel between the southern factions were unsuccessful, and violence between them continued. SPLA-United killed thousands of Dinkas and captured or slaughtered their cattle. At the time, Garang's SPLA forces were tied down in western Equatoria and could not defend the Dinka. Tens of thousands fled the violence. Garang's forces countered SPLA-United's advances and in 1993 attacked Lafon and seventeen villages to the south of it in reprisal for the region's support for the SPLA-United faction. In all, about 43,000 displaced sought refuge in the Imatong Mountains.[39] Throughout the year, the southern Sudanese were battered by fighting between the government and the SPLA, and between the mainstream SPLA and the SPLA-United factions.

In late 1993 the two southern factions participated in face-to-face meetings facilitated by the U.S. government. Both agreed to the "Washington Declaration," which called on the two factions to contain hostilities and to begin discussing whether the south should become independent. Despite the declaration, however, fighting continued.[40]

Because widespread insecurity prevented aid workers from making reliable estimates of the number of displaced persons, in May 1994, USAID supported a significant effort to count the displaced. In what was the most ambitious effort to compile a census of the internally displaced in the southern Sudan, large numbers of field reporters enumerated 1.5 million displaced at 112 sites. Those data, however, soon became irrelevant when an attack by the Sudanese military forced hundreds of thousands of displaced to flee toward Sudan's borders with neighboring countries.

In September 1995 the SPLA-United group changed its name to the South Sudan Independence Movement/Army (SSIM/A) and in October clashed with SPLA forces. At about the same time, a new Sudanese government offensive that continued into the early months of 1995 targeted SPLA-held areas along Sudan's southern border with Uganda.

An SPLA counterattack in October 1995 indicated that the rebels, while badly injured, were hardly defeated. The agony of eastern Equatoria was about to be repeated, and as the SPLA scored victories in the regions of Torit and Kapoeta, observers felt a sense of déja vu as refugees and internally displaced began to return to their villages.

Also in late 1995, after discussions with the government, former U.S. president Jimmy Carter announced a cease-fire between the government and the SPLM/SPLA that, while aimed at enabling a Carter health initiative, some observers hoped might contribute to a resolution of the conflict. But the cease-fire was often broken, was not in effect in the Nuba Mountains, and broke down entirely when government forces attacked and captured Kaya, a key town on the Ugandan border.[41] The agreement had lasted only four months.

In April 1996, following several rounds of talks, the SSIM/A appeared to establish closer links with the Khartoum government. It signed a "Political Charter" with the NIF government that called for the resolution of the conflict through peaceful means and for southern Sudanese to hold a referendum, at a later date, "to determine their political aspirations." The SPLM/SPLA rejected the charter, which an editorial in the *Sudan Democratic Gazette* labeled a "formal surrender to Khartoum" by the SSIM/A.

Continued Harassment of Displaced Southerners in Khartoum

Shortly after the NSRCC coup that brought the NIF to power, the government warned that all "squatters" (meaning displaced southerners) found in "planned areas" in and around Khartoum would be removed. The government then moved quietly but purposefully to carry out its threat. In September 1989 the government informed NGOs that it had begun organizing fifteen so-called Peace Camps in White Nile and Upper Nile provinces. The government planned to force "140,000 displaced persons in Southern White Nile and another 52,000 in Renk and Wada Kona," as well as untold numbers of others from the north, to provide labor battalions for official "agricultural schemes."[42] In July 1992, Human Rights Watch reported that the Sudanese government had "bulldozed and burned the homes of about 500,000 of its poorest citizens in a forcible and often violent program of expulsions from Khartoum to new camps located outside the city." Human Rights Watch noted that in one incident Sudanese soldiers killed twenty-one displaced persons who resisted relocation. It added that conditions in the new camps were poor and that deaths from exposure had been reported.[43]

An independent review of OLS carried out in 1996 found that thirty-nine people had been killed during the government's demolition program, that the government forcibly had relocated more than 600,000 displaced persons by 1992, and that in early 1996 the government continued to destroy the houses of some 850 displaced families per month.[44]

In May 1994, reports from Khartoum indicated that the government recognized no internally displaced persons in the capital region. Somehow, the 1.8 million southerners were "officially" gone. The government only acknowledged 250,200 internally displaced persons in the Khartoum area, all outside of the capital proper. Khartoum was, again, the Arab and Muslim city that the government had envisioned in 1989.

The Characteristics of Displacement in the Sudan

When the first Sudanese civil war concluded in 1972, out of an estimated southern Sudanese population of more than 5 million, nearly 500,000 were internally displaced and more than 180,000 were refugees in neighboring countries.[45] Between 1972 and 1982, relative calm permitted many of those uprooted by the first civil war to return home.

The best data on the internally displaced are available from late 1988 through 1990, the period of greatest NGO activity in both the northern and southern Sudan.[46] A census conducted by the Sudanese government in October 1989 found that there were some 1.8 million internally displaced Sudanese within the three towns (Khartoum, Khartoum North, and Omdurman) that make up the Sudan's capital region.[47] The vast majority were southerners, but the number also included some drought-displaced persons from western Sudan. By 1991, more than 2 million displaced southerners were living in 48 "camps" in greater Khartoum. The largest camp, Zagalona, was home to 377,000 displaced southerners; three other camps had populations of more than 100,000 displaced persons each.[48]

Of the estimated 4 million Sudanese displaced in mid-1996, some 1.8 million were living in and around Khartoum in the north, several hundred thousand were located in South Kordofan and South Darfur, and 1.5 million remained within the southern Sudan. Some 600,000 were in areas under SPLA and SSIM control in the southern Sudan, including 235,000 in the Bahr al-Ghazal region, 125,000 in the Upper Nile region, 110,000 in Equatoria west of the Nile, and 120,000 in Equatoria east of the Nile. An estimated 250,000 displaced persons were living in the southern Sudan's largest city, Juba, which was held by the government but surrounded by the SPLA.

The Government Response

Much of the problem of internal displacement in the Sudan has resulted from the policies of the government toward the southern Sudanese. It has done little to respond to the needs of the internally displaced and much to exacerbate their suffering and increase their numbers. It has bombed displaced person camps, attacked civilian villages, prohibited relief efforts, and forced people out of their homes at gunpoint.

Following a visit to the southern Sudan in 1990, USCR director Roger Winter said:

> The Sudan government, as a party to the conflict, and with a horrible record regarding actual, effective delivery of relief supplies to displaced people in need, has forestalled operation of much of the international relief efforts in Sudan. It has consistently refused to allow relief efforts to proceed during the dry season, when transporting food is less costly, then agreed to allow transport when the rainy season is imminent—a time, observers

say, when transportation costs rise substantially, which benefits northern Sudanese merchants, particularly those with ties to the government.[49]

Besides being criticized for its poor record in providing relief for the internally displaced, the Sudanese government has been criticized for its poor human rights record by the UN special rapporteur on human rights in the Sudan, Dr. Gaspar Biro, among others.[50] The U.S. government's deputy assistant secretary of state for African affairs, Edward Brynn, called Khartoum's human rights record "abysmal."[51]

According to Human Rights Watch, the Sudanese government also has been particularly guilty of human rights violations against internally displaced children. Human Rights Watch says that the government removes displaced children from their families against their will, forces them to undergo Islamic religious training, and makes them adopt Arab names, thus suppressing their heritage.[52] As if these abuses were not enough, many southern and Nuba children have been forced into unpaid labor and even slavery. These findings were reinforced in an article by reporters from the *Baltimore Sun* who traveled to the Sudan undercover and demonstrated that it was possible to buy southern Sudanese children. While the government vehemently has denied that forced labor and slavery exist in the Sudan, it has refused the assistance of international organizations in investigating such allegations. [53]

In April 1993 the UN Commission on Human Rights adopted a resolution regarding the Sudan that expressed deep concern about:

> activities such as slavery, servitude, the slave trade and forced labor, the sale and trafficking of children . . . especially but not exclusively affecting displaced families and women and children belonging to racial, ethnic, and religious minorities from southern Sudan, the Nuba Mountains, and Ingessana [sic] Hills areas. . . . [reportedly] frequently carried [out] by agents acting under government authority or taking place with the knowledge of the Government of Sudan.[54]

Within the north, the NIF government is opposed by the Umma Party and the Democratic Unionist Party, both of which have previously been in power and are led mostly by the Sudan's traditional elite. The opposition also includes a loose coalition of professional associations, trade unions, women's groups, students, and others who oppose both the fundamentalists and the traditional elite.[55] In December 1994 the Umma party, the SPLA, and all other members of the National Democratic Alliance signed the Asmara Declaration, an agreement that endorsed the Inter-Governmental Authority for Development (IGAD, a group that promotes conflict resolution in the region) Declaration of Principles, including the south's right to self-determination.[56]

The International Community's Response

Throughout the 1980s, annual rainfall in the Sudan was far below average. The first serious crisis occurred in western Sudan in 1983 and resulted in the terrible famine of 1984–85, which brought many foreign humanitarian agencies to the Sudan. By the mid-1980s, drought had struck the south, where attacks from Kordofan by *murahileen* (Arab militia) compounded the problems of crop failure and scarcity of forage. Relief for the displaced and the starving came almost solely from the foreign humanitarian agencies.[57]

By 1986, primarily in response to the effects of drought and famine and the presence of large numbers of Ethiopian and Chadian refugees in the Sudan, more than 100 Western humanitarian agencies representing all ideological and religious persuasions were operating in the Sudan, primarily in government-controlled areas.[58] NPA and World Vision were among the few organizations assisting civilians within the SPLA-held areas. Their operations saved thousands of lives.[59]

Despite these operations, an estimated 500,000 Sudanese lost their lives between 1986 and 1988, mainly from conflict-related famine in the south and the international community's unwillingness to assist displaced persons in a rebel-held zone. Apart from some NGOs, the world long ignored the humanitarian emergency in the Sudan, even though the spectacle of tens of thousands of emaciated Dinka boys making an extraordinary trek to Ethiopia in early 1988 was a hard indicator for the international community to miss. These boys marched hundreds of miles from Bahr al-Ghazal to western Ethiopia, leaving thousands of their companions dead along the route.[60]

Despite its poor track record with the displaced, in June 1988 the Sudan asked the UN to appeal to the international community for assistance to the Sudanese government so that it could assist displaced persons in and around Khartoum. In response, the UN General Assembly adopted Resolution 43/8 on October 18, 1988, calling on all states to contribute to relief operations, rehabilitation, and reconstruction in the Sudan.[61]

In response to the 1988 tragedy, in 1989 the international community succeeded in getting Khartoum to agree to the UN's Operation Lifeline

Sudan, discussed earlier in this chapter. Although OLS initially succeeded in delivering large quantities of food aid to civilians at risk and
became a model for other international efforts to assist displaced and
other vulnerable populations in situations of conflict, it ultimately did not
live up to its own groundbreaking ideal.

In 1993 the representative of the secretary-general on internally displaced persons, Francis Deng, visited the Sudan and made a number of
proposals aimed at improving the situation of internally displaced Sudanese that the government agreed to implement. In September 1994,
Deng wrote to the Sudanese authorities to inquire about its progress. In
its response, the government reaffirmed its commitment to implement
the proposals in the representative's report, although in reality it had
done little or nothing.[62] The UN has not taken any stronger measures to
ensure these recommendations are implemented beyond the adoption of
resolutions.[63]

In a February 1995 report to the UN Commission on Human Rights,
Deng said that "the situation of the internally displaced in the Sudan
remains grave" and noted a report to the UN General Assembly by the
special rapporteur on the human rights situation in the Sudan, which
expressed concern about the "government's indiscriminate bombing of
places where there are concentrations of the internally displaced" and
described a "deteriorating health and food situation in some camps."[64]
Despite Deng's and the special rapporteur's reports, however, neither
the Commission on Human Rights, the secretary-general, nor the General Assembly ever directly asked Khartoum to implement the recommendations in the reports.

The OLS charter was renegotiated in 1994 with the concurrence of
both the Sudanese government and the SPLM/SPLA.[65] Since then, however, the NIF government has bent the rules in its own favor, without any
effective opposition from OLS's managers. An independent review of
OLS undertaken in 1996 at the request of the UN Department of Humanitarian Affairs (DHA) found that the principle of permitting OLS
access to war-affected people irrespective of who controlled the territory
in which they were located had "never been fully implemented . . . especially in GOS [government of the Sudan–controlled] areas." The review noted that while OLS agreements continue to refer to the principle
of free access, in reality "UN coordination is confined to those non-
government [controlled] areas that the GOS is willing to agree are both
'war-affected,' and beyond its control."[66] Between September 1995 and

July 1996, the government blocked OLS from using large, Hercules C-130 cargo airplanes, the only effective means of reaching some areas, to airlift food into some SPLA-held areas. The government only relented following criticism from the newly appointed director of the UN's World Food Programme, who said that the government's "cruel" position was putting hundreds of thousands of civilians at risk in Bahr al-Ghazal and other areas.[67]

OLS's failure to remain a neutral, effective tool for assisting all displaced Sudanese is largely due to the international community's lack of commitment and staying power and its timidity in challenging governments. The review of OLS for DHA concluded, "In essence, the critical weakness of OLS is that, through the astute exercise of its political authority, one of the warring parties has retained and augmented its ability to define the humanitarian space that OLS occupies."[68] When the international community has the interest, it not only supports OLS but also stands up for its neutrality. When international interest and commitment waver, however, Khartoum is ready and eager to seize control and manipulate the humanitarian effort.

According to the United Nations High Commissioner for Refugees (UNHCR), the experience of OLS in the Sudan shows that if serious efforts to deal with the root causes of displacement are not undertaken, the belligerents will continue fighting, while leaving the international community to care for the civilian population.[69]

Regional Implications of the Conflict

The continuing crisis in the Sudan had major implications for the entire region. The exodus of more than 445,000 southern Sudanese refugees into Uganda, Zaire, Ethiopia, Kenya, the Central African Republic, and Egypt has strained local resources and people in the areas where the refugees have settled.

Of perhaps greater concern to the Sudan's neighbors, however, are indications that the NIF is promoting the spread of Islamic fundamentalism in neighboring countries. Beyond such reports, there are clear indications that the Sudan and some of its neighbors are now actually supporting each other's internal enemies, including armed insurgencies, in the perception that doing so is in their own interest.

The government of recently independent Eritrea, which has a population almost evenly divided between Christians and Muslims, has accused the Sudan of supporting attacks on Eritrean territory by the Sudan-based Eritrean Islamic Jihad. In December 1994, Eritrea became the first of the Sudan's neighbors to break diplomatic relations with Khartoum.[70]

Khartoum's support for violent opposition groups in neighboring countries has been most overt in Uganda. The Sudanese military has harbored and trained members of the Lord's Resistance Army (LRA), a Ugandan rebel group that espouses its own form of alternative Christianity. Sudanese soldiers have joined Ugandan LRA rebels in attacks on villages in northern Uganda, including an attack in early 1995 that left 250 Ugandan villagers dead. Following that attack, the Ugandan government also broke diplomatic relations with the Sudan.[71] By mid-1996, the LRA had fundamentally changed. With support from the government of the Sudan, it was openly able to attack major targets, presenting a serious threat to the Ugandan People's Defense Forces. In July 1996 the LRA massacred Sudanese refugees in northern Uganda.[72]

Khartoum's support for radical Islamic fundamentalists in Egypt has created tensions with that country's government. Egyptian President Hosni Mubarak accused the Sudanese government of backing an attempt on Mubarak's life while he attended an Organization of African Unity (OAU) meeting in Addis Ababa. For its part, the Ethiopian government was furious over the attempted assassination that took place in its capital. It has spearheaded OAU and UN attempts to pressure the Sudan to extradite three of the suspects in the attempted assassination, who it claims are hiding in the Sudan.[73]

The Ugandan government has been the most conspicuous supporter of the SPLA, but other regional governments, including those of Eritrea and Ethiopia, may be considering extending or increasing support to the SPLA.[74]

A Regional Peace Initiative

In 1994, IGAD adopted a "Declaration of Principles" aimed at providing a basis for discussions on peace in the Sudan. All four IGAD members—Kenya, Uganda, Eritrea, and Ethiopia—are neighbors of the Sudan. Their peace initiative has met with international support. The U.S. government and the UN sent observers to IGAD talks and, on February 8, 1995, the Netherlands, the United States, Norway, Canada, and Italy formed a "Friends of IGAD" group to support the regional peace initiative.[75]

The Sudanese government, however, has refused to continue to participate in IGAD-sponsored peace talks because it vehemently rejects the call in the 1994 Declaration of Principles for the Sudanese government to address the issues of self-determination and separation of religion and state in peace talks.

Drought Exacerbates Displacement

Terrible droughts in 1982, 1983, and 1984 struck the Sudan's Sahelian belt from Darfur in the west to the Red Sea in the east. In a pattern that would be repeated again and again, the government spurned those who were affected, who were largely marginalized northerners. By the time the drought finally ended in 1986, an estimated 250,000 Sudanese had died and more than 500,000 others had become internally displaced.

In 1989, scant rains limited harvests in North Darfur and Kordofan. The drought continued in 1990, once again placing more than a million people in the Sudanese Sahel at risk. Untold thousands starved and more than 100,000 were internally displaced in the west, Bahr al-Ghazal, Red Sea province, and Khartoum, where the government allegedly treated them better than the displaced southerners with whom they lived side by side.

The crisis coincided with the beginning of the Persian Gulf War. For months, Khartoum adamantly denied the need for international relief efforts, both because it would not request aid from the anti–Saddam Hussein coalition and because it was reluctant to admit failure in its domestic self-sufficiency efforts. President al-Bashir criticized international relief agencies for "begging on behalf of the Sudanese people." After the end of the Gulf War, Khartoum reached a quiet agreement with the UN to allow limited international relief efforts. By then, thousands of people had starved to death.[76]

The Displaced Sudanese in the Late 1990s

Many of the displaced in the SPLA-controlled areas live near their places of origin, in camps or temporary locations where they can farm or herd until the next attack. Others have moved to more distant towns.

Those in the government-controlled garrison towns live under the command of the Sudanese military, which views the displaced as little more than hostages. Some of those in the garrison towns are members of southern ethnic groups that either fear or dislike the Dinka-dominated SPLA.

There were an estimated 4 million internally displaced persons in the Sudan in mid-1996. However, the total number of vulnerable populations was much higher. For example, in Bahr al-Ghazal, more than 1.2 million were feared to be hungry and starving in mid-1996.

Since 1994, internally displaced persons in some areas of the southern Sudan have required less food aid, while in other areas delivery of food aid has not kept pace with need. In 1994, donors and relief groups delivered just over 65,000 metric tons of food aid (excluding the aid to Juba town). In 1995, after a normal harvest in late 1994, the total food aid supplied was only about 46,000 metric tons. Projected food aid needs for 1996 remained at about the 1995 level.

In early 1996, however, there was a shortfall in food deliveries to Bahr al-Ghazal and Upper Nile, primarily due to the lack of air transport capacity and the difficulties in gaining access to Bor county. A grave situation was expected to develop in the latter part of 1996, with the main famine areas being those least accessible.

Previously, when famine struck the south, the military had allowed tens of thousands of displaced southerners supposedly under its care to die, though its soldiers have never been seriously affected. The hundreds of thousands of displaced persons in the government-controlled towns who have survived have done so because of the efforts and funds expended by Western aid agencies.[77]

The Situation in Equatoria

With the exception of the Dinka in Manglatore camp, most of the displaced on the west bank of the Nile River have been forced to flee their homesteads, but are still staying near their areas of origin, in areas familiar to them and often within their ethnic group's geographic boundaries. These people are generally highly motivated to manage on their own, and although they welcome food relief, they consistently stress their preference for agricultural tools and seeds with which they can help themselves. Norwegian People's Aid remains one of the main NGOs involved in assistance to the displaced on the west bank. Others include Action Africa in Need, the American Refugee Committee, the International Rescue Committee, Médecins sans Frontières/Holland, and World Vision.

In 1995 and the first half of 1996, the main problem that NGOs faced was a significant increase in transport costs, because all NGO convoys that originated in Kenya and normally traversed northern Uganda en route to the southern Sudan were forced to detour through Zaire to get to western Equatoria and Bahr al-Ghazal. That was due to insecurity in northern Uganda and the Sudanese Army's blocking of direct access from Uganda to western Equatoria. Because NGOs also found it difficult to obtain sufficient funding for agricultural projects, the process of establishing self-sufficiency among the displaced was slowed. In spite of the various difficulties in reaching the displaced on the west bank, their health status and situation in general remained at acceptable levels throughout 1995–96.

Beginning in mid-1995, a slow flow of people left Juba, heading toward the west and settling in areas east of the Yei River. By mid-1996, the total number of displaced in these areas reached close to 15,000, including some locally displaced people from areas outside Juba. Because of the problems of getting food through Zaire and across the Yei River, and significant looting of relief food from NPA in this area, very little relief was distributed to the east bank of the Yei River after September 1995.

In mid-1996, Sudanese were still moving toward the Zairian border. At the same time, Sudanese refugees from northern Uganda were returning to the Sudan as a result of the push-pull effect of the instability on the Ugandan side and the SPLA's recapture of large areas on the east bank. Some refugees also were returning from the camps in Zaire, allegedly because of poor services in those camps.

In eastern Equatoria, east of the Nile, the majority of the displaced are Dinka from the Bor region, virtually all of whom have been displaced two or three times since they were first driven out of their home areas by the Nuer raid in October 1991 and by the Sudanese army's 1992 offensive. Most of those displaced have received agricultural support in addition to food relief since 1993. Despite the hopelessness generated by their frequent displacement, displaced Bor Dinka generally have responded positively to attempts to reduce their food aid dependency. Still, because of the insecurity in the areas of their camps before the SPLA offensive in October 1995, and because of insufficient rains in most seasons since 1993, food aid continues to account for as much as 80 percent of the group's needs.

The main food relief agencies assisting displaced populations in Eastern Equatoria are Catholic Relief Services and NPA. Both of these organizations also are involved in significant agricultural projects in their target areas. The overall nutritional status of the displaced in eastern Equatoria has been mostly satisfactory, although some groups of displaced have experienced insufficient or much delayed supplies periodically as a result of the insecurity in northern Uganda, extremely difficult road conditions during the wet season, and delayed shipments of food to Kenya, where most cross-border relief operations into the southern Sudan are based.

In Upper Nile, the displacements in the Nuer areas are mainly the result of internal tensions caused by Riek Machar's SSIM signing an agreement with the Sudanese government, and the other SSIM faction, under the leadership of John Luk, signing a reunification declaration with the SPLM/SPLA. The outbreak of fighting between these parties in the Akobo area in mid-1996 may result in further displacement.

In the SPLA-controlled areas of Upper Nile, Bor county still receives Dinka returnees, especially from the Maridi area and Yirol. At the end of May 1996, the estimated number of returnees to the Bor area had reached 22,000. The returnees' presence exacerbated an already precarious situation caused by a combination of late rains and flooding.

The Situation in Bahr al-Ghazal

Displaced people in Bahr al-Ghazal have received much less food relief in relation to their identified needs than displaced persons in other areas of the southern Sudan. That is largely because they are inaccessible by road and because there is inadequate air transport capacity. But, as mentioned above, the food deficit is not limited to the displaced. Much of the total population in Gogrial, Aweil, and the northern part of Wau also experience great problems. The rains that normally start in early April in these areas had still not arrived in June 1996, causing large-scale crop damage. Attacks and harassment by the Sudanese military and armed militia also prevented the population from growing crops.

The Situation in Khartoum

Most of the 1.8 million displaced in Khartoum and nearby areas still reside in cardboard *tukuls* (huts) in shantytowns—some built atop garbage mounds—that pass for displaced persons' camps. The camps' residents endure grossly inhumane conditions. They are despised by the local community and ignored by the government, which does not provide them with health services, education, or other basic amenities. The few displaced who are able to find temporary or part-time work as laborers receive only subsistence wages.

According to a 1995 report by African Rights on internally displaced persons in the Khartoum area:

> The tragedy of these 'displaced people' is on a scale with few parallels. . . . They are systematically oppressed by their government and shunned and ostracized by the majority of the Northern townspeople. . . . The international community has made no serious or sustained efforts to protect them. . . . [The government's] programme of forced relocation . . . is one of the largest relocation programmes in the modern world, and one of the most abusive. . . . To date the programme has not slowed. . . . Displaced people are systematically blocked from access to adequate health services.[78]

In a separate report, Human Rights Watch said that "the government is creating a permanent underclass through its policies of marginalizing and segregating displaced southerners." It added that "while feigning a show of concern for the displaced and making small concessions following substantial diplomatic efforts, the government is single-mindedly pressing ahead with its Islamization/urban removal plans which punish the displaced."[79] The independent review of OLS carried out for DHA in 1996 strongly criticized the UN's role regarding the Khartoum displaced. It said:

> The continuing crisis among war-displaced populations in greater Khartoum, the largest concentration of internally displaced people in Sudan, represents the greatest failure of OLS in the Northern Sector. . . . Indeed, in 1995, three years after their formal incorporation [under the OLS umbrella], the nutritional status of displaced populations in Khartoum was reported to be deteriorating."[80]

The review team concluded that, in the face of pressure from the government of the Sudan, the UN largely had given up trying to protect or assist the vast number of displaced persons in the north in order to preserve OLS in the south. The review said:

In exchange for a transient UN coordination in the south, OLS humanitarian principles have never been robustly and openly pursued in the north.
The equivocal autonomy of OLS in the south has thus been purchased at
the expense of displaced and war-affected populations in the north.[81]

Forced Displacement in the Nuba Mountains

According to USCR director Roger Winter, who visited the Nuba
mountains in 1995 along with an African Rights team (among the few
outsiders to be able to do so in recent years), the Sudanese government
has pursued a "strategy of liquidation" of the Nuba people since 1985.[82]
The Nuba Mountains region includes not only the Nuba Mountains themselves but also a large stretch of fertile plains. The more than 1 million
Nuba people are in fact a conglomeration of a large number of distinct
groups that speak more than fifty different languages.[83] The Nuba population, which includes Muslims, Christians, and followers of traditional
religions, is known not only for its religious diversity but also for religious
tolerance. Unlike in other areas of the Sudan, religion has not been a
barrier to the evolution of a Nuba identity.

According to African Rights, a human rights group that provided the
first on-site documentation of the Sudanese government's abuses in the
Nuba Mountains in its 1995 report, *Facing Genocide: The Nuba of Sudan*,
"The Government of Sudan is actively engaged in a campaign against
the Nuba people that, if followed through to its conclusion, will mean
that there is no society recognizable as Nuba remaining in existence."[84]

The Sudanese government's war against the Nuba began in 1985 when
the Sudanese government armed militias of Baggara Arab nomads to
fight the SPLA, which had attacked a Baggara camp. These militia,
known as *murahileen*, became a powerful, ferocious force that targeted
both Dinkas and Nuba.[85]

To rid Bahr al-Ghazal and Upper Nile of *murahileen*, the SPLA began
to recruit north of the Bahr al-Arab in 1987. In South Kordofan, it
enlisted both Christian and Muslim Nuba. By 1988, there were reports
of an SPLA force including indigenous Nuba—the New Kush Brigade—
actively engaging the Sudanese military in the Nuba mountains and the
fertile plains near Kadugli, the capital of South Kordofan.[86]

After the NIF came to power in 1989, it began a campaign not only
to defeat the SPLA forces there but also to drive the Nuba into submis-
sion through hunger, destitution, and demoralization.[87] In September

1990, government security forces systematically arrested educated Nuba. The UN, Amnesty International, and Pax Christi-Netherlands reported extensive violations of human rights, including massive attacks on Nuba villages, the killing of large numbers of civilians, the rape of Nuba women and girls, and the forced relocation of tens of thousands of Nuba.[88]

In January 1992 the governor of Kordofan announced a *jihad* in the Nuba Mountains. The Sudanese military surrounded the Nuba Mountains, denied entrance to any outsiders, and began the wholesale destruction of Nuba villages. Between June and August the military transported some 30,000 Nuba by truck to desert wasteland in North Kordofan and herded them into government-controlled, so-called Peace Camps. The government claims that the Peace Camps are relief centers for civilians who have fled or been "liberated" from the SPLA. But according to African Rights, "The truth is very different." In its 1995 report on the government's actions in the Nuba Mountains, the group said:

> Inmates are kept there against their will, they are forced to work for low wages or no wages, men are forced to become members of the PDF [People's Defense Forces], women are raped, and children have their identities changed. It is all part of the program for dismembering Nuba society. . . . It is also widely held that the peace camps are kept as a 'human shield' to discourage SPLA attacks.[89]

By September 1992, 143,000 displaced Nuba had been forced into eighty-nine Peace Camps. Tens of thousand of others fled to SPLA-controlled areas.[90]

According to African Rights, beginning in late 1993 and continuing through 1995, the government "followed a new military-political strategy. There are no frontal assaults on the SPLA positions, and fewer large massacres. But . . . the combination of practices employed by the Sudan government are still aimed at . . . obliterating Nuba society as it has existed up to now. It is genocide by attrition."[91]

The new strategy, labeled "combing," includes soldiers attacking Nuba villages, stealing whatever there is to steal, destroying everything else, and burning the village to the ground. Sometimes, the soldiers abduct the villages' residents and force them into Peace Camps. Other times, the soldiers simply rely on the villagers' being left with no possessions to drive them into the camps.[92]

The Sudanese government's campaign against the Nuba people has drawn little international attention or response. The government has not permitted OLS assistance in the Nuba Mountains, and the UN has never challenged the government's position. Cease-fires have excluded the Nuba Mountain region. IGAD has failed to include the issue of the Nuba Mountains on its agenda. In short, according to African Rights, "The international role [in the Nuba Mountains] is one of omission—almost nothing has been done internationally either to expose the crime [of genocide] or prevent it from relentlessly progressing towards its completion."[93]

Recommendations

Conflict and displacement in the Sudan are not new. Since the 1960s, and particularly since the inception of the second civil war in 1983, hundreds of thousands of Sudanese have died. Many have been direct victims of violence; others have starved, often as a result of famine engendered or exacerbated by the conflict. Millions of others have been uprooted from their homes, in some cases temporarily, in others for many years. Many of the uprooted fled as refugees to neighboring countries, but a majority became internally displaced—refugees in their own land.

The international community has provided protection and assistance to Sudanese who fled to other countries. That has largely been possible because of the existence of a formal international mandate and a well-established system (primarily through UNHCR) for protecting and assisting refugees.

In part because there is no comparable mandate or system for internally displaced persons, the international community, overall, has failed to help protect and assist internally displaced Sudanese.

Not that it hasn't tried: the international community has promoted negotiations, arranged cease-fires, appointed special representatives, provided food aid and other humanitarian assistance, and—to get that assistance to all those in need—arranged safe corridors and emergency airlifts, undertaken cross-border relief operations, and more. In many situations of internal displacement, recommendations to protect and assist the internally displaced probably would include urging the international community to take many of the above steps. In the Sudan, however, these steps and others have already been tried, all too often unsuccessfully.

As long as the conflict continues, attempts to control and manipulate humanitarian aid for military, political, or economic advantage will also continue, and the displaced and other affected civilians will continue to suffer. While it does, the international community must continue to try to improve its present humanitarian efforts on behalf of the victims of the conflict while continuing to press Khartoum to respect the human rights of all of its citizens.

Most important, the UN needs to reassume control over OLS and implement it as intended: as a neutral, humanitarian effort undertaken with the cooperation of the government of the Sudan and the SPLA.

At a meeting in Geneva in September 1996 in which the government of the Sudan, the three southern factions, UN agencies, and NGOs working in the Sudan met to discuss the future of OLS, most participants agreed to the creation of a new OLS agreement in which all parties would "commit themselves to principles of humanitarian rights and access by OLS" and would grant the UN and OLS the "final authority to determine needs." The Sudanese government, however, expressed reservations about the proposal.[94]

Second, humanitarian aid should go to those in need regardless of their location. Assistance can only reach many displaced persons and other affected people in the south through cross-border relief operations from neighboring countries. This can be done by expanding the carrying capacity of cross-border operations deeper into the Sudan and opening new cross-border channels. Although land-based efforts entail risks, they work even in the most difficult of conditions.

The government of the Sudan has ultimate responsibility for the care and protection of its internally displaced citizens. However, if it forsakes that responsibility and instead targets the displaced as enemies, the international community cannot simply pretend that the fate of those at risk is solely the internal affair of the sovereign government of the Sudan. When the rights of human beings to survive confront the sovereignty rights of a government of questionable legitimacy, the international community should act on behalf of innocent people.

Third, the government should give humanitarian and human rights organizations free access throughout the country, in particular in the Nuba Mountains and the towns of the southern Sudan. The parties should grant monitors access to locations where they can improve information flow and independently verify reports on human rights.[95]

Finally, the international community also should take all possible steps to stop the Sudanese government from deliberately targeting displaced persons and other civilians, not only through its direct military operations, including bombing raids, but also through its use of ruthless armed militia.

However, even if the international community succeeded in implementing all of the above, that would not be a solution. A solution requires that the international community do more than provide humanitarian assistance: it must try to help remedy the root cause of the human suffering, the conflict itself.

Clearly, that will be very difficult. According to U.S. Deputy Assistant Secretary of State Brynn:

> The Government of Sudan has shown no inclination toward positive change. Indeed, the regime's reaction to outside pressure has been to reinforce NIF domination of the government. . . . [U.S. representatives have] consulted extensively with the IGAD partners, the parties to the conflict, and the international community on ways toward a peaceful settlement. Unfortunately . . . both the Khartoum regime and the southern rebels have been unresponsive to our concerns.[96]

Even though there may appear to be little hope for progress, old avenues must be reexplored and new ones found and pursued.

The four members of IGAD, all neighbors of the Sudan, are trying to help resolve the Sudanese conflict. The international community should strongly support the IGAD framework for peace in the Sudan, not only between south and north but also between the rival southern factions.

The UN Security Council should include in its consideration of Sudanese policies the official practices that inhibit aid to the internally displaced. If the government continues to obstruct relief agencies' access to internally displaced persons, the international community should impose an arms embargo (the European Community has already done so), an energy embargo, and sanctions on Sudanese exports, which would reduce the amount of foreign exchange available to the government of the Sudan to finance the war.[97]

Notes

1. Millard Burr, "The Internally Displaced Issue in the Sudan," unpublished manuscript, U.S. Committee for Refugees (USCR), Washington, D.C., June 1996.

2. Ibid.

3. Roger P. Winter, on behalf of USCR, "War and Famine in Sudan," testimony before the U.S. House of Representatives Committee on Foreign Affairs, Subcommittee on Africa, October 25, 1990.

4. Burr, "The Internally Displaced Issue in the Sudan."

5. USCR, *World Refugee Survey 1997* (Washington, D.C., 1997).

6. Ibid.

7. Burr, "The Internally Displaced Issue in the Sudan."

8. Kevin Vigilante, M.D., on behalf of Puebla Institute, "Crisis in Sudan," testimony before U.S. Senate Subcommittee on Africa, March 22, 1995; World Vision, "Sudan, Cry the Divided Country," Federal Way, Wash., Spring 1996, p. 3; African Rights, "Sudan's Invisible Citizens: The Policy of Abuse against Displaced People in the North," London, 1995.

9. For information on the enslavement of displaced women and children, see Frank Wolf, "Facing Genocide: The Nuba of Sudan," testimony before U.S. Senate Subcommittee on Africa, March 22, 1995; African Rights, "Facing Genocide: The Nuba of Sudan," London, July 1995; and World Vision, "Sudan: Cry the Divided Country," pp. 3–4. For information on the government's profiteering, see World Vision, "Sudan: Cry the Divided Country," p. 12. For information on the prevention of aid from reaching displaced people in need, see Report to the General Assembly of the UN Special Rapporteur on the Human Rights Situation in the Sudan (A/49/539), cited in Francis M. Deng, *Report on Internally Displaced Persons*, E/CN.4/1995/50 (United Nations, Commission on Human Rights, February 2, 1995); and USCR, *World Refugee Survey 1992* (Washington, D.C., 1992), p. 53.

10. Human Rights Watch/Africa, "Behind the Red Line: Political Repression in Sudan," Washington, D.C., May 1996, p. 78.

11. Francis M. Deng, *War of Visions: Conflict of Identities in the Sudan* (Brookings, 1995).

12. Ibid.

13. World Vision, "Sudan: Cry the Divided Country."

14. Ibid.

15. Famine Relief Committee, "Famine and Drought in Upper Nile," Malakal, July 10, 1985; SUDANAID/Sudan Council of Churches, "Emergency Assistance Needs, Bahr al-Ghazal and Upper Nile," Khartoum, September 28, 1986.

16. Sudan Council of Churches, "Regional Situations: Special Report on South Sudan," Khartoum, February 3, 1986.

17. Governor's Office, "Famine Situation in Bahr al-Ghazal Administrative Area," BGAA/19.A.1, Wau, Bahr al-Ghazal, November 19, 1986, cited in Burr, "The Internally Displaced Issue in the Sudan."

18. "Mass Starvation Imminent in Southern Sudan," *Arab News*, August 29, 1986; "John Garang: A New Sudan," *Africa Report*, July–August 1989, p. 46.

19. Nick Roberts, "Visit to Juba and Yei," *Emergency Aid Monitor*, CART Juba, November 14, 1989.

20. Francis M. Deng and Larry Minear, *The Challenges of Famine Relief: Emergency Operations in the Sudan* (Brookings, 1992), p. 15.

21. Winter testimony, October 25, 1990.

22. Deng and Minear, *The Challenges of Famine Relief.*

23. Barbara Hendrie, ed., and Ataul Karim, team leader, "Operation Lifeline Sudan: A Review," July 1996, p. 59.

24. J. Millard Burr and Robert O. Collins, *Requiem for the Sudan: War, Drought, and Disaster Relief on the Nile* (Boulder, Colo.: Westview, 1995).

25. Deng and Minear, *The Challenges of Famine Relief*.

26. Burr, "The Internally Displaced Issue in the Sudan."

27. Winter testimony, October 25, 1990; Africa Watch, "Denying the Honor of Living, Sudan: A Human Rights Disaster," New York, March 1990; Amnesty International, "Sudan: A Permanent Human Rights Crisis: The Military's First Year in Power," New York, August 1990.

28. African Rights, "Sudan's Invisible Citizens," pp. 1–4.; U.S. Rep. Gary Ackerman in House of Representatives hearing, March 22, 1995; Millard Burr, "A Working Document: Quantifying Genocide in the Southern Sudan 1983–1993"; "Nuba," *Sudan Update*, London, August 7, 1995, p. 1.

29. Roger P. Winter, "War and Famine in Sudan," testimony before the U.S. House of Representatives, Select Committee on Hunger International Task Force, March 15, 1990.

30. Deng and Minear, *The Challenges of Famine Relief*.

31. Ibid.

32. Winter testimony, March 15, 1990.

33. Deng and Minear, *The Challenges of Famine Relief*.

34. Burr, "The Internally Displaced Issue in the Sudan."

35. Roger P. Winter, on behalf of USCR, testimony before the U.S. Senate Committee on Foreign Relations, Subcommittee on African Affairs, February 23, 1989.

36. Theodore Dagne, "Sudan: Current Conditions, Peace Efforts, and U.S. Policy," Congressional Research Service, Washington, D.C., November 1995.

37. Information provided to USCR by Norwegian People's Aid.

38. U.S. Agency for International Development (USAID), Office of Foreign Disaster Assistance (OFDA), "Sudan: Civil Strife/Displaced Persons," Washington, D.C., December 1, 1993.

39. USAID, OFDA, "Weekly Situation Report for South Sudan, June 9 through June 15, 1993," Nairobi, Kenya, June 1993.

40. *Africa Confidential* (January 7, 1994); *Sudan Newsletter*, vol. 3, no. 4, p. 9.

41. Human Rights Watch/Africa, "Behind the Red Line," p. 78.

42. Lt. Gatluak Deng Garang, "Points for Discussion with H.E., the U.S. Ambassador," Upper Nile Region, Governor's Office, Report REC/UNR/69.A.1., September 20, 1989, cited in Burr, "The Internally Displaced Issue in the Sudan."

43. Africa Watch, "Sudan: Refugees in Their Own Country," New York, July 10, 1992.

44. Hendrie and Karim, "Operation Lifeline Sudan," p. 190.

45. Estimates of the southern Sudanese population vary significantly. Most estimates range between 3.5 million and 8 million. See also Burr, "The Internally Displaced Issue in the Sudan."

46. Burr, "The Internally Displaced Issue in the Sudan."

47. 1995 UN estimate, reported by Human Rights Watch in 1996.

48. Burr, "The Internally Displaced Issue in the Sudan."

49. Based on winter testimony, March 15, 1990.

50. "In Spite of NIF Provocation, IGADD Broadens the Search for Peace," *Sudan Democratic Gazette*, vol. 57 (February 1995), p. 4.

51. Testimony of Edward Brynn, principal deputy assistant secretary for African Affairs, U.S. Department of State, before the U.S. House of Representatives Subcommittee on Africa, March 22, 1995.

52. Human Rights Watch /Africa, "Special Report on Sudan's Children: Children of Sudan, Slaves, Street Children and Child Soldiers," Washington, D.C., 1995, p. 2.

53. *Baltimore Sun*, June 16, 1996, p. 1.

54. Commission on Human Rights Resolution 1996/73 on "Situation of Human Rights in the Sudan," United Nations, April 23, 1996.

55. World Vision, "Sudan: Cry the Divided Country," p. 10.

56. Bona Malwal, testimony before the U.S. House of Representatives Subcommittee on Africa, March 22, 1995.

57. Burr and Collins, *Requiem for the Sudan*.

58. Ibid.

59. Winter testimony, February 23, 1989.

60. Ibid.

61. Nathan M. Belete, "Operation Lifeline Sudan: A Humanitarian Mission," *Africa Notes* (March 1996), p. 3.

62. Deng, *Report on Internally Displaced Persons*.

63. The General Assembly, for example, has called on the government of the Sudan to carry out the recommendations of the special rapporteur. See General Assembly Resolution 51/112, "The Situation of Human Rights in the Sudan," United Nations, December 12, 1996.

64. Deng, *Report on Internally Displaced Persons*.

65. "How the UN-OLS Has Become a Potent Weapon of War for Khartoum," *Sudan Democratic Gazette*, vol. 75 (August 1996).

66. Hendrie and Karim, "Operation Lifeline Sudan," p. 60.

67. See "How the UN-OLS Has Become a Potent Weapon of War," *Sudan Democratic Gazette*.

68. Hendrie and Karim, "Operation Lifeline Sudan," p. 61.

69. UNHCR, Division of International Protection, *UNHCR's Operational Experience with Internally Displaced Persons* (Geneva, September 1994), p. 161.

70. USCR, *World Refugee Survey 1995* (Washington, D.C., 1995).

71. World Vision, "Sudan: Cry the Divided Country."

72. According to SPLM/SPLA representatives.

73. World Vision, "Sudan: Cry the Divided Country."

74. Ibid.

75. Brynn testimony.

76. Roger P. Winter, on behalf of USCR, "War and Famine in Sudan," statement before the U.S. Senate Committee on Foreign Relations, Subcommittee on African Affairs, May 14, 1991.

77. Burr, "The Internally Displaced Issue in the Sudan."

78. African Rights, "Sudan's Invisible Citizens," pp. 1–2.

79. Human Rights Watch, "Sudan 'In the Name of God': Repression Continues in Northern Sudan," New York, 1994.

80. Hendrie and Karim, "Operation Lifeline Sudan," p. 193.

81. Ibid., p. 60.

82. Roger P. Winter, "The Nuba People: Confronting Cultural Liquidation," unpublished manuscript, USCR, 1996.

83. Ibid.

84. African Rights, *Facing Genocide: The Nuba of Sudan*, p. 1.

85. Ibid.

86. Burr, "The Internally Displaced Issue in the Sudan."

87. "Nuba," *Sudan Update* (August 7, 1995), p. 1.

88. Burr, "The Internally Displaced Issue in the Sudan."

89. African Rights, *Facing Genocide: The Nuba of Sudan*, p. 243.

90. Danish Church Aid, "Sudan Focal Point," January 18, 1996, p. 3.

91. African Rights, *Facing Genocide*, p. 137.

92. Ibid.

93. Ibid., p. 331.

94. Department of Humanitarian Affairs, "OLS Review: New Thinking on Sudan," *Humanitarian News*, United Nations, New York.

95. UN Commission on Human Rights, *Situation on Human Rights in the Sudan*, E/CN.4/1995/58 (United Nations, January 30, 1995), p. 18.

96. Brynn testimony.

97. Winter testimony, March 15, 1990.

CHAPTER SIX

Dealing with the Displacement and Suffering Caused by Yugoslavia's Wars

Thomas G. Weiss and Amir Pasic

THE FUNDAMENTAL LESSON to be learned from displacement in the former Yugoslavia is to avoid the tragic conflation and confusion of humanitarian and political issues. There are five internationally recognized states in the erstwhile Socialist Federal Republic of Yugoslavia (see map). The causes and consequences of involuntary displacement and war-inflicted suffering in the five units are so intertwined that they are best analyzed as a single case, particularly for the focus of this essay: Croatia, the Federal Republic of Yugoslavia (Serbia/Montenegro), and Bosnia-Hercegovina.

Though the major dramas of violent displacement have ended with efforts to implement the Dayton Peace Accords of November 1995, the problem of displacement continues to haunt Bosnia and its neighbors. The return of refugees and internally displaced persons (IDPs) continues to be one of the major unfulfilled provisions of the Dayton Accords.[1]

The authors are grateful to UNHCR's chief statistician, Béla Hovy, who helped generate data for this chapter and made other useful comments on the overall approach, and to Larry Minear, who helped sharpen its conclusions.

Former Socialist Federal Republic of Yugoslavia

Certainly the military forces in the former Yugoslavia have been silent since the arrival of the NATO and partner troops in Bosnia in December 1995. There has been no distressed movement of large numbers of people since the early 1996 exodus of Serbs from Sarajevo during the early stages of implementing the military part of the Dayton Accords.[2] Nonetheless, the subsequent analysis, with its focus on the origin and trajectory of human displacement before the end of 1995, supports the emerging reality that displacement promises to be a major impediment to achieving a lasting peace. Understanding the political context of displacement becomes more crucial than ever.

The political roots of violence in the Yugoslav case indicate that the lessons are overwhelmingly related to actions that should be, and should have been, taken in the political arena. Humanitarian measures cannot address fundamentally political problems. As in other complex emergencies, misplaced humanitarianism and political ineffectiveness often combined in the former Yugoslavia to make a bad situation worse.[3] Future humanitarian efforts must avoid such a syndrome of negative reinforcement.

In many ways, this case study highlights efforts by the United Nations High Commissioner for Refugees (UNHCR) to alleviate the suffering of all displaced—both refugees and IDPs—and besieged populations. We argue for a principled extension of this ad hoc practice for all the victims of war. This is a logical extension not only of using UNHCR as the UN's "lead agency" in the former Yugoslavia—that is, the agency in the driver's seat for the international humanitarian response—but also of the general concern for IDPs that has found official expression by the UN secretary-general and his special representative on the matter.[4] Though the specific needs of people who have been uprooted appropriately draw our attention, the specific needs of all those who require care and refuge should be dealt with flexibly and without discrimination, regardless of the most appropriate institutional form for humanitarian action. UNHCR's designation as lead agency extended its mandate to assist and protect all those who can no longer count on any state for their security and provided a glimmer of hope in the humanitarian travesties of the former Yugoslavia.

This case was, in Secretary-General Boutros Boutros-Ghali's words, a "rich-man's war," drawing an exceptionally massive dedication of resources and sustained international concern. As such, we consider it to be instructive as an extreme case. It is hard to imagine that other endangered populations would receive similar treatment. Because the international attention devoted to the former Yugoslavia may be highly unusual, it suggests the limits of what can be reasonably expected. This case also dramatically reveals the vital importance of the political context and its enmeshment with humanitarian efforts. Indeed, responsibility for fellow humans implies a political act that either directly contravenes or significantly adjusts the political lives of suffering populations who are supposed to be separate, whole, and distinctive as a result of the sovereignty of their country.

Characterizations of Yugoslavia's wars and the role of displaced and besieged populations have been profoundly political. The three most common characteristics of sovereignty—territory, authority, and identity—have been in continuous flux and contested at every turn. The situation in the former Yugoslavia may be the most extreme example of the inappropriateness of distinguishing "refugees" and "internally displaced persons." These terms have been called into question because of their lack of operational significance, although in other cases there are more obvious needs to separately identify IDPs.[5] Adding to the problematic nature of conceptual and operational distinctions between these two categories are persons "affected" by war itself—or "war victims" in the terminology of UNHCR. Those not uprooted but in dire need of humanitarian assistance and protection composed over 40 percent of the refugee agency's beneficiary population in 1993, 1994, and 1995.[6]

In analytical terms, "displacement" may in many cases be an inappropriate policy guide unless it is conceived in the broadest sense to encompass the conditions of those who have crossed a border or stayed behind—all those who have been literally or figuratively uprooted from the conditions of humane survival. This is a humanitarian adaptation of "the end of geography"—which originally signified the lack of salience of borders because of modern international finance and communications, but which increasingly applies also to comprehensive coverage to all those affected by war regardless of their physical location.[7]

When the bounds of territory, authority, and identity—of borders, political arrangements, and collective solidarities—are both ambiguous and uncertain, they serve as poor guides for action. In other words, it is conditions of deprivation and not categories of victims that should be addressed. Although categories of victims are discernible and classifications are possible, all of those who suffer are victims. They should receive attention strictly in consideration of their specific needs, whether or not they have been displaced. The special requirements and specific contexts of particular victims—for example, some IDPs may have more immediate nutritional needs than others—should be taken into account rather than their legal status.[8]

In the former Yugoslavia, additional problems arose simply because uprooted people were categorized as belonging to an ethnic group; their group membership was used to determine whether and when they received aid or other consideration by the international community. Adding to the complexity of defining victims in circumstances where identities are intensely politicized is the related disagreement over "international" and "internal" borders. Because the boundaries of citizenship did not coincide with those of ethnic identity, external recognition of boundaries became a key feature in shaping not only the prolonged horror of displacement in the former Yugoslavia but also domestic and international responses, in ways that did not reflect the intentions of the act of recognition or the purpose of the institution of recognition.[9] Such action implies a form of participation in the "ethnification" of peoples whose country has been decimated largely through a political process that destroyed interethnic trust and led to the degeneration of an existing multiethnic society as a result of manipulating ethnic differences, making them the basis for spreading fear and divisiveness.

All census data can be used for political purposes, but one of the most graphic illustrations of how extreme this phenomenon has become is the widely distributed color map of Croatia and Bosnia-Hercegovina in which there is a breakdown, commune by commune, of the three major ethnic groups on the basis of the 1991 census. This indicated the raw material for displacement, even before the triumph of nationalism and "ethnic cleansing." Catering to the needs of those who had the greatest potential to be displaced before the conflict would have been preferable to alleviating their suffering after ethnic homogenization.

Knowing that afflictions that often accompany war and displacement can be diverse and highly specific to regions, peoples, gender, and age, one would prefer to be able to practice preventive medicine. Unfortunately, there is no mobile hospital with a well-delineated and managed ward that could be appropriately designed to accommodate IDPs in all situations. Sometimes they are the most needy; at other times they are the relatively privileged. Displacement is manifested differently in different countries and also within locations in a country. Given current resource constraints and the fluid conditions facing actually or potentially threatened populations, devising a full-fledged public health approach to IDPs is infeasible. The metaphor of triage might serve us better; it allows for flexibility to determine acute needs and provide tailored responses in light of the capacities of international institutions to protect and assist victims.

Categorizing persons is appropriate only when it facilitates protection or the delivery of needed assistance. Indeed, the case of Yugoslavia demonstrates the need to proceed with caution and to adopt longer-term perspectives about the impact of humanitarian assistance, which has political consequences that should not be obscured by the well-intentioned rush to rescue the afflicted. In particular, humanitarian efforts affect both the mental well-being and the basic political orientations of local populations. The broadening of concern toward IDPs—and toward endangered populations—implies a commitment to the political evolution of a society that is in need of immediate rescue and subsequent rehabilitation.

This chapter proceeds in six sections. First, we begin with a survey of the causes of the armed conflicts in the former Yugoslavia, paying particular attention to international factors in the political manipulation of identities. Second, we offer a statistical and chronological overview of the scope of displacement in the former Yugoslavia, which reflects major political and military developments. We discuss the specific difficulties faced by IDPs and other endangered populations, especially the deep political involvement in traditions and cultures whose autonomy has been respected more in normal times.

Third, we discuss international responses to the conflicts, illustrating their effect on IDPs; this is the most lengthy and complex part of the argument. We begin with recognition—diplomatic, pragmatic, and media—and then proceed to both military and humanitarian responses, explicating the enmeshment of politics and humanitarianism. We analyze the leadership role of UNHCR, which suggests that although general efforts at protection failed, its successful delivery of assistance was an organic outgrowth and a coherent extension of its concern for those without refuge who have crossed an international boundary.

Fourth, we discuss the hallmarks of the Yugoslav case and the lessons that might be drawn from it. Fifth, we consider the politics of rescue and argue for an articulation of, and engagement with, the political implications of humanitarian action.[10]

Last, we advocate reactivating the abandoned (since 1992) practice of designating a lead agency to orchestrate the international community's rescue efforts. Although a lead agency could not be as comprehensive in its undertakings as a completely new unit dedicated to the task, we believe this to be a pragmatic approach that could lead to greater international responsibility and a more comprehensive public health approach in complex emergencies.

The Causes of Yugoslavia's Wars

A deteriorating economy provided the background for nationalist and ethnic dissatisfaction and mobilization as well as its subsequent manipulation.[11] Initially, certain members of the Serb elite were the strongest supporters of the unrest; they had the most to lose from a devaluation of their predominant role in state bureaucracies.[12] Beginning with the suppression of ethnic Albanians in Kosovo in the early 1980s, widespread politicization of both ethnicity and the ethnodemographic history of certain portions of the territory became commonplace. Also relevant were the role of the Yugoslav military as a failed all-Yugoslav institution and the cumbersome constitution bequeathed by Marshal Tito—both became forces for separation rather than unity.[13]

The internal economic, political, legal, and ethnic structure of Yugoslavia created conditions and a climate within which neighbors could slaughter one other. Yet such conditions had existed for some time before the actual explosion of ethnic violence, and they also exist in countries that have not undergone such social upheaval. The most salient explanation lies in the radicalization of perceptions about differences, inequalities, and the role of neighbors in perpetrating injustices. These perceptions changed the course of Balkan history. The recourse to a politics of fear based on ethnicity drove many men (and very few women) to pick up arms lest their homes and identities fall prey to the designs of neighbors who were suddenly recast as threatening strangers.[14]

If any consensus is emerging from the scholarship on Yugoslavia's demise, it may be one that runs directly counter to the ethnic/religious/primeval hatreds that underlie many media treatments and popular understandings of what Susan Woodward has called the "Balkan tragedy." There is general agreement that leaders and intellectuals within Yugoslavia more or less consciously employed divisive language and accentuated past episodes of intra-Yugoslav armed conflicts for political purposes. More than simply reflecting the sociopolitical realities in their country, leaders stirred the cauldron of ethnic tensions and added fuel to the embers underneath it; they calculated that their hateful messages would serve political goals by mobilizing support.[15] At the same time, many who formulated or condoned malicious national and ethnic ideology never fully contemplated the possibility that their ideas would bring back genocide as a policy option on the European continent, but international organizations nonetheless abetted matters by eagerly recognizing actions that favored ethnic identity over other forms of identity.[16]

One important reason that ethnic and nationalist discourse flourished in Yugoslavia was its international resonance among numerous observers who expected ethnic divisions to assert themselves in the Balkans, sooner or later. Consequently, the international context added to the significance of the malicious domestic hatreds that were first acted on by para-military groups whose entrance onto the political scene brought a new and dangerous tenor to local political processes. Moreover, politicians and political parties who first constructed and then stressed the presence of dangerous ethnic threats added to the damage by confronting ethnic swaggering with jingoistic bravado. Those who tried to counter the hysteria of ethnic menace by calling for tolerance and coexistence found little support. Their voices were dampened initially because they emanated from a confused left that was experiencing the defection of key personalities to nationalist causes at the same time that socialism was losing its luster. In a time of general crisis and despair, ethnic ideologies met with popular acclaim, and because they reflected aspirations to national self-determination they also received international encouragement.[17]

An element of social breakdown that is particularly relevant in this case was the creation of a "moral ambiance" that sanctioned the inhumane treatment of those who until shortly before had been viewed as trustworthy neighbors.[18] The perpetrators of such acts first had to be desensitized by long and intense exposure to dehumanizing ideas about those on whom they would vent their frustrations.[19] The absence of mercy for those known rather intimately accounted for some of the most bewildering and inhumane episodes of displacement.[20] Outside organizations and negotiators unwittingly participated in condoning and perhaps enabling the initial "ethnification" of politics in Yugoslavia and then in advancing ethnic solutions by framing the options in essentially ethnic terms.

Yugoslavia unraveled so completely and quickly because it arrived at a time when the world was undergoing profound economic and political transformations. Deadly ideas were intensifying and preparations were being made for armed hostilities in the Balkans at the moment when the Berlin Wall and the Soviet bloc collapsed and Iraq invaded Kuwait. There were warnings of an impending conflagration in the Balkans, but Europe was giddy about the enhanced prospects for European unification in the aftermath of the Maastricht Treaty. The Conference on (now Organization for) Security and Cooperation in Europe (CSCE, now OSCE) was just setting up its institutional capacity for emergencies at the time, and the United States did not consider that its national interests were significantly affected by Balkan machinations.[21]

Overview of Displacement: June 1991–December 1995

More precise data about what we call the "casualties of war"—all of the victims of armed conflict including refugees, internally displaced persons, returnees, and war victims—would be useful for scholarly analysis as well as for planning, budgeting, fundraising, and programming. Yet conceptual and practical problems abound. In the prose of *The State of the World's Refugees 1995*, in spite of "the constant demands on UNHCR for facts and figures. . . . [it is] difficult to answer such queries with any real degree of accuracy."[22]

Displacement and suffering in the former Yugoslavia can be divided into three periods, which roughly correspond to major political changes resulting from the application of military force and armed intimidation. The significant changes in effective military control that served as the proximate causes of displacements since 1991 are the Croatian War (June 1991–November 1992); the Bosnian Wars (March 1992–August 1995); and the offensive by Croatia and the Bosnian-Croatian federation in tandem with NATO air power against the Croatian and Bosnian Serbs (August–November 1995). These military engagements were the proximate causes for the preponderance of involuntary displacement, even though it continued steadily throughout the period under review.[23]

The well-known difficulties of compiling accurate statistics within war zones should not prevent efforts to understand how data, however sketchy or exaggerated, are used both by warring parties and by the international humanitarian system. As one UN official close to the operation put it, "Numbers were used and abused by all parties during the war."[24] The statistics for each of the three periods present different snapshots of displacement and suffering depending upon the point of departure: political authority as gauged from Belgrade/Knin/Pale, Zagreb, and Sara-

Figure 6-1. *Asylum Applications in Western Europe by Citizens of the Former Yugoslavia, 1991–95*[a]

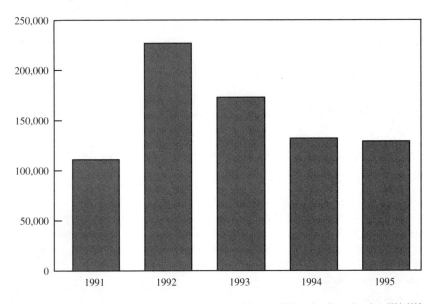

Source: UNHCR, *Refugees and Asylum-Seekers in Europe: A Statistical Overview of Citizens from Former Yugoslavia 1991–1995* (Geneva: UNHCR, 1996).

a. Western Europe includes Austria, Belgium, Denmark, Finland, France, Germany, Greece, Italy, the Netherlands, Norway, Portugal, Spain, Sweden, Switzerland, United Kingdom.

jevo; identity as measured from inclusion in Serb, Croat, or Muslim categories; and territorial claims using the internal administrative boundaries of the former republics of Yugoslavia that became the de jure international borders.

The latter juncture is where we begin because this is where the most comprehensive and viable data exist. There are few if any accurate flow statistics available. However, approximately 700,000 refugees moved to Western Europe—over half to Germany—who to date have been cared for mainly by host countries after being moved by the International Organization for Migration (IOM), but who become part of UNHCR's caseload as repatriation proceeds. These statistics are accurate and reliable (unlike many provided by belligerents). Global flow statistics for the over 4 million persons displaced in the territory of the former Yugoslavia, if available, would no doubt mirror the patterns depicted in figure 6-1 (the annual summaries of displacement in Europe). These data indicated that the overall displacement pressures faithfully reflected changes in the political and military situation on the ground during the wars.

The first major period of displacement was the war in Croatia from June 1991 to January 1992.[25] This resulted in Serb rebels laying claim to about one-third of Croat territory and the displacement of some 200,000 Croats, Hungarians, and others from Baranja, Slavonia, and what came to be known as Serb Krajina. Measuring the conflict's consequences in February 1992, UNHCR estimated that there were 605,000 displaced people in all the countries of the former Yugoslavia: 324,000 in Croatia, about 100,000 each in Bosnia-Hercegovina and Serbia proper, and 60,000 in Vojvodina.[26] The lull in hostilities was to be short-lived, reflected in UNHCR's switch from issuing a "Situation Update" to an "Emergency Report" in April 1992.

The second major period of displacement was the war in Bosnia (March 1992–August 1995). The war may be over, but migration continues. Most displacement took place in 1992 through a series of territorial shifts and incidents of "ethnic cleansing," which generated more than 1 million internally displaced persons and some 1.1 million refugees who left the territory of Bosnia-Hercegovina but remained on the territory of the former Yugoslavia.[27] Approximately 500,000 people emigrated out of the area and may or may not choose to be repatriated. It is also within Bosnia that the most intense "nonethnic" warfare took place: Fikret Abdic, the rebel strongman, fought against Bosnian government troops to maintain his hold over the political and economic entity in Bihac. He was allied with the Serbs in spite of his own Muslim background. Continual movement into and from the Bihac pocket marked an important exception to the general rule that displacement in the former Yugoslavia only mirrored ethnicity.

The final major period of displacement began in August 1995 and resulted in a mass migration of nearly 150,000 civilian and 50,000 soldiers from the Krajina region—Serbian "expellees" in Belgrade's view. In addition, there were incidents of designed expulsions of tens of thousands of non-Serbs from the Banja Luka region controlled by Bosnian Serbs. The continuing spillover from what was the largest involuntary displacement of Europeans since the Soviet invasion of Hungary in 1956 took place in the six months immediately preceding the Dayton negotiations and is shown in table 6-1. The Federal Republic of Yugoslavia estimates that about 750,000 refugees had arrived from other former republics by

Table 6-1. *Population Displaced in the Former Yugoslavia,*
May–October 1995

Month	Sector	Number
May	Sector west	12,000
July	Srebrenica	30,000
	Zepa	5,000
	Men of Zepa in RFY	800
August	Sectors north and south	170,000
	Stayed in Banja Luka	30,000
	Veika Kladusa	25,000
	Banja Luka minorities	20,000
September	Western Bosnia	80,000
October	Western Bosnia	50,000
	Banja Luka minorities	6,500
Total		429,300

Source: International Committee of the Red Cross, "Operations in Ex-Yugoslavia," January 30, 1996.

mid-October 1995.[28] This essay is not the place to do more than note that the humanitarian burden on the displaced populations in the Federal Republic of Yugoslavia was exacerbated by the sanctions that had been imposed by Security Council Resolution 820 of April 1993.[29] Additional refugees heightened the impact of the sanctions on the general populace because a remarkable number, some estimate 90 percent, of refugees in Serbia/Montenegro were accommodated in private households.

The future of Bosnia portends more displacement. Annex 7 of the peace settlement is designed to bring refugees and internally displaced persons back to their pre-war homes to claim property that was destroyed or occupied by voluntary or involuntary migrants from other parts of the former Yugoslavia.[30] It will take some time to straighten out the chain of illegal property transfers that accompanied "ethnic cleansing," in spite of the establishment of the Commission for Displaced Persons and Refugees. So much housing and infrastructure have been destroyed that it is unclear to what extent returnees and the persons whom they will displace (that is, the illegal occupants who themselves may have been chased from their own property) can be accommodated. Again, displacement will be a part of the policy landscape for international and local officials for decades.

At the moment that the Bosnian, Croatian, and Serbian presidents initialed the first agreement of the Dayton accords at Wright-Patterson

Air Force Base in November 1995, the government of Croatia claimed to be caring for almost 400,000 displaced persons. It estimated that 130,000 could return to their original places of residence as soon as the reconstruction process allowed them to do so. To this end, the government set up a program of reconstruction loans, the use of which changes the displaced person's status to that of a "returnee."

In Serbia, displacement also promises to remain an ongoing problem. The government claims that its resettlement policies are intended to achieve an equitable distribution of displaced persons across municipalities. Those displaced from the Krajina are being resettled in Vojvodina, often in housing from which Croats, Hungarians, and other non-Serbs were evicted. A similar but more contentious policy seems to be in progress in Kosovo; most Krajina Serbs probably do not want to go to serve as a form of ethnic currency in Belgrade's attempt to alter the demographic balance where ethnic Albanians constitute some 90 percent of the population. This may be one of the reasons why some Serbs have even expressed their desire to return to Croatia, despite the possibilities for retaliation against them.[31]

In Bosnia, the obsession with the ethnic categorization of victims continued as the official peace agreement was signed in Paris. The map that appears here as figure 6-2 was dropped from UNHCR's monthly "Information Notes" after December 1995. Yet the comparison of prewar and postwar categories of populations according to the breakdown into three ethnic categories illustrates the extent to which the casualties of the war in Bosnia also were "ethnified" as part of the international response.

The preceding data suggest the difficulty of attempting to differentiate refugees, IDPs, returnees, and war victims in armed conflicts like those in the former Yugoslavia. In addition to the operational pull to merge the four categories, the analysis of the human toll from Yugoslavia's wars leads us to argue for a single category of "casualties of war" on conceptual grounds as well. Efforts to place persons in one category or another depend on the analyst's or policymaker's assumptions about the acceptability of particular claims to territory, to authority, and to identity. Rather than take sides in this unseemly exercise, why not straightforwardly help all those who are suffering because they are entitled to human solidarity and protection by international norms? As explained below, comprehensive coverage without discrimination was precisely the basis for UNHCR's actions in the area.

Figure 6-2. *Pre-War Census and Wartime Population Estimates*

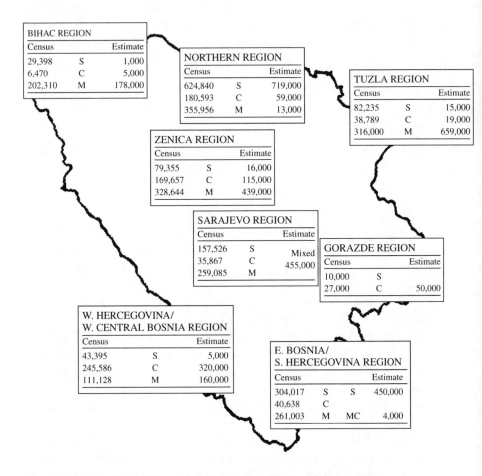

BIHAC REGION		
Census		Estimate
29,398	S	1,000
6,470	C	5,000
202,310	M	178,000

NORTHERN REGION		
Census		Estimate
624,840	S	719,000
180,593	C	59,000
355,956	M	13,000

TUZLA REGION		
Census		Estimate
82,235	S	15,000
38,789	C	19,000
316,000	M	659,000

ZENICA REGION		
Census		Estimate
79,355	S	16,000
169,657	C	115,000
328,644	M	439,000

SARAJEVO REGION		
Census		Estimate
157,526	S	Mixed
35,867	C	455,000
259,085	M	

GORAZDE REGION		
Census		Estimate
10,000	S	
27,000	C	50,000

W. HERCEGOVINA/ W. CENTRAL BOSNIA REGION		
Census		Estimate
43,395	S	5,000
245,586	C	320,000
111,128	M	160,000

E. BOSNIA/ S. HERCEGOVINA REGION			
Census			Estimate
304,017	S	S	450,000
40,638	C		
261,003	M	MC	4,000

Source: UNHCR Office of the Special Envoy for former Yugoslavia, External Relations Unit, December 1995.
Notes: The pre-war population figures are from the 1991 census. Wartime estimates are derived from various sources and have not been reconciled. The figures are related to total population, not to UNHCR's planned beneficiary population. The pre-war population and wartime estimates cannot be directly compared because front lines crisscross municipalities; thus the data represent only general population shifts.
In the boxes, S stands for Serb, C for Croat, and M for Muslim.

This case study does not focus on the current needs of displaced peoples and other threatened populations in the former Yugoslavia but rather on the four-year period during which hostilities and the threat of death and radical destitution were constant and real possibilities for many civilians. It is in this context that our stress on the politics of humanitarian engagement should be read because an explicit clarification of principles would allow multilateral policy to tackle the political environment more vigorously in conflicts like the former Yugoslavia. Rather than clinging steadfastly to an illusory middle ground that often requires inaction, we argue that all victims should be protected and assisted without differentiating among them.

Although identifying the specific needs of displaced and other afflicted populations is important when devising appropriate intervention strategies, it was extremely difficult in the former Yugoslavia because populations and boundaries shifted continuously. When would it have been appropriate to consider precise population distributions as given and stable in order to constitute a statistical gauge against which to measure the need for protection and assistance? Nonetheless, certain public health efforts were launched. For example, the World Health Organization helped to support surveillance of infectious diseases during the war in Bosnia. Public health advocates have argued since that such humanitarian aid should be sensitive to the future needs of the communities at war.[32]

Data are scarce, but there is much anecdotal and some systematic evidence regarding the special needs of the displaced and various categories of victims that tend to be disproportionately represented in their ranks. Women, children, and the elderly faced particularly acute hardships in the former Yugoslavia, as in all wars. In addition, the impact of the turmoil on their identities has rarely received adequate attention. Perhaps the international community can help facilitate the political conditions in which identities can be actively reconstructed by the victims of war. Indeed, one medical report has commented on the psychosocial problems that emerged in Sarajevo, including the dislocation and bewilderment shared by both doctors and patients regarding the West's perception that they were "Muslim fundamentalists."[33]

This phenomenon points to the profound importance of carefully considering the manner in which contact between the victims and those who seek to relieve their plight is established and sustained. Categories and characterizations are not only key for targeting the problems and delivering the goods; they also provide an indication to the afflicted of how the "outside world" sees them and the nature of the international commitment to the shared humanity that is said to motivate assistance.

Because women and children figure prominently as casualties, focusing on women seems to be a way of supporting peace and empowering those who generally do not directly participate in hostilities or the abuse of international norms. The usual victimization of women in war was taken to an extreme in Bosnia where rape was an explicit war aim.[34] A recent report has emphasized the particular needs of women in the former Yugoslavia, not only because of a general lack of response to date but also because of their vital role in reconciliation.[35] Also, in the former Yugoslavia as in other societies, women's displacement disrupts their capacity to support their families and subsequently to reconstruct the war-torn communities that they undergird. After a war that killed an estimated 250,000 people, mostly men, thousands of widows are now their families' sole breadwinners, and many have few skills with which to support themselves and their children.

The study by the Women's Commission for Refugee Women and Children draws attention to the fact that women are not being integrated effectively into the postwar economy and that local governments and international aid agencies are not adequately addressing women's needs. While many programs aim to create jobs for demobilized soldiers, the study warns that this should not come at the price of excluding widows and female heads of household from taking part in the economic reconstruction. Although their integration into international programs might meet local resistance, both international standards and the rehabilitation needs of a war-torn society make it essential.

In Sarajevo, a relatively large cadre of scientifically capable personnel have made it possible to monitor needs systematically. One study of the nutritional situation during the winter of 1993–94 concluded that the elderly were the most nutritionally vulnerable group. Meanwhile, displaced people housed in collective centers were the most "food insecure" because they were completely dependent on aid, had fewer relatives outside Sarajevo who could help, and did not have access to gardens where they could grow fruits and vegetables.[36] The study nonetheless concluded that the winter did not bring a nutritional disaster.

A similar conclusion was reached regarding the general success of preventing major nutritional shortcomings in Bosnia during 1993.[37] Again, in Sarajevo, a study of trends in birth weight during the war concluded that babies were adequately protected in part because of the efforts of UNICEF to promote breast-feeding and to distribute food supplements to mothers and babies.[38]

Regarding the elderly, the London-based Institute of Child Health reported in 1995 that one in seven elderly people in Bosnia's urban areas suffered from malnutrition. The institute suggested that even though women and children have been traditionally seen to be at risk from malnutrition in war zones, in Bosnia they were not as significantly afflicted as the elderly by actual or threatened malnutrition.[39]

Finally, there is also some evidence that aid deliverers and so-called protectors often contributed to exacerbating the problems of victims. Peacekeepers around Sarajevo are widely reported, for example, to have engaged in smuggling, recruiting women for prostitution, and selling aid shipments illegally.[40] Although the behavior of the vast majority of international personnel is beyond reproach, outsiders often become a negative presence in the lives of endangered populations.

International Responses to Displacement

International responses to the massive displacements in the former Yugoslavia can be analyzed under three rubrics: various acts of recognition, military operations, and humanitarian action.[41] They are interrelated and their effects are often difficult to disentangle, but their understanding is especially critical for purposes of the present analysis. The hasty and often haphazard process of recognizing the former republics of the Socialist Federal Republic of Yugoslavia as states, without realistic guarantees for minorities, represented the international community's initial attempt to influence the course of the conflict. Subsequently, international responses consisted of military and humanitarian action, which were often counterproductive with respect to the stated political intentions of the international community. These responses merit in-depth examination as part of our attempt to understand the contribution of humanitarian politics to displacement and suffering in the Balkans from 1991 to 1995.

Formal and Informal Recognition as Responses

By uprooting people from their habitual residences, displacement calls identity into question; but often pre-existing differences in identity, however defined, inadequately explain the causes of violence.[42] Displacement severs that aspect of identity tied to a residence, possibly leading to an intensification of those aspects of a person's identity that can accompany the movement of an involuntary migrant. For the sedentary war victim, his or her place of residence becomes transformed and is no longer able to sustain the normal activities that produced a livelihood. Besieged populations, especially in an atmosphere that transforms neighbors into enemies, become isolated and functional refugees in their own homes. Finally, the notion of collective identity is crucial, which is why aspirants to statehood eagerly anticipate its validation by established states.

A key feature of personal and collective identity is how others perceive identity, as well as how it is "imagined."[43] It is also important to recognize the efforts that are expended to maintain identities, often outside the ambit of official institutions. Thus the issue of recognition amidst displacement should be viewed more broadly than the concerns of state-to-state recognition under international law.[44] Although the precipitous official recognition by Bonn and Washington of Slovenia, Croatia, and Bosnia are generally seen as crucial for precipitating Yugoslavia's unraveling, other types of recognition were crucial for the evolution of Yugoslavia's wars and the resulting displacement.[45]

Formal recognition is well developed in state practice and legal scholarship, but considerably less analytical work has been done to understand the profound consequences of nonstate recognition on the plight of displaced peoples and the conduct of the conflicts that victimize them. The first supplement to official practice is pragmatic recognition by humanitarians, and the second is media recognition that informs local and international actors about how they are perceived. In the same way that the location of state authority in the economic arena has moved from states toward corporations, economic blocs, and even crime syndicates, so too has the locus of effective political recognition been released from the narrow confines of state-to-state relations. Pragmatic and media recognition are important supplements to formal recognition because they reflect the unsettled and "constructed" nature of sovereignty.[46] As such, sovereignty is better viewed as a continuous, fluctuating process rather than as a final and perpetual symbol of unassailable majesty tied to a specific geographic location.[47]

DIPLOMATIC RECOGNITION. Formal state recognition was meant to confirm and reflect the existence of effective control over a population and territory, signaling the finality of political settlements that could be taken for granted once official recognition had been conferred. The leaders of the former Yugoslav republics that were to become five separate states understood the importance of legal recognition by states outside the Balkans.

Although it does not exhaust the ways in which outsiders affected Yugoslavia, the issue of formal recognition by other states, separately and collectively through intergovernmental bodies, turned out to be an especially important factor in massive involuntary displacement. Many citizens of the former Yugoslavia were either ethnic minorities in a post-Yugoslav state that claimed territorial jurisdiction over their original place of residence, or they were minorities in a state to which they fled—even when they fled to the state that was the "homeland" of their nationality or ethnicity. A Croat from Mostar who found himself in Zagreb and a Serb from Knin who found herself in Belgrade soon found that there were other nonethnic distinctions that could make one a minority and marked for discrimination, even in the capital of one's ethnic or national heartland.

Legal recognition acquired additional importance because of the explicit conditions imposed by the European Community (EC), now the European Union (EU). The Badinter Commission, a panel of prominent international jurists, was asked to determine a set of criteria for recognizing new states, and more specifically whether states that had seceded from Yugoslavia fulfilled these explicit criteria. The three essential characteristics that a state had to exhibit in order to be deemed worthy of recognition were protecting individual and minority rights, respecting democratic processes, and demonstrating a commitment not to change internal borders by force.[48] In December 1991, the EC foreign ministers expressed their commitment to recognize Slovenia and Croatia pending the Badinter Commission's findings regarding the aspirant states' observance of the requisite criteria.[49] The panel of experts also suggested that Bosnia could demonstrate its democratic will by engaging in a nationwide referendum, which was promptly scheduled for February 29 and March 1, 1992—even though Serbs boycotted the process and used the occasion to justify the erection of their own rebel state within a state.

INFORMAL RECOGNITION: PRAGMATIC. Aside from diplomatic recognition from individual states and the EC, there was also the ongoing process of pragmatic recognition of various claimants to authority. How do humanitarian agencies—be they governmental or intergovernmental organizations or nongovernmental organizations (NGOs)—designate those whom they are helping? Do they view exchanges of ethnic hatred with equanimity, or do they shame those who express jingoism? By immediately negotiating with those who claim control and prevent access to victims, do humanitarians legitimize thugs and encourage victims to see criminals in a new light? For instance, many of the men controlling vital roadways were, until they were given arms and uniforms, unemployed adolescents with little constructive activity to fill their time.[50] Outsiders' treatment of them as officers of a responsible political entity enhanced their authority but increased the despondency and resignation of the victims.

The political ramifications of this kind of pragmatic recognition result from the mundane task of classifying victims for administrative purposes. To some extent, identifying people by their ethnicity implies an endorsement, albeit an unwitting one, of the political dynamics or the political agendas that benefit from deepening such identifications. UNHCR mainly used geographical boundaries and resisted pressures for the most part to gather or publicize statistics on the basis of ethnic groups, a practice that was more widespread among NGOs because of its obvious fundraising potential.

One prominent illustration of the importance of pragmatic recognition can be seen from the way that UN forces became instruments to symbolize the recognition of territorial claims. It is as if the warring parties hoped to elicit eventual official recognition for their territorial claims by accumulating as much pragmatic recognition as possible. Among belligerents, international actors' acknowledgment of or acquiescence to control over territory in itself constituted an important sign of legitimacy. The implication was that this eventually would lead to official confirmation.

For example, activities on Croatian territory, at least for much of the first two years of the war, highlighted this tactic. Both the rebel Serbs and the Zagreb government believed that their incompatible and exclusive claims to the so-called United Nations Protected Areas (UNPAs) within the Krajina and western Slavonia were being strengthened by the UN's presence. Both the Croatian government and the rebel Serbs tried to interpret the mandate of the United Nations Protection Force (UNPROFOR) in the UNPAs as implying a recognition of their exclusive claims to this territory.[51] As misinterpreted symbols of recognition, peacekeepers were perceived by both sides as advancing their case. UN soldiers separated belligerents and often prevented conflict, but they did not serve as a catalyst for the kind of political negotiations that the international community had hoped would resolve the Serb insurgency in Croatia. In fact, peacekeepers became pawns whose presence was manipulated.

In Bosnia, UNHCR and UNPROFOR found themselves in the ironic position of partially facilitating war aims (that is, "ethnic cleansing") in order to protect endangered civilians from the "wrong" ethnic group who found themselves in freshly conquered territory. Susan Woodward has argued that "Bosnian Serb military tacticians were particularly adept at getting UNPROFOR II to pacify an area they had seized once they were ready for a cease-fire."[52] Thus there was a presumption that the presence of the UN flag in an area over which one side had achieved a strategic hold would cease to be a military threat and perhaps also become more legitimately a bargaining chip for future negotiations.

That people gamble with the symbolic resource of recognition does not mean that they always win their wagers. Pragmatic recognition did not always serve as a stepping stone to the official variety. This was certainly a disappointment to the Krajina Serbs who lost their proto-state, and the Bosnian Serb leadership ultimately did not benefit from having been dubbed "High Contracting Parties" at various international conferences on the former Yugoslavia from 1991 to 1995. As a result of the Dayton agreement, the rebel Serb state in Croatia no longer exists; and the Republika Srpska in Bosnia has lost its autonomy. But it would be imprudent to discount the role of pragmatic recognition in affecting the behavior of belligerents during four years of war.

Bosnia provided numerous demonstrations of the destructive potential of apparently apolitical, benign recognitions of peoples by humanitarian actors. Although indispensable for access, international actors should carefully consider how they alter, and occasionally even transform, the status and capacity of local actors chosen as interlocutors or partners. In addition, the categories that are used to identify people for administrative purposes should be examined for their effect both on displaced peoples whose tattered identities have lost the important moorings of their homes and on those who were not uprooted but found themselves vulnerable in their homes. There is clearly a vast difference between the kind of recognition bestowed upon a Radovan Karadzic and a Ratko Mladic, the leaders of the Bosnian Serbs, on the one hand, and the procedure used to select a local driver for an aid convoy, on the other. Nonetheless, the experience in Bosnia has demonstrated the importance for humanitarian actors of treading carefully and consciously where their footsteps alter the terrain.

INFORMATION RECOGNITION: MEDIA. Media recognition served as a mirror for local and outside actors to evaluate not only what was taking place but also how the world perceived it. In the former Yugoslavia, images of the conflict in the Western media were critical of how local citizenry understood the conflict—from crude conspiracy theories, to despondency regarding the absence of a meaningful response to aggression, to the disbelief that their own people could be seen as the villains. Reactions often were sustained by what the media said and how they said it. States and proto-states within the former Yugoslavia tailored their propaganda to speak to the concerns about the region as they were framed by CNN or the *New York Times*. There is no doubt that the Bosnian Serb belligerents were the worst human rights violators. At the same time, because journalists were denied access to Serb-held territories, their portrait was almost universally negative.

Outside and local media thoroughly adopted the practice of ethnic designations. Journalists generally referred to "Croats," "Serbs," and "Muslims" rather than the political regimes that were in power, whose nature was usually presumed to be "ethnic" or "religious," somehow reflecting centuries of inscrutable Balkan hatreds. There were bold and prominent exceptions who sought to alter the tenor of coverage as the conflicts wore on.[53] But the media generally used "Bosnian" as an adjective to designate a territory rather than a people; thus, there were Bosnian Serbs, Croats, and Muslims. Yet in Croatia there were no Croatian Serbs or Croatian Muslims because that would have implied a mixture of ethnic labels violating the media's conventional presentations of what "the war was all about." Those who struggled to avoid the complete ethnification of their identity or the reduction of a multi-ethnic background to a single ethnicity rarely saw their self-images reflected by the media. Undeniably, those political actors whose power and appeal were based on clashes of unitary ethnicities benefited.

THE IMPORTANCE OF INFORMAL AND FORMAL RECOGNITION. This discussion suggests the extent to which recognition by actors other than states can change what actually constitutes sovereign recognition. States—separately or collectively, for instance, through the United Nations or the European Union—formally recognize the claims of other states to assume ultimate responsibility over a population and territory.[54] Becoming a recognized sovereign entity serves as a legal culmination to the process through which a state demonstrates the appropriate integrity of a population and territory and adequately justifies its claim to assume responsibility for them.

Often, observers overlook the extent to which there are ongoing domestic and international sociopolitical processes that amount to recognition, and indeed that recognition is not reducible to a single fixed event. This kind of constancy in less troubled states and societies is understandable because of assumptions about the normal continuity that undergirds sovereignty. But as a case of radically uncertain and unsettled sovereignty, the former Yugoslavia demonstrates the extent to which nonstate actors are involved even in sovereignty's putatively domestic side. This case reveals a multiplicity of informal acts and avenues of recognition that undermined the conventional image of self-contained, local dynamics that, once settled, are then presented to the community of states for ratification.

As political authorities lose or abandon responsibility for the uprooted, international actors assume responsibility for them. What amounted to groping with the phenomenon of displacement in the former Yugoslavia demonstrated the extent to which recognizing sovereignty was decentralized and distributed among various nonstate and state actors. The result was blurred conventional, conceptual, and legal divisions, including those that separate domestic and international affairs.

Military Responses

The other international responses that circumscribed and contributed to displacement were outside military forces. However, even before the actual wars in Croatia and Bosnia, a pattern of extreme rhetoric and threats of violence had already developed around perceived demographic imbalances. The rise of Slobodan Milosevic and his strong-armed intimidation to install his "greater Serbia" cronies to head the governments of Kosovo, Vojvodina (two formerly autonomous provinces of Serbia), and Montenegro established the precedent that violence was an acceptable and effective instrument for political intimidation. The stratification of the army according to ethnic categories doomed the one actor that otherwise might have reined in the lawlessness that brought fear of ethnic conspiracies into everyday life.[55] Once hostilities erupted, many armed groups, including significant segments of the former Yugoslav People's Army, considered one of their primary goals to be the "ethnic cleansing" of territory.[56]

Because of its genocidal implications, "ethnic cleansing" elicited a number of international legal responses, including the establishment of the International Criminal Tribunal for the former Yugoslavia. More important and in spite of the arms embargo, outsiders altered the military balance on the ground in numerous ways. Even before Croatia's stunning Blitzkrieg in the summer of 1995 that eliminated Serbs as a political force in Croatia, there had been much speculation about the West's (primarily Washington's) clandestine support for Croatia and Bosnia despite the arms embargo. It subsequently has come to light that the Clinton administration had turned a blind eye to arms shipments to Bosnian Muslims by Iran and other countries, including sending a message to Zagreb that it would not stop shipments through Croatia, or Zagreb's "commission" for permitting them.[57]

However, the failure of legal efforts, the brazen manipulation of humanitarian efforts, and the relatively feeble position of the Bosnian-Croat Federation until late 1995 also had led to a greater willingness by the international community to deploy troops and use military force. The history of European and American military efforts to address the breakup of the former Yugoslavia is rife with examples of wishful thinking and piecemeal action.[58] The 14,000 UN blue helmets initially authorized in early 1992 to act as a buffer between the Croats and the Serbs in newly independent Croatia never achieved the two most critical objectives of their mandate: collecting heavy arms from the Serbs in the UNPAs and facilitating the return of the Croatian refugees who had been "cleansed" from the protected areas.

The initial deployment of UN troops in Croatia was accompanied by a token presence in Sarajevo. The troops were of limited value in staving off atrocities in the Balkans. Some 1,000 blue helmets were initially deployed to Bosnia and were followed by a steadily growing number of additional troops, mainly from NATO countries; no-fly zones were imposed but not fully enforced; other forms of saber rattling, including low-altitude sorties over Serbian positions and warnings about possible retaliatory air strikes were tried; the Security Council passed what the *Economist* called "the confetti of paper resolutions"; and numerous cease-fires were negotiated.[59] As Lawrence Freedman observed, the Security Council "experimented with almost every available form of coercion short of war."[60]

UN peacekeepers in Croatia were unable to implement their mandate because they received no cooperation from the Croats or Serbs in the UNPAs. In Bosnia, the situation was even more problematic. The UN force there was under Chapter VII, with the coercive authority of the

UN Charter, but it lacked the capability to apply coercive force across a wide front. Unable to create the conditions for its own success, UNPRO-FOR was not militarily credible. Shortly before resigning in January 1994 from a soldier's nightmare as UN commander in Bosnia-Hercegovina, Lt. Gen. Francis Briquemont lamented the disparity between rhetoric and reality: "There is a fantastic gap between the resolutions of the Security Council, the will to execute those resolutions, and the means available to commanders in the field."[61]

The international unwillingness to react militarily in the former Yugoslavia until August 1995 provides a case study of what not to do. In the words of international legal scholar Rosalyn Higgins, who has since become a member of the World Court, "We have chosen to respond to major unlawful violence not by stopping that violence, but by trying to provide relief to the suffering. But our choice of policy allows the suffering to continue."[62] This inaction left many inhabitants of the region mistrustful of the United Nations and lent a new and disgraceful connotation to the word "peacekeeping." Bound by the traditional rules of engagement (fire only in self-defense, and only after being fired upon), UN troops never fought a single battle with any of the factions in Bosnia who routinely disrupted relief convoys. The rules of engagement led to the appeasement of local forces rather than to the enforcement of UN mandates. Among the most unsafe locations in the Balkans, indeed in the world, were the so-called safe areas. The provisions for economic and military sanctions in the UN Charter were designed to back up international decisions to counteract aggression and to halt atrocities in just such situations as the one in Bosnia. Yet, with apt gallows humor, many in Zagreb and Sarajevo referred repeatedly to the UN soldiers as "eunuchs at the orgy."

Thus armed force was central in the drama of displacement in Yugoslavia. It was employed by the warring parties, whose violence directly caused rapid displacement and led to involuntary migration as the consequence of continuous military activity. The use of force under United Nations auspices also contributed to displacement, albeit in different ways, by facilitating nonforceful emigration and deterring changes in the status quo among belligerents. In addition, the arms embargo coupled with the no-fly zone was meant to prevent any faction from achieving military advantage, so that belligerents would be compelled to hammer out their differences at the negotiating table. In fact, a much heavier dose of NATO bombing and U.S. arm twisting proved necessary to compel the belligerents to attempt to reach a political settlement, sequestered at Ohio's Wright-Patterson Air Force Base.

The international military responses to the former Yugoslavia can be seen as a protracted yet steady escalation against the Serbs. Ironically, much of the earlier displacement was a result of feeble Western military actions, whereas the largest single episode of involuntary migration in Europe since the 1956 Soviet crushing of the Hungarian uprising took place after robust Western military action was combined with the Croatian-Bosnian offensive in August and September 1995. The deployment of NATO-led forces after Dayton—first through the Implementation Force (IFOR) and then the Stabilization Force (SFOR)—was considerably more realistic.

Humanitarian Responses and UNHCR's Role

From the outbreak of violence and the first involuntary displacements, the primary international responses to Yugoslavia's wars were humanitarian. As the peace agreements went into effect, external humanitarian organizations were providing assistance for almost 4 million civilian war casualties within the borders of the former republic. UNHCR as lead agency was spending about $500 million in the region annually, and various other governmental, intergovernmental, and nongovernmental organizations another $1 billion.[63] It might be assumed that it would be easier in the humanitarian than in the military arena for the United Nations first to reconcile principles with political and operational realities, and hence to mount coherent and effective programs of action to mitigate the suffering from massive displacement. Yet in the former Yugoslavia, international actors begged ethical and operational questions, with distinctly negative consequences for the shape and impact of UN operations on behalf of the displaced and other war victims.[64]

There are operational implications for dealing with displacement that arise from sustaining the shibboleth of UN Charter article 2(7), with its emphasis on nonintervention in "matters which are essentially within the domestic jurisdiction of any state." Some UN practices themselves were antihumanitarian, including the decisions to prevent civilians from leaving Sarajevo and other besieged areas in Bosnia and from entering or leaving protected areas. The conscious restriction of activities precluded UN staff from confronting political authorities about human rights abuses as a routine part of their missions. The need to reinforce the neutrality of the United Nations is the most sanguine explanation. The world organization's leadership routinely wishes to sidestep confrontations with states, move ahead with negotiations, and be seen as an impartial partner once cease-fires are in effect. The promotion of human rights is a victim of such well-intentioned evenhandedness.

In the former Yugoslavia, UN personnel acted as if the most, and sometimes the only, essential undertaking was the delivery of relief goods—a recent manifestation of myopic do-goodism that one prominent and disillusioned activist has called "two centuries of ambiguous humanitarianism."[65] The world organization downplayed such tasks as protecting fundamental rights, gathering information about war crimes, and assertively and routinely investigating alleged abuses. Dealing mainly with the products of war rather than with its causes, the United Nations ignored opportunities for at least documenting and publicly denouncing some of the causes. The main exception was the UN High Commissioner for Refugees, whose staff fairly consistently exposed abuse. However, treating human rights more as nonessential luxuries than as central elements in UN operations caused Human Rights Watch to lament the "lost agenda" that has "led to a squandering of the UN's unique capacity on the global stage to articulate fundamental human rights values and to legitimize their enforcement."[66] Tadeusz Mazowiecki, the UN's special rapporteur on human rights in the former Yugoslavia, resigned in protest.[67]

Moreover, potentially significant innovations in meeting human rights challenges in the former Yugoslavia have received so little financial and political support from governments as to be the subject of ridicule.[68] Among these innovations were a first-ever emergency session by the UN Commission on Human Rights after the discovery of concentration camps in western Bosnia; the appointment of a commission of experts to report on breaches of the Geneva Conventions; the deployment of field monitors by the UN Centre for Human Rights and the assignment of human rights responsibilities to UNHCR protection officers; and, most significant, the convening of an ad hoc international war crimes tribunal. About the latter, one observer has concluded: "Lacking the political will to act decisively to curtail abuses of prisoners and civilians, they endorsed or went along with the creation of the Tribunal," a lamentable charade that constituted a "black eye."[69] The lack of political will and leadership undermines the utility of these initiatives, with repercussions not only for today's victims in the former Yugoslavia but also for the victims of tomorrow's armed conflicts. However, their potential value, not simply as moral statements but also as effective deterrents, should not be minimized.[70]

Some senior officials, in interviews both in the field and in Geneva, argued that UNHCR should never again become involved in providing emergency relief in an active civil war, a task better left to the International Committee of the Red Cross (ICRC). However, the ICRC is skeptical about institutionalizing IDPs as a special category of concern. Its expressed institutional preference is to protect threatened ethnic minorities in situ and to focus instead on disseminating and strengthening international humanitarian law, of which it is the custodian, and more especially to enhance the coverage for civil wars—530 articles apply to international armed conflicts, but only 29 to intrastate armed conflicts.[71]

At the same time, the ICRC has expressed its concern that protection activities in the former Yugoslavia have been carried out so much less effectively than the delivery of assistance. An independent evaluation of efforts in the former Yugoslavia by a former staff member acknowledges "a record of solid achievement" in emergency delivery but admits that the "scales tip sharply to the wrong side" in terms of protection.[72] Moreover, ICRC President Cornelio Sommaruga has indicated that his institution is grappling with "the extent to which international humanitarian law covers the various categories of personnel involved in the different types of actions undertaken by the United Nations and the furnishing of assistance and protection in extreme situations by resorting to military means."[73]

Humanitarian action requires effective management of inevitable political pressures rather than maintaining the fiction that humanitarianism and politics occupy separate spheres. What was especially vital about UNHCR's actions in the former Yugoslavia was its principled adaptation of its guiding mission beyond supporting the right of asylum to aiding all those with a well-founded fear of prosecution whatever their location. From its inception, the refugee agency has operated at the interstices of sovereignty, catering to the one human right that is both national and international.[74] In the process of expanding its mandate to cover IDPs and even the sedentary war-afflicted, it extended the legitimate purview of international organizations, although the debate will continue as to whether states have consented or been unable to mount an effective protest.[75]

UNHCR has been struggling to square its mandate, which is confined to conventional refugees, with the stark reality that other persons involuntarily displaced by wars are "refugees in all but name," while still others live in "refugee-like conditions." With IDPs outnumbering refugees worldwide and UNHCR having been requested by the UN secretary-general and donors to assume increasing responsibility for assistance to and protection of both categories of displaced people, UN High Commissioner Sadako Ogata commissioned a study to evaluate past experience with a view to spelling out a "comprehensive approach to coerced human displacement."[76]

There is clearly a need for newer thinking about the beneficiaries of UNHCR's humanitarian action in the former Yugoslavia (see table 6-2). IDPs, depending upon the year, are three or four times as numerous as refugees. For an agency whose primary clients cross international boundaries, the adaptation to IDPs is logical, albeit controversial. IDPs are on the move, and UNHCR's institutional culture is based on movement and serving those who have no alternative refuge from political calamity.

As UNHCR has progressed from dealing with a restricted scope of refugees under the 1951 Convention to the broadening of its initial regional competence with the 1967 protocols, it expanded its attention to IDPs in the 1990s. In the former Yugoslavia, the most numerous beneficiaries of UNHCR's attention were persons who did not move at all. Approximately 85 percent of UNHCR's half-billion-dollar budget for the former Yugoslavia was allocated to victims who were outside the boundaries of its official mandate. In the most visible crisis area of Bosnia-Hercegovina that was driving international policy, virtually no UNHCR beneficiary was legally a refugee.

According to program officials, differences in assistance benefits did not result from the category in which a person was classified. Per capita expenditures on assistance for each category were approximately the same. Displacement creates a legitimate presumption of the need for assistance and protection and, in fact, is prima facie evidence of vulnerability. In the former Yugoslavia, however, besieged populations that had remained in their communities oftentimes were as or even more vulnerable.

Assistance varied according to logistical or damage-related differences—for example, transport and insurance varied with distance from distribution centers, and winterization materials reflected the extent of destruction.[77] Differentiation in relief benefits resulted not from classification but from assessed caloric needs, which for the most part reflected

Table 6-2. *Populations of Concern to UNHCR, 1991–95*

Recipients of UNHCR assistance	1991	1992	1993	1994	1995
Bosnia-Hercegovina					
Refugees	0	0	0	0	0
IDPs	0	0	1,290,000	1,282,600	1,097,800
War victims	0	0	1,450,000	1,456,700	1,442,800
Total	0	810,000	2,740,000	2,739,300	2.540,000
Croatia					
Refugees	0	0	280,000	183,600	188,600
IDPs	0	0	344,000	307,000	198,700
War victims	0	0	176,000	0	60,000
Total	0	648,000	800,000	490,600	447,300
Former Yugoslav Republic of Macedonia					
Refugees	0	0	15,000	14,900	9,000
IDPs	0	0	0	0	0
War victims	0	0	12,000	0	0
Total	0	32,000	27,000	14,900	9,000
Federal Republic of Yugoslavia					
Refugees	0	0	479,100	195,500	650,000
IDPs	0	0	0	0	700
War victims	0	0	150,000	0	0
Total	500	516,500	629,100	195,500	650,700
Slovenia					
Refugees	0	0	45,000	29,200	22,300
IDPs	0	0	0	0	0
War victims	0	0	0	0	0
Total	0	47,000	45,000	29,200	22,300
Total					
Refugees	0	0	819,100	423,200	869,900
IDPs	0	0	1,634,000	1,589,600	1,297,200
War victims	0	0	1,788,000	1,456,700	1,502,800
Total	500	2,053,500	4.241,100	3,469,500	3,669,900

Source: UNCHR's annual statistical surveys.

whether persons were totally or partially dependent upon outside succor. In the middle of 1993, after nutritional surveys were completed, estimates of food needs were modified to reflect the fact that IDPs, refugees, and war victims who were on their own or with families—irrespective of their legal status—required less help than those living in collective centers.[78]

Refugees received more protection than IDPs or war victims. This was not because of a lack of desire to help out the latter, but because they were removed from the war zone. UNHCR's well-established conventions and mechanisms apply to refugees outside war zones, whereas IDPs and war victims must rely upon the application of *jus in bello* and human rights norms.[79] Weak international mechanisms to help ensure compliance meant that in-country protection for them was considerably more problematic, and formal and informal protestations by UNHCR and ICRC generally proved inadequate. Although the law relating to the conduct of armed conflicts and to human rights should have applied to the numerous victims of Yugoslavia's wars, there were no enforcement mechanisms, and local political authorities ignored this law.

UNHCR truly acted as the "lead agency" in the former Yugoslavia—UN jargon for being in the humanitarian driver's seat. It played what a growing number of observers see as a vital role, namely that of "UN humanitarian organization for casualties of war." In many ways, this ad hoc adaptation responded to long-standing complaints about the largely uncoordinated UN system in complex emergencies. After the embarrassing slowness and disorganization of international humanitarian responses to the various Persian Gulf crises, donor countries finally pushed the General Assembly in December 1991 to authorize the appointment of a humanitarian coordinator and the creation of the Department of Humanitarian Affairs (DHA).[80] However, DHA has made no appreciable difference in emergencies since its establishment in 1992. This is hardly surprising when the coordinator—in 1996, Yasushi Akashi became the third in four years, following Jan Eliasson and Peter Hansen—has no real budgetary authority and does not outrank the heads of the agencies that he is supposed to coordinate.

Thus a different approach is moving into the mainstream of intergovernmental discussions, one whose rationale is highlighted in the former Yugoslavia: the urgent requirement for a single body to set priorities, to raise and distribute resources, and to coordinate emergency inputs. Disparate views remain among Western governments about the exact shape of such a mechanism. But U.S. Secretary of State Warren Christopher tabled a proposal at the July 1995 session of the Economic and Social Council (ECOSOC) to consider "whether and how to consolidate the emergency functions of UNHCR, the World Food Programme (WFP), UNICEF, and DHA into a single agency."[81] This was also one key option, albeit controversial, emanating from the unprecedented multinational, multidonor evaluation of the international response to the Rwandan tragedy.[82] Such a consolidation would build upon recent proposals by seasoned practitioners for dramatic centralization.[83] Unfortunately, momentum in this direction evaporated from the early drafts of the secretary-general's much heralded but lackluster report on UN restructuring in mid-1997.[84]

UNHCR's enterprising adaptation in the former Yugoslavia helps to contextualize calls for consolidation of the emergency capabilities of the United Nations. Although there were real risks and even potential disaster lurking in such a large and complex venture, seizing an opportunity to expand an institution's financial base is, for idealists as well as cynics, an important explanation for organizational behavior.

Ogata became high commissioner in February 1991 when UNHCR was at a low point: recovering from the unceremonious departure of Jean-Pierre Hocké, suffering low morale, and trying to compensate for the embarrassment of having been caught totally off-guard in the Persian Gulf. The Yugoslav crisis that began in June 1991 was a proving ground for Ogata's call for "emergency preparedness" and helped overcome what one senior staff member described as an image of being "irrelevant in Europe and the former Soviet Union." Her agency responded quickly and well, and its budget doubled virtually overnight. Expenditures in the former Yugoslavia reached $500 million, or half of the institution's budget in 1993. In programmatic terms, the program for the Balkans became what one official called "a state within a state," an image that mirrored the high commissioner's self-deprecating self-description as "the desk officer for the former Yugoslavia."

The former Yugoslavia compelled UNHCR to act and overcome two important impediments to undertaking responsibility for IDPs: what its internal study had identified as the primary "reasons most frequently invoked against UNHCR getting involved—or involving itself more—in such cases."[85] In the former Yugoslavia, nothing could have been farther from the truth than "others are doing the job." No other agency of the UN system had more operational expertise or was better prepared to take up the gauntlet.

Furthermore, donors—particularly Europeans whose own asylum policies were getting tighter as a result of the migration pressures after the collapse of the Soviet bloc—pushed UNHCR to help stem the hemorrhage of refugees on the continent. The internal study also had pointed to "proved or putative lack of donor interest . . . as a major constraint to extending UNHCR's programs in favour of the internally displaced." In fact, as more than one senior staff argued, "money was never a problem." When comparing the statistics from 1995's UN Consolidated Inter-

Agency Humanitarian Assistance Appeals, the former Yugoslavia received more than 100 percent of requirements, as it had in previous years, unlike such other countries as Angola, Sudan, Somalia, Afghanistan, Iraq, and Sierra Leone, which received less than 50 percent.[86]

The availability of resources meant that there was little pressure to register accurately the various types of victims in the former Yugoslavia; it was never a priority for UNHCR. Normally, donors insist upon better and more accurate numbers in order to control the number of beneficiaries. But because of donor largesse, there was really no reason to distinguish refugees from "affected nationals" (that is, IDPs and war victims). The casualties of Yugoslavia's wars received benefits simply because they needed them and not because of their legal classification. However, more resources did not necessarily translate into adequate protection.

In spite of these valorous efforts, humanitarian "assistance" in the former Yugoslavia, especially in Bosnia-Hercegovina, often was a double-edged sword that both helped and injured the victims of displacement. Assistance to refugees no doubt decreased their suffering, but it also fostered "ethnic cleansing" by facilitating the movement of unwanted populations, one of the central war aims of both Serbs and Croats. Air drops of food may have had some positive impact, but they also helped to dissipate political pressure for more vigorous action. It has been reported that in many instances massive shipments of food and medicine intended for civilians were diverted to soldiers. Although exact percentages are virtually impossible to verify, there is no doubt that too many concessions were made to belligerents in Yugoslavia's wars. As in other war zones, a more principled approach with fewer "deals" might have led to less extortion, a subject to which we return in the penultimate section.

Hallmarks of the Case

Six characteristics of Yugoslavia's wars suggest limits for the lessons from this case, both as a generalizable instance of displacement as well as an example of dealing comprehensively with displacement through mainly humanitarian means. Nonetheless, the Yugoslav case can at least be instructive.

The first peculiarity is the region's proximity to western Europe and the relative socioeconomic privilege of its victims. This geopolitical position of the countries of the former Yugoslavia had consequences for a variety of issues ranging from military logistics and journalistic coverage, to emigrant destinations and humanitarian access. Distances, logistics, the literacy of the populations, and available infrastructure were only obstacles because they became part of the political conflict.

In a related manner, the second hallmark is the precipitous unraveling of the economic and social fabric of an industrialized county into unspeakable living conditions and chaos.[87] The siege of complex urban areas demonstrates the degree to which their populations can be more vulnerable than their counterparts in less economically advanced and urbanized countries because so much of their survival depends on imports of foodstuffs, an industrial base, and public utilities that can all be relatively easily disrupted or destroyed.

In this respect, however, Yugoslavia does not seem destined to remain an exception. There are a growing number of candidates for help in the former second world because nine of the fifty-three member states of the OSCE have been actively involved in shooting wars in the post–cold war era.[88] Yugoslavia was, however, the first on the international agenda. As such, it exposed both intergovernmental and nongovernmental humanitarian organizations as ill-prepared to work in areas where until recently they had recruited expatriate staff and raised money. There were no country files, expertise, or language skills. Now that the third world no longer has a monopoly on complex emergencies, humanitarian organizations have much to learn from their unusual first exposure to a new range of problems in the former Yugoslavia.

The third feature is that the case represented an extreme instance of the politicization of displacement. Moving people was not simply a side effect of armed conflict; it was the explicit aim of both political and military actors in the region. Visible and vituperative political crises, with displacement as the major theme, preceded the actual uprooting of groups and individuals. A general perception of being "in the wrong political place" accompanied political developments, which situated "ethnic" or "national" groups within legal and political jurisdictions that they or their leaders found unacceptable.[89]

Perceptions of political displacement preceded physical displacement, the latter then becoming a direct result of the former. When people became aware that they were in the wrong political space, their actual displacement often seemed to be the logical conclusion to a steady buildup of hostility and isolation. The political process that reconstructed the relations between their places of residence and made an issue of "who" would govern, rather than "how," eliminated the trust that allows political processes without violence. For too many people, even those who did not suffer physical displacement, there was a severe dislocation because the social environment generally deteriorated into fear and hatred, in which certain kinds of people were simply excluded from a common social and political space.

The fourth peculiarity is that physical displacement, however involuntary, was not always unwelcome or inhumane, especially when it alleviated more suffering than it caused. Involuntary migration was often the alternative to outright extermination in the former Yugoslavia. Indeed, it allowed "ethnic cleansers" to style themselves as humanitarian saviors of the populations whom they threatened to slaughter. One political commentator went so far as to argue that "ethnic cleansing was a prerequisite for peace."[90] Although many observers attack separation as immoral, there is a growing literature on the potential positive impact of ethnic homogeneity on conflict resolution. One scholar has pointed out in relationship to the Balkans, for example, that "as the progress of the war has left fewer and fewer unmoved people still to move, more realistic proposals have gradually emerged."[91]

Occasionally, those who moved or were forced to move attracted far more attention and relief than those who remained in besieged enclaves. Given the various kinds of physical displacement experienced by the peoples of Bosnia and their different fortunes at different stages of the wars, the relative desirability of being displaced and herded into a concentration camp as in Omarska or staying in one's hometown and being shelled or massacred as in Srebrenica is not always clear-cut. There may even be long-term political and economic benefits from such migration.

Needless to say, such unsentimental realism is not without problems. Involuntary displacement clearly violates human rights norms and the prohibition against forcing civilian migration under international humanitarian law. The definition of the public interest is torn between accepted notions pertaining to a club of states and those pertaining to humanitarians. Empirical and normative knowledge is continually evolving, but the Yugoslav case suggests an uncomfortable tentative hypothesis: In certain circumstances—and the intractable political conflict within the former Yugoslavia is one because demographic distributions were fundamental war aims—tolerating distressed migration, while preventing its worst consequences, may involve less suffering than ineffective protection efforts without displacement. This line of argument about separating ethnic populations at war is especially apt if there is no political will to implement effective prevention or to sustain long-term outside military occupation and trusteeship. In the demonstrated absence of political will, it is prudent to acknowledge straightforwardly the failure to protect norms but to try nonetheless to minimize suffering.

The fifth characteristic, unique to date in complex emergencies, is the prevalence and salience of international security organizations in the conflicts of the former Yugoslavia. The densely populated environment included the EC (later, EU), NATO, CSCE (later, OSCE), and the Western European Union. Such a formidable array of politically powerful and resource-rich actors is unusual in humanitarian emergencies. It is hard to imagine such a range and depth of involvement by the West or other powerful military actors in future cases of displacement elsewhere.

The operational implications alone are remarkable. For instance, UNHCR as lead agency for the first time in the midst of armed conflict was obliged to innovate with military liaison and personnel. Seconded military personnel in headquarters helped plan the air lift, and large numbers of new recruits in the field who had previous military experience were a first. Subsequently, a recently retired Western military officer was engaged as an adviser to the high commissioner, and UNHCR published a manual for staff working side by side with outside military forces.[92] Nonetheless, despite the organizational innovations that were effected to deliver aid, the density of formidable military capabilities proved irrelevant until there was political will to use them to stop the killing of civilians.

The sixth and final distinguishing feature of the crisis is the extent to which UNHCR as lead agency, with the blessing of donors, provided succor to all casualties of Yugoslavia's wars, whatever their juridical status or physical location. As detailed earlier, UNHCR moved away from its preoccupation with categorizing refugees as distinct from other civilian victims. With the urging and financial support of donors, UNHCR helped everyone who needed help. It is worth underlining that "populations of concern" to the refugee agency included all the casualties of Yugoslavia's wars, 85 percent of whom fell outside the mandate of the refugee agency.

There was no question of a shortage of resources, other than political ones. The generosity and longevity of the international response—four years with more than adequate resources—is unlikely to occur in other areas. Nonetheless, this allows the case to serve as an indicator of what can be accomplished by humanitarian assistance without serious resource constraints. Moreover, UNHCR can be viewed as a symbol of the international community's willingness to assume responsibility where political authorities of the former Yugoslavia had failed.

The Politics Of Rescue

Distinctions between humanitarian and political concerns are instructive, reflecting the difference between the goals of rescue and of stability.[93] In spite of lofty rhetoric in the post–cold war world, our analysis of the former Yugoslavia suggests more reflections and fewer visceral responses to humanitarian tragedies. Removing superpower rivalry has been insufficient for the international humanitarian system to move from merely pursuing rescue toward instituting political order.

There are inevitable tradeoffs between the two goals. Pursuing rescue seeks the immediate and unconditional alleviation of human suffering. Instituting stability seeks to create and sustain viable social institutions that will forestall the need for subsequent rescue. Political strategies to create an enduring sociopolitical order may even require temporarily attenuating the absolute humanitarian impulse to save lives and alleviate the suffering of noncombatants with all available means. In the prescient prose of Alain Destexhe, the former secretary-general of the International Office of Médecins sans Frontières:

> All over the world, there is unprecedented enthusiasm for humanitarian work. It is far from certain that this is always in the victims' best interests. . . .
>
> In dealing with countries in ongoing wars of a local nature, humanitarian aid has acquired a near-monopoly of morality and international action. It is this monopoly that we seek to denounce. Humanitarian action is noble when coupled with political action and justice. Without them, it is doomed to failure and especially in the emergencies covered by the media, becomes little more than a play thing of international politics, a conscience-solving gimmick.[94]

To complicate matters, there is a much more philosophically loaded trade-off lurking within the concept of stability that emerges from the use of "peace" as a synonym for "stability." No one is willing to sacrifice everything for peace, and not all political orders are worth preserving no matter how apparently stable. Thus we confront the age-old tensions between order and justice. As demonstrated by twentieth-century struggles against colonial domination, there are situations in which increased suffering and disorder are justifiable to fashion a more equitable and sustainable political order. How and under which circumstances is it possible and justifiable to calculate the costs and benefits of such endeavors is, of course, by no means obvious. Moreover, the conflict between order and justice has been temporarily obscured by a superficial consensus about the values of democratization and liberalization.[95]

What makes the problems of rescue, order, and justice stand out so vividly is the conventional wisdom regarding the "impulse"—some, such as the ICRC, would say the "imperative"—of rescue even where sovereignty presents a legal prohibition.[96] Most humanitarian endeavors without the consent of a state take place in areas of turmoil supposedly governed by weak or even failed and collapsed states. However intrusive, the subordination of sovereignty to rescue is still less problematic than the moral and operational implications of assuming responsibility for the consequences of rescue efforts. Even where effective political authority is absent, humanitarian intervention implies an obligation to assume a longer-term commitment to the sustainability and health of a society rather than merely a short-run episode of rescue.

No matter how intense and heroic an intervention to deliver food, resettle people, or eliminate an irresponsible tyrant or an armed threat, it is only a start. Declaring that sovereignty presents no bar to outside intervention when the human suffering reaches intolerable levels only begins to pose extremely thorny questions about obligations across borders.[97] Not only do we not know how the international humanitarian system might work to maintain long-term order after an intervention, we also do not even know what normative criteria might be appropriate to trigger interventions that are more consistent, or perhaps less selective, in giving reign to the humanitarian impulse.[98]

"Ethnic cleansing" is a poignant example of how ideas move people figuratively and can also serve to displace them literally. In situations where people are not threatened at gunpoint, the thought of fear can move them, whether or not the fear is warranted. In the Yugoslav context, ethnic identity became a potent tool even for those national and international actors who most wanted to stop hostilities and were appalled by the disappearance of a multiethnic society. As Susan Woodward wrote of the September 1991 peace conference in The Hague, convened under the auspices of the European Community: "No pro-Yugoslav parties were represented in the formulation, nor were the representatives of non-ethnic parties, the civilian population, or the many civic groups mobilizing against nationally exclusive states and war consulted."[99] Genocidal extermination, distressed migration toward ethnic purity, and national animosity did not fester in a vacuum. They were clearly and faithfully reported and legitimated by the international community's actions even before violent hostilities commenced.

The overarching lesson from this analysis of involuntary displacement and the lot of war victims in the former Yugoslavia is the extent to which humanitarianism and politics were inextricably intertwined. Should policy aim to keep the two as separate as possible or, alternatively, recognize the inevitable enmeshment of politics and humanitarianism while seeking to understand how they should be addressed simultaneously?

The former—largely visceral and apolitical—approach advocates keeping the issue of who decides for those at risk largely their own affair. As such, humanitarians provide relief to those in need, making whatever compromises are required. Aid providers respond viscerally to massive human suffering, which may require military force to secure immediate and direct access to civilian victims as the highest priority. Issues of sustainable order, much less its quality, are so distant that even thinking about them detracts from the immediacy of the life-saving task at hand.

The latter—more calculating and political—approach recognizes that virtually all humanitarian agencies, even the 125-year-old International Committee of the Red Cross, have had to compromise in many complex emergencies of the post–cold war era.[100] For example, they relied upon armed escorts, including the infamous "technicals" in Somalia, because sometimes only such private mini-armies or gangs could secure access and protect humanitarians in areas of turmoil. By actually diverting a portion of aid as bribes to those who control infrastructure, or allowing themselves to be extorted, humanitarian efforts are already deeply involved in political affairs.[101] All humanitarian delivery has distributional effects with political consequences. As High Commissioner Ogata has stated, ignoring the political consequences of humanitarianism is not an option: "Mass displacement of the most cruel kind imaginable has become a conscious objective of the combatants in many armed conflicts. Humanitarian assistance is used as a weapon of war."[102]

Perhaps an incident in Bosnia can serve as a particularly poignant illustration of the politicization of humanitarian efforts—despite the fervent desire by its purveyors to remain neutral and impartial. At the beginning of 1993 the UN was unable to cajole the Bosnian Serbs to let humanitarian convoys through to besieged towns in eastern Bosnia, where people were faced with imminent starvation. Radovan Karadzic, the Bosnian Serb president, guaranteed "humanitarian corridors" of safe passage to the Muslims of Gorazde, Srebrenica, and elsewhere provided that they removed themselves from their besieged towns and thus from their islands in Bosnian Serb–occupied territory. Responding with indignation to what they saw as a proposal for "ethnic cleansing" under humanitarian auspices and for emptying their political commitment to eastern Bosnia, the Bosnian government banned all aid deliveries in Sarajevo with the intention of goading the UN into a more aggressive stance toward the Bosnian Serbs. Viewing this as blackmail and as a clear indication that the warring parties were unwilling to respect internationally sanctioned procedures, Ogata suspended all relief in Serb-held Bosnia and ordered staff to withdraw from Sarajevo. On the next day, February 19, UN Secretary-General Boutros-Ghali reversed her decision.

This incident illustrates the degree to which humanitarian endeavors often become part of the local political landscape, especially when they help to change the ethnic composition of an area. Although Karadzic's plan for eliciting humanitarian endorsement for "ethnic cleansing" was not accepted, on many occasions international staff have indeed greased the wheels of ethnic resettlement in less visible ways. This has been especially the case, understandably, when the apparent alternative was the possible death of civilians had they chosen to stay where they were.

"Ethnic cleansing" is an utter abomination. At the same time, would accepting Karadzic's offer have been sensible? Doing so would have required accurate knowledge of local and international contexts. The latter would have included appreciating that the alternative would have been unmentionably worse because the West was unwilling to use military force. With the advantage of hindsight, we now know that Srebrenica and Zepa were overrun by Bosnian Serbs in the summer of 1995, leading to the haphazard and dangerous flight of tens of thousands from the area, which included a massacre in Srebrenica under the watch of Dutch UN soldiers.[103] Our humanitarian impulse would have us turn back the clock and accept Karadzic's "humanitarian corridor." This would have been clearly the right thing to do for the people who were massacred in Srebrenica. Or would it?

This perspective and calculation are incomplete because Srebrenica's citizens were not the only victims who would have suffered from an acceptance of Karadzic's proposal. The movement out of the enclaves in eastern Bosnia would also have dramatically changed the strategic situation by creating what the Serbs had long sought, an ethnically homogeneous swath of territory bordering on Serbia itself. Thus the delicate balance on the ground that was being maintained by the interaction of the various actors would have been altered. The moral justification for order is conservative, reflecting fears that tampering with established procedures could bring about an even worse state of affairs. The rejection of Karadzic's proposal seems to have embraced the argument regarding the need to preserve the strategic order, but it also went beyond to considerations of justice and morality.

Sometimes the need to preserve order does not seem to be the dominant norm. We often are confident that improvements can be made without risking chaos, that dramatic changes are imperative. In such situations, people sacrifice themselves for a collective good. Although the Bosnian government and the UN literally did not have to sacrifice themselves, they did face the almost certain prospect of institutional failure if eastern Bosnia turned into even bloodier killing fields. They could not bow to Karadzic even though he seemed to have the capacity to realize his implied threat.

The justifiable rejection of Karadzic's proposal involved a political judgment by both the United Nations and the Bosnian government that subordinated the normal impulse to rescue the Muslims of eastern Bosnia. The implication is that there was a greater value to be gained or protected by not rushing to provide immediate succor to victims. There was also the outright rejection of the terms of reference of the choice proposed by Karadzic. His implied threat that aid would not be allowed was met with a momentary stiffening of NATO resolve. His proposal also made him seem even more of a pariah because the consequences that he implied were beyond what was considered imaginable abuse even by the deteriorating standards for official behavior in the Balkans.

It took some time for the UN and the West to realize that negotiating with Karadzic was not fruitful even if at loggerheads with the rescue impulse. How can we make explicit the implicit political judgments according to which this proposal was set aside and Karadzic rejected? Can we find a way of systematically considering relevant factors? Are there ways to analyze conflicts and leaders more quickly and more directly, so that we do not waste so many lives and resources in the process of blundering our way into situations where help is counterproductive?

A logical starting place would be to spell out "terms of disengagement"—political and ethical principles that define in advance points beyond which compromise would be so egregiously out of kilter with enunciated principles as to be unthinkable. It is not so much the separation of humanitarianism and politics that presents a challenge for the future but rather their contextualization and conscious management. From a global perspective, the dilemmas that attend the scarcity of resources and the burgeoning demands for rescue have been compared to triage in medical emergencies.[104] Such decisions regarding who gets first attention and scarce medical resources are based on a stock of medical knowledge and a corpus of medical ethics supported by a substantial body of practice. In the rapidly changing field of politically conscious humanitarian engagement, however, we have only begun to digest the profound implications of "humanitarian war" and some of the limits of multilateral military efforts.[105]

We can continue to assume the appropriateness and applicability of an apolitical humanitarian impulse to earthquakes or other natural disasters even if the organization of those who have suffered or been made homeless has political consequences. Complex humanitarian emergencies are totally different. Domestic decisions and actions, not nature's vagaries, have overwhelmed local capacities to cope. It is necessary to contemplate the need, rationale, and consequences of lending outside helping hands in such circumstances. The developments that bring about the deterioration in the human condition, cause international outrage, and catalyze international responses are also part of the social fabric that outside assistance is supposed to mend. Into this maelstrom, outside humanitarians must proceed with care, reflecting before responding viscerally. They must recognize that they are not simply mending a rent fabric, but they are also participating in a domestic process through which it is either rewoven or frayed further.

Conclusion

The prominent role of refugees and internally displaced persons in the peace plan initialed in Dayton and signed in Paris highlights the policy implications of the preceding analysis. The problem of displacement, broadly construed here to include all those whose places of livelihood have been destroyed, serves as a very human indicator of the failure of politics in the Balkans. And the problem has only begun. What is to be done with all those who need a place to resume productive lives and the even greater number who will remember displacement with bitterness or look to avenge their suffering? As developments since the end of 1995 aptly demonstrate, continued displacement and jockeying for territory are hardly things of the past.

Dealing with all the casualties of armed conflict—refugees, internally displaced persons, returnees, and besieged populations—is the ultimate challenge to stylized notions of sovereignty that assume states to be the natural and exclusive locus of responsibility and authority. International responses to the plight of Yugoslavia's civilian victims demonstrate that sovereignty is continually redistributed and promises to go through even more alterations, especially if humanitarians abandon some of the naïveté that often characterizes their rescue mission. In international society, as in all societies, responsibilities can be embraced boldly or shirked, authority can receive greater luster or be corrupted. The choice is triage or dealing comprehensively with the crisis of displaced populations.

The ideal for humanitarian action would be to have the equivalent of a full-fledged, completely staffed and equipped mobile field hospital with well-designated wards for all of the victims. Whether they moved involuntarily or their conditions for survival were removed from them in their own communities, there would be appropriate medicine (relief) and care (protection). However, even in the former Yugoslavia where resource constraints were absent, there was no coherently administered public health approach that took into consideration the long-term nature of needs generated by the region's wars. Acute needs took over, no matter who or where the victims were, which was perhaps wise, especially because the specificity of individual needs for IDPs, refugees, and other victims varied greatly. Indeed, how could it be otherwise as outside humanitarians do their best to cater to military and political transformations, as the populations whom they support are continuously manipulated and reconfigured in direct contravention of the fundamental norms that guide humanitarians?

In the absence of the type of sustained engagement that would be implied by the actualization of the above public health metaphor, the case of the former Yugoslavia was still a humanitarian accomplishment. UNHCR as lead agency managed to assist those with the most acute needs, whose relative satisfaction was remarkable given the politically hostile terrain. Nonetheless, international responses to Yugoslavia's wars demonstrate that triumphalism in the garb of humanitarian rescue is out of place. If there are adequate resources and a competent lead agency, at least a successful triage-based provision of emergency assistance can occur.

Such a conclusion should not be taken lightly because it is essential to comprehend the limits of humanitarian action in war zones until the international community is prepared to move beyond rescue and institutionalize a more comprehensive public health approach. At the same time, we should be clear about the implications of moving beyond rescue, which would constitute a thorough political enmeshment in the domestic lives of the displaced and other victims whose social health a sustained humanitarianism would be seeking to rehabilitate. Displacement is a symptom and not a disease.

We doubt that additional legal and normative coverage for internally displaced persons and associated victims would have any appreciable influence on rogue authorities because the violation of norms is integral to achieving their war aims. Those who appreciate human rights and international humanitarian law are those who try to assuage the horrors witnessed in the former Yugoslavia. Outsiders affect political perceptions of belligerents and their victims. Therefore, humanitarians must be aware of the ramifications of their actions.

This case study reinforces the argument that identifying the host of problems associated with displacement inevitably forces the analyst to confront the ongoing trials and tribulations of sovereign responsibility.[106] The focus on UNHCR was critical, not only because it was the lead agency but also because its narrow mandate as the caretaker of people who are exiled from state protection points ironically in the direction of a concern for all those who suffer, whatever their location, who have no access to state protection. If authorities provide no protection, the only alternative is to jump wholeheartedly into the political fray.

There is no overarching structure that will necessarily lead to a more comprehensive approach on behalf of those suffering the consequences of war. Thus the central challenge posed by displacement for sovereignty is the assumption of responsibility. Displacement is usually a signal that those in charge of the social order have washed their hands of responsibilities or are simply overwhelmed by their magnitude. That outsiders feel a sense of responsibility is suggested by the robustness of the humanitarian impulse to rescue. Whether the humanitarian impulse will be extended beyond rescue to assume responsibility for populations and publics in distress is the challenge posed by successful rescue in the former Yugoslavia.

Reinventing UNHCR to confront the tragedy of the former Yugoslavia was a useful and necessary adaptation to the emerging humanitarian needs of post–cold war disorder. In many ways it was a microcosm of institutional identity crises, both of the UN system as a whole and of UNHCR, in confronting modern humanitarian dilemmas.

There is little support at present for an international convention on behalf of the internally displaced to complement the 1951 Convention and the 1967 Protocol for Refugees. An extension to IDPs of the international community's legal obligations would institutionalize a principle that straightforwardly gives victims priority over sovereigns. It would go beyond the fiction that states only occasionally fail to act responsibly toward their populations. A system to succor and protect victims wherever they are found would extend informal normative coverage and operational outreach to those who have not crossed an international border but who are ever more frequently victimized by the failure of so-called sovereigns to assume responsibility for what takes place within their borders.

Mainstream policy debates frequently ignore the significant differences between the well-developed conventions and mechanisms for the protection of refugees and the gap for affected nationals, especially in terms of an international institution capable of intervening on behalf of IDPs and other war victims. Although host countries have pressured UNHCR to pursue "in-country protection" to prevent displacement, the organization is unable to intervene equally effectively for both IDPs and refugees.[107]

What nervous potential host countries fail to appreciate is that the humanitarian principles under which they want to "internalize" refugees and thus prevent them from showing up on their doorsteps contradict sovereignty. Refugees have always been an embarrassing phenomenon for sovereign authorities. But as long as they appeared to constitute sporadic and small-scale "failures" of sovereignty, asylum was an acknowledgment of the need for occasional corrections.

However, moving toward an internalization of the refugee problem, which was the effective result from the donor practice to provide UNHCR with sufficient resources to keep migrants confined to the Balkans, implies a dramatic deepening of the humanitarian impulse. Endangered persons are becoming an international concern even if they do not cross a boundary but are victims of a nominal sovereign's failure to exercise minimal stewardship over its population and territory. Although there has been no codification, the separation and autonomy that sovereignty supposedly guarantees to states over their populations has been weakened. Humanitarianism expresses its concern and brings its relief to humanity—not to nations, ethnicities, or political systems. Thus we are drawn again toward a medical analogy because medical professionals commit themselves to action because a victim is a human, not a particular kind of human.

Humanitarianism necessarily jumps the fences of sovereignty because borders that have previously mediated the relations of peoples become defective when they no longer circumscribe a distinctive and integral political society. Populations lose their distinctiveness when they become of "humanitarian concern"; they are no longer separated by boundaries. Their plight has connected them to the rest of humanity because their condition signals their common, and often imminent, mortality.[108] Humanitarain assistance in the former Yugoslavia, however politically misguided, implicitly reflected precisely such principles.

Although there is significant room for strengthening the international safety net, emergency assistance can be—and is to a remarkable degree—delivered to casualties of wars through the workings of the present international humanitarian system. Protection is a different matter. Despite some rhetorical progress, the ICRC is an inadequate mechanism to ensure compliance with international humanitarian law for IDPs and other war victims. There is only limited effective internationalization of human rights.[109]

Furthermore, UNHCR is not presently keen to become the universal institutional solution for the problems of displacement writ large. High Commissioner Ogata has repeatedly made it clear that the task is overwhelming. Thus there is a danger in letting governments off the hook when speaking indiscriminately of delivery and protection as if both were equal responsibilities of the so-called international community. Emergency assistance for everyone and protection of refugee rights are widely seen as general human concerns, whereas only governments are responsible for the human rights of their own citizens, albeit with prodding from the ICRC as custodian of *jus in bello*. At present there is no effective global mechanism to which to address the human rights claims of IDPs and other war victims who remain within their country of origin. As one philosopher has noted, "The international community may help rescue, but it is not a possible addressee of human rights," and "The UNHCR cannot be and does not want to be the addressee of the harassed human rights."[110]

In the absence of intergovernmental decisions about conventions or the establishment of a new agency with a dedicated capacity to respond to the urgent needs of all civilian victims, UNHCR effectively assumed the ad hoc rescue role of a "UN humanitarian organization for casualties of war" along with its traditional role as protector of refugee rights. Because of their capacities in both delivery and protection, the only realistic candidates for assuming these expanded rescue responsibilities are UNHCR and UNICEF. They should be encouraged to assist and protect victims—irrespective of whether they are refugees, IDPs, or others who are equally affected by war—when a commensurate tragedy develops, as it is certain to do within the present world disorder.

Although the UN secretary-general declined to name UNHCR a "permanent lead agency" in his disappointing mid-1997 proposal for reform, the humanitarian institution that is the most operational in a particular region should be named by the secretary-general to head a coalition of UN agencies and be given the authority to exercise leadership. In spite of the compelling logic and some political support, consolidating the UN's emergency capabilities within a new institution appears for the moment to remain largely a visionary proposal, as does any substantial restructuring.

Although one case does not a general theory make, the lessons from the former Yugoslavia suggest that the United Nations should revive the standard mode of humanitarian operations during the cold war. Set aside since DHA's establishment in 1992, the nomination of a lead agency to take charge would be more efficacious than relying upon feeble or untested coordinating mechanisms. Operationally, the most practical course in the former Yugoslavia at war was to deal comprehensively with all those in need without discrimination. It was preferable to identify and supplement institutional capacities rather than building bureaucracies in the sky. UNHCR shed some light on the Balkan gloom by pragmatically and responsibly embracing the challenge of displacement in its largest sense.

In sum, the salience of politics in the displacement and related suffering resulting from Yugoslavia's wars is indisputable. To neglect this insight is to make humanitarianism a substitute for a clear strategy to end violence, and more particularly, to exert robust diplomacy and military efforts. "Doing something," meaning salving consciences, becomes a convenient excuse to ignore political realities, the neglect of which leads to greater suffering in the long run. In the words of José-Maria Mendiluce, UNHCR's first special envoy to the former Yugoslavia and now a member of the European Parliament, humanitarian action served as "a palliative, an alibi, an excuse."[111] Our analyses of statistics, the variety of international responses (recognition, military, humanitarian), the UNHCR's role, the hallmarks of humanitarian action, and the politics of rescue in the former Yugoslavia from 1991 to 1995 reinforce the conclusion that " 'the age of innocence' is over."[112] If humanitarians recognize the profound challenge that they pose to sovereignty, they will be better able to evaluate their seriousness about a commitment to go beyond rescue.

The resources and attention devoted to violence, human rights abuse, and involuntary displacement in the former Yugoslavia may represent the outer limits of a response from the international humanitarian system— not only as measured by resources but also by the extent and duration of engagement by publics, parliaments, and pundits in industrialized countries.[113] The energy devoted to the former Yugoslavia would have been better spent had the fundamental political nature of the wars received more emphasis rather than attempts to address the intractable mystery of the Balkans through humanitarian action. This would have required decisions, actions, and a thorough engagement with politics. Mysteries are there to behold in awe as we pray and give alms, in vain we think, hoping that they do not impinge on our normalcy.

Notes

1. See UNHCR, Office of the Special Envoy, "Information Notes: Bosnia and Hercegovina and Regional Reports," No. 5–6/97, Sarajevo, May/June 1997.

2. See Dick A. Leurdijk, *The United Nations and NATO in Former Yugoslavia, 1991–1996: Limit to Diplomacy and Force* (The Hague: Netherlands Atlantic Commission, 1996).

3. See Rakiya Omaar and Alex de Waal, "Humanitarianism Unbound? Current Dilemmas Facing Multi-Mandate Relief Operations in Political Emergencies," Discussion Paper 5, African Rights, London, November 1994.

4. See Francis M. Deng, *Protecting the Dispossessed: A Challenge for the International Community* (Brookings, 1993); and Francis M. Deng, "Internally Displaced Persons: An Interim Report to the United Nations Secretary-General

on Protection and Assistance," UN Department of Humanitarian Affairs and Refugee Policy Group, December 1994.

5. See Roberta Cohen and Jacques Cuénod, *Improving Institutional Arrangements for the Internally Displaced* (Washington, D.C.: Brookings Institution–Refugee Policy Group Project on Internal Displacement, 1995).

6. These and other statistics, unless otherwise noted, are drawn from UNHCR's *Populations of Concern to UNHCR: A Statistical Overview* (Geneva: United Nations), published annually since 1993.

7. Richard O'Brien, *Global Financial Integration: The End of Geography* (London: Pinter, 1992).

8. See Roberta Cohen, "Protecting the Internally Displaced," *World Refugee Survey 1996* (Washington, D.C.: U.S. Committee for Refugees, 1996), pp. 20–27.

9. See Tom J. Farer, "How the International System Copes with Involuntary Migration: Norms, Institutions and State Practice," *Human Rights Quarterly*, vol. 17 (February 1995), pp. 72–100.

10. See Larry Minear and Thomas G. Weiss, *Humanitarian Politics* (New York: Foreign Policy Association, 1995).

11. Susan Woodward traces the deteriorating economic context to the global economic crisis of 1979 in *Balkan Tragedy: Chaos and Dissolution after the Cold War* (Brookings, 1995). For other explanations, see David Owen, *Balkan Odyssey* (New York: Harcourt Brace, 1995); and Laura Silber and Allan Little, *Yugoslavia: Death of a Nation* (New York: TV Books, 1996).

12. See Ivo Banac, "The Fearful Asymmetry of War: The Causes and Consequences of Yugoslavia's Demise," *Daedalus*, vol. 121 (Spring 1992), pp. 141–74.

13. See James Gow, *Legitimacy and the Military: The Yugoslav Crisis* (New York: St. Martin's, 1992). See also Robert Hayden, *The Beginning of the End of Federal Yugoslavia: The Slovenian Amendment Crisis of 1989*, Carl Beck Papers in Russian and East European Studies, no. 1001 (University of Pittsburgh, 1992).

14. As in most wars, men engaged in most of the destruction, while women featured prominently as victims. See Alexandra Stiglmayer, ed., *Mass Rape: The War against Women in Bosnia-Herzegovina*, trans. Marion Faber (University of Nebraska Press, 1994).

15. See Norman Cigar, *Genocide in Bosnia: The Policy of "Ethnic Cleansing"* (Texas A&M Press, 1995), pp. 22–37; V. P. Gagnon, "Ethnic Nationalism and International Conflict: The Case of Serbia," *International Security*, vol. 19 (Winter 1994/95), pp. 130–66; Branka Magas, *The Destruction of Yugoslavia: Tracking the Breakup 1980–92* (London: Verso, 1993); and Slavko Curuvija and Ivan Torov, "The March to War (1980–1990)," in Jasminka Udovicki and James Ridgeway, eds., *Yugoslavia's Ethnic Nightmare: The Inside Story of Europe's Unfolding Ordeal* (Chicago: Lawrence Hill, 1995).

16. See Susan Woodward, "Redrawing Borders in a Period of Systemic Transition," in Milton Esman and Shibley Telhami, eds., *International Organizations and Ethnic Conflict* (Cornell University Press, 1995), pp. 198–234.

17. Susan Woodward expresses the argument forcefully: "By accepting the principle of national self-determination for the independence of states—without regard to the Yugoslav conditions of multinationality and the shared rights to national sovereignty of the Titoist system, or a willingness to enforce their unilateral decision on borders—Western powers were making war over territory inevitable." Woodward, *Balkan Tragedy*, p. 198.

18. Primo Levi articulated the notion that genocide requires a kind of permissive "moral ambiance" to sanction and make routine what would otherwise have been unspeakable acts of cruelty and transforms them into sacred rituals of "cleansing" impurities from the social body. See Primo Levi, *Survival in Auschwitz: The Nazi Assault on Humanity* (New York: Collier, 1961).

19. See Cigar, *Genocide in Bosnia*, pp. 22–37.

20. See *Final Report of the U.N. Commission of Experts pursuant to SCR 780*, S/1994/674/Add.2 (United Nations, December 28, 1994); and Helsinki Watch, *War Crimes in Bosnia-Hercegovina* (New York: Human Rights Watch, 1992).

21. See James Steinberg, "The Response of International Institutions to the Yugoslavia Conflict," in F. Stephen Larrabee, ed., *The Volatile Powder Keg: Balkan Security after the Cold War* (American University Press, 1994), pp. 201–18.

22. See Annex I, "The Problem of Refugee Statistics," in UNHCR, *The State of the World's Refugees 1995: In Search of Solutions* (New York: Oxford University Press, 1995), pp. 244–46, quotation at p. 244.

23. For a visual depiction of displacement for most of the period under review, see four maps of "Conflicts, Displaced Persons and Refugees in Former Yugoslavia," in François Jean, ed., *Populations in Danger 1995* (London: Médecins sans Frontières, 1995), pp. 146–49.

24. The accuracy of numbers varies with their origins and possible impact. Registration in Croatia proceeded smoothly on top of what was already a developed statistical service. The Office for Displaced Persons and Refugees in Zagreb produced frequent and accurate numbers used by international organizations, which also was part of the government's public relations effort against Serbs and particularly the Federal Republic of Yugoslavia. The latter spent little effort in putting forward its case and routinely exaggerated the number of Serbian victims and downplayed those of other ethnic groups. Data for Serbia and Montenegro are always discounted by humanitarian agencies and roughly summarized in statistical tables. The government of Bosnia was unable to conduct a serious registration program because of the insecurity of the war, which means that international organizations themselves produced estimates only.

25. The Implementation Accord signed in Sarajevo on January 2, 1992 ended hostilities (endorsed by Security Council Resolution 727 of January 8). It marked the end of significant military engagements in Croatia until the spring of 1995.

26. See UNHCR, "The Displaced in Yugoslavia," Situation Update 2, February 18, 1992, p. 4.

27. The number of internally displaced is drawn from UNHCR estimates, while the number of refugees outside the country is based on Bosnian government

estimates (via fax letter to the authors from the Ministry for Refugees and Social Policy, February 23, 1996). The same fax mentions that 60 percent of the Republic's population has been displaced by "war, hostile acts, persecution, and ethnic cleansing."

28. Annex to General Assembly, *Letter from the Mission of Yugoslavia to the UN*, A/50/710 (United Nations, November 3, 1995), para. 2.

29. See Susan Woodward, "The Use of Sanctions in Former Yugoslavia: Misunderstanding Political Realities"; and Sonja Licht, "The Use of Sanction in Former Yugoslavia: Can They Assist in Conflict Resolution," both in David Cortright and George A. Lopez, eds., *Economic Sanctions: Panacea for Peacebuilding in a Post–Cold War World?* (Boulder, Colo.: Westview, 1995), pp. 144–60. See also Julia Devin and Jaleh Dashti-Gibson, "Sanctions in the Former Yugoslavia: Convoluted Goals and Complicated Consequences," in Thomas G. Weiss and others, eds., *Political Gain and Civilian Pain: Humanitarian Impacts of Economic Sanctions* (Lanham, Md.: Rowman and Littlefield, 1997), pp. 149–87.

30. "General Framework Agreement for Peace in Bosnia and Herzegovina," http://www.nato.int/ifor/gfa-home.htm.

31. Government of the Republic of Croatia, Office for Displaced Persons and Refugees, "Refugees and Displaced Persons in Croatia," Zagreb, Croatia, November 1995, p. 9. (Original in Serbo-Croat–Bosnian: Vlada Republike Hrvatske, Ured za Prognanike i Izbjeglice, "Prognanici i Izbjeglice u Republici Hrvatskoj," Studeni 1995.)

32. Julius Weinberg and Stephanie Simmonds, "Public Health, Epidemiology and War," *Social Science and Medicine*, vol. 40 (June 1995), pp. 1663–69.

33. L. Jones, "On a Front-Line," *British Medical Journal* 310 (April 22, 1995), pp. 1052–54.

34. Dorothy Q. Thomas and Ralph E. Regan, "Rape in War: Challenging the Tradition of Impunity," *SAIS Review* (Winter/Spring 1994), pp. 81–99.

35. Women's Commission for Refugee Women and Children, Washington, D.C., "The Struggle for Peace and Recovery in Former Yugoslavia: Move Women from Background to Foreground!" Delegation Visit to Bosnia and Croatia, April 9–16, 1996.

36. F. Watson, I. Kulenovic, and J. Vespa, "Nutritional-Status and Food Security: Winter Nutrition Monitoring in Sarajevo 1993–1994," *European Journal of Clinical Nutrition*, vol. 49 (October 1995), pp. S23–S32.

37. A. Robertson and others, "Nutrition and Immunization Survey of Bosnian Women and Children during 1993," *International Journal of Epidemiology*, vol. 24 (December 1995), pp. 1163–70.

38. D. Moro, "Birth-Weight And Breast-Feeding of Babies Born during the War in One Municipal Area of Sarajevo," *European Journal of Clinical Nutrition*, vol. 49 (October 1995), pp. S37–S39.

39. Reuters, "Old Worst Hit by Malnutrition in Bosnia: Study," London, September 7, 1995.

40. Dzenita Mehic, "We Are Dying of Your Protection," *Bulletin of the Atomic Scientists*, vol. 51 (March/April 1995), pp. 41–44.

41. This argument first appeared in lengthier form in Amir Pasic and Thomas G. Weiss, "Humanitarian Recognition in the Former Yugoslavia: The Limits of Non-State Politics," *Security Studies*, vol. 7 (Autumn 1997), pp. 194–228.

42. See Francis M. Deng, *War of Visions: Conflict of Identities in the Sudan* (Brookings, 1993).

43. Benedict Anderson, *Imagined Communities* (London: Verso, 1991).

44. See Hersch Lauterpacht, *Recognition in International Law* (Cambridge: Cambridge University Press, 1947); Lhasa Oppenheim, *International Law*, 6th ed. (London: Longmans, 1944); and James Crawford, *The Creation of States in International Law* (Oxford: Clarendon Press, 1973). For a consideration of the role of governmental (not state) recognition, see M. J. Peterson, "Recognition of Governments Should Not Be Abolished," *American Journal of International Law*, vol. 77 (1983), pp. 31–50.

45. See Woodward, *Balkan Tragedy*, pp. 185–88, 277–78; Zoran Pajic, "The Former Yugoslavia," in Hugh Mall, ed., *Minority Rights in Europe: Prospects for a Transnational Regime* (New York: Council on Foreign Relations, 1994), pp. 56–65; and Flora Lewis, "Reassembling Yugoslavia," *Foreign Policy* 98 (Spring 1995), pp. 132–44.

46. See Thomas Biersteker and Cynthia Weber, eds., *Sovereignty as Social Construct* (New York: Cambridge University Press, 1996).

47. For an argument that stresses the process of legitimation that is involved in the claim to sovereignty, see Amir Pasic, *Sovereignty as Authority in World Politics,* Ph.D. diss., University of Pennsylvania, 1995.

48. See Steinberg, "The Response of International Institutions," pp. 244–45.

49. Germany prematurely declared its intention to recognize Croatia regardless of the panel's finding and set up ties with Croatia that amounted to de facto recognition of the new state. For a critical reading of the Badinter panel's presumption that no possible form of Yugoslav unity was a viable option, see Woodward, "Redrawing Borders," pp. 212–13.

50. See Susan Woodward, *Socialist Unemployment: The Political Economy of Yugoslavia, 1945–1990* (Princeton University Press, 1995).

51. Only a few hours before the expiration of the mandate of what had been known as the United Nations Protection Force (UNPROFOR) on April 1, 1995, the Security Council decided to split the operation into three separate contingents: UNPROFOR would henceforth apply only to the operation in Bosnia; the peacekeeping tasks in the Krajina would be handled by the UN Confidence Restoration Operation in Croatia; and the efforts in Macedonia would be handled by the UN Preventive Deployment Force (UNPREDEP). Zagreb formerly served as the headquarters for UNPROFOR and became the United Nations Peace Forces Headquarters (UNPF-HQ). In this chapter, UNPROFOR normally refers to the UN operations in Bosnia, Croatia, and Macedonia, as was actually the case for most of the period under review. In autumn 1995 at the maximum of its

numerical strength, the deployment was as follows: 1,100 in Macedonia; 22,000 in Bosnia along with 12,500 in the rapid reaction force; and 13,000 in Croatia.

52. Woodward, "Redrawing Borders," p. 229.

53. See Roy Gutman's coverage for *Newsday*. See also Roy Gutman, *A Witness to Genocide* (New York: Macmillan, 1993).

54. See Francis M. Deng and others, *Sovereignty as Responsibility* (Brookings, 1995).

55. See Gow, *Legitimacy and the Military*.

56. The UN Commission of Experts defined "ethnic cleansing" to mean "rendering an area ethnically homogenous by using force or intimidation to remove from a given area persons from another ethnic or religious group." *Final Report of the U.N. Commission of Experts pursuant to SCR 780*, S/1994/674/Annexes, p. 17, para. 84.

57. See Elaine Sciolino, "U.S. Aid to Bosnia: Secret Plan Boomerangs in Congress," *New York Times*, April 26, 1996, p. A6.

58. The discussion of military and humanitarian responses draws on Thomas G. Weiss, "Collective Spinelessness: UN Actions in the Former Yugoslavia," in Richard H. Ullman, ed., *The World and Yugoslavia's Wars* (New York: Council on Foreign Relations, 1996), pp. 59–96.

59. "In Bosnia's Fog," *Economist*, April 23, 1994, p. 16.

60. Lawrence Freedman, "Why the West Failed," *Foreign Policy*, vol. 97 (Winter 1994–95), p. 59.

61. "U.N. Bosnia Commander Wants More Troops, Fewer Resolutions," *New York Times*, December 31, 1993.

62. Rosalyn Higgins, "The New United Nations and Former Yugoslavia," *International Affairs*, vol. 69 (1993), p. 469.

63. This argument first appeared in lengthier form in Thomas G. Weiss and Amir Pasic, "Reinventing UNHCR: Enterprising Humanitarians in the Former Yugoslavia," *Global Governance*, vol. 3, no. 1 (1997), pp. 41–57.

64. For a discussion, see Larry Minear and others, *Humanitarian Action in the Former Yugoslavia: The U.N.'s Role 1991–1993*, Occasional Paper 18 (Providence, R.I.: Thomas J. Watson Jr. Institute for International Studies, 1994).

65. Alain Destexhe, *L'Humanitaire Impossible: Deux Siècles d'Ambiguïté* (Paris: Ammand Colin, 1993).

66. See Human Rights Watch, *The Lost Agenda: Human Rights and U.N. Field Operations* (New York, 1993); and *Human Rights Watch World Report 1995* (New York, 1994), p. xiv. See also Paul LaRose-Edwards, *Human Rights Principles and Practice in United Nations Field Operations* (Ottawa: Department of Foreign Affairs, September 1995); and Alice H. Henkin, ed., *Honoring Human Rights and Keeping the Peace: Lessons from El Salvador, Cambodia, and Haiti* (Washington, D.C.: Aspen Institute, 1995).

67. See Bernard Osser and Patrick de Saint-Exupéry, "The UN's Failure: An Interview with Tadeusz Mazowiecki," *New York Review of Books*, vol. 42 (September 21, 1995), pp. 38–39.

68. See Roberta Cohen, "Strengthening International Protection for Internally Displaced Persons," in Louis Henkin and John Lawrence Hargrove, eds., *Human Rights: An Agenda for the Next Century* (Washington, D.C.: American Society of International Law, 1994), pp. 17–49.

69. David P. Forsythe, "Politics and the International Tribunal for the Former Yugoslavia," *Criminal Law Forum*, vol. 5, nos. 2–3 (1994), p. 403; and David Forsythe, "The UN and Human Rights at Fifty: An Incremental but Incomplete Revolution," *Global Governance*, vol. 1 (September–December 1995), p. 314.

70. See Thomas Schelling, *Arms and Influence* (Yale University Press, 1966), pp. 99–105.

71. See ICRC, "The ICRC and Internally Displaced Persons," *International Review of the Red Cross*, vol. 305 (March 1, 1995), pp. 181–91. For the texts, see the Geneva Conventions of August 12, 1949, and Protocols Additional to the Geneva Conventions of August 12, 1949, ICRC, Geneva, 1989; and an explanatory text, "Basic Rules of the Geneva Conventions and Their Additional Protocols," ICRC, Geneva, 1983.

72. See Michele Mercier, *Crimes without Punishment: Humanitarian Action in Former Yugoslavia* (London: Pluto Press, 1995), p. 166.

73. Cornelio Sommaruga, "Preface," in Umesh Palwankar, ed., *Symposium on Humanitarian Action and Peace-keeping Operations* (Geneva: ICRC, 1994), p. 6.

74. Ernst Tugendhat, "The Moral Dilemma in the Rescue of Refugees," *Social Research*, vol. 62 (Spring 1995), pp. 127–41.

75. See Michael S. Teitelbaum and Myron Weiner, eds., *Threatened Peoples, Threatened Borders: World Migration and U.S. Foreign Policy* (New York: Norton, 1995); and Myron Weiner, ed., *International Migration and Security* (Boulder, Colo.: Westview, 1993).

76. UNHCR, Division of International Protection, *UNHCR's Operational Experience with Internally Displaced Persons* (Geneva, September 1994), p. iv.

77. Evidence from the first year of the war suggests that the humanitarian effort to prevent serious hunger and malnutrition in Bosnia was remarkably successful. See A. Robertson and others, "Nutrition and Immunization Survey of Bosnian Women and Children during 1993," *International Journal of Epidemiology*, vol. 24 (December 1995), pp. 1163–70.

78. See, for example, the footnote on "Revised Planning Figures (January–April 1996)" on p. 7 of UNHCR, "Information Notes on Former Yugoslavia," January 1996, which reads: "The figure 2,700,000 is given in this table which represents the population in Bosnia and Hercegovina who receive some form of UN assistance. The food deficit met by WFP is 23,000 MTs [metric tons] per month, which is equal to 1.4 million full food rations. This food ration is targeted to the higher number of beneficiaries who receive full or partial rations according to assessed needs."

79. See Hilaire McCoubrey and Nigel D. White, *International Law and Armed Conflict* (Aldershot, U.K.: Dartmouth, 1992).

80. See Larry Minear and Thomas G. Weiss, "Groping and Coping in the Gulf Crisis: Discerning the Shape of a New Humanitarian Order," *World Policy Journal*, vol. 9 (Fall/Winter 1992–93), pp. 755–88; and Larry Minear and others, *United*

Nations Coordination of the International Humanitarian Response to the Gulf Crisis 1990–1992, Occasional Paper 13 (Providence, R.I.: Thomas J. Watson Jr. Institute for International Studies, 1992).

81. U.S. Permanent Mission to the United Nations, "Readying the United Nations for the Twenty-First Century: Some 'UN-21' Proposals for Consideration," undated "non-paper" of July 1995. This theme also permeated the Address by Secretary of State Warren Christopher to the 50th Session of the United Nations General Assembly, September 25, 1995.

82. See *Humanitarian Aid and Effects,* vol. 3, pp. 159–61, and *Synthesis Report,* vol. 5, p. 58, of *The International Response to Conflict and Genocide: Lessons from the Rwanda Experience,* Joint Evaluation of Emergency Assistance to Rwanda (Copenhagen, March 1996).

83. See, for example, Erskine Childers with Brian Urquhart, *Renewing the United Nations System* (Uppsala: Dag Hammarskjöld Foundation, 1994); and Gareth Evans, *Cooperating for Peace* (London: Allen and Unwin, 1993). An even more radical proposal for a single agency, an "internationalized" ICRC, was made by James O. Ingram as he was leaving the post of executive director of the WFP, in "The Future Architecture for International Humanitarian Assistance," in Thomas G. Weiss and Larry Minear, eds., *Humanitarianism across Borders: Sustaining Civilians in Times of War* (Boulder, Colo.: Lynne Rienner, 1993), pp. 171–93. In the same volume, see the criticisms of the disorganized humanitarian system by the late Frederick C. Cuny, "Humanitarian Assistance in the Post–Cold War Era," Intertect, Dallas, pp. 151–69.

84. General Assembly, *Renewing the United Nations: A Programme for Reform,* Report of the Secretary-General, A/51/950 (United Nations, July 1997).

85. *UNHCR's Operational Experience with Internally Displaced Persons,* p. 75, following quotes on pp. 75–76.

86. U.S. Mission to the United Nations, "Global Humanitarian Emergencies, 1996," New York, February 1996, p. 24. The periods vary slightly, and there may be some needs and some disbursements not reflected in the data. The accuracy of the broad comparative data and of the privileged position of the former Yugoslavia, however, are clear.

87. The World Bank estimates that at the end of 1995, 63 percent of Bosnia's housing stock had been damaged and 90 percent of the population in the federation was "at least partly dependent on humanitarian food aid." See http://www.worldbank.org/html/extdr/exteme/bhgen.html.

88. See Jarat Chopra and Thomas G. Weiss, "Prospects for Containing Conflict in the Former Second World," *Security Studies,* vol. 4 (Spring 1995), pp. 55283; and Antonia Handler Chayes and Abram Chayes, eds., *Preventing Conflict in the Post-Communist World: Mobilizing International and Regional Organizations* (Brookings, 1996).

89. See Bogdan Denitch, *Ethnic Nationalism: The Tragic Death of Yugoslavia* (University of Minnesota Press, 1994), pp. 173–85.

90. George Will, "Morality and Map-Making," *Washington Post,* September 7, 1995, p. A19.

91. Chaim Kaufmann, "Possible and Impossible Solutions to Ethnic Civil Wars," *International Security,* vol. 20 (Spring 1996), p. 167.

92. See UNHCR, *A UNHCR Handbook for the Military on Humanitarian Operations* (Geneva, January 1995).

93. This argument first appeared in lengthier form in Amir Pasic and Thomas G. Weiss, "The Politics of Rescue: The Humanitarian Impulse and Yugoslavia's Wars," *Ethics and International Affairs*, vol. 11 (1997), pp. 105–50. See special journal issue "Rescue: The Paradoxes of Virtue," *Social Research*, vol. 62 (Spring 1995), especially Michael Walzer's "The Politics of Rescue," pp. 53–66. See also David Rieff, "The Humanitarian Trap," *World Policy Journal*, vol. 12 (Winter 1994–95), pp. 1–11. For a review of the limits of the post–cold war ambitions of humanitarian intervention, see Stephen John Stedman, "The New Interventionists," *Foreign Affairs*, vol. 72, no. 1 (1993), pp. 1–16. For a normative argument in the opposite direction, see Nigel Rodley, ed., *To Loose the Bonds of Wickedness: International Intervention in Defence of Human Rights* (London: Brassey's, 1992).

94. Alain Destexhe, "Foreword," in Jean, ed., *Populations in Danger 1995*, pp. 13–14.

95. See Ed Mansfield and Jack Snyder, "Democratization and the Danger of War," *International Security*, vol. 20 (Summer 1995), pp. 5–38. For a general argument regarding the priority of order over justice, see Hedley Bull, *The Anarchical Society* (Columbia University Press, 1977).

96. See Thomas G. Weiss and Jarat Chopra, "Sovereignty Is No Longer Sacrosanct," *Ethics and International Affairs*, vol. 6 (1992), pp. 95–117; Marianne Heiberg, ed., *Subduing Sovereignty: Sovereignty and the Right to Intervene* (New York: St. Martin's, 1994); Gene M. Lyons and Michael Mastanduno, eds., *Beyond Westphalia? National Sovereignty and Intervention* (Johns Hopkins University Press, 1995); and Paul A. Winters, ed., *Interventionism: Current Controversies* (San Diego: Greenhaven Press, 1995).

97. See Stanley Hoffman, *Duties beyond Borders: On the Limits and Possibilities of Ethical International Politics* (Syracuse University Press, 1981).

98. See Mark Prutsalis, "Humanitarian Aid: Too Little, Too Late," in Ben Cohen and George Stamkoski, eds., *With No Peace to Keep: United Nations Peacekeeping and the War in the Former Yugoslavia* (London: Grainpress, 1995), pp. 77–85. For a more general argument about such difficulties, see Thomas G. Weiss and Cindy Collins, *Humanitarian Challenges and Intervention: World Politics and the Dilemmas of Help* (Boulder, Colo.: Westview, 1996).

99. Woodward, "Redrawing Borders," p. 213.

100. See David P. Forsythe, *Humanitarian Politics* (Johns Hopkins University Press, 1977); James A. Joyce, *Red Cross International and the Strategy for Peace* (New York: Oceana, 1959); and John F. Hutchinson, *Champions of Charity: War and the Rise of the Red Cross* (Boulder, Colo.: Westview, 1996).

101. Writing in mid-1994, Age Eknes stated: "The accusation that the United Nations has indirectly legitimized ethnic cleansing and territorial aggression does not bite as much today—not because it is less true but because it has become a fact of life" see "The United Nations Predicament in the Former Yugoslavia," Thomas Weiss, ed., *The United Nations and Civil Wars* (Boulder, Colo.: Lynne Rienner, 1995), p. 124. For a discussion of the possible manipulation of aid agencies by

belligerents, see Gayle E. Smith, "Relief Operations and Military Strategy," in Weiss and Minear, eds., *Humanitarianism across Borders*, pp. 97–116.

102. Quoted by Christopher S. Wren, "Resettling Refugees: U.N. Facing New Burden," *New York Times*, November 24, 1995, p. A15.

103. See O. van der Wind, *Report Based on the Debriefing on Srebrenica* (Assen: Netherlands Ministry of Defense, October 4, 1995).

104. Thomas G. Weiss, "Triage: Humanitarian Interventions in a New Era," *World Policy Journal*, vol. 11 (Spring 1994), pp. 1–10.

105. See Adam Roberts, "Humanitarian War: Military Intervention and Human Rights," *International Affairs*, vol. 69 (1993), pp. 429–49. For an extreme statement of the supposedly insuperable problems associated with such efforts, see John Mearsheimer, "The False Promise of International Institutions," *International Security*, vol. 19 (Winter 1994–95), pp. 5–49.

106. See Francis M. Deng, "Frontiers of Sovereignty," *Leiden Journal of International Law*, vol. 8 , no. 2 (1995), pp. 249–86.

107. See UNHCR, *The State of the World's Refugees: The Challenge of Protection* (New York: Penguin Books, 1993), and UNHCR, *The State of the World's Refugees 1995*. For a discussion of this and other factors in recent humanitarian interventions, see Tom J. Farer, "Intervention in Unnatural Humanitarian Emergencies: Lessons of the First Phase," *Human Rights Quarterly*, vol. 18 (February 1996), pp. 1–22; and Thomas G. Weiss, "Overcoming the Somalia Syndrome: 'Operation Rekindle Hope?'" *Global Governance*, vol. 1 (May–August 1995), pp. 171–87.

108. This theme is under development by Amir Pasic, "Humanitarian Rescue and the Process of Sovereignty" (forthcoming).

109. See David P. Forsythe, *The Internationalization of Human Rights* (Lexington, Mass.: Heath, 1991); and Jack Donnelly, *Universal Human Rights in Theory and Practice* (Cornell University Press, 1989).

110. Tugendhat, "The Moral Dilemma in the Rescue of Refugees," pp. 136–37.

111. Quoted by Stanley Meiser, "U.N. Relief Hopes Turn to Despair," *Washington Post*, October 25, 1993, p. A1.

112. Thomas G. Weiss, "Military-Civilian Humanitarianism: The 'Age of Innocence' Is Over," *International Peacekeeping*, vol. 2 (Summer 1995), pp. 157–74.

113. For example, the UNHCR operation in the Balkans ate up nearly half its budget in 1993 and led to much tension within the organization. See David Reiff, *Slaughterhouse: Bosnia and the Failure of the West* (New York: Simon and Schuster, 1995), pp. 197–99.

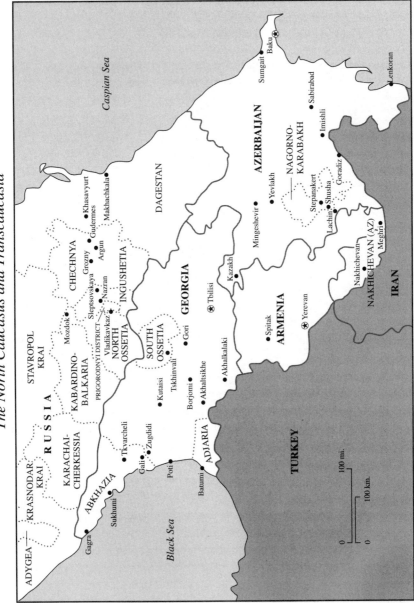

The North Caucasus and Transcaucasia

ADYGEA

KRASNODAR KRAI

R U S S I A

STAVROPOL KRAI

KARACHAI-CHERKESSIA

KABARDINO-BALKARIA

PRIGORODNYI DISTRICT

NORTH OSSETIA

SOUTH OSSETIA

INGUSHETIA

CHECHNYA

DAGESTAN

Caspian Sea

Mozdok

Khasavyurt

Gudermes

Makhachkala

Grozny

Argun

Sleptsovskaya

Nazran

Vladikavkaz

Tskhinvali

GEORGIA

Gori

Akhalkalaki

Akhaltsikhe

Borjomi

Kutaisi

Tbilisi

Kazakh

Mingeshevir

AZERBAIJAN

Sumgait

Baku

Lenkoran

Sabirabad

Imishli

Yevlakh

NAGORNO-KARABAKH

Stepanakert

Shusha

Lachin

Goradiz

Spitak

ARMENIA

Yerevan

NAKHICHEVAN (AZ)

Nakhichevan

Meghri

IRAN

TURKEY

ABKHAZIA

Gagra

Sukhumi

Gali

Tkvarcheli

Zugdidi

Poti

Batumi

ADJARIA

Black Sea

100 mi.

100 km.

0

0

CHAPTER SEVEN

Internal Displacement in the North Caucasus, Azerbaijan, Armenia, and Georgia

Thomas Greene

WELL OVER a million people have become internally displaced in the Caucasus. Azerbaijan has the largest number of internally displaced persons (IDPs), with more than 600,000. Next is Chechnya with between 320,000 and 370,000, many of them in the process of returning to their homes. Georgia has around 275,000, Armenia 65,000–72,000, and Ingushetia approximately 30,000. The causes of displacement have their roots in policies pursued by the Soviets though not new to them. The post-Soviet Russians have also contributed to displacement, notably in Chechnya.

Any account of displacement in Transcaucasia should take emigration from the area into consideration. The IDP figures, of course, do not include refugees (e.g., the Armenian refugees from Azerbaijan, and Azerbaijani refugees from Armenia, both numbering between 200,000 and 300,000), victims of natural disaster (most notably the 1988 earthquake in Armenia), or those who have quietly left the area for Moscow, St. Petersburg, or the Krasnodar and Stavropol Districts of southern

During the course of his research the author traveled to Georgia, Armenia, and Azerbaijan in June and July 1996.

233

Russia. Since 1987, when people were allowed to move around within the Soviet Union, perhaps as many as half a million have left Georgia. Probably a larger number have left Armenia. Large numbers have left Azerbaijan as well, many in search of economic opportunities. In addition to Georgians, Armenians, and Azerbaijanis, those who have left include Russians, Ukrainians, Jews, and others. The number of those leaving the region grew after independence in 1991, as the region suffered from international war, wars of secession, and rapid economic downturn.

Background

The Caucasus is an area of many nationalities and languages. Situated between the Black and Caspian Seas at a major historical crossroads, the area comprises the North Caucasus, at the southern reach of the Russian Federation, and the Transcaucasus or Transcaucasia, to the south of the Caucasus Mountains. Both the North Caucasus and Transcaucasia are divided by religion and by language. The Georgians, Armenians, Ossetians, and Russians are largely Christian (Orthodox and Apostolic); the Azerbaijanis are mostly Shia Muslim; and the Chechens and the other indigenous people of the North Caucasus are for the most part Sunni Muslim. The dozens of languages spoken in the area belong predominantly to the Iranian, Turkic, and Ibero-Caucasian language groups. Society in the Caucasus has remained heavily traditional, centering on clan and social group even in urban areas. The many ethnic groups share codes of honor, folklore, and history. The North Caucasus, part of the Russian Federation, is divided from east to west into the following republics: Dagestan (itself composed of more than twelve different ethnic groups), Chechnya, Ingushetia, North Ossetia, Kabardino-Balkaria, Karachai-Cherkessia, and Adygea. Transcaucasia comprises the three independent republics of Azerbaijan, Armenia, and Georgia.

Of the three major nationalities of Transcaucasia, the Azerbaijanis are Turkic, the Armenians are Indo-European, and the Georgians are neither.[1] Armenia is the most homogeneous of the three. All three date their cultures to ancient times. All cite history to buttress their territorial claims in the region, including the conflicting claims of Armenia and Azerbaijan to Nagorno-Karabakh. In Georgia two important non-Georgian nationalities, the Ossetians and the Abkhaz, have revolted against Georgian domination since independence. The early attempts of the Georgian leadership to make Georgian the only valid national identity contributed to fear among these groups that they would be absorbed into the "little empire."[2] With help from Russia, this conflict spawned two wars that displaced thousands of citizens of Georgia.

In both the North Caucasus and Transcaucasia the corrupt bureaucracy, which grew in Soviet times as a way of circumventing the omnipresent control of Moscow and the Communist Party, has resisted reform. Only in the mid-1990s did some of the economies of the area stabilize to the point that post-communist economic reconstruction could start. The entry of the Transcaucasian republics into the international arena and the development of direct ties with the outside world after generations of dealing exclusively through Moscow have subjected all three (Azerbaijan, Armenia, and Georgia) to special pressures. These in turn have had a direct bearing on how the republics have dealt with the displacement of people within their borders.

In the Caucasus as elsewhere, Stalin and his successors did not eliminate local nationalism but forced it underground. As long as the USSR held together, all decisions of importance were made in Moscow, even though local cadres governed. The local power structure in the North Caucasus and Transcaucasia, based on immediate family, kinship, and clan, was remarkably resistant to Communist Party controls. Patronage networks were carefully maintained and adapted to the requirements of an economy of scarcity. These networks were basic to the "black" (illegal) economy. The corrupt networks, set up to bypass Soviet channels of authority during the long years of communism, have made the region prone to gangsterism and cronyism.

During the Soviet period, especially under Stalin, all three Transcaucasian republics were favored by the authorities in Moscow for economic development. The hold of the three titular nationalities in their respective republics was strengthened by the national power structures and buttressed by relative economic well-being. Endowed with agricultural wealth as well as important industries, Transcaucasia enjoyed a higher standard of living than many parts of the Soviet Union. However, Azerbaijan, Armenia, and Georgia remained hobbled by bureaucracy and the client mentality that pervaded the Soviet Union, and were highly vulnerable to changes in the central economy.

All three Transcaucasian republics should have been among the most successful post-Soviet states. They had been independent for a short period after World War I and therefore had traditions of modern statehood on which to base their revival. Their people were highly skilled and industrious. But the legacy of seventy years of Soviet rule more than offset those advantages. The sudden collapse of the Soviet Union did not afford the population of Transcaucasia time to train itself for responsible administration and to develop realistic political judgment. Consensus and trust were in short supply in the Caucasus. The pernicious effects of Soviet "divide and rule" policy proved powerful. Confrontation became the order of the day when independence was thrust on the Transcaucasian republics and led to the displacement of hundreds of thousands of people.

It is difficult to overstate the effect of the breakup of the Soviet Union on the Caucasus. On the political and institutional side the Soviet Union was extremely underdeveloped. The Soviet republics were less well prepared for independence than were many third world countries that have been granted their independence since World War II. Before 1991 all decisions of importance were made in Moscow. A strong dependency attitude developed during this long period. Production in the Caucasus was interlocked with production in many other parts of the USSR, some of them thousands of miles away. Even if factories are able to start up, the markets have been lost. Statistics tell part of the story. In Georgia, for example, although only 60,000 unemployed are officially registered, there are probably as many as a million unemployed, hundreds of thousands of them former employees of closed factories.[3] The quality of goods produced in the North Caucasus and Transcaucasia is not good enough for most export markets. The concept of productivity is virtually unknown. To cap it off, the breakup has been accompanied by a severe energy crisis. Where everyone is poor, it is extremely difficult to eliminate economic hardships that exacerbate problems of internal displacement.

Economic collapse and demands for democratic change hastened the breakup of the Soviet Union and the breakdown of public life. In the Caucasus, as economic collapse added to the sense of desperate instability, demands for democracy and independence became intertwined with bloody ethnic conflict. Concerns about human rights seemed unworthy of attention, resulting in countless human rights violations. All warring ethnic groups in the North Caucasus (and in Transcaucasia) have committed such violations.

Displacement

Some of the most brutal Soviet displacement took place during World War II. After the Soviets had driven the Nazi army back, several national groups were deported en masse in 1944, all accused of collaborating with the Nazis. Some of them, including the Chechens, were uprooted from areas that had not been occupied by the Germans. Four North Caucasian nationalities (the Chechens, Ingush, Karachai, and Balkars) were deported, along with the Volga Germans (who had been uprooted in 1941), Koreans, Crimean Tatars, Meskhetian Turks, Kalmyks, and Kurds from other parts of the Soviet Union.[4] The deportations, from which the ethnic groups were "rehabilitated" in the 1957, have been a powerful impetus to nationalism.

Playing one ethnic group against another was a constant theme in the Soviet Union, preparing the ground for the conflicts that led to displacement in the early 1990s. Early in the Soviet period Stalin considered attaching the Armenian-majority area of Nagorno-Karabakh to Armenia but in the end left it part of Azerbaijan. The Abkhaz, a Caucasian people in western Georgia, were given an Autonomous Republic but constituted only 17 percent of the population in 1989. The Ossetians were divided between Georgia and Russia. Some North Caucasian ethnic groups (e.g., the Circassians) found themselves separated from closely related groups and combined with others with whom they had little in common (e.g., Kabardinians, a Circassian people, with the Turkic Balkars in Kabardino-Balkaria).

With perestroika, the North Caucasus and Transcaucasia witnessed an explosion of "bourgeois nationalism." Its intensity varied from region to region. Initially, perestroika was not greeted with enthusiasm in Azerbaijan or Georgia. Throughout the area a number of independent political groups had been founded in the late 1980s. In the crisis of the Soviet system in the North Caucasus and Transcaucasia indigenous political groups had to struggle with the communist establishment, at the same time responding to movements in the area for greater autonomy. Some of the groups that evolved were truly independent, while others were manipulated by elements of the communist establishment. With the flowering of nationalism in the final years of the Soviet Union it was inevitable that groups of all sizes, not only the Armenians, Azerbaijanis, and Georgians but also the Abkhaz, Chechens, Ingush, Ossetians, and others should be affected.

The alliance of nationalism and territory became an underlying principle of the Soviet Union; countless nations and national groups were allotted a titular territory with limited language and cultural rights. A continuing problem for much of the former Soviet Union is how to prevent territorial disputes from turning into mini-wars such as that in the Prigorodnyi District in the North Caucasus or major wars like the war between Armenia and Azerbaijan and the Russo-Chechen War. Areas with multiple nationalities such as Dagestan face real problems in affording all ethnic groups access to the political system.

Independence and the opening of the political system brought with it competition for access to power and privilege throughout the former Soviet Union. The demise of the old system of insider promotions brought to power many politicians who subscribed to nationalist ideologies and focused on ethnically defined electorates. Personal and clan loyalties contributed to displacement when they transcended loyalties to the nation as a whole. When he was president of Georgia, Zviad Gamsakhurdia played on these forces with disastrous effects for his country.

Most displacement in the Caucasus has taken place on the basis of ethnicity. The dividing lines of the wars in South Ossetia and Abkhazia, both part of Georgia, were almost exclusively ethnic. For too long ethnicity had been the principal determinant of access to political spoils in Georgia. Georgia suffered from its own mini-imperialism, making the minorities formerly favored by the Soviets feel "double discrimination." When war came the Georgians, who resented the nationalism of the Ossetians and Abkhaz, were the first to be displaced from South Ossetia and Abkhazia.

Virtually all of the movement of populations between Azerbaijan (including Nagorno-Karabakh) and Armenia has also been prompted by ethnic strife. Nagorno-Karabakh, nearly 30 percent of whose population was Azeri, has been "cleansed" of all Azeris. Almost all Azeris have been forced to flee most of the districts that surround Nagorno-Karabakh and have been forced out of Armenia. Almost all Armenians have been forced out of Azerbaijan.[5] Armenia and Azerbaijan also have large refugee populations, owing to the animosity between them. Despite the ethnic overtones of this conflict, Human Rights Watch/Helsinki believes that "much of the animosities were artificially created by governments through irresponsible and inflammatory propaganda that blamed the country's problems on a scapegoat ethnic group."[6] Armenia, Azerbaijan, Georgia, and Russia all have focused on the ethnic component of problems and not on the loss of markets and mass emigration.

The Role of Governments

Each of the Transcaucasian republics has established organizations to deal with IDPs, refugees, and other vulnerable populations. All of them focus on IDPs as only one of many categories of needy people. Azerbaijan's organizations seem somewhat unwieldy and fragmented, resulting in a relatively passive role in dealing with IDPs. More and more of the planning is left to the international community. In Armenia the offices that deal with vulnerable populations, including IDPs, are in the Ministry of Social Security, Labor, Migration, and Refugees. Their location there emphasizes the relatively small number of IDPs in Armenia but ensures coordination of assistance to all vulnerable groups. Georgia tracks IDPs through its Committee on Refugees in the Ministry of IDPs. In 1995, Georgia established a coordination bureau for humanitarian aid, which improved coverage of assistance to all vulnerable groups.

Russia's Role

Relations with Russia have been a major foreign policy problem for the three Transcaucasian republics. Inevitably "there has been a direct linkage between events in Moscow, most notably power struggles both during and after the Soviet era, and events in the periphery, including the fate of national political movements."[7] In the long run much depends on what Russia wants as it plays its cards in the region.

In Georgia, Gamsakhurdia's approach to relations with Russia was naive and imprudent. His intense nationalism was bound to irritate Russia, and he made a fatal mistake in underestimating the centrality of Russia in the West's political and strategic calculations. The former Soviet foreign minister Eduard Shevardnadze has done somewhat better. In return for Russia's recognition, on paper at least, of Georgian territorial integrity and support against the followers of Gamsakhurdia, Shevardnadze joined the Commonwealth of Independent States (CIS). He also agreed to the continued presence of Russian bases in Georgia and to having Russian troops guard the frontier with Turkey. Many people in Georgia believe Russia will continue to play an ambiguous role in the Caucasus but still think that Georgia has benefited politically from Russian embroilment in Chechnya.

Armenia and Azerbaijan each have unique relations with Russia. Traditionally Armenia has been the closest of the Transcaucasian republics to Russia. Azerbaijan has had a somewhat prickly relationship with Russia, seeking to avoid hosting Russian troops and yearning for the financial independence it is counting on oil revenues to provide.

Chechen relations with Russia are a question mark. The Chechens believe they have won their independence and certainly will try to keep

Moscow at arm's length. Russia does not have the resources to contribute much to the reconstruction of Chechnya, despite promises it made during various electoral campaigns. Meanwhile, Russia insists that Chechnya is still part of the Russian Federation.

The International Community

International organizations and NGOs have undertaken assistance programs that have helped broad categories of vulnerable people in the Caucasus, including the displaced. These programs have blurred the mandates of many organizations, particularly the UN High Commissioner for Refugees (UNHCR). Although mandated to deal with refugees, UNHCR early became involved with assistance to IDPs. This was a calculated strategy of preventing further impoverishment and out-migration, in which IDPs would have become refugees. In Chechnya this was taken one step further: help went to all vulnerable groups in the hope that fewer would become displaced.

In all parts of the former Soviet Union, the need to undertake bureaucratic reform, find an ideological alternative to communism, and cope with a collapsed economy made the transition to independence exceedingly difficult. Displacement compounded these difficulties. In each of the four regions of the Caucasus displacement is unique. All of the displacement problems, however, are interrelated. Resolution of one conflict can set a precedent for settlement of the others. The history of each displacement, the effectiveness of national institutions, and the role of the international community will all provide lessons for dealing with the problem of internal displacement. The rest of this chapter focuses in turn on the North Caucasus (both Chechnya and the Prigorodnyi District), Azerbaijan, Armenia, and Georgia.

The North Caucasus (Chechnya and Its Neighbors)

Displacement in the North Caucasus has largely come from conflicts in two areas: Chechnya and the Prigorodnyi District of North Ossetia. The displaced from Chechnya lost their homes during the 1994–96 Russo-Chechen War. They number between 320,000 and 370,000 and are located primarily in Chechnya, in the neighboring republics of Ingushetia, Dagestan, and North Ossetia, and in the southern reaches of the Russian Federation.

The Prigorodnyi District had been part of the Chechen-Ingush Republic before the mass deportation of Chechens and Ingush from the area in 1944. After the deportations the Chechen-Ingush Republic ceased to exist. Large pieces of its territory were attached to Georgia and North Ossetia. When the republic was reconstituted and the deported peoples were able to return starting in the late 1950s, Georgia relinquished areas that had been part of the pre-war republic, but North Ossetia did not. Some 30,000 Ingush were displaced from the Prigorodnyi District, driven out by the Ossetians with Russian help in 1992.

The number of displaced from the Russo-Chechen War is far greater. During the war, hundreds of thousands of persons, members of all ethnic groups, fled the indiscriminate bombing and shelling of Grozny and many other population centers, big and small. Chechens frequently were taken into the homes of their relatives and friends in outlying parts of Chechnya and neighboring Ingushetia and Dagestan. The Russian civilians, with fewer relatives in the mountains and villages nearby, and often with extremely limited financial resources, became a disproportionately large percentage of the victims.

The population of Chechnya before the war was estimated at 1.2 million, more than 400,000 of them in the capital city of Grozny. Then and now the population was about two thirds ethnic Chechen, one quarter Russian, and the rest various Caucasian nationalities.[8] Probably a third of the population, some 400,000, died or fled. Estimates of the dead range from 30,000 to 80,000,[9] leaving the number of IDPs between 320,000 and 370,000. It is unlikely that the exact number of displaced will ever become available. Not all of the IDPs were displaced at the same time. As fighting surged across the countryside, some people returned to their homes while others fled from wherever they were at the moment. Because virtually all those who fled the conflict stayed within the Russian Federation, they remained IDPs rather than becoming refugees.

The first rush of IDPs fled from Grozny in December 1994 and January 1995 to the villages of Chechnya. As the shelling and fighting broadened, they moved to the neighboring republics. For the most part the displaced took refuge in Dagestan and Ingushetia, with some in the neighboring Stavropol *krai* (Russian Federation), North Ossetia, and Kabardino-Balkaria. By the first week of March 1995, some 200,000 people, a majority of them women, children, and elderly, had been displaced to the neighboring republics: 84,000 to Dagestan, 112,000 to Ingushetia, and 7,000 to North Ossetia.[10] Thousands remained in Chechnya. In 1995–96 some 150,000 became displaced inside Chechnya (many for the second or third time), and 27,000 sought refuge in Ingushetia, Dagestan, and North Ossetia. In addition, as many as 70,000 IDPs, most of them ethnic Russians, were reported to have sought refuge in Stavropol *krai*.[11] There were also significant numbers in Astrakhan, as well as substantial numbers in Moscow. Many of the IDPs, particularly the Chechens, returned to their homes, or what was left of them, when the fighting ended in August 1996. At the end of September 1996 it was estimated that there were 78,000 IDPs from Chechnya in the nearby republics (42,000 in Ingushetia, 2,000 in North Ossetia, and 34,000 in Dagestan) and 8,000 in Kabardino-Balkaria. Fifty-two thousand IDPs and refugees were reported in Stavropol *krai*.[12]

The numbers of displaced in Chechnya were greater than in Georgia and less than in Azerbaijan. There were no camps set up for the IDPs from Chechnya, either within Chechnya or in the neighboring regions. Most IDPs took refuge with friends or relatives in Chechnya and the neighboring republics. Some were lodged in public buildings (schools, hostels, and sanatoriums). With the signing in 1996 of the cease-fire and other agreements between Moscow and Grozny, the capital of Chechnya, IDPs started returning. Those who remain outside but near Chechnya are mostly from towns that have been demolished. More than sixty thousand IDPs from Chechnya temporarily living in Ingushetia and Dagestan voted in the January 27, 1997, election in special polling places set up along the borders of Chechnya.[13]

At the end of September 1995 there were reported to be 29,845 IDPs from the Prigorodnyi District (North Ossetia) in Ingushetia.[14] It is unlikely that more than a handful of these have returned to their homes. Probably most have little prospect of doing so because Russia helped North Ossetia drive them out in the brief war in 1992.

Russia's Troubled Relations with the Peoples of the North Caucasus

The peoples of the North Caucasus have resisted Russian (tsarist, communist, and post-communist) efforts to absorb them in varying degrees. Displacement is not new to the area. The North Caucasus was taken by Russia in stages from the Ottoman Empire and from local princes and khans, a process of acquisition that ended in the nineteenth century. In the first part of the nineteenth century, Russia waged a long war against the Caucasian peoples.[15] Thousands of Circassians, Abkhaz, and other nationalities from the northwestern Caucasus were deported or emigrated to Turkey, and their lands were colonized by Cossacks and other Russians. Russia consolidated its control in Transcaucasia by taking much of what are now Azerbaijan and Armenia from Iran in two wars in the first third of the nineteenth century, then set about absorbing the North Caucasian peoples. The nationalist Shamil, a member of the Avar ethnic group, led a guerrilla war against the tsarist authorities for more than thirty years.[16] When the area was finally incorporated into the Russian Empire, a policy of assimilation began that continued under the Soviets.

The North Caucasus was the scene of much fighting in the civil war in Russia that followed the 1917 Revolution. After the foreign intervention in Russia had ended and the communists had won the civil war, the Soviets consolidated their control over both the North Caucasus and Transcaucasia. Under Stalin, "administrative structures were imposed which divided the mountain people and prevented them from acting in their own interest." Communist rule "magnified the differences of dialect to build up the idea of separate nations, and then confirmed the split by concocting separate literary languages."[17] Administrative reshuffling continued until the outbreak of World War II. Three related groups of Circassians, the Kabardinians, the Cherkess, and the Adygei, found themselves in three separate administrative units. The Ossetians were divided between Russia and Georgia. The closely related Chechens and Ingush had separate autonomous units until 1934, when they were combined.

DEPORTATIONS AND RETURN. During World War II, German armies reached the western edge of Chechnya. After the Soviets had driven the Nazi forces back, several national groups, including four from the North Caucasus (the Chechens, Ingush, Karachai, and Balkars) were deported en masse. All were accused of collaborating with the Nazis. The Chechens were uprooted from areas that had not been occupied by the Nazis. Between a quarter and a third of the deportees died in the deportation to Kazakstan and Uzbekistan.[18] Thousands perished in the unheated boxcars used to transport them, and more died in the inhospitable steppes where they were left to fend for themselves. In late 1948 they were sentenced to remain in areas of "special settlement," which they were forbidden to leave for life.[19] As a result of the deportation, most

Chechens who are today over forty years old were either born or lived in exile, a collective trauma that has fueled resistance to the Russians. That deportation has been a powerful factor in the reassertion of ethnic identity in the 1990s.

In his famous speech at the Communist Party Congress in February 1956, Khrushchev mentioned by name five ethnic groups that had been deported, including the Chechens. The deported nationalities were officially rehabilitated in 1957. They were allowed to return to the areas from which they had been deported. By the time the USSR fell apart, all of the groups that had been deported had been allowed some measure of repatriation save for the Meskhetian Turks. The Chechens, Ingush, Karachai, and Balkars had their territories restored as administrative units; but because they did not always get back as much land as they had had before World War II, disputes continued to plague the region.[20] In no cases have the victims of deportation been given material compensation for the loss of their family members or homes. The issue of repatriation of deported peoples was discussed in detail at the Geneva Regional Conference on refugee and migration issues in the CIS, May 30–31, 1996.[21]

Meanwhile, in 1991 the Supreme Soviet of the Russian Federation, following up on the "official rehabilitation" granted the deported North Caucasians in 1957, had passed a poorly conceived law allowing for the return and territorial compensation of territorial groups exiled by Stalin, but creating no mechanism to carry it out.[22] The law stated that the borders between republics of the Russian Federation should be restored to their status at the time the "repressed peoples" were deported. It was the catalyst for a brief war.

FROM REHABILITATION TO THE PRIGORODNYI DISTRICT WAR. After their rehabilitation, the Ingush went back to the North Caucasus only to find Ossetians in their former homes in the Prigorodnyi District.[23] The Ingush pressed for return of the Prigorodnyi District, but Moscow left it attached to North Ossetia. In 1992 the Ingush and Chechens divided the Chechen-Ingush Republic into the Republic of Chechnya and the Republic of Ingushetia. The Ingush, unlike many of the Chechens, did not want to leave the Russian Federation and hoped Moscow would support their attempt to reclaim the Prigorodnyi District.

In 1990–92, while the Ingush were pressing for the return of the Prigorodnyi District, they obtained arms from Chechens, while the North Ossetians got arms from Russia and from the South Ossetians in neighboring Georgia. In October 1992 the dispute over the Prigorodnyi District turned into war. Atrocities were committed on both sides. The war was brief, and by the end of 1992 fighting had virtually ended. Russian Interior Ministry troops and army units sent to the region to "restore order" helped North Ossetian forces defeat the Ingush.[24] Nearly all of the Ingush population of the district (numbering between 34,500 and 60,000) was displaced to Ingushetia.[25] Ingush sources claim that 60,000 were deported, but according to the 1989 census, only 32,000 Ingush inhabited the district.[26] Thousands of homes, mostly Ingush, were destroyed.

An agreement between Ingush, North Ossetian, and Russian authorities for the return of the IDPs to the Prigorodnyi District was concluded in 1993 but has not been implemented. An estimated 9,000 Ossetians were displaced from the Prigorodnyi District, but most have returned. Only a very small number of Ingush were able to return to the region before the outbreak of hostilities between Russia and Chechnya in 1994 added new waves of displacement to the region. Approximately 10,000 Ingush from the Prigorodnyi District live in group settlements in Ingushetia. The rest of the Ingush displaced from the district are scattered throughout Ingushetia. North Ossetia is host to some 30,000 Ossetians from South Ossetia and at least as many from other parts of Georgia.

CHECHNYA DECLARES INDEPENDENCE. The communist leadership of Chechnya welcomed the August 1991 coup attempt against Soviet president Mikhail Gorbachev. When it failed, they found themselves discredited. General Dzhokar Dudayev, a Chechen who had risen through the ranks of the Soviet military to become commander of the Soviet Air Force Base in Tartu, Estonia, and had returned to Chechnya, condemned the coup. The communists were ejected from office and Dudayev came to power as head of the Chechen National Congress. Chechnya under Dudayev's leadership declared its independence in October 1991.

Chechen independence was never recognized by Russia. In November 1991 Moscow sent in troops. A strong Chechen response and public outcry in Moscow forced President Boris Yeltsin to withdraw the troops without a fight. By early 1992 all but two of the twenty-one republics in the Russian Federation had signed a new union treaty. Tatarstan and Russia reached an accommodation in 1994, leaving only Chechnya.[27]

Negotiations between the Russians and Chechens continued intermittently throughout 1991–94. During this period there was a general failure in Chechnya to appreciate how seriously the authorities in Moscow took

Chechnya's bid for secession. Dudayev did not tolerate open discussion and dissolved the Chechen Parliament in 1992, an action that many Chechens opposed. Parts of Chechnya, particularly the north, were far less independence-minded than the south. However, using heavy-handed tactics, Russia pushed Chechens who wanted accommodation with Russia to support Dudayev.

In late 1994, impatient hard-liners in Moscow apparently overcame efforts to resolve the crisis by negotiation. Moscow saw this conflict as a template for its struggle with groups throughout the Russian Federation who wanted more autonomy. The war party was influenced by Russian perceptions of the North Caucasus rooted in historical and literary accounts of Russians fighting against the "evil Chechen."

December 1994: All-Out War

After months of negotiating with Dudayev and an unsuccessful attempt to stage a coup d'état with a party of pro-Russian Chechens, the Russians decided to attack. On December 11, 1994, Soviet armed forces crossed the borders of Chechnya and planes bombed Grozny. Then-defense minister Pavel Grachev promised that Chechen resistance would be eliminated in a week. The war continued for twenty-one months.

The Russian campaign quickly engulfed the civilian population. Tens of thousands were killed or wounded and hundreds of thousands displaced. Many humanitarian centers, including hospitals and orphanages, sustained direct hits. By the end of the war many of Chechnya's largest population centers lay in ruins, and most of the towns and villages in Chechnya had been subject to at least some bombardment and shelling. One of the outstanding features of the war was the indiscriminate and disproportionate use of force. Civilians were often strafed as they tried to get out of population centers to the countryside or to flee to neighboring Ingushetia and Dagestan. Usually very circumspect in describing conflicts, the International Committee of the Red Cross (ICRC) repeatedly called on the warring parties to respect international humanitarian law and noted that civilians had been deliberately targeted by the Russians.[28]

In February and March 1996, Russian federal forces pressed an offensive designed to end the war before Yeltsin faced the presidential election in June. It was not successful. A lightning takeover of Grozny by Chechen fighters in August 1996 finally defeated the Russians.

On August 22, Alexander Lebed (as secretary of the Security Council of the Russian Federation) and Aslan Maskhadov, Chechen chief of staff, signed a cease-fire and several additional agreements. The Khasavyurt Agreement, a statement of principles signed on August 31, stipulated that Russian federal forces would be withdrawn shortly. Discussions on the political status of Chechnya were delayed for five years, to be resolved by December 31, 2001. A pro-Moscow Chechen administration installed by Moscow in Grozny disappeared. With these agreements, Moscow recognized the government of Chechnya de facto, and after the January 27, 1997, elections de jure, while stating that Chechnya was still part of the Russian Federation.

It will be a difficult job to reconstruct Chechnya. The center of Grozny resembles Dresden in 1945. Many areas of the country are mined. Several decrees that had promised large amounts of money to rebuild Chechnya, made before and during the election campaign in Moscow, have been revoked. Russia is short of funds. Meanwhile, the Chechens consider that they have won their independence.

CONDONING RUSSIAN ACTION. Within weeks after the Russians attacked, Turkey, Iran, and a number of CIS states urged an end to military action in Chechnya and a peaceful solution to the crisis. The Western countries characterized the war as an internal Russian affair and from the start called for restoration of order "with a minimum of bloodshed and violence."[29] The pinnacle of the Western countries' eagerness not to alienate Russia was reached in April 1996. Before the April 1996 G-7 meetings in Moscow, Médecins sans Frontières (MSF)/Belgium prepared a paper outlining atrocities committed by Russian forces in Chechnya and emphasizing their disregard for the most basic humanitarian considerations. The paper, circulated to all of the G-7 embassies in Moscow, was greeted by a resounding silence. Not a word about Chechnya was said at the time of the G-7 meeting in Moscow or at the subsequent summit meeting between Yeltsin and U.S. President Bill Clinton. This lack of response effectively encouraged the Russian Federation to pursue a military solution.

Who Is Doing What and with What Degree of Effectiveness?

The needs of the hundreds of thousands of IDPs have been vast both within and outside Chechnya. All assistance to the IDPs within Chechnya has been subject to the ebb and flow of the conflict. On many occasions it was impossible to help the IDPs. The already difficult water and sanitation conditions in Grozny became catastrophic with the termination of ICRC assistance in early 1997. Security is a major issue for everyone in Chechnya, both the displaced and those who have somehow remained in their homes. Since the Russians withdrew, robberies, kidnappings, and murders have multiplied. Order and stability were seen as the main issue in the 1997 presidential campaign, independence being taken as a given.[30]

In December 1996, six expatriate ICRC delegates were murdered at the recently established ICRC hospital in Novyye Atagi, near Grozny. It was clear that the foreign nationals were targeted. The murders and the deteriorating security environment have had far-reaching consequences for the provision of international humanitarian aid in Chechnya. Following the murders, ICRC and all other foreign humanitarian organizations working inside Chechnya turned their operations over to local staff and pulled out their expatriate staff.

THE GOVERNMENT OF THE RUSSIAN FEDERATION. The Russian government secured help for the IDPs from a number of quarters. Early in the conflict, Russia's Federal Migration Service asked several international organizations to assist IDPs from Chechnya in Dagestan, Ingushetia, and North Ossetia. IDPs within Chechnya were not included in the request made to UN agencies because Russia apparently wanted to avoid the impression that any of its sovereignty in Chechnya had been alienated. Russia allowed fewer international organizations and NGOs to assist IDPs than did the governments of Georgia, Armenia, and Azerbaijan with their respective IDPs. Assistance arranged through Moscow was somewhat fragmented, but most observers felt that the coordination on the ground in Dagestan, Ingushetia, and North Ossetia was good. Both ICRC and the International Organization for Migration (IOM) set up programs within Chechnya, at the request of the Russian Federation.

THE INTERNATIONAL COMMUNITY. Although hampered by the ever-shifting fighting, political uncertainty, and lack of security, the international community was able to make a difference for the people displaced by the conflict in Chechnya. The United Nations humanitarian assistance program for IDPs from Chechnya located in Dagestan, Ingushetia, and North Ossetia began in January 1995, following a request from the Russian Federation. The UN agencies involved in relief work included

UNHCR, the World Food Programme (WFP), the United Nations Children's Fund (UNICEF), the World Health Organization (WHO), and the UN Department of Humanitarian Affairs (DHA). The UN, as earlier noted, was not present in Chechnya itself. In 1997 the UN agencies provided limited nonfood assistance for Chechnya. UN agencies were expecting and planning for the return of many IDPs in 1997, with gradual phasing out of the UN interagency humanitarian assistance program by the end of the year. Following are some highlights of the assistance supplied by the international community.

UNHCR. UNHCR's programs for victims of the Chechnya conflict began in January 1995. UNHCR supported programs for shelter, water and sanitation, and the food and health sectors and undertook a number of protection-related activities. These included assessment of the causes of displacement, monitoring and documenting human rights issues, promoting durable solutions, and facilitating access to displaced persons and their areas of residence.[31] Other UNHCR activities included assisting local governments with capacity-building through the donation of vehicles and computer equipment. UNHCR chose a number of NGOs as implementing partners, including MSF/Belgium, Relief International, the International Rescue Committee, Radda Barnen, Equilibre, and some Russian NGOs. UNHCR also worked closely with Russia's Federal Migration Service.

In 1997 UNHCR provided packages to returning IDPs and small-scale rehabilitation assistance in villages of origin. This assistance was to encourage the return of IDPs to Chechnya. UNHCR also assisted the integration of IDPs (mostly non-Chechens) who do not intend to return to Chechnya, located in Dagestan, Ingushetia, North Ossetia, Kabardino-Balkaria and Stavropol.

ICRC. ICRC was actively engaged inside Chechnya starting in 1995. Early in the conflict ICRC launched an appeal to assist 400,000 victims of the conflict, emphasizing medical needs and protection against the cold. Throughout the conflict ICRC appealed to all parties to respect humanitarian rules and to provide good treatment of civilians and people detained in connection with the hostilities. ICRC also provided important assistance to the people who remained in Grozny, and to more than 250,000 IDPs in Chechnya, Dagestan, Ingushetia, Kabardino-Balkaria, North Ossetia, and elsewhere in the region.[32]

ICRC was active throughout the war in many fields in Chechnya. It was the sole provider of drinking water for Grozny, producing a million liters of chlorinated water daily. Thousands of food parcels, wheat flour, and other relief items were distributed to more than 50,000 vulnerable people in Grozny, Argun, and Gudermes and in villages in southern Chechnya. Essential school equipment was provided to thousands of children in Chechnya, Dagestan, and Ingushetia.

After the signing of the cease-fire in August 1996, the ICRC established a field hospital at Novyye Atagi, twenty kilometers south of Grozny. ICRC was eager to introduce the concept of a neutral and protected area in a conflict zone in the Russian Federation. On the night of December 16–17, 1996, six expatriate delegates at the Novyye Atagi hospital were murdered by a group of unidentified gunmen. To date, the Chechen authorities have not determined who did it. ICRC has concluded that the murders were carried out by professional killers and were planned in advance.[33] Following the murders, ICRC suspended all programs that required the presence of expatriates in Chechnya, Dagestan, and Ingushetia.

IOM. Acting on a December 1994 request from the Russian Federal Migration Service for humanitarian assistance, IOM set up field offices in Vladikavkaz (North Ossetia) and Sleptsovskaya (Ingushetia) to assist IDPs who had fled there.

IOM's Chechnya Emergency Project began in January 1995 and ended in May 1996. It provided IDPs with emergency transportation (evacuation, secondary movement, and return), temporary shelters, heating, and health care. IOM also assisted the local migration service in capacity-building. IOM established a bus route for evacuating vulnerable individuals (the elderly, women, and children) directly from the center of Grozny, and more than 45,000 persons were given emergency transportation assistance. By May 1995, IOM had an office in the center of Grozny. IOM and ICRC were the only international organizations to establish offices inside Chechnya. In May 1996, IOM handed over its shelter facilities to the local migration service, after obtaining guarantees from the Chechen civilian authorities that they would protect the shelters from vandals and support the local migration service in managing the shelters.[34]

Security was an ongoing problem for IOM, as it was for all agencies working in Chechnya. In March 1995 an IOM local staff member and nine evacuees were killed when the bus in which they were riding hit a land mine. In December 1995 a Finnish national working with IOM to install prefabricated shelters donated by Finland was murdered. These events led IOM to relocate its international staff from Chechnya to Vladi-kavkaz (North Ossetia).

WFP. WFP supplied food rations including flour, pasta, bulk cereal, sugar, and cooking oil for distribution to IDPs by UNHCR. Its target beneficiaries were IDPs from Chechnya and the Prigorodnyi District and refugees from Georgia. Because IDPs had some access to other food supplies, including food available erratically on the local market, WFP assistance was supplementary rather than basic. In 1996, WFP stated that it did not plan to distribute food inside Chechnya because ICRC's vulnerable feeding projects were expected to cover local needs.[35]

NGOs. Several NGOs assisted IDPs in Chechnya and the neighboring republics as implementing partners of international organizations. As earlier noted, UNHCR's implementing partners included MSF/Belgium, Relief International, International Rescue Committee, and some Russian NGOs. IOM worked with six NGOs in a program to winterize shelters. After the murder of six ICRC delegates in December 1966, all international NGO personnel were withdrawn from Chechnya.

Conclusions and Recommendations

With the end of the war the three constants in Chechnya's future seem to be privation, crime, and Russia. A special challenge for the Chechens will be learning to live with their neighbors as the euphoria of their "victory" wears thin. Parts of the Russian Federation (Ingushetia, North Ossetia, Stavropol *krai*, and Dagestan) border Chechnya to the west, north, and east. Russia is largely responsible for the upheaval of the 1990s, yet Russia is short of funds to repair the huge amount of damage inflicted on Chechnya. It will cost billions of dollars to reconstruct Chechnya. The euphoria of the Chechens at having "won" the war will help them reconstruct their country, but it will not be enough.

The overriding requirement for solving the problem of internal displacement in Chechnya is that there be a permanent political settlement. The Chechens are behaving as if independence has already been won, while the Russians insist that final determination of Chechnya's status can wait until the end of 2001. Any uncertainty on the subject will hamper a return to normalcy in the North Caucasus, and with it a return for IDPs. Meanwhile, Chechens entertain lingering suspicions of the Ingush, and Chechnya needlessly alienated Georgia, its immediate neighbor to the south, by participating in the battle of Sukhumi.

Resolving internal displacement in the North Caucasus requires a regional approach. IDPs from Chechnya, IDPs from the conflict in the Prigorodnyi District, and refugees from Georgia (mostly from South Ossetia) in North Ossetia have overlapped. Some IDPs from Prigorodnyi who took refuge in Chechnya became IDPs again. Thousands of IDPs in Chechnya were displaced more than once. Assistance to the victims of the war in Chechnya was required in a wide area including Dagestan, Ingushetia, North Ossetia, Kabardino-Balkaria, and Stavropol. The fact that the international community recognized all of the North Caucasus as being part of the Russian Federation presented a special challenge.

For the Russians, what happened in 1994–96 will, one hopes, lead to some introspection. The Soviet Union, and since 1991 the Russian Federation, have been major agents of displacement in the North Caucasus. All of the peoples of the Caucasus, but particularly the Chechens, have been victims of Russian racism. It is difficult to imagine the Russians bombing and strafing Slavs in the way they did the Chechens. If Russia is to avoid further tragedies with its enormous non-Slavic population it must overcome its feelings of ethnic superiority. The non-Russian nationalities throughout the Russian Federation cannot fail to have been alienated by Russia's military intervention, although it can be argued that they have been taught to avoid actions leading to secession.

Among the lessons provided by the crisis in the North Caucasus are the following:

- UNHCR's role in IDP crises has broadened. In many places (e.g., Georgia and Tajikistan) UNHCR assistance to and protection of IDPs made it possible for them to remain in their countries of origin. In a parallel manner, in the North Caucasus UNHCR assistance to the vulnerable resulted in their not becoming IDPs. Treating all of the vulnerable in the conflict zone in the same manner was not always possible because of the ongoing war, but this posture represents a major broadening of the mandate of international organizations. This new assistance strategy has raised the standards for assistance provided to all categories of vulnerable persons, including the internally displaced.
- Chechnya demonstrated the convergence of needs between IDPs and other vulnerable groups. Assistance to the vulnerable in order to prevent them from becoming IDPs underlined the identity of needs between IDPs and other vulnerable groups in

Chechnya. Dealing simultaneously with all categories of vulnerable persons should improve the ability of the international community to cope with complex emergencies, in which internal displacement often plays a large part.

- Reluctance to condemn Russia encouraged it to pursue a military solution. Outspoken criticism of the disproportionate use of force and targeting of fleeing civilians would have put Russia's brutality in Chechnya in high relief. Because of their concern over relations with Russia, G-7 countries were reluctant to criticize Russia for this heavy-handed policy. They thereby encouraged harsh Russian actions in the war. In future crises, G-7 countries and others should not hesitate to be critical. Doing so might exert pressure to bring the conflict to an end.
- Proper mechanisms for official discussion of issues and for public dialogue are essential if IDP crises are to be averted. Dudayev might have heard some warnings about Russia's intentions if he had been willing to listen. He was so intent on pushing for independence that he suspended the Chechen Parliament rather than listen to compatriots who did not share his views. Ironically the Chechen clan structure, which Dudayev ignored when he took power, traditionally encouraged discussion at many levels before political decisions were made. Since Dudayev was martyred in the conflict, it will be difficult for Chechens to appreciate the negative influence he had on their political system.
- Providing assistance should have been made conditional. The Russo-Chechen War represented a total breakdown of law and order. International organizations and NGOs can make their help conditional on actions of the belligerents, and in this case should have done so. In contrast, the ICRC, which is mandated to help all victims of war, cannot. Russia asked for assistance for persons displaced from Chechnya. The international community was correct to respond but should have demanded that Russia give basic protection to civilians in the conflict zone. Lives would have been saved if assistance had been conditioned on not targeting unarmed civilians.
- Imperial wars are as destructive of human rights and as damaging to IDPs as civil wars. There has been a tendency to think that civil wars (e.g., those in Somalia and Sudan) are more destructive of human rights than imperial wars are. The Russo-Chechen War

was fundamentally an imperial war, with religious overtones. It was highly destructive of human rights and led to immense problems of displacement. Only when the imperial power suffered a defeat that it could not reverse, the takeover of Grozny in August 1996, did it move to end the war.

- The means and methods of warfare used in Chechnya were the direct cause of displacement. International observers characterized the warfare in Chechnya as "completely disproportionate, indiscriminate, and unacceptable in terms of international humanitarian norms."[36] The outright attacks on civilian targets and blanketing of towns and cities alike made it impossible to flee. Virtually everyone in zones of conflict was displaced, and many had nowhere to go but into the path of destruction.

Azerbaijan

The more than 600,000 displaced Azerbaijanis constitute the largest group of IDPs in the Caucasus. The displaced include the entire Azeri population of Nagorno-Karabakh and a wide area surrounding it. They comprise a broad range of professionals, farmers, and workers and include men, women, and children of all ages.[37] Because of the ethnic basis of displacement in Azerbaijan, the IDPs there are virtually all Azeri (Turkic) peoples. Most of them are nominally Shia Muslim, but many of those from Lachin and Kelbajar Provinces are Sunni Muslim Kurds.[38]

When UNHCR first sent an emergency response team to Azerbaijan in December 1992, there were 53,000 IDPs in Azerbaijan. By the summer of 1994 they numbered 653,000. This number has remained more or less constant.[39] International organizations and NGOs working in Azerbaijan believe there are 620,000–650,000 IDPs in Azerbaijan.[40] According to data prepared for the May 1996 CIS Conference in Geneva, there are 668,000 IDPs and 233,000 refugees or persons in refugee-like situations in Azerbaijan.[41]

The biggest wave of IDPs came in 1993 as Armenian forces from Nagorno-Karabakh, with support from the Republic of Armenia, forced out the Azeri civilian population successively from seven provinces (Lachin, Kelbajar, Agdam, Fizuli, Jibrail, Qubatli, and Zangelan) adjacent to Nagorno-Karabakh. An early 1994 Armenian offensive displaced another 50,000 Azeris.[42] Some of Fizuli Province was reconquered by the Azerbaijanis in the months before the May 1994 cease-fire. Twenty to thirty thousand IDPs have returned there, to an area where all the infrastructure was looted and burned and 95 percent of the houses had only their damaged walls standing.

UNHCR reported in 1994 that with the exception of about eleven camps (housing some 15,000–20,000 families, or 75,000–100,000 individuals, based on average family size of five), and 1,600 families housed in railway wagons, most of the IDPs were scattered throughout Azerbaijan in many types of accommodation. Many IDPs resided in small encampments along roads or took over facilities designed for other use, such as factories and sports stadiums.[43] UNHCR commissioned a survey of IDPs in 1996. It indicated that 67 percent of Azerbaijan's IDPs lived in urban areas and 33 percent in rural areas. The average IDP family size was 5.37 people.[44] A health and nutrition survey completed in 1996 indicated that 63.8 percent of the IDPs sampled were housed in dormitories or other public buildings. The remainder lived in railroad cars (4.7 percent), camps (5 percent), houses (8.5 percent), apartments (10.2 percent), or "other" accommodations (7.8 percent).[45]

IDPs are dispersed throughout Azerbaijan. With the exception of IDPs living in Baku and Sumgait, far from the areas from which the IDPs were displaced, IDPs have moved to areas fairly close to their region of origin. For example, IDPs from Fizuli are mostly located in Imishli and Sabirabad, and those from Agdam are in Mingeshevir, Yevlakh, and Sheki. Several hundred IDPs (many from Shusha, Nagorno-Karabakh) live in former vacation hotels in the Apsheron Peninsula north of Baku. Many others are in school buildings in cities such as Mingeshevir and Ganja.

In 1998 the number of IDPs in camps is probably between 75,000 and 100,000. Many of the camps are located in southern Azerbaijan near the Aras River. These include Sabirabad, two camps at Saatli, and four camps at Bilasuvar. In January 1996 the population of these four camps was 44,000.[46] The Sabirabad camp alone, one of the least salubrious, and located at some distance from towns and villages, housed 12,000 IDPs. The number of IDPs in tented camps has declined since 1994 as many of them have been transferred to other accommodations, including prefabricated one-room houses furnished by the European Community Humanitarian Office (ECHO). Most of the IDPs who returned to Fizuli had been in camps. The April 1996 UNHCR survey stated that approximately 5 percent of its respondents were in camps. Only a small percentage of the people who became displaced in 1993–94 have merged into the communities where they live.

When people flooded out of the Fizuli and Zangelan areas into Iran in 1993–94, some 32,000 refugees were transported along the Aras River to a point where they could be returned to Azerbaijan. Iran constructed camps for them at Imishli, in Azerbaijan, where they were relocated as IDPs. Iran was host to more than 2 million refugees from Afghanistan and did not want to find itself in a similar situation with refugees from Azerbaijan. These IDP camps, initially administered by the Iranian Red Crescent Society, were turned over to the Azerbaijani Red Crescent Society, with assistance from the International Federation of Red Cross and Red Crescent Societies (IFRC), in 1995.

Background

The term *Azerbaijan* as used here refers to the independent Republic of Azerbaijan, the successor state to the Soviet Socialist Republic of Azerbaijan. Before the advent of Christianity and Islam in the region, Azerbaijanis were Zoroastrians. Now between 70 and 75 percent of the Azerbaijanis are at least nominally Shia Muslims. A substantial Sunni Muslim minority exists, as well as small groups of Jews and Christians.[47] Azerbaijan also has some ethnic minorities. Before 1988 the Armenians of Azerbaijan numbered more than 300,000. Since their departure, the largest ethnic minorities are the Lezghins in the north along the border with Dagestan (Russian Federation) and the Talysh near the Iranian border.[48] In 1993, when things were turning bad on the battlefield, separatist tendencies briefly appeared among the Lezghins and Talysh. The Armenians of Nagorno-Karabakh remain the only the minority in Azerbaijan that has taken up arms to secede.

Like Armenia and Georgia, Azerbaijan has been subject to foreign rule for much of its history. In relatively recent times Iran ruled most of the area, alternating with the Ottoman Turks and Russians. Russian power extended only to the Caucasus range until the nineteenth century, when two Russo-Iranian wars secured for them "Transcaucasia," a name that reflects the Russian perspective on the area. The first war placed eastern Azerbaijan, including Baku and Lenkoran, in Russian hands. The second war was followed by the transfer of Yerevan and Nakhichevan from Iran to Russia in 1828. These wars left both the Armenian and Azerbaijani people divided. The Azerbaijanis found themselves split between Iran and Russia, while the Armenians were split between Turkey and Russia. Only one third of the Azerbaijani people were in the Russian

Empire; two thirds remained in Iran, a ratio that still holds between the Azerbaijanis in independent Azerbaijan and those in Iran.

With the collapse of the Ottoman and Russian Empires in World War I, Azerbaijan and the two other Transcaucasian states proclaimed their joint independence as the state of Transcaucasia in 1917, only to split up in May 1918. In 1918–21 violence, much of it interethnic, spread throughout the region. Both Turkish and British troops were active in Transcaucasia. In 1919–20 the British established a military hold in Transcaucasia (in Baku and Batumi). After their withdrawal in 1920, independent Azerbaijan, weakened by interethnic strife and a collapsing economy, was no match for the Red Army. The Soviets seized power in Baku and established the Soviet Republic of Azerbaijan in April 1920. In 1920–21 the Soviets also absorbed Armenia and Georgia.

Azerbaijani nationalism was relatively slow to develop under the communists. "Rather than imagining themselves as part of a continuous national tradition, like the Georgians and Armenians, the Muslims of Transcaucasia saw themselves as part of the larger Muslim world, the *umma*."[49] Soviet Azerbaijan, a major source of oil, contributed much more to the Soviet economy than it received in the form of capital investment. Like the other two Transcaucasian republics, Azerbaijan was hobbled by networks of clans and personal ties and by networks of bureaucrats resistant to reform. Perestroika was not embraced enthusiastically in Azerbaijan, unlike in Armenia, because the entrenched communist power structure was content with the status quo. The local power apparatus was led by Heydar Aliyev, whom Gorbachev fired for corruption. When the movement for independence from the Soviet Union first appeared to gain momentum in 1988, it was largely as a reaction to the movement for self-determination in the Armenian-majority enclave of Nagorno-Karabakh. Armenian claims to Nagorno-Karabakh had to be met with counterclaims. Thus the Nagorno-Karabakh issue, spurred by the determination of the Armenians of Nagorno-Karabakh to join Armenia, became midwife to the Azerbaijan national movement.

Nagorno-Karabakh: The Black Garden

Nagorno-Karabakh is a mountainous enclave southwest of Baku.[50] Three-quarters of its population was Armenian in the late 1980s. It had been linked administratively with Baku to its east since Russia took the area from Iran in the early nineteenth century. In spite of Armenian calls for it to be joined with Armenia when the borders of the Soviet republics were drawn in the 1920s and 1930s, Nagorno-Karabakh was made an autonomous oblast within Azerbaijan. Nakhichevan, which contained a large Armenian minority and was separated from the rest of Azerbaijan by an arm of Armenian territory, was made an Autonomous Soviet Socialist Republic within Azerbaijan. With some justification, both Azerbaijan and Armenia have accused Stalin of deliberately making trouble when he drew their frontiers.

Conflicting claims over Nagorno-Karabakh are the underlying cause of the conflict between Azerbaijan and Armenia, and thus of displacement in both countries. The dispute has left hundreds of thousands displaced after first precipitating a forced exchange of populations between Armenia and Azerbaijan. The constitutions of the Soviet Union of 1922 and 1936 upheld two principles that have been at the heart of the conflict over this Armenian-majority enclave: national self-determination and the inviolability of borders. However, as long as the communist grip on Armenia and Azerbaijan remained strong, claims and counterclaims relating to Nagorno-Karabakh remained under control. Perestroika and glasnost changed that.

Violent conflict between Armenia and Azerbaijan over Nagorno-Karabakh broke out in 1988. In February of that year there were mass demonstrations in Yerevan and Stepanakert (the capital of Nagorno-Karabakh, called Khankendi by the Azerbaijanis) centering on a purported ecological theme. The demonstrations in Stepanakert quickly turned into a nationalist demonstration, with Nagorno-Karabakh calling for union with Armenia. Two Azerbaijanis were killed and a substantial number wounded.[51]

Word of the Azerbaijani deaths in Stepanakert reached Baku and Sumgait, an industrial city north of Baku. On February 27, 1988, thousands of Azeris protested against Armenian demands and alleged Armenian atrocities. A pogrom targeting Armenians in Sumgait killed at least thirty-one people, some in their apartments, some dragged from buses. Sumgait "rekindled memories of persecution branded on the Armenian collective consciousness."[52]

Armenians and Azerbaijanis agree on one thing: that the pogrom was organized. One survivor noted that Armenian houses had been marked with crosses.[53] From there their views diverge: Armenians see the Sumgait pogrom as an organized signal to all Armenians to get out of Azerbaijan; Azerbaijanis see it as a conspiracy involving Armenian extremists and the KGB designed to turn world sympathy against Azerbaijan. One author believes the pogrom was probably organized by local authorities in collaboration with the KGB. The local police stood idly by, and troops did not arrive to restore order for three days.[54]

The situation deteriorated during the remainder of 1988. Demonstrations in many cities in Azerbaijan in November 1988 endangered all ethnic Armenians in Azerbaijan. Soviet armed forces began organizing a massive forced exchange. Ethnic Azerbaijanis were transferred from Armenia to Azerbaijan, and ethnic Armenians were transferred from Azerbaijan to Armenia. These transfers in the 1988–90 period achieved rough parity, with around 250,000 ethnic Azerbaijanis leaving Armenia and Nagorno-Karabakh, and some 300,000 Armenians leaving Azerbaijan.[55] The two shifting populations, however, were very different. The Armenians leaving Azerbaijan were for the most part urban, and the Azerbaijanis leaving Armenia were for the most part rural. It was thus virtually impossible to have one group of refugees take over the houses and apartments of those who had fled.

In late February the district soviet of Nagorno-Karabakh urged annexation to Armenia. Moscow refused to acknowledge it and placed Nagorno-Karabakh under direct rule from July 1988 to November 1989. However, Moscow was unwilling or unable to take decisive action on Nagorno-Karabakh and ended direct rule in frustration in late 1989. Shortly thereafter, a joint session of the Supreme Soviet of Armenia and the National Council of Nagorno-Karabakh declared Armenia and Nagorno-Karabakh to be the "United Armenian Republic." In Azerbaijan a push toward democratization broke down over the Nagorno-Karabakh issue, since no important Azerbaijani could agree to self-determination for that area.

Early in 1990 violence spread to Baku, the capital of Azerbaijan. Newly arrived Azerbaijani IDPs from Nagorno-Karabakh and refugees from Armenia attacked the Baku Armenians starting on January 13. This attack led to a mass exodus of most of the remaining Armenian population. As in Sumgait, many of the attacks on Armenians appeared to be carefully planned. Dozens were killed, and thousands of Armenian residents of Baku were evacuated, many of them directly across the Caspian Sea to Turkmenistan, from where they got flights to Yerevan.[56]

Martial law was declared in Baku. Several days after the rioting, on January 19, Soviet troops intervened. By this time there were few Armenians left. The troops came in with considerable force anyway and went on a killing spree. Dozens of people, virtually all Azeris, were shot or crushed by tanks in the streets. The military action crystallized years of resentment against Moscow and galvanized a push for independence. In spite of this, Ayaz Mutalibov, head of a faction in the Communist Party, was installed in power following the Soviet military intervention and remained in power for two years. Azerbaijan finally declared its independence on October 18, 1991, at which time it was still run by this communist faction.

One of the final Soviet acts in the area before the breakup of the USSR was "Operation Ring," undertaken with the participation of the Soviet army and Azerbaijani Special Function Militia troops. Officially this was a campaign to search for arms in and around Nagorno-Karabakh, but it resulted in the deportation of thousands of Armenians from rural villages in the area.[57]

A FULL-SCALE WAR. By the time the Soviet Union broke up in 1991, the conflict between Azerbaijan and Armenia had turned into a full-scale war. It helped the warhawks on each side that Soviet army equipment was transferred or allowed to get into the hands of Azerbaijani and Armenian forces. Following the independence of Armenia and Azerbaijan, the Armenians of Nagorno-Karabakh proclaimed the "Republic of Nagorno-Karabakh" on January 6, 1992. Although Armenia continued to support Nagorno-Karabakh economically and militarily, it did not recognize it as a separate republic, and neither did anyone else. Nevertheless, Armenia has continued to provide massive support for Nagorno-Karabakh. The war has become a contest between Azerbaijan and "Armenian forces." The latter is a deliberately ambiguous term, including as it does Armenians and supplies from Nagorno-Karabakh, from other parts of Azerbaijan, from Armenia proper, and from the Armenian diaspora.[58]

At various times in 1992–93 each side was convinced that it could win on the battlefield. In February 1992, Armenian forces overran Khojali, the second largest Azerbaijani-populated city in Nagorno-Karabakh. This was followed by a massacre of Azerbaijani civilians that left at least 159 dead.[59] A few weeks of unsuccessful attempts at mediation of the dispute by Iran, France, the United Nations, and the Conference on Security and Cooperation in Europe (CSCE) followed. In May, Armenian forces captured both Shusha, the largest ethnic Azerbaijani town in Nagorno-Karabakh, and Lachin, thereby taking control of the corridor linking Nagorno-Karabakh with Armenia. The fall of Shusha created a political crisis in Baku and brought the Azerbaijan Popular Front (APF) to power.

In June 1992 the APF announced that its main objective was to regain lost ground in Nagorno-Karabakh. Azerbaijani military went on the offensive and initially had some successes. They captured about a third of Nagorno-Karabakh, displacing about 40,000 Armenians. By the winter of 1992–93 the military situation began to turn against the Azerbaijanis. Armenian forces carried the war well beyond the bounds of Nagorno-Karabakh. Taking advantage of the political crisis in Baku in 1993, Armenian offensives took the city of Kelbajar northwest of Nagorno-Karabakh in April and May; the Azerbaijani city of Agdam east of Nagorno-Karabakh in July; Fizuli, southeast of Nagorno-Karabakh near the Iranian border in August; and much of the Zangelan region in the southwestern corner of Azerbaijan in October and November. As the last ex-Soviet Army troops left Azerbaijan in May 1993, their weapons, instead of being used against the Armenian advances, were turned on Baku. In June 1993 the army ousted Abulfazl Elchibey, the APF president of Azerbaijan. He was replaced by Heydar Aliyev from Nakhichevan, who is still the president at this writing in 1998.

Four successive resolutions adopted by the UN Security Council in 1993 called for the withdrawal of occupying (Armenian) forces from territories taken from Azerbaijan. The third of these, resolution 874, reaffirmed the sovereignty and territorial integrity of Azerbaijan, expressed its grave concern over the human suffering caused by the conflict, in particular the displacing of large numbers of civilians in Azerbaijan, and called on all parties not to violate the latest cease-fire and to refrain from violations of international humanitarian law.[60] These resolutions had little if any effect and did not prevent a further push by Armenian forces that resulted in the occupation of the remainder of Zangelan Province and the city of Goradiz.

CEASE-FIRE BUT NO SOLUTION. After protracted negotiations, a cease-fire among Azerbaijan, Armenia, and Nagorno-Karabakh (whose separate participation represented a major concession by the Azerbaijanis) went into effect on May 12, 1994. It left 20 percent of Azerbaijani territory in Armenian hands. The cease-fire has held since then, with not infrequent violations on both sides.[61] Various mediation efforts have attempted to resolve the Nagorno-Karabakh conflict, without much success, but those efforts continue. The principal venue for peace negotiations has been the Minsk Group under the Organization for Security and Cooperation in Europe (OSCE).[62] It seems impossible to reconcile the opposing principles of self-determination and the nonviolability of existing frontiers.

Since gaining independence in 1991, Azerbaijan has been dominated by the Nagorno-Karabakh conflict. The Azerbaijanis believe that separation of Nagorno-Karabakh would be the beginning of Azerbaijan's disintegration. They are afraid that "if the principle of the inviolability of territorial borders is tampered with, other Azeri minorities may also want to separate from the republic."[63] Given separatist tendencies among the Lezghins and Talysh, this fear is not unreasonable.

Azerbaijan's Neighbors and Displacement

RUSSIA. Russia does not have a clear, unified position on the Nagorno-Karabakh dispute but wants a central role in the solution, that of peace broker, on its own terms. There is a strong anti-Caucasian sentiment in Moscow, highlighted by its Chechnya policy. At the start of the war in Nagorno-Karabakh, Russia appeared to support Armenia. Later Russia appeared more balanced in its approach to Azerbaijan, perhaps because when Aliyev came to power in 1993 he joined the CIS. There were reports as recently as 1997 of Russian arms shipments to Armenia. Many Azerbaijanis believe that Russia wants their country to remain in continuous turmoil to give Moscow an excuse for intervention.

IRAN. Early calls from Baku for the "reunification of the Azerbaijani people" caused concern in Tehran because they represented a push for the Iranian provinces of East and West Azerbaijan to unite with the Republic of Azerbaijan. At this writing in 1998, Azerbaijan has a reasonably good relationship with Iran, and there is a substantial amount of trade between the two countries. At the same time, Iran is assisting Armenia with oil and possibly with weapons. The Iranians have opened a direct route to Armenia with a new bridge over the Aras River.

TURKEY. Turkey and Iran vie for influence in Azerbaijan, especially in Nakhichevan, which has a very short common border with Turkey and a long frontier with Iran and Armenia. Azerbaijan has had a cordial relationship with Turkey since independence.

GEORGIA. There are reported to be more than 50,000 Meskhetian Turks from Fergana in Azerbaijan who hope to return to Georgia.[64] In November 1944, Stalin deported the Meskhetian Turks from the Akhaltsikhe-Akhalkalaki region of Georgia near the Turkish frontier. Originally they were IDPs, but the breakup of the Soviet Union has turned them into refugees. The deportation of the Meskhetians is relatively poorly documented, but one Soviet source says 115,000 were deported.[65] They were deported to Central Asia, most of them to Uzbekistan. Thousands perished in the deportation. The Meskhetians were not allowed to return when the Chechens and other deported peoples were rehabilitated in the 1950s. In 1989 ethnic riots broke out in the Fergana Valley, where most of the Meskhetian Turks had resettled, and thousands were relocated to Russia, elsewhere in Central Asia, and Azerbaijan. As part of a pilot resettlement program, the government of Georgia is trying to return thirty-five to forty Meskhetian families from Azerbaijan to a district in eastern Georgia. Larger repatriation programs face strong local resistance and budgetary constraints.

Who Is Doing What and with What Degree of Effectiveness?

Security in some of the IDP camps has been a problem, and an NGO reported that one of its staff had been beaten at a camp assisted by ECHO near Yevlakh. Resentment of foreign presence and assistance has increased, along with a sense of dependency.[66]

According to the 1996 survey of IDPs commissioned by UNHCR, food is the most important need of most IDP families. Food aid is an important component of assistance to IDPs because of the IDPs' low incomes and their inability to earn money. Urban areas with a higher concentration of IDPs receive better and more food aid than rural areas.[67] In November 1993, WFP began distributing food to approximately 450,000 IDPs throughout Azerbaijan, using donations from the EC, the Netherlands, Italy, Sweden, Switzerland, United Kingdom, Canada, and the United States. Several NGOs also have food assistance programs for the IDPs, many of them supported by the U.S. Department of Agriculture (USDA).

The most prevalent accommodations for IDPs, according to UNHCR's 1996 survey, are public buildings (e.g., schools, administrative buildings, hostels, sanatoriums). The worst shelters are railway wagons, tents, mud houses, and dugouts. The UNHCR-sponsored survey highlighted a number of problems with accommodations for IDPs including lack of heat, erratic electricity supply, lack of bathing facilities, and cramped conditions. Construction of permanent housing for IDPs would not be acceptable to the government of Azerbaijan because it would "weaken the declared political statement of return" of the IDPs to the communities from which they had fled.[68]

Water is a systemic problem in Azerbaijan, as it is elsewhere in the former Soviet Union, but the quality of water is no worse for IDPs in public buildings than for the general populace. IDPs in urban areas generally have better access to water supplies than those in rural areas, although some of the camp population have clean water from new wells. One third of IDPs have received water or had their water source repaired by a humanitarian organization or the government. One third of IDP families have received a latrine from a foreign assistance organization.

IDPs report an increase in sickness since their displacement. Because most IDP shelters have no bathing facilities, scabies is common among IDP children. Respiratory diseases and mental illness are also common problems for IDPs, particularly in camps. WHO has focused on immunizations, particularly for diphtheria and polio. About one fifth of IDPs receive treatment from Mobile Health Units and receive free drugs.

A nationwide health and nutrition survey was conducted in 1996, with the aim of providing baseline information about the health status of IDPs and resident populations and identifying vulnerable populations to determine priorities for humanitarian assistance.[69] The survey did not find evidence of broad-based acute emergency situations among the IDPs but noted that chronic malnutrition rates are elevated in children and the elderly, and rates of anemia and iodine deficiency are unacceptably high.

The 1996 survey indicated that many IDP children do not attend school at all or attend irregularly. In contrast, a high percentage (76 percent) of adult IDPs in the same survey have finished secondary education, and only 13 percent of adult IDPs have no education at all.[70] UNICEF, UNHCR, and UNESCO (the United Nations Education, Scientific, and Cultural Organization) are working with NGOs (Relief International and World Vision International) to improve school facilities, supplies, and textbooks.

THE GOVERNMENT OF AZERBAIJAN. The government of Azerbaijan has established several organizations to deal with IDPs, refugees, and related problems. These organizations are somewhat unwieldy and fragmented, and it is not always clear which ones have clout. Government officials are the first to acknowledge this.

At the top of the "IDP organization hierarchy" is the Republican Commission on International and Technical Assistance, headed by a deputy prime minister. It was created in December 1994 against the advice of the Baku UNHCR office, which noted that a similar commission already existed, at least on paper, but had become moribund. The commission meets at least once a month. Its head is essentially a figurehead.

In 1995 the commission established a seven-person Working Group to deal with humanitarian issues on a day-to-day basis. Each member of the Working Group is responsible for dealing with specific agencies (international organizations, NGOs) and for coordinating all programs in designated provinces of Azerbaijan. In 1996, using a new registration system for IDPs in the Baku area, the Working Group determined that the number of IDPs there had dropped from 196,000 to 123,000. A substantial number of IDPs had moved out of Baku, and the new system eliminated many double registrations. One NGO official described the Working Group as having "control without responsibility." Nevertheless, the Working Group appears to have important coordinating functions. Despite the uncertainty generated by the absence of prospects for peace, and with it the return of IDPs, the Working Group encourages income-generation projects. It also deals with issues such as the problems created by a rise in the level of the Caspian Sea, which has forced 2,000 families out of their homes in Lenkoran, south of Baku.

As a result of this fragmented administrative structure, the government of Azerbaijan leaves much of the planning to the international organizations and NGOs. An official from an international organization described the government as friendly and helpful in its dealings with the international community but concluded that "Azerbaijan is not doing anything for the IDPs, leaving it to the NGOs. The more the NGOs are here, the less the GOA [government of Azerbaijan] has to do."[71]

The government has also created a Department of Refugees and IDPs, which in 1996 was described as inactive. The Humanitarian Department of the Ministry of Foreign Affairs deals with foreign assistance to refugees and IDPs. IOM and other organizations can offer suggestions on administrative improvements, but only the government can decide what structures are best suited to its needs.

A further issue is the extent to which the government sells itself short on matters relating to IDPs and humanitarian assistance. For example, the UN Department of Humanitarian Affairs held a regional meeting in April 1996 in Tbilisi. Georgia and Armenia had a good level of participation but Azerbaijan, whose 600,000 IDPs give it by far the largest humanitarian needs in the Caucasus, made a poor showing.

According to an international organization official, the government pays too much attention to administrative organization and not enough to the human dimension of displacement, especially in Baku. Overall, the government's top priorities appear to be (1) staying in power, (2) supporting the petroleum industry, and (3) maintaining the city of Baku.

THE INTERNATIONAL COMMUNITY. Azerbaijan, like Chechnya and Georgia, had few resources to devote to the care of refugees and IDPs when massive displacement occurred. Reeling from military defeats, it welcomed help and was happy to receive the large-scale assistance offered by UNHCR and other international organizations. Following are some highlights of selected programs for the benefit of IDPs and other vulnerable groups of international organizations and NGOs in Azerbaijan.

UNHCR. UNHCR arrived in Azerbaijan in December 1992 as the lead organization in helping IDPs. [72] Initially, UNHCR programs focused on responding to the emergency, providing tents, plastic sheeting, blankets, heaters, food, clothing, medicines, and household utensils. Early programs included a substantial amount of support for education because at least two hundred school buildings in Azerbaijan were occupied by IDPs.[73] In 1995, UNHCR shifted its focus to improving the living conditions of the IDPs and started some income-generating programs. Its goal has become to provide "semi-permanent shelter," which serves the objective of keeping the status quo visible in the absence of a political settlement. In 1996, UNHCR constructed several hundred one-room limestone houses and repaired accommodations for a large number of families living in public buildings. Several hundred families returning to the liberated part of Fizuli Province in 1996–97 were given construction materials to repair their houses.

UNHCR has contracted with NGOs for specific assistance projects, including the Adventist Development Relief Agency, the International Rescue Committee, Oxfam, Relief International, and World Vision International. UNHCR has suggested to the government of Azerbaijan that it create humanitarian corridors to get assistance into Nagorno-Karabakh, similar to the corridors set up in Sri Lanka, but it did not receive a positive reply. "On Nagorno-Karabakh the government is blinded by the political issues," commented an international organization official.[74]

ICRC. The ICRC provides food parcels to 3,500 families living near the cease-fire line in the Fizuli area. It also furnishes water pumps to some damaged villages that are being repopulated by returning Azeri IDPs. ICRC has seed distribution programs and programs to develop awareness of land mines in Nagorno-Karabakh and Fizuli. It is one of the few nonindigenous organizations working in Nagorno-Karabakh, to which it gets access from Yerevan. ICRC's 1996 appeal indicated plans to restore a measure of self-sufficiency in several villages in the enclave.[75] ICRC has arranged a number of prisoner exchanges since the start of the conflict.

IFRC. The International Federation of Red Cross and Red Crescent Societies has a program of food assistance in seven IDP camps in southern Azerbaijan. It distributes assistance through its local partner, the Azerbaijan Red Crescent Society. It also distributes food parcels to some 150,000 vulnerable people in areas that are not considered part of the conflict zone. Donors to the IFRC programs are USAID/USDA, ECHO, governments, national societies, and NGOs.

IOM. Since the May 1996 CIS Conference, UNHCR and IOM have been working on a joint strategy in the Caucasus. IOM established a migration management program in Azerbaijan similar to programs operating in Georgia and Armenia.

NGOs. More than forty NGOs actively assist IDPs in Azerbaijan. Representatives of the NGOs meet monthly in Baku and on an ad hoc basis as specific questions arise. Far fewer NGOs operate in Azerbaijan than in Armenia. Most of the more recent arrivals have been created by private Azerbaijani groups. Many of the NGOs are shifting from emergency assistance to development-related activities, taking care to be sensitive to government concerns that their programs not imply permanency in the IDPs' status.

Section 907 of the Freedom Support Act severely hampers U.S. aid to nongovernmental organizations in Azerbaijan. It provides that "United States assistance under this or any other act . . . may not be provided to the Government of Azerbaijan until the President determines, and so reports to the Congress, that the Government of Azerbaijan is taking demonstrable steps to cease all blockades and other offensive uses of force against Armenia and Nagorno-Karabakh."[76] Section 907 was opposed by the executive branch of the government but adopted by Congress at the urging of Armenian groups in the United States. Section 907 puts constraints on humanitarian assistance, as a result of which many NGOs have decided not to set up programs in Azerbaijan.

As originally interpreted, Section 907 barred governmental and private agencies from aiding or working with institutions or facilities even indirectly controlled by the government of Azerbaijan. Revised guidelines have made it somewhat easier to carry out programs in compliance with Section 907; it is now possible to work with officials in the government of Azerbaijan under some circumstances. The fact that all of Azerbaijan's public health system is state controlled, however, has severely limited the ability of U.S.-government-funded NGOs to assist in this important sector. Under the terms of Section 907, the United Methodist Committee on Relief (UMCOR) was only able to assist a dispensary serving IDPs in a hotel that had been taken over by IDPs because the hotel was owned by a trade union and not the government.

Save the Children. Through March 1998, Save the Children/US, under an agreement with USAID, managed an umbrella grant that provided funding for several U.S. NGOs working in Azerbaijan. Among the subgrantees of Save were World Vision, the American Red Cross, Relief International, the International Rescue Committee, and Care. ISAR has a Save grant for general capacity-building with local NGOs. In April 1998, Mercy Corps International took over management of USAID's umbrella grant.

Conclusions and Recommendations

Despite the intractability of the Nagorno-Karabakh conflict in Azerbaijan and Armenia, there have been some accomplishments. First and foremost, Azerbaijan has managed to cope with the burden of more than 600,000 IDPs without violence and epidemics. The herculean task of housing 600,000 people was successfully accomplished, even though much of the housing created was substandard. Second, some reconstruction has taken place in the liberated part of Fizuli Province. These accomplishments could not have been brought about without generous financial input from abroad, from governments, international organizations, and NGOs. Reconstruction in Fizuli will offer a number of useful lessons when more people return. The task of de-mining these liberated areas and reconstructing heavily damaged infrastructure will drive home the lesson that even with the advent of peace, the IDPs will not be going home in a hurry.

The Azerbaijanis are frustrated that the international community has not been able to put sufficient pressure on Armenia to withdraw from occupied territories, in spite of four Security Council resolutions to that effect. Resentment feeds on the feeling that foreign hands were involved in Nagorno-Karabakh from the start.

Until the Nagorno-Karabakh dispute is settled, the vast majority of IDPs in Azerbaijan will not be able to return to their homes. Because of its large IDP population, Azerbaijan alone of the Caucasian republics has IDP camps. The psychological effects of long-term displacement both on the IDPs and on the communities in which they live are understandably negative. Faced with this immense IDP problem, the government of Azerbaijan has adopted an almost passive role. Other organizations have filled in to do what is immediately necessary.

Among the lessons provided by the crisis in Azerbaijan are the following:

- Assistance makes a difference. Without generous financial assistance from abroad, Azerbaijan could not have become host to 600,000 IDPs and given them basic support without violence and epidemics.
- Ethnic commonality between IDPs and their hosts is beneficial to everyone concerned. The basic needs of the IDPs have been met without mass social unrest. The Azerbaijanis see the IDPs as brothers and sisters and have received them with hospitality, even if it is wearing thin in the absence of progress toward resolution of the displacement. Everyone has benefited from this ethnic solidarity.
- The government of Azerbaijan needs to exert leadership. The government should contribute more dynamic administrative direction. This is even more necessary than assistance in kind and money. Although highly structured on paper in dealing with the displaced, the government exerts control without taking full responsibility for the challenges facing the country. In this situation, both a dependency mentality and resentment against foreign assistance have developed.

- Local participation and input are essential. As a corollary to the above, more input is needed in many localities, especially active planning and direction. Some local officials earn high marks for their involvement in IDP issues. However, in a number of areas international organizations do much of the work that one could reasonably expect local governments to do. Needs are being provided for, but mostly by the international community. This assistance is passively accepted by local governments. The result is growing resentment, even when the government does not have the resources to cope with problems on its own.
- The government of Azerbaijan needs to take more initiative in soliciting international organizations and NGOs for assistance with health and education. Both areas need more funding. WHO, UNESCO, and UNICEF all have received less than they need. These two areas are particularly important because they affect the long-term well-being of IDPs.
- A lingering attachment to a military solution will undermine the push for peace. Azerbaijan has the disadvantage of the prospect of an enormous increase in its oil revenues in the early part of the twenty-first century. That makes some Azerbaijanis think that they will be able to purchase weaponry to recapture Nagorno-Karabakh, taking the pressure off the need to reach a political settlement now. Moreover, the expectation of great wealth has led Azerbaijan to take a casual attitude toward the need for restructuring its society along equitable lines to ensure that the wealth will benefit everybody.
- The government of Azerbaijan needs to focus on step-by-step improvement of IDP conditions. Absent resolution of the Nagorno-Karabakh dispute, the best that can be hoped for is gradual improvement of IDP conditions. Although integrating them into the society is anathema to the government of Azerbaijan, a certain amount of integration has already taken place and will be to everyone's benefit. A number of programs point in this direction, including (1) income-generating activities, (2) programs under which UNHCR and other organizations are building houses, and (3) the return of IDPs to the liberated part of Fizuli Province.
- Azerbaijan (and Armenia) should redouble their search for a political settlement to the Nagorno-Karabakh dispute. This is the

ultimate solution for the problem of displacement in both countries.

Armenia

Displacement within Armenia is relatively small. Armenia has an IDP population of approximately 72,000, according to government of Armenia sources, and somewhat fewer according to UNHCR, which believes that many of the IDPs have returned to their homes. The figure of 72,000 was first used in 1992.[77] Sixty-five thousand is probably a closer estimate of the number of IDPs. The IDPs in Armenia were evacuated from villages adjacent to the border with Azerbaijan. They are from the mountainous area northwest of Kelbajar, the part of Azerbaijan to the west of Nagorno-Karabakh taken by Armenian forces in the spring of 1993. The border villages have been subjected to intermittent rocket and artillery barrages by Azerbaijani forces, in spite of the cease-fire.

The Armenian IDPs are a homogeneous lot. Virtually all of them are ethnic Armenian farmers and villagers from the frontier area. Some have returned home to cultivate their orchards and vineyards, while others have been unable to return to the frontier area because of the shelling.[78] The IDPs are for the most part lodged with friends and relatives in nearby towns and in public buildings. Many of the border villages are populated by day by Armenian farmers, who retreat to nearby towns and cities at night. The governor of Taush in northeastern Armenia, one of the districts where there has been some displacement, has talked with the mayor of Kazakh in nearby Azerbaijan in an effort to get on with life in the border area.

Not included among the IDPs are the populations that were exchanged between Armenia and Azerbaijan during the years 1988–90. The 300,000 or so Armenians who left Azerbaijan and the 250,000 or so Azerbaijanis who left Armenia are properly classified as refugees rather than as IDPs.[79] The Azerbaijanis who left Nagorno-Karabakh are counted among Azerbaijani IDPs. All the people interviewed in Armenia emphasized the burden of the refugees, though a large number of the refugees either did not come to Armenia or did not remain there.

While not considered IDPs by the government, there are still thousands of Armenians in refugee-like circumstances resulting from the December 1988 earthquake that devastated the town of Spitak and much of northwestern Armenia. The earthquake left thousands dead and many more homeless. Thirty percent of Armenia's industrial capacity and half of its schools were destroyed or heavily damaged, and it is no exaggeration to say that Armenia has still not recovered. The head of the government of Armenia's Migration Department called those made homeless by the earthquake "ecological migrants." He estimated their number at 500,000.[80] This figure seems high, but the fact remains that, distracted by the war with Azerbaijan and the blockade, and suffering economic downturn, Armenia has not been able to construct permanent dwellings and provide jobs for all the victims of the earthquake. In its factsheet prepared for the CIS Conference, Armenia did not list the ecological migrants.[81]

Background

Armenia is an Indo-European, Christian country surrounded by Turkey, Azerbaijan, Georgia, and Iran. Like many of the nationalities of the Caucasus, the Armenians have a long history. Armenians were mentioned in Persian and Greek sources as early as 500 B.C. Historic Armenia, the Armenian homeland, was located on the southern edge of the Caucasus in northeastern Anatolia, in an area where great empires contested for domination. Armenia enjoyed independence for only relatively short periods. Armenians have lived for centuries under foreign dominion, at different times as part of the empire of Alexander the Great and of the Roman, Byzantine, Persian, Ottoman, and Russian empires.

In the first half of the nineteenth century, Russia took Yerevan, Nagorno-Karabakh, Baku, and adjacent areas from Iran. Armenians were in a large majority in Yerevan and Nagorno-Karabakh and played an important role in the commercial development of Baku and Tbilisi. From then until after World War I, Armenians found themselves largely in the Ottoman and Russian Empires. Before the spread of modern nationalism to the Ottoman Empire, the Armenians there, like the Greeks and Jews, benefited from the rights of *millet*, communal self-government enjoyed by non-Muslims. With the spread of nationalism in the nineteenth and early twentieth centuries, relations between Armenians and Turks soured. During World War I hundreds of thousands of Armenians were killed or deported from eastern Anatolia. The death toll of this ethnic cleansing was enormous; estimates range from 600,000 to 1.1 million.[82] As many as half a million Armenians became refugees.[83]

The tragic events of this period and a sense of vulnerability and encircle-ment still drive Armenian policy, both domestic and international. Russia (and later the Soviet Union) came to be looked on as the protector of Armenia, a reflection of Russia's declared permanent interest in the Caucasus and of the absence of an articulated interest of countries out-side the area.

THE FIRST ARMENIAN REPUBLIC. With the collapse of the Ottoman and Russian Empires during and immediately after World War I, Armenia, together with Azerbaijan and Georgia, enjoyed a brief period of inde-pendence. The weak and inexperienced governments of the three repub-lics were beset by infighting between communists and nationalists and among each other. The Paris Peace Conference in 1919 supported the independence of Armenia, but support from abroad to protect Armenia against Russia and Turkey was not forthcoming. Meanwhile the Red Army, having established the Soviet Republic of Azerbaijan in Baku in 1920, continued its westward advance to Nakhichevan.

Foreign military intervention was a continuing threat to Russia, and the Soviets were eager to conclude peace with the Turks. For their part, fearful of ethnic cleansing by Turkish armies, the Armenians felt, in cold war language, that their choice was "better Red than dead." Soviet Ar-menia was proclaimed.[84] Ataturk and Lenin, both confronting foreign intervention, were eager to establish peace. The Soviet Union and Turkey concluded two treaties in 1921 in which the present border was drawn between Georgia, Armenia, and Azerbaijan (Nakhichevan) on one side and Turkey on the other. Ardahan and Kars Districts (which had been taken by Russia in the Russo-Turkish War of 1878), and Armenia's na-tional symbol, Mt. Ararat, have since been in Turkey.

ARMENIA AS PART OF THE USSR. The Armenian Soviet Socialist Re-public represented only one tenth of the area of historic Armenia and a reduction in size from the independent Armenia of 1918–20. It was the most homogeneous of the Soviet republics, with Armenians constituting over 85 percent of the population. After the bloody years of World War I, there was a sense of relief that the Armenian nation had somehow survived.

When Bolshevik forces initially moved into the area in 1920, it was decided that the three regions of Nakhichevan, Zangezur, and Karabakh would be part of Armenia. In 1921 this decision was reversed in part,

and Nakhichevan and Karabakh were made part of Azerbaijan.[85]
Throughout the Soviet period, both the Armenians of Armenia and those
of Nagorno-Karabakh pressed in vain for a change in that area's status.
A number of population changes occurred during the Soviet period. The
percentage of Armenians in the Nagorno-Karabakh Autonomous Oblast
declined from 94 percent when the oblast was established to 76 percent
in 1979. The percentage of Armenians in Nakhichevan declined steeply.
The Armenian population of Zangezur, the arm of Armenia that sepa-
rates Nakhichevan from the rest of Azerbaijan, increased while the Azeri
population of that area declined.[86]

When Gorbachev instituted his policies of perestroika and glasnost,
Armenian nationalists embraced them, linking them to their drive for
self-determination for Nagorno-Karabakh. With perestroika:

> The development of civil society and coherent, conscious nations within
> the USSR inexorably transformed Gorbachev's efforts at state-building into
> a liberating process of state-dismantling. The first mass resistance that
> could not be contained within the metamorphosing Soviet system, the crisis
> that precipitated the unraveling of central Soviet authority, came from an
> Armenian enclave in the republic of Azerbaijan.[87]

It was in Armenia, when faced with an early surge of nationalist
aspirations, that the contradictions of Gorbachev's policy of perestroika
first became apparent. The lessening of Communist Party control led to
the emergence of many political forces and a mushrooming of armed
militias. Armenia condemned the hard-liners' coup attempt against Gorbachev in August 1991, but many other Soviet republics were ambivalent.
In a referendum on September 21, 1991, Armenia overwhelmingly approved independence.

Crisis in Armenia

The Nagorno-Karabakh dispute is notable for both its longevity and
its seeming intractability. Both Armenia and Azerbaijan assert that Nagorno-Karabakh has been part of their country for at least 3,000 years.
The Armenians see Nagorno-Karabakh as "the last remaining part of
what they consider as the historical Armenia, where the Armenians' right
to self-determination should be preserved at all costs."[88] Under tsarist
rule the region became economically integrated with what is now independent Azerbaijan. Under the Soviets, Nagorno-Karabakh remained
part of Azerbaijan. As long as the communist grip on both Armenia and

Azerbaijan remained tight, tensions and counterclaims relating to Nagorno-Karabakh remained under control. The causes of the dispute have been attributed variously to religious animosity (Muslims versus Christians), ethnic enmity (Turks versus Armenians), Soviet mismanagement of the nationality issue, and manipulation by outside forces.[89]

ARMENIA FACES INDEPENDENCE. The two principal political groupings in Armenia as it faced independence were the Armenian National Movement (ANM) and the nationalist Dashnak Party. With the spread of glasnost, Armenia called for full independence from the Soviet Union, and the Karabakh Armenians for union with Armenia. ANM leader Levon Ter-Petrossian, president of Armenia until 1998, has emphasized the need for Armenia to have a civil relationship with Turkey in order to survive.

The second major political force in Armenia at independence was the nationalist Armenian Revolutionary Federation, known as the Dashnak Party from its Armenian name, Dashnaktsutiun. It originated in the nineteenth century and played an important role in the short-lived first Armenian republic (1918–20). It is influential both in Armenia and among Armenian communities of the diaspora. Its stance differs from that of the ANM primarily on matters of foreign policy. It insists on including the 1915 genocide and Armenian claims to part of Turkey as part of the negotiating process that would lead to normal relations with Turkey. Dashnaks also believe that Armenia should recognize an independent "Republic of Nagorno-Karabakh," with whose interest they insist there is no difference. Their position on Nagorno-Karabakh has made a possible compromise with Azerbaijan more difficult for the government of Armenia.

THE ROLE OF THE DIASPORA. Unlike the other two independent Caucasian republics, Armenia has a large diaspora, numbering some 1.8 million outside the former Soviet Union. The Dashnak Party is particularly strong in the diaspora.[90] The most influential communities of the Armenian diaspora are in the United States and France. "The willingness of Armenians abroad to support the newly independent republic gave it the possibility of rapid economic expansion to a level of prosperity no other ex-Soviet republic could have attained so soon. . . . Unfortunately, the existence of a large Armenian diaspora has been as harmful as it has been helpful."[91] After independence, many Armenians of the diaspora returned to take prominent positions in Yerevan "as if they had a greater right to them than Armenians who had endured life under Soviet communism. They intensified the militarization of the Karabakh campaign."[92] The Armenians of the diaspora have encouraged territorial demands against Turkey and left Armenia with nowhere to turn for international support but to Russia.

ECONOMIC DISASTER. The economic blockade that has been part of the Armenian-Azerbaijani confrontation has caused terrible hardship in both countries. Azerbaijan was Armenia's principal source of oil before the war, as well as the transit point for its natural gas. Exceptionally cold winters from 1992 to 1995 left people freezing. Chaos in Georgia in 1992–94 added to Armenia's energy problems by disrupting the flow of gas through a pipeline in Georgia. Inflation, unemployment, and low salaries have depleted the savings and purchasing power of people in Armenia's cities, particularly Yerevan.

A UNDP report published in May 1996 states that Armenian society has become stratified into a rich elite and "a vast army of poor and deprived."[93] The latter include Armenia's well-educated but now poverty-stricken professionals and intellectuals. The number of people registered as unemployed, about 4 percent, clearly represents only a fraction of the true number. Foreign assistance is all that has kept the people from starvation, and it has brought with it a dependency mentality.

The transition from the Soviet command economy to a market economy would have been extremely difficult even without the blockade. The Armenian economy recorded a cumulative decline in measured output of 75 percent from 1990 to 1993. Land privatization and the cease-fire have led to modest sectoral growth since then. However, factories throughout the country have lost their markets in far-away parts of the former Soviet Union and have had to close because of lack of fuel and investment. When Ter-Petrossian promised during his 1996 campaign that the next five years would be "incomparably better than the last five," a newspaper pointed out that of the fifty-nine industrial enterprises in the region, half were closed or running at less than 10 percent of capacity, leaving thousands unemployed.[94]

EMIGRATION. Faced with the downward-spiraling economy and long heatless winters, hundreds of thousands of Armenians have left Armenia. Many of those with draft-age sons have either left or sent their sons away.

Some have gone to Moscow and St. Petersburg, others to the nearby Stavropol and Krasnodar Oblasts, to the north of the Caucasus in the Russian Federation. Others have gone to the United States and Europe. Armenia has lost at least 700,000 citizens through emigration since independence, more than 20 percent of its population. The radical Armenian nationalists have been slow to recognize that "Armenians will not endlessly endure policies that put abstract nationalistic aspirations above the welfare of the population."[95]

Nagorno-Karabakh and Displacement

The more immediate causes of the Nagorno-Karabakh conflict have been linked with several levels of power struggle: power struggle in Moscow, power struggle within Azerbaijan and Armenia, and regional and international struggles for influence in the Caucasus.[96] In Armenia the domination of Nagorno-Karabakh's political establishment by the Dashnaks has limited the influence of those like Ter-Petrossian who would have been more inclined to compromise on the Karabakh issue. In addition, negotiations remain the exclusive focus of the OSCE, excluding the UN. Russia has wanted to be the sole peacekeeper and mediator. All these factors have worked against finding a compromise solution to the conflict. Resolution of the Nagorno-Karabakh conflict "is likely to remain hostage to the vagaries of Transcaucasian regional politics, international politics, and, above all, Russian objectives."[97]

There are many similarities among Armenia, Georgia, and Azerbaijan in the way in which displacement has run its course. As they did in the early years of Georgia's displacement, armed groups played an important role in the early confrontation with Azerbaijan as Armenia drifted into war. These included Armenian army soldiers, Russian soldiers who participated in the fighting (some directly, some by selling their weapons), soldiers and militias from Nagorno-Karabakh, and Armenians from the diaspora. In the late 1980s, Armenian political and military groups, as in Georgia, struggled with the communist establishment. The communists totally underestimated the strength of Armenian feeling about Nagorno-Karabakh and hoped the issue would go away, even as arms and fighting proliferated.

The relatively small number of IDPs in Armenia cannot be considered separately from the much larger number in Azerbaijan. Resolution of the difficulties of Armenian IDPs depends on an overall political solution. Nagorno-Karabakh is an actor in the struggle with Azerbaijan and was recognized as a party to the dispute in the May 1994 cease-fire. Yet few believe the somewhat disingenuous claims that the army of Nagorno-Karabakh is "independent" and not subject to Yerevan's will. Although Yerevan cannot dictate to Stepanakert on all points, especially on matters relating to the ultimate status of Nagorno-Karabakh, there are some areas where Yerevan can put pressure on Stepanakert, if it will.

FOREIGN ACTORS IN ARMENIAN DISPLACEMENT.

Russia. As elsewhere in the Caucasus, the role of Russia is key to understanding internal displacement in Armenia. The territorial gerry-mandering of the Caucasus has been the Soviet Union's most enduring and damaging legacy. Without Russian support, the conflict cannot be resolved. Russia will remain the most important foreign actor in Armenia's foreign relations. Armenia's political and strategic options are limited by its small size and landlocked position, its war with Azerbaijan, and its hostile relationship with Turkey. At this writing, Russia keeps more than 10,000 troops and border guards on Armenian soil and helps guard its borders, especially those with Turkey and Iran.[98] Russia has shown in many ways that it has an interest in maintaining tensions between Turkey and Armenia.[99] Russia does not seem to be in a hurry to find a solution to Nagorno-Karabakh, which would reduce its leverage in the Caucasus. As the former imperial power, Russia needs to define its role, which may be difficult given continuing political uncertainties in Moscow.

Turkey. Both Turkey and Armenia need to adapt to realities and seek mutually advantageous ways to cooperate. Turkey recognized Armenia's independence in 1991, but the massacre of Azeri civilians at Khojali and the push of Armenian forces well beyond the boundaries of Nagorno-Karabakh derailed attempts to normalize relations between the countries. Rapprochement has proven elusive even though leaders of the ANM Party wanted to put Turkish-Armenian relations on a new footing.

Questions arise from time to time about the Turkish-Armenian border, although Armenia insists that in joining CSCE it recognized Turkey's borders. As Turkish foreign policy has sought close relations with Georgia, Ukraine, Azerbaijan, and the countries of Central Asia, it has aroused past fears in Yerevan of an alliance against Armenia. Russia has been concerned about Turkish policy not only in the Commonwealth of Independent States but also in Chechnya and Tatarstan, which are parts of the Russian Federation. These concerns have led Russia and Armenia to gravitate toward each other. If the Turkish government were to lift the ban on commerce transiting Turkey for Armenia, all Armenians, including the IDPs, refugees, and other vulnerable groups would benefit immediately.

Iran. Iran's hostility to the West and its meddling in religious affairs keep Caucasians on their guard.[100] Russia has also discouraged closeness between Yerevan and Tehran because it wants to remain the arbiter of regional politics. There is substantial and increasing trade between Armenia and Iran, and a permanent bridge over the Aras River at Meghri has been constructed between the two countries. The effects of this trade on the economy and on the well-being of vulnerable elements of Armenian society may increase.

Georgia. Georgia has sizable Armenian and Azerbaijani minorities, both of which could be a source of difficulty between it and Armenia. The area in southern Georgia where much of its Armenian population lives, Akhalkalaki and Ninotsminda, was disputed between the two countries during their brief first republics (1918–20/21). Georgia's Azerbaijani population lives in its eastern Marneuli region, and Georgian efforts to accommodate Azerbaijan so it will not lay claim to this territory may be viewed with hostility by Armenia. Different attitudes toward Russia as well as different views of relations with Turkey could also cause friction between Armenia and Georgia.

Who Is Doing What and with What Degree of Effectiveness?

Because Armenia's IDPs constitute only a fraction of the needy in the country, they have received relatively little attention. "We have a refugee program but no program for IDPs; the latter is a big need," said an Armenian government official.[101] Available assistance goes to all categories of vulnerable people, including IDPs, rather than being specifically earmarked for a particular group.

The IDPs are located in northeastern Armenia at some distance from most of the major cities and towns. Most are in rural areas that receive food through WFP distributions. Basic shelter and health needs are being met by various government, international organization, and NGO programs. IDP children generally attend school with nondisplaced populations in the areas where they live. It appears that the basic needs of Armenia's IDPs are being met, and they are no worse off than most of the permanent population of those areas.

THE GOVERNMENT OF ARMENIA. Armenia established the State Department for Refugees on November 5, 1991, shortly after gaining independence but nearly three years after refugees had started arriving in
large numbers from Azerbaijan. The Department of Refugees had basic
responsibility for registration of refugees and IDPs and cooperated with
all governmental and nongovernmental organizations dealing with refugees.[102] It prepared identity cards for refugees and IDPs, including a
special card for people from Nagorno-Karabakh. In September 1995 the
Department for Refugees was combined with other offices and integrated
into the Ministry of Social Security, Labor, Migration, and Refugee
Issues.

The ministry works closely with many international organizations,
particularly UNHCR, in assisting all categories of vulnerable people.
Two other departments that frequently deal with IDPs (as well as refugees
and the needy) are the Ministry of Economics and the office of the
Coordinator of Humanitarian Aid and Development. Assistance for refugees and IDPs is implemented by city and regional councils. In its
statement for the CIS Conference, the government noted: "Armenia will
elaborate, adopt and implement legislation on migration, repatriation,
refugees, internally displaced persons, entry and exit and free movement
within the national territory. . . . Armenia will continue its cooperation
with the UN in order to provide humanitarian assistance to displaced
persons."[103]

THE INTERNATIONAL COMMUNITY. Faced with refugees, war, an economic blockade, loss of markets. and massive outmigration, Armenia
needed immediate international assistance when it regained its independence in 1991. Fortunately, large-scale international assistance was available. International organizations and NGOs are present in large numbers
in Armenia. Save the Children/US was the umbrella organization for
many USAID-funded NGO programs until April 1998, when it was replaced by Mercy Corps International. UNHCR, DHA, WFP, and several
other international organizations have programs that assist several categories of needy people, including IDPs. By 1996 most of the organizations
furnishing assistance to several categories of Armenians, recognizing that
there was no longer an emergency, began providing assistance to the
vulnerable and elderly and developing income generation and capital
formation projects.

The following are examples of organizations providing programs of assistance to IDPs and other needy groups in Armenia.

UNHCR. In Armenia, as elsewhere in the Caucasus, UNHCR's broad assistance strategy covers refugees, IDPs, and vulnerable groups. UNHCR started its aid programs in Armenia in 1992 with emergency assistance—kerosene, clothes, and food. Because of their numbers, refugees have been the largest group to receive UNHCR aid. The mid-1990s saw a switch from aid to income-generating activity.

UNHCR has participated in all of the United Nations Department of Humanitarian Affairs Consolidated Inter-Agency Appeals for the Caucasus. These appeals have been issued annually since 1992 and target all vulnerable groups. The largest funding requirements in the Inter-Agency Appeal are for WFP, UNHCR, UNICEF, and WHO. WFP's Caucasus Logistics Advisory Unit headquartered in Tbilisi coordinates relief shipments and regional logistics and has played a key role in keeping the assistance pipeline to Armenia from Georgia open.

ICRC. The ICRC participates in Minsk Group discussions on Nagorno-Karabakh when humanitarian questions are on the agenda.[104] In 1996 an ICRC program for vulnerable groups affected by the conflict gave food parcels and seed kits to 9,000 families living in the northeastern border districts of Armenia, where most of Armenia's IDPs are concentrated.

IFRC. The International Federation of Red Cross and Red Crescent Societies opened its delegation in Armenia after the December 1988 earthquake. It is a key distributor of food and medical aid, working with a broad range of beneficiaries, among them families with five or more children, single pensioners, preschool children, and the elderly. The IFRC carries out its programs in collaboration with a number of Red Cross Societies, including the Armenian Red Cross Society, which became a member of the federation in 1995.

NGOs. More than thirty-five expatriate NGOs are currently working in Armenia. They do not single out IDPs as such, but their programs are of direct assistance to them and to other needy groups. The Armenian Assembly of America has encouraged the establishment of dozens of Armenian NGOs that deal with all aspects of assistance there.[105]

Save the Children/US. Encouraging the development of a legislative and regulatory environment that would enable NGOs to operate more effectively was one of Save the Children's principal goals in Armenia during its period as the umbrella organization for USAID (1993–98), similar to its role in Azerbaijan and Georgia. Save the Children's primary function was managing NGO grants for USAID. It mobilized and supported U.S. NGOs to meet the urgent needs of the most vulnerable populations (including IDPs) and to address longer-term rehabilitation and development needs. Save the Children also sought to develop a broad base of self-sufficient Armenian NGOs.

Armenian Assembly of America. The Yerevan office of the Armenian Assembly of America (AAA) facilitates contact between the government of Armenia and Western governments. Through its NGO centers in Yerevan and Gyumri, the AAA has trained more than a hundred local NGOs, many of which have been awarded grants from USAID, UNHCR, and other organizations for their projects.

Conclusions and Recommendations

Displacement in Armenia differs in important ways from displacement in Azerbaijan and Georgia. The number of IDPs is much smaller, they are less spread out than in the other two republics, and they represent a smaller percentage of vulnerable populations. Nevertheless, until the conflict is resolved, shelling in the border area is likely to continue and most of Armenia's internally displaced will be unable to return to their homes. Armenia's special challenge is to look for imaginative ways to resolve the conflict with Azerbaijan. This will require Russian support. As the conflicts in Chechnya and Georgia move toward resolution, precedents may be found for encouraging at least partial settlement of the Nagorno-Karabakh dispute.

Among the lessons Armenia provides for dealing with the problems of displacement are the following:

- The religious nature of the conflict makes it doubly intractable. Nagorno-Karabakh has assumed a quasi-religious significance for many Armenians. They identify the Azerbaijanis with the Turks of the Ottoman Empire and see Nagorno-Karabakh as the last piece of historical Armenia from which they have been unjustly driven over the centuries. Religion has added a degree of intensity to what would otherwise be "merely" an ethnic conflict. Recognizing this is a first step toward resolution of the conflict, which will also impose major political risks for all involved.

- Favorable conditions may be undermined by hostilities. Armenia's homogeneity and the relatively small number of IDPs have not simplified the task of finding a political solution to the dispute with Azerbaijan. The resources channeled into Armenia by the diaspora have tended to solidify the military situation rather than contribute to dialogue and conflict resolution. The persisting hostilities with Azerbaijan color every aspect of Armenia's economic and political situation, undermining conditions that might be favorable to peace.

- Protection and assistance alone are not enough. Protection and assistance for IDPs and other vulnerable groups are not a substitute for determined action to resolve disputes politically. Ambivalence toward a political settlement in Armenia and in Nagorno-Karabakh has grown with the realization that peace will mean giving up a large swath of Azerbaijani territory occupied by Armenian forces. Armenia is faced with the dilemma of land for peace, with its appetite for holding on to conquests increasing with each passing year.

- Every effort should be made to find at least a partial resolution of the Nagorno-Karabakh dispute. This could provide the climate in which Turkey would open its borders with Armenia. When this does occur, it will have an immediate positive effect on the political climate as well as the economy. This, in turn, will strengthen the transition from aid to sustainable development that is already evident in many assistance programs in Armenia.

- For the United States to maintain credibility with both sides of the Nagorno-Karabakh conflict, it should repeal Section 907. Doing so would remove the appearance of taking one side in the dispute and would enable the United States to try to play an active role in the Minsk peace process, currently the most promising venue for resolution of this conflict.

- Armenia (and Azerbaijan) should redouble their search for a political settlement to the Nagorno-Karabakh dispute. This is the ultimate solution for the problem of displacement in both countries.

Georgia

The dividing lines of the wars in South Ossetia and in Abkhazia that gave rise to displacement in Georgia have been almost exclusively ethnic. Large numbers of Georgians (as an ethnic group, not as citizens of

Georgia) were displaced from South Ossetia and Abkhazia, as were members of virtually all the area's non-Abkhaz populations. Most of the Georgians, the largest group to flee Abkhazia, went to Tbilisi and other parts of Georgia. Many Russians, Armenians, and Greeks went to nearby areas in the Krasnodar and Stavropol Districts (*krais*) in southern Russia. Many of the Greeks emigrated to Greece and many of the Jews to Israel. It is unlikely that all the Abkhaz have remained, although no figures are available. The displaced from South Ossetia included both Georgians and Ossetians. Most of the Georgian displaced went to Tbilisi. Those Ossetians who did not remain in South Ossetia or elsewhere in Georgia went to North Ossetia. Ossetians living elsewhere in Georgia became displaced as well. Nearly 350,000 people were displaced in the two conflicts in Georgia, more than a quarter million from the fighting in Abkhazia in 1992–93 and the rest from the war in South Ossetia in 1991–92. The number of IDPs in Georgia at this writing is probably around 275,000.

In the war in Abkhazia, both the Georgian authorities and the Abkhaz forcibly displaced people on the basis of their ethnicity. Both sides terrorized civilians to force them out of areas of strategic importance. Human Rights Watch/Helsinki has reported that most of the displaced Abkhaz have been able to return (not infrequently to set up house in formerly Georgian homes), while most of the ethnic Georgians have been "cleansed" from Abkhazia.[106] More than 25,000 IDPs, virtually all ethnic Georgians, have unofficially returned to the Gali District of Abkhazia along the Inguri River, in spite of security hazards in the area. The Inguri River, which forms the eastern border of Abkhazia, is the center of a twenty-four-kilometer security zone. The area is infested with land mines. In contrast to unofficial repatriation, only 311 people officially returned to Abkhazia under the abortive Quadripartite Plan in 1994.[107] The ICRC reports that more than 250,000 who fled Abkhazia in September 1993 after the capture of the capital, Sukhumi (referred to as Sukhum by Abkhaz), have still not returned.[108]

As a result of the war in South Ossetia, approximately 100,000 Ossetians in South Ossetia and other parts of Georgia were forced out of their homes. Perhaps 40,000 of the Ossetians who lived all over Georgia fled to neighboring North Ossetia in the Russian Federation, where some of them played a significant role in further ethnic fighting, this time between Ossetians and Ingush in North Ossetia's Prigorodnyi region. Some 23,000

Georgians fled South Ossetia.[109] Unofficially, the displaced from South Ossetia are gradually returning home.

Unlike Azerbaijan and many other countries with large IDP populations, Georgia has no camps for IDPs. At the beginning of displacement, the bulk of the IDPs from Abkhazia stayed in regions of western Georgia (Mingrelia, Kutaisi, and Tskhaltubo), not far from the Inguri River border with Abkhazia. They were often lodged with relatives and friends. They were redistributed to collective centers (hotels, hostels, sanatoriums, hospitals, schools, and other public buildings) over the course of a year or more, during which many moved to Tbilisi. IDPs are usually grouped in such centers according to their place of origin, which has the advantage of facilitating day-to-day existence but further isolates them from the local populations in the communities where they have settled.[110]

In April 1995 the Norwegian Refugee Council (NRC) published a survey taken among IDPs from Abkhazia.[111] Most of the survey respondents saw their principal difficulties as economic. Their desire to support themselves is a measure both of being displaced and of the economic situation facing all Georgians. Nearly 53 percent of the IDPs interviewed in the NRC survey lived in collective centers; 38 percent lived in private homes with host families. Two large hotels in Tbilisi, the Ajaria and the Iberia, which used to house foreign tourists, are now entirely occupied by IDPs, whose laundry on the balconies has become a city landmark. Thousands of IDPs are living with relatives in cities in Georgia, particularly Tbilisi, Kutaisi, and Zugdidi. The author of the NRC survey emphasized the need for a centralized database in order to generate a comprehensive profile of all IDPs.[112]

Background

Georgia, like the two other independent Transcaucasian republics, has been confronted with severe challenges since independence. Together they have almost overwhelmed the newly independent state. Since 1991, Georgia has had to define its national identity, find an ideological alternative to communism on which to base national life, undertake bureaucratic reform, and build a viable economy.

The Georgians, an ancient people living in the western part of Transcaucasia, have lived through periods of independence from and attachment to adjacent empires (the Byzantine, Ottoman, Iranian, and Russian). Georgia was incorporated into the Russian Empire in the early nineteenth century. It enjoyed a brief period of independence from 1918 to 1922. This first Georgian Republic was recognized de facto if not de jure by a number of countries and the League of Nations. It fended off threats from pro-tsarist White Russian forces, rebellious local minorities, and Armenian incursions before falling to the Red Army.

After Georgia was incorporated into the Soviet Union, the Soviets instituted their own program of limited self-determination for parts of Georgia by giving special status to three areas within the country. Thirty percent of the population spoke languages other than Georgian as their mother tongue, including Abkhaz, Armenian, Greek, Ossetian, and Russian. The Abkhaz, a small minority population in northwestern Georgia, were given a large Autonomous Republic in 1931, as were the predominantly Muslim (though culturally and ethnically Georgian) people of Ajaria in southwestern Georgia. The Ossetian minority was given the South Ossetian Autonomous Oblast. The Caucasian minorities, typified by the Ossetians and the Abkhazians, have historically been subject to demographic manipulation by Russia and Georgia, two of the region's "imperial powers."[113]

Soviet nationality policies played one ethnic group against another within gerrymandered borders. When Gorbachev's policy of perestroika led to the loosening of Moscow's grip in the late 1980s, tensions rose in Georgia, as in several other parts of the Soviet Union. Regionalism had always been strong in Georgia. With relaxation of some of the tight controls from the center, there was an explosion of nationalism. Two ethnic groups in particular, the Abkhaz and the Ossetians, felt alienated by the dominant Georgians and held a series of nationalist demonstrations in late 1988. The Abkhazian Popular Front called on Moscow to recognize Abkhazia as a full Union Republic. This demand in turn led to demonstrations by Georgians, who were against Abkhazian independence. The demonstrations quickly evolved from calls for rejecting Abkhazian independence to calls for Georgian independence.

On April 9, 1989, Moscow dispatched military forces to Tbilisi to counter demonstrations that had been going on for several days. This intervention resulted in substantial death and destruction in central Tbilisi. It also marked the beginning of the end of communism in Georgia as the disparate political groups united around one cause—independence. Although the incumbent Communist Party chief was dismissed, the Communist Party's subsequent unwillingness to share power prevented the creation of a broad-based reform coalition and a gradual approach to independence.

In 1989–90, Georgia adopted a new electoral law that led to parliamentary elections in October 1990. The supporters of nationalist Zviad Gamsakhurdia won the election handily, earning 155 seats in a 250-member Parliament. The Communist Party did best in areas where ethnic minorities were concerned about the rise of Georgian nationalism. Gamsakhurdia was elected chairman of the Supreme Soviet in November. A referendum was held on the issue of independence in March 1991, with an overwhelming majority voting in favor. The Parliament declared Georgia's independence on April 9, 1991. On May 26, 1991, Gamsakhurdia won Georgia's first presidential election.

There is no doubt that Gamsakhurdia was an undemocratic, even dictatorial president. During the period leading up to and after the victory of his coalition, military forces in Georgia fragmented and private armed groups emerged as a major force. At the time of the abortive coup against Gorbachev in August 1991, Gamsakhurdia had issued an appeal to all Georgians asking them to remain calm. The appeal went unheeded. The fractured nature of Georgian society and fierce personal rivalries between Gamsakhurdia and his political opponents led to fighting between the factions. After several weeks of clashes between forces loyal to him and the opposition, Gamsakhurdia fled Tbilisi in January 1992, going first to Armenia, then to Chechnya, and finally returning to western Georgia, where he died under somewhat murky circumstances in late 1993.

After Gamsakhurdia's departure, two key military personalities, Dzhaba Ioseliani, head of the Mkhedrioni militia, and Tengiz Kitovani, head of the splinter section of the National Guard, disbanded the Parliament and established a Military Council to prepare for early parliamentary elections. They invited Eduard Shevardnadze (foreign minister of the USSR under Gorbachev and former Georgian Communist Party boss) to return and head a government of national reconciliation. Shevardnadze's return in March 1992 unfortunately did not signal the end to Georgia's troubles.

Chaos enveloped Georgia during the presidency of Gamsakhurdia and continued well into Shevardnadze's administration. All sorts of groups became active, including armed bands, Georgian army soldiers, Russian soldiers who took part in the fighting (either directly or by selling their weapons), free-lance gangsters, and organized militia such as the Mkhedrioni. Some were nationalists, and some were separatists. Ioseliani and

Kitovani, two of the biggest warlords, had criminal records. Smaller warlords sprang up everywhere. A nearly successful attempt on the life of Shevardnadze in August 1995 led him to imprison the notorious Mkhedrioni leader, Ioseliani. Since then the country has experienced improved political and economic stability. Shevardnadze survived another attempt on his life in February 1998.

As nationalism grew under perestroika and in the first heady months of independence, Gamsakhurdia set the tune with his slogan "Georgia for the Georgians." His heavy-handed policy of intense Georgian nationalism aggravated the situation and gave domestic and foreign enemies leverage. Not surprisingly, the rebirth of Georgian nationalism led to a similar renaissance of nationalistic feelings and fear of the Georgians among the non-Georgian population. "Interethnic tensions closely interacted with other elements in Georgian politics, notably power struggles among its key political figures and external meddling, in a pattern that evolved into a vicious circle of violence."[114] Gamsakhurdia's policy also worried the 400,000-strong Armenian minority, the majority of whom live in the Akhalkalaki and Ninotsminda Districts near the frontier with Armenia. Finally, his provocative anti-Russian attitude, combined with paranoia about Russian plots against him and Georgia, became self-fulfilling.

War in South Ossetia

The first sign of Ossetian assertiveness began in April 1988, after the publication of a letter from the leader of the Ossetian Popular Front in an Abkhaz paper supporting Ossetian independence. In 1990, Gamsakhurdia had been quoted as stating, "The Ossetians are a wild, uneducated people who must be made to fear the Georgians, just as the Abkhazians now fear us."[115] After he was elected president of Georgia, Gamsakhurdia dissolved the Autonomous Oblast of South Ossetia, which he viewed as a Soviet legacy that threatened Georgia's territorial integrity. The Ossetians, like other groups considered "double minorities" in the USSR, no longer able to count on Moscow, challenged their diminished status. Gamsakhurdia's extremism made moderate Abkhaz and Ossetians align with their own extremists. He has been credited by a number of people with starting the South Ossetian war.

The Ossetian Popular Front first demanded that it be united with North Ossetia (part of the Russian Federation), then that it become an

Autonomous Republic (on the same footing as Abkhazia). Gamsakhur-dia's Parliament reacted by abolishing South Ossetia's autonomous oblast status in late 1990. South Ossetia was renamed the Tskhinvali Region after its capital. Shortly thereafter South Ossetia declared itself a Union Republic within the USSR, an action tantamount to a declaration of independence from Georgia.

Although violent incidents had occurred as early as November 1989, the war in South Ossetia is considered to have begun in January 1991, when street fighting broke out in Tskhinvali. Military operations aided by North Ossetia (part of the Russian Federation) continued until June 1992. In July 1992 a cease-fire was signed and a mixed CIS peacekeeping force of Russians, Ossetians, and Georgians was deployed in the area. As a result of the war, approximately 100,000 Ossetians in South Ossetia and other parts of Georgia were forced out of their homes. Many of the Ossetians who lived all over Georgia fled to neighboring North Ossetia, where some of them played a significant role in the ethnic fighting be-tween Ossetians and Ingush in North Ossetia's Prigorodnyi region. Some 23,000 Georgians fled South Ossetia.[116] An estimated hundred villages were destroyed in South Ossetia, although a substantial number of Geor-gian villages remained intact in the area. Between 1988 and 1992 the North Ossetian–Georgian border was virtually uncontrolled. The result-ant free passage of weapons, fighters, and ammunition contributed im-portantly to continued conflict.

According to UNHCR, at the end of 1995 there were 30,000 IDPs from South Ossetia in Georgia (largely in the region of Gori, south of Tskhinvali), and 37,000 South Ossetians in North Ossetia.[117] Human Rights Watch/Helsinki estimated in 1996 that approximately 20,000 peo-ple, for the most part Georgian, were unable to return to their homes in South Ossetia for fear of reprisals.[118] Although fighting came to a halt, the area has since been plagued by criminal gangs and the economy has remained sluggish. In 1997–98 a limited amount of unofficial repatriation took place, as some ethnic Ossetians returned to their homes elsewhere in Georgia (e.g., Borjomi), and many ethnic Georgians returned to villages around the South Ossetian capital, Tskhinvali.

The South Ossetia conflict, according to Professor George Khutsish-vili, head of the International Center on Conflict and Negotiation in Tbilisi, is more easily resolved than the Abkhaz conflict because South Ossetia is not fundamentally opposed to remaining part of Georgia.[119] The OSCE has taken a leadership role in conflict resolution in South

Ossetia, which has helped stabilize the situation on the ground and led to an agreement to reduce the number of peacekeepers there.

Shevardnadze, meanwhile, returned to Georgia in March 1992 and became president of the State Council, created after the dissolution of the Military Council. It was hoped that he would be able to bring an end to the ethnic conflicts in Georgia, but his return was not enough to save Georgia from what one expert in the area has termed "an accelerated descent into chaos."[120] He did oversee the arrival in South Ossetia of a Russian peacekeeping force in mid-1992 that ended the fighting there, but war broke out in Abkhazia in August 1992.

War in Abkhazia

In 1922, the year the Soviets secured control over Georgia, Abkhazia became a Union Republic and a signatory to the formation of the USSR. Abkhazia drew up its own constitution in 1925, and in 1931 was incorporated into the Transcaucasian Federation as a Soviet Socialist Republic, the same status enjoyed by Georgia. When the federation was dissolved in 1936, under Stalin's direction Abkhazia became an Autonomous Soviet Socialist Republic within Georgia rather than resuming its status as a Union Republic, which would have kept it on an equal juridical footing with Georgia. Stalin pushed the border of Abkhazia southeast to include a section of the traditional Georgian region of Mingrelia, thereby increasing the percentage of ethnic Georgians living in the new Abkhaz Autonomous Soviet Socialist Republic. Large numbers of non-Abkhaz migrated to Abkhazia under Stalin, making the Abkhaz a minority in their own land. By 1989 only 17 percent of the population was Abkhaz. Georgians constituted the largest ethnic group, with 46 percent of the population.[121]

Following an outburst of protest and anti-Georgian activities in Abkhazia in 1978 (Georgians say it was directed from Moscow), Moscow directed that a university be established in Sukhumi, capital of Abkhazia, an action the Georgians resented.[122] By the time of perestroika, the Georgians and the Abkhaz were already deeply suspicious of each other. In 1990–91, Sukhumi was declared the capital of the North Caucasian Federation, which included all of the North Caucasian Autonomous Republics (then Autonomous Soviet Socialist Republics) and autonomous oblasts from Adygea on the west to Dagestan on the east, in the Russian Federation. Georgia saw this as a further threat to its territorial integrity.

In July 1992 the Abkhaz, with the support of the other non-Georgian peoples of Abkhazia, together constituting 54 percent of the population, declared the reinstatement of the 1925 constitution. This became the casus belli. Hostilities lasted from August 1992 through 1993. Many Georgians thought that because Shevardnadze had supported Yeltsin, a deal had been struck that would end Russian support of separatism in Georgia. They were disappointed. Russia appeared to be determined to bring Georgia to its knees. The war was most intense in the capital, Sukhumi, and in and around Tkvarcheli in eastern Abkhazia. Fighting continued for sixteen bloody months. The population declined dramatically. Some 350,000 of Abkhazia's 540,000 inhabitants fled the region between August 1992 and late 1993.[123] Several thousand were killed.

War in Abkhazia began on August 14, 1992, when Shevardnadze sent in troops. It pitted the central government of Georgia, in the form of the National Guard, paramilitary groups, and volunteers, against Abkhaz irregulars, volunteers, and mercenaries from the North Caucasus (including some Chechens, Circassians, and Ossetians) and, of key importance, Russian military. A cease-fire negotiated in Moscow in July 1993 called for withdrawal of Georgian troops from Sukhumi and "a restitution of the legitimate government."[124] The cease-fire did not last. "Abkhaz separatists, supplied and encouraged by conservative Russian military leaders and neocommunist imperialists, persisted in their efforts to separate this rich and attractive region from Georgia."[125] Sukhumi fell to the Abkhaz on September 3, 1993, and by the end of September 1993 the last government troops were forced out of Abkhazia. The region was officially declared "liberated" from Georgia.

The war resulted in a military victory by the Abkhaz and was seen as a defeat for the Georgians. In trying to negotiate with the Abkhaz, Shevardnadze was frustrated by the military actions of Georgian warlords who ignored most directives from Tbilisi. Taking advantage of Tbilisi's defeat in Abkhazia, militias under the recently returned Gamsakhurdia began taking towns in western Georgia. With no forces to prevent them from eventually marching on Tbilisi, Shevardnadze agreed to Moscow's insistence that Georgia join the CIS, a move he had opposed. In exchange, the Russians made a show of military force in western Georgia, scaring off the militias of Gamsakhurdia, who died in December 1993.

The UN Security Council called for deployment of military observers in Abkhazia after the establishment of a cease-fire.[126] Later the Security Council established a UN Observer Mission in Georgia (UNOMIG) comprising eighty-eight military observers, plus support staff.[127] Later resolutions have changed UNOMIG's mandate and expanded the number of observers to 136.[128] The Security Council was unwilling to grant the CIS (i.e., Russia) a peacekeeping mandate given Russia's active participation in the conflict, but many see the deployment of observers as international approval of Russian actions anyway. Since June 1994, approximately 3,000 Russian peacekeeping troops, nominally under CIS auspices, have monitored the cease-fire. At this writing, no major hostilities have broken out since the cease-fire between Georgia and Abkhazia became effective in late 1993, replacing the September 1993 cease-fire that did not last. However, incursions by Georgian partisans into Abkhaz territory have claimed the lives of civilians and Russian peacekeepers alike. Both sides have taken hostages. The cease-fire as well as the buffer zone along the Inguri River are monitored by CIS peacekeeping forces under the supervision of UNOMIG.

"Abkhazia has always been a problem for Georgia," said one of the leading Georgian intellectuals looking for a peaceful way out of the conflict.[129] Because the Georgians acknowledge the existence of Abkhazia in history and the Abkhaz language and people, it should have been less difficult for them to accept special status for Abkhazia than for Ossetia. However, Abkhazia's strategic position made it difficult for them to contemplate any loosening of control over the area. Two comments are illustrative of the current Georgian/Abkhaz impasse. One interviewee said former Georgian minister of defense Karkarashvili had suggested genocide as a way of "solving" the Abkhaz problem, saying it would be worth sacrificing 100,000 Georgians to kill 100,000 Abkhazians and eradicate their culture.[130] Another maintained that the Abkhaz "will fight for anything" and have a strong interest in staying under Russian domination. With such strongly held opinions, it is not surprising that Abkhaz-Georgian negotiations are deadlocked over the issues of the status of Abkhazia and IDP return. However, since the visit of Abkhaz president Vadislav Ardzinba to Tbilisi in August 1997, there have been increasing bilateral contacts dealing with reconstruction and other issues, with the facilitation of Russia and the UN.

In Abkhazia, Russian forces effectively sided with the separatists and transformed the conflict into a protracted war. The war in Chechnya has underlined Russia's determination to keep the Russian Federation together, and it is possible that this will make Russia more likely to support the unity of Georgia.

Repatriation: The 1994 Quadripartite Agreement

On April 4, 1994, in Moscow, Georgia, Abkhazia, Russia, and UNHCR signed an agreement for peace and repatriation in Abkhazia, known as the Quadripartite Agreement.[131] The Quadripartite Agreement stated that repatriation of the IDPs would start with the Gali District along the eastern border of Abkhazia. Between April and September 1994, UNHCR chaired meetings on repatriation and established a transit center. Repatriation started slowly in September 1994 under intense pressure from Russia, the United Nations, and individual Georgians. UNHCR decided it could only repatriate IDPs to Gali city, where infrastructure for food distribution was in place.

At the time it signed the agreement, Abkhazia supported the plan for rapid repatriation of IDPs to the Gali region. It saw the plan as a prerequisite to the next stage in Abkhaz normalization, a referendum on the status of Abkhazia, which it hoped could lead to international recognition of the independence of Abkhazia. The Abkhaz also supported repatriation, expecting the returnee labor to restart the tea plantations and other agricultural enterprises in Abkhazia.

But statements and actions of Abkhaz officials on the ground contradicted their approval of the agreement. UNHCR presented the Abkhaz authorities with a list of names to clear for repatriation, and the Abkhaz took a month to approve it. IDPs were required to submit applications for repatriation on an individual basis. The Abkhaz authorities claimed that any other method would allow terrorists to return. They drew up a list of thousands of Georgians who they claimed fought against Abkhazia and therefore could not return. Ethnic Georgians who tried to return to their homes in the Gali region were subjected to harassment. Hard-liners had the upper hand and torpedoed the agreement. Its breakdown heralded an end to prospects for repatriation to most of Abkhazia, except for small numbers of Abkhaz who have trickled back to towns and villages throughout the area (there is no accurate tally of their number), and for ethnic Georgians who have unofficially returned to the Gali region.

By mid-1995 it was clear that the agreement was a dead letter. UNHCR consequently changed its program to focus on helping IDPs, especially the 20,000 or so who had unofficially returned to Gali city and the southern part of the Gali District. UNHCR's experience with the Quadripartite Agreement shows that there are limits on the extent to which repatriation can take place when the parties are not ready for a political settlement.[132] UNHCR has been faulted for not sufficiently surveying the displaced population in Georgia and the resident population in Abkhazia into which the IDPs would have to be reintegrated. Yet UNHCR's involvement was part of a comprehensive conflict resolution scenario that in April 1994 appeared to have a reasonable chance of succeeding. The agreement itself was accompanied by a declaration signed the same day "on measures for a political settlement of the Georgian-Abkhaz conflict." UNHCR had every reason to believe that all parties fully accepted the envisaged repatriation. That this was not so was made clear in March 1995, when President Ardzinba reiterated his goal of independence for Abkhazia.

Georgia's Neighbors and Displacement

RUSSIA. The role of Russia is essential to understanding displacement in Georgia. Without outside (Russian) encouragement, neither the Ossetians nor the Abkhaz would have been able to mount a war of secession. Georgians blame Russia for causing the war in Abkhazia and for wrecking the repatriation envisaged by the 1994 Quadripartite Agreement. Many Georgians believe that Moscow encouraged separatism in Georgia both to maintain leverage over Russia's strategic underbelly in the Caucasus and to get even with Shevardnadze for his part in the breakup of the Soviet Union.

IRAN. For Iran, as for the West, relations with Georgia are less important than ties with Russia. Iran has played a cautious role in the Caucasus, taking care not to antagonize Moscow. In January 1993, Shevardnadze traveled to Tehran, hoping to improve commercial exchanges and to solicit support for Iranian assistance in improving Georgian infrastructure. Commerce between Georgia and Iran grew in the 1990s but is still relatively insignificant.

TURKEY. Relations between Georgia and Turkey have been cordial, although the Georgians remain wary of Turkey's long-run objectives. Since the collapse of the Soviet Union, the two countries have eased border crossings, and there is important truck traffic across Turkey and Georgia to Azerbaijan and Central Asia. Georgia is concerned about the long-run relations between Turkey and Ajaria, the Georgian Muslim autonomous republic that borders Turkey.

ARMENIA AND AZERBAIJAN. Shevardnadze is doing all he can for regional cooperation in the Caucasus, and both Armenians and Azeris meet on "neutral ground" in Tbilisi. Georgia is watchful of possible separatism within its own Azeri and Armenian minorities, fearing Russian encouragement of separatism and action by Armenian nationalist Dashnaks.

Conflict Resolution: Inching toward Peace in Ossetia and Abkhazia

Students of the Abkhazian and Ossetian disputes have been actively looking for ways to assist in resolving the conflicts, thereby bringing about an end to the internal displacement generated by these conflicts. Those interested in conflict resolution (or, as some people prefer to call it, conflict transformation) need to create a model that will be attractive to the authorities both in Tbilisi and in the breakaway regions. The laborious process seems agonizingly slow at times.

In January and May 1996, Georgians, South Ossetians, and North Ossetians participated in two seminars on conflict resolution in Oslo. Sponsors of the seminars were the government of Norway (with the close collaboration of the Conflict Management Group of Harvard University) and the Norwegian Refugee Council. Participants in the first seminar included professors and opposition leaders; the second seminar included six Ossetians and six Georgians as well as officials of the Georgian Ministry of Foreign Affairs and KGB. Its purpose was "to generate ideas and options on political status and other issues that might help official negotiators settle the differences between Georgia and the unrecognized Republic of South Ossetia."[133] Following the second seminar, Shevardnadze wrote a letter to the sponsors thanking them for making "a notable contribution to overcoming controversies between Georgians and Ossetians."[134]

While the process of conflict resolution is moving more slowly with regard to Abkhazia, economic hardship in partially blockaded Abkhazia may have pushed the Abkhaz authorities to initiate high-level bilateral talks with the Georgians in late 1996. Earlier, in May 1996, the ambassadors from five countries, "friends of Georgia" (the United States, the United Kingdom, Germany, France, and Russia), met with President Ardzinba in Sukhumi. Because the ambassadors are accredited to Georgia, their trip to Abkhazia indicated a willingness on Ardzinba's part to have Abkhazia considered in some sense part of Georgia. President Ardzinba stated in an interview with Georgian television in 1996 that "the Abkhaz problem cannot be solved through [the] use of force."[135]

One result of recent efforts of conflict resolution in Georgia was the signing on May 16, 1996, of a memorandum that looks to an eventual political settlement of the dispute. It was signed by Georgia and South Ossetia, with the guarantee of North Ossetia–Alania (a member of the Russian Federation), Russia, and the OSCE.[136] It refers to South Ossetia by name, a concession by the Georgian hard-liners, who would have preferred "Inner Kartli" (Shida Kartli), Samachablo (fiefdom of the Machabeli clan), the Tskhinvali region, or "the so-called region of South Ossetia." The May 1996 memorandum recognizes the need of step-by-step confidence-building measures and looks forward to continuing conversations leading to an overall political settlement. The OSCE is cautiously optimistic because the memorandum, together with subsequent talks, demonstrates continuing slow but sure progress in defusing the South Ossetian dispute. Some Ossetians and even some Georgians have returned to South Ossetia, and some Ossetians have also returned to cities elsewhere in Georgia, such as Borjomi and Tbilisi.

Who Is Doing What and with What Degree of Effectiveness?

Lawlessness in the former war zones in Abkhazia and Ossetia, as well as in other parts of Georgia, has been a problem for IDPs as for all elements of Georgian society.

Food assistance for IDPs and other vulnerable people is provided by a number of organizations including WFP, ECHO, and USDA. Assistance is distributed throughout Georgia, including Abkhazia, where it is administered by Aide Internationale Contre la Faim (AICF), ICRC, and Première Urgence; and the Armenian-majority Akhaltsikhe District in southern Georgia, where it is administered by International Orthodox Christian Charities (IOCC). The WFP allotment is 200 grams of food per person per day. Most IDPs are able to get at least a minimal water supply from facilities where they are lodged.

In an interview in June 1996, the director of the Coordination Bureau for International Humanitarian Aid (see below) emphasized that people were still hungry in spite of humanitarian aid, particularly in the summer, when food aid was cut.

There are no camps for IDPs in Georgia. After initially being lodged with relatives and friends, many of the IDPs from Abkhazia were redistributed to hotels, hostels, sanatoriums, hospitals, schools, and other public buildings. While the basic shelter needs of most IDPs have been met, IDPs interviewed in an Oxfam survey perceived the lack of their own permanent dwelling as their main difficulty.[137]

Since independence, Georgia has seen an alarming decline in levels of health in all population groups, and infant mortality has risen; in 1994 it was estimated that there were 25.2 deaths per 1,000 live births.[138] In principle, all vulnerable persons, including IDPs, receive a combination of free and patient-cofinanced basic health services. The state of the government budget, however, is such that only around 100,000 people enjoy this benefit, and the health care system in Georgia depends on external assistance. Medical assistance comes from ECHO, organizations in the MSF family, UNICEF, USAID, and others. It is implemented by a number of agencies, including Médecins du Monde, UMCOR, IFRC, MSF, and UNICEF in districts all over the country.

IDP children are generally able to attend school in the areas where they live. Schools attended by IDPs will only be improved as part of general improvement of the national education system, which is unlikely considering that education expenses as a proportion of GDP in 1995 amounted to only about 2 percent of their 1990 level. UNICEF has supplied chalk to all primary schools in Georgia, including Abkhazia. AICF is running a school-based meal program for 15,000 school children in Abkhazia's Sukhumi area. UNHCR financed the rehabilitation of twenty-eight schools in the Gali District with AICF as its implementing partner. South Ossetia has not received significant assistance for the education sector.[139]

THE GOVERNMENT OF GEORGIA. The government of Georgia's Coordination Bureau for International Humanitarian Aid (CBIHA), established in April 1995, coordinates all international organization and NGO programs in Georgia, in the process ensuring that IDPs and other vulnerable groups are targeted. The CBIHA was created with IOM and USAID funds as part of a capacity-building project for Georgia. It has received additional funding from DHA and Save the Children. Its director reports directly to the state minister and the president. The CBIHA publishes a monthly report that reviews all aid programs in Georgia and includes useful commentary on the state of assistance.[140] Its March 1996 issue, for example, noted increasing attention to humanitarian assistance. The CBIHA performs a wide range of tasks, including introducing new legislation governing aid, developing programs, and creating jobs.

The Committee on Refugees in the Ministry of IDPs is the organ of the government of Georgia that tracks the internally displaced and the relatively few refugees in Georgia. Set up with UNHCR assistance, it was the chief point of contact in the government during the lifetime of the Quadripartite Agreement. The Ministry of Labor and Social Affairs takes care of pensioners and the elderly, many of whom are IDPs. In 1996, IOM, UNHCR, and UNDP agreed to assist the government on a priority basis to develop a unified migration management system.[141] In the absence of a law on refugees, the migration process is regulated by decrees and regulations, more than 130 of which have been passed since independence.

Most of the people interviewed believe that coverage of IDPs is reasonably comprehensive and that such gaps as exist are not extremely serious. When the director of the CBIHA referred to the "terrible conditions" the IDPs live in, he was referring primarily to their psychological outlook. It appears that virtually all of the IDPs receive at least minimal assistance. IDPs and other vulnerable groups have existed at roughly the same level, which some would term poverty, thanks to the downturn in the economy. The economic situation began to improve in 1996, with currency stabilization; however, the economic turnaround had not reached many IDP-affected areas by 1998.

THE INTERNATIONAL COMMUNITY. When Georgia reemerged as an independent state in 1991, the government recognized that it did not have the resources to help IDPs and welcomed help from all quarters, including UNHCR and other international organizations.

The following are examples of international and nongovernmental organizations that provide assistance to IDPs and other needy groups in Georgia.

UNHCR. UNHCR has a wide range of programs in the Caucasus that focus on the needs of vulnerable groups. It has participated in several Inter-Agency Appeals for the Caucasus to address the continuing need for assistance to IDPs.

UNDP. UNDP is one of the participants in the Inter-Agency Appeals for the Caucasus. In its concern with longer-run development, it emphasizes energy, economic growth, and banking issues, all of which will affect IDPs.

ICRC. ICRC has a delegation in Tbilisi, an orthopedic center there and in Gagra (Abkhazia), and a smaller presence in Sukhumi and Zugdidi. About two thirds of those requiring orthopedic assistance are victims of land mines. ICRC is concerned with the situation of non-Abkhaz groups living in Abkhazia. It has distributed medical supplies and food parcels in Abkhazia and has provided food parcels in South Ossetia.

OSCE. OSCE monitors the situation in South Ossetia, looking to the ultimate repatriation of all people displaced from that area. The May 1996 memorandum of understanding signed by South Ossetia, Georgia, North Ossetia–Alania, and Russia recognizes that the IDPs can only return to their homes when there is an overall peace agreement.

DHA. Together with ECHO and Save the Children/US, DHA has conducted a vulnerability study of IDPs and others in Georgia.

IOM. IOM has been actively engaged in capacity-building activities in the Caucasus since 1993, often in collaboration with UNHCR. In 1995 the government of Georgia established a program for migration management, with IOM as the lead agency and UNHCR and UNDP as collaborating partners. IOM sponsored a workshop on institutional capacity-building in the Transcaucasus in Geneva in April 1996.

NGOs. An increasing number of NGOs are actively assisting IDPs and other vulnerable groups in Georgia.[142] The following are illustrative: Caritas/Denmark has taken over ICRC programs in South Ossetia. The International Rescue Committee has been active in Georgia since late 1993 and assists IDPs in Tbilisi, Imereti, and Mingrelia, particularly with basic repairs of IDP collective centers. IOCC has distributed food to some 40,000 beneficiaries (most of them local vulnerable populations) in an area near the Turkish and Armenian frontiers where the population is largely Armenian. Since 1995, many NGO implementing agencies have included income-generation activities in their programming. A number of potential constraints on the implementation of income-generation activities exists, including the need to ensure that there is a market for the products and services produced by the target beneficiaries.[143]

Conclusions and Recommendations

A host of problems confronted Georgia at independence. Though many Georgians had yearned for freedom, Georgia was totally unprepared for it. Georgia lacked a civil society and had a limited tradition of self-government. In Georgia the transition away from the Soviet system was complicated by three civil wars, two of which led to massive displacement. Russian support was a key factor in the wars in both South Ossetia and Abkhazia. Neither region could have aspired to full independence without unofficial Russian backing.

Most of Georgia's IDPs have not returned to their homes. With few exceptions, those who are still lodged in temporary quarters have not integrated into the communities in which they live. Their use of public buildings as living quarters that could otherwise be put into service for the local communities is a constant reminder that Georgia has a long way to go before the problem of internal displacement is solved.

In reviewing the programs of assistance to IDPs in Georgia, one is struck by the immensity of the needs. With the establishment of the CBIHA, the government of Georgia has been able to bring about greater coordination and cooperation between international organizations and NGOs. With this assistance, Georgia will be able to expand into new areas with programs carefully designed for the most vulnerable, including IDPs. The creation of the CBIHA has been a big step forward in ensuring the equitable distribution of assistance throughout Georgia and in assisting with the transition to sustainable development. This will in turn assist Georgia as it takes further steps toward a political settlement of the disputes that led to displacement.

Among the lessons Georgia provides for dealing with the problems of displacement are the following:

- The restoration of law and order is essential. As the international organizations and NGOs move from assistance to sustainable development, they need to emphasize the role of civil society and support institutions that will create a new and more equitable structure of law and order for all citizens of Georgia, including IDPs.
- Leaders must address multiple ethnic loyalties. The nature of Georgia's conflicts underlines the need for programs, possibly including quotas and affirmative action, to strengthen minority representation in the national power structure and in the cultural area.[144] Such policies are a useful tool for addressing disputes over multiple loyalties, provided they are accompanied by educational efforts that promote *national* rather than *ethnic* identity. They must be accompanied by greater disengagement on the part of Russia.

- Regional (autonomous republic, autonomous oblast) borders should not be changed unless all parties agree. In order to avoid international conflict, many of the nations of the former Soviet Union have decided that they will not tinker with frontiers. To prevent Russia from making the most of ethnic divisions caused by Stalin's cartography, autonomous republic and autonomous oblast borders should also not be changed unless all parties agree.
- Protection and assistance must be accompanied by efforts to resolve disputes. Protection and assistance are essential in situations involving internal displacement. But because protection and assistance are responses to the symptoms of conflicts, not their causes, they alone are not enough to solve difficult political disputes. With protection and assistance ensured, conflict resolution (conflict transformation) has played an important role in bringing the conflicting parties to an accommodation in South Ossetia.
- For the return of IDPs to succeed, the parties must be ready for it. UNHCR's experience with the Quadripartite Agreement in Abkhazia shows that the parties must be ready for repatriation (and even for a political settlement) for it to work. Unofficial return of IDPs has had considerable success both in the Gali District of Abkhazia and in South Ossetia.

Conclusion

Solving the problems of displacement in the Caucasus requires political settlement of the disputes that caused them. The governments concerned will have to make difficult political decisions for peace to break out. They must not underestimate the difficulties involved. Peace will require a mechanism for resolution of conflicts. Peace will need to be accompanied by political and economic incentives. It will require turning the economies of the area around. Only with peace will the continual outflow of people from the Caucasus come to a halt. Armenia will need to recognize that the loss of hundreds of thousands of people through emigration is far greater than any gain that can be realized from holding on to all the territories occupied since the start of the war with Azerbaijan.

Political compromise will require a willingness to make step-by-step progress that falls short of giving the warring parties everything they want. Conflict resolution offers such a gradualist approach. The international community should urge all parties to disputes to apply the techniques of conflict resolution. Unfortunately there has been little use made of conflict resolution in most of the conflicts leading to displacement in the Caucasus. In Chechnya, Russia was sure it could win a victory on the battlefield. There seems to be no interest in conflict resolution in the Nagorno-Karabakh dispute. For Azerbaijan it would require some kind of political compromise on the status of (i.e., sovereignty over) Nagorno-Karabakh, and for the Armenians a compromise on the issue of occupied territory. Armenia's special challenge, since it has the upper hand militarily, is to explore imaginative ways to resolve this conflict.

A prerequisite of conflict resolution is the willingness to talk and to compromise. All facets of the disputes must be open to discussion. The opposing parties must be willing to engage in talks at all levels. Given the geopolitical importance of Russia in the area, Russia should be involved at some point. Another salient feature of conflict resolution is the significance of small steps, essential on the road to an overall settlement, even as bigger questions remain unresolved. Small steps are contested by parties to a dispute that do not want anything less than a complete settlement. A case in point is the vested interest of the government of Azerbaijan in keeping people displaced until there is broad political settlement.

Conflict resolution has been most successful in South Ossetia. Georgia and South Ossetia have taken cautious steps in the direction of a political settlement, as judged by the memorandum of understanding signed in May 1996. The memorandum is a statement of intent that looks to a permanent settlement of the dispute but recognizes that this is not it. It recognizes that the peace process will take time. It requires compromise on both sides. The Georgians recognized the distinctiveness of South Ossetia, and the South Ossetians recognized tacitly that they are part of Georgia. Georgia agreed to use the term South Ossetia, an accommodation that its militants opposed. The memorandum was signed by the Russian Federation as guarantor and by OSCE and North Ossetia–Alania. Thus it recognized the role of Russia in the area. Combined with the unofficial return of several thousand IDPs to South Ossetia and to other parts of Georgia, including Tbilisi, these are grounds for optimism.

The role of the international community is of great importance, both politically and economically . The silence of the G-7 countries during the Russo-Chechen War can be credited with encouraging Russia to use disproportionate force in Chechnya, driving thousands of people into displacement, many of them more than once as war surged across the countryside. In dealing with the Transcaucasian republics, the desire of Western countries not to overcommit themselves left the field to Russia, which has often seemed to be more interested in turmoil than in resolution of problems.

An exception to what might have been perceived as Western indifference to the Caucasus is the tilt of the United States toward Armenia, represented by Section 907 of the Foreign Assistance Act. This removes the United States from a possibly useful mediatory role in encouraging settlement of the Nagorno-Karabakh dispute. The Azerbaijanis remain frustrated that the international community has not persuaded Armenia to withdraw from occupied lands, in spite of Security Council resolutions. Discussions aimed at resolving this dispute under OSCE, the so-called Minsk Process, have produced little apparent result, although the parties to the dispute have met periodically to try to iron out their differences.

The international community can contribute to the economic betterment of the area by encouraging trade and monetary policies that will help raise standards of living. The economies of all the countries need to be strengthened. Ethnic conflicts diminish where people do not have to struggle over scarce resources. The IMF helped Georgia launch its own currency, which has brought a measure of stability to the economy. UNHCR and IOM are assisting in institutional capacity-building in the Caucasian republics. Other international organizations should follow their lead by encouraging programs that advance economic well-being and relieve ethnic tensions.

Donor countries—particularly the United States, Western European counties, and Japan—should coordinate their politics and programs in support of displaced persons. They should actively encourage adversaries in the Caucasian disputes to reach peaceful solutions. Diplomacy, publicity, and economic assistance are all essential tools.

The pervasive role of Russia is essential to understanding displacement in both the North Caucasus and Transcaucasia. Both the Soviet Union and its successor, the Russian Federation, have been major agents of displacement. First came gerrymandered boundaries between political units in the Soviet Union, often dividing like peoples and combining unlike peoples. Russia's post-Soviet actions have also often led to displacement. Since independence, Russia has often acted as if it had carte blanche in the Transcaucasian republics. Secessionist groups in Georgia, particularly in Abkhazia, staked out their claims with former Soviet arms, as well as with the active military support of Russia. Russian armed support enabled the North Ossetians not only to hang onto the Prigorodnyi District but also to expel the Ingush from it.

Without Russian support, displacement in the North Caucasus and Transcaucasia will not end. Russia's continuing involvement in the Caucasus needs to be defined. Much will depend on Russia's willingness to support stable, independent countries in Transcaucasia and a wide measure of autonomy, approaching independence, in Chechnya. Russia must actively encourage the peaceful resolution of disputes in the Caucasus and refrain from provoking conflicts among the groups in the area. Other countries in the region, particularly Turkey and Iran, which border the area to the south, need to be discouraged from taking sides in the disputes.

Resolving internal displacement in the Caucasus requires a regional approach. The May 1996 CIS Conference in Geneva recognized the interdependence of all the countries of the area and the desirability of avoiding sudden surges of migration. Its discussions focused on a wide range of migrant categories: refugees, IDPs, repatriants, persons involuntarily relocated, ecological migrants, and illegal transit migrants.

International organizations and NGOs can continue their constructive role in the Caucasus. The mandates of UNHCR have broadened to include virtually all categories of vulnerable people. The international organizations and NGOs helped the Caucasian republics survive difficult times in their first years of independence. Now is the time to direct continued assistance toward development and to make it contingent on working toward political resolution of disputes. By insisting on resolution of conflicts and directing assistance to this goal, the international community can help bring about political settlements that will avoid future displacement.

Notes

1. Shireen T. Hunter, *The Transcaucasus in Transition: Nation-Building and Conflict* (Washington, D.C.: Center for Strategic and International Studies, 1994), p. 3.

2. For a view of the often strained relationship between Georgians and other ethnic groups in that country, see B. G. Hewitt, "Demographic Manipulation in the Caucasus (with Special Reference to Georgia)," *Journal of Refugee Studies*, vol. 8, no. 1 (1995).

3. Interview, Tbilisi, June 30, 1996.

4. See Human Rights Watch, "'Punished Peoples' of the Soviet Union: The Continuing Legacy of Stalin's Deportations," New York, September 1991.

5. A number of sources indicate that there are probably a few thousand Armenians still in Azerbaijan who are married to Azeris, and a few thousand Azeris in Armenia married to Armenians.

6. Human Rights Watch/Helsinki, "The Commonwealth of Independent States: Refugees and Internally Displaced Persons in Armenia, Azerbaijan, Georgia, the Russian Federation and Tajikistan," New York, May 1996, p. 13.

7. Hunter, *The Transcaucasus in Transition*, p. 116.

8. Alessandra Stanley, "Chechens Crowd Polling Places in a Vote for 'Freedom,'" *New York Times*, January 28, 1997, p. 3.

9. Lee Hockstader, "Moscow Weighs Costs of War in Chechnya," *Washington Post*, January 3, 1997, p. 27.

10. Ibid.

11. "Mid-term Review of the 1996 United Nations Humanitarian Programme for Persons Displaced as a Result of the Emergency Situation in Chechnya, Russian Federation, and Programme Strategy for 1997," United Nations, November 1996, p. 5.

12. Department of Humanitarian Affairs, "United Nations Inter-Agency Humanitarian Programme for Persons Displaced as a Result of the Emergency Situation in Chechnya, Russian Federation," *Situation Report of the DHA Coordinator* (based on field reports and covering the period August 20–September 30, 1996).

13. Stanley, "Chechens Crowd Polling Places."

14. UNHCR statistics cited in Hrair Balian, "Armed Conflict in Chechnya: Its Impact on Children," Case Study for the United Nations Study on the Impact of Armed Conflict on Children, Arlington, Va., Covcas Center for Law and Conflict Resolution, 1995, p. 29.

15. See Paul B. Henze, *The North Caucasus: Russia's Long Struggle to Subdue the Circassians* (Santa Monica, Calif.: Rand, 1990).

16. The Avars, a nationality comprising fourteen tribal groups, are the most populous single group in Dagestan. See Suzanne Goldenberg, *Pride of Small Nations* (London: Zed Books, 1994), p. 176.

17. Goldenberg, *Pride of Small Nations*, p. 176.

18. Paul B. Henze, *Russia and the Caucasus* (Santa Monica, Calif.: Rand, 1996), p. 12.

19. Vera Tolz, "New Information about the Deportation of Ethnic Groups under Stalin," Radio Liberty, Report on the USSR, April 26, 1991, cited in Human Rights Watch/Helsinki, "'Punished Peoples' of the Soviet Union," pp. 8–9.

20. Goldenberg, *Pride of Small Nations*, p. 176.

21. See UNHCR, IOM, and OSCE, *Report of the Regional Conference to address the problems of refugees, displaced persons, other forms of involuntary displacement and returnees in the countries of the Commonwealth of Independent*

States and relevant neighbouring States, CISCONF/1996/6, July 4, 1996. Paragraph 79 of this report states, "The orderly return of repatriants and persons belonging to formerly deported peoples . . . should be facilitated."

22. Supreme Soviet of the Russian Federation, "Law on the Rehabilitation of Repressed Peoples," April 1991.

23. See Human Rights Watch/Helsinki, "The Ingush-Ossetian Conflict in the Prigorodnyi Region," New York, 1996.

24. See Anatoly M. Khazanov, *Interethnic Relations in the North Caucasus* (Washington, D.C.: National Council for Soviet and East European Research, 1995), pp. 5–6.

25. Human Rights Watch/Helsinki, "The Ingush-Ossetian Conflict," p. 36.

26. Balian, "Armed Conflict in Chechnya," p. 7.

27. "Treaty on Mutual Delimitation and Delegation of Authority," signed between Russia and Tatarstan in February 1994. Cited in Fiona Hill, *Russia's Tinderbox: Conflict in the North Caucasus and Its Implications for the Future of the Russian Federation* (John F. Kennedy School of Government, Harvard University, 1995), p. 33.

28. See, for example, International Committee of the Red Cross (ICRC), Communication to the Press 96/23, July 11, 1996; and "Northern Caucasus: 'Enough Is Enough!'" *ICRC News*, vol. 10, March 13, 1996.

29. Balian, "Armed Conflict in Chechnya," pp. 8, 10.

30. Alessandra Stanley, "Chechen Voters' Key Concerns: Order and Stability," *New York Times*, January 24, 1997.

31. Balian, "Armed Conflict in Chechnya," p. 25.

32. ICRC, *Annual Report*, 1995 (Geneva, 1996), pp. 204–6.

33. ICRC, "Update on ICRC Activities in the Russian Federation/Northern Caucasus," no. 1, Geneva, January 10, 1997.

34. International Organization for Migration (IOM), "Chechnya Emergency Project: Final Report," Geneva, 1996, pp. 1, 7.

35. "Mid-term Review of the 1996 United Nations Humanitarian Programme," p. 7.

36. Balian, "Armed Conflict in Chechnya," p. 40.

37. The most common profession of IDPs questioned in a recent UNHCR-sponsored survey was collective farming. Others included drivers, teachers, civil servants, builders, health professionals, and shop owners.

38. Center for Strategic and International Studies (CSIS), *Azerbaijan, a Sociological Study on Internally Displaced People: Humanitarian Aid, Needs and Survival Strategies* (Baku: UNHCR, 1996), p. 5. Before 1991, Kurds in Azerbaijan were centered in Lachin Province, which in the 1920s was a Kurdish Autonomous Republic.

39. UNHCR and Government of Azerbaijan, "Factsheet" prepared for the 1996 CIS Conference, Geneva, p. 1.

40. Interviews, Baku, June 24–27 and July 8–10, 1996.

41. The 233,000 figure includes 46,000 Meskhetian Turks, one of the "formerly deported peoples," deported by Stalin from Georgia to Kazakhstan and

Uzbekistan in 1944, who are in Azerbaijan awaiting return to Georgia, which may be years away.

42. Human Rights Watch/Helsinki, "The Commonwealth of Independent States," p. 13.

43. UNHCR, Programme and Technical Support Section, "Azerbaijan: Technical Mission to Assess the Need for Semi-Permanent Shelter for Internally Displaced Persons and Refugees," October 21–November 4, 1994, p. 3.

44. CSIS, *Azerbaijan, a Sociological Study*, p. 5.

45. World Health Organization, Centers for Disease Control and Prevention, and UNICEF, in collaboration with Relief International and Médecins sans Frontières/Holland, "Health and Nutrition Survey of Internally Displaced and Resident Population of Azerbaijan," Baku, April 1996, p. 65.

46. International Federation of Red Cross and Red Crescent Societies (IFRC), Fact Sheet on Azerbaijan, Baku, 1996, p. 3.

47. Hunter, *The Transcaucasus in Transition*, p. 5.

48. The Lezghins speak a Caucasian language and are Muslim. In the 1989 Soviet census they numbered 466,000, with 50 percent living in Azerbaijan and 44 percent in Dagestan. See Helen Krag and Lars Funch, "The North Caucasus: Minorities at a Crossroads," Report 94/5, Minority Rights Group, London, 1994, p. 16. The Shia Muslim Talysh, who speak an Iranian language, number an estimated 150,000–200,000. They live in the Lenkoran area near the Iranian frontier; the 1989 Soviet census said their population was 21,000, but "this is thought to reflect a campaign of assimilation from the Soviet era and their true numbers are believed to be ten times that." See Goldenberg, *Pride of Small Nations*, p. 128.

49. Ronald Grigor Suny, *The Revenge of the Past: Nationalism, Revolution and the Collapse of the Soviet Union* (Stanford University Press, 1993), p. 39.

50. The term Nagorno-Karabakh derives from Russian (Nagorno = mountainous), Turkish (kara = black) and Persian (bakh/bagh = garden).

51. The circumstances of the deaths remain a matter of dispute. See Bill Frelick, "Faultlines of Nationality Conflict: Refugees and Displaced Persons from Armenia and Azerbaijan," U.S. Committee for Refugees, Washington, D.C., March 1994, p. 10.

52. Goldenberg, *Pride of Small Nations*, p. 154.

53. Frelick, "Faultlines of Nationality Conflict," p. 11.

54. Egbert G. Wesselink, "Human Rights Violations in Azerbaijan and Armenia," *Soviet Refugee Monitor*, vol. 1 (February 1992), p. 4.

55. Frelick, "Faultlines of Nationality Conflict," p. 11.

56. According to the KGB, forty-eight persons, of whom forty-six were Armenian, were killed outright, and twenty died subsequently from their injuries (ibid., p. 13). See also Helsinki Watch/Memorial Report, "Conflict in the Soviet Union: Black January in Azerbaijdzhan," May 1991, p. 7.

57. Frelick, "Faultlines of Nationality Conflict," p. 14; interview, Yerevan, July 4, 1996.

58. This term deliberately leaves the origin of the Armenians somewhat ambiguous. See Frelick, "Faultlines of Nationality Conflict."

59. Ibid., p. 22.

60. Security Council Resolutions 822 (April 30, 1993), 853 (July 29, 1993), 874 (October 14, 1993), and 884 (November 12, 1993), dealt respectively with the Kelbajar Province; Agdam; Jibrail and Fizuli near the Iranian border (and included a reaffirmation of Azerbaijani territorial integrity); and Zangelan Province and the city of Goradiz.

61. See ICRC, *Annual Report*, 1995, p. 209.

62. The Minsk Group includes Armenia, Azerbaijan, Belarus, the Czech Republic, Finland, France, Germany, Italy, Russia, Sweden, Turkey, the United States, and "interested parties in Nagorno-Karabakh." The group takes its name from the capital of Belarus. See Human Rights Watch/Helsinki, "The Commonwealth of Independent States," p. 13.

63. Hunter, *The Transcaucasus in Transition*, p. 105.

64. Interview, Tbilisi, July 2, 1996.

65. Kh. Panesh and L. B. Ermolov, "Turki-Meskhetintsy," *Sovetskaya Etnografiya*, no. 1 (1990), p. 16, quoted in Human Rights Watch/Helsinki, "'Punished Peoples' of the Soviet Union," p. 51.

66. Interview, Baku, June 26, 1996.

67. CSIS, *Azerbaijan, a Sociological Study*; WHO, Centers for Disease Control and Prevention, and UNICEF, "Health and Nutrition Survey," p. 1.

68. CSIS, *Azerbaijan, a Sociological Study*.

69. WHO, Centers for Disease Control and Prevention, and UNICEF, "Health and Nutrition Survey."

70. CSIS, *Azerbaijan, a Sociological Study*, p. 13.

71. Interview, Baku, June 25, 1996.

72. See UNHCR, "UNHCR in Azerbaijan: Three Years of Helping the Displaced People in Azerbaijan and Plan of Activities in 1996," Baku, February 1, 1996.

73. Thomas Greene, "Dimensions of Migration in Russia and the Caucasus," Refugee Policy Group, Washington, D.C., 1995, p. 26.

74. Interview, Baku, June 24, 1996.

75. ICRC, "ICRC Emergency Appeals for 1996," Geneva, 1995, p. 148.

76. Revised Section 907 Guidelines for assistance activities in Azerbaijan funded by the United States Department of State, the United States Agency for International Development (USAID), the United States Information Agency (USIA), and the United States Department of Agriculture (USDA), October 1, 1996.

77. Interviews, Yerevan, July 3 and 4, 1996. The figure of 72,000 was also cited in the factsheet drafted by the government of Armenia and CIS Conference Secretariat in May 1996.

78. Interview, Yerevan, July 4, 1996.

79. UNHCR and Government of Armenia, "Factsheet," p. 1.

80. Interview, Yerevan, July 4, 1996.

81. UNHCR and Government of Armenia, "Factsheet."

82. Historian Justin McCarthy cites the lower figure, while Johannes Lepsius uses the higher number. Cited in Gerard Chaliand and Jean-Pierre Rageau, *The Penguin Atlas of Diasporas* (New York: Penguin Books USA, 1995), p. 85.

83. David Marshall Lang and Christopher J. Walker, "The Armenians," Report no. 32, Minority Rights Group, London, 1987, p. 8.

84. Ronald Grigor Suny, *Looking toward Ararat: Armenia in Modern History* (Indiana University Press, 1993).

85. Hunter, *The Transcaucasus in Transition*, p. 98.

86. Frelick, "Faultlines of Nationality Conflict," p. 9.

87. Suny, *The Revenge of the Past*, p. 132.

88. Hunter, *The Transcaucasus in Transition*, p. 105.

89. Ibid., p. 104.

90. Chaliand and Rageau, *The Penguin Atlas of Diasporas*, p. 89.

91. Paul B. Henze, *Georgia and Armenia: Troubled Independence* (Santa Monica, Calif.: Rand, 1995), p. 7.

92. Paul B. Henze, *Turkey and Armenia: Past Problems and Future Prospects* (Santa Monica, Calif.: Rand, 1996), p. 4.

93. David Hoffman, "After Grim Times, Armenia Lightens Up," *Washington Post*, September 18, 1996, p. 21.

94. Ibid.

95. Henze, *Turkey and Armenia*, p. 5.

96. Hunter, *The Transcaucasus in Transition*, pp. 105–6.

97. Ibid, p. 109.

98. "Yet It Moves," *Economist*, September 21, 1996.

99. Henze, *Turkey and Armenia*, p. 9.

100. Henze, *Georgia and Armenia*, p. 12.

101. Interview, Yerevan, July 4, 1996.

102. Greene, "Dimensions of Migration in Russia and the Caucasus," p. 18 and the following pages.

103. UNHCR and Government of Armenia, "Factsheet," p. 2.

104. ICRC, *Annual Report*, 1995, p. 209.

105. See Rouben P. Adalian, ed., *Armenia and Karabagh Factbook* (Washington, D.C.: Armenian Assembly of America), p. 55 and the following pages.

106. Human Rights Watch/Helsinki, "The Commonwealth of Independent States," p. 17.

107. For a critical discussion of this plan, see Open Society Institute, "Forced Migration: Repatriation in Georgia," New York, 1995.

108. ICRC, "ICRC Emergency Appeal 1996," Geneva, December 1995, p. 150.

109. The Republic of North Ossetia–Alania is a former Autonomous SSR in the Soviet Union and now a member of the Russian Federation. The Ingush were deported from the Chechen-Ingush Autonomous Republic in 1944 along with the Chechens. When the Ingush returned, they found that the Prigorodnyi District, where they had constituted 90 percent of the population before the deportation, had been attached to North Ossetia and colonized by Ossetians. North Ossetia has not been willing to

relinquish this area. See Human Rights Watch/Helsinki, "The Ingush-Ossetian Conflict," p. 11.

110. Julia Kharashvili, "Psycho-Social Examination of IDP Children and Women: Victims of Military Conflicts on the Territory of the Republic of Georgia," survey sponsored by Oxfam, Tbilisi, December 1995, p. 11.

111. Norwegian Refugee Council, "Survey on Internally Displaced People in Georgia," report sponsored by UNICEF and the NRC, Geneva, April 1995.

112. Interview, Tbilisi, July 2, 1996. The NRC figures are useful working figures, although they are at odds with two earlier surveys cited in the NRC survey that found the IDPs living in significantly different locations. The Tbilisi survey of March 1994 indicated that about 84 percent of the IDPs lived in private residences. March 1995 data from the government of Georgia Committee on Refugees (COR) indicated that about 35 percent of IDPs in Tbilisi and 17 percent on a national average lived in collective centers. As the NRC regional representative wrote in the introduction to the survey, "The difficulties encountered by interviewers, particularly in the regions, in locating IDPs using lists from the central COR office, underline the lack of systematic registration data on the IDPs in Georgia."

113. Hewitt, "Demographic Manipulation in the Caucasus," p. 48.

114. Hunter, *The Transcaucasus in Transition*, p. 122.

115. Gamsakhurdia said this in an interview with a Dutch journalist that was published in *NRC Handelsblad's Zaterdags Bijvoegels*, February 3, 1990; cited in Hewitt, "Demographic Manipulation in the Caucasus," p. 60.

116. Human Rights Watch/Helsinki, "The Ingush-Ossetian Conflict," pp. 11, 25.

117. Open Society Institute, "Forced Migration," p. 36.

118. Human Rights Watch/Helsinki, "The Commonwealth of Independent States," pp. 16–17.

119. Interview, Tbilisi, June 29, 1996.

120. Hunter, *The Transcaucasus in Transition*, p. 129.

121. According to the 1989 Soviet census, the ethnic makeup of the 540,000 people in the Abkhazian Autonomous Republic was as follows: Georgians 45.7 percent, Abkhaz 17.8 percent, Armenians 14.6 percent, Russians 14.2 percent, Greeks 2.8 percent, Ukrainians 2.2 percent, Belarusians 0.4 percent, Jews 0.2 percent, Ossetians 0.2 percent, other 1.6 percent. Figures quoted in Open Society Institute, "Georgia: The Georgian-Abkhaz Conflict," *Forced Migration Monitor* (November 1994), p. 1.

122. Hunter, *The Transcaucasus in Transition*, p. 125.

123. Open Society Institute, "Georgia: The Georgian-Abkhaz Conflict," p. 1.

124. Hewitt, "Demographic Manipulation in the Caucasus," p. 62.

125. Henze, *Georgia and Armenia*, p. 4.

126. Security Council, Resolution 849 on Abkhazia, United Nations, July 9, 1993.

127. Security Council, Resolution 858 on Abkhazia, United Nations, August 24, 1993.

128. Security Council, Resolutions 881 and 937 on Abkhazia, November 4, 1993, and July 21, 1994.

129. Interview, Tbilisi, June 29, 1996.

130. Interview, Tbilisi, July 1, 1996.

131. The full name of the agreement was "Quadripartite Agreement on the Voluntary Return of Refugees and Displaced Persons." For a review of how this agreement worked out on the ground, see Open Society Institute, "Forced Migration."

132. Greene, "Dimensions of Migration in Russia and the Caucasus," p. 25.

133. Norwegian Refugee Council, Press Statement, May 28, 1996.

134. Letter of Eduard Shevardnadze to Conflict Management Group and Norwegian Refugee Council, June 24, 1996.

135. Quoted in International Center on Conflict and Negotiation, Tbilisi, *Conflicts and Negotiations*, nos. 6–7 (March–April 1996).

136. The full title of this memorandum, translated from Russian, is "Memorandum on measures for guaranteeing security and increasing mutual trust between the parties in the Georgian-Ossetian conflict."

137. Kharashvili, "Psycho-Social Examination of IDP Children and Women," p. 12.

138. IOM and UNHCR, "Workshop on Institutional Capacity Building Strategies in the Trans-Caucasus," Geneva, 1996, p. 48.

139. IOM and UNHCR, "Workshop on Institutional Capacity Building Strategies," pp. 50–52.

140. Coordination Bureau for International Humanitarian Aid, "Humanitarian Assistance in Georgia," monthly reports published with support of IOM and UNDHA/Norwegian Government.

141. IOM, in partnership with UNHCR and UNDP, "Program Description and Appeal, Capacity Building in Migration Management: Republic of Georgia," Tbilisi, 1996.

142. For a full listing, see the CBIHA monthly reports.

143. IOM and UNHCR, "Workshop on Institutional Capacity Building Strategies," pp. 53–54. When this report was written, there were about twenty income-generation projects delivering services to approximately 20,000 people, a number that represented less than 5 percent of the population living below the poverty line.

144. Valery Tishkov, "Perspectives on Ethnic Accord in Post-Soviet Space," *Cultural Survival Quarterly* (Summer/Fall 1994), p. 54.

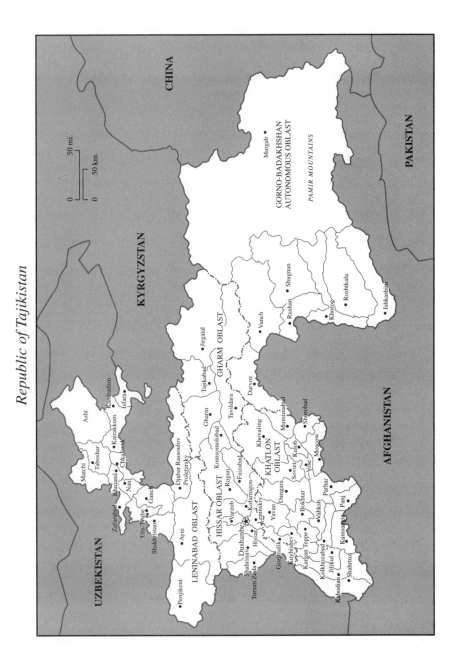

Republic of Tajikistan

CHAPTER EIGHT

Turmoil in Tajikistan: Addressing the Crisis of Internal Displacement

Jennifer McLean and Thomas Greene

TAJIKISTAN IS THE POOREST and most remote of the former Soviet republics. During the short but brutal civil war that erupted months after the country declared independence in 1991, as many as 60,000 persons were killed and at least 600,000 internally displaced.[1] After a coalition of opposition parties bid for power and failed, hundreds of thousands were driven from their villages, their homes looted and burned behind them by pro-government forces, and were forced to flee to other parts of Tajikistan or across the border to Afghanistan. Although most internally displaced persons (IDPs) and refugees have returned since the war ostensibly ended in early 1993, subsequent fighting has resulted in new waves of internal displacement.[2]

Tajikistan's civil war was "the bloodiest conflict in the aftermath of the Soviet collapse, until Chechnya."[3] The case of Tajikistan exhibits features common to many problems of internal displacement: civilian suffering and flight against a backdrop of internal conflict, human rights abuses perpetrated by both government and opposition forces, and efforts by international agencies—in this case initially by the United Nations High

Commissioner for Refugees (UNHCR) and the International Committee of the Red Cross (ICRC)—to provide assistance and protection.

Several other characteristics set Tajikistan apart. Most Tajik IDPs sought refuge in the Gharm Valley and Gorno-Badakhshan, their former homelands, and thus were accommodated, albeit in miserable conditions, by their extended families and in public buildings among those of their own ethnicity rather than in camps or special settlements. Moreover, the Tajik government cooperated with the international community, particularly in the early stages of the humanitarian operation, in a markedly effective manner. The various reasons for this cooperation and its deterioration are considered below. This case study also discusses the implications of the Soviet Union's sudden disintegration, the continued flareups in some areas in contrast to the urgent need for development in others, the sometimes shaky coordination between the international organizations, UNHCR's handover of protection responsibilities to the Organization for Security and Cooperation in Europe (OSCE), and the remarkably fast return of most IDPs. Furthermore, the study examines the course and underlying causes of the war, the displacement that was a manifestation of the war, the international community's response, and the continuing attempts to help IDPs return and reintegrate.

The Causes of Displacement

Formerly the Tajik Soviet Socialist Republic, Tajikistan covers 143,100 square kilometers in Central Asia—roughly the size of Nicaragua—and is bordered by Uzbekistan to the west and north, Kyrgyzstan to the north, China to the east, and Afghanistan to the south. Most of its 6 million citizens are Sunni Muslims and speak the Tajik language, a variety of the Indo-European Persian language. Tajikistan was historically part of the Persian Empire. Later, after the Mongol invasions of the thirteenth century, Tajikistan, like much of Central Asia, was ruled by the khans of Bukhara.

Like the other Central Asian republics, when Tajikistan became independent it had no strong sense of national identity and no organized security forces. Tajikistan's political life as a Soviet Socialist Republic had been divided along regional, ethnic, and clan lines, which stunted the growth of a sense of common identity. When the Soviets divided Central Asia into new states in the 1920s, they deliberately drew the new borders to encompass minorities on each side, thereby ensuring dependence on Moscow. Stalin's cartographers gave Bukhara and Samarkand, traditional Tajik cultural centers, to neighboring Uzbekistan and cast the small town of Dushanbe as the capital of the new Tajik Republic. Tajikistan also inherited mountainous areas with no urban centers. None of the pre-tsarist Central Asian khanates, of which Tajikistan and Uzbekistan are the heirs, had been established along ethnolinguistic lines. Where different groups once had intermingled—Tajiks, Uzbeks, nomads, and town and city dwellers—"Soviet policy had ripped a vibrant human tapestry into pieces and then attempted to sort the resulting threads by their primary colors."[4]

Under Stalin, perhaps one third of Tajikistan's population was displaced or liquidated. In the 1930s, thousands of members of the Tajik intelligentsia, many of whom had been loyal supporters of the Soviets during their suppression of the *basmachi* rebellion, were purged.[5] Often they were replaced in the administration with illiterate peasants. The effects of the purges were still being felt in 1991 in the diminished quality of the governing elite.

After the collapse of the Soviet Union, newly independent Tajiks could not identify with any clearly united territory. In 1992 only 62 percent of the nation's 5.8 million people were ethnic Tajik; the rest were Uzbeks (about 24 percent), Russians (about 5 percent), and Kyrgyz, Kazak, Turkmen, Ukrainian, Byelorussian, Tatar, German, and Caucasian minorities.[6] The word "Tajik" itself had a number of designations, the most common being a Persian-speaking Sunni Muslim living in Central Asia, and included several million Tajiks in northern Afghanistan. Absent a well-developed sense of national consciousness, the state and its institutions were seen as plums to be snatched by groups from various regions within Tajikistan, in pursuit of their parochial interests. With the state being run like a private fiefdom of local leaders, the ruling elite was regarded as representative of a particular part of the country, the Kulob region, and not of the nation as a whole.[7]

The collapse of the Soviet Union forced independence on an unprepared, impoverished republic completely dependent on Moscow. The government of Tajikistan had lived on subsidies from its Soviet benefactor, which in 1991 alone paid for more than 40 percent of state expenditures. Earlier during the Soviet era, subsidies had accounted for up to 60 percent of Tajikistan's budget. In addition, Tajikistan ran a large trade deficit with other Soviet republics. The loss of subsidies and the breakup of the USSR forced the Tajik communist elite to search for new sources of political support, which it quickly found in "regionalism" and patron-client relations. Regionalism "translated in local politics into the distri-bution of power and privilege based on regional loyalties. It was a form of nepotism in which the kin, in this case formed around a geographical location, played an important role in the placement of cadres, and in lobbying for the allocation of resources."[8] More than an ideological con-frontation, the Tajik civil war was a regional power struggle between the communist-led government and emerging opposition forces for access to political and economic spoils.[9]

Tajikistan had no unifying nationalist movement seeking indepen-dence, and consequently no such movement proved strong enough to fill the ideological vacuum left by the demise of Soviet rule.[10] The "forced divorce" from the USSR was critical: "on the one hand, it deprived the ruling elite of communist support in political and ideological terms, rig-idifying it into uncompromising positions. On the other hand, the system-atic change gave the new emerging political forces hopes of political liberalisation."[11] To opposition groups, consisting largely of persons of Gharmi and Pamiri origin, the disintegration of Soviet power and the simultaneous deterioration of the traditional Khojand-Kulobi ruling al-liance meant that all was up for grabs. Antigovernment protests in Du-shanbe, starting in late 1991 and continuing into 1992, quickly spread to other parts of the country. The combination of political protests, regional rivalries, and economic difficulties made an explosion hard to avoid. Compounding the crisis, Tajikistan had no developed civil society, its security forces were split along regional lines, and weapons were easily available from the former Soviet military.[12] In addition, shortly after Tajikistan's independence, the collapse of the Kabul government in neighboring Afghanistan accelerated the disintegration of state authority in that country and facilitated the flow of arms and drugs into former Soviet Central Asia.

Geography

Tajikistan is divided into five topographically and culturally diverse regions, or oblasts: Hissar, Leninabad, Gharm, Gorno-Badakhshan, and Khatlon. This diversity, and the corresponding interplay of political, eth-nic, religious, and economic factors, were crucial in determining loyalties during the war and shaping patterns of displacement.

The capital, Dushanbe, lies in the western-central Hissar Oblast, which contains a sizable Uzbek minority. Hissar is primarily an agricultural region and is also the site of Tajikistan's strategically important aluminum industry.

To the north, in the Ferghana Valley, is the Leninabad Oblast. Separated from the other regions by the Zarafshan mountain range, this area came under Russian domination as early as the 1860s and was the chief source of Communist Party elites who dominated Tajik politics during Soviet days. It is the most economically developed region and also contains a large Uzbek population. The capital city of this region is Khojand.

The Gharm Oblast east of Dushanbe, in the central section of Tajikistan, is a mountainous and agricultural region whose Sunni Muslim inhabitants, known as Gharmis, are among the most religious in Tajikistan.[13] Intensive bouts of fighting, which have erupted sporadically since 1993, have centered on the strategically important town of Tavildara in the Gharm Valley, from which thousands of persons were displaced by fierce fighting during the summer of 1996. Tavildara lies along the one route between Dushanbe and the eastern parts of Tajikistan.

Southeast of Gharm is the large Gorno-Badakhshan Autonomous Oblast, the last area in Tajikistan to be brought under Soviet control in the 1920s. Dominated by the ruggedly beautiful Pamir Mountains, this is the most distinctive region from an ethnic point of view and the least developed economically. Most activity in Gorno-Badakhshan takes place in the valley of the Amu Darya River (also known as the Panj and the Oxus), which forms the border with Afghanistan. The inhabitants of Gorno-Badakhshan, known as Pamiris, are mostly Ismaili Muslims who speak various eastern Iranian dialects distinct from the Tajik language.

In the 1930s and 1940s, as areas in lowland Tajikistan were opened for cultivation, Stalin forcibly moved thousands of Gharmis and Pamiris to the new collective farms in southwestern Tajikistan, a district then known as Kurgan Teppe. The cotton these irrigated farms produced, as well as the aluminum produced in now nearly idle plants, formed the backbone of the Tajik economy. Although the Gharmis and Pamiris who had been transported to Kurgan Teppe intermarried with the local population to some extent, especially in urban areas, "many Gharmis and Pamiris remained acutely aware of their status as 'immigrants' to the area," and "many villages and towns retained distinct neighborhoods defined by area of family origin."[14] Having retained their ethnic distinction, these groups became targets during the civil war. Southwestern Tajikistan became the site of the war's greatest violence outside of Dushanbe. In late 1992, as Tajik government forces were consolidating their victory over the opposition, the Supreme Soviet voted to combine Kurgan Teppe with the adjacent district of Kulob, whose inhabitants, known as Kulobis and traditionally allied with Khojandi communist leaders from the north, by then had come to dominate the Tajik political scene. This move, which resulted in the creation of Tajikistan's fifth oblast, Khatlon, solidified Kulobi control over southwestern Tajikistan.

During the civil war, the opposition drew its primary support from the Gharm and Gorno-Badakhshan Oblasts and from Gharmis and Pamiris originally from those regions who had been relocated to Kurgan Teppe and the capital. The opposition comprised a loose coalition of democratic, nationalist, and Islamist parties and movements. Having been excluded from governing during the communist period, the Gharmis and Pamiris succeeded in coming to power for a few months in 1992 as part of a coalition government. Their bid to change the status quo ended in failure, however, and thousands of Gharmis and Pamiris were forcibly displaced. The old communist elite from Khojand and the Khojandis' traditional partners, the Kulobis, were determined to retain control of the levers of power, to the continued exclusion of the Pamiris and Gharmis. With the help of Tajikistan's ethnic Uzbek population, they succeeded.

Since 1993 the victorious Kulobis have dominated the government and have included a small number of Khojandis in their administration.[15] Today, although few consider the government to be representative of the country as a whole, under the terms of the 1997 peace accord the government is making an effort to broaden its base.[16] Opposition representatives are now included in the government, although small armed clashes continue. Moreover, since the civil war thousands of educated Tajiks, as well as Russians and Volga Germans, have left for destinations abroad. Absent the glue of a uniting nationalist framework, it is understandable that a conflict on clan and regional lines broke out. The government has not succeeded in cementing the country together well enough so that war and displacement cannot occur again.

Fundamentalism?

Just as internal displacement in Tajikistan has been a manifestation of civil conflict, the root causes of the displacement are equated to a great extent with the causes of the war itself. Not surprisingly, different observers and parties assign blame to different causal factors. Some brand the entire opposition fundamentalist. Others contend that the opposition never had as its primary objective the establishment of an Islamic regime and even question the degree to which outside Islamic powers such as Afghanistan and Iran have backed the opposition fighters.

During the war, the Kulobi-dominated government publicly associated the opposition with Islamic fundamentalism and insisted that its own electoral law, constitution, and parliamentary elections be respected. For their part, opposition leaders, at least when speaking with outsiders, dismissed government fears of a fundamentalist takeover as unfounded and argued that the government was hiding its unwillingness to share power.[17]

Although fundamentalism has been a factor, the causes of the civil war and displacement are more complex. They lie in the breakup of the USSR and its consequences for a weak state, and in the internal structure of Tajik society, including the lack of a cohesive national identity. These factors not only brought about the war and massive displacement; they also influenced the ways in which the Tajiks have treated IDPs since the displacement occurred. In addition, the characteristics of the war itself and the resurgence of ethnicity as a feature of political rivalry accounted for the viciousness of the attacks against civilians. For the government forces and their allies, victory was not a straightforward operation of defeating opposition militia but a matter of driving out persons of the same regional origins as the opposition, whether or not they had been associated with the rebel cause.

Economic Crisis

The collapse of the USSR brought with it the disappearance of the "social contract," conditions and policies fostered by the government in Moscow in exchange for stability. Price stability, the absence of inflation, and job security vanished overnight. Monetary transfers from Russia virtually disappeared, and Tajikistan imported hyperinflation through the ruble zone. Tajikistan's extremely high birth rate, which produced an annual population increase of 2.99 percent, was an added pressure.[18] Employment opportunities also disappeared for the vast majority of the population. To the extent that Kulobis and Khojandis could make jobs available to anyone, they favored their own. After the civil war, unemployed displaced persons returning home found it next to impossible to retrieve their former jobs. Moreover, the unstable economy militated against the return of many who remained internally displaced, as well as others who had left Tajikistan.

Compounding these misfortunes, the lack of diversity in agriculture rendered the economy vulnerable. Soviet leaders had designated nearly all of Tajikistan's arable land for growing cotton; with the collapse of the Soviet barter system and the ensuing civil war, cotton production proved unable to support the economy. The switch from cotton to wheat and other food crops, moreover, has been problematic. Farms lack fertilizers, fuel and spare parts, and good quality seeds. Uzbekistan is reluctant to export these items to Tajikistan, and deteriorating relations between the two nations have added to supply difficulties. Many areas are uncultivated. Cotton harvesters in Khatlon have been forced to work under almost serf-like conditions, although this practice has decreased over the past few years. The overwhelming majority of these forced laborers are returning refugees and internally displaced persons.[19] The control of agriculture and industry is a continuing source of friction between independently operating military commanders and the government. The Kurgan Teppe district (now part of Khatlon Oblast), with its cotton gins and railroad network connecting it to Uzbekistan and the outside market, was fought over fiercely during the war and was long a hot spot.[20] In 1997, rival warlords skirmished over the city of Tursunzade in the Hissar Oblast, home to Central Asia's largest aluminum factory.

In addition to political disarray, then, Tajikistan's economic turmoil since independence has heightened the nation's crisis. The economy of post-Soviet Tajikistan has been characterized by a breakdown of responsibilities, decentralization at all levels, a search for new markets, and economic regionalism.[21] Economic activity has fallen in virtually all spheres. Business enterprises in Tajikistan have to operate in a precarious environment. Credit is unavailable. Purchasing power in the local economy is low, except in some population centers. Raw materials and supplies are difficult to locate. The legal environment is characterized by labyrinthine confusion, with little recourse to business-related litigation. The scarcity of resources has accelerated the fragmentation of society and pushed people to rely upon their traditional regional and clan networks, strengthening the very localism that is at the root of the national identity crisis.

The Tajik Identity Crisis

Unlike several other former Soviet republics, such as Armenia, Georgia, and the Baltic States, Tajikistan did not have a well-developed sense of national identity when independence was thrust upon it. The word "Tajik" has different meanings for different people. Each of the country's five regions thinks of itself in different terms. Moreover, "the fact that the boundaries of the republic are reflected neither by a traditional polity nor by the distribution of the Tajik population . . . within Central Asia or beyond is a further reason why Tajik national consciousness has been hindered from growing properly."[22]

Despite the fact that outside powers became involved in Tajikistan, the conflict was first and foremost a civil war with roots in the nature of Tajik society. As analyst Julien Thöni discusses in his study The Tajik Conflict, the traditional organization of Tajik society along regional and clan lines has made it difficult to establish a sense of nationhood and is the fundamental cause of the Tajik conflict. Independence from the Soviet Union confronted the nation with the problem of defining a comprehensive identity and, in the context of a heterogeneous population, settling the difficult issues of political and economic control or power-sharing. Nevertheless, some sense of Tajik national consciousness is apparent throughout the country; at the very least, there are no serious bids for regional independence.[23] The civil war was not about secession.

An early Conference on Security and Cooperation in Europe (CSCE) report on Tajikistan notes that "ethnic, religious, and political/ideological differences among the warring parties should be taken into account, but these are eclipsed in significance by more historic—and pervasive—differences based on region, tribe, and clan."[24] The motivating factor behind the bloodshed, deep-seated resentment against those regions and clans in power by those excluded from power, remains alive. Today, as at the beginning of the civil war, the real issue is the redistribution of power and property at the local level. The government, lacking a vision to develop the nation, desires first and foremost to maintain its domination and avoid redistribution.

In the absence of an overarching national identity, geographic provenance and "localism" became the prime determinants of self-identification and loyalty in Tajikistan. Thöni defines localism as "a cultural-political attitude and process consisting of recruiting and promoting the elites in the framework of solidarity networks of political patronage according to religious, blood, regional, friendly or social affiliations." The Soviet period reinforced this process by entrenching the power of the Khojandis and their Kulobi supporters. The force of localism helps account for the war's swift brutality and "the rapid development of the conflict from political confrontation to armed clashes, for under the rule of localism power is an indivisible asset."[25] Believing itself to have "won" the war by crushing all alternative bids for power, the government has been loath to share the spoils, although this is slowly changing.

External Actors

External interactions, particularly between the Tajiks and Russian, Uzbek, Afghan, and Iranian players, also have had important bearings on displacement. While Uzbekistan feared a fundamentalist spillover and strongly supported Tajik government forces during the war, relations between Tashkent and Dushanbe have since cooled. Iran has provided a base for part of the Tajik political opposition and has hosted rounds of the Inter-Tajik Talks (see below). Northern Afghanistan served as a base for the armed Tajik opposition and as a refuge, however insecure considering its own state of unrest, for some 60,000 Tajik refugees. Tajik opposition parties have been able to procure arms and train guerrilla fighters among the refugees in Afghanistan. The Afghan government under President Rabbani, however, wielded scant control over the border area and probably had little incentive to fan the flames of the Tajik war.[26] In 1997–98, fighting in northern Afghanistan between the Taliban and groups resisting the Taliban's drive northward has raised concerns about long-run stability in the region.

The Russian role, of course, has been key. In 1992, Russian intervention tipped the balance of the civil war in favor of the procommunist Kulobi forces. In August 1992, the Tajik coalition government asked the Commonwealth of Independent States (CIS) division stationed in Dushanbe to help guard important installations, thereby providing the legal basis for Russian intervention. CIS peacekeeping forces, composed of 25,000 troops from Russia, Kyrgyzstan, Kazakstan, and Uzbekistan, guard essential infrastructure. The Russian Border Forces (RBF), composed mostly of Tajik troops, are present allegedly to guard the sensitive Tajik-Afghan border, prevent gunrunning, and curtail drug smuggling. The RBF limited the opposition's capacity to engage in large-scale military action on Tajik territory. Nevertheless, the opposition succeeded in making many attacks across the border from Afghanistan and for some time remained in control of part of Tajikistan.

Some analysts interpret the Russian presence and active military involvement in a different light and question Russia's stated "neutrality." One convincing view is that because Tajikistan is Russia's last foothold in Central Asia, Russia wants "an unsettled, slightly chaotic situation" there and is "not pushing for a real settlement to the conflict." Russian soldiers, who occasionally exchange fire with Afghan troops across the border, have an incentive to exaggerate accounts of border skirmishes to justify their high salaries in a "war zone."[27] According to some sources, the RBF has perpetrated human rights abuses against the local population in Gorno-Badakhshan. Moscow has hosted some sessions of the Inter-Tajik Talks, which have been taking place intermittently since April 1994. Overall, however,

> The Russian troops' inclination for pro-communist militias [during the war] . . . discredited Moscow as a potential neutral third party. . . . Russian partisan intervention firstly legitimated and enhanced the PF [pro-government Popular Front] role in Tajik society along with their reprehensible war methods and their uncompromising search for political domination. . . . Secondly, it excluded the opposition forces from the political scene, thereby pushing them to resort to guerrilla warfare from across the border.[28]

According to analyst Igor Rotar in 1996, "the current Tajik regime is good for the present Russian leadership . . . because it is fully oriented to the former parent state and is willing to serve Moscow's geopolitical interests."[29] Other sources, however, raised the possibility that Moscow was seeking to broaden the Tajik government. The emergence in mid-1996 of a trio of Tajik ex–prime ministers in Moscow, who called for a new coalition government of national reconciliation and increased power-sharing among Tajikistan's regions, was a possible sign of a Russian policy reassessment.[30] Indeed, Moscow played a constructive role in the negotiations that led to the 1997 peace accord.

From Tension to Civil War

The mid-1980s ushered in expanded freedom of expression and gave rise to the development of opposition parties with various causes, including a more democratic government (the goal of the Democratic Party of Tajikistan), the renewal of Tajik culture (the Rastokhez, or Rebirth,

Party), a moderate or fundamentalist Islamic government (the Islamic Revival Party), and greater autonomy for Gorno-Badakhshan (the Lale Badakhshan Party). These four parties attracted followers, principally Gharmis and Pamiris, who tended to see the opposition as a mechanism for redressing the regional power disparities of the communist period.[31] Moreover, the abortive coup in August 1991 against Gorbachev called into question the legitimacy of the Communist Parties in the USSR, Tajikistan, and other republics and led to the resignation of Kakhar Makhkamov, leader of the Communist Party of Tajikistan. Demonstrations protesting government corruption and demanding reforms heightened tensions in Dushanbe during the early 1990s. Many Russians and members of other minorities left the country.[32] Since these groups constituted a large number of Tajikistan's skilled workers and administrators, their departure further contributed to the general economic recession. Following declarations of independence by neighboring Uzbekistan and Kyrgyzstan, Tajikistan declared independence on September 9, 1991.

Any elation over Tajikistan's new statehood must have been shortlived. Rakhmon Nabiyev, a Khojandi who had led the Communist Party before Makhkamov, assumed the presidency after elections in November (the Kulob and Khojand regions, forming 60 percent of the nation's population, were easily able to elect a Khojandi communist to power) and a month later made the country a founding member of the CIS.[33] In March 1992, members of the opposition parties gathered in the center of Dushanbe, where they remained camped for nearly two months, and demanded the resignation of Nabiyev and his government. Nabiyev, in turn, accused the opposition parties of trying to establish a fundamentalist Islamic state. Government supporters demonstrated blocks away. Within weeks, violent clashes broke out between paramilitary groups supporting each side, paralyzing the capital. After opposition forces seized Dushanbe's television station and claimed control of the city, Nabiyev negotiated a truce. On May 7, 1992, he formed a compromise Government of National Reconciliation with opposition members appointed to some key ministerial positions, including interior, defense, and foreign affairs.[34]

Although the fighting halted temporarily in Dushanbe, it erupted in the Kulob region to the south between pro-communist Kulobi forces, who opposed the new coalition government, and opposition Islamic and democratic groups. As the situation further polarized and both sides committed atrocities, the first movements of internally displaced persons commenced.

Opposition forces seized the initiative during the early phases of the war and reportedly subjected the town of Kulob to a blockade, which resulted in famine.[35] From Kulob the fighting spread west and south to the Kurgan Teppe region, which supported the coalition government, and where a Kulobi militia called the Popular Front turned against the local opposition forces. By the beginning of September, the violence between the Kulobis, supported by their Uzbek allies, and the Pamiris and Gharmis, backed by the coalition government, escalated into pitched battles with heavy armor. Human rights abuses, including summary executions and the torture and massacres of civilians, were attributed to both parties to the conflict.

As pro-government forces began to gain ground, Kulobi militias and former neighbors "began a systematic campaign to expel or exterminate the region's entire Gharmi and Pamiri population," ransacking and torching their villages.[36] In the words of Davlat Khudonazarov, an unsuccessful presidential candidate in 1991, "people were shot in the streets . . . bodies were thrown out of windows into courtyards; entire families were killed, from children to grandparents. It was like the fascist terror."[37] Although the motive for the massive destruction of property was ostensibly to prevent the return of the displaced, an accompanying incentive was the opportunity for pro-government forces to loot with impunity and to harass particular ethnic groups.

The coalition government gradually proved unable to rule. On September 7, 1992, it forced Nabiyev to sign a letter of resignation and named Akbarshah Iskandarov the acting president. This move was not accepted by Parliament, however, which had remained dominated by the old communists. Parliament held a special session in Khojand in November and elected Imomali Rakhmonov, a Kulobi, the new president.[38] At that time, Parliament decided to merge the districts of Kurgan Teppe and Kulob, thereby forming the new Khatlon Oblast, in order to consolidate its control over the entire south. The coalition government's refusal to cede power led to a week of severe fighting in the capital, during which Uzbek paramilitary forces from Hissar came to the assistance of the procommunist forces, allowing them to enter Dushanbe in mid-December and form a new government. With the coalition government's defeat in Kurgan Teppe (now part of Khatlon) and Dushanbe, Gharmi and Pamiri civilians and the remaining members of the coalition government fled to the mountains. The four major opposition parties eventually were banned and in exile formed the United Tajik Opposition (UTO). A military offensive toward the Gharm Valley in early 1993 moved on the opposition's last stronghold within Tajikistan. Armed gangs continued to commit serious human rights abuses in the aftermath of the war.

In December 1992 and January 1993, after the government instigated an intense crackdown against opposition sympathizers and Kulobi warlords mounted further attacks against Gharmis and Pamiris in Khatlon, another large wave of displacement took place, including the flight of at least 60,000 Tajiks to Afghanistan. Long after these incidents, the crumbling mud walls of roofless houses in many Gharmi and Pamiri villages formed a stark contrast to the untouched Kulobi neighborhoods nearby and bore testimony to the selectivity of destruction and the exile of specific populations.

Displacement and Response

According to a UNHCR protection officer in Tajikistan, whether a displaced person became an IDP or a refugee was largely an academic distinction. People fled via whatever road was safe; they did not make political decisions about where to go. The movements of pro-government armed forces divided Khatlon in such a way that targeted civilians were forced to flee either southward to Afghanistan or northward to Dushanbe and on to the eastern parts of the country. Whether civilians became refugees or IDPs, the cause of their flight was the same. Moreover, refugees and IDPs faced similar problems, in terms of material support and security, upon returning to Khatlon.

The final destinations of displaced persons, however, were dictated by perceived safety: "IDPs in Tajikistan didn't merely flee the scene of disturbance or armed conflict; they fled having a destination of perceived security."[39] The vast majority of IDPs fled to their original homelands in Gharm and Gorno-Badakhshan. In addition, at least 15,000 fled to Dushanbe. Others went to the northern city of Khojand. A further 140,000 IDPs massed at the Afghan border during the harsh winter of 1992, some on islands in the Amu Darya River. In total, some 600,000 persons—individuals, families, and entire neighborhoods and villages of Gharmis and Pamiris—became internally displaced during the war. Entire districts in Khatlon were largely depopulated, and many villages remain empty.

UNHCR's list of figures for Khatlon districts is illustrative: in Bohktar District 90–95 percent of the population was displaced, most to the Gharm area; in Vakhsh District more than 95 percent of the population was displaced; in Shahrtuz District more than 40 percent of the population fled, many to Afghanistan. In Kurgan Teppe town, the regional capital of Khatlon, 60 percent were displaced.[40]

While the major period of displacement was brief, ongoing conflict in central Tajikistan generated new displacement in subsequent years during warm weather offensives by pro-government and opposition forces. The fighting focused on the strategically located Tavildara District astride the only road from Dushanbe to Khorog, the regional capital of Gorno-Badakhshan. Fighting during the summer of 1996, which UN Secretary-General Boutros Boutros-Ghali called the "worst and most volatile since the end of the civil war of 1992," resulted in new IDP emergencies.[41] The International Organization for Migration (IOM) reported in June 1996 that some 2,200 IDPs had fled Tavildara for Kalaikhumb on the Amu Darya River.[42] Later in the summer, ICRC reported a mass exodus of 11,000 persons fleeing both east toward Gorno-Badakhshan and west toward Dushanbe.[43] Others were displaced from the Karategin Valley east of Dushanbe. In early 1997, according to UNHCR and IOM, there were 30,000 IDPs in Tajikistan.[44]

The vast majority of those who were internally displaced in 1992 and 1993 returned home remarkably quickly, most of them spontaneously within the first year. By March 1993, 70 percent had returned to their villages in Khatlon and near Dushanbe. By the end of 1995, an estimated 98 percent had returned.[45] Many IDPs who remain in Gorno-Badakhshan wish to stay there permanently or seem ambivalent about returning home. UNHCR, the lead agency in Tajikistan until the United Nations Development Programme's (UNDP) resident representative began serving as the UN resident coordinator in February 1996, provided material assistance and protection to the returnees. Other international organizations contributed to this assistance effort as well (see below). Nevertheless, the displacement and destruction that took place in Gharmi and Pamiri villages is still evident today.

The estimate that 98 percent of those displaced in 1992–93 returned to their home communities should be qualified. Since the recorded number of returnees in different districts merely represents the number of persons moving into those areas, temporarily or permanently, it is hard to say whether those returning are the same as the original population that was displaced. For example, a number of people from Kulob have moved into the Vakhsh District.[46]

During the 1992–93 war, the combination of a large influx of IDPs and the deterioration of the national economy proved a tremendous hardship for receiving areas. Gorno-Badakhshan, with its mountainous terrain and harsh climate, was not agriculturally self-sufficient even before the war. This region received an influx of at least 100,000 persons, an obvious burden to an impoverished area with a pre-war population of fewer than 200,000.[47] Extended families absorbed most of them, and the overflow took shelter in public buildings such as schools and motels. Although the IDPs and their hosts lived in miserable conditions, often with many persons crowded into single rooms, most were at least surrounded by relatives. Many who took refuge in Gorno-Badakhshan found jobs and settled there permanently.[48] Although protection problems for IDPs in Gorno-Badakhshan have not been significant, malnutrition, starvation, and epidemics have indeed occurred, affecting IDPs and locals alike.[49] Both populations have become heavily dependent upon assistance from the international community.

International Response to Displacement: Patterns of Relief Assistance

The fact that IDPs and refugees were motivated to flee for similar reasons implies that the international community should assess each group's needs equally and without discrimination. UNHCR recognized this implication: "A major effective contribution was made when UNHCR stood its ground and declared its unwillingness to make an artificial distinction between those who had fled their homes for other parts of Tajikistan and those who crossed the border into Afghanistan."[50]

The allocation of responsibilities among the leading international agencies, initially ICRC, UNHCR, and the World Food Programme (WFP), was fairly straightforward and smooth. Activities among the agencies were divided both regionally and according to the services rendered. ICRC, the first international agency in Tajikistan, split its humanitarian mission to the internally displaced with UNHCR.[51] Soon after UNHCR's arrival, ICRC relinquished its protection and assistance activities in Khatlon and concentrated on assisting IDPs during their period of displacement in Gorno-Badakhshan, as part of the agency's humanitarian mission to the population at large. ICRC also continued to care for the 140,000 IDPs on the river border with Afghanistan until UNHCR was able to intervene some three months later.[52] UNHCR, present in Tajikistan from January 1993 and acting as humanitarian coordinator on behalf of the UN Department of Humanitarian Affairs (DHA), spearheaded efforts to care for Tajik refugees in northern Afghanistan.[53] UNHCR also provided protection and assistance to IDPs once they returned to Khatlon. Cooperation between UNHCR and ICRC apparently was strong. A supportive role has been played by the United Nations Mission of Observers in Tajikistan (UNMOT), which, under the leadership of the UN special representative of the secretary-general for Tajikistan since 1996, monitors cease-fires, assesses the military and security situation on the ground, and facilitates communication.

On the whole, coverage of the IDPs' emergency needs appears to have been fairly comprehensive. Many IDPs did not receive international assistance before they returned to their homes. For most, the consequences of their flight were mitigated by extended kinship relations. The immediate problems of those displaced to Gorno-Badakhshan became little different from the problems of the local Gharmis and Pamiris, though the sheer numbers of people exacerbated hardship for everyone. Given the region's poverty, of course, IDPs had to worry whether their extended families could afford to keep them. In 1997, 3,500 persons who had been displaced during the 1992–93 war decided to remain in Gorno-Badakhshan, and the resources of extended families were stretched thin.

Several other agencies provided relief assistance to IDPs during their period of displacement without distinguishing them from the local population. The Aga Khan Foundation stepped in after the war and the Soviet collapse cut off 80 percent of Gorno-Badakhshan's food supply to provide wheat flour and other food to the entire population there.[54] Médecins sans Frontières (MSF) distributed medical assistance to IDPs and locals throughout the region since April 1992. WFP managed the largest food assistance program in the country since mid-1993. The agency initially targeted 140,000 IDPs and other "seriously war-affected persons" in Khatlon in cooperation with UNHCR. By the end of 1993, however, after most IDPs displaced by the fighting in 1992 had returned home, it became apparent that a much larger number of people were in need of relief food. Confronted with the choice of serving the specific population of returning displaced persons or expanding its operations, WFP decided to shift to a country-wide vulnerable group program.

> This reflected the deteriorating conditions for all vulnerable groups, not only those directly affected by the civil war of 1992–1993. It also served to

reduce regional tensions because the relief food resources became targeted on vulnerability and poverty criteria whereas the war-affected criteria effectively concentrated most relief food in one Oblast [Khatlon].[55]

While it continued its distributions in Khatlon, WFP started working outside of Khatlon with implementing partners such as German Agro Action and the International Federation of Red Cross and Red Crescent Societies (IFRC) and began direct distributions in Gorno-Badakhshan. It targeted 400,000 persons in "vulnerable groups" throughout Tajikistan, including pensioners, the disabled, and households with no breadwinners. IDPs and returning displaced persons were among these groups but were no longer specifically targeted.

Government Attitudes toward the International Community

In its work as the lead international agency in Tajikistan, UNHCR concluded that it had "been able to gain the Government's confidence and respect in a manner that ha[d] made the organization much more influential than in most country situations." This also added to UNHCR's "making a more significant contribution to peace and general stabilization of the country than is customary."[56]

After the fighting in 1992–93, the Tajik government made the decision that it indeed wanted stability and wished to demonstrate that to the international community. It accepted UNHCR's role: the agency had a substantial presence, having opened eight field offices in addition to its headquarters in Dushanbe and employing at its peak more than fifty national and international staff. The government lacked resources, whereas UNHCR was able to provide large-scale return and reintegration assistance. Moreover, once the central government had decided to promote the repatriation of IDPs and refugees as a serious policy, UNHCR was in a position to halt its repatriation operations from Afghanistan if militia, police, or local government officials threatened the returnees. UNHCR "played this card rarely," but that option always existed. [57]

UNHCR did have to earn its acceptance in the field:

From January to March 1993, UNHCR's activities in Tajikistan focused on tough negotiations with the authorities to be granted full access to the areas of potential return of Tajik refugees [and IDPs] and to agree on the assistance measures to these areas. Likewise, UNHCR worked hard to influence the authorities to adopt measures that would ease the tensions between Tajikistan's various communities.[58]

The very weakness of the government encouraged its cooperation with the international community. Having lost its Soviet benefactor, the government desperately needed assistance. For UNHCR, one of the first international organizations to have contact with the government, this permitted a greater emphasis than usual on protection activities and human rights coverage in a country of origin. It was able to intervene actively in cases of abuse against returnees and monitor human rights.[59] December 1993, said one international official, was "emergency at its best" because the government was open to any and all assistance. The government's subsequent consolidation of power, however, made it more reluctant to cooperate with international humanitarian organizations, especially in war zones where the government believed aid organizations might interfere with its military objectives.[60]

There were several positive signs of government cooperation. The Tajik Central Refugee Department, created in July 1992, gave UNHCR a focused contact within the Tajik government. The existence of this agency, which falls under the Labor Ministry, made communicating with the government much easier for UNHCR than it would have been if the office's functions were spread across several agencies. UNHCR has been trying to encourage the creation of similar "focal agencies" in other countries as well.[61]

Another important measure was the passage of a national law on "forced migration" in June 1994 (often called the "Law on Internally Displaced Persons"). This law regulates registration procedures and provides government protection and assistance for IDPs and returning refugees and displaced persons. However, "the promised benefits to IDPs required funds which the government did not have, and the assistance clauses of the law have proven largely aspirational."[62] IDPs and returnees say that government assistance has been minimal, if not nonexistent, and unevenly distributed.

In spite of a stated desire to cooperate with international organizations, the extent to which different segments of the government of Tajikistan coordinated with each other and communicated with the public, and the intent of some local officials, was open to question. In the summer of 1996, some IDPs in Gorno-Badakhshan were told that their "IDP status" had expired and that they should vacate the public buildings in which they had been living. An official at the Central Refugee Department in Dushanbe, however, maintained that a new decree adopted in August 1995, entitled "Additional Measures of Repatriation of Citizens and IDPs to Places of Origin," had abolished all time limits on "IDP status."[63]

A closer examination indeed reveals that the whole picture was not so rosy. At lower levels of government, many local officials proved unresponsive to the protection needs of returning refugees and internally displaced persons, and police and military units harassed certain communities. Both the government and the opposition questioned the humanitarian neutrality of international organizations. Local officials frowned at convoys moving into areas of presumed resistance, while the opposition suspected that humanitarian agencies were supporting the army and thus, indirectly, the government. In short, government attitudes were mixed.

Coordination within the International System and with the Government

In 1996, a senior government official, when asked about the government's relations with the international agencies present in his country, claimed not to understand what any of them were doing save for UNHCR and UNDP. This remark, although flippant, was revealing. At first, coordination among the few international bodies that were present and between aid agencies and the government seems to have been effective. After an initial period marked by the absence of NGOs, the arrival of a plethora of humanitarian agencies bewildered the government and weakened the cohesion and impact of the international community's humanitarian response. While the major organizations were known to the entire government, many were known only to officials with whom they worked directly and not to other branches of government that had nominal authority over relief agencies. This disarray was due to shortcomings in organization within both the government itself and the international system.

A notable disappointment in the international community's response to the crisis in Tajikistan was the UN's failure to achieve the "integrated response" that it originally had envisaged. In November 1992, the secretary-general dispatched a joint Good Offices Mission to Tajikistan that included UNHCR, DHA, the Department of Political Affairs, and the Department of Peace-keeping Operations. It was hoped that by combining peacemaking efforts with the provision of humanitarian aid, this coordinated approach could prevent future displacement.[64] Despite the fact that other relief and development agencies were expected to join the overall effort, the burden for carrying out assistance and protection activities in the field soon fell almost entirely upon UNHCR and ICRC. UNHCR performed effectively as lead agency and humanitarian coordinator. However, when it came to the turnover of responsibilities, coordination proved weak, partly because UNDP, other UN agencies, and NGOs were slow to become involved in Tajikistan.[65]

On a more positive note, communication between most of the international agencies appeared to be fairly strong. In the summer of 1996, UNDP hosted weekly meetings in Dushanbe for agency representatives to exchange information and share experiences, although some organizations chose to remain on the periphery of this group.

The Tajik government, for its part, was slow to establish a central point of contact through which international agencies could communicate.[66] Moreover, when UNHCR handed over its field offices and protection responsibilities to OSCE in 1995, the government did not fully understand the differences between the organizations. While UNHCR demanded protection for returnees *and* provided assistance, which the government viewed as its "reward" or stake in cooperating with UNHCR, OSCE provided only protection.[67] The public, including IDP returnees, saw the same local staff working in the same buildings UNHCR used to occupy and mistakenly thought OSCE might have material assistance to distribute.

Some questioned the need for so many agencies to be present. One international official bemoaned the emphasis on humanitarian assistance at the expense of conflict resolution efforts:

> We find it tragic that there are ever more institutions trying to find themselves mandates and only creating confusion. . . . People have the illusion that because they want to be effective and cannot make any political headway, they can all turn to the humanitarian field. But this field is no less frustrating or difficult than the political field. This situation confuses the government and creates opportunities for the government and other forces to play institutions against each other.[68]

According to another international official, too much attention was focused on the humanitarian agencies themselves, which eagerly discussed their objectives and individual programs with donors in order to gain high visibility and further contributions from donors. He regretted that too little attention was paid to efforts to promote the sustainable development of Tajikistan. If the large number of international organizations and their lack of a coordinated thrust were confusing to someone familiar with the UN system, he asked, how must it appear to the government?[69] If one goal of international humanitarian assistance is to help fill a gap in support for vulnerable persons until the national government resumes full responsibility, does it not make sense for international agencies to present a coordinated front to that government and to openly communicate about their programs and the needs of vulnerable citizens?

Lack of coordination between international agencies and the government has several negative, self-perpetuating repercussions. Some international relief officials, for example, work as quietly and independently as possible because they fear that open communication might endanger their operations. While this course may reap immediate gains for needy beneficiaries, it is likely to heighten government suspicion and defensiveness, which in turn may lessen the government's willingness to cooperate. By 1996, cooperation had, in fact, deteriorated. One example can be found in the experience of an international NGO in Khatlon that produced cement tiles to help returnees rebuild their roofs. The local police chief reportedly had installed two men on the NGO's payroll to keep an eye on the organization. When the NGO discovered this and fired the two men, the police chief insisted that he be informed of the NGO's schedule of activities each week in advance. The chief also was said to have removed two loads of expensive, hard-to-find cement from the operation.[70]

The government also did not comprehend international humanitarian principles and goals and perceived some programs as threatening or interfering with its own activities. In the summer of 1996, the government obstructed ICRC's access to the contested Tavildara area from which thousands of internally displaced persons were fleeing. This forced the agency to reroute humanitarian aid and delayed the delivery of that aid. Moreover, the government interfered with a soap production facility in Khatlon run by an international NGO. The project succeeded in turning local cottonseed oil into high-quality, low-cost soap, until various "cotton barons" connected with the government had the plant shut down.[71] In addition, the government issued a new order in May 1996 for all international agencies to provide prior notification of any travel outside Dushanbe—a clearly restrictive move that the agencies hotly protested and reportedly agreed to ignore.

Relations between the international organizations and the government, then, have been difficult at times. The Tajik government had strong reasons to encourage the return of displaced persons after the war and thus was motivated to cooperate with key agencies such as UNHCR. But the government is loath to support activities that it believes might undercut its political or strategic positions. These include aid distributions to war victims in militarily sensitive areas as well as development projects that benefit returnees but challenge entrenched economic interests.

Solutions: Return and Reintegration

After government troops and other pro-government militia had unleashed a brutal campaign against the Gharmis and Pamiris, it seems startling that 90 percent of all IDPs returned home within a year, beginning as early as January and February of 1993.[72]

Factors Favoring Return and International Involvement

One reason for this rapid return had to do with the expectation that government policy was changing. Once the Kulobi-dominated government had won the war, it recognized that normalization and stability were necessary to overcome the country's economic disintegration and ongoing political unrest. At the international level, the government needed legitimacy and external support for reconstruction; to obtain this, it had to demonstrate a sense of responsibility for the entire population. The Russian Federation, Uzbekistan, and the UN also exercised pressure and influence to this end.[73] At the national level, the depopulation of Khatlon meant labor shortages and plummeting income for the cotton industry. The government also feared that the opposition would recruit persons who remained displaced and thereby strengthen its ranks. Indeed, the longer Tajik refugees remained in Afghanistan, the greater the suspicion with which the government viewed them. Thus it was no surprise when, in March 1993, the central government told local officials throughout the country that they were "to welcome the return of our Tajik brothers."[74] If the government had good reasons to encourage return, the dismal living conditions in Gorno-Badakhshan and Afghanistan and the demonstration of increasing stability in Khatlon, strongly promoted by the UNHCR field presence, were enough to convince most IDPs and refugees to go home.

Government-encouraged returns in 1993 were hardly organized with a soft touch, however. Some IDPs who had fled to Dushanbe during the war were forcibly relocated to the Kabodian District of Khatlon:

> Once dumped in their villages, these people had nowhere to go; their houses were either destroyed or, if they remained intact, they were taken over by those on the winning side of the war, i.e. Kulobis and Uzbeks. UNHCR came to their rescue by launching an immediate emergency airlift of tents from Peshawar, Pakistan.[75]

Returnees near Kabodian related their own story: about 500 IDPs who had fled to Dushanbe were loaded onto trains and transported south to their village, where an angry mob blocked the returnees from their homes. During a two-week standoff, while UNHCR, ICRC, and the UN Department of Peace-keeping Operations negotiated with local authorities, sixteen people died of cold and hunger. Following a joint UNHCR-ICRC protest, the government halted these forced returns. Article 8 of the Tajik Law on Internally Displaced Persons, adopted the next year, states that "a forced migrant [IDP] cannot be returned against his will to the place of his previous permanent residence." However, international involvement was clearly needed to aid and protect the thousands of returnees and to prepare local communities to receive them.

In the summer of 1996, UNHCR and others helped the government establish three reception centers with dormitories and food for newly displaced IDPs on the road west from Tavildara. In August, some 300 IDPs were returned to Tavildara by the government, allegedly voluntarily. The government planned to continue such return transports, despite the ongoing hostilities, the large number of land mines placed by both opposition and government forces, and the fact that international organizations had been denied access to the areas. International organizations did not consider conditions in central Tajikistan safe enough to warrant return and were prevented from assessing the returnees' safety and providing relief assistance.[76]

Despite difficult traveling conditions, most IDPs who had fled to Gharm and Gorno-Badakhshan returned spontaneously. One exception occurred during the summer of 1995, when UNHCR, IOM, ICRC, and UNMOT arranged for a series of return convoys with the consent and cooperation of the government and opposition. UNHCR told local authorities in Khatlon and Dushanbe how many IDPs would be returning and, working from government registration lists of returnees, urged the authorities to investigate cases of illegal house occupation before the returnees arrived. Despite careful planning and hopes to move 500 persons weekly, however, only three convoys (containing a total of some 1,700 persons) were completed before the onset of winter. The poor condition of government-supplied vehicles and the harassment of some returnees during prearranged arms searches also undermined the operation's success.[77] The opposition was against the convoys from the start; it claimed that convoy participants were subjected to human rights abuses en route and that some people registered as IDPs only to travel to Dushanbe to visit family or friends. In June 1996, fighting in Tavildara rendered the road west from Gorno-Badakhshan inaccessible. After some delays, in 1997 IOM airlifted more than 1,300 of the remaining IDPs who had registered to return.

Factors Militating against Return

Although the presence of UNHCR, OSCE, and other international bodies in Khatlon and Dushanbe improved the environment for returning IDPs, ethnic violence was not eliminated. In 1997, for newly displaced IDPs from Tavildara and other areas, as well as for the estimated 9,000 IDPs who remained in Gorno-Badakhshan and Gharm, protection issues overshadowed the desire to return home. Problems with insecurity were particularly difficult in the spring of 1993, following the heaviest period of fighting. The government's capacity to provide security was limited because it had been brought to power by irregular forces that operated to some extent outside its control and did not reflect a unified coalition. These forces, many connected with the Popular Front, were responsible for serious human rights abuses. "When the civil war ended . . . various armed, pro-government paramilitary groups continued to attack with impunity Gharmis and Pamiris throughout the country."[78]

The situation improved in the intervening years, and some paramilitary groups were brought under control, but the ability and inclination of Tajik authorities to provide protection remained questionable for some time. In the summer of 1996, ethnically motivated harassment of civilians continued to take place, though killings had become infrequent. Word of this violence, as well as cases of illegally occupied houses and forced conscription, continued to spread from Khatlon and Dushanbe to villages throughout Gorno-Badakhshan, discouraging the return of the remaining internally displaced.

Human Rights Watch/Helsinki reported on these and other hardships awaiting returnees, including arguments over occupied houses, the forced recruitment of returnees to provide labor on collective farms, the lack of building materials (particularly roofing timbers), discrimination in employment, and the confiscation of humanitarian assistance.[79] As mentioned above, IDPs felt alienated from the Kulobi-dominated national government and had little faith in the government's inclination to address these problems. The comment of an IDP woman near Rushan, Gorno-Badakhshan, was echoed in many interviews with IDPs and returnees: "We have no leaders in Dushanbe."[80]

In 1996, at the time of the visit of the representative of the secretary-general on internally displaced persons, the human rights environment in Tajikistan continued to discourage return and undermine stability.[81] Security problems remained a strong concern of returnees and other citizens. Hostilities in central Tajikistan had resumed and intensified, and government forces were recruiting new combatants by conducting raids at night, searching buses and houses, and arresting young men who were allegedly beaten if they resisted.[82] Although those recruited in the Khojand region were said to receive adequate training before being sent into combat zones, young men taken from Gharmi and Pamiri communities in Khatlon and Dushanbe reportedly did not. Moreover, these groups often were singled out for drafting. According to IDP returnees in a Gharmi village near Dushanbe, it was not safe for young men to leave their neighborhoods even in daylight. Many young men disappeared, having fled or been seized by the military, leaving the women behind with the difficult task of supporting their families.[83] Other returnee communities suffered similar experiences during the war but did not seem to face such dire threats upon return, an indication that the level of protection provided by local authorities varied considerably.

In addition to these security problems, other human rights violations have persisted. Freedom of movement, provided by Tajik law, has been hampered by the numerous security checkpoints set up along roads throughout the country, at which military forces reportedly harass civilians and confiscate goods. In addition, the state of the education system reflects wider problems in Tajik society. Teaching materials and money to pay teachers' salaries are lacking, and many of the most qualified teachers have emigrated. School attendance is also affected by the need for children to work and earn money and by the practice, in the Kurgan Teppe region, of forcing teachers and children to provide labor in the fields during the cotton harvesting season. Furthermore, although the Tajik constitution protects freedom of expression, the government severely restricts the voicing of public criticism. A number of journalists have been murdered by unknown groups, generally without charges being brought against any suspects.[84] Harassment and dismissals of journalists have led to a high level of self-censorship in the few newspapers that remain.

The Tajik constitution provides for protection against ethnic discrimination and also explicitly states that men and women have equal rights. Discrimination continues, however, in employment and housing. Although government officials have made efforts to settle some cases of the illegal occupation of returnees' houses, authorities have failed to prevent de facto ethnic (or clan) discrimination in cases where the alleged perpetrator was a relative or warlord who could pressure the authorities not to take action. As a result, the formerly displaced often hesitate to bring cases of discrimination to the authorities.

Members of Garmi and Pamiri communities also complain of having lost their employment to persons of a different ethnic origin. The risks and consequences of losing employment are even more serious for the women of those communities and for female-headed households, who suffer from both minority and gender discrimination. Women also have greater difficulty establishing alternative sources of livelihood because credit is unavailable. Because IDPs and minorities are often overlapping categories in Tajikistan and the problems facing them are similar, the improved protection of minorities would increase protection for formerly and currently displaced persons as well.

A related human rights issue is the independence of the judiciary. Although the Tajik constitution states that judges are independent and prohibits interference in their activities, these principles are routinely violated. Strengthening the rule of law is crucial for returnees and others to feel safe. OSCE and UNHCR have provided some assistance, in the form of financial support, capacity-building, and the training of court personnel and law enforcement officials. OSCE regards legislation on the judicial system, passed in March 1996, as a step in strengthening the independence of the judiciary, although the issue still needs attention.

Protection issues and human rights problems are not the sole reason that remaining IDPs have not returned. Throughout 1996, fighting in the Tavildara region in central Tajikistan made it impossible for IDPs who wished to return from Gorno-Badakhshan to do so by land. Many who remain decided to stay because Gorno-Badakhshan is their original homeland, from which they were displaced during the 1930s. Their return to the region evoked a sense of attachment.

Dependence on aid is another reason for staying. Although poverty in the mountains motivated many IDPs to return to Khatlon and Dushanbe, those who remain in Gorno-Badakhshan seem to be holding out for a better life in that region. One senses the hope (on the part of government officials as well as IDPs) that someone will continue to care for them, that some new order will fill the void left when the Soviet system crumbled. IDPs and locals alike benefit from, and depend on, food aid from the Aga Khan Foundation and WFP and other assistance from the government and the international community. The extent to which local officials have helped IDPs is unclear, but certainly some IDPs have found jobs, and village officials have provided some with land. Conditions are hard, but many wish to stay in Gorno-Badakhshan as long as humanitarian aid continues and the future holds a chance of improvement. Resettlement, then, is an alternative to return.

The tensions surrounding the issue of return are readily apparent. The central government, seeking stability after winning the war, welcomes return but has little assistance to offer. Many local authorities and former neighbors have been antagonistic or unaccommodating. IDPs and refugees have their own reasons for and against returning, which the international community has respected. Moreover, the opposition has at times discouraged return. In reference to the return convoys organized in 1995, one opposition member maintained in 1996 that in the face of continued discord in Khatlon it was "dangerous and premature to encourage the return of IDPs. We do not agree with this policy of the international organizations." Indeed, returnees have faced many problems. Only recently have these started to subside.

Relief Assistance and Protection for Returnees

GOVERNMENT AND INTERNATIONAL RELIEF ASSISTANCE. The immediate needs of returning IDPs and refugees were obvious. As discussed above, many Gharmis and Pamiris found their houses occupied or destroyed. Local populations were often hostile, and although the violence has diminished since then, murders, beatings, disappearances, and harassment were common during the early stages of return. Returnees felt alienated from local officials and security forces and claimed that the authorities did not represent their interests. Moreover, food, housing, and employment were in short supply. Women were often left with the responsibility of supporting their households after the men had been killed, had gone into hiding to avoid forced conscription, remained in Afghanistan, or had joined the armed opposition. For those women it was especially difficult to find employment and the resources to survive. However, the situation by 1998 improved, particularly with regard to the more egregious protection problems.

The government's refugee department, under the Law on Internally Displaced Persons, was supposed to provide monetary compensation for displacement and an allotment for rebuilding houses, but it is difficult to say how many actually were paid and how much. In 1994 the government dropped displacement compensation and substituted home repair payments with credit toward the purchase of food at government stores. The Law on Internally Displaced Persons also grants returnees temporary rent-free housing, medical services, and either work equivalent to their previous experience or training courses. Furthermore, the law entitles returnees to assistance placing their children in schools and to a pension or limited salary according to their period of absence.[85] Many returnees, however, claimed in 1996 that they had received no government assistance. Certainly the value of the Tajik ruble has plunged dramatically since its introduction in May 1995, and the devastation of the economy has precluded major government assistance programs.

UNHCR, the lead international organization assisting and protecting returnees in Khatlon and Dushanbe, organized the distribution of non-food items, such as tents and cooking fuel, and set up an emergency water and sanitation program. In addition, UNHCR provided a one-time seed distribution and later funded an implementing partner, Save the Children/US, to continue this project. With ICRC, UNHCR surveyed Khatlon and initially estimated that 17,000 houses were destroyed. This figure was later revised to more than 18,000 houses. Through a reconstruction program that was plagued by funding constraints and procurement and logistical delays associated with "realities in the newly independent states of the former Soviet Union," UNHCR was able to provide building materials for 18,500 homes in a three-phase operation that ended in April 1996.[86] In June 1996, however, many neighborhoods remained in ruins, and the agency continued to fund Save the Children/US to carry on the project. At that time, the international community's assistance program in Khatlon was still focused on emergency food and housing needs, while a few agencies were introducing development-oriented projects in the same region. WFP food continued to be distributed to returnees and others in need. German Agro Action, CARE International, IFRC, Save the Children/US, and Mercy Corps International also participated in the vulnerable group feeding program in areas of return.

Significantly, UNHCR directed aid to local populations as well as returnees. Its expanded involvement stemmed from the need for stability in Khatlon communities, where tension between the different population groups remained high and protection problems were critical, before the repatriation of refugees and IDPs could succeed.

> As a refugee agency, it is logical for UNHCR to design its programme and tasks in relation to the number of displaced people of concern to the Office. However, in Tajikistan as in other country-of-origin operations, neither protection nor assistance could logically be restricted to returning refugees without this being considered as undue favouritism by other community members in equal need. The scope of UNHCR's activities would, therefore, have to be formulated and justified in relation to a clearly defined qualitative objective of reintegration and reconciliation.[87]

One international official, however, expressed reservations about UNHCR's enlarged role and maintained this should not become a pattern. It is true that UNHCR's involvement should be clearly defined in order to clarify goals, distinguish its mandate from those of other agencies, and keep the government informed about its programs. Agency mandates must be clear during the transition from relief to development assistance, for example, which is discussed below. Yet despite these qualifications it makes sense for UNHCR, which is sensitive to the needs of refugees and IDPs—often society's most vulnerable people—to address the needs of larger populations, including those who were not displaced, when the post-conflict peace is as shaky as it was in Tajikistan and when unbalanced aid could rekindle the resentment that brought on the civil war.

PROTECTION. International presence in areas of return was key to helping calm a dangerous situation in which local hostility gave rise to a host of protection problems. The cornerstone to UNHCR's success in Khatlon was its country-of-origin protection activities. Its large field presence comprised officers who did not hesitate to get involved with individual cases, taking an active approach "whereby Field Officers confronted authorities and forcefully insisted that existing legislation be applied fairly to all segments of the population."[88]

One key role for UNHCR field officers was in listening to and acting on complaints from people who had suffered human rights abuse or whose houses had been occupied. Fearful of the local administration, which was dominated by the Kulobis, these people needed the help of an international agency to bring their complaints to the authorities. UNHCR's presence was also important in ensuring that local authorities did not remain passive. Keeping the central government informed helped ensure that local authorities responded to complaints, especially at times when they might have been reluctant to act for the reasons discussed above.[89] Although the problems did not vanish, the marked decrease in violence against returnees between 1993 and 1996 was due in large part to the active international presence. Greater stability, in turn, further encouraged return.

After most IDPs had returned home and the rate of repatriation from Afghanistan had slowed, UNHCR began searching for an agency that could pick up the human rights protection work it had begun. In a unique transition in the fall of 1995, UNHCR handed over three of its eight field offices—replete with computers and a functioning local staff—to OSCE, which was already known to the Tajik government through its diplomatic mission in Dushanbe. OSCE took up UNHCR's monitoring and intervention activities and has fostered contacts with local and national government officials, prosecutors, security officers, and police. Pleased with the smooth turnover, UNHCR reported that it might view this transition as a precedent, even though OSCE, traditionally more active in the political than the humanitarian field, got the job simply because no one else, not even UN human rights bodies, stepped forward.[90] Since then, UNHCR has shifted from a country to a regional focus, although it continues to fund some projects within Tajikistan. In November 1997, the agency also repatriated the last of the Tajik refugees in northern Afghanistan.

Like UNHCR, OSCE saw a direct link between protection and reintegration, between urging local authorities to investigate returnees' complaints fairly and averting outbreaks of ethnic hostility (UNHCR called this "preventive protection"). Accordingly, OSCE's field officers considered individual cases of illegal house occupation, often issuing statements for court cases, and brought cases of mistreatment in prisons and police harassment to the attention of local and national authorities. They also provided a communications link by radio and letter between Tajik refugees in Afghanistan and family members in Khatlon. Although IDP and refugee returnees were the main focus of its efforts, OSCE also addressed human rights issues for the general population, including ethnic Uzbeks and Russians. The organization was encouraged to monitor human rights more comprehensively in Dushanbe and throughout Khatlon.[91]

OSCE's involvement in Tajikistan seems promising. As a regional political organization of which Tajikistan is a member, OSCE had established a working relationship with the government before taking over human rights monitoring and is in a position to support the development of the entire democratic process. The combination of political influence in Dushanbe with a field presence that is willing to intercede should benefit returnees.

REINTEGRATION AND DEVELOPMENT PROGRAMS. An outsider viewing both areas of return and regions of continued displacement in Tajikistan sees a striking paucity of development initiatives. Most international organizations maintain a presence in Khatlon only and have concentrated on relief assistance or relief in the context of reintegration, rather than development assistance. Although some international staff members recognize the dire need for longer-term development in all parts of the country, it may be difficult for agencies to switch gears when the emergency requirements of so many people are so obvious. Thousands of families continue to require emergency food and shelter. In March 1998, the UN issued a consolidated inter-agency appeal to widen humanitarian programs in Tajikistan. Still, while the country has many problems and few resources, and security remains a concern, military activity in areas of return has largely ended.

What is clear to most of the international community, if not to the Tajiks, is that outside resources are not infinite. Officials at the central and local levels have emphasized that they would like to provide more support for returnees but lack the resources, even though most IDPs returned several years ago. In response to a question about how long Tajikistan will continue to require assistance, one local official in Khatlon replied "as long as the international community can give it."[92] The Soviet legacy is a contributing factor to this dependency syndrome. During the Soviet era, the welfare state provided for the needs of everyone without any particular initiative being necesssary. Today, it appears that this role has been taken over in part by the international community, given the expectations of beneficiaries and government officials. As long as international assistance continues to be doled out with compassion, if not foresight, the motivation and ability of the Tajiks to help themselves is likely to remain low. Given the decreasing availability of international funding, however, continuing dependency will inevitably result in disappointment.

To help consolidate the growing stability in areas of return and improve conditions in Gorno-Badakhshan, international organizations need to design programs with an eye toward sustainable development. As one official succinctly stated, people must not be made passive recipients; they must be given a role in "managing their own misery . . . [for] to cover the whole place with a blanket of western 'do-goodism' is a costly and dubious undertaking."[93] If such a blanket of relief aid were to smother the country's initiative, Tajikistan would lose an opportunity to replace fighting with peaceful development.

Tajikistan does contain a wealth of untapped natural resources, notably water and minerals. The country also has inherited infrastructural assets from the Soviet era, including roads and railways, a network of irrigation channels, and a high degree of electrification, although maintenance is sorely needed. Given the traditionally high value placed on education, Tajikistan has the potential to develop its human capital as well; before the war, an estimated 98 percent of the population was literate.[94] Depending on the state of the economy, if the international community can help mobilize remaining capacities, people may develop a stake in working instead of fighting.

Some organizations already have implemented development-oriented programs in Tajikistan; others are planning to do so. Such initiatives include food-for-work programs run by WFP and NGOs, including Mercy Corps International and Save the Children/US, which aim to improve long-term food security. UNICEF and WFP have designed joint food-for-work projects to help restore public health facilities. UNICEF also has introduced a "peace education" training project for teachers throughout Tajikistan "to give useful positive messages regarding local geographic and ethnic diversity . . . as well as messages about peaceful conflict resolution."[95] In Gorno-Badakhshan, the Aga Khan Foundation funds the Pamiri Relief and Development Programme, which hopes to strengthen the agriculture and education sectors, provide technical advice and credit to new businesses, promote preventive health care, and launch afforestation projects. UNDP's $20 million Rehabilitation, Reconstruction, and Development Programme, which commenced in March 1996 and is to be implemented over four years, aims to further stabilize postwar Tajikistan. Among its other activities, UNDP runs nine youth clubs in Khatlon to promote reintegration. None of these programs targets returnees exclusively, but the enhanced stability the programs aim to foster should benefit returnees as well as the general population.

As in other countries, UNHCR implemented a regimen of quick-impact projects (QIPs) designed to promote speedy reintegration in areas of return that, after the war, were almost devoid of economic activity. Relief International and the International Rescue Committee (IRC) served as implementing partners. Relief International's projects, whose direct participants were almost exclusively women, focused on the small-scale production of household goods such as *chapans* (men's traditional coats), *kurpachas* (warm mattresses), yarn, Pamiri socks, and school bags. Other activities included rabbit farming and a revolving loan fund.[96]

Insofar as the participants received income and sewing machines and were able to produce some much-needed items, these QIPs were successful. Once under way, the rabbit-raising QIP also flourished. The QIPs largely failed as long-term projects, however. The procurement of supplies was complicated and costly, thus making the final products too expensive to sell for profit. In addition, machinery never functioned properly, and Tajik men objected to the women's loan program. Most important, the participants themselves did not learn new business skills that could help them after the internationally funded projects ended.[97]

Drawing lessons from these experiences, UNHCR decided to recast the IRC-implemented QIPs as "Small Enterprise Development Projects," or SEDs. Subsequently, IRC focused its activities on producing scarce commodities such as soap and shoes, which were in high demand, and revitalizing poultry farms. In its attempt to convert the QIPs into SEDs, UNHCR was acknowledging that the international community could not support these projects indefinitely and that they would need to be "privatized."[98]

Transforming QIPs into SEDs was not an easy undertaking. As an independent evaluator observed, the QIP design put a premium on speed and efficiency, but this may have undercut longer-term goals, such as achieving ethnic reconciliation. Although workers at IRC's production sites came from many backgrounds, the agency's core staff was composed predominantly of Russians who were recruited quickly and chosen for their technical qualifications.[99] The projects also did not pay adequate attention to gender issues and beneficiary participation, important aspects of sustainable development. In IRC's projects in Khatlon, for example, all of the sixty-two beneficiaries who operated the shoe and soap production facilities were men. To UNHCR, the Tajik experience highlighted the importance of addressing longer-term development objectives alongside short-term QIPs.

Problems inherent in the shift from a command to a market economy complicated the efforts of international agencies to carry out development projects and the efforts of returnees to resume normal lives. UNHCR's experiences, and those of other organizations, underline facets of the Tajik economy that hinder development: state ownership of most productive assets, corruption and entrenched political and economic interests, limited access to capital, and lack of production inputs. One international staff member, remarking on the large loans international financial institutions have provided the Tajik government, maintained it would be more effective to provide Tajik officials with a crash course in market economics.[100] In 1996 the lack of markets led returnees in Khatlon to ask UNHCR officials if international organizations would buy their latest wheat harvest.[101]

The unanswered question is where UNHCR's role with returnees (indeed with entire populations in areas of return) should end, and where the roles of other development agencies, especially UNDP, should begin. Both UNHCR's immediate relief response to returnees' needs and its longer-term, more development-oriented program increased the organization's credibility and influence with Tajik authorities, which facilitated its protection work. In addition to the QIPs and SEDs, UNHCR engaged in a number of development-oriented projects that bear an indirect relation to its assistance and protection work with refugees and returnees: a judicial assistance program to strengthen Tajik judiciary and law enforcement institutions, an art and culture program to promote peace and reconciliation, an NGO capacity-building training program, a survey of bazaar and household economies in Tajikistan, a feasibility study on small- and medium-sized enterprise development, and a women's economic survey.[102]

UNHCR's programs appear to have been creative and valuable, and the lessons learned have been constructive, including the lesson that "the focused parameters of the QIP concept are obviously inadequate when applied to development projects."[103] However, in light of the importance attached to "bridging the gap" from relief to development, and considering that UNHCR has been scaling back its mission but continues to fund development-related activities, attention should be paid to its coordination with UNDP. UNHCR and UNDP signed a memorandum of understanding in July 1995. Under this agreement, UNDP assumed responsibility for a number of UNHCR's ongoing projects. It discontinued others, however, judging that they could not become economically viable. An evaluation of the SED program found that the transfer to UNDP would have been easier if the projects had been conceived from the outset as part of a long-term development program, which would have allowed UNDP to provide complementary support.[104] At the same time, it was pointed out that UNDP's slow start in Tajikistan rendered this difficult.

The Quest for Peace

Reintegration and development programs are essential in helping Tajikistan recover and assisting returnees in reestablishing themselves. However, the original cause of displacement—the exclusion of certain groups from power-sharing—has not been resolved. Although a general peace accord was signed in June 1997 and represents a hopeful milestone in the resolution of the conflict, ethnic and regional antagonism has not been overcome. Ultimately, a lasting solution to the crisis of internal displacement in Tajikistan requires addressing the root causes of unrest and resolving the conflict.

Neither the government nor the opposition forces are truly unified. Considering the opposition's complicated web of ideological, ethnic, regional, and political motives, it should not be surprising that it conducted the war on several different tracks: conventional fighting in central Tajikistan, hit-and-run guerrilla tactics against government convoys along the mountainous northeast road toward Kyrgyzstan, and a "phony" war of propaganda in Khorog. Nevertheless, the opposition's political front, the UTO, has continued to insist that the Kulobis share power with other regions and form a transitional coalition government. In February 1998, the first representatives of the UTO were in fact appointed by presidential decree to five ministerial posts as provided for by the general peace accord. An important opposition leader, Akbar Turajonzada, was appointed first deputy prime minister.

The government forces also have not been able to retain control over all their former military units. In February 1996, for example, an ethnic Uzbek from the south, Colonel Makhmood Khodayeberdiev, led his followers in a blockade of Kurgan Teppe town and threatened to march on Dushanbe if the government did not reduce corruption and make certain changes, including giving him a special position in Dushanbe. The government did made concessions, and the colonel later took part in the Tavildara conflict on its behalf. Still, many in the government fear his popularity, and attempts on his life have been reported. In August 1997, Khodayeberdiev's troops clashed with forces of the presidential guard, leading President Rakhmonov to relieve the colonel of his duties.

In December 1996 and February 1997, an outlaw gang led by brothers Bahrom and Rizvon Sadirov, a formerly pro-opposition group that turned pro-government and then became independent, took several dozen foreigners hostage, including Russian journalists and UN workers, for whom they demanded ransom and the free passage of some gang members from Afghanistan. In March 1997, in a joint operation by forces of the Tajik government and opposition, members of the outlaw gang were captured or killed. This action was notable for being the first instance in which government troops worked together with UTO forces.[105] Several outlaw bands that are not loyal to the UTO operate outside the government's control as well, and terrorist activities by rogue warlords continue to present a threat. A kidnapping in November 1997 led to the death of a French aid worker.

Although there is little unity among either the government or the opposition forces, one can still generalize about their overall stances. Mediation carried out by the UN secretary-general's special envoy for Tajikistan, as well as pressure from external actors, gradually led to a series of high-level negotiations held under UN auspices and with the assistance of other interested observer governments. The first round of these Inter-Tajik Talks produced a cease-fire in April 1994, which has been extended through several subsequent rounds of talks. The talks also led to prisoner exchanges, other confidence-building measures, and the establishment of a joint commission to monitor adherence to the agreements by both parties. UNMOT monitored and supported this process as well.

Each cease-fire agreement was violated, however, and each side blamed the other for the resumption of fighting. During the course of these hostilities, military commanders on both sides gained increased political influence, leaving less room for negotiators to compromise. Both the government and the opposition seemed fearful of each other's real motives and suspicious that the stated objectives were not sincere. Nonetheless, the Inter-Tajik Talks laid the groundwork for the general peace accord.

On June 27, 1997, President Rakhmonov and UTO leader Said Abdullo Nuri signed the General Agreement on the Establishment of Peace and National Reconciliation in the presence of representatives from observer nations, including Russian president Boris Yeltsin, and organizations, including OSCE. The accord gives the UTO a 30 percent share of seats in the central government, provides amnesty for former opposition fighters, and lifts a ban on opposition mass media and UTO political parties. It also establishes a Reconciliation Commission, composed of an equal number of representatives of the current government and the UTO, which will recommend changes to the national constitution in preparation for parliamentary elections scheduled for 1998. The agreement furthermore paves the way for the completion of repatriation of refugees from strife-ridden northern Afghanistan. The accord is a hopeful sign in the midst of ongoing political uncertainty; however, as noted above, the peace process continues to face serious threats.

The United Nations, other organizations, and outside governments can do much to alleviate human suffering, promote reintegration and development, and try to persuade the Tajik government to respect international human rights standards. Beyond this, the international community must encourage the government of Tajikistan to carry out all provisions of the 1997 peace accord, including power-sharing.

Conclusions

The study of internal displacement in Tajikistan is significant both as a historical experience that offers lessons applicable to other situations and as a problem area with demonstrated potential to flare up again. The lessons the international community learned from the Tajik crisis also can be applied in its response to the continuing unrest in the country.

In comparative terms, although the Tajik civil war was intense and the resulting displacement massive, the government on the whole cooperated effectively with the international community. This stands in contrast to some displacement emergencies in which national governments may not welcome outside assistance or may even impede humanitarian intervention. The government's interest in promoting the return of IDPs and refugees, and its need to pull the displaced population away from the opposition and to demonstrate some degree of stability to gain national and international legitimacy, proved helpful in the aftermath of the war. The Tajik case demonstrates that when a national government perceives the return of its displaced citizens to be in its own interest and sees a convergence of its goals with those of the international community, the plight of the displaced likely will be ameliorated.

That the Tajik crisis of national identity has not been resolved is evident both in the manner of governance and in the degree of protection and assistance that the government—especially local officials—has accorded the affected population. Discrimination and abuse continue, and IDPs and returnees continue to feel that the government does not represent them. Although the Tajik government has promoted the return of IDPs and the repatriation of refugees, its actions at times have vitiated this policy.

National and international response to displacement, though adequate in many respects, also has been constrained by problems of coordination among the international agencies and between the agencies and the government. Initially open, the government became increasingly suspicious of the growing number of international agencies. The agencies may have had legitimate reasons for wanting to carry out their relief and development activities with a minimum of government interference. At the same time, the absence of coordinated communication with the government understandably made officials question the presence of so many outsiders. It is to be hoped that the creation of a new focal point within the government for coordination with international organizations will enable the government and the international community to interact with greater cooperation, openness, and understanding.

The economy of Tajikistan remains in shambles. Even at this writing in 1998, roughly five years after the 1992–93 war, Tajikistan's grain production meets less than one third of domestic consumption needs. The production of cotton and aluminum, the country's main barter commodities, has fallen sharply. Foreign currency reserves are low, and within two years of its introduction in May 1995 the value of the Tajik ruble plummeted from an exchange rate of 50 to nearly 600 rubles to the dollar. Given this ongoing need for outside support, the roles of external regional players and Russia in particular have become vitally important to the security of the state and to the strength of the opposition. Outside organizations and governments working in both political and humanitarian spheres must recognize the regional aspect to this conflict.

Whether the remaining IDPs in Gorno-Badakhshan decide to return home will depend largely on the extent to which the state provides essential services, including protection, assistance, and employment. Ultimately it is the state that determines whether "home" is secure or insecure and economic opportunities are present or lacking. It is clear that Tajikistan will continue to need international support for some time to meet the needs of IDPs, returnees, and the masses of population also affected by war and poverty. And yet, despite the conspicuous dependency on external support, it is unlikely that the international community will continue to render relief assistance in areas of return when there is no obvious emergency. The need for development in these areas, as well as in the poor mountainous regions to the east, could not be clearer. The World Bank and International Monetary Fund have stepped into this void with large loans, and the government in return has pledged to privatize its holdings, but much more can be done at the community level. In order to help returnees feel economically secure in their homes and encourage the remaining IDPs and refugees to return, UN agencies and international NGOs must continue to redirect their relief efforts toward development work. Government officials must support these efforts instead of shutting down promising initiatives or helping themselves to the raw materials international agencies have procured.

For the Tajik government, increased international legitimacy also will depend on a cleaner human rights record. The protection role initially played by UNHCR and assumed by OSCE is encouraging. Both agencies have stepped beyond their traditional mandates, and this has benefited returnees in Khatlon. UNHCR and OSCE field officers have devoted attention to individual cases. Both organizations have fostered contacts with local Tajik officials and have used their strong political presence in the capital to maintain relations with the national authorities. The presence of UNMOT, while aimed at monitoring cease-fire agreements and not human rights specifically, also has enhanced stability in Gorno-Badakhshan and other areas, despite occasional attacks on UNMOT soldiers.

Although overlapping mandates among agencies risk causing confusion and interagency competition, monitoring and protection efforts might work better on the ground if there were multiple efforts toward attaining the same goals. An additional human rights monitoring mission or even an assessment mission by UN human rights bodies or other interested organizations could benefit Tajikistan. In this regard, the UN Commission on Human Rights could provide assistance with human rights monitoring and, through the technical assistance and advisory services program, with institution-building.[106] The need for human rights monitoring is particularly acute in central Tajikistan and along the Tajik-Afghan border in Gorno-Badakhshan, where there are abundant complaints of abuse by the Russian Border Forces, whose presence is viewed as tantamount to occupation.[107]

In Tajikistan, international agencies decided, with sound reasoning, to address IDPs not as a specific beneficiary group but in conjunction with entire needy populations. Some aspects of humanitarian assistance could have been improved, such as the transition from relief to development and coordination among agencies and with the government. Overall, however, the international community has good reason to view many of its activities as successes, particularly its relief operations and efforts to protect and assist the returning displaced population.

Notes

1. Estimates of the number of casualties and displaced persons vary. Estimates of the number of deaths range from 20,000 to more than 60,000. Between 60,000 and 80,000 persons became refugees in Afghanistan. A further estimated 20,000 fled to Kyrgyzstan (mostly ethnic Kyrgyz) during the war; by mid-1997 the estimate was 40,000 to 45,000 (RFE/RE Newsline, vol. 1, no. 39, pt. 1, May 27, 1997). In addition, an unknown number of ethnic Russians, Uzbeks, and Tajiks migrated or fled to Uzbekistan, Russia, and other parts of the CIS. See UNHCR, "Report on Tajikistan, January 1993–March 1996," Geneva, p. 1. UNHCR consistently estimates that between 400,000 and 600,000 persons were internally displaced. In its March 1996 report, UNHCR cites the upper figure of 600,000, which we use in this chapter. For purposes of comparison, Human Rights Watch reports consistently cite a figure of 800,000 total displaced and 500,000 to 700,000 IDPs. The U.S. Committee for Refugees places the peak number of IDPs at 520,000. See U.S. Committee for Refugees (USCR), *World Refugee Survey 1996* (Washington, D.C., 1996), p. 105. In early 1995 the government of Tajikistan claimed that 697,653 people became "wanderers in their own country, i.e. internal refugees" after the war. See "Report of the Republic of Tajikistan on the International Conference on the Problems of Refugees, Displaced Persons and Migrants on the Territory of the Former USSR," March 1995, pp. 2, 4 (hereafter "Report of the Republic of Tajikistan").

2. Dr. Francis Deng, representative of the UN secretary-general on internally displaced persons, visited Tajikistan in May and June 1996. This study incorporates many of the findings from that visit. The authors also wish to thank Daniel Helle of the UN Centre for Human Rights for his insights and contributions to this case study.

3. United States Institute of Peace, "Special Report: The War in Tajikistan Three Years On," Washington, D.C., 1995, p. 1 (hereafter USIP Special Report).

4. Thomas J. Barfield, "Prospects for Plural Societies in Central Asia," *Cultural Survival Quarterly* (Summer/Fall 1994), p. 49.

5. The term *basmachi* refers to the local guerrilla fighters who took up arms to oppose the Soviet takeover of Central Asia.

6. "Report of the Republic of Tajikistan," p. 1.

7. Shirin Akiner, *Political and Economic Trends in Central Asia* (London: British Academic Press, 1994), p. 182.

8. Shahrbanou Tadjbakhsh, "Economic Regionalism in Tajikistan," Former Soviet South Project, London, Royal Institute of International Affairs, March 1996, p. 4.

9. USIP Special Report, p. 1.

10. Andrew Meier, "Yeltsin's Next Quagmire?" *New York Times*, January 2, 1995, p. 23.

11. Julien Thöni, *The Tajik Conflict: The Dialectic between Internal Fragmentation and External Vulnerability, 1991–1994* (Geneva: The Graduate Institute of International Studies, Programme for Strategic and International Security Studies, 1994), p. 13.

12. See Barnett R. Rubin, "The Fragmentation of Tajikistan," *Survival 35*, vol. 35 (Winter 1993–94).

13. Human Rights Watch/Helsinki, "Return to Tajikistan: Continued Regional and Ethnic Tensions," New York, May 1995, p. 4.

14. UNHCR, "Internally Displaced Persons in Tajikistan: A History and Analysis and UNHCR's Response," Briefing Note, Dushanbe, May 1996 (hereafter UNHCR Briefing Note).

15. The civil war did result in a reshuffling among the dominant groups. From the 1930s until the Tajik civil war, the Khojandis, from the prosperous Ferghana Valley in the north, were Tajikistan's leaders. The poorer Kulobis from the south were their junior partners. The civil war effectively reversed this role, making the Kulobis the senior partners. This in turn has kindled resentment and demonstrations in the north.

16. Even several years after it "won" the war, the central government was extremely hesitant to diversify its power base. However, the leadership has been encouraged by the international community and by demonstrations in Khojand to open some government positions to persons outside of Kulob, and in some cases it has responded positively. However, the placement of a few non-Kulobis in government positions usually is perceived by outsiders as mere window dressing.

17. General Assembly, Report of the Representative of the Secretary-General on Internally Displaced Persons, Francis M. Deng, *Profiles in Displacement: Tajikistan*, A/51/483/Add. 1, Annex (United Nations, October 24, 1996), p. 54 (hereafter Deng Report).

18. This figure represents the natural increase in population for the years 1985–1990. See "UN World Population Prospects," United Nations, 1996.

19. Human Rights Watch/Helsinki, "Return to Tajikistan," p. 20.

20. United Nations Development Programme, *Tajikistan Rehabilitation, Reconstruction and Development Programme*, TAJ/95/002 (United Nations, 1995), p. 6.

21. Tadjbakhsh, "Economic Regionalism in Tajikistan," p. 2.

22. Thöni, *The Tajik Conflict*, p. 15.

23. Even the region of Gorno-Badakhshan prefers autonomy within a Russian-dominated system to outright separation from Tajikistan, which would open it up to influence from the Uzbeks and Chinese (UNMOT Briefing, Dushanbe, June 2, 1996). Khojand in the north is strongly tied to Uzbekistan but also has a Tajik identity and does not want to be swallowed up by Uzbekistan (interview with senior U.S. official, Dushanbe, June 2, 1996).

24. CSCE, "Mission Report to the Republic of Tajikistan," April 1993, p. 2, quoted in Thöni, *The Tajik Conflict*, p. 13.

25. Thöni, *The Tajik Conflict*, pp. 20–25.

26. In 1995, according to Olivier Roy, former head of the OSCE mission in Tajikistan, Kabul was not pressing for an Islamic regime in Tajikistan and had little interest in giving military support to the Tajik opposition, because that would only prolong the conflict (USIP Special Report, p. 9). The Kulobis have alleged that the Tajik opposition received support from various Afghan *mujahedin*. However, both Kabul prior to the Taliban takeover and Tehran, which also granted asylum to opposition leaders, may have viewed friendship with Russia as more important than support of the Tajik opposition. See Sergei Strokan, "Tajikistan: All Eyes on Latest Round of Peace Talks," *Peacenet* (July 8, 1996).

27. USIP Special Report, pp. 9, 7.

28. Thöni, *The Tajik Conflict*, p. 41.

29. See Igor Rotar, "Tajikistan and Russia's Presidential Election," *Prism: A Monthly on the Post-Soviet States*, vol. 2, pt. 2 (Jamestown Foundation, July 1996).

30. Jamestown Foundation, *Monitor,* July 31, 1996.

31. Tadjbakhsh, "Economic Regionalism in Tajikistan," p. 2.

32. Before the war, some 300,000 ethnic Slavs lived in Tajikistan. By July 1996, only 60,000 remained, mainly the elderly. See Rotar, "Tajikistan and Russia's Presidential Election."

33. Aziz Niyazi, quoted in Thöni, *The Tajik Conflict*, p. 22.

34. Europa Publications Limited, *The Europa World Year Book 1993*, vol. 2, pp. 2750–51.

35. Deng Report, p. 9.

36. UNHCR, "Report on Tajikistan, January 1993–March 1996," p. 3–4; UNHCR Briefing Note.

37. Davlat Khudonazarov, quoted in "A Passion for Peace," *PeaceWatch*, vol. 1 (April 1995), p. 7.

38. President Rakhmonov was reelected in November 1994 in elections that some, such as Human Rights Watch/Helsinki, claimed were unfair and fraudulent. Rakhmonov subsequently banned all opposition parties and issued death sentences and arrest warrants for opposition leaders.

39. UNHCR Briefing Note, p. 3.

40. Ibid.

41. Security Council, *Report of the Secretary-General to the Security Council on the Situation in Tajikistan*, S/1996/412 (United Nations, June 1996), para. 28.

42. Interview with International Organization for Migration official, Dushanbe, June 1996.

43. "Tajik Refugees Pose Growing Problem in Kyrgyzstan and in Own Country," Jamestown Foundation, *Monitor*, July 3, 1996.

44. UNHCR-IOM Joint Appeal for the CIS, 1997.

45. UNHCR, Division of International Protection, *UNHCR's Operational Experience with Internally Displaced Persons* (Geneva, September 1994), p. 54; UNHCR, "Report on Tajikistan, January 1993–March 1996," p. ii.

46. UNHCR, "Report on Tajikistan, January 1993–March 1996," pp. 17, 18.

47. UNHCR Briefing Note, p. 3.

48. According to local government officials in Gorno-Badakhshan, in 1996 close to 4,500 people wished to remain in the region permanently (interview, June 1, 1996). It is likely that this figure is inflated.

49. See World Food Programme, "Appeal for Tajikistan: Food and Cash Resources Requirements," April 1, 1996–March 31, 1997, p. 11. During the war, starvation occurred in remote mountainous areas.

50. UNHCR, "Report on Tajikistan, January 1993–March 1996," p. 23.

51. ICRC arrived in Tajikistan toward the end of the war in October 1992, which one representative considered late by ideal standards. Interview with ICRC official, Dushanbe, June 1, 1996.

52. UNHCR, *UNHCR's Operational Experience with Internally Displaced Persons*, p. 54.

53. DHA led a humanitarian assessment mission to Tajikistan in conjunction with a November 1992 UN Good Offices Mission (see below). However, DHA did not establish a presence in Dushanbe and asked UNHCR to play the role of humanitarian coordinator. UNHCR became fully operational in March 1993. Tajik refugees in Afghanistan were gathered into three large camps in the north. UNHCR frequently has had difficulty reaching these camps.

54. Interview with Hakim N. Feerasta, chief executive officer, Aga Khan Foundation, Khorog, June 6, 1996.

55. World Food Programme, "Appeal for Tajikistan," pp. 35–36.

56. UNHCR, "Review of UNHCR Activities in Tajikistan," EVAL/TAJ/14, September 1994, p. 4.

57. Interview with UNHCR official, Dushanbe, June 2, 1996.

58. UNHCR, *UNHCR's Operational Experience with Internally Displaced Persons*, p. 55.

59. UNHCR, "Review of UNHCR Activities in Tajikistan," p. 5.

60. Interview with OSCE official, Tajikistan, June 9, 1996.

61. Interview with UNHCR official, Dushanbe, June 10, 1996.

62. UNHCR Briefing Note, p. 4.

63. Interview with Tajik Central Refugee Department official, Dushanbe, June 11, 1997.

64. See "Tajikistan: An Integrated Approach," in UNHCR, *State of the World's Refugees: The Challenge of Protection* (New York: Penguin Books, 1993), p. 134; UNHCR, "Tajikistan: Lessons Learned from a Country of Origin Operation," SWANAME Bureau/CDR lessons-learned seminar on Tajikistan, Geneva, March 1996; and UNHCR, "Report on Tajikistan, January 1993–March 1996," pp. 5–8.

65. UNDP's resident representative began serving as the UN resident coordinator, the representative of DHA in Tajikistan, only in February 1996.

66. According to the Tajik prime minister in June 1996, a government department had been established to deal with international organizations. The prime minister was to chair roundtable discussions with the representatives of all these agencies and convey to them the government's priorities for coordination. Several previous attempts at coordination between the government and the international agencies present in Tajikistan were unsuccessful.

67. Interview with UNHCR official, Dushanbe, June 2, 1996.

68. Interview with ICRC official, Dushanbe, June 2, 1996.

69. Interview with senior UN official, Dushanbe, June 11, 1996.

70. Activity report of an international organization operating in Khatlon, June 1996.

71. Interview with UN official, Dushanbe, June 5, 1996.

72. UNHCR, "Report on Tajikistan, January 1993–March 1996," p. 10.

73. Deng Report, p. 12.

74. UNHCR official, June 1996.

75. UNHCR, *UNHCR's Operational Experience with Internally Displaced Persons*, p. 55.

76. In August 1996, Francis M. Deng, the representative of the secretary-general on internally displaced persons, and Bacre Waly Ndiaye, special rapporteur on extrajudicial, summary, or arbitrary executions, sent a joint urgent appeal to the government of Tajikistan, drawing its attention to the relevant provisions of international law and requesting information on the steps taken to prevent the occurrence of such incidents in the future.

77. UNHCR, "Update on IDP Return Convoys from Gorno-Badakhshan," interoffice memo, July 28, 1995; IOM Regional Bureau for Europe and North America, "Update on IOM Activities in the CIS/Baltic Region," no. 2 (1995) and no. 3 (January 1996).

78. Human Rights Watch/Helsinki, "Return to Tajikistan," p. 13.

79. See, for example, ibid., pp. 17–23.

80. Interview with IDPs, Gorno-Badakhshan, June 7, 1996.

81. See Deng Report, pp. 22–28.

82. Interviews with returnees, Dushanbe, June 1996. Accounts of beatings and torture in custody also are found in United States Department of State, *Country Reports on Human Rights Practices for 1995*, chapter on Tajikistan, March 1996, section 1(c).

83. Interviews with returnees in Myaskombinat, June 5, 1996.

84. OSCE, Office for Democratic Institutions and Human Rights (ODIHR), *Central Asia and Transcaucasia Newsletter*, vol. 1, no. 2, p. 6.

85. See Deng Report, p. 13.

86. For information on UNHCR's relief and reintegration programs, see UNHCR, "Report on Tajikistan, January 1993–March 1996."

87. UNHCR, "Tajikistan: Lessons Learned from a Country of Origin Operation," pp. 3–4.

88. UNHCR, "Report on Tajikistan, January 1993–March 1996," p. 36.

89. Daniel Helle, "Enhancing the Protection of Internally Displaced Persons," in *Rights Have No Borders: Worldwide Internal Displacement* (Norwegian Refugee Council, 1998), p. 39.

90. Interview with UNHCR official, Dushanbe, June 2, 1996.

91. Human Rights Watch/Helsinki, "Tajik Refugees in Northern Afghanistan: Obstacles to Repatriation," New York, May 1996, pp. 3, 26–27.

92. Interview with Tajik government official, Shahrtuz, June 10, 1996.

93. Interview with senior UN official, Dushanbe, June 11, 1996.

94. This estimate is from 1989 and is the most recent available (CIA World Factbook, "Tajikistan," 1996). See also Deng Report, p. 34.

95. UNICEF, "UNICEF Peace Education Activities in Tajikistan," project overview, Geneva.

96. See UNHCR, "Report on Tajikistan, January 1993–March 1996," pp. 43–48.

97. Presentation on the implementation of QIPs in Tajikistan, Society for International Development meeting, Washington, D.C., May 16, 1996; UNHCR, "Report on Tajikistan, January 1993–March 1996," p. 45.

98. UNHCR, "Report on Tajikistan, January 1993–March 1996," pp. 44–45.

99. Ibid., p. 47.

100. In June 1996 the World Bank was preparing a $10 million credit for a "poverty alleviation" program. In May 1996 the International Monetary Fund approved a $22 million loan to address macroeconomic issues such as inflation and the budget deficit (interview with Mohammad Reza Ghasimi, chief economist, World Bank, June 11, 1996).

101. Meeting with IDP returnees near Kolkhoz Kommunism, Kabodian, June 10, 1996.

102. For further information on NGO, OSCE, IOM, and UNHCR activities, see UNHCR, "Report on Tajikistan, January 1993–March 1996," pp. 36–56.

103. See ibid., p. 46.

104. Carolyn S. Peduzzi, "Independent Evaluation of the UNHCR Small Enterprise Development Projects in Tajikistan," UNHCR, Geneva, December 14, 1995, pp. 5–6.

105. *OMRI Daily Digest*, part 1, no. 40 (February 26, 1997), no. 53 (March 17, 1997), and no. 61 (March 27, 1997).

106. Deng Report, p. 35.

107. Interview with human rights advocate, Dushanbe, June 11, 1996.

CHAPTER NINE

Sri Lanka's Vicious Circle of Displacement

H. L. Seneviratne and Maria Stavropoulou

THIS CHAPTER PRESENTS the paradox of the case of Sri Lanka: the deterioration of the situation of the internally displaced under a government that is ideologically, and to all appearances sincerely, committed to bringing peace and thereby eradicating the root of the problem of internal displacement.

The chapter has three parts. The first part deals with the background to the ethnic conflict that is the cause of displacement and that needs to be resolved in order to achieve a lasting solution. The second, which constitutes the bulk of the empirical material regarding the displaced, is a revised version of Francis Deng's report on his 1993 field visit to Sri Lanka as the representative of the UN secretary-general on internally displaced persons. The third part of the chapter focuses on the state of the displaced under the present regime (elected in 1994), in particular after the resumption of war in late 1995 and the ensuing new displacement of large numbers of people, especially in the northern part of the country.

The authors wish to acknowledge the generous cooperation of the relevant government officials of the Ministry of Welfare, Rehabilitation, and Social Welfare and the Office of the President. Invaluable research assistance was provided by Lalitha Gunawardena.

Democratic Socialist Republic of Sri Lanka

Displacement has affected the whole country, but the largest single group of affected persons are the Tamils from northeastern Sri Lanka. According to government statistics, at the end of September 1995 there were 141,992 displaced families consisting of 570,453 persons.[1] Of those, 37,532 families (152,275 persons) were housed in 483 welfare centers, and 104,460 families (418,178 persons) were with friends and relatives.

There was a dramatic rise in the number of the displaced during the Riviresa military operation of October 1995, which was launched by the government to regain control of Jaffna, the rebel stronghold and the political and cultural center of the Tamils. That campaign caused a massive exodus of about 400,000 persons, most of whom had returned to their original homes by mid-1996.[2] Large numbers, predominantly Tamil refugees, have left the country in search of asylum abroad, especially in India.

In nearly the same plight as the displaced are persons affected by the war but not displaced, and families "resettled" in their original homes or elsewhere. Such persons are assisted by the government according to specific criteria.

Historical Background

The population of Sri Lanka is about 17 million. It is estimated, with slight variations, that 74 percent of the population are Sinhalese, 18 percent Tamils, and 7 percent Muslims. Nearly all Sinhalese are Buddhist and speak Sinhala. Tamils are mostly Hindu and speak Tamil; they consist of "Ceylon" or "Jaffna" Tamils (69 percent), who have a long history on the island, and "Indian" or "estate" or "plantation" Tamils, descendants of laborers brought from southern India under British rule to work on coffee, tea, and rubber plantations. The Muslims speak mostly Tamil but distinguish themselves by their religion. There are a few Christians in both the Sinhalese and the Tamil communities.[3]

In most of the country, the Sinhalese form the majority. In the northern districts (including the Jaffna Peninsula), the Ceylon Tamils are the largest community. The Indian Tamils reside mainly in the hill country in the central part of Sri Lanka. In the east, things are more complicated: while Tamils and Muslims inhabited this area until the twentieth century, today all three communities are equally represented. There are substantial Tamil and Muslim communities in the rest of the country, although they are in the minority there.

Two opposed nationalisms, Sinhala and Tamil, are the underlying cause of the present conflict between the two groups. The popular view has it that the conflict is ancient, but most scholars trace it to the radical social changes brought about primarily in the twentieth century, in particular the explosion of population, the stagnation in the economy, the resulting competition for economic resources, and the influence of Western ideas about nationalism.

The different ethnic groups in Sri Lanka have a long history of social and cultural intermixture. For instance, although the Sinhala and Tamil belong to two different language families, their long historical contiguity has led the Sinhala language to borrow from Tamil a good deal of grammar, syntax, and vocabulary. At the same time, the Tamil language has borrowed extensively from Sanskrit, the parent language of Sinhala, which is indispensable to Hinduism (the religion of most Tamils). A significant part of popular Buddhism is borrowed from Hinduism. Through the centuries intermarriage between the two groups has been common, a practice that continues. This mixed ethnic and cultural picture contrasts with the puristic conceptions of identity and ethnic separateness that extremists of both groups promote today.[4]

In 1815 the last independent kingdom of the island was ceded to the British by agreement between the local chiefs and the British governor. The treaty, known as the Kandyan Convention, included a clause that required the British government to patronize Buddhism. By the 1840s, however, it was clear that British ideologies of separation of church and state on the one hand and missionary pressures on the other prevented the British government from keeping its promise. By the 1850s, neutrality in religious affairs had become a part of state policy. The prestige of the Buddhist monkhood suffered when the state withdrew its recognition. Moreover, the establishment of secular schools with modern curricula by the British, primarily designed to train personnel for their increasing administrative needs, deprived the monks of their traditional role as teachers. This was aggravated by the fact that these schools were run by missionaries, a foreign and rival clergy.

Because the missionary organizations were concentrated in Jaffna, the capital of the Tamil heartland, proportionately more Tamils were educated in English than in Sinhalese. And because agricultural work in Jaffna was more demanding, more and more Tamils sought education and state employment in the capital, Colombo, and other "Sinhala" areas—that is, in the south. Tamils were represented in university admissions, the public service, and the professions in significantly higher proportions than the Sinhalese. Sinhala activists claimed that a community constituting less than 12 percent of the population held more than 85 percent of the higher-level professional positions.

Colonialism spurred a nationalist movement that espoused Sinhala Buddhist hegemony based on the theory that the majority of the population of the island, the Sinhala Buddhists, have been oppressed and outdone by both the imperialist rulers and the Tamil minority. For their part, Tamils developed a nationalism of their own inspired by the South Indian cultural nationalism, which challenged North Indian Brahmanic dominance and advocated a separate Tamil state in India. The central claim of Tamil nationalism is to a separate Tamil state in the north and the east, first conceived of as a solution to the ethnic crisis but later imagined to have always existed until the Westerners brought it within the compass of the larger nation.[5]

Ethnic divisiveness grew in the twentieth century because of arbitrary territorial demarcations and rival claims for water rights, arable lands, and natural resources. Muslims have been discriminated against by both other communities over the past fifty years, although much more by the Tamils, because they reside in areas mainly populated by the Tamil community.

Political Developments since Independence

Sri Lanka's transition to independence in 1948 was relatively calm. The Soulbury Constitution of 1947 established a bicameral legislature within a monarchical framework in which a resident governor-general represented the king of England. Universal adult franchise was introduced in Sri Lanka in 1931, and since independence the country has held elections every five to seven years. In 1972 a new constitution replaced the monarchical system with a republic; and in 1977 still another constitution established an executive presidency with an elected parliament and also introduced proportional representation. Sri Lanka has a vigorous political opposition. Although members of each ethnic community can be found in many of the political parties, the two most influential ones generally draw their support from the Sinhalese community.

When the British departed, both Tamils and Sinhalese were left in positions of authority, partly because the colonial education system had produced an intercommunal elite. Nevertheless, the Soulbury Constitution, which laid down the terms of decolonization, established the principle of majority rule and a highly centralized political system. It provided few protections for the rights of the minorities. Although section 29(c) prohibited legislation that discriminated on the basis of religion or participation in any community, no other basic protections or detailed provisions for an independent judiciary were elaborated.

After 1948 the country was initially ruled by the United National Party (UNP) under the leadership of Don Stephen Senanayanake. During this time two significant policies were set in place. The first was the denial of citizenship to approximately a million Indian Tamils; the second was the opening up of agricultural opportunities for the landless Sinhala peasants in undeveloped areas in the north and east.[6] The immediate consequence of the first was to provide a political advantage for the Sinhalese electorate in the hill country; the second made possible a process of colonization in lands that the Tamils considered to be "theirs" from ancient times, which ultimately would alter the demography (and the electoral constituency) of those areas.[7] Both caused deep resentment in the Tamil community and aggravated fears of a majority dictatorship.

In 1956 the Sri Lanka Freedom Party (SLFP), led by S.W.R.D. Bandaranaike, won the election by effectively tapping the resentment of the nationalist forces against the Westernized elite. An important segment of these forces was the Buddhist clergy led by an outspoken and radicalized minority of urban monks. They defined their role as "social service," a thinly veiled designation to justify political activity, and were committed to the task of enthroning the Sinhala language and Buddhism.

Almost as a means of affirmative action, Bandaranaike's government adopted the "Sinhala only" policy in order to facilitate access of the Sinhalese to public sector employment and university education. For the Tamils this action was not only offensive but it also eliminated an important source of income and infringed upon their educational opportunities and advantages. Following his election, however, Bandaranaike tried to soften the effects of the "Sinhala only" policy. He sketched out an arrangement together with the federalist Tamil leader S. J. V. Chelvanayagam that included modifications to the centralized system and a degree of political and cultural autonomy for the minorities. The UNP, under the leadership of J. R. Jayewardene, used the occasion to present itself as even more radically nationalist, and the proposed agreement was abrogated. In this, Bandaranaike lost the opportunity to nip in the bud the ethnic crisis that later grew into a separatist struggle.

In 1959, Bandaranaike was assassinated by a Buddhist monk and was succeeded immediately by his wife, Sirimavo Bandaranaike. During her tenure, an extensive education campaign was initiated, in the course of which the state took control of most Christian schools. In addition to reducing Christian influence over schools, this represented another victory for the nationalist forces. Buddhist-Christian relations worsened to the extent that an unsuccessful coup d'état was staged in 1962 by Christian military and police officers. A notable consequence was the elimination of Christians from the security forces, which thereafter largely remained in Sinhalese hands.

After a five-year period of UNP rule, the SLFP returned to power and two years later, in 1972, adopted a new constitution, which severed legal links with the United Kingdom. The Constituent Assembly had rejected the Tamil Party proposal for a federal structure and had dropped even the inadequate minority safeguards of the previous constitution (section 29(c)). The new constitution adopted Sinhala as the one official language; the use of Tamil was to be determined by statute. The constitution also provided for Buddhism the "foremost place" in Sri Lanka. The Tamil Federal Party walked out of the Constituent Assembly, and the UNP voted against the adoption of the constitution.

The constant marginalization of the Tamil community and its politicians, and the fact that none of their demands for minority protection were accommodated, allegedly led to the creation of the Tamil United Liberation Front, which in a formal resolution issued in May 1976 advocated for the first time a separate Tamil State in Sri Lanka, the Eelam Tamil nation. Thus the demand for rights became a demand for a separate state. The government responded by asking all members of Parliament to take an oath of allegiance; when the Tamil members refused, they lost their seats, thus depriving the legislature and the governing party of a democratic Tamil opposition with which they could negotiate. Further, the Tamil people were left with no representation other than the separatist movement of the armed rebels, which by then had emerged.

In 1977 the UNP returned to power with the promise to reform economic and social policy. One of its first acts was the adoption of a new constitution that accorded official status to the Tamil language. Although Tamils supported the UNP, they were soon disappointed by what they saw as half-hearted attempts at devolving power and ensuring cultural autonomy. They were further disturbed by the new administration's pursuit of the Accelerated Mahaweli Project, which was seen by the Tamil community as a further encroachment upon their lands. The government maintained that these lands were not inhabited and that economic considerations had triggered these irrigation and agriculture schemes; nevertheless, it appeared that the measure undermined the economic and political security of the Tamil community.

The politicization of education in the 1970s was another major factor in the deterioration of relations between the Sinhalese and the Tamils. With the change in the medium of instruction in schools in the mid-1950s from English to Sinhalese and Tamil, and the rapid growth in secondary education, competition for university admission, based on the nationally conducted "A-level" examinations, intensified. Because examinations were from then on conducted in either Sinhalese or Tamil, Tamil examiners were accused of grade inflation. The populist government elected in 1970 resorted to a procedure known as "standardization," namely the selection of students for admission proportional to the ethnic ratio between the Sinhala and Tamils.[8] Under this system, the percentage of places in the sciences the Tamils held fell from 35.3 percent in 1970 to 20.9 percent in 1974 and to 19 percent in 1975. The new government elected in 1977 abandoned this system, but its ghost kept reappearing in different forms. And its effect on ethnic relations was disastrous. According to one Sri Lankan historian, "few issues have contributed more substantially and so dramatically to the sharp deterioration of ethnic relations in the last decade, and to radicalizing the politics of the Tamil areas in the north and east of the island, more than the question of university admissions."[9] This educational policy became an important basis of the Tamils' contention that they were being discriminated against.

Finally, the general climate of insecurity that prevailed after the rise, by 1971, of an ultra-left organization, the Janatha Vimukthi Peramuna (JVP), and the sporadic but violent ethnic confrontations, added to the polarization of the ethnic groups. Following violent incidents in 1977, the Jayewardene government adopted the Prevention of Terrorism Act in 1979 in an effort to contain what by then amounted to civil war. Instead, its unusually broad provisions only contributed to increased tensions.

The Prevention of Terrorism Act (which became permanent law by Act No. 10 of 1982) and the Emergency Regulations, both of which give security forces wide powers (e.g., preventive and incommunicado detention) remain in effect in the whole of the country and continue occasionally to be the cover for extrajudicial killings, disappearances, abuse of detainees, and arbitrary arrest and detention. Various law-enforcement forces such as the army, intelligence units, the police force, and civil defense groups operating under military or police control or acquiescence have been accused of human rights abuses.

Economy and Social Welfare

Although Sri Lanka's very low per capita income places it among the thirty-six poorest developing nations in the world, it has a high level of literacy and education, low infant mortality rates, and a relatively high average life expectancy. Its major problems of poverty and unemployment, however, have affected in particular the farmers in the south. The implications of the structural adjustment programs of the World Bank and the "open-market" economic policies of the government led to even greater disparities between the rich and the poor.

The Armed Conflict

By 1983 the elements for an explosive combination were already in place. The armed campaign for an independent Tamil state had become persistent; some Tamil groups were thoroughly committed to violence, and in response, the Prevention of Terrorism Act provided sweeping powers against antistate actions. In July of that year, Tamil militants killed thirteen soldiers in Jaffna. Widespread internecine strife between Sinhalese and Tamils living in southern areas followed. Extremist elements among Sinhalese nationalists in urban areas attacked the Tamil population and destroyed their properties. The security forces seemed unwilling to act to bring the riots under control. Tamils in the south fled to the north, increasing pressure on resources in that area, including land, water, food, and employment opportunities, and reinforcing separatist sentiments. The Liberation Tigers of Tamil Eelam (LTTE) gradually emerged as the dominant guerrilla force and unleashed a cycle of brutal violence against army outposts and Sinhalese, and later also against Muslim civilians. Tamils in greater and greater numbers began to perceive the government as the enemy; conversely, many in the government and the army started to believe that the only way to reestablish peace was to "solve" the "terrorist" problem.

The Role of India

In 1987, after the Sri Lankan forces had called a halt to an offensive on Jaffna, the governments of India and Sri Lanka signed an agreement (the so-called Indo-Lanka Accord) that provided for concerted political and military action with a view to putting an end to the conflict in the north.[10] The accord made some concessions to the Tamils, and it declared that Tamil and English would also be official languages. It also provided for a scheme for devolving administrative powers to the northern and eastern provinces. The accord called for the temporary union of the two provinces for one year, after which the inhabitants of the eastern province might (at the discretion of the president) decide in a referendum whether they should form a separate administrative unit. As a result of the Indo-Lanka Accord, the Indian Peace-Keeping Forces (IPKF) landed in Sri Lanka with a mandate to disarm the Tamil militants and to maintain law and order in the north and northeast. Some Tamil militants went along with the accord. The LTTE did not and soon was fighting the IPKF and other Tamil militants, who then joined in to try to defeat the LTTE. The IPKF failed to subdue the LTTE, and its attempts to do so led to accusations of widespread human rights abuses.[11]

Political Terrorism

More ominously, many among the Sinhalese came to regard India's role as a threat to Sri Lankan sovereignty. The JVP, which came to the political forefront by staging a student demonstration in 1971 and later was ruthlessly suppressed and outlawed, regrouped at this time and resorted to extreme violence. In early 1988 it launched a campaign of murder against members and activists of the ruling UNP and government employees. In retaliation, paramilitary vigilante groups, possibly connected with the armed forces, engaged in "exemplary killings" and other atrocities. In July 1989 the fighting escalated when the JVP made a final thrust toward capturing state power. The state launched a general counterinsurgency campaign, and by the end of November 1989 the armed forces put down the revolt when they succeeded in arresting and executing the nucleus of the JVP leadership.

After a relatively peaceful one and a half years in the south, in 1992 both pro-government and antigovernment elements again began resorting to political violence. Violence or threats of violence were directed against participants in political rallies and demonstrations, members of the academic world, the media, the legal profession, human rights groups, and Buddhist monks. Several national leaders, including President Ranasingha Premadasa, were assassinated.

Peace Initiatives and Failures

President Premadasa, who came to power in December 1988, had always opposed the Indo-Lanka Accord and the presence of foreign troops on Sri Lankan soil. In April 1989 the president undertook negotiations with the LTTE that resulted in a mutual cease-fire, though the LTTE continued fighting the IPKF. The Sri Lankan government actually supplied arms to the LTTE in order to expedite the withdrawal of the IPKF. In September of that year, the Indian government agreed to pull out its troops. They eventually left the country in March 1990. A few arms were turned in by the LTTE to the Indians; the rest may have been used later in opposition activity.

The north remained relatively peaceful during most of 1989 and 1990, while the army was occupied with the JVP insurgents. In mid-1990, however, heavy fratricidal fighting was reported between the LTTE and the Tamil National Army, a combat unit forcibly recruited by Tamil factions with the help of the Indian forces. Hundreds of persons were reported to be killed, and thousands of Tamils fled to India and other countries. The LTTE took effective control in the north and east after the retreat of the Indian army. In June 1990 the LTTE, breaking a fourteen-month cease-fire, attacked police stations and army camps and killed a number of soldiers before retreating into the jungle. The army retaliated ferociously, allegedly against mostly unarmed Tamil civilians. Local Muslims, angered by the killing of Muslim policemen, sometimes accompanied soldiers in order to point out Tamils. The death and destruction of the summer of 1990 were referred to in many discussions between the representative of the secretary-general on internally displaced persons and the local population in the east. Displaced persons living in camps were among the most frequent victims: if they were not killed or "disappeared," they often would be displaced yet again.

In September 1990 an all-party conference was convened on the issue of the devolution of power in the north and east with the intention of resolving the ethnic conflict. After much negotiation, the Tamil and Muslim groups participating in the conference failed to reach agreement regarding equal status and power or the merging of the two provinces. The Muslims are said to fear the merger, in which case they would become the clear minority in that area.

Despite President Premadasa's efforts throughout his term to promote consultations and negotiations as a solution to the ethnic conflict, the violence continued unabated in the north. It is estimated that between June and September 1990 more than a million people were displaced by the fighting in the northeast. By January 1991 more than 210,000 people had fled to southern India and more than 5,400 had been killed. In August 1991 the army carried out Operation Balavegaya, entering the besieged Elephant Pass army camp. The Jaffna Peninsula was thereby cut off from the rest of the island. Since then, the army has maintained camps around the Jaffna Peninsula, which it intermittently bombed and shelled during 1992.

During 1992 and 1993, as the intensity of violence between the Sri Lankan armed forces and the LTTE continued, attacks by the LTTE and reprisals by the military victimized hundreds in the civilian population, including children and elderly people. Muslim communities were the most frequently targeted. Muslims were expelled from their homes in the north, while in the east they were often caught in the crossfire between the army and the rebels. The army had armed and trained groups known as Muslim Home Guards, which acted as civil defense units in the Muslim villages. This "cooperation" provoked retaliatory action by the Tamil insurgents against Muslim villagers and the Home Guards; but the Home Guards also have been accused of arbitrary violence and human rights abuses. It is against this background that the People's Alliance (PA) government of President Chandrika Kumaratunga was elected to power in 1994.

The Conditions of the Displaced in 1993

This section provides an overview of the state of the displaced as observed by the representative of the secretary-general during his field visit in 1993. The representative visited camps and welfare centers housing Tamil, Muslim, and Sinhalese displaced in the western, north-central, and eastern parts of the country, as well as in Colombo. He also visited resettlement sites, to which the displaced had returned, and transit camps for returning refugees from abroad. The representative was not able to visit Jaffna, despite the large numbers of displaced living there, because of the sudden escalation of the armed confrontation during his visit.[12]

Subsistence

Internally displaced persons in Sri Lanka are housed either in so-called welfare centers (or camps) or outside such centers if they can find private accommodation—with friends or relatives, for example.

FOOD. The most important thing the government provided the internally displaced was food. Most displaced persons received coupons that entitled them to dry rations from the local state cooperative shop, which they cooked individually. People living outside welfare centers obtained their coupons from local officials (the additional government agents). Except for certain districts supported by the World Food Programme (WFP), the bulk of the expenditure on dry rations was borne by the government. The government provided dry rations without discrimination to the whole affected population on the island. In LTTE-controlled areas, the food was transported with the assistance of the International Committee of the Red Cross (ICRC) and was then distributed by government agents in cooperation with international and local agencies and the LTTE. The government has been complimented repeatedly for assuming this huge financial burden and responsibility, especially with regard to the Tamil population, although food assistance trickled to the rebels. Even more striking were the pragmatic arrangements between the government and the rebel forces, which amounted to a form of devolution of administrative power in the midst of the armed conflict. Some argued that the government accepted these arrangements in order not to alienate the Tamil population entirely, but others argued it did so out of a genuine sense of duty toward its people.

Some of the displaced voiced complaints about the inadequate nutritional value of the dry rations; many NGOs also suggested that although there was no food security crisis, the nutrition provided, when not supplemented, was low in proteins and vitamins. The most serious problems existed in Jaffna, where the blockage of the Elephant Passes and the Jaffna Lagoon had kept prices high, despite the government's provision of food for sale at controlled rates.

SHELTER. Most centers consisted of huts covered with cadjans (coconut thatch for temporary roofing), built with varying degrees of stability. In some places, as in one of the Sinhalese camps, the walls were solid and the floor cement, and, were it not for the cadjan roofing, they looked rather like houses. In others, as in a Tamil camp in Trincomalee, the huts were built right on the sand, near or on the beach. Most huts consisted of one room in which whole families lived. Most centers had no electricity, so people cooked in the huts using firewood and kerosene lamps. Cadjans frequently caught fire; a Muslim camp in Puttalam had once been burnt to the ground. During the monsoon season cadjans leaked, and some whole camps were flooded.

Some camps were particularly overcrowded and congested, especially when people were housed in preexisting buildings meant for different purposes (for instance, Clapenburg, in Trincomalee, which had been a supply depot for the British during World War II, and Saraswathy, a former theater in Colombo). In such buildings, people made partitions using their belongings (cartons, trunks, etc.) or pieces of cloth. In Clapenburg and the camps in Colombo, overcrowding and the total lack of privacy were considered the causes of serious psychosocial problems.

In resettlement villages the huts looked the same, although they were more spread out. People often built cadjan huts right next to the ruins of their old homes. As emergency assistance, the government and international and local NGOs provided the cadjans for the roofing or assisted in putting up the welfare centers and the huts.

SANITATION. Sanitation was more problematic. Inadequate facilities and scarce drinking water were among the most common complaints in most camps. The representative was told that in one transit camp in Batticaloa there was no drinking water at all when the first group of persons to be resettled arrived in June 1993. When the representative inquired, the coordinating officer (the brigadier) told him that soon afterward a well had been built. The same person said that in any event that camp was no longer being used. In one of the centers in Colombo, only one toilet was available for all the women. In a Tamil camp in Trincomalee (Nilaveli), there were no latrines at all.

HEALTH. Health problems such as respiratory tract infections, scabies and fungal infections, worsening cases of anemia, chronic malnutrition, and mental health problems associated with traumatic experiences were attributed to the inadequate shelter and sanitation facilities. Health facilities, though, appeared to be generally available. The area where medical supplies were lacking was, not surprisingly, the Jaffna Peninsula. Because the areas controlled by the LTTE were under partial economic blockade, items such as drugs and all fuel and lubricants apart from kerosene were closely monitored. Drugs were supplied to the government hospitals, with the exception of strong painkillers, anesthetics, and antibiotics. Some persons voiced serious concern that in order to gain access to the state-run medical facilities they had to pass through army checkpoints. Some NGOs said that for security reasons they also had been denied access to certain areas where there were internally displaced persons, for instance in Mutur (in the district of Trincomalee) and in Kilinochchi.

Self-Reliance

EDUCATION. The number of schools and the number of children attending them in the areas visited were impressive and illustrated the strong education tradition of the country. Nevertheless, some parents complained that they had no money for uniforms and books, and although the Ministry of Education had issued a notice saying that displaced children were not required to wear uniforms, discriminatory practices at the level of each school continued. In one of the schools in Batticaloa district it seemed that at least some teachers were unable to get to the schools because of the lack of public transportation.

EMPLOYMENT. Most grievances concerned employment. Some displaced persons could find work in rice paddies (notably in Ampara) or in onion cultivation (in Kalpitiya), but there was a general shortage of employment opportunities. People who could not work were unable to supplement the dry rations, and unemployment also contributed to the breakdown of traditional social roles, especially for men. In some cases, the displaced said that the local population did not welcome their presence in the local labor market. Others said that they were not given any land to cultivate, although they believed that land was available nearby or in other areas where they would be happy to resettle.

The displaced were also eager to start self-help projects and often expressed the hope that the state or an NGO would make the necessary arrangements. For many single-parent families (overwhelmingly headed by women) the lack of income was a serious problem: women whose husbands had either died or disappeared had serious difficulties raising their children while at the same time trying to earn a living for their families. Many said that without knowing whether their husbands were dead they could not even remarry. Government officials acknowledged that the problems of women and children (especially widows and orphans) were daunting but expressed the hope that the NGOs would help address them. In addition, women of little education, or those not experienced in dealing with officials, had difficulty complying with complicated administrative procedures. Government policies with regard to these target groups, if they existed, did not seem to be implemented effectively at the local level.

The Administration of Relief Assistance

The government attempted to carry out the great majority of its own relief operations through its regular administrative structures. The civilian authorities were responsible for the provision of relief aid by the government itself and the coordination of the overall relief effort. For instance, the purchase of food rations was financed by the central government; then the food rations were transported through a complex system of private transport and assistance by the ICRC and NGOs. They were then distributed at the local level, mostly through the government cooperative infrastructure under the supervision of the government agent (at the district level), additional government agents (at the division level), and others designated by them. The government also was responsible for the provision of essential services in the affected areas.

The provision of relief supplies and other assistance differed somewhat in the north and the east. The main problem for the north was moving relief supplies from the southern areas to the main centers in the north, not their local distribution. This contrasted with the situation in the east, where reaching the main centers was not as difficult, but local distribution was more complicated. The assistance of the United Nations High Commissioner for Refugees (UNHCR), ICRC, and NGOs was instrumental in both instances.

The military had considerable say over how goods were provided. At the national level, the Operational Headquarters at the Ministry of Defense was designated to set policies for what kinds of relief could be provided and where it could be transported and to set up procedures for clearing the transport of relief. In practice, it appeared that the local commanders had a great deal of de facto discretionary power over what relief could actually be provided.

On the whole, relief assistance was considered in 1993 to reach most groups satisfactorily. The problem of inadequate resources, however, compounded by a tacit policy not to encourage settlement in the camps, limited the government's support to the displaced. Lack of cash in the Treasury was a serious constraint with immediate repercussions for the displaced. There were also allegations of corruption—namely, that assistance meant for the displaced and the affected got lost on the way and that resources were wasted. The LTTE also helped itself to a portion of the supplies.

LIFE, PERSONAL SECURITY, AND PERSONAL LIBERTY. Security conditions in Sri Lanka varied considerably from area to area. In a few places it appeared that people had reverted to their normal, peaceful lives. Nevertheless, the violence and the related atrocities (arbitrary executions, arbitrary detentions, disappearances, rapes, harassment, mistreatment of prisoners and civilians, etc., recorded in the past by groups in and outside Sri Lanka) were forever imprinted on the memories of the people who had survived them and profoundly affected how they perceived their future.

Furthermore, the conflict has been so volatile that conditions of security change fast. Many areas in the east were at the time of the visit said to be pacified, or "cleared," in the terminology of the government. In the urban centers (the town of Trincomalee, for instance) life was in full swing. In Anuradhapura people walked in the streets well after dark, seemingly without fear. Yet it was considered necessary for the representative to be accompanied by a heavily armed escort in the east, which was not the case in Puttalam or in Colombo. A senior army commander in the east said that the army had fought its way step by step in the district of Batticaloa and that the rebels had been confined to the jungles in the interior. Other officials, though, said that many areas still remained to be "cleared." People resettled in Alankany (in Trincomalee) could not cultivate their fields a few miles away because the area was not yet "clear."

These were results of the LTTE's low-intensity, guerrilla-style war in the east, mainly in rural areas. After dark much of the countryside was at its mercy; killings of soldiers in outposts were not uncommon. The

LTTE continued to recruit among the local population, although opinions differed as to the scale and voluntary nature of the recruitment. Nevertheless, it was not disputed that there were many instances of LTTE infiltration. The local population often was asked to provide other types of assistance to the rebels, risking retaliatory activities if it did not comply with such requests. The Muslim community felt particularly threatened in these cases. Nonetheless, compliance with LTTE requests put civilians at risk of being seen as sympathizers by the security forces.

There is a heavy military or police presence near or around many camps and resettlement villages, especially in border areas and disputed territories. One such place was Thanthirimale in Anuradhapura, where the representative was told that the people went during the day to cultivate their lands north of the center and at night returned to the center, which was next to a Buddhist shrine and an army camp, because they felt safer there. Thanthirimale was a so-called Sinhalese "border area"; the war front was a few miles to the north. The purpose of settling people near or around army camps, according to the authorities, was to protect them. There were allegations, however, that the army used some such villages as "human shields" because in some places the civilians surrounded the army camp rather than vice versa.

Also present in some camps and resettlement villages were paramilitary units such as Muslim Home Guards or other volunteer forces and Tamil paramilitary groups opposed to the LTTE (the People's Liberation Organization of Tamil Eelam, or PLOTE; the Tamil Eelam Liberation Organization, or TELO; and the Eelam People's Democratic Party, or EPDP). In the past, they had been accused of committing serious human rights abuses.

By the time of the representative's visit the armed forces and paramilitary groups were making an effort to "win the hearts and minds" of the people: government and military officials repeatedly said that they were trying to restrain abusive behavior by the soldiers and the policemen and to educate the army in the laws of war. They did acknowledge that the rapid expansion of the army in the previous few years had resulted in a gap in their education. One minister said that, wherever possible, security responsibilities were transferred from the army to the police (which employs people from the local population). In his talks with the displaced, the representative did not hear any serious allegations contesting these claims, although people's relations with the army and the police were said to depend heavily on the personal disposition of their local leaders.

As expected, those who felt more vulnerable with the tight security around the camps were potential suspects as rebel supporters. A serious grievance expressed by many displaced persons was having to go through the numerous checkpoints on the roads, where they were subjected to questioning and thorough checks. If on a bicycle, they had to get off and walk through; if in a car or bus, they had to step out. Female army officers were not always present to check women, although this problem was being increasingly rectified. These procedures obviously affected the daily lives of everyone, but for people in suspect categories, such as young Tamil men, the procedures were serious threats. Others, such as those who had lost their identity cards (not uncommon among persons displaced in a hurry), had to provide alternative explanations for their presence. The point of view of the army was that people had to become "security-conscious," as one brigadier phrased it, because the security reasons for retaining the checkpoints were compelling. The local people would have to learn to go on with their normal lives while the army continued its operations.

In some places, such as Talavai, and Erravur in Batticaloa, people spoke of roundups, beatings, and detentions. In Sorikalmunai the women recalled "visits" by "men in uniforms" who would come and "take" them. Others spoke more explicitly of incidents of rape. The men said they had sometimes been taken to do work in the Special Task Forces camp; that some of them had to report regularly to the police; that after 6 P.M. they could not stay outside the village; and that they had not always been able to protect the women.

The general impression was that in the previous few months things had improved and that such instances had decreased in frequency. The relationships between the security forces and the local population and between the communities themselves remained very tense, however, reflecting the hostilities and bitter memories of the ten-year-long conflict.

Resettlement: Return and Alternative Settlement

In 1992 the government embarked on an ambitious resettlement and rehabilitation project, essentially consisting of the return of displaced persons to their original places of residence when these areas were "clear." As central and local government authorities explained, after the military "clears" an area and declares it safe, civilian authorities are authorized to go ahead with their resettlement projects. In some cases families were to be transferred from their camp to a "transit" camp where under normal circumstances they would stay for a few days until transportation to their original area of residence could be arranged. When a family "resettled" in their area of origin, the government had undertaken to provide, inter alia, a "settling-in allowance" of Rs. 2,000 and an amount of Rs. 15,000 for housing construction. (These amounts were not adequate and were doubled by the new government elected in 1994.) The government also provided three months' dry rations to those who chose to return to their communities; that grant was extendable to six months in exceptional circumstances. Within the civil administration, the focal point for the implementation of the resettlement and rehabilitation program was the Ministry of Reconstruction, Rehabilitation, and Social Welfare (MRR&SW).

The military played a large role in effecting resettlement. Apart from "clearing" the area, it had to ensure security thereafter. It appeared that the extent of the military's involvement depended on the security situation in a given area. In some cases it seemed that the army was the driving force in the implementation of the government's resettlement policies.

ATTITUDES TOWARD RESETTLEMENT. Whenever asked, government and military officials repeatedly stressed that resettlement was always voluntary and that no one was forced to return to his or her home area. Officials also said that the displaced from Vavuniya, who were being sheltered in LTTE-held areas, wanted to go back to their villages but that the LTTE would not allow them to do so.

Some of the displaced, when asked, expressed a clear reluctance to return to their areas. Many Tamil displaced said that it was not safe to go back, especially for young men, and that in the camps they were closer together and therefore felt more secure. They also said that their fields were being occupied by the Muslims so that "there was nothing for them back there." Displaced Muslims said that they wanted Tamil villages to be established between them and the LTTE before they would decide to go back; others preferred not to go back, fearing confrontations with their Tamil neighbors. Women said that they would be too insecure to return to their villages without their sons and husbands. They also said they could not consider returning if the security situation were not considerably improved. In Colombo displaced people reported that relatives who had returned to Batticaloa were harassed at checkpoints and that they would consider returning to Batticaloa only if the conflict ended and conditions improved.

Many government officials, however, candidly expressed their conviction that the war would be hard to end in the near future. Although the army was large, the LTTE remained strong. Its power derived from the Tamil community who perceived the LTTE forces as the only ones capable of defending the "Tamil cause"; therefore, recruitment and mobilization were massive and frequently voluntary. Steady financial assistance to the LTTE was apparently also not lacking.

Some of those who had already been resettled said that conditions were so awful in their camps that they preferred to be back in their villages, although they still lived in cadjan huts and could not go to cultivate the fields for security reasons. Others said they had been brought back by the Special Task Forces a year earlier; at the time they were not very happy about it but "felt they had to come back." In many camps people mentioned that the authorities had threatened to cut the rations once the government decided they could return to their homes. The brigadiers also had visited the camps and had tried to convince the displaced that their home areas were safe. Some people said the appearance of the brigadiers was not particularly reassuring; others said they could not trust the officers of the army who had attacked them in the past and killed their relatives.

A consistent grievance was that the authorities did not provide the financial assistance they had promised. Although dry rations were supplied to the resettled, the settling-in allowance, the funds for reconstructing houses, and the productive enterprise grants frequently did not materialize.

NGOs reported that resettlement was not always voluntary and that occasionally it had been conducted under harsh conditions; that it was taking place despite the fact that there was no end to the conflict in sight; and that coercion could take subtle forms. They expressed concern that the government did not always comply with its own 1993 guidelines (discussed below), which stressed that resettlement should be voluntary.

On the other hand, many displaced persons expressed their wish to return to their areas of origin once they received some financial assistance. Of those who had already been resettled, many said that conditions were better in their own village than in the camp and that although they had originally been reluctant to return they had become less so. Also, many NGOs had agreed to assist only those who returned voluntarily to their homes and were involved in providing rehabilitation assistance to the resettled. Their presence undoubtedly had a moderating and monitoring effect both on the authorities and on the local population, which the government acknowledged. While recognizing that the government naturally perceived the fulfillment of basic needs as its first priority, many NGOs expressed concern at the lack of realistic and detailed long-term plans.

Although the government had been implementing its resettlement program for those who were displaced from the so-called cleared areas, it had made fewer plans for the communities that would be formed from "uncleared" areas. Both Sinhalese and Muslim displaced persons who had fled the fighting or who were evicted by the rebels, and whose prospects for returning to their home areas in the near future were slim, expressed the wish that the government would devise a scheme of granting or leasing them land to cultivate.

With regard to the possibilities of integration with the local community for those whose prospects of returning to their home area did not seem feasible, this did not appear to be excluded outright, although many sources cited conflicts and disagreements over job opportunities. One observer suggested creating joint committees of the displaced and the host population, in which NGOs or the clergy and the local authorities would participate, which would attempt to find solutions to such disputes. There did not appear to be a lack of agricultural opportunities, at least in the areas the representative visited, but the displaced would need capital in order to begin working, in addition to the cooperation of the local community and local officials. Other measures could also be taken: for instance, in a Sinhalese camp in Puttalam the people said they hoped that the government would "fill in" the marsh around their camp, so that they could start some cultivation.

THE DILEMMAS OF IMPLEMENTATION. There is no doubt that the government was faced with serious dilemmas. Officials appreciated the fact that assistance with resettlement and rehabilitation meant saving expenses for dry rations in the future. They also believed that people could not stay forever in the camps. When the majority of a camp decided to return to their villages and a minority refused, the officials could see no good reason to maintain the camp and continue supplying food assistance. Officials also expressed the suspicion that some of those housed in welfare centers had developed a dependency syndrome or found it lucrative, particularly if living in Colombo, because they received rations while also working outside the camp. One senior army official even thought that some relief NGOs were "living off" the displaced and preferred the perpetual existence of the camps. NGOs, for their part, felt that conditions in the camps were too bad to allow the displaced to develop a dependency syndrome.

Some officials said that it was often hard to determine who was from which area and that the tensions between the communities complicated the allocation of land. It also was not contested that propaganda was in play: in Madhu Open Relief Center, for instance, where UNHCR distributed food, the displaced staged demonstrations because the government stopped distributing rations to those originating from "cleared" areas in Vavuniya. The LTTE had discouraged, if not actually prohibited, those contemplating return from doing so. It was also possible that the government placed too much emphasis on persuading the first ones to resettle on the premise that those who took the first difficult step would be followed more willingly by the rest.

The most serious problem, as the authorities saw it, was that the government did not have enough money to fulfill its promises to the resettled. Lack of funds made it impossible for the government to design and implement special projects or projects directed toward target groups. Both government and military officials said that unless infrastructure were built, especially schools and medical facilities, and employment opportunities were developed, people could not be expected to return to their homes.

On the question of the voluntary nature of return, the officials' responses were not very illuminating: they said either that the people themselves would express their will to be resettled, or that the authorities would manage to convince them by providing the necessary information. On the question of how safe an area needed to be in order to be declared "clear" or how "permanently clear" it had to be before resettlement could begin, some officials said that the potential for violence could not be excluded altogether in any area.

In addition, there appeared to be regional patterns to the whole issue of resettlement. The government was actively promoting the resettlement of the displaced in the east and in Vavuniya in the north. It had declared its goal to accomplish this resettlement before the end of 1993 so that it could hold local elections for the provincial councils early in 1994. In addition, it was planning to conduct a referendum in the east, provided for in the Indo-Lanka Accord of 1987, on the issue of the "merger" between the east and the north. NGOs and other sources privately expressed serious doubts about the feasibility (and fairness, should they take place at that time) of the elections and the referendum. They also voiced concerns about the genuineness of heightened efforts to "normalize" the area. MRR&SW officials and military authorities said that their job was to implement the government policy as fast and efficiently as possible.

In light of the complicated issue of settlement of landless Sinhalese farmers in the past, resettlement of the local population in the east for the purpose of voting had become a highly politicized issue. Reports alleged that Tamils were not being resettled as quickly as Muslims and that they had not received equal assistance from the government. Some individuals expressed the fear that the LTTE was going to do anything possible to jeopardize the referendum (not excluding, of course, violence).[13] This "resettlement by date" rendered the prospects of maintaining peace for those already resettled rather precarious.

The International and the Nongovernmental Community

Generally, there is much activity regarding Sri Lanka on the international level; this, however, remained low-key and geared mostly toward humanitarian and development assistance rather than high-profile interventions on the political level. United Nations agencies and international and local NGOs provided housing and related assistance to displaced persons. Much donor assistance was channeled to the displaced through the NGOs, which composed a well-established community. Among the international actors providing support for the internally displaced were UNHCR, UNICEF, ICRC, NGOs, and the donor community.

UNHCR was involved with the repatriation of refugees and to that extent dealt also with internally displaced persons. It had an open dialogue with both the government and the LTTE and was the most substantive United Nations operation in the north and the east. It had established two so-called open relief centers (ORCs) and several subcenters, the history of which was connected with the Tamil movements between Sri Lanka and India. In the period from 1983 to 1987, many Tamils fled conditions of insecurity in the north and east and sought asylum in India. Following the Indo-Lanka Accord of July 1987, many were encouraged to return home; UNHCR and the government of Sri Lanka signed a Memorandum of Understanding in August 1987 regarding UNHCR's monitoring of its assistance for the rehabilitation and reintegration of returnees. After hostilities resumed in June 1990, a large number of persons crossed the Palk Strait to seek refuge in South India, and even more fled their homes for other destinations. Mannar District (on the mainland) was the home area of the largest number of returnees and thus had become the focal point of the UNHCR-assisted reintegration program. At the same time, Mannar provided the shortest, safest, and cheapest crossing to India, thus attracting most of the persons fleeing the conflict. UNHCR found itself, perhaps for the first time in its history, with a field presence in a country of origin amidst a mass exodus. Its need to help the returnees went hand in hand with the opportunity to defuse the causes for departure. It was also assumed that UNHCR would be in a better position to promote conditions for the spontaneous voluntary repatriation of refugees from Tamil Nadu. But most compelling was the fact that it was impossible to draw a legal distinction between categories of persons with respect to their entitlement to basic humanitarian assistance.

It was against the backdrop of these considerations that UNHCR decided to establish its ORCs. These have been defined as temporary places where displaced persons on the move can freely enter or leave and obtain essential relief assistance in a relatively safe environment. But they were not closed camps or government welfare centers or legal "safe havens."

There were two ORCs in Mannar District: one at Pesalai, a fishing village on the northern coast of Mannar Island that is under the control of the Sri Lankan armed forces, and one at the Madhu shrine, deep in the forests of mainland Mannar, an area largely dominated by LTTE militant forces. The presence of UNHCR field staff at the ORCs provided the opportunity to monitor the situation and to show that some effort was being made to observe international standards. It also can be said that the UNHCR presence was a restraining influence on the combatants.

Several problems were encountered in the operation of the ORCs. One was that UNHCR never formally obtained consent for their establishment from one of the combatant parties, the LTTE. This oversight threatened to undermine the whole operation in Madhu because the

LTTE was not inclined to accept that Madhu was supposed to remain a zone of tranquillity. Another was that a phasing out of the ORC program did not seem feasible, since the need for it persisted and no agency was prepared or able to take over from UNHCR.

UNHCR, in close cooperation with the government, also had been establishing transit and reception centers on Mannar Island, in Trincomalee and in Vavuniya. UNHCR implemented micro-projects at the sites where the returnees eventually resettled and monitored their conditions to some extent.

Some sources were critical of UNHCR's involvement in the repatriation/return exercise, which they saw as sending a false signal to governments with large Sri Lankan refugee populations, and they welcomed the cautious approach of the return program from India. They stressed the need for UNHCR and NGOs to gain access to the camps hosting returnees and for the refugees to be provided with valid and accurate information about the situation in their home areas.

UNHCR did not have a presence in the rest of the country and did not extend its protection and assistance activities to any other area or group outside the north. Despite the beneficial effects of the UNHCR presence, many observers deemed that an extension of its operations to the rest of the country would considerably undermine what it was already doing.

The United Nations Development Programme (UNDP) had been providing management support to the Ministry of Reconstruction, Rehabilitation, and Social Welfare, which handled the relief programs. The resident representative, in his capacity as resident coordinator, had recruited an adviser on humanitarian programs. This officer was responsible for advising the UN agency team in Sri Lanka on humanitarian issues related to the conflict and for preparing analytical reports that the government, donors, and NGOs could use to make the provision of humanitarian needs more effective. The resident coordinator convened monthly meetings between donors and the United Nations; he also participated in a monthly meeting of government officials and NGOs, which was convened by the NGOs.

A number of obstacles prevented the initiation of a more active resident coordinator function in Sri Lanka and elsewhere: some government officials would have seen this as a public declaration that the government was not able to adequately handle the relief situation on its own.

UNICEF had been the conduit for the procurement of medical supplies and equipment funded by contributions from several bilateral donors. This assistance had helped maintain immunization coverage at high levels and prevent epidemics in all the affected areas. It also had provided school kits to displaced children and in so doing helped them continue their schooling and reduce the effects of psychosocial trauma. In general, however, UNICEF was not highly active.

The ICRC primarily addressed protection issues: it worked with persons detained by the government and operated a tracing program to help reunite families. Red Cross trucks and ships helped deliver food to the areas where the government did not have uninhibited access. The ICRC assisted the Sri Lankan Red Cross in its medical operations (such as the mobile clinic that visits camps), and, together with the Sri Lankan Red Cross, it ran the hospital on the Jaffna Peninsula. Many NGOs expressed gratitude for the presence of the ICRC, which enabled them to operate also.

The World Health Organization, the Food and Agriculture Organization, the World Food Programme, the International Monetary Fund, the World Bank, and the International Labor Organization also were involved in one way or another with issues related to the internally displaced.

A large number of NGOs were involved with relief, rehabilitation, and development programs in Sri Lanka, which traditionally has had a pluralistic and vigorous NGO sector. Most were small village-level groups, although a few were quite substantial. A number of international NGOs also operated in the country, and others provided funds to local partners. Much of their work was done in education, health, and agriculture. Some observers had found that local, community-oriented projects implemented by NGOs had beneficial effects for the local population. In addition, a human rights NGO community had been developing over the previous twenty years, although it had become less active in the face of increased threats to the security and life of its members.

The activities of the NGOs were of great importance to the relief effort because government funds were not sufficient to maintain all camps and NGOs had much greater freedom of action in applying funds. Government officials at all levels, including the military, expressed appreciation and gratitude for the work of the international and local NGOs with the internally displaced. In Ampara, where the NGO sector was not as large, many among the government and the displaced expressed the wish that a greater NGO presence would be established. On the whole, there was agreement on the fact that NGOs provided a significant degree of de facto protection to the displaced population by the mere fact of their presence for humanitarian reasons.

Members of the donor community expressed the view that it was the responsibility of the government of Sri Lanka to provide protection and assistance to its internally displaced and that they were keen not to undertake any measures that might undermine that responsibility. They thought that channeling assistance to UNHCR or to the NGOs was beneficial; they also reported that the government had not specifically approached them on the question of assistance to those displaced or resettled. The opinion also was expressed that donors were not inclined to fund the resettlement and rehabilitation project because they felt that not enough was being done to resolve the conflict.

The Post-1994 Era

The government of President Chandrika Kumaratunga was elected in 1994 on a platform that included as one of its fundamentals achieving a peaceful solution to the ethnic problem in which the question of internal displacement is rooted. The PA coalition and the president campaigned on a moral platform as much as on any other and were sincere in their desire to bring about peace. The new government contrasted with the outgoing one, which had been unwilling to acknowledge the existence of an ethnic problem and was associated with hegemonic politics.

The new government's early actions were encouraging. After the representative's mission, it responded comprehensively to his request for information on developments regarding the internally displaced. The government reiterated that it adhered to a principle of voluntary resettlement and reported improvements in the security situation and the signing of Protocol II Additional to the Geneva Conventions. It also noted the establishment of a Human Rights Commission for the promotion of human rights of minorities and disadvantaged groups. It further undertook protective measures for the internally displaced, such as minimizing military and security operations near the welfare centers and investigating thousands of cases of "disappeared" persons.[14] In January 1995, the LTTE and the government entered into a "cessation of hostilities."

As its first act after assuming office, the PA government unilaterally lifted a ban on the delivery of items to Jaffna that were considered potentially useful in making explosive devices and entered into preliminary negotiations with the LTTE. There was jubilation in Jaffna when the first team of negotiators arrived there, and widespread hope that the conflict was drawing to an end. This optimism proved premature, however. In April 1995 the LTTE abruptly violated the cease-fire; skirmishes between LTTE forces and government troops continued throughout the summer of 1995. In August 1995 the government made public its plan for a settlement by means of a comprehensive devolution of power to the regions.

Ironically, the developments from this point onward contributed to a worsening of the plight of the displaced. Apparently convinced that the LTTE would not negotiate without a military victory, the government launched a military campaign in October 1995, known as Riviresa, to gain control of the city of Jaffna, the rebel stronghold. In early December 1995 the government troops achieved this objective; their victory was a hollow one, however, since the LTTE ordered (and in some cases coerced) civilians to leave, turning the city into a ghost town.

This created a new displacement of 400,000 people: approximately 170,000 stayed in the LTTE-controlled eastern part of the peninsula, while 230,000 crossed the lagoon to the LTTE-controlled Vanni region south of the peninsula ("Vanni" means forest or jungle and includes the northern provinces of Mullaitivu, Mannar, and parts of Vavuniya). In May 1996 another 30,000–50,000 people were displaced in the course of operation Riviresa II, during which the military took control of the whole Jaffna Peninsula. A further offensive in Killinochchi in July 1996 caused the Jaffna displaced as well as most of the area's residents to flee to other parts of the Vanni.

By mid-1996 many of the displaced in the military-controlled peninsula returned to their homes, but those in the Vanni were largely stuck there, mainly because of restrictions on civilian movements imposed by both the LTTE and the government. According to various reports, they were mainly from poorer backgrounds, unlike those displaced in the peninsula. Many had been displaced before. Another offensive in July 1996, Sathjaya, resulted in a substantial turn for the worse for the displaced. The proportion of those staying with friends and relatives in Killinochchi decreased significantly, and more people moved to welfare centers (schools and temples), as well as crude shelters. The relief organizations linked to the LTTE left Killinochchi, leaving the displaced to fend for themselves.

The Displaced in the Vanni, Jaffna, and Vavuniya

War effectively continued in the north throughout 1996, trapping civilians and the displaced in its cycle of violence. Even where the armed forces clearly controlled an area (at the time of this writing, the cities of Jaffna and Vavuniya and most parts of the Jaffna Peninsula), the LTTE still could make incursions, jeopardizing the safety of noncombatants. In addition, constant tension between the non-Tamil-speaking soldiers and local people, especially in Jaffna city, often resulted in human rights abuses. "Disappearances" were again reported, as well as numerous incidents of rape, allegedly committed by drunken soldiers who entered houses after the 6 P.M. curfew and dragged out women and girls. Checkpoints, whether manned by soldiers or the LTTE, greatly restricted the movement of the displaced, whether toward refuge or toward their own homes, and posed constant security threats for "suspects." The LTTE carried out attacks throughout this period, allegedly to keep the population ill at ease so that they would resent the military's presence. The LTTE also targeted military officers and civilians and engaged in exemplary killings. In the Vanni the danger of continued shelling and the fear of another military offensive were the main security problems. Recruitment of children by the LTTE continued unabated.

It was reported, however, that the government planned to establish a national Human Rights Unit to investigate human rights abuses by the armed forces and the police and that the Ministry of Defense was going to appoint a Board of Investigation consisting of senior officers to investigate the "disappearances."

Subsistence needs were only partially fulfilled. Although there was no widespread malnutrition reported in any of the northern areas, nutrition was not considered adequate. In several of the "uncleared" areas of the Jaffna Peninsula and the Vanni, the transportation of food items was restricted. In addition, land mines planted in fields and a ban on fishing greatly increased the dependence of the population on government relief. In the Vanni in particular, serious distribution and entitlement issues remained unresolved, and many displaced persons were denied food aid. Water shortages were also frequent: during the dry season, as many as 300 persons might have to share one well. Shelter conditions were no better: in Jaffna city, where many displaced squatted in the homes of those who had fled, there was little electricity and minimal telephone or postal service. In the Vanni, most people lived in public buildings in crowded and unsanitary conditions. Conditions in the Vavuniya "detention" centers were similar (see below).

Serious shortages of medical personnel and equipment, delays in the delivery of medicine and only few and partly functioning hospitals meant that the population of Jaffna city and in the Vanni did not have access to adequate health care. Epidemics of malaria and typhoid occasionally erupted and an increase in psychological trauma was reported. Very poor health and sanitation conditions were reported in the detention centers in Vavuniya; diarrhea, dysentery, malaria, and typhoid spread rapidly among the detainees.

As to education, it appeared that schools functioned best in Jaffna city. However, staff shortages, a lack of teaching materials, and safety hazards for some students contributed to a low level of attendance. Few classes were held in the Vanni and in Vavuniya because most schools had been converted into emergency shelters.

The situation of the displaced in the eastern part of the country and in Colombo did not improve after the representative's visit, because security significantly deteriorated after the breakdown of the cease-fire. The LTTE attacked many Sinhalese villages and key installations in Colombo; a suicide bomber attacked the Colombo business district, killing ninety people, all civilians, and injuring about two thousand others. Tamil residents in Colombo, including displaced persons, were increasingly harassed as the conflict intensified. Minor bombings in the east marked the slow destabilization there, and some people who originally had resettled in their home villages had to flee again and return to the larger towns, such as Trincomalee, fearing for their safety.

The government's main form of relief assistance continued to be the provision of food rations to all those in need, including those in areas under LTTE control. Nevertheless, grievances were expressed that the government did not provide enough assistance to meet the needs and that what assistance it did provide was slow in coming. In the Vanni it was alleged that the government purposely provided less assistance than required in order to keep criticism at bay and lure the displaced into government-controlled areas. It also was reported that the government, in particular the military, greatly restricted operations of international and local NGOs and limited their ability to deliver relief supplies. The government did set up a "focal point" within the Ministry of Ethnic Affairs in Colombo to coordinate the relief operation, which facilitated the efforts of NGOs. Meetings were held regularly between NGOs, international agencies, and government officials in Colombo in which questions of access and distribution permits and of the overall humanitarian situation were frequently discussed.

The government was less receptive to initiatives from higher levels of the international community to address the humanitarian situation. A statement by the secretary-general expressing his concern was not welcomed by the government, which stated that it did not "wish to permit outside agencies, including the United Nations, to run any independent relief work in the country."[15]

Freedom of Movement, Return, and the "Detention" Centers in Vavuniya

Freedom of movement was highly restricted in Jaffna. Many of those who did not flee to the Vanni before the military's capture of the city were thereafter trapped there because the only routes south were by ship or military plane, and only a few people were given permission to use them. Movement also is restricted in and out of the Vanni. It was reported that although some of the displaced might have wanted to return to Jaffna, others feared the security situation there.

It appeared that a variety of strategic motives, sometimes conflicting, on the part of both the government and the LTTE determined whether the displaced would be allowed to return or move to safer areas of the country. This was made evident in the case of those displaced who were promised increased relief assistance if they left the Vanni and entered into the government-controlled Vavuniya city, only to find themselves held up at the checkpoint, while the military determined who and how many could cross into Vavuniya. Once there, however, most of the displaced were held in "welfare centers" (a euphemism for detention centers), which they were not allowed to leave. Observers speculated that the government wanted to reduce support for the LTTE, or that it wanted to reduce civilian numbers in the Vanni in order to carry out further offensives, but that it did not intend to allow more civilians to resettle in Jaffna.

On the whole, resettlement efforts were curtailed severely after the representative's visit; nevertheless, ironically, the government improved and strengthened its resettlement guidelines.

Resettlement Guidelines

The guidelines remain another area of apparent disjunction between government policy and practice. After the election of the new government in 1994, resettlement policy was redefined as one of "bringing the population affected by ethnic violence and terrorist activities back to productive life by providing basic amenities to live with dignity, paying compensation for the loss and damage sustained and to create a physically, economically and socially sustainable environment for their progress."[16] Relief, rehabilitation, and construction were to be treated as an "exercise integrated with the development process." The new policy reiterated that resettlement should be voluntary and should consist of two "phases." In phase one, a resettling family would be provided with a temporary hut and a settling-in allowance. Food assistance would be provided until the family was able to recommence economic activities of its own. Thereafter, a productive enterprise grant would be provided and food assistance continued for up to six months from the date of the grant. At the minister's discretion, an extension of this might be possible. Resettled communities would be provided with infrastructure facilities such as school buildings, health facilities, and a community center.

In phase two, each family whose house had been destroyed would be given a grant to construct a permanent house. Phase two also envisaged the rebuilding of community life with social, economic, and infrastructural aid. These included the establishment of a Reconstruction and Rehabilitation Bank to assist the affected population, the appointment of appropriate officials, and the rebuilding of damaged public and private assets (such as places of worship, hotels, and guest houses). Other elements included payment of compensation to affected families and persons not covered by existing schemes, assistance to rehabilitate affected industries, and enhancement of existing vocational training programs. Thus, the program envisaged not only economic support that would markedly improve the situation of the displaced but also community rebuilding integrated with development.

While these guidelines are laudable, there is little evidence that they have been translated into practice. In the context of renewed hostilities, they are likely to remain unimplemented in the near future.

Devolution Proposals

A lasting solution to the problem of the displaced can be achieved only through peace. A political solution to the conflict should address the three major concerns of the Tamils: colonization, language, and the merger of the northern and eastern provinces. Although a major cause of the crisis initially was competition for jobs, this is no longer true. Fewer educated Tamils seek state employment, and many are interested in independent employment in commerce or the private sector. Focus has now shifted to land. Settlement of Sinhalas on lands populated by Tamils is seen by the latter as an encroachment. Second, although Tamil is an official language in law, in practice Tamils are disadvantaged. This is compounded by the significance that the Tamil language has for its speakers. Finally, the question of the merger is a thorny one: Tamils would be a clear majority in the case of the merger and for this reason support it, but Sinhalas and Muslims fear it because they would become minorities. Dispute on this issue has for years blocked progress on reconciliation and peace.

The devolution proposals face considerable opposition, but that should not be insurmountable. For example, the clergy is vocal but not a serious threat because it wields no power. Besides, the clergy is divided: there is a sophisticated section that supports the proposals. The nonclerical extremist elements are also in themselves a powerless minority. Any resistance by these elements could be easily overcome with opposition support. Such support should be sought, since the opposition, unlike the clergy and the extremists, are a mainstream force and can be expected to respond with reason. Furthermore, considering the national importance of the proposals, they should receive bipartisan support.

The government, however, has gone out of its way to antagonize the opposition and is instead following a policy of appeasement of the clergy and the extremists. The opposition, for its part, has so far lacked the sense of responsibility and national purpose to ignore petty politics and support the government on the proposals. There is an enlightened faction in the opposition that supports the package, but the government has failed to harness the potential of this group.

Conclusions

The government of Sri Lanka has often been commended for assuming responsibility for its internally displaced and civilian population, even for those living in territories it did not control. It has primarily provided food and medicines, but there is little evidence that it has fully committed itself to alleviating the plight of the displaced: many basic needs are not being adequately met, and in some cases, such as in the Vavuniya centers, the provisions are thoroughly inadequate. In the Vanni, even food assistance does not reach all those in need. Furthermore, the government, especially the military, restricts the activities of international and local NGOs, which could assist the displaced where the government's resources are not sufficient. Consequently, many displaced persons are suffering. It is necessary that the government continue to provide food aid to all those who need it and allow the international community to deliver nonfood items, in particular those related to shelter, sanitation, medicines, and education. Long delays in the delivery of assistance and any discriminatory practices in the provision of assistance or other benefits should be avoided. In view of the government's limited resources, the possibility of switching some of the food aid to income-generation projects should be considered, in particular where security is not an issue.

Security

There has been a gradual subordination to military priorities of commitments and obligations made by the PA government as well as by the Sri Lankan state as a signatory to international human rights instruments. Life and personal security of the displaced and other noncombatant populations in Jaffna, the Vanni, and other areas of the north and east are frequently threatened by the escalation of the conflict and the presence of the military. Human rights violations such as "disappearances" and rape, whose frequency had decreased at the time of the representative's visit, began being reported again after 1996, despite the government's pledges to uphold human rights. To the extent possible, the administration in Jaffna and in the east should be placed in the hands of civilian authorities, and allegations of human rights violations by soldiers should be investigated promptly. Those accused of rapes, "disappearances," arbitrary detentions, and executions should be prosecuted. Tensions between the army and the displaced must be reduced, if necessary by decreasing the number of checkpoints and easing security measures around the welfare centers. Military presence and operations in or near welfare centers and resettlement sites must be avoided. The LTTE also must be given a strong message that targeting civilians is illegal under humanitarian law and may call for international criminal prosecution.

Holding people in the Vavuniya welfare centers against their will may amount to arbitrary detention. If security screenings are required, those should be promptly carried out so that innocent civilians can resume their lives in destinations of their own choosing.

The Issue of Resettlement

Resettlement, plans for which were very ambitious during the representative's visit, has slowed significantly. Many persons who had returned to their areas of origin have had to flee again in response to the ongoing conflict and the destabilization of "cleared" areas. Unless the security of the people can be guaranteed, and unless they themselves decide to return, resettlement may be premature and disruptive. Any type of coercion, including the threat of withdrawing food assistance to induce return, should be avoided. Conditions in the camps should not be allowed to become so perilous or dehumanizing that the displaced prefer the fear of being persecuted or victimized to remaining in the camps. Where resettlement does take place, accurate information about security in the area of original residence should be provided to those to be resettled, and procedural safeguards for voluntary resettlement should be developed. The government's resettlement guidelines should be complied with, and promises of benefits following resettlement should not be misleading.

At the same time, restrictions on freedom of movement that impede return, especially from Vavuniya town and the Vanni to the Jaffna Peninsula, should be significantly eased, and people who wish to return to their homes should not be prevented from doing so.

The Search for Durable Solutions

Despite the promising beginning of the new government in working toward peace and the protection of the rights of minorities, Sri Lanka has not been able to break the cycle of violence that has engulfed it since the early 1980s. Extremists on both sides have managed once again to undermine the wishes of the overwhelming majority of the Sri Lankan population that craves an end to the conflict. Genuine efforts to reach a negotiated peace agreement therefore should restart, and the government's devolution proposals should receive the support they merit. If the war continues for much longer, the prospects for maintaining peace and security even in those areas that are relatively peaceful may be seriously jeopardized. Increased freedom of information and expression of opinion may facilitate the spread of peace initiatives, publicize the plight of the displaced, and give an accurate picture of the magnitude of the war and its consequences.

Because the projects for population settlements in the east are particularly controversial, their careful reconsideration may be necessary. Members of the communities who originate from that area should be given special attention in the settlement process. In addition, alternative long-term solutions need to be found for communities that will not be able to return to their original areas of residence in the foreseeable future, such as the Muslim communities who were forcibly evicted from Jaffna.

The Role of NGOs

Both the government and the LTTE have accepted the significant role of international and local NGOs in providing emergency relief to the displaced and victims of conflict. Their role, therefore, should be given unequivocal support. In addition, they should be given full and free access to the displaced population and be allowed to deliver food, non-food items, and essential services to them. A greater NGO presence in Jaffna would add to civilian participation in the city. The government should further strengthen its dialogue with NGOs, clarify its stance toward them, and modify its restrictions on access. Given the military's important role in those areas where there are large concentrations of displaced populations, it might be useful to consider establishing an NGO liaison office in the Ministry of Defense and at the district level, where access and delivery permits could be easily obtained.

The Role of the International Community

International agencies and NGOs in Sri Lanka so far have maintained a relatively low profile in relief operations. Given that the conflict has been going on for so many years, however, and that the human rights situation still requires many improvements, it may be timely to consider alternative forms of international activity and intervention. One area in which Sri Lanka seems to be in need of external assistance is in mediating peace; there appears to be no military solution to the conflict, and all political efforts to come to a negotiated solution have failed. Hundreds of thousands of people have been victimized for the sake of extremist elements on both sides.

In the area of human rights, monitoring by human rights organizations and publication of their findings would contribute to the security of the people. UNDP and the UN High Commissioner for Human Rights should consider establishing a human rights and humanitarian liaison office to process such information and advise on common strategies to be adopted by the resident agencies, and where appropriate, by NGOs and donors as well. Advocacy on human rights issues should become a central element of the work of United Nations agencies and international NGOs.

Notes

1. Government of Sri Lanka, Ministry of Shipping, Ports, Rehabilitation, and Reconstruction, "Report on Implementation of the Development Programmes," Colombo, September 1995, p. 1.

2. The exception is those who crossed the Jaffna Lagoon to Kilinochchi, who were displaced once more when the government forces took the town in September 1996.

3. Another group one finds in Sri Lanka are the Burghers, who are descendants of the Dutch, either in direct line or intermarried with other groups.

4. See also Bernard Anderson, *Imagined Communities: Reflections on the Origin and Spread of Nationalism* (London: Verso Editions/NLB, 1983), p. 26.

5. Sri Lanka has been described as the "island of the two minorities": while the Sinhala are a majority on the island, they form a minority in relation to the 50 million Tamils of neighboring South India. Each ethnic group constantly feels under siege by the other.

6. In 1964 an agreement was reached between India and Sri Lanka by which India would take back 575,000 Indian Tamils who had not opted for Sri Lankan citizenship in 1948 and thereafter had become disenfranchised, while Sri Lanka would grant citizenship to about 300,000 of them. The agreement was only partially carried out. By 1988, however, Sri Lanka had promised to grant citizenship to the remaining 250,000 stateless plantation Tamils.

7. By disenfranchising the Indian Tamils, the government also sought to weaken the left-wing parties, which drew considerable support from the former. Tamils claimed this was a deliberate attempt to "colonize" strategic areas of the

North in order to break up geographical continuity and build physical and electoral buffer zones. For instance, according to one report, almost 400,000 Sinhalese were settled in the North by 1971, with 40,000 carving out a new electorate in the Seruwila area of Trincomalee; Sinhalese in Trincomalee rose from 3 percent to 30 percent of the population. The same happened in Batticaloa district, which was divided in 1963 to create a predominantly Sinhalese Amparai district. The government claimed that much of the disputed territory was underdeveloped Crown land and that the Tamil community could not "reserve" uninhabited territory in perpetuity in the face of the growing need for development. The momentum, according to one source, grew in the 1970s as need for land increased in Trincomalee and Batticaloa districts with the development of two large irrigation and settlement schemes at Mahaveli and Madura Oya funded by the United Kingdom and Canada. Tamils saw Sinhalese settlers as the civilian "shock troops" guarded by government soldiers with a mandate to drive out Tamil civilians in surrounding areas.

8. See C. R. de Silva, "The Politics of University Admissions: A Review of the Admissions Policy in Sri Lanka, 1971–1975," *Sri Lanka Journal of Social Sciences*, vol. 2, pp. 85–123.

9. K. M. de Silva, "University Admissions and Ethnic Tension in Sri Lanka, 1977–82," Cross-National Workshop on Preference Policies and Programs, Trincomalee, Sri Lanka, March 7–14, 1982.

10. Earlier, the Indian government had encouraged the separatist movement by training and arming the rebels; later it tried unsuccessfully to disarm the militants and persuade them to accept a political solution. There were two reasons for India's early support to the rebel groups. First, the anti-Tamil riots of July 1983 had led the Tamil Nadu government to urge New Delhi to intervene. Second, and perhaps more important, the government of India had watched with displeasure and alarm the dramatic turn Sri Lanka took in 1977 in rejecting socialism and opting for a pro-Western market economy. India, a major trade and security partner with the Soviet Union, was keen to maintain its regional hegemony and viewed Sri Lanka's economic and foreign policies with suspicion. Thus in 1987, when a decisive victory of the Sri Lankan forces over the rebels was imminent, India violated Sri Lankan air space and dropped "relief supplies." Sri Lanka, wisely deciding not to take on the world's fourth largest army, had to agree to the truce imposed by India. See Francis M. Deng, *Profiles in Displacement: Sri Lanka*, E/CN.4/1994/44/Add.1 (United Nations, Commission on Human Rights, January 25, 1994).

11. Another result was the fragmentation of the separatist movement. Splinter groups such as the Tamil Eelam Liberation Organization (TELO) and the People's Liberation Organization of Tamil Eelam (PLOTE) appeared at that time.

12. In the western district of Puttalam, the representative visited Sinhapura, the one Sinhalese camp in the area, and a few Muslim camps in Alankuda and Kalpitiya. In the district of Anuradhapura he visited Thanthirimale, a so-called border Sinhalese area; a Sinhalese camp (including one Muslim family) in Kahatagasdigiliya; and a few Muslim and Sinhalese camps in Morawewa and Horowpotana. In the eastern district of Trincomalee the representative visited Alles

Gardens, where UNHCR was hosting returnees from India; Nilaveli and Clapenburg camps, housing Tamil displaced persons; Alankany village (in the division of Kinniya), where Tamils had resettled; and one Muslim camp, also in Kinniya. In the district of Ampara he went to a Tamil resettlement village, Sorikalmunai, and a Tamil "transit" camp (where people are housed pending resettlement to their villages) in Karativu. In Batticaloa, he visited Thalavai, a Tamil resettlement village, and two camps in Erravur, one Tamil and one Muslim. Finally, while in Colombo, the representative visited the Maligawatte welfare center, which housed Muslim displaced persons, and Saraswathy Hall, which housed Tamil displaced persons.

13. The LTTE subsequently did escalate violence in the area, and the referendum was never held.

14. See Francis M. Deng, *Internally Displaced Persons*, E/CN.4/1995/50 (United Nations, Commission on Human Rights, February 2, 1995); and General Assembly, *Internally Displaced Persons*, Note by the Secretary-General, A/50/558 (United Nations, October 20, 1995).

15. See Hiram A. Ruiz and Katie Hope, "Conflict and Displacement in Sri Lanka," U.S. Committee for Refugees, Washington, D.C., March 1997; and Mario Gomez, "The People in Between: Sri Lankans Face Long-Term Displacement as Conflict Escalates," U.S. Committee for Refugees, Washington, D.C., March 1996.

16. Government of Sri Lanka, Ministry of Shipping, Ports, Rehabilitation and Reconstruction, "Performance, Policy, Strategies and Programmes 1994–1995," Colombo, 1995, p. 27.

CHAPTER TEN

In Search of Hope: The Plight of Displaced Colombians

Liliana Obregón and Maria Stavropoulou

DISPLACEMENT IN COLOMBIA has been primarily the result of political violence, which in some areas of the country has degenerated into armed conflict among insurgents, the military, and various paramilitary groups and private agents. More than a million people were displaced between 1985 and 1998, and they have little hope of resolving their situation in the near future. The representative of the United Nations secretary-general on internally displaced persons visited Colombia in June 1994, and his findings are included in this chapter.[1] Information collected by the authors since then, including during subsequent visits, indicates that the situation of the internally displaced has continued to deteriorate despite the formal commitments undertaken by the Colombian government.

In 1995 the government developed a "National Program for Integrated Attention to the Population Displaced by Violence."[2] The program accepts the Permanent Consultation on Internal Displacement in the Americas (Consulta Permanente para el Desplazamiento Interno en las Américas, or CPDIA) identification of violence as a main cause of displacement.[3] The government further took into account the findings of the Colombian Conference of Bishops' 1995 Report on Violence and Internal Forced Displacement and accepted the Consultation for Human

Republic of Colombia

Rights and Displacement Report (Consultoría de Derechos Humanos y Desplazamiento, or CODHES), which determined the main cause of displacement to be political violence.[4] In May of 1997, the program was restructured as a "system" with specific attention to institutions, information systems, and financial resources.[5]

Until recently, the phenomenon of displacement in Colombia was different from that in other countries: internally displaced persons typically moved individually, with their immediate families or in small groups. They frequently relocated in silence to neighboring rural areas and from there to urban centers, often to join relatives or friends originating from the same area. The displaced mingled with the local population, generally the poorest layer of society, which includes other migrant and displaced persons. They did not wish to be identified and therefore avoided contacting authorities or aid organizations.

Although these patterns of movement are long-standing, concern about the humanitarian dimensions of the problem have sharpened. Since 1992, political violence has increased, and displacement is more frequent and affects larger groups of people. Since 1996 several events of collective forced displacement have demonstrated that the practice continues to be an instrumental part of the government's counterinsurgency strategy and of the drug traffickers' and guerrillas' territorial control. In some regions the violent actors have forced the displaced into neighboring Panama and Venezuela; those two countries have undertaken forcible repatriations, thereby bringing an international dimension to the problem. The plight of the displaced has become another of Colombia's daily stories of violence.

THE CONTEXT. Colombia is a country of flux and stagnation, where modernity has clashed with traditional patron-client relations and an exclusionary political system. Though it claims to be the oldest democracy in Latin America, elections since the 1960s have been paralleled by troubled political life and violence. At the root of these problems lie the enormous disparities in the distribution of land and wealth, a loss of government legitimacy, the ineffectiveness of established institutions, an oligarchic political and social system based on clientism, the state's use of terrorist methods, a breakdown of social relations, the inaccessibility of power for the majority of Colombians, the physical absence of the state in many regions, and a highly militarized society.[6]

In the 1980s the violence-stability paradox became especially manifest as the brutality increased without breaking down the economic and political system. A government-commissioned study, which is regarded as definitive, posits that violence in Colombia has been traditionally used as a mechanism for dealing with social problems.[7] As such it has become "institutionalized," empowered by its own dynamic and creating its own reality.[8] *La Violencia* in its present form remains inherent to Colombia's social and political relations.[9] Colombia may have met electoral standards and institutional and economic stability criteria, but the country's endemic violence has called into question the legitimacy of its formal institutionalized democracy. Impunity for crime and the enormous wealth generated by illegal activities also have generated ambiguous legal and ethical standards that feed the cycle of violence.

In the 1990s, Colombia has one of the highest homicide rates in the world, a yearly average of 89.5 murders per 100,000 inhabitants. In 1996 the number went down to 66 per 100,000, but murder was still the number one cause of death in Colombia; there were a reported 26,142 murders among a population of approximately 36 million.[10] Of these, 3,173 (13 percent) were considered to be caused by political violence, meaning they were "combat related deaths, murder of noncombatants by the guerrillas and the army, 'social cleansing' killings (whose targets are beggars, prostitutes, drug addicts, and the homeless), massacres and selective murders of political adversaries committed by paramilitary forces and by the Army or police forces of Colombia."[11] Though rural inhabitants constitute only one third of Colombia's total population, the majority of the victims of violence are from this sector.

Political Background

A BIPARTISAN SYSTEM. Colombia's political history reads like a chronicle of confrontations between the Liberal and Conservative parties, or as the struggle of an oligarchy to retain power. During the civil wars of the nineteenth century, the elites remained strong with the military under their control. Clientism characterized the early evolution of local political systems, later reflected in the national scheme of voting. Mass participation in politics was limited to following one of the parties according to the "patron's" vote and to family ties. Such a relationship institutionalized a bipartisan or "consociational" coalition: an agreement between the elites to share power. The oligarchical character of a negotiated democracy became characteristic of Colombia's political solution to national crisis.[12]

FROM HEGEMONY TO HEGEMONY. From 1890 to 1930, Conservative governments ruled. 1930 marked the start of a transition, with the Liberal Party assuming power for several years. The federal bureaucratic slate was wiped clean, with the replacement of Conservative officials by Liberal ones. The Liberals continued to win the presidency until they were divided in the presidential campaign of 1946 between two candidates: Gabriel Turbay and Jorge-Eliecer Gaitán. Their division allowed Mariano Ospina Pérez, a moderate Conservative, to win. Gaitán, a radical liberal and a mestizo of the lower middle class, continued to promote his ideas in the hope of winning the 1949 elections.

Gaitán represented a challenge to the dominant political elite: he was the first candidate with popular support who did not come from the traditional ruling families. The party hierarchies considered him a radical and a populist, though he played within the rules of the bipartisan system. His charismatic leadership, his humble origins, and his speeches against the political ruling class appealed to a vast mass of the middle and lower classes, both urban and rural.

Gaitán's defiance of the status quo shook the reactionaries, led by Laureano Gómez, a hard-line Conservative presidential candidate, who virtually declared war on the Liberal Party. The polarization of those two groups led to extreme violence in the rural areas. Finally, Gaitán was assassinated in Bogotá on April 9, 1948. Violent demonstrations quickly spread throughout the country. This was the beginning of the period known as *La Violencia* (1948–65) during which more than 300,000 civilians (mainly poor peasants) were killed and approximately 2 million people fled to the cities in order to escape the bloodbath.

The Liberals boycotted the 1950 election, and Gómez, the only candidate, was elected president. *La Violencia* rose to its peak during the Gómez presidency. Gómez's administration is considered a "civil dictatorship" because he isolated Congress, used the police to persecute his opposition (Liberals, Communists, and Protestants alike), and implemented many authoritarian measures.[13] As the violence increased, members of his own party realized the need for an alternative to his authoritarian regime. Thus on June 15, 1953, the only military coup in Colombia in the twentieth century materialized under General Gustavo Rojas Pinilla with the support of both the Conservative and the Liberal elites.

Unlike other dictatorships in Latin America, Rojas weakened the military apparatus and decreed a general amnesty in order to restore a degree of stability to the country. Rojas did not try to create control mechanisms or a new legal system to give his regime legitimacy. He obtained power as a consequence of the crisis in the system and the pact between the elites, not to institutionalize military rule.

Indeed, the Rojas regime lasted only until the general attempted to consolidate military rule by forming a "third force," which would compete in elections against the two traditional parties. Confronting the bipartisan system through his populist actions made the traditional ruling classes apprehensive, and their opposition to his government grew.

THE NATIONAL FRONT. In May 1957 the Liberal and Conservative leaders agreed to a temporary military junta to remove Rojas and direct the presidency until August 1958 in order to allow the transition to a "National Front": they agreed to alternate in government for a period of sixteen years. Such an agreement is the basis of Colombia's "democracy by pact," already an informal custom among the ruling elite.[14]

One immediate effect of the pact was to pacify the country and return the military to the barracks. A 1957 referendum approved a "restricted democracy," which institutionalized Liberal and Conservative Party rule and purposely excluded other political initiatives from any legitimate participation in the system. Opposition forces could now legally exist, but only if controlled or co-opted under the banners of the traditional parties.

Under the National Front agreement, made between the heads of the two parties that had incited the massacre of thousands of peasants, the poor did not gain access to the nation's economic resources. Neither did income and quality of life improve significantly during this period. Although the 1961 agrarian reform was initially intended to restore social harmony by addressing the problems of the rural population, it was never fully implemented. Clientism thrived and became the pillar of the system, obstructing the process of reform and change.[15] Guerrilla movements in Colombia surged, led by middle-class urban students, professors, intellectuals, and political leaders inspired by the Cuban Revolution.

THE AD HOC CONTINUATION OF THE NATIONAL FRONT (1974–84). After sixteen years of exclusionary politics, the 1974 elections were declared open to other political groups. By then the state machinery was well conditioned to work in favor of the two traditional parties. The missed opportunity of the elites to address historical inequalities such as land tenure and the provision of basic necessities for the poor during this period provoked social uprisings throughout the country. Land invasions and popular protests became everyday news. Guerrilla groups continued to grow while the Communist Party and the Left failed to take effective advantage of this situation to become a strong opposition movement.[16]

Violence became a form of resolving problems in geographically marginalized regions where the presence of the state was almost nonexistent.[17] Guerrilla groups easily filled the vacuum in such areas. The two traditional parties had become subcultures in themselves without allowing significant political challenges to the system.

Also prevailing during the post–National Front period were the exceptional procedures legalized during the State of Siege (Estados de Sitio). Through these procedures, the military gradually acquired greater power and the authority to "maintain public order," becoming involved in repressing social movements and grass-roots organizations as part of its counterinsurgency strategy.

The National Front had created a clientist machinery that perpetuated the power of the traditional parties.[18] Smaller voter turnouts in elections and the low percentage of voting for third parties strengthened the bipartisan hegemony even after the formal years of the National Front ended.

The weakness of institutional controls allowed violence to penetrate all sectors of society. It became the dominant form of relationship as well as an instrument of the political game. Though attempts were made during the administrations of Belisario Betancur (1982–86) and Virgilio Barco (1986–90) to pacify the country through dialogue with the guerrillas, the lack of a permanent national commitment to peace and the opposition of the elites and military throughout both processes prevented a successful outcome.

FROM THE ASSASSINATION OF LARA TO THE ASSASSINATION OF GALÁN (1984–89). After 1984 the drug trafficking trade emerged on the political stage, adding even more complexity to the tangled web of democratization and violence. Before then, commerce in illegal drugs was seen as an additional element of common crime, even tolerated because it seemed beneficial for some impoverished sectors of the society and harmless to the social and political stability of the country. The government had turned its back on the problem because at that time the guerrilla groups seemed to be the most politically dangerous element of destabilization. But when Minister of Justice Rodrigo Lara Bonilla was killed on the streets of Bogotá in 1984, the frailty of the state became evident at one of its most vulnerable points: the judicial system.

Initially the drug traffickers were worried about defending their economic interests, but gradually they became involved in politics as their influence extended into other areas of society. The traffickers began to territorialize their power by buying enormous tracts of land from traditional landowners who were tired of being pressured by peasant mobilizations and guerrilla groups. This in turn gave them social and political influence. They contributed to the existing paramilitary groups by financing sophisticated training and armaments. Most of the massacres of 1988 and 1989 took place in the areas of major mafia influence.[19]

On August 18, 1989, the popular and charismatic presidential candidate Luis Carlos Galán was murdered by the drug mafia, marking the climax of a period in which bloodshed was an everyday reality. Three presidential candidates were murdered before the 1990 presidential elections. The homicide total reached 25,000. Cesar Gaviria was elected president by default.

CHANGING THE RULES OF THE GAME: THE NEW CONSTITUTION. At the worst moment of the crisis the political actors of the system, including forces as radical as the guerrillas and the drug traffickers, decided to combine efforts and agree on social and political reconstruction based on a new constitution, peace talks with the guerrillas, and certain concessions to those drug traffickers who would turn themselves in to the authorities. A Constituent Assembly, made up of members from the most varied social, economic, and political origins, was elected by the Colombian people in December 1990. Political tolerance had to be learned and practiced in this forum since it was necessary to combine efforts from different groups to reach agreements that would appeal to the majority.

On July 4, 1991, full of hope, Colombians thought themselves to have embarked on a different phase of history, under the rule of a new constitution. They thought it was rid of many of the old flaws that had supported bipartisan politics and the excessively centralized presidential system. Because the constitution provided for significant new human rights protections, many citizens began to hope for peace despite the context of political turmoil. However, the military structure remained the same as in the constitution of 1886.

LOSS OF HOPE: THE CRISIS CONTINUES. By 1992 the peace talks foundered again under pressure from extremists at both ends of the political spectrum. The development of narco-terrorism in the 1980s and narco-corruption in the 1990s limited the possibilities of further peace negotiations between the guerrillas and the government, both of whom have had to deal with and have been corrupted by the drug wars. Optimism for the future prospects of the country, which were running high after the adoption of the new constitution, has diminished significantly since then.[20]

Only 32 percent of the voting population participated in the presidential elections of June 1994 in which Ernesto Samper Pizano, the Liberal Party candidate, was elected. Samper began his administration with accusations from the opposing candidate that his campaign had been financed in part with money contributed by drug traffickers. This developed into a major political crisis.[21] Though Samper made some positive advances in human rights policies during the first year of his administration, as the political crisis deepened and his legitimacy to govern was increasingly questioned by public opinion, he turned to the armed forces for support; the result was to strongly reinforce the military's power and create additional opportunities for paramilitaries to act with impunity. As a consequence, guerrilla groups also increased their violent acts and carried out repeated and grave violations of international humanitarian law. Samper was absolved by Congress, but his political legitimacy and credibility—both nationally and internationally—continues to be questioned.

In 1998, Colombia continues to be one of the most violent countries in the world. Murders had increased from around 10,000 in 1980 and 20,000 in 1988 to an average of 30,000 a year since 1994. Generally, between 7 and 15 percent of the total were calculated to be "political" assassinations, and the rest a result of "common violence" (settling of accounts, fights, theft, etc). However, both types of violence are mutually reinforcing and have become part of how society has learned to function.[22] Thus attempts to find a peaceful resolution to the conflict have failed because each political actor is more interested in a military victory, and there is no clear idea how the rest of society should participate. The issue of most concern is that civilians are the majority of the victims. During 1996 alone, approximately 180,000 people were displaced from their homes. And finally, impunity is almost 100 percent for human rights violations (97 percent for all other crimes).[23]

The Socio-Economic Context

Despite its political turmoil, Colombia is the only country in Latin America that had continuous economic growth throughout the 1980s; it also had the highest cumulative rate of economic growth (34 percent; the Latin American average was 14.2 percent). In the 1995 UNDP (United Nations Development Programme) Human Development Index, it ranked 57 out of 173 countries, had a GNP per capita amounting to US$1,260, and enjoyed very high literacy rates. Nonetheless, the current political crisis has affected economic growth.[24] Two thirds of the population still live between the poverty and misery levels, and a 1997 World Bank study of the relation between crime, violence, and development in Latin America estimates that Colombia's homicide rates cost the country about two percentage points annually in the rate of growth and gross domestic product.[25] According to the study, were it not for murders, individual incomes might be as much as 32 percent higher. It also estimates that the direct costs of crime and violence in the country are twelve times greater than the net profits of the fifty largest industrial enterprises in the country.[26]

Land distribution continues to be at the heart of social conflict in Colombia. Agrarian reform encountered many obstacles and has languished, mainly because it implies a change in land rights and in local politics and encounters strong opposition from members of Congress, many of whom are themselves wealthy landowners. Thus, invasions and conflicts associated with land continue as peasants resort to occupation and are forced out by landowners. This process is known as "colonization," but in areas where land distribution has been carried out, settlements tend to be more peaceful. Colonization also affects the environment because it often entails clearing the jungle to establish a field or a pasture. Wealthy drug traffickers have pushed their own process of "counteragrarian reform" through several years of buying or appropriating land abandoned by peasants who fled from paramilitary groups or by landowners exhausted from guerrilla pressures. This process has shifted the concentration of land from the traditional elites to the emerging narco-businessmen.[27]

The economic reasons for migration include the concentration of land in a few hands and the need for labor in the major agro-industrial centers and mining zones of the country. Traditionally, however, Colombians linked to organized labor and social protest movements in these regions have been forced into displacement; in 1928, for example, the military murdered hundreds of striking banana workers in Magdalena, and around 12,000 peasants fled the region.[28] In the 1960s and 1970s there was another wave of economic migration to the cities, also related to violence in the rural areas. During this period, peasants formed groups to defend their lands and lives against military persecution. By 1965, many of those groups had turned into armed guerrilla movements known as the Revolutionary Armed Forces of Colombia (FARC) and the National Liberation Army (ELN), which are still active today.

From then to the present, sectors of the government and political elements of the extreme right have treated many social organizations as facades for subversive groups. Colombia's elites have been highly intolerant of parties or movements other than the Liberal and Conservative ones. Community movements and peasant organizations are seen as forms of rebelliousness and not of legitimate popular organizing. Several have been persecuted by the military, polarized, and excluded.[29] Many members of community groups and NGOs have become victims of displacement as well.

Displacement and Its Consequences

The CPDIA defines the internally displaced as

every person who has been forced to migrate within the national territory, abandoning his place of residence or his customary occupation, because his life, physical integrity or freedom has been rendered vulnerable or is threatened due to the existence of any of the following man-made situations: internal armed conflict, internal disturbances or tensions, widespread violence, massive violations of human rights or other circumstances originating from prior situations that can disrupt or drastically disturb public order.[30]

Until the survey undertaken by the Bishops' Conference at the parish level in most areas of Colombia, there were no methodologically acceptable attempts to estimate the number of the internally displaced based on this definition.[31] The Bishops' Conference report, published in March 1995, used the CPDIA definition, and through a survey of 1,170 people estimated that a maximum of 650,000 people (108,301 homes) had been displaced from January 1985 to August 1994 (table 10-1). The CODHES used a survey of 760 people throughout the country to calculate the number of displaced from September 1994 to November 1995. This study had a broader participation of NGOs, the Catholic Church, and governmental entities concerned with the situation of the displaced. It registered 89,906 people (21,312 homes) who had to leave their homes involuntarily in 1995 and included more information on the socioeconomic aspects of displacement.[32] It must be recognized that neither study took into account individuals who had fled in silence or who had been displaced from regions that were difficult to access.

For the 1995–96 period, new studies focused on the regional and local character of displacement. The district mayor's office of Barranquilla studied displacement on the Atlantic Coast, and the Support Group for the Displaced (Grupo de Apoyo a Desplazados, or GAD) concentrated its efforts in Urabá. These efforts attempted to study the socioeconomic, cultural, and psychological characteristics and consequences of the violation of fundamental rights of those displaced by violence. Furthermore, the CODHES and the United Nations Children's Fund (UNICEF) calculated that an additional 181,000 people (36,202 households) fled their homes in 1996. This estimate means that four households were being displaced by violence every hour and that 2 percent (approximately 900,000 people) of the total population of Colombia has been forced to migrate in the previous ten years because of factors relating to violence.[33] The 1998 U.S. State Department Report on human rights in Colombia calculates the total number of displaced persons between 1995 and 1997 to exceed 525,000.

Violence as the Main Cause of Displacement

Since violence is the main cause of displacement in Colombia, both the 1995 Bishops' Conference report and the CODHES report single out the agents of violence. Displaced people were asked how many armed actors intervened in their migration. Sixty-eight percent said only one actor was responsible, 21 percent blamed two actors, and 7 percent said that they had been affected by more than three actors.[34] Displacement

Table 10-1. *The Displaced Population in Colombia*

Year	Homes	Individuals
1985–94	108,301	586,261
1995	21,312	89,510
1996	36,202	181,010
1997	51,400	257,000
Total	217,215	1,113,781

Sources: Conferencia Episcopal de Colombia, *Desplazados por la violencia en Colombia* (Bogotá Kimpres, 1995); Consultoría para los Derechos Humanos y el Desplazamiento (CODHES), *Sistema de Información de Hogares Desplazados por Violencia en Colombia* (Santafé de Bogotá: SISDES 1, April 1996).

was attributed by 32 percent to guerrillas, 21 percent to paramilitary groups, 20 percent to the armed forces, 10 percent to others—neighbors, hired killers (known as *sicarios* in Colombia), family members, landowners, and unidentified authors, 5 percent to the police, 5 percent to drug traffickers, 4 percent to popular militias, 2 percent to emerald buyers, and 2 percent to security police—Department of Administrative Security (Departamento Administrativo de Seguridad, or DAS). The CODHES update covering 1994–95 presented some changes in these statistics: 32 percent attributed their displacement to the paramilitary, 26 percent to guerrillas, 16 percent to the armed forces, 3 percent to the police, 3 percent to self-defense groups, 2 percent to drug traffickers, and 2 percent to militias.[35]

According to the updated report, the factors that motivated displacement from 1994 to 1995 were threats (50 percent), murders (15 percent), violent coercion (8 percent), torture (4 percent), disappearances (3 percent), aerial attacks (1 percent), and other acts of intimidation (21 percent).[36]

PARAMILITARY GROUPS. In many regions of the country, paramilitary groups sprang up as small private armies to protect interests and carry out much of the "dirty work" of the armed forces, or to protect the properties of the drug traffickers, who began acquiring land during the marijuana boom of the 1970s.

Even though paramilitary groups have existed since the 1960s, their operations are perhaps the most hotly debated issue in the country.[37] Academics and national and international NGOs have extensively researched their history, current existence, alliances, and strategies.[38] According to these sources, well-structured, -financed, -armed, and -organized paramilitary groups continue to operate in Colombia and are considered responsible for most of the political killings, disappearances, cases of torture, and death threats.[39] These groups generally work in areas of high military presence with impunity and with hardly any reported confrontations with the armed forces.

The UN special rapporteur on extrajudicial, summary, or arbitrary executions reported on his visit to Colombia in 1989 that paramilitary groups were the greatest source of violations of the right to life and that they had contributed to widespread impunity. The report also noted that violence by paramilitary groups was increasingly affecting militants of the Liberal and Communist Parties despite their status as public officials.[40] Almost a decade later, these allegations continue to be relevant. Human rights groups allege that the pattern of assassinations of human rights activists, public officials, and popular leaders demonstrates that one objective of these groups is to extinguish opposition.[41] Government and military officials often assert that such groups act autonomously and declare that in any event they are illegal, and that those from within the army who collaborate with them exceed their authority and are subject to sanctions.

Despite the criticism, since 1994 the government has promoted a new source of paramilitarism, this time with its official authorization and blessing. Decree 356/1994 created the "Cooperatives for Rural Security" known as the *Convivir*. The *Convivir* are associations of civilians that provide "special vigilance and security services" with authorization to obtain and use arms usually restricted to the armed forces.[42] Although they are supposedly under state control, there is no credible information about the number of *Convivir* in the country, the arms they have, or the number of people belonging to them. Government sources state that there are anywhere from 200 to 1,000. Some of these groups have been linked to displacement.[43]

GUERRILLA GROUPS. The guerrilla groups initially were engaged in land struggles. They multiplied and strengthened their presence in many areas of the country throughout the 1960s and 1970s. These groups were the Revolutionary Armed Forces of Colombia, or FARC, made up initially of peasants demanding land; the People's Liberation Army, or EPL; the National Liberation Army, or ELN; the M-19 Movement, created after allegations of fraud during the 1970 presidential elections; the Quintín Lame Armed Indigenous Movement; the Ricardo Franco Commando; and others. Today, only the FARC, ELN, and a faction of the EPL remain active; however, they are estimated to have 10,000–15,000 guerrillas, organized in more than 100 groups and present in more than half of the country's municipalities.

The prolonged guerrilla warfare, the closed political spectrum of the National Front, and the ineffectiveness of the state in resolving social unrest in rural areas created the conditions for the consolidation of a "chronic insurgency."[44] By the 1990s, guerrilla forces became fractured and no longer had any unifying political goals but continued to have a stronghold in several regions of the country. If initially the movement represented valid political and ideological claims, it now suffers from debilitating problems and lack of internal control, demonstrated by increasing violations of international humanitarian law, forced recruitment of minors, and lack of commitment to democratic participation. The continuation of war has diminished the popular support it enjoyed in some areas and strained relationships with the peasants. However, unlike other Latin American insurgencies, the Colombian guerrilla "was born and has thrived under elected civilian governments, with which it has had successful negotiations. The insurgency has not only survived the fall of communism but has actually prospered—the rebels are now more numerous and more powerful."[45] Since the FARC declared a "general insurrection" in August of 1996, Colombians have seen an escalation of war with increased presence of both guerrillas and the army.

There is a widespread feeling of increasing intolerance from those who would like to see the forty-year conflict end and have come to believe that the guerrillas offer no solution. At the same time, peace processes have not been fully implemented, and many demobilized guerrillas have been targeted and killed, leaving a serious economic and social problem unsolved and a lack of trust in peace efforts.[46]

ARMED FORCES. Though responsible for a percentage of extrajudicial executions, disappearances, "social cleansing," and torture, the armed forces in Colombia, as in the rest of Latin America, continue to play a prominent role as defenders of the state.[47] Moreover, many Colombians take pride in the fact that, unlike in other countries in the region, the armed forces have not held state power (apart from the period 1953–57). However, the military have overwhelming authority to direct internal security with little civilian oversight. It thus has the best of both worlds: power and civilian support without political responsibility. It has no need to take the form of outright intervention through a coup d'état, since alliances among the military, counterinsurgents, and economic interests give it the authority to determine much of the political agenda.[48] The mainstream media and influential sectors of public opinion also support military power and contribute to an evolving mentality that regards excesses as justified when employed in the fight against guerrillas, subversives, and drug traffickers.[49]

POLICE. The police and security agents (DAS) are the main actors in urban displacements through an excess of authority, torture, forced disappearances, and threats. One of the most disconcerting and outrageous forms of urban violence and displacement is that known as "social cleansing." This term denotes the extermination or subjugation of petty thieves, street children, homosexuals, prostitutes, drug addicts, and all others considered "disposable" elements of society. NGOs have counted more than 2,000 victims killed by death squads in which members of the police or state security agents participated.[50]

DRUG TRAFFICKERS. Most Colombians agree that drug trafficking has added another dimension to the historical problems of corruption, violence, and political animosity in Colombia. The penetration of drug money into different sectors of the economy and the political system is complex and has been analyzed from many perspectives.[51] Its implications for the continuation of violence and therefore of displacement in Colombia are particularly insidious. Drugs have become the subject of mutual accusations of corruption by all sides in the Colombian conflict.[52] The U.S. government has isolated Colombia as a "narco-democracy" by "decertifying" it in 1996 and 1997.[53] Sectors of the right accuse the Colombian guerrilla groups of being a third cartel (the narco-guerrillas).[54] Human rights NGOs and sectors of the Left have denounced the narcos' alliances with the armed forces.[55] This vicious circle of mutual accusations, however true, makes any type of political solution practically impossible in a context where all actors are "narcotized."

Regardless of the facts outlined above, with anticommunist propaganda and a land expansion agenda the drug traffickers and their paramilitary alliances have obtained extensive property by killing or threatening the local population and forcing them to sell their land cheaply or abandon it altogether.[56] Through this method they have managed to "cleanse" entire areas of the country and repopulate them with those who are more receptive to their economic and political agenda. This would explain why drug traffickers are directly responsible for only 2 to

4 percent of the displacement but indirectly, through their alliances, for much more.

COMMON CRIMINALS. Criminal and social violence accounts for at least 80 percent of the total number of murders committed each year. Permanent political violence, a weak judiciary, social intolerance, and the availability and proliferation of guns have contributed to the high murder rate. Other causes are said to include the consumption of alcohol, poverty, and few educational and employment opportunities for middle- and lower-class youth.[57]

The Bishops' and CODHES reports attribute civilian responsibility for displacement to neighbors, hired killers (*sicarios*), family members, landowners, and unidentified actors. These actors account for a very high percentage of the displacement caused by violence (10 percent between 1985 and 1994 and 21 percent between 1994 and 1995).

Patterns and Consequences of Displacement[58]

ZONES OF EXPULSION. The map of forced displacement in Colombia can be divided into areas of *expulsion* and areas of *reception*.[59] The Bishops' Conference report divides the expulsion zones into three categories: "traditional zones," where there has been an internal armed conflict for many years and the presence of guerrilla and paramilitary groups is well established; a "temporary or junction zone" (*zona de coyuntura*), affected by concrete actions such as air raids and ground searches, which often force people to move temporarily or permanently; and "expansion zones," where the new presence of armed actors intimidates the civilian population.[60] Both the junction and expansion zones are related to the presence of new guerrilla fronts, coca leaf or poppy flower cultivation, and new paramilitary groups.[61] Expulsion zones are characterized by little or no access to channels of political participation, persecution of social or political dissidents, criminalization of popular protest, discrimination against indigenous or Afro-Colombian communities, armed conflict, drug cultivation or trafficking, lack of basic public services like running water or electricity, enormous disparities in wealth, and a disorganized process of colonization, among other complex social and economic problems.[62] Some regions have been particularly affected, such as

Los Llanos, Urabá, Magdalena Medio, Norte de Santander, and most recently Chocó.

The Meta department and the eastern Llanos (plains) are very rich in natural resources and good for agriculture and cattle raising. They have been areas of poor peasant colonization as well as of enormous extensions of privately owned farm property. The Unión Patriótica emerged here after the 1985 peace agreements. Paramilitary groups, the FARC, and the ELN have strong bases in this region. In January of 1995, 1,200 peasants marched to protest the militarization of their lands and the control of their movements. Human rights monitors have also been continuous targets.[63] In July of 1997, paramilitary groups took over the town of Mapiropán in Meta, executing more than twenty people and forcing the exodus of thousands.

Urabá, the banana plantation region in the northwest, of strategic importance because of its access to the Atlantic and Pacific Oceans as well as the Darien Gap, is rich in natural resources and a thoroughfare for arms and drug contraband. In 1995, Urabá recorded the largest number of massacres, targeted killings, and forced displacements in the country. The Ombudsman's Office (Defensoría del Pueblo) calculated that more than 4,000 families (25,000 people) were displaced between December 1994 and May 1995. They estimated that the number doubled in the 1995–96 period. The peasant Self-Defense Groups of Córdoba and Urabá, created in the late 1980s by Fidel Castaño, are the strongest paramilitary groups in the country, with an army of around a thousand men and a network of sophisticated informants. They control the region and through ruthless killings and constant threats have forced a mass exodus of people.[64] In 1997 the many paramilitary groups coalesced under a national umbrella organization: the United Self-Defense Groups of Colombia. Guerrillas have committed several retaliative executions and raided towns in search of military supporters.[65]

Paramilitary pressure is especially severe in the Magdalena Medio region (which includes parts of Santander, Cesar, Antioquia, and Bolívar). This region has been characterized by permanent migrations of groups of people for the last five decades.[66] However, much of this movement is involuntary and worsens during heightened political strife and violence. The presence of paramilitaries has grown since the late 1980s, and now more than thirty groups operate in this area, issuing death lists that target union and community leaders. Many times the threats are carried out, pressuring the victim's family and related neighbors and/or coworkers to leave the region.

Norte de Santander is an oil-rich and commercially important region, where the peasant unions have been strong and where the guerrillas (ELN, FARC, and EPL) have been present since the 1970s. Guerrilla groups in the area commit kidnappings, condemn people to death through "popular trials," perform "social cleansing" murders, and blow up public property such as oil wells, electric cables, and buses in violation of humanitarian law.[67] Retaliations by the armed forces are usually indiscriminate and disproportionate, causing many civilian casualties. Drug cartels are not as established in Norte de Santander as in Córdoba or Meta, but there is a strong presence of the paramilitaries and the Mobile Brigades. Combined with a weak presence of the state, the violations by those actors have made this into another area of grave and massive displacement.

The Chocó department, on the Pacific coast of Colombia, is inhabited mainly by Colombian citizens of African heritage. Despite the wealth of natural resources and the Afro-Colombian Law of 1993 recognizing their rights to communal lands, this region continues to be one of the most impoverished and neglected areas of the country.[68] Because it is so isolated, Chocó lived in relative peace, though staggering poverty, until recently. Guerrilla forces and paramilitary groups have moved into the Chocó area of the Urabá region. From December 1996 to April 1997 an estimated total of 15,000 poor black Colombians from the municipality of Riosucio, Chocó, were forced to leave their homes. A year later, many of them were still living in temporary shelters. Around 300 reached Panama, where they stayed for a few weeks until they were forcibly returned to Colombia.[69] This was the first reported episode of mass movement from Colombia into a neighboring country.

ZONES OF RECEPTION. Displacement usually takes place in small family units. Poor peasant families fleeing violence move first to a nearby rural area or town, trying to work in their fields during the day and returning to where they have fled at night. However, once they flee to an urban center, displacement often acquires a permanent character. In 12 percent of the cases displacement occurs collectively, integrating family, friends, and neighbors, and typically happens when there is an extreme confrontation between a guerrilla group and military forces.

Individual displacement occurs when the head of the family is threatened and must leave immediately. The rest of the family usually follow. In many cases, individuals or small groups move from one urban center to another to avoid persecution, giving rise to a phenomenon termed "urban displacement." More than 80 percent of the displaced relocate in urban areas. Only 9 percent remain in the rural zones.[70]

The cities most of the displaced flee to are Bogotá, Medellín, Cali, Barranquilla, Bucaramanga, Barrancabermeja, Girón, Montería, Villavicencio, Apartadó, Cartagena, Cúcuta, and smaller cities in the departments of Cundinamarca, Antioquia, Santander, Córdoba, Atlántico, Boyacá, Valle del Cauca, Norte de Santander, Sucre, and Cauca.[71]

VICTIMS. The majority of the victims of displacement are members of the poor peasant, indigenous, and black populations living in areas of guerrilla or paramilitary influence and victimized by counterinsurgency activities or caught in the cross fire. Almost 60 percent of the displaced are women (often widows or single mothers) and their children. The men who flee alone or with their nuclear families are characteristically leaders of political movements, social advocates (such as members of teachers' and peasant unions), and government officials (such as judges and attorneys).[72]

Women. Research on the impact of political violence on Colombians tells how the rape and murder of women (especially pregnant ones) during the period of *La Violencia* was used as a symbolic demonstration of hatred toward the opposing political party. In the 1970s, urban women were more active in political and social movements and therefore became victims of selective murders in order to eliminate political opposition. In the late 1980s, violence toward rural women increased. Women became victims of the war between guerrilla and the military-paramilitary groups and were killed in bombings and random confrontations and were detained and tortured to obtain information about their partners or sons.[73] In 1997, women's groups documented the increase of rape and sexual abuse of women and girls in areas of former guerrilla presence as a strategy of intimidation by paramilitary groups.

The scarce information available indicates that direct violence committed by women is relatively rare and generally related to their membership in guerrilla groups. There seems to be no record of armed women as part of the drug trafficking, military, or paramilitary combat groups, though women are known to be used as informants.

Many displaced women, separated from their partners, become the economic providers for the whole family.[74] They must adapt to an urban environment in which they no longer play a domestic role but are forced to assume new responsibilities for which they were not prepared. Their origins in rural communities make this process very disruptive to their cultural, psychological, and social structures. Women who come from indigenous groups and black communities must face additional class and racial discrimination. Low levels of education and marked regional differences also add to the obstacles they must face in the city.[75]

The involuntary causes of displacement and its generally isolated and individual character force many rural women to work as maids in the houses of the urban middle and upper classes. Because of the high supply of poor women willing to do domestic work, their lack of education, isolation from other workers, and need to become anonymous for fear of reprisals from the originating violence, this type of employment is especially abusive and denigrating. House maids usually have long work days (twelve hours is normal), few or no social benefits, and very low wages because a large part of their salaries may be paid as room and board. It is also well known that many of them suffer sexual abuse from the male residents of the houses where they work and sometimes even become the source of sexual initiation for the young boys.[76] Apart from prostitution, this type of work is perhaps the only option for women with little or no education and few skills for the job market in the city.

Children. Children are the forgotten victims of violence in Colombia, although they are perhaps the ones that suffer the most abuses.[77] Of the 121,000 homicides in Colombia between 1991 and 1995, 41,000 were of young people.[78] Children are also victims of child prostitution, homelessness, "social-cleansing" killings, forced recruitment in both the armed forces and guerrilla groups, land mines, kidnappings, and domestic violence. According to UNICEF, 55 percent of the displaced are under eighteen, and 13 percent are under five years of age. A large number of children live in extreme poverty, an issue that has been addressed by the Committee of the Rights of the Child.

Indigenous and Black Communities. The indigenous (approximately 800,000 among eighty-two distinct ethnic groups) and black (2 million) populations of the Chocó are especially vulnerable to forced displacement. In the past, these communities often were forced to abandon their lands and have suffered from further economic discrimination. Today the indigenous communities are accorded special protection under the new constitution, which vests them with legal, political, and resource-management authority over certain areas of the country. Yet they have been moving farther into the mountains because of slash-and-burn farming by *colonos* (colonizers) and have found themselves in areas of guerrilla presence where they are victimized both by the armed forces and by the guerrillas. Also, various incidents of violence by paramilitary forces have been reported in recent years. In addition, relocation due to oil extraction, industrial, and development projects continues to generate concerns.[79]

Human Rights and Humanitarian Law Issues

It should be mentioned at the outset that the human rights situation and internal armed conflict in Colombia are not consistent with the country's record of signing and ratifying international instruments.[80] This fact has been recognized and documented by national and international NGOs as well as Colombian and foreign governmental institutions. Since 1989, national and international human rights organizations also have documented and denounced the grave violations of international humanitarian law committed by the guerrilla groups.[81]

Pervasive impunity contributes to the country's poor human rights record. According to government reports, 97 to 99.5 percent of all crimes go unpunished.[82] It is estimated that 74 percent of all crimes are not reported to the authorities. Various studies on the mechanisms of impunity have pointed out obstruction by the military justice system, the permanent state of emergency or internal commotion, weak investigations, threats and intimidation, lack of sufficient resources, the faceless courts (now called regional courts), and the lack of a political will to recognize the link between a weak judiciary and the perpetration of violence.[83]

LIFE AND PERSONAL SECURITY. Both the guerrilla groups and military forces have disregarded the distinction between combatants and noncombatants in their war, and neither side strictly abides by Protocol II Additional to the Geneva Conventions, which was ratified by the government in 1995.

Guerrillas force civilians into displacement when they carry out political killings or assassinations or use threats, extortion, recruitment of minors, kidnappings, land mines, and attacks on civilian targets. In areas of guerrilla influence, peasants have been forced to cooperate with the insurgents, have been forcibly recruited, or have been subjected to "popular trials."[84] Landowners and their families and members of the armed forces and the police have been assassinated by guerrilla members or kidnapped for ransom, or have lost or been forced to abandon their properties.

The paramilitary and self-defense groups, when in control of a zone, exercise authority through terror. They are responsible for multiple massacres, homicides, forced recruitment, threats, forced disappearances, mutilations, torture, and cruel and degrading treatment of civilians. Paramilitaries target anyone they believe is a guerrilla member, sympathizer, relative, or aide or friend. Serious displacements occur when peasants withhold their full support of paramilitary activities.

When the displaced refer to the armed forces as a single actor they generally mean the military (especially the Mobile Brigades), the police, and the security services (DAS). Their actions include abusive treatment, threats, extrajudicial executions, torture, joint actions with paramilitaries, bombings, and indiscriminate fire, theft, and forced disappearances. In the name of the struggle against subversion, the armed forces frequently kill civilians and say they have died in combat in order to justify the excessive use of force and claim guerrilla casualties. Some have testified that those who tried to flee were threatened or actually prohibited from doing so, either because they were suspected of being insurgents or sympathizers (attempting to flee would be positive proof) or because they would be able to report on the abuses committed by the army or paramilitary groups.[85]

In 1995 the government gave power to the governors and mayors to evacuate the civilian population in areas where the military was going to carry out counterinsurgency operations.[86] The Constitutional Court declared the measure to legalize forced displacement unconstitutional in 1996, because it was not connected to the reasons why the government had declared the state of emergency. Nevertheless, in 1996 Decree 717 authorized governors to create "special public order zones." Military authorities in such zones have special powers to restrict individual movements in and outside of the zone, declare curfews, and force residents and visitors to register and inform the military officials of their movements.

SUBSISTENCE. As noted earlier, a big part of the rural and urban population in Colombia is very poor. Displaced persons in both rural and urban areas share in the poverty of the local population. Immediately after displacement people need food, shelter, and security. After they have relocated more permanently, secure housing and basic services, employment and education opportunities, and safety from future persecution are the priorities.

Mass displacements have exacerbated the problems of relocation. During the peasant mobilization from the Chocó many children died, already weakened from deprivation and poverty and forced to move to some of the most inhospitable areas of the country. In the camps that have been set up to house the displaced, sanitary conditions are poor and diseases spread easily. One of the gravest concerns is the mental health of individuals who have lived in an environment of constant fear and violence and who are rejected by the local governments and communities to which they are displaced because they are seen as "problematic" or "suspicious."

PROPERTY. When peasants flee from violence, they generally lose most if not all of their property. In several regions, abandoned land is occupied or bought very cheaply by drug traffickers in an effort to increase territorial control and political power; they frequently use agro-industry and cattle ranching for money-laundering purposes. The displaced have little or no access to legal services and do not know how to protect their properties. In the cities they become squatters or must pay rent while constantly under the threat of eviction.[87]

COMMUNITY AND FAMILY VALUES. Emotional trauma among the displaced is common. Movement from a rural area that shares values of security, reciprocity, trust, collaboration, and solidarity to an urban one where individualism, consumerism, class discrimination, and crime exist affects the vital identity and stability of the individual and his or her community. Families lose their support networks and are subjected to crime and violence, while their often meager resources vanish.[88]

Real and functional illiteracy is high among displaced people. According to the Bishops' Conference Report, those who had any education at all had only reached elementary school level. As earlier noted, 55 percent of the displaced are younger than eighteen, and 13 percent are under five years of age. Two out of every five children who have to move do not have the chance to go to school again. A large number of children, especially rural and indigenous, are socially marginalized and have limited or no access to health care and education.[89] In urban areas, the lack of employment and income-generation opportunities has serious psychosocial effects, especially on the younger generations, who have grown up in the climate of violence and crime that unemployment fosters.

PARTICIPATION IN POLITICAL LIFE. More often than not, displaced persons feel compelled to flee in absolute silence, because a displaced person is considered to have a "problematic" past. This is exacerbated by the fact that the most "visible" displaced are those who have some links with a political or social organization. Those who had a prominent role in local society or politics before being displaced actually have to hide their achievements for fear of renewed persecution when they arrive in the cities.

Moreover, their political or social organizations frequently will not support them in the process of displacement. A consequence of their suffering and isolation is a loss of trust and confidence in their country's social, legal, and political institutions and apathy about participating in politics. This problem should be seen as a collective rather than an individual one because it affects the essence of democratic government. Out of fear and disappointment displaced people are less likely to once again express their political ideas, vote, participate, or form associations for political or social causes.[90]

The Government's Response to Displacement

Until roughly 1993, the government did not recognize that there was a problem of internal displacement in the country, either because it was seen as an indistinguishable part of a process of colonization and internal migration or because it perceived the problem as a consequence of the violence for which it repeatedly had denied responsibility. Government officials believe that the issue was too politicized in the past, seen in the context of human rights "extremism" and not in its humanitarian dimensions. They also think that part of the problem is that the state is not consolidated, which in some areas means that the civilian government is not fully represented.

Since 1993, the Colombian government has officially recognized the humanitarian and human rights dimensions of displacement. It is one of the few governments in the world to provide information on internal displacement to the representative of the secretary-general, despite the fact that, as mentioned above, it was not in a position to do so with much accuracy. In 1995 the first CONPES document incorporated many of the recommendations included in the UN representative's report and elaborated a number of mechanisms to address the needs of the displaced.

The political crisis surrounding the Samper government has blocked efforts to carry out many of the measures set forth for the protection and assistance of victims of violence and other vulnerable populations. These setbacks are described in the following paragraphs.

Protection Measures

Little progress has been made in the protection of human rights in Colombia, and most human rights institutions have remained ineffective. The 1991 constitution includes extensive references to human rights and creates a number of mechanisms for their protection, but the situation has only deteriorated since then.

The Ombudsman's Office (Defensoría del Pueblo) has been characterized as an intermediary body between the state and the citizen. Its work with NGOs in advising victims and in channeling information on human rights abuses has had positive results. However, it has lacked the resources to do more thorough reporting and critical analysis of the gravest human rights situations, the actors involved, and the government's position toward these problems.

Another protection measure introduced in 1991 was the legal remedy of the *tutela*, a private right of action when constitutional rights have been or are in danger of being violated. It can be initiated in any court, and there is a right of review by the Constitutional Court. Owing to its initial effectiveness and success, the use of the *tutela* has become widespread and has created a culture of judicial activism. There have been as a result several proposals to limit the scope of the *tutela*. However, people most affected by displacement rarely use this and other judicial mechanisms for lack of guidance and knowledge of the system or for fear of bringing a claim against a state actor.

A third ground for optimism was the constitutional requirement that the minister of defense be a civilian and accountable to Congress. In late 1993 the government passed a police reform law establishing a civilian Police Commissioner's Office and a National Advisory Board. The ministry also started a human rights awareness campaign, creating a special office staffed by civilians to advise the joint chiefs of staff on human rights issues and to develop training materials and programs. Regardless, in 1994 the ministry promoted the creation of rural defense groups of armed civilians (the *Convivir*), which have sprung up all over the country and contributed to intensifying the war by augmenting the number of armed actors.

A fourth measure was the reorganization of the judiciary, which under the 1991 constitution is largely independent of the executive and legislative branches. The 1991 constitution modified the structure of the judicial branch by creating the Office of the Prosecutor General (Fiscalía) as an independent prosecutorial body. This agency is vested with the judicial authority to investigate human rights violations under the accusatory system. However, a former prosecutor's role in exposing drug corruption at the highest level of government, including that of the president, has made this office a target of criticism as well as praise.

The Attorney General's Office (Procurador General) is a separate independent body that investigates and requests disciplinary actions in cases where public officials have violated the law. The political crisis also has affected this institution. Two successive top officials faced criminal charges for corruption, and the offices of the delegate for human rights and special investigations were largely dismantled. These events, as well as proposals for reform of its role so that this body cannot investigate members of the armed forces, have diminished its ability to control human rights violations.[91]

Another significant reform in the 1991 constitution was the elaboration of different types of emergency situations in which "neither human rights nor fundamental freedoms may be suspended." This measure's purpose was to break the permanent state of emergency that had been in place in Colombia for thirty-six of the previous forty-four years. However, the situation has not changed much, and in 1996 and 1997 the government operated under declared states of emergency that enabled the executive to rule by decree in broad areas of the country. The decrees frequently limit due process rights and freedom of movement. Sadly, this provision, like many others, is virtually ignored by the Colombian government.[92]

On the other hand, the Office of the Presidential Adviser for Human Rights, which was established in 1987, continues to provide an institutional opening by working with NGOs and supporting promotion and protection activities, though its profile is very low in the current government. This office has undertaken several activities relating specifically to the internally displaced. It worked with NGOs to develop the second CONPES document, and it contracted with the CODHES to update information from the Bishops' Conference Report for the period 1995–96. The office has also actively collaborated with international organizations. Despite these positive activities, in March 1997 a new Presidential Advisory for the Displaced was created by decree. It remains to be seen whether the offices will carry out simultaneous functions or be centralized in the new one.

The government elaborated the National Strategy against Violence in 1991, as a result of which peace dialogues with the guerrillas were initiated along with measures for drug traffickers to turn themselves in through a "subjection to justice" policy (a type of plea bargaining). Despite these measures, peace dialogues have been suspended while rehabilitation projects for demobilized guerrillas are said to have been left incomplete. The current government's high commissioner for peace, Daniel Garcia-Peña, declared in late 1996 that "the country is at war and a negotiated peace cannot be expected in the next couple of years."[93]

One positive development has been the establishment and upgrading of reserves for indigenous groups and the granting of collective management of traditional lands to the Afro-Colombian communities, in accordance with the constitution of 1991. Between 1987 and 1992, 15,000 million hectares of land were allocated for the former.[94] However, despite the passage of the Afro-Colombian Law in 1993, little concrete progress has been made in expanding public services and private investment in the Chocó or other predominantly black regions.

Serious setbacks in the area of human rights protection and the fact that all armed perpetrators of violence seem to be getting stronger leads to the unavoidable conclusion that the situation of the displaced will only get worse.

Assistance to the Internally Displaced

On the basis of the representative's recommendations on September 9, 1994, Colombia's National Human Rights Day, President Samper formally recognized the problem of internal displacement and the state's responsibility to address it.[95] Four years later, after surviving a turbulent political crisis and with an additional half-million displaced people, President Samper reannounced his administration's interest in dealing with the problem as if it were a new phenomenon.[96]

In June 1995, a Mediation and Follow-up Commission to develop guidelines on displacement was formed with the participation of NGOs, the Church, the Defensoría, the Procuraduría, the National Planning Office, and the Presidential Adviser for Human Rights. In September 1995, the government sent a draft of the National Program to the NGOs for their comments three days before its final approval. Though the document incorporates many of the representative's recommendations and those of the CPDIA, it did not have the input of the NGO community, international agencies, or the Church, all of which had grass-roots and administrative experience with displaced populations. By 1997, many of the structural problems of the program became evident and the government had to present a self-critical second CONPES document, this time referring to the displaced as a "system." This document is signed by representatives of the Ministry of the Interior, the (new) Presidential Adviser for the Displaced, the Presidential Adviser for Human Rights and Social Policy, as well as the National Department of Planning.

The Ministry of the Interior had been restructured and under Law 0372 of February 1996 began operating the Special Administrative Unit for the Protection of Human Rights. This unit was responsible for carrying out the program established by the first CONPES document but did not receive sufficient human or financial resources to deliver all that was projected. The official in the Ministry served as a "coordinator" who had to depend on the good will of government officials in other institutions and their quick and efficient disbursement of resources. The first person in charge of the office not only had difficulties obtaining support from other institutions but received death threats and had to leave the country. The second CONPES recognized that the different government institutions involved did not accept responsibility for carrying out the policy or create the normative structures necessary to do so.[97] Therefore it modified the existing institutional structure to cover all levels of government, from the president to local institutions and agents with the objective of giving more ample assistance to the displaced.

The original program established a budget of 10,000 million pesos (approximately 1 million dollars), an insignificant amount for dealing with a problem of its dimensions. The money must be secured from different institutions. The government is counting on international support for the rest of the budgeted money ($5 million). The new system created one centralized account in which to deposit all the funding obtained from national and international sources.[98]

The program is centered on four strategies: prevention, emergency assistance, consolidation and socioeconomic stability, and communication. The plan is to carry out these strategies through a complex structure of project elaboration by all entities involved, identification of the displaced, territorial committees for assistance, a National Council for Integral Attention to the displaced (composed of several ministers and other institutional representatives), and a presidential adviser who will coordinate all of the above.[99] The Ministry of the Interior was left with the function of carrying out specific tasks of prevention and protection.

The prevention strategy focuses on early analysis and early communication of potential risk factors that may cause displacement, so that the system may react and supply services before displacement occurs. The strategy emphasizes the need to educate the general public about humanitarian law, to combat impunity, and to generate community tolerance. However, the plan accepts the context of violence as a fact of life that needs to be studied in order to prevent further damage. Only 3 percent of the resources were distributed for this strategy between January 1996 and April 1997.

The emergency assistance strategy has been implemented by the National System for the Prevention of and Attention to Disasters. Personnel are responsible for assisting in the provision of immediate food, health, personal hygiene, medical and psychological needs, transportation, and temporary housing in cases of collective displacement. In the first stage, 83 percent of the resources have been put into emergency relief.

The consolidation and socioeconomic stabilization strategy may be restricted by its dependence on funds from other bureaucracies in the system. According to the plan, displaced persons have priority and additional guarantees to obtain access to a number of governmental programs dealing with agrarian reform, micro-enterprises, education, and job training. Existing programs are designed to help poor and needy people gain access to basic services. Their implementation depends on local and/or regional authorities who distribute the funds and who might not be willing to help the displaced because of their presumed political sympathies.[100] This system could also falter because it relies on the governors' and mayors' clientist, political, and bureaucratic institutions.

The Institute of Agrarian Reform (INCORA) is charged with purchasing/expropriating and redistributing land and providing other types of assistance. The government lacks the resources to extend credits to farmers or to invest in education or major development projects targeting the peasant population; nevertheless INCORA committed $15 million to buy eighteen lots for 605 displaced families. In 1997 the National Institute for Social Housing and Urban Reform (INURBE) designed an urban action plan for the displaced that includes housing, jobs, protection, and education.

Finally, on July 18, 1997, both CONPES documents were incorporated into Law 387. This law takes the position that violence is the main cause of displacement and lists a set of important guiding principles: the right to receive international aid, the right to enjoy internationally recognized civil rights, the right not to be discriminated against because one is displaced, the right to be reunited with family members, the right to find durable solutions to displacement, the right to return to the place of origin, the right not to be displaced, and the obligation of the state to promote the conditions that will facilitate coexistence, equality, and social justice among Colombians.

Law 387 must be recognized as an important governmental effort to create an integrated policy on the issue of displacement. Unfortunately, like many other well-intentioned laws in Colombia, its effectiveness depends on the actual resources and the political will of many for it to be carried out and implemented. Interestingly, article 35 of the law sets forth the right of NGOs, state entities, and victims to use the newly regulated "compliance action" to request the effective judicial implementation of what is promised in the law.[101]

The Role of the Nongovernmental Community

In Colombia the nongovernmental community, which is understood here to include the Church, local NGOs, and the university, plays a very important role in protecting and assisting internally displaced persons. Local groups provide training and legal services and raise funds from national and international groups based in Bogotá.

The work of local NGOs can be divided into four categories: those oriented toward providing specialized assistance to the displaced, those that provide assistance but are primarily political organizations, those that promote social organization, and the general human rights NGOs. The first category includes NGOs whose premise is that the displaced need to be served, irrespective of the cause of displacement;

typically, they provide one type of assistance—for example, funds for small income-generation projects, psychological/psychiatric services, shelter, projects for return to the home area, and technical assistance. The second includes groups with ties to existing political and other organizations that provide emergency assistance. The third includes groups that work with local grass-roots organizations such as human rights committees, workshops, and projects to prevent violence and human rights violations, and the like. The fourth comprises organizations that specialize in the protection of human rights, legal services, research, advocacy at the international level, and mobilization and support for victims of human rights violations.

It is important to underscore that the work of these organizations is vital in view of the limited response of the state and the entrenched distrust between the displaced and the state. Some of them perform activities in more than one of the sectors mentioned above. However, because they operate on different premises and have different specializations, their work has been fragmented and inefficiently coordinated. For instance, some groups have no expertise in development, others "politicize" all the problems of displacement, and many are good at approaching the community but have little effect in promoting long-term solutions. For all these reasons, efforts to work together, such as the June 1993 seminar and GAD, are beneficial for coordination, exchange of ideas, experiences and expertise, and rapid mobilization.[102] They coordinate the provision of assistance and protection for the displaced.

The hostile attitude of the state toward the nongovernmental community is frequently a cause of friction and in some cases has reached serious levels. The tendency of government officials to perceive NGO workers as "guerrilla allies" has led to threats against human rights lawyers and activists, and in some cases death or displacement.[103] Despite the fact that human rights organizations publish and denounce the violations of the law of war that the guerrilla groups have committed, because they continue to be seen as collaborators it is dangerous for them to work with the displaced. Though most of the NGOs are small, underfunded, and lack the expertise and capacity to undertake major projects, their knowledge of the regions and their direct contact with the people and problems should make the government consider directing some funds through them.

The Church is the most important social institution throughout Colombia. It has shown an active interest in the problem of internal displacement precisely because many of the displaced look for a church as their first shelter in a new area. The yearlong project of the Bishops' Conference to document the number of internally displaced at the parish level is the most comprehensive documentation of internal displacement in the country to date. The Church is able to lend credence to the claims of the displaced community without arousing political suspicions. Funds from the international community for protection of human rights and assistance work have been channeled to the Church. In many areas the Church also is implementing "pastoral dialogue for peace" projects.

The involvement of universities and think tanks in studying displacement and its causes is also welcome: they not only produce much needed comprehensive information but also concentrate intellectual and social forces and provide a forum for discussion.

The Role of the International Community

There is only a small international presence in Colombia dealing with the internally displaced and, more generally, the victims of violence and persecution. The International Committee of the Red Cross has a delegation in the most affected areas, which undertakes protection and assistance activities for the victimized civilian population (including visits to detainees, dissemination of humanitarian law, material assistance to those recently displaced, and support for the national Red Cross). An NGO consortium, the Project Counseling Service for Latin American Refugees, and Oxfam have established offices that distribute resources and work with the displaced. Peace Brigades International has accompanied human rights groups in most areas of the country since 1994. However, Amnesty International and the Swedish agency Dia Konig had to close their offices in 1997 after receiving death threats to their employees.

Other NGOs from Europe and the United States have visited Colombia sporadically but do not have the mandate or resources to establish a permanent presence. Some European governments channel assistance and protection funds to the displaced directly through local NGOs. The international NGO presence has helped put the issue of the internally displaced on domestic agendas (including those of the government and the Church) and has encouraged national NGOs to work together in a less sectarian and more professional way.

Many UN and inter-American agencies are present in the country but give little support to the internally displaced. UNICEF has held several events on the impact of war on children and has written a report on displacement in Colombia. It also has a fund for displaced women and children. UNDP supports five human rights officials. The United Nations High Commissioner for Refugees (UNHCR), which until 1998 was not present in the country, has begun to pay attention now that displacement has led to more sizable external refugee flows and some of the temporary locations have developed problems similar to those of refugee camps.

During the representative's visit in June 1994, NGOs consistently proposed that a UN special rapporteur on human rights in Colombia be appointed. In their view this would maintain a level of pressure that is vital for the protection of human rights. The government expressed concern that a special UN representative could paralyze current efforts to address human rights violations and to enhance cooperation with the NGOs: it deemed that international pressure could be counterproductive and that a low-key presence, if any, would be a better option. Government officials did support a continued role for a representative in the area of internally displaced persons.

In March 1996 the Colombian government successfully blocked the appointment of a special rapporteur by the UN Commission on Human Rights. However, as a consequence of the pressure by national and international human rights groups, the government finally agreed to accept the establishment of a UN human rights office in Colombia. The UN high commissioner for human rights appointed a Spanish diplomat as director of the office, which opened in March 1997 with a one-year mandate. The European Union provided five experts for the staff and is helping to finance the office. Though it has already been criticized by some government officials and politicians as lacking neutrality and violating the country's sovereignty, many Colombians are hopeful that a permanent UN presence will help reduce some of the violence. In February 1998 more than fifty NGOs and social groups wrote a letter to the UN stating that the office's role should be less directed at promoting a peace agreement between warring parties and more focused on the implementation of policies and programs that would help protect human rights and prevent violations by addressing their structural causes. The groups requested that the high commissioner maintain the office in Colombia and give it additional support. The groups also again expressed support for a special rapporteur on human rights in Colombia.

Conclusions and Recommendations

Protection of the civil, political, economic, social, and cultural rights of all citizens, including the internally displaced, irrespective of their ideology, is the duty of any government. Obviously, strengthening democratic institutions results in better protection for the displaced and decreases the probability of future displacement. It is worrisome that the steps the Samper administration began to take to strengthen human rights protection were set back by authoritarian measures and restrictive policies intended to control the political crisis. Those early steps, modest and tentative though they were, were acknowledged within the country and by the international community and needed to be further supported and enhanced. The delay has only helped to increase the number of the displaced and the problems associated with displacement.

Any developments toward "depoliticization" of the issue of internal displacement would be welcome. Depoliticization in this context means that the study of the causes of displacement must be methodologically sound and not turned into a political weapon; and the displaced themselves must be seen as victims, not political pawns. Awareness-raising campaigns to that effect seem indispensable. Victims of human rights violations (and those who support and defend them) should also be seen in the same way regardless of their political, historical, geographical, or other background. Political organizations should approach the issue of displacement in the same humanitarian light, for the sake of the displaced.

Human rights and humanitarian NGOs should be perceived by the government as partners in its efforts to care for the displaced. Since the arm of the government cannot reach everywhere, those who possess local knowledge and enjoy the trust of the displaced should be entrusted with funds and given the guarantees (and the security) to do their work. This would allow a better streamlining of the few resources available and a more efficient distribution of tasks. It is, furthermore, beyond doubt that the work of human rights NGOs that provide legal assistance for victims of human rights violations must be fully supported by the government.

Measures to strengthen the protection of human rights have to be further enhanced. Attention should be drawn to recommendations made by previous human rights missions to the country and their expressions of concern about human rights abuses in Colombia. Evidence suggests that despite the government's stated good intentions the human rights situation has worsened since the representative's visit in 1994, and it is feared that even more political pressure and violence are ahead. The internal armed conflict and corruption among prominent government officials have limited the possibility of carrying out a comprehensive, coherent policy of human rights protection and attention to the displaced. Understanding of and cooperation on the human rights and humanitarian dimensions of the displacement problem must be a matter of consensus within the government itself. With regard to internally displaced persons, it is fundamental to underline the importance of strengthening protection of the following: land and property rights; humanitarian laws that prohibit displacement; and the right to life and physical integrity, especially during and immediately following displacement. Provisions should be made for special protection of the rights of women, children, and indigenous and black communities.

The internally displaced, especially women, need support from their communities to defend their rights and to cope with their plight. They should be encouraged to become more involved in existing organizations at the local level. Whether that will be possible or whether they will need to create their own separate organizations is something that they themselves will have to assess.

Projects to provide emergency humanitarian assistance, shelter, financial support, health care, and psychological assistance during the post-displacement emergency phase, designed specifically for the displaced, need to be significantly improved. These should have the objective of rapid response without negatively affecting the community of reception. Continued cooperation between the state and the nongovernmental community, especially the Church and the Red Cross, is indispensable. The few organizations founded by women to provide relief assistance and support for income-generating projects have already shown impressive potential; they should serve as models for other similar organizations. Legal assistance and guidance to the various state mechanisms that can provide relief is also necessary and could be achieved to some extent through publications and leaflets. Returning displaced persons to their home areas does not seem feasible in most regions at this moment but should be pursued wherever possible. The settling of the displaced in the slum belts around the cities is not a good solution but has become the main option in light of the continuing internal conflict. Measures to help the displaced remain near their homes and lands, where appropriate, should be implemented.

At later stages, provision of assistance to the displaced would seem to be more appropriate in the context of general public policies addressing inequality, poverty, and marginalization, both locally and nationally. If the country can continue its economic growth, then some of the new wealth must reach the poorest layers of the society in more concrete ways than it now does. Apart from the obvious need for basic public services in some urban zones, there is a serious need for social and economic projects that increase employment opportunities, especially for youth, and for income-generation projects both in urban and in rural areas. These policies should contain elements of priority and special treatment for the displaced. They should further promote gender equality, eliminate discrimination based on economic or ethnic differences, and encourage the development of skills that will allow the displaced to support themselves.

Social and economic programs and emergency assistance projects run by government institutions need more money, more coordination, and simpler procedures in order to respond to the needs of the potential beneficiaries. Finally, the government of Colombia should take steps to implement Law 387 as a positive step in the right direction, in close coordination with NGOs.

Addressing the Causes of Displacement

In the context of this report it would be presumptuous to try to make detailed recommendations for solutions to problems as complex as those in Colombia. Yet it is beyond doubt that peace in the country and the full guarantee of basic human rights is the prerequisite for a decrease in the level of displacement and for the alleviation of the plight of the victims. Peace requires not only demobilization of all armed groups but also the alleviation of some of the fundamental socioeconomic problems. The question is whether the government is able and willing to address them.

The government is not monolithic in its approach to the fundamental problems of the country. There is much sincerity on the part of many government officials in discussing these issues, although a more collective willingness to tackle them seems to be lacking. What efforts have been undertaken, as one government official put it, have been largely of an ad hoc nature and detached from reality. There appears to be a wide disparity between the numerous ideas and projects and their actual implementation in almost every sector of the administration (whether it be human rights, humanitarian assistance, housing projects, or land reform). By way of explanation, officials often emphasize the complexities of the situation, implying that complexity is a rationalization for helplessness. Although their concern appears to be sincere, complexities do not absolve the government of its responsibilities.

The government must take effective action to address the causes of displacement. More should be done to end the impunity with which the actors of violence operate, paramilitary leaders should be arrested, and the role that military institutions play in society must be minimized. The "drug war" policies also must be reevaluated. In addition, the government must treat social protest as a legitimate form of political expression and open channels for political involvement and mobilization of society (as happened, for instance, around the 1991 constitutional reform). Furthermore, electoral politics must be reorganized, including the public financing of political campaigns, broader ownership of the means of communication, and free access to the media by political parties and social movements. Moreover, the government must give priority to reform programs that will adopt the institutional changes necessary to bridge the social and economic inequalities that foment violence and should involve the business community in the democratization process. Less priority should be given to episode-specific legislation (such as that which reacts to specific internal disturbances).

Strong institutional and educational reforms need to give citizens access to active political discussion through a culture of civility, tolerance, respect, understanding, and solidarity. Citizens should explore peaceful alternatives for resolving disputes, oppose the culture of revenge and hatred, reject support for any of the armed actors of violence, and promote the right not to take part in the war (that is, there should be the right of conscientious objection to all legal or illegal armed institutions). Citizens should be encouraged to protect and support each other and each other's property, especially in the adverse circumstances of conflict. Preventive activities of this type should be implemented as a matter of urgency in areas where displacement can be expected.

Human rights promotion and protection at the local level are very important forms of prevention, especially in areas where the central government has little influence. Indeed, the defense of human rights must be seen as the essence of democracy. The work of local human rights committees, wherein local ombudsmen and representatives of social organizations, unions, local businesses, and the Church participate, must be strengthened. Police and the military need to be trained not to view all of those who are poor, underprivileged, ethnically different, and/or active in their communities as guerrillas or guerrilla supporters. The police and military institutions should rethink their roles in defending and cooperating with the most disadvantaged members of society and should not be identified as sole protectors of elite interests or the business community. They should accept responsibility openly in cases of human rights violations and publicly purge institutions of human rights violators in order to regain a legitimate standing in society.

A rough assessment of the situation suggests that (1) there is no widespread sense of politics as a public matter of collective interest that allows for democratic forms of opposition and participation; (2) the current political system, which attracts only a third of the electorate, has not allowed for the full inclusion of all citizens in the democratic and political processes; (3) the two parties (and their respective governments) have adopted national security legislation and a modus vivendi with the armed forces that in effect have resulted in their complicity in human rights violations; and (4) the unending spiral of violence supports allegations to the effect that violence itself has come to play a social function in Colombia. Unless the socioeconomic and political causes of the violence are dealt with, the pretext of violence can be used for ever-increasing repression and for more violence.

The government of Colombia has to face its country's problems and take immediate action on several fronts with what resources it has. The most obvious need is to embark on an extensive "project of tolerance," starting with the continuation of peace dialogues. Many in Colombia, including government officials, suggest that the guerrillas have a political role to play and must be allowed to do so; they must be seen as political actors rather than just criminals and drug traffickers, in order to allow for a peaceful settlement. Some of the guerrillas' positions have been acknowledged by the government in the past and would have to be taken into account. Were a peace agreement to be reached, the next step would be to disband the paramilitary groups, whose role would be of lesser value, and to purge the ranks of the military. In addition, however, there is a need to "depoliticize" the role of the civilian authorities in the country. As one government official said, the civilian government is caught in the middle: if one defends human rights one is called a guerrilla, but if one defends the army one is called a paramilitary. This "project of tolerance" needs to be extended to every citizen, and peace should be a national effort in which all sectors of society participate.

Another step would be to open up spaces for legitimate social action primarily at the micro-level. Grass-roots projects and the local organization of citizens seem to have helped local populations and should be promoted and supported rather than attacked. For instance, grass-roots reconciliation initiatives should be strengthened in order to provide a firm basis for peace agreements at the local level. The government's recognition of the need for serious land reform, strengthening of the judiciary, decentralization, and better internal control of the military creates a certain accountability to make these reforms.

Finally, since Colombians have come to accept that the narcotics business permeates all levels of society and corrupts the ideological spectrum, measures have to be taken to decrease its influence in ways other than through military actions. The "war on drugs" as it is conceptualized at present may be a further obstacle to political negotiations. Labeling all political and armed actors in the conflict as drug traffickers can be a major barrier to any sort of transformative political project. Since the drug war is impossible to win but must be fought militarily because of international pressures, it should be rethought so that it will not be the underlying obstacle to prospects for peace in the country. It would be beneficial for all sectors of society to begin understanding the link between the drug policy and the ongoing conflict and to openly discuss possible alternative ways of dealing with the problem.

The Involvement of the International Community

There is no doubt that in Colombia, as in any other country, solutions to the problems described herein can be found only within the country itself. However, in any "project of tolerance," support by and involvement of the international community will be beneficial, if not indispensable, if internal resources have been exhausted. For instance, in the negotiations with the guerrillas that have been going on for the past decade, the international community could be invited to play a more active role—for example, as a mediator, to assist the government with the implementation of its peace commitments.

So far, the international community has done much to increase security for potential victims (which, in turn, is a sine qua non for return projects and for peace). Support from the international community for the work of human rights and humanitarian NGOs in the country has shown beneficial results and should be enhanced.

Two areas of international assistance are particularly appropriate. The first is financial assistance and technical support for the nongovernmental organizations in Colombia that work directly with the displaced. The second, closely linked to the first, is training of administrators of human rights and humanitarian NGOs, so that they will be in a position to document and analyze the problems professionally and work toward solutions. The representative of the secretary-general also recommended that international human rights missions continue to take place in order to document the implementation of the results of previous missions to the country.

The new UN office in Colombia for the supervision of human rights should play an important role in monitoring the situation of the forcibly displaced. It should also provide technical assistance to the government with regard to international human rights standards and other protection needs. In addition, an international humanitarian/human rights liaison officer could provide advice to the resident UN agencies in and outside the country and thereby promote more effective international efforts. The human rights office also could help to keep open channels of communication among the government, nongovernmental organizations, and the international community and promote longer-term solutions to the human rights problems in the country.

The greater involvement of UNICEF with displaced populations would also be welcome, in particular with internally displaced children living in substandard conditions. In addition, UNHCR should be expected to play a role with the internally displaced, specifically to help ameliorate the conditions that could result in potential refugee flows. It would be useful for UNHCR to systematically monitor the protection and assistance needs of the internally displaced, serve as an advocate to improve their conditions, and provide technical assistance to government officials, NGOs, and local communities that deal with the displaced.

Development assistance could also acquire an additional dimension in Colombia: this could take the form of the establishment of microenterprise projects to benefit the displaced, as proposed in the first CONPES document. In this respect, an exchange of ideas and experiences with international organizations active in Central America (such as UNDP and UNHCR), perhaps with the support of CPDIA, would be valuable. The government, the international community, and the local

nongovernmental community have a common goal in providing protection, assistance, and development for the internally displaced. It is to be
hoped that with increased cooperation and political will on all sides the
plight of the displaced of Colombia will improve in the near rather than
the far-distant future.

Notes

1. Francis M. Deng, *Profiles in Displacement: Colombia*, E/CN.4/1995/50/
Add.1 (United Nations, Commission on Human Rights, October 3, 1994).

2. República de Colombia, Departamento Nacional de Planeación, *Docu-
mento CONPES 2804: Programa nacional de atención inmediata a la población
desplazada por la violencia* (Santafé de Bogotá: Planeación Nacional, September
13, 1995 (hereafter "first CONPES").

3. This replaced a previous government definition that included "natural or
man-made disasters, or other circumstances originating from prior situations
likely to drastically disturb public order." Consulta Permanente para el Desplazamiento Interno en las Américas (CPDIA), *Informe Final*, Misión *in situ* de
asistencia técnica sobre desplazamiento interno en Colombia (Costa Rica, November 1993). In a letter dated November 16, 1994, to Francis Deng, the government used the previous definition of displaced persons.

4. Conferencia Episcopal de Colombia, *Desplazados por la violencia en Colombia* (Bogotá Kimpres, 1995) (hereafter Bishops' Conference report); Consultoría de Derechos Humanos y Desplazamiento (CODHES), *Sistema de información de hogares desplazados por violencia en Colombia* (Santafé de Bogotá:
SISDES 1, April 1996) (hereafter CODHES report).

5. República de Colombia, Departamento Nacional de Planeación, *Docu-
mento CONPES 2924: Sistema nacional de atención integral a la población desplazada por la violencia* (Santafé de Bogotá, May 28, 1997) (hereafter "CONPES
1997.")

6. Some of these reasons were first addressed by Paul Oquist, *Violence,
Conflict and Politics in Colombia* (New York: Academic Press, 1980).

7. Comisión de Estudios sobre la Violencia, *Colombia, violencia y democracia: informe presentado al Ministerio de Gobierno* (Bogotá: Centro Edit, Universidad Nacional de Colombia, 1987).

8. "The actors disappeared, motivations disappeared and . . . responsibility
was eluded," in Alvaro Camacho and Alvaro Guzmán, "Violencia, democracia
y democratización en Colombia," *Nueva Sociedad*, no. 101, Bogotá (May–June
1989), p. 64.

9. The first serious intent of a global analysis of violence in Colombia was the
groundbreaking *La violencia en Colombia: estudio de un proceso social*, by
Germán Guzmán, Orlando Fals Borda, and Eduardo Umaña Luna Bogota (Bogotá: Ediciones Tercer Mundo, 1962, 1964). Since then, a broad range of historical
and theoretical approaches to violence in Colombia have been published. See

Gonzalo Sánchez and Ricardo Peñaranda, eds., *Pasado y presente de la violencia en Colombia*, 2d ed. (Santafé de Bogotá: CEREC, 1991); Marco Palacios, *Entre la legitimidad y la violencia: Colombia 1875–1994* (Santafé de Bogotá: Grupo Editorial Norma, 1995).

10. Statistics from the Health Situation Analysis Program of the Pan American Health Organization, 1997, cited in World Bank, "Crime and Violence as Development Issues in Latin America and the Caribbean," paper prepared for the Conference in Urban Crime and Violence, Rio de Janeiro, March 2–4, 1997. See also Comisión Colombiana de Juristas (CCJ), *Colombia, derechos humanos y derecho humanitario: 1996* (Santafé de Bogotá: Opciones Gráficas Editores, 1997), p. 9.

11. Americas Watch, "Political Murder and Reform in Colombia: The Violence Continues," New York, 1992.

12. The "consociational" denomination was coined by Daniel Levine, who defined consociational democracies as those based on "elite cooperation and compromise in which elites develop new norms and operational codes for the regulation of partisan and interest disputes." See Daniel Levine, *Religion and Politics in Latin America: The Catholic Church in Venezuela and Colombia* (Princeton University Press, 1981), p. 19. See also Alexander W. Wilde, "Conversations among Gentlemen: Oligarchical Democracy in Colombia," in Juan J. Linz and Alfred Stepan, eds., *The Breakdown of Democratic Regimes: Latin America* (Johns Hopkins University Press, 1978).

13. Daniel García-Peña, "Democracias pactadas y política exterior: las experiencias de Colombia y Venezuela 1957–1962," in *Documentos Ocasionales*, no. 19 (Bogotá: Centro de Estudios Internacionales–Universidad de los Andes, January–February 1991).

14. According to John A. Peeler, this was how traditional elites reasserted control of citizenry "without formally abandoning liberal democracy's commitment to universal suffrage and a political system." See Peeler, *Latin American Democracies: Colombia, Costa Rica, Venezuela*, 2d ed. (University of North Carolina Press, 1986), p. 38. Alfred Stepan considers it "a case of redemocratization in which party pacts and even some consociational practices—mutual guarantees, vetoes, and purposeful depolitization—were crucial." See Stepan, "Path towards Redemocratization: Theoretical and Comparative Considerations," in Woodrow Wilson International Center for Scholars, *Transitions from Authoritarian Rule: Comparative Perspectives* (Johns Hopkins University Press, 1986), p. 80.

15. See León Zamosc, "Peasant Struggles of the 1970s in Colombia," in Susan Eckstein, ed., *Power and Popular Protest: Latin American Social Movements* (University of California Press, 1989); and Francisco Leal Buitrago and Andrés Dávila Ladrón de Guevara, *Clientelismo: el sistema político y su expresión regional* (Bogotá: TM Editores–IEPRI–Universidad Nacional, 1990).

16. Daniel Pecaut, "Presente, pasado y futuro de la violencia," *Análisis Político*, no. 30 (Santafé de Bogotá: IEPRI, Universidad Nacional, January–February, 1997), p. 13.

17. Fernán Gonzaléz, "Hacia un nuevo colapso parcial del Estado? Precariedad del estado y violencia en Colombia," en *Documentos Ocasionales*, no. 50 (Bogotá: Centro de Investigación y Educación Popular [CINEP], September 1988).

18. On clientism, see Francisco Leal Buitrago and Andrés Davila Ladrón de Guevara, *Clientelismo: el sistema político y su expresión regional*, n. 23.

19. Rafael Pardo Rueda, *De primera mano: Colombia 1986–1994, entre conflictos y esperanzas* (Santafé de Bogotá: Editorial Norma, 1996), p. 177.

20. A survey taken by the weekly magazine *Semana* in November 1996 showed that the level of pessimism was higher than ever before. Eighty-six percent of Colombians surveyed feared that the country's situation could only get worse. What distinguished this pessimism from previous attitudes was the collective feeling that there were no alternatives in sight. See "Pesimismo," *Semana*, November 4, 1996.

21. For an analysis of the origins and consequences of the Samper crisis, see Francisco Leal Buitrago, ed., *Tras las huellas de la crisis política* (Santafé de Bogotá: TM Editores–FESCOL–IEPRI, 1996).

22. On this thesis see Pecaut, "Presente, pasado y futuro de la violencia."

23. See Comisión Colombiana de Juristas (CCJ), *Colombia, derechos humanos y derecho humanitario: 1995* (Santafé de Bogotá: Opciones Gráficas Editores, 1996).

24. UN statistics are from United Nations Development Programme (UNDP), *Human Development Report 1995* (New York, 1996). In 1996 unemployment reached 12.1 percent, its highest level in ten years. Inflation, which had been decreasing steadily, changed course and increased to 21 percent a year. Economic growth was only 2.5 percent in 1996; it had been 5.2 percent in 1995. See "Pesimismo," *Semana*, November 4, 1996.

25. According to Colombian official analysis, a person is considered to be living in poverty when one of the five basic necessities is not satisfied (food, health, housing, education, or utilities), and in misery when two or more of those needs are not met. Although unemployment is around 12 percent, a figure that misleadingly does not include the temporarily employed and the underemployed, each of which accounts for around 20 percent of the active population, only 20 percent of the population benefits from social security.

26. See Mauricio Rubio, "Crimen y crecimiento en Colombia," in Inter-American Development Bank, *Hacia un enfoque integrado del desarrollo: ética, violencia y seguridad ciudadana, encuentro de reflexión* (Washington, D.C.: IDB, 1996), cited in World Bank, "Crime and Violence as Development Issues in Latin America and the Caribbean," p. 7.

27. Alfredo Molano, "La tierra ha cambiado de dueño," *Revista Número*, no. 7 (Santafé de Bogotá, August–October, 1995), p. xv. The new geography of violence has been extensively studied by Alejandro Reyes Posada, both from the traditional social conflict perspective as well as from that of the more recent land distribution through paramilitary pressures. See "Conflictos agrarios y luchas armadas en la Colombia contemporánea," *Análisis Político*, no. 5 (Bogotá:

IEPRI, September–December, 1988), pp. 6–27; and "Paramilitares en Colombia: contexto, aliados y consecuencias," *Análisis Político*, no. 12 (Bogotá: IEPRI, January–April 1991), pp. 35–41.

28. As described in Jorge Villegas Arango and Jorge Yunis, *La guerra de los mil días* (Bogotá: Carlos Valencia Editores, 1978).

29. See Marion Ritchey-Vance, *The Art of Association: NGOs and Civil Society in Colombia* (Roslyn, Va.: Interamerican Foundation, 1991).

30. Revised definition, approved in the course of the Technical Meeting of CPDIA on April 15, 1993.

31. Because displaced people fear for their safety and in general do not speak out, it is impossible to make an accurate census of the displaced population. Studies generally use surveys to calculate the number of displaced. A national registration system is being set up to allow displaced families to register voluntarily. See Jorge E. Rojas, "Elementos para un sistema de información sobre desplazamiento y derechos humanos en Colombia," faxed memo (on file with author), March 11, 1997. See also CPDIA report, p. 5.

32. CODHES report.

33. Reuters, "Colombian Violence Said Creating Army of Homeless," March 11, 1997.

34. Bishops' Conference report, p. 55.

35. CODHES report, p. 3.

36. Ibid.

37. "The lack of a unified government position, the absolute impunity that did not allow for serious investigations of the accusations against the armed forces, the unexplainable silence surrounding this phenomenon, and the obvious cases of military complicity with these groups in various regions implied the executive branch's responsibility. . . . The participation of the armed forces, in my opinion, was clear in promoting these self-defense groups in the 1960s, but they never controlled them or actively promoted their growth; neither were they the nucleus of the counterinsurgency strategy. On the other hand, they were not unauthorized, nor were the cases of clear complicity sanctioned, nor was the high command able to explain why these groups existed" (authors' translation of comments by Rafael Pardo, former minister of defense, referring to the surge of paramilitary groups in the late 1980s in *De primera mano*, p. 57.

38. Government documents: Manuals published by the army command that encourage paramilitary activity include Imprenta de las Fuerzas Militares, "Reglamento de combate de contraguerrillas," EJC 3-10 Reservado, Bogotá, 1969; Imprenta de las Fuerzas Militares, "Instrucciones generales para operaciones de contra-guerrillas," Bogotá, 1979; and Imprenta de las Fuerzas Militares, "Manual EJC 3-101 de combate contra bandoleros o guerrilleros," Bogotá, 1982. Academic studies: Carlos Medina Gallego and Mireya Téllez Ardila, *La violencia parainstitucional, paramilitar y parapolicial en Colombia* (Santafé de Bogotá: Rodríguez Quito Editores, 1994); and Mauricio Romero, "Transformación rural, violencia política y narcotráfico en Córdoba, 1953–1991," in *Controversías*, no. 167 (Bogotá: October–November, 1995), pp. 94–121. NGO reports: Ediciones NCOS,

"Terrorismo del Estado," Brussels, 1992; Americas Watch, "The Killings in Colombia," Washington, D.C., 1992; Justicia y Paz, "El proyecto paramilitar en la regióndel Chucurí," Santafé de Bogotá, August 1992; Amnesty International, "Colombia: Political Violence, Myth, and Reality," London, 1994.

39. For an extensive history of paramilitary-military relations, see Human Rights Watch, "Colombia's Killer Networks: The Military-Paramilitary Partnership and the United States," Washington, D.C., 1996; and NCOS and others, *Tras los pasos perdidos de la guerra sucia: paramilitarismo y operaciones encubiertas en Colombia* (Brussels: Ediciones NCOS, 1995).

40. UN Commission on Human Rights, *Report on the Visit to Colombia by the Special Rapporteur on Summary or Arbitrary Executions*, E/CN.4/1990/22/Add. 1 (United Nations, January 24, 1990), para. 64.

41. "From their inception in the 1960s, paramilitaries and their military patrons have enjoyed an impunity that is nothing short of breathtaking. . . . To the impunity of evasion and denial is added the additional barrier of impunity from prosecution. . . . The Government's failure to aggressively investigate and prosecute those responsible for organizing, directing, and tolerating paramilitaries has contributed to the consolidation of the tie between the military and paramilitaries and represents a virtual guarantee that such activity will continue to be tolerated." Human Rights Watch, "Colombia's Killer Networks," p. 61.

42. When asked about the existence of a certain *Convivir*, the chief of the armed forces confirmed that these groups were used to protect private business interests, although the initial reason for their creation was to protect defenseless peasants. According to General Bonnet, "In the south of Bolívar there is not even an [economic] capacity to create self-defense groups or *Convivir*, because there are no businessmen in that region; that is the poorest zone of Colombia. It would be a mistake to say there are self-defense groups or private organizations when there is nothing there to defend" (authors' translation as quoted in the journal *El Tiempo* of Santafé de Bogotá, August 21, 1997, p. 9-A). In the same sense, President Samper remarked that "for their part, the groups that are up in arms and the defenders of human rights themselves, must clearly understand that kidnapping, extortion and cattle rustling were largely responsible for the formation of these cooperatives, and that if the *Convivir* are outlawed but kidnapping and extortion and cattle rustling continue, the people would seek out new methods of self-defence, both within and without the boundaries of the law" (BBC translation, found in British Broadcasting Corporation, "Samper Addresses Congress on Human Rights, Drugs, Violence," available through Lexis/Nexis, July 24, 1997).

43. See "Convivir: The New Disguise of Paramilitarism" in the bilingual edition of *Exodo: Boletín sobre desplazamiento interno en Colombia*, no. 4 (February–March 1997), pp. 3–6.

44. This is the underlying thesis of Eduardo Pizarro's book, *Insurgencia sin revolución* (Santafé de Bogotá: TM Editores, 1996), which analyzes Colombia's guerrilla movements and concludes that these groups continue to exist because conditions for their disappearance have not been made possible. At the same

time, their existence has eroded much of the democratic process and impedes any resolution of the conflict.

45. See Gabriel Escobar, "Colombian Insurrection Becoming Civil War; Guerrillas Chronically in Hills Take On Army—Which Turns to Bogotá for Funds," *Washington Post,* October 28, 1996, p. A15.

46. For example, human rights groups have documented the assassination of more than 3,000 members of the Patriotic Union (Unión Patriótica) since 1985, after the peace process and the demobilization of former FARC guerrillas. Many members of a faction of the EPL that in 1990 converted into the political movement "Hope, Peace, and Freedom" (Esperanza, Paz y Libertad) have also been murdered. Urban displacement also was said to be caused in 3.42 percent of the cases by "popular militias," urban leftist armed groups formed to "protect" neighborhoods. They are active in the cities of Medellín, Cali, Bogotá, and Barrancabermeja. See Bishops' Conference report, pp. 51–52.

47. Several NGOs have noted that the number of murders attributed to state agents declined from around 50 percent in 1993 to around 5 percent in 1996 and 1997. This drop is attributed by some to the overwhelming increase in killings committed by paramilitary and/or self-defense groups (77 percent in 1997), which have been linked to the armed forces and reportedly are carrying out a good part of their "dirty work." See Human Rights Watch, "Colombia's Killer Networks"; and U.S. Department of State, *Country Reports on Human Rights Practices for 1997,* chapter on Colombia, 1998.

48. Dietrich Rueschemeyer and others, *Capitalist Development and Democracy* (Cambridge, UK: Polity Press, 1992), p. 196.

49. During a meeting of the National Assembly of Financial Institutions (ANIF) in October 1996, presidential candidate Rudolph Hommes proposed that the military budget be increased to 6 percent of total expenses and that the military be increased by 200,000 soldiers. Juan Manuel Santos promoted himself as a future Colombian Alberto Fujimori (the current president of Peru), who would close the corrupt Congress and promote a liberating campaign across Colombia headed by the armed forces in order to "cleanse" the country of poverty and violence. He also proclaimed the need to form an "army of diplomats that would combat the guerrillas' foreign policy," because "every time they want to they win human rights claims in international tribunals and make Colombia look very bad in terms of human rights." Unsurprisingly, these candidates received the most support from the public. (As described by Antonio Caballero, "Un tambor y una corneta," *Revista Semana,* October 22–29, 1996.)

50. See Juan Pablo Ordoñez, *No Human Being Is Disposable: Social Cleansing, Human Rights, and Sexual Orientation in Colombia* (Washington, D.C.: Colombia Human Rights Commission, 1995); Elizabeth F. Schwartz, "Getting Away with Murder: Social Cleansing in Colombia and the Role of the United States," *University of Miami Inter-American Law Review,* vol. 27 (Winter 1995–96), p. 381; CCJ, *Colombia, derechos humanos y derecho humanitario: 1995,* p. 25.

51. Studies have been done on the impact of the drug trade on micro- and macro-economics, social relations, culture, ethics, local and national politics,

international relations, and law. For a good summary of these perspectives and their relation to President Samper's political crisis, see Francisco Leal Buitrago, ed., *Tras las huellas de la crisis política*.

52. The "Drug War" approach was first proclaimed by President Richard Nixon. In 1973, Nixon declared an "all-out global war on the drug menace" in Message from the President of the United States Transmitting Reorganization Plan No. 2 of 1973, "Establishing a Drug Enforcement Administration," H.R. 69, 93 Cong. 1 sess. (1973). President Clinton's strategy reflects the same tendency: "Continued U.S. leadership in international narcotics control and the U.S. support and cooperation with other nations is critical to the efforts to stem the flow of illicit drugs across our borders. . . . The Government has made it clear that the United States sees international criminal narcotics organizations as a threat to our national security" *(National Drug Control Strategy*, Washington, D.C., 1996, p. 34).

53. William J. Bennett and Jesse Helms, "Colombia, America's Favorite 'Narco-Democracy,'" *Wall Street Journal*, February 6, 1996, op-ed. In the words of Madeleine Albright, "We must work together to eradicate crops, disrupt trafficking, break up cartels and punish those who would enrich themselves by selling poison to our children. The United States drug certification law has become part of our strategy of cooperation. . . . It requires difficult up or down judgments to be rendered in a public manner that engenders in some cases deserved embarrassment, in others unhelpful resentment." Albright made those comments on CNN, "Secretary of State Albright Announces the Clinton Administration's Decision of Who to Recertify in the War on Drugs," CNN Breaking News, Transcript #97022803V00, February 28, 1997. The certification process was implemented during the Reagan administration. "Section 490 of the Foreign Assistance Act requires the President to certify annually that each major drug producing or transit country has cooperated fully or has taken adequate steps on its own to meet the goals and objectives of the 1988 UN Convention, including rooting out public corruption. Governments that do not pass the test lose eligibility for most forms of U.S military and development assistance; they also face a mandatory 'no' vote by the U.S. Government on loans in six multilateral developments banks" (Bureau for International Narcotics and Law Enforcement Affairs, U.S. Department of State Policy and Program Overview for 1996, Washington, D.C., 1997).

54. "The concept of 'narco-guerrillas' was . . . coined in 1984 by former U.S. Ambassador Lewis Tambs [consultant on Latin America for the National Security Council and protégé of Senator Jesse Helms, R-N.C.]. Tambs was trying to undercut the effort of Belisario Betancur, then Colombia's president, to negotiate a peace with the left-wing insurgents." See Randolph Ryan, "Colombia's Other War: Political Suppression by Assassination Has Been as Violent as the Battle Against Drugs," *Boston Globe*, November 26, 1989. "There is general agreement that guerrillas are involved in some regions in the initial cultivation of crops and in the protection of peasant growers from herbicide fumigation and abuse by the traffickers. . . . However, they do not have the same business profile as the Medellin or Cali cartels, and have many times been in direct confrontation with the

cartels and their paramilitary groups over the control of the cultivation process" (authors' translation). See Alejandro Reyes Posada, "La erradicación de cultivos: un laberinto," *Análisis Político*, no. 24 (Bogotá: IEPRI, January–April 1995).

55. See Human Rights Watch, "Colombia's Killer Networks," pp. 17–26; Carlos Medina Gallego, *Autodefensas, paramilitares y narcotráfico en Colombia* (Santafé de Bogotá, 1990); NCOS, *Tras los pasos perdidos de la guerra sucia: paramilitarismo y operaciones encubiertas en Colombia* (Brussels, 1995).

56. Alejandro Reyes, researcher at the Institute of Political Studies and International Relations (IEPRI) of the National University, estimates that drug traffickers have investments in more than 400 of the 1,051 municipalities in Colombia. The drug traffickers now own more than half of the country's best agricultural lands. These findings recently were incorporated into a UNDP report and served as the basis for the asset forfeiture law 333 of December 19, 1996, which targets expropriation of lands that have been acquired with illegal incomes. Former minister of defense Rafael Pardo has noted that "the entrepreneurs of the drug trade could become the dominant economic group in the country" (María Isabel García, "Colombia-Economy: Drugs and the Narco-Revolution," Inter Press Service, December 23, 1996).

57. Justicia y Paz, "Behind Colombian Violence: Economic, Social and Political Conditions," *A Magazine of Human Rights for Colombia*, vol. 1 (Fall 1996), p. 4.

58. See Jorge E. Rojas, ed., *Desplazamiento, derechos humanos y conflicto armado* (Santafe de Bogotá: CODHES, 1993).

59. Rural areas are the expulsion zones in 53 percent of the cases. The Bishops' Conference report lists the following departments in the order of largest to smallest number of people displaced: Antioquia, Santander, Meta, Córdoba, Boyacá, Cauca, Bolívar, Norte de Santander, César, Arauca, Magdalena, Cundinamarca, Caquetá, Valle, Tolima, Sucre, and Caldas. The CODHES report registered 127,875 people displaced between September 1994 and November 1995 in the following proportions: Antioquia 31 percent, Santander 15 percent, Cesar 7 percent, Sucre 5 percent, Meta 4 percent, and Boyacá 4 percent. CODHES, *Informe Presentado a la Consejería Presidencial para los Derechos Humanos*, Seguimiento del Informe de Desplazados Presentado por la Conferencia Episcopal en Diciembre de 1994, mimeo, Santafé de Bogotá, December 1995.

60. See also UN Commission on Human Rights, E/CN.4/1990/22/Add.1, para. 47; Robin Kirk, "Feeding the Tiger: Colombia's Internally Displaced People," U.S. Committee for Refugees, Washington, D.C., 1993, p. 3.

61. Bishops' Conference report, p. 48.

62. Comisión Colombiana de Juristas, "Desplazamiento forzado en Norte de Santander," December 1995, p. 7.

63. The Meta Civic Committee for Human Rights was dismantled because of the murder and displacement of its members. Josué Giraldo, the founder of the committee, who did not leave the region, was shot on October 13, 1996, while playing with his two young daughters in front of his home. Both human rights

and humanitarian law violations have forced hundreds of people to flee from Meta.

64. See Grupo de Apoyo a Organizaciones de Desplazados (GAD), "Urabá: el mayor exodo de los últimos años," June 2, 1995.

65. In May 1996, FARC guerrillas killed at least sixteen persons, including two children, and burned numerous houses in the fishing town of Turbo, Urabá. In September members of the fifth FARC front summarily executed four rural community leaders near Apartadó, Urabá. The FARC continued its campaign of assassination against the Hope, Peace, and Freedom Movement (formerly known as EPL, when it was a guerrilla group), whose members had left the EPL in the early 1990s and become active in the National Syndicate of Agro-Industry Workers in Urabá. See U.S. Department of State, *Country Reports on Human Rights Practices for 1996*, chapter on Colombia, February 1997.

66. For details on the specific situation of this region, see *Monografía-estudio sobre el desplazamiento forzado en la región del Magdalena Medio colombiano*, Barrancabermeja, March 1996.

67. Comisión Colombiana de Juristas, "Desplazamiento forzado en Norte de Santander," p. 17.

68. The Afro-Colombian Law was designed to benefit the descendants of African slaves, who formed Maroon communities in the rain forests of the department of the Chocó. The 1991 constitution recognized that Colombia was "pluricultural and multiethnic." This led to the recognition of the community of black Colombians in the Chocó as a unique ethnic group with communal property rights in an area of that department.

69. Yadira Ferrer, "Colombia-Human Rights: Thousands of Peasant Farmers Flee Violence," Inter Press Service, March 31, 1997; "Repatriarán a los desplazados que huyeron a Panamá," *El Tiempo*, April 15, 1997.

70. CODHES report, p. 9.

71. The metropolitan area of Bucaramanga in the Santander department has seen a 30 percent increase in the displaced population since the publication of the Bishops' Conference report. The displaced are said to be fleeing from the northeast of the country. The Governor's Office for Peace and Human Rights reported that 160,000 displaced people (20 percent of the city's population) are living in areas surrounding the city. See "Aumentan desplazados por violencia en Santander," *El Tiempo*, February 17, 1997. Cúcuta, with a population of 600,000, was a peaceful city until 1990. Between 1991 and 1995 squatters seized land in more than twenty-five sites around the city and built additional marginal housing in slums. It is estimated that there are around 30,000 people from Norte de Santander, Montería, and Córdoba now living in these misery belts around the city. See CCJ, "Desplazamiento forzado en Norte de Santander," p. 25. See also CODHES report, p. 4.

72. See also CPDIA report, pp. 10 and 17 and the following pages; Bishops' Conference report, pp. 58–60.

73. See Donny Meertens, "Mujer y violencia en los conflictos rurales," *Análisis Político*, no. 25 (Bogotá : IEPRI, January–April, 1995), pp. 42–43.

74. Flor Edilma Osorio, *La violencia del silencio: desplazados del campo a la ciudad* (Santafé de Bogotá: CODHES–Universidad Javeriana, 1993), p. 195.

75. Bishops' Conference report, p. 44. For policy on women in situations of displacement, see Roberta Cohen, "Refugee and Internally Displaced Women: A Development Perspective," Brookings Institution–Refugee Policy Group Project on Internal Displacement, Washington, D.C., November, 1995.

76. According to figures provided by the International Labor Organization (ILO), the situation is alarming. Twenty percent of all Colombian girls between the ages of ten and fourteen work as domestics. See Zoraida Portillo, "Latam-Children: Cinderellas without a Prince Charming," Inter Press Service, February 28, 1997.

77. As defined by the United Nations Convention on the Rights of the Child (Article 1), a "child" is understood to be anyone under the age of eighteen.

78. Pan American Health Organization (PAHO), *La violencia en las Américas: la pandemia social del Siglo XX*, Washington, D.C., 1996, p. 24. See also Human Rights Watch, "Generation under Fire: Children and Violence in Colombia," New York, November 1994.

79. See CERD/C/SR.944-945. During the discussion of the fifth periodic report of Colombia, the Committee on the Elimination of Racial Discrimination was concerned about loss of land, invasions by colonists, and the right to life and personal safety of the indigenous. The ILO Committee of Experts, in a "direct request" to Colombia concerning the implementation of ILO Convention no. 107 in 1992, noted the extreme difficulty of protecting the civilian population and referred to the threats received by the community in Totoró (in the department of Cauca). The committee also noted its concern for groups who in 1992 allegedly were being threatened with displacement and relocation: the Wayuu in Manaure (from the Industrial Promotion Institute), the Embera (from the dam in Alto Sinú), and the communities of the Pijao de Ataco-Tolima. (See comments made by the Committee of Experts of the International Labor Organization on the application of ILO Convention no. 107 by Colombia.) The U.S. State Department has pointed out that most threats, killings, and intimidation of indigenous and black communities are related to land rights and territorial disputes. (See U.S. Department of State, *Country Reports on Human Rights Practices for 1996*, chapter on Colombia.)

80. Colombia has ratified the International Covenant on Economic, Social, and Cultural Rights; the International Covenant on Civil and Political Rights; the Optional Protocol to the International Covenant on Civil and Political Rights; the International Convention on the Elimination of All Forms of Racial Discrimination; the International Convention on the Suppression and Punishment of the Crime of Apartheid; the Convention on the Prevention and Punishment of the Crime of Genocide; the Convention on the Rights of the Child; the Convention on the Elimination of All Forms of Discrimination against Women; the Convention on the Political Rights of Women; the Convention against Torture and Other Cruel, Inhuman, or Degrading Treatment or Punishment; and the Convention and Protocol Relating to the Status of Refugees. Colombia became a party to

International Labor Organization Convention no. 169 (Indigenous and Tribal Peoples Convention) in 1991. Previously, it was also a party to ILO Convention no. 107, which was replaced by Convention no. 169 in 1989. Colombia is also a party to the American Convention on Human Rights. With regard to international humanitarian law, Colombia has signed the four Geneva Conventions and on May 18, 1995, the Constitutional Court formally declared Law 171 of 1994 to be constitutional; this law ratified without reservation Protocol II to the Geneva Conventions. Article 3 common to the four Geneva Conventions establishes minimum rules to be adhered to in the case of situations of armed conflict not of an international character. These provisions are binding on all parties.

81. See, for example, UN Commission on Human Rights, *Report of the Special Rapporteur on Extrajudicial, Arbitrary or Summary Executions*, E/CN.4/1994/7 (United Nations, 1993), especially paras. 220–38. See also UN Commission on Human Rights, *Report of the Working Group on Enforced and Involuntary Disappearances*, E/CN.4/1994/26 (United Nations, 1993), para. 167; *Report of the Special Rapporteur on Torture*, E/CN.4/1994/43 (United Nations, 1993), para. 188; and General Assembly, *Report of the Human Rights Committee*, A/47/40 (United Nations, 1992). The Inter-American Commission on Human Rights of the Organization of American States has found the Colombian government responsible in twelve cases of serious human rights abuses. See Annual Reports of the Inter-American Commission on Human Rights 1993–1997. On December 8, 1995, the Inter-American Court of Human Rights issued a finding of government responsibility in the 1989 disappearances and presumed deaths of Isidro Caballero and María del Carmen Santana. This was the first Colombian case to reach the court. On October 27, 1995, the UN Committee on Human Rights formally declared the government responsible for the 1987 arrest, disappearance, torture, and subsequent murder of Nydia Erika Bautista.

See also the following reports: Hiram A. Ruiz, "Colombia's Silent Crisis: One Million Displaced by Violence," U.S. Committee for Refugees, Washington, D.C., 1998; Javier Giraldo, S.J., *Colombia: The Genocidal Democracy* (Common Courage Press, 1996); CCJ, *Colombia, derechos humanos y derecho humanitario* (1996 and 1997 reports); U.S. Department of State, *Country Reports on Human Rights Practices for 1994-1997*, chapters on Colombia; Human Rights Watch/Americas, "Generation under Fire"; Procuraduria General de la Nación, *Informe sobre derechos humanos, 1993–1994* (Santafé de Bogotá, July 1994); Edición ADAI, *Derechos humanos en Colombia: Mito y realidad* (Bogotá, 1994); Amnesty International, "Political Violence in Colombia," New York, March 1994; Human Rights Watch/Americas, "State of War: Political Violence and Counterinsurgency in Colombia," Washington, D.C., December 1993; Washington Office on Latin America (WOLA), "The Colombian National Police, Human Rights and U.S. Drug Policy," Washington, D.C., 1993; Americas Watch, "Political Murder and Reform in Colombia: The Violence Continues," Washington, D.C., 1992; WOLA, "Clear and Present Dangers: U.S. Military and the War on Drugs in the Andes," Washington, D.C., 1991; Americas Watch, "The 'Drug War' in Colombia: The Neglected Tragedy of Political Violence," Washington, D.C., 1990.

82. Over the past thirty years, an estimated 1.2 to 2 percent of all crimes have been resolved with the prosecution and sentencing of a guilty party. See Michael Pahl, "Wanted, Criminal Justice: Colombia's Adoption of a Prosecutorial System of Criminal Procedure," *Fordham International Law Journal*, vol. 16 (1992), pp. 608–34. In June 1996 the Superior Council of the Judiciary reported that 74 percent of all crimes go unreported, and between 97 and 98 percent of all crimes go unpunished. The government commission on public spending placed the impunity rate for all crimes at 99.5 percent. The Colombian Commission of Jurists claimed the impunity rate for politically motivated crimes is virtually 100 percent.

83. See "Strategy of Impunity," in Human Rights Watch, "Colombia's Killer Networks," pp. 61–83. See also CCJ, *Colombia, Derechos Humanos y Derecho Humanitario: 1995*; Robert Weiner, "War by Other Means: Colombia's Faceless Courts," in NACLA, *Injustice for All: Crime and Impunity in Latin America*, vol. 30 (September/October 1996).

84. See Kirk, "Feeding the Tiger," pp. 13–14.

85. See U.S. Department of State, *Country Reports on Human Rights Practices for 1993*, chapter on Colombia, 1994.

86. The powers were given through the "state of internal commotion" decree 2027 of 1995.

87. Bishops' Conference report, pp. 78–82.

88. Kirk, "Feeding the Tiger," p. 10.

89. "One out of every 40 Colombians is forced to move by violence," *Agence France Presse*, March 12, 1997. See also Human Rights Watch/Americas, "Generation under Fire."

90. See Henry Steiner, "Political Participation as a Human Right," *Harvard Human Rights Yearbook*, vol. 1 (Harvard University, 1988), p. 78; Tom Farer, "Human Rights and Human Wrongs: Is the Liberal Model Sufficient?" *Human Rights Quarterly*, vol. 7 (1985), p. 189; Universal Declaration of Human Rights, Article 21; International Covenant on Civil and Political Rights, Article 25; and American Declaration, Articles 20, 38, and 32.

91. Human Rights Watch, *World Report* (New York, 1996).

92. "During the first half of 1996, President Samper governed Colombia under a 'state of internal commotion,' invoked after the killing of Conservative leader Alvaro Gómez on November 2, 1995, and extended through August. Although the measure never produced the capture of Gómez' killers, its stated goal, it did suspend key rights, like freedom from unwarranted search and seizure. The military was also authorized to circumvent local civil authority and petition the executive directly to declare 'special public order zones' where rights such as free movement were suspended. By the end of May, over one-third of Colombia was a 'special public order zone.' The governor of the department of Guaviare publicly criticized the executive for failing to notify him that his state would be placed under *de facto* military rule. After the Constitutional Court overturned President Samper's August 1995 declaration of a state of internal commotion, its members were barraged with anonymous death threats. Subsequently, the court did not

challenge the November declaration of a state of internal commotion, limiting its actions instead to striking down a few measures imposed in its wake. In what was considered a public rebuke, in July 1996 President Samper introduced to Congress a constitutional reform bill that would bar the court from reviewing states of internal commotion in the future and eliminate time constraints on such declarations, making them indefinite." See Human Rights Watch, *World Report*.

93. "His comments were made in the wake of the worst guerrilla violence in Colombia's recent history. The current offensive has its roots in massive peasant demonstrations against the Government's U.S.-backed coca eradication program. When the Army moved in to control 150,000 angry farmers in southern Colombia, members of the Revolutionary Armed Forces of Colombia—or FARC, the country's largest guerrilla group—were quick to come to the peasants' defense. Two months of skirmishes came to a head in late August, when 500 of the guerrilla rebels stormed the Amazon Army base of Las Delicias, reducing it to rubble. Thirty soldiers were killed; 60 more were taken prisoner. The attack on Las Delicias sparked a wave of violence nationwide. Farmers and guerrillas mobilized in 15 of Colombia's 31 provinces, attacking Army installations and crippling transportation systems. Nearly 200 police and soldiers have been killed, officials say. For much of the last two months, half the country has effectively been isolated from central government control." Jeremy Lennard, "Peace with Guerrillas Unlikely, Colombian Authorities Report," *Dallas Morning News*, September 29, 1996.

94. According to the fifth periodic report of Colombia submitted in 1991 to the Committee against the Elimination of Racial Discrimination, the 1991 constitution guaranteed the rights of eighty-one indigenous groups who inhabit 25 percent of the country. See CERD/C/191/Add.1. See also UN Commission on Human Rights, Working Group on Indigenous Populations, Information Submitted by Colombia, E/CN.4/Sub.2/AC.4/1991/4 (United Nations, June 5, 1991).

95. As mentioned in Nelson Viloria Larios, "Exposición de motivos: Proyecto de ley; por el cual se dictan medidas especiales de apoyo a los desplazados forzosos en Colombia," July 1995.

96. "Armed violence in various regions of the country is causing a worrying phenomenon whereby large segments of the population are displaced. Almost 34,000 families have been displaced. This relatively recent phenomenon must be quickly eradicated from the root. The government understands this and has legally created . . . the National System for the Treatment of People Displaced by Violence, to face the various phases of displacement, the initial phase, temporary stabilization, consolidation and, finally, the definitive return or relocation" (BBC translation). "Samper Addresses Congress on Human Rights, Drugs, Violence," available through Lexis/Nexis, July 24, 1997.

97. CONPES 1997, p. 3.

98. Ibid., p. 12.

99. The committees are to be integrated by the local governor or mayor, the local head of the military brigade, the head of the police, the director of the social health services, the director of the institute for family welfare, a represen-

tative of the ICRC, of the civil defense, and of the Church, and two representatives from the displaced population.

100. The well-known *Hacienda Bellacruz* case, in which hundreds of families living on the property of a former ambassador were displaced after paramilitary persecution, is a good example of what happens when political conflict continues in the consolidation process. When 150 families were assigned by the government to a piece of land in a suburban area, the mayor of the city said he had not been informed of the plan and that he would provide no assistance to the families. See Esperanza Paez, "Ibagué, nuevo gogar de desplazados," *El Tiempo*, December 30, 1996.

101. Law 393 of July 29, 1997, regulates compliance. It is anticipated that its effect will be similar to that of the *tutela* because it has its origin in the constitution (Article 87) and is a quick and effective mechanism that can be used to enforce rights.

102. The GAD was formed by various organizations (Centro de Investigación y Educación Popular, Comisión Colombiana de Juristas, Justicia y Paz, Instituto Latinoamericano de Servicios Legales Alternativos, Movilidad Humana, Fundación para la Educación y el Desarollo) to inform the general public about displacement, to support government projects, to lobby for laws on displacement at the national and international level, and to give emergency relief.

103. Three groups working with families displaced by paramilitaries, including the National Association of Peasant Smallholders–Unity and Reconstruction, were described as "manipulated by the guerrillas" in an army report. Human rights activists often are charged with slander by army officers. Although the courts rarely have acted on these cases, the tactic is widely seen as an effort to silence critics. Even international intervention—like the invocation of precautionary measures by the Inter-American Commission on Human Rights—has resulted in more, not less, danger for monitors. See Human Rights Watch, *World Report*, 1997.

Republic of Peru

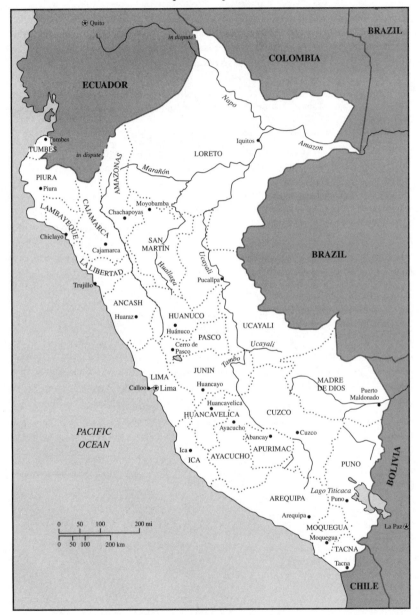

CHAPTER ELEVEN

Will Peru's Displaced Return?

Maria Stavropoulou

DISPLACEMENT IN Peru has been largely the result of armed opposition to the government, which escalated into rampant terrorism in the 1980s. Most of the violence has been suppressed and a return to relatively normal conditions has made return possible for some internally displaced persons, but some 600,000 people were still displaced in late 1996. The need to protect and assist them has become increasingly recognized as a priority for the government. Accordingly, the representative of the secretary-general on internally displaced persons undertook a mission to Peru from August 12 to 25, 1995. This chapter describes the main findings of that mission.

Since the representative's visit, the government has taken a number of steps to ameliorate the situation of the displaced, all of which were recommended in the representative's mission report.[1] In March 1996 an ombudsman was appointed, whose office began examining individual allegations of human rights abuses in late 1996. One of the first steps taken was to ensure the release of some hundred alleged "terrorists" by recommending that they be "pardoned." It is envisaged that the ombudsman's office will monitor developments in the area of provision of documentation to the displaced and help improve relations between the government and the NGO sector. More attention is being devoted to those among the displaced who do not want to, or cannot, return to their home areas, while the Proyecto de Apoyo para el Repoblamiento (PAR,

455

or Support Project for Returnees) reportedly has been given more funds to implement its projects for returnees. But because the security crisis has not been resolved, and displacement of the population is likely to continue, a follow-up visit by the representative would be useful to assess progress and recommend further steps to address the problems of the displaced.

The Context

The forced displacement of almost a million people has been the result of a sixteen-year armed conflict between armed opposition groups and the armed forces of Peru. A factor contributing to the birth of the armed opposition, in turn, has been the existence of socioeconomic disparities between different geographic areas and socioethnic groups.

Ethnic and Socioeconomic Background

Peruvian territory is geographically complex, both climatically and ecologically, and the economies of different regions are varied as well. Access to some regions, because of the lack of transportation infrastructure, is very limited. The Andes mountain chain creates three natural "strips" that run from the north of the country to the south: the coastal strip; the Sierra (the Andean mountains, frequently referred to as the highlands); and the *selva* (jungle). The total population is approximately 22,128,000. Apart from the Peruvians of European ancestry and the small number of Asian or African ancestry (3 or 4 percent), official sources distinguish between the "indigenous communities" of Quechua and Aymara origin, living in the Sierra (in particular the departments of Cuzco, Puno, Apurimac, Ayacucho, Huancavelica, Junin, and Pasco), and the "native and peasant communities" (numbering a few hundred thousand), living in dispersed settlements in the *selva* (in the departments of Loreto, Junin, Ucayali, Amazonas, Cuzco, and Madre de Dios) and representing some fifty-five ethnolinguistic groups belonging to more than twelve linguistic families.[2]

Ever since the sixteenth century, when the Spanish conquered the territory of what is today Peru, the indigenous and native communities have held an inferior status. The Spanish and their descendants initially gained control over the Inca communities and their lands and subjected them to serfdom. After independence (July 28, 1821), General José de

San Martín abolished the tribute payments and labor services of the native communities and decreed that native people should enjoy the full rights of Peruvian citizenship. Nevertheless, the non-Spanish population remained subordinate and continued to be perceived as inferior; their territories have always been marginalized and abandoned. Socioeconomic indicators show a clear pattern of historical discrimination, and derogatory terms used in particular for the Quechua-speaking populations have survived to this day. As for the members of the native communities of the *selva*, which retain many elements of their traditional lifestyle, they are often still treated as third-class citizens.

It is estimated that between 1970 and 1990 the Peruvian population increased by 60 percent. Although the labor force grew, in the 1980s GDP had a negative growth rate. International investment stagnated. Salaries dropped significantly between 1973 and 1988, while unemployment and underemployment rose. Poor families became poorer as the economic structure deteriorated. The hardest hit were the poorest departments, such as Ayacucho, which had never benefited from international or local investment. Some areas in the southern Andes consequently share more characteristics with some "fourth world" countries in Africa than with the coastal cities of Peru.[3]

A principal cause of poverty is the shortage of fertile land. An estimated 37 percent of the land is unusable for agricultural purposes without large quantities of fertilizers or long periods of rest. In the Sierra, this problem is compounded by the lack of modern technologies, high population density, and in some cases, unequal land distribution. In some areas of the *selva*, the highly acidic topsoil can be cultivated only by slash-and-burn techniques. In both cases, neither one-product cultivation to achieve economies of scale nor intensive cultivation is appropriate. In fact, both types of cultivation tend to increase the vulnerability of the peasants by creating higher dependence on the market prices of the crops or the necessary fertilizers.

To offset some of their subsistence problems, many poor families have migrated to urban centers, where they have become self-employed in the so-called informal sector. According to 1981 estimates, this sector of the monetized economy represented 60 percent of the urban labor force.[4] But since the expansion of the informal sector is affected by the same pressures as the formal, ultimately many of its members have seen their incomes decline. For the same reasons, coca-growing has become the only means of subsistence for many peasants in rural areas; however, with the sharp drop in the price of coca, following the breakup of the Cali cartel, serious economic hardships and related conflicts are expected.

Since 1992, President Alberto Fujimori has taken severe austerity measures that have reversed the negative growth and reduced inflation dramatically. Although the immediate effects on the poorest segments of the society were negative because of entrenched extreme poverty, it is generally acknowledged that the president's popularity is due largely to his economic policies. At the same time, the government took steps to reduce poverty, such as the creation of a social emergency fund, FON-CODES (Fondo Nacional de Compensación y Desarrollo Social, or National Fund for Compensation and Social Development). These, however, have been far from adequate in meeting actual needs.

Until the 1940s, roughly 65 percent of Peru's population lived in the Andes. In the late 1990s, only 29.6 percent of the population is rural, and Lima's population has grown twelvefold. Urbanization has not been a result of industrialization, but of the precarious rural situation.[5] The poorest departments—Ayacucho, Apurimac, and Huancavelica—have sent most migrants to the cities and the *selva*. The first arrivals in the cities settled on empty lots and farm land and built rudimentary structures; today these areas constitute vast shantytowns, constantly expanding to accommodate new arrivals. It is estimated that 70 percent of the metropolitan population of Lima lives in shantytowns.

The Conflict and the Pacification Process

SHINING PATH AND THE OTHER ARMED OPPOSITION MOVEMENTS. Poverty and the neglect of entire areas contributed to the birth of armed opposition in Peru. The Shining Path (Sendero Luminoso, or Communist Party of Peru), a strict Maoist political party, was founded by philosophy professor Abimael Guzmán in 1968 at Ayacucho's National University of San Cristóbal de Huamanga. It concentrated its activities in the countryside, starting first in provincial universities and later creating "cells" among local communities. Its leaders capitalized on the extreme poverty of the Ayacuchanos, caused by the serious shortage of fertile land and the economic imbalances in the country.

The Shining Path's first attacks occurred in 1980 and continued throughout the decade. The terrorist and indiscriminate nature of its attacks mirrors the preference of its leaders for violence over politics and its ideology of "total revolution," leading some observers to compare the movement to the Khmer Rouge of Cambodia.[6] Soon the movement alienated many of its initial supporters, especially with the introduction of attempts to institute collective farms, the forcible recruitment of young women and children, and "popular trials" of local officials.

In 1984 a second armed opposition group emerged, the Tupac Amaru Revolutionary Movement (MRTA). Unlike the Shining Path, the MRTA started its violent activities in urban centers before gaining control of some rural areas in Junin, Pasco, Huanuco, and San Martín. During the late 1980s the MRTA had lost control over parts of these areas to the Shining Path. In December 1996, however, it showed its strength by invading the Japanese embassy in Lima and holding more than seventy persons hostage for many weeks.

THE ARMED CONFLICT. It is now generally accepted that the state, when first confronted with armed opposition, initially neglected the problem because it affected only remote areas. In December 1982 the government of Belaunde Terry (1980–85) placed nine provinces under a state of emergency and entrusted control to a political-military command, which operated as an occupation army. This act not only did not stem armed opposition activity but gave rise to the first allegations of massive human rights violations committed by the military. The first two years of the government of Alan Garcia (1985–90) were hopeful: the military presence in the emergency zones was restricted, and fewer allegations were made. After 1988, however, the area of hostilities expanded significantly, as the armed dissidents escalated their terrorist activities in urban centers and self-defense committees increasingly became involved in counterinsurgency tactics. Civilians were caught in the cross fire, and the volume of denunciations and the numbers of the displaced spiraled upward.

With the election of President Alberto Fujimori, countersubversive strategies were consolidated, including the organization of the rural population in self-defense committees under the control of the military and the intensification of police and military control in marginal urban areas. Severe antiterrorist legislation and the activation of the central intelligence branch of the police facilitated the capture of the Shining Path leadership in September 1992 and a number of other major victories.

It is estimated that during the fourteen years of war, 27,000 Peruvians were killed and almost a million were displaced.[7] Political violence had detrimental effects on the agricultural economy, and many development projects, schools, health clinics, and markets were destroyed. Official sources estimate that material losses amounted to $21 billion, a figure equivalent to the entire foreign debt.[8]

Pockets of both the Shining Path and MRTA remain in some parts of the country, and armed skirmishes, in particular in the coca-growing valleys and in some of the more isolated highlands, still are being reported.[9] One faction of the Shining Path, led by "Feliciano," is thought to be among the strongest and most radical and to maintain bases in the Río Mantaro and Río Apurimac valleys. Car bombings in Lima and the Japanese embassy hostage crisis show that security is still fragile. Military operations have diminished significantly and security has improved considerably, but active army officers are still in charge of the Ministry of the Interior and the Ministry of Defense, which supervise the counter-insurgency operations. Local commanders remain the paramount authority in the emergency zones.

RONDAS CAMPESINAS AND SELF-DEFENSE COMMITTEES. Peasants traditionally organized themselves in self-defense groups (*rondas*) to fight against cattle rustling. In the 1980s the military started providing official recognition and arming these groups in an effort to consolidate power in rural areas and to fight the armed opposition groups. It also started creating new groups known as *comités de autodefensa*, or self-defense committees. Some interviewees in 1995 noted that in the past the security forces had practically forced peasants to participate in the self-defense committees and that those who refused to participate were immediately suspect. Full military authority over both the *rondas* and the self-defense committees was conferred on the army in early 1993. One NGO estimate placed the number of *ronderos* at more than 100,000; in Ayacucho alone there were 35,000 *ronderos*, and the Political-Military Command was at the time of the representative's mission about to recognize a substantial number of new self-defense committees, some of which belonged to returnees. In all the communities the representative visited, a number of *ronderos* were present. For the most part they had no uniforms and were lightly armed, sometimes with traditional weapons such as spades and knives.

In many instances, especially in isolated areas and native communities in the *selva*, the self-defense committees have been the only source of security and the main fighting force against the armed opposition groups. At the same time, the necessity of organizing in self-defense committees has disrupted subsistence activities. In addition, self-defense committees themselves occasionally have been involved in illegal activities, including drug trafficking, or have used their arms to settle personal disputes. In some cases they have become the nucleus of the communities, militarizing social life and assuming leadership.[10]

RECENT POLITICAL DEVELOPMENTS. On April 5, 1992, President Fujimori, with the full backing of the Armed Forces Joint Command, dissolved Congress, suspended the Political Constitution of 1979, and set up an emergency government. From then until the end of 1992, the president and the Council of Ministers ruled the country by decree. They issued wide-ranging antiterrorism decrees that allowed for summary proceedings against persons accused of terrorism and treason. Furthermore, the president suspended civilian courts and removed from office the members of the Tribunal of Constitutional Guarantees, Supreme Court judges, the attorney general, and other judges and members of the judiciary.

In December 1992 the Democratic Constituent Congress (Congreso Constituyente Democrático) was inaugurated; it approved a law confirming the constitutionality of the president and the continued applicability of all laws enacted by him, as well as a motion that the Peruvian state did not have a policy of systematically violating human rights. It also established a Commission on Human Rights and Pacification. The Congress promulgated a new constitution that was ratified by a referendum on December 27, 1993.

In the general elections of April 9, 1995, President Fujimori won a clear majority over his rival, former UN secretary-general Javier Pérez de Cuéllar. Published and private sources have suggested that his success in combating the Shining Path and lowering inflation accounted for his reelection, despite the 1992 "self-coup" and his authoritarian governance.

THE 1993 CONSTITUTION. The constitution of 1993 provides that the government shall be unitary, representative, and decentralized and organized in accordance with the principle of the separation of powers. The executive branch is composed of the president and two vicepresidents of the republic and the Council of Ministers. By means of emergency decrees having the force of law, and with the obligation to report to Congress, the president has the power to order that extraordinary measures be taken on economic and financial matters and whenever required by the national interest.

According to the letter of the constitution, legislative authority lies with Congress, while the judiciary is made up of jurisdictional organs determined by the constitution. The state guarantees to judges their independence and permanency of tenure. The constitution grants certain judicial powers to the rural and native communities so that they may execute their customary law.

There is, however, a discrepancy between the provisions of the constitution and the practice, as some of these constitutional provisions have not been implemented. There is general acknowledgment that the president and the legislature interfere with the judiciary and that the government remains heavily centralized and bureaucratic. The state of the judicial system is a cause of concern for all Peruvians, including the leadership of the country.

The Human Rights Dimension

INTERNATIONAL INSTRUMENTS. Peru's pledge to protect and promote the human rights of its citizens is reflected in its ratification of most major international human rights and humanitarian law instruments. The extent to which Peru complies with this commitment has direct relevance to the issue of displacement because it influences both whether displacement occurs and whether persons already displaced can return to their homes.

The Peruvian constitution of 1993 includes many provisions for the protection of human rights, and by virtue of Article 55 gives domestic legal force to international instruments ratified by Peru (not constitutional force, however, which the previous constitutions did). By virtue of the fourth transitory provision of the constitution, human rights provisions are to be interpreted in light of the Universal Declaration of Human Rights and the other international human rights instruments. The new constitution's first provisions relate to the fundamental rights of the individual, its first article stipulating: "The defense of the individual and respect for his dignity constitute the supreme purpose of society and the State." In addition, the government on several occasions has stated that it is committed to the protection of human rights.

Despite these international and constitutional guarantees, Peru has been the object of criticism for its human rights record since the early 1980s. The main reasons are discussed below.[11]

STATE OF EMERGENCY AND ANTITERRORIST PROCEDURES. Most serious human rights violations have occurred, and are still occurring, in emergency zones.[12] A state of emergency was declared for the first time in 1981 and since then has been in force off and on in many parts of the country.[13] As soon as the military assumed the direction of the counterinsurgency war in 1982, thousands of people "disappeared" or were massacred, raped, or tortured by military and police forces. These acts appear to have been part of the strategies to erase the threat of "communism," but they were underpinned by racism and contempt. Forcible conscription by the military in rural areas is thought to be still going on at this writing, and it is estimated that 4,000 minors are members of the self-defense committees. In the emergency zones the judiciary seems to be particularly constrained, and the possibility of obtaining an effective legal remedy is practically nonexistent. This judicial vacuum is filled by the "law" of the self-defense committees, the armed opposition groups, or the military authorities.

Although under both the 1979 and the 1993 constitutions the declaration of a state of emergency does not suspend the exercise of habeas corpus or *amparo* proceedings, in practice these proceedings were rendered ineffective.[14] During the days following the 1992 coup d'état, the entire judicial system was brought to a halt and the right to habeas corpus was practically suspended. In 1998 the judiciary has regained neither its permanent tenure nor its independence.

In addition, the government of President Fujimori resorted to antiterrorist substantive and procedural legislation for two types of offenses: ordinary terrorist offenses and the offense of treason. Those charged with treason, even civilians, are tried by military "faceless courts."[15] Civilians accused of terrorism are tried by civilian "faceless courts." At the time of the representative's visit, this practice was scheduled to ease in October 1995, although a new law postponed the change.[16] Military courts also try officers of the armed forces when they are accused of having violated human rights, even though, in principle, common crimes fall under the jurisdiction of civilian courts.

One decree, the so-called "repentance law" (no. 25499), repealed in November 1994, allowed for anyone except armed opposition leaders to "clear their past" by "repenting" and "cooperating" with the authorities. As a result, those eager to absolve themselves implicated as many as 3,000 reportedly innocent civilians in terrorism cases. Many *requisitoria-*

dos, as those who have pending cases against them are known, are internally displaced persons.[17]

These procedures drew severe criticism of the government for not conforming with fair trial standards, for permitting the unjustified arrest, conviction, and prolonged detention of civilians, and for applying different standards to army officers, who are rarely prosecuted, tried, or sentenced for crimes.

In addition, in the summer of 1995 Congress promulgated two laws, collectively known as amnesty laws, which (1) granted general amnesty to the staff of security forces implicated, or even already tried and sentenced, for acts related to the fight against terrorism since 1980; and (2) prohibited judges from declaring the law unconstitutional. These two laws have been heavily criticized by international human rights organizations and the local human rights community for entrenching impunity, impairing the rule of law and the principle of equality of all citizens before the law, and undermining the independence of the judiciary.[18] Government leaders have pointed out that the law was justified by the need for reconciliation and the psychological trauma suffered by individuals in the army and the police during the war. They have claimed that such amnesty laws have contributed to reconciliation in other countries and are in line with previous actions by the government to pardon 5,000 terrorists (through the "repentance law").[19] They also have noted that no one has criticized the pardoning of the terrorists and in this connection have expressed mistrust of the human rights and other international organizations who, they say, did not denounce the brutality of the Shining Path during the first twelve years of the war but were always keen to defend the "human rights" of the terrorists.[20]

Others have pointed out that in the long run the amnesty laws do not contribute to reconciliation. They are not blanket amnesties for the entire population, as amnesty laws are usually understood to be, but benefit specific individuals in the military. In addition, the "repentance law," which was repealed in the meantime, did not automatically grant amnesty to those suspected of or sentenced for terrorism, but required them to "prove" their repentance through questionable means. Moreover, it did not apply to the leaders of the armed opposition groups. Polls conducted at the time of the representative's visit estimated that 66 percent of the population was opposed to the amnesty laws.

Aside from all of the legal and moral arguments that can be invoked against the amnesty laws, all measures that tolerate human rights violations and encourage a climate of impunity and insecurity impair efforts to bring peace and discourage the internally displaced from returning to their areas of origin.

Peruvian human rights NGOs recognize that political violence, including extrajudicial executions and disappearances, has decreased significantly since 1993. Nevertheless, violations of the right to life by law enforcement personnel and members of the self-defense committees have been reported.[21] Arbitrary detention of persons suspected of "subversion" and "terrorism" continue to occur, and there are fears that torture is being used widely in violation of constitutional and procedural guarantees.[22] It has been reported that minors have also been subjected to such procedures.[23] Government leaders, while expressing sympathy for some of these concerns, dismiss others and maintain that the critics are interested in defending the human rights of terrorists without regard for the welfare of the rest of the population.

General statements by the leadership of the state implying that human rights monitors, journalists, academics, political activists, environmental activists, defense lawyers, NGOs, and social leaders are implicated with "terrorists" have greatly increased the chances that such persons may be prosecuted unfairly and condemned or otherwise persecuted.[24] Those who raise human rights issues continue to be harassed, and people are being effectively silenced.[25]

Officials stress the role of the Office of the Attorney General (Fiscalia) in protecting human rights, in particular through its computerized registry of detainees and its power to visit police stations and military bases to monitor the conditions in which the detainees are held. They also mention the importance of the role of the ombudsman, an office created by the 1993 constitution, whose legal framework has been defined in Legislative Decree no. 52, passed in August 1995.

However, members of the government and other officials, including the president, observed that the judicial system had always been corrupt and inefficient and that little had changed. The sheer backlog of cases pending in the courts accounts for lengthy detentions and the unfair treatment of many innocent citizens.[26] The Fiscalia has limited powers and capacity, and judges are not encouraged to act independently. For instance, judges who enforce human rights law themselves risk prosecution.[27]

ECONOMIC, SOCIAL, AND CULTURAL RIGHTS.[28] Although large segments of the population continue to live in poverty, especially in the interior of the country, there have been some signs of improvement since the early 1990s. For instance, inflation that had been higher than 7,000 percent was at 15 percent during the representative's visit in 1995, and the negative growth in GNP of the 1980s had been replaced by a positive growth of 12 percent. Unemployment and underemployment, however, had soared because of the downsizing of the public sector and the lack of absorption by the private sector. It is estimated that, in real terms, per capita GDP was equal to that in 1961.[29]

The disparities between urban and rural areas in the enjoyment of economic, social, and cultural rights are striking. For instance, in 1995 there were approximately 18,707 health workers (doctors and nurses) in Lima, but only 1,268 in Junin and 315 in Ayacucho, to mention two of the departments the representative visited.[30] Insufficient health care in some departments has resulted in the persistence, and in some areas an increase, of cholera, tuberculosis, and other infectious and parasitic diseases.

Infant mortality rates have improved significantly, although they remain high in the central Sierra. It is estimated that 60 percent of all families in these areas have between six and nine children.[31] More than one third of the population are minors, and this group has increased by 2 million since the 1970s, making demand for food, health services, and education even more critical.

The illiteracy rate in Peru decreased from 58 percent in 1940 to 18 percent in 1981. Nevertheless, as pointed out by NGOs and supported by a government report, illiteracy has not decreased in the departments of Ayacucho, Huancavelica, Cuzco, and Puno, where most of the population are Quechua speakers.[32] Since 1989 some Ashaninka communities have received no education at all. Also, women are disproportionately illiterate, particularly in the rural areas.[33]

Despite the fact that 5 million Peruvians speak Quechua, it is not an official language. That those people have little access to state mechanisms, including the judicial system, has been pointed out by government officials: it is sometimes difficult to find interpreters, let alone judges and public attorneys who speak Quechua. Similar problems exist with regard to the other languages. No policies exist on bilingual education. As a result, children grow up being taught only in Spanish, and parents avoid speaking to their children in their mother tongue because the use of indigenous languages is frequently ridiculed by the rest of society. Women speak Spanish less frequently than men and for this reason suffer disproportionate discrimination in their encounters with the authorities or when searching for work, including domestic work and petty trading.

The government has introduced social welfare projects to counterbalance the effects of structural adjustment and has attempted to improve living conditions in the rural and marginalized areas by ameliorating its transportation and communications infrastructure and building schools and health centers. The president personally has taken the lead in this effort to reach out to those segments of the population that were for centuries abandoned and exploited. Officials stress that once peace has been achieved, development is the next task of the government and that the government's political will to address the needs of the citizens is firm. They emphasize, however, that the government's resources are not sufficient.[34] Leaders of civil society and NGOs told the representative that frequently what had been pledged by the central government was prevented from reaching the communities by bureaucratic structures and attitudes that contribute to corruption and mismanagement. They also mentioned that the government's measures are for the most part sporadic and populist.[35]

CONSEQUENCES OF ARMED OPPOSITION ACTIVITIES FOR THE ENJOYMENT OF HUMAN RIGHTS. International law applies only in certain limited instances to nonstate actors, such as insurgents, and establishes individual responsibility only for certain war crimes and crimes against humanity, as well as certain violations of international humanitarian law, in particular of common Article 3 of the Geneva Conventions of 1949 and Protocol II Additional to the Geneva Conventions. Even so, the Shining Path has declared its opposition to the concept of human rights, which it labels reactionary, counterrevolutionary, and bourgeois weapons of revisionists and imperialists.[36]

As local and international human rights NGOs have observed repeatedly, the Shining Path is generally considered to be alone among Latin American guerrilla groups in its ferocious treatment of a population whose interests it claims to promote. Its members have been responsible for numerous massacres; its leaders are known to target communities that have refused to take sides or have joined (voluntarily or not) civil defense patrols. Community leaders have been executed after being summarily "tried" in "popular trials." Villages are reported to have been burned to the ground, and the inhabitants, including women and children, tortured and brutally killed.[37] Sexual violations have also been reported. Forcible recruitment is still practiced, and it is estimated that a thousand minors are attached to subversive groups. Attacks against security forces and civilians by the Shining Path and the MRTA continue to be reported, particularly in the central *selva*.[38] The Shining Path's treatment of the Ashaninka and other native communities has been particularly harsh. Entire communities were forcibly relocated or placed in virtual slavery.[39] In the province of Satipo, the Shining Path caused intraethnic and intratribal conflicts and managed to divide some of the communities. In the words of a community worker, there were times when people were either "Ashaninka-*senderos* or Ashaninka-*ronderos*."

Between 1988 and 1992 the Shining Path became increasingly active in metropolitan Lima. It spread terror among the population with several attacks, including car bombs that caused heavy casualties and killings of its opponents in the shantytowns.[40]

The government has labeled all members of the Shining Path and the MRTA terrorists and continues its relentless efforts to track them down and eradicate the movements. This strategy is supported publicly by many members of the civil society; privately, however, some point out that the Shining Path rose out of the structural problems of the country and that the merciless treatment of those suspected of being affiliated with it is frequently unfair. Although the government, especially in the person of the president, appears to be reaching out to the poor and the marginalized communities, there is no willingness to recognize the link between rebel violence and the structural problems and inequities of the system.

The Internally Displaced

Displacement in Peru is a direct consequence of conflict, poverty, ethnic divisions, and disrespect for human rights. The poorest and most violent departments, Ayacucho, Huancavelica and Apurimac, as well as the *selva* of the Río Ene and the Río Huallaga valleys, are those from which people fled in the greatest numbers.[41]

Estimated Number of Displaced, Zones, and Phases of Displacement

The consensus is that there are several hundred thousand internally displaced persons. The most commonly quoted figure is 600,000, although some believe it may be as high as a million.[42] Most are women and children.[43] According to official sources, 54 percent of the persons displaced during the twelve years between 1981 and 1993 moved within their own departments, and the rest moved elsewhere.[44]

Today, the internally displaced are more willing to identify themselves as such. Previously, they avoided being singled out for fear that they would be suspected by both the army and the armed opposition as deserters who had joined the other side. They are more inclined to say where they come from, especially when they might benefit from programs designed to address their needs.[45] NGOs working with internally displaced persons in the cities have been able to "map" the most significant concentrations.

As mentioned previously, rural to urban migration and to the *selva* due to the poverty and marginalization of the rural areas has been extensive in the past fifty years. Increasingly, however, especially after 1980, many of the persons who moved were compelled to because of the violence and persecution they faced. In the conflict zones, large areas were depopulated and many villages and settlements were abandoned or razed. In the Sierra, the displaced tend to move first to areas near their communities or to the provincial capitals, and as a last resort to the capital. In the *selva* they tend to gather around larger communities. Those with relatives in the cities were among the first to arrive in the shanty towns, creating clusters of families with the same geographic origin. Today, entire neighborhoods maintain many of the customs and community structures of their inhabitants' native regions.

There are seven main zones of displacement:[46]

- The departments of Ayacucho, Huancavelica, and Apurimac, in particular the northern provinces of Ayacucho: these were highly conflictive areas, and among the poorest in the country. Ayacucho was the epicenter of violence and the department in which most displacement occurred. People have fled to the provincial capitals of Huamanga, Huancayo, Huancavelica, and Ica, or to Lima. At this writing, most of these areas are relatively peaceful, although pockets of armed dissidents are still present.
- The Alto Huallaga valley: This is one of the most dangerous areas because of the infiltration of the Shining Path and its increasing control over coca trafficking. Displacement affects mostly small landholders and traders. It is estimated that 70 percent of all displaced from the area have left their homes between 1993 and 1995.

- The Valley of the Río Mantaro and the zone of Viscatán: for a time, this zone was under the virtual command of the armed dissidents. One Shining Path faction still retains a presence. Forced migrations to Huancayo began in 1988 and still continue, although to a lesser extent.
- The valleys of the Río Ene and the Río Tambo: populated by native peoples, in particular the Ashaninkas, this area of the *selva* came under the control of the Shining Path, who practically enslaved the population. Those who managed to escape (approximately 5,000) gathered around the communities that had been able to defend themselves or fled to Huancayo and even Lima.
- The so-called *corredor norte*, which includes areas of various departments in the north of the country.
- The *corredor sur-andino*, which covers areas of the Cuzco and Puno departments.
- Lima, and some areas north of the department of Lima, where subversive and countersubversive activity was frequent in the last few years of the conflict.

Each area has a different "scenario" of displacement. The protection needs of the displaced and returning communities, as well as needs associated with shelter, food, and health, vary from region to region and require specific approaches.[47]

Until 1986 most of the displaced came from the southern highlands and were peasants from isolated villages. Some were also town dwellers and professionals from small towns. After 1986 violence spread to a much wider area, displacing people from a variety of ethnic and geographic backgrounds.

The capture of Guzmán in 1992 and the general weakening of the Shining Path, as well as intolerable living conditions in some receiving cities, encouraged many people to return to their areas of origin or to start making plans to do so. Those most willing to return have been persons who remained closer to their homes or left them only a short time earlier. Most returns have taken place in the departments of Ayacucho and Huancavelica, and to a lesser extent in Apurimac and Junin. The representative visited communities of returnees both in Ayacucho and in Junin and noted their satisfaction with having returned; he also observed, however, their apprehension about their future, in particular the precariousness of their security and economic welfare.

Issues Related to the Human Rights of the Displaced

EQUALITY AND NONDISCRIMINATION. According to official sources, 70 percent of all internally displaced persons in Peru belong to indigenous and native communities.[48] These communities have been traditionally disadvantaged in Peru, and their social conditions have not improved. Those who have taken refuge in the cities, where the environment is alien and the language spoken is not one in which they are fluent, suffer even greater prejudice and social marginalization. Very little integration takes place in the cities because most of the displaced and the migrants from the rural areas live in shantytowns. In addition, displaced peasants from the "red zones" (areas with a large presence of guerrilla groups) have been prime suspects of terrorism by the police. When the Shining Path was active in Lima, these persons were suspected by the armed dissidents of being government sympathizers as well. Native communities in the *selva* that the representative visited were particularly bitter about the state's disinterest; the chief of one displaced community pointed out that the government had called them to fight the Shining Path but had no interest in getting to know them and their customs, did not encourage education in, and use of, their language, and supported only the Spanish-speaking *colonos* (settlers, or persons migrating to the *selva* from other areas, usually the highlands).

Women especially have difficulty finding employment, in particular because they usually have no education and no command of Spanish. One study undertaken in a Lima slum showed that 89 percent of the displaced who were completely illiterate were women.[49] Most of these women remain isolated in the shantytowns.[50] NGOs providing assistance to the displaced noted that the cultural barriers between them and the displaced women make it difficult to provide psychosocial support.

PERSONAL SECURITY. With the reduction in armed opposition activity, the displaced generally enjoy greater security, both in their areas of refuge and in their areas of origin (if they return). Concerns remain, however, about personal security, mostly relating to occasional abuses of authority by the security forces or the self-defense committees, killings and other violations by the Shining Path, and the high incidence of domestic violence.

Many persons still remain unaccounted for, in particular those who were forcibly recruited by the armed opposition groups. In the central *selva*, entire communities disappeared.[51] Many who have reappeared escaped from the Shining Path or were "retrieved" by the *rondas*. These so-called *recuperados* return in a deplorable state of physical and mental health and relate stories of servitude and inhuman treatment at the hands of the Shining Path. Nevertheless, many are perceived as "repentant terrorists." There also remain outstanding cases of persons who "disappeared" during the war. The representative met with a number of persons in Ayacucho whose relatives "disappeared" and who have been unable to find out what has happened to them since the early 1980s. They said that initial investigations implicating the military had been blocked and that the prosecutor handling them had fled the country.

Since the beginning of the war, women have been perceived as "less useful" or "dangerous" by the agents of violence. At the same time, many women have been in the forefront of the fight for better protection of the human rights of their husbands, sons, and daughters, for which they have paid dearly. In areas of refuge, displaced women are continuously exposed to abuse and sexual aggression.[52] During the first decade of the conflict, both sides raped and abused women in the emergency zones and during detentions and interrogations.[53] In some areas, women who work in the fields still face significant security risks. Women who belong to indigenous and native communities, human rights activists, members of teachers' and students' unions, and leaders of displaced communities are at high risk of being targeted and victimized by both sides to the conflict.

Domestic violence among displaced and returnee families was routinely mentioned as a problem during the representative's visit, even though the topic is extremely sensitive among the indigenous and peasant communities. Women attributed such violence to the unemployment of their husbands and to alcoholism. Alcoholism and violence among children are becoming increasingly evident; of particular concern is the extremely aggressive behavior of minors who were forcibly recruited by the armed opposition groups or the self-defense committees.

Rape and domestic violence were, and continue to be, chronic problems. However, there have been very few denunciations filed at the office of the Fiscalia, probably because of the strong social stigma attached to the victims of such acts.[54]

PERSONAL LIBERTY. During the representative's mission, it was repeatedly mentioned that many displaced persons were being held arbitrarily in prisons either without formal charge or while awaiting trial. Others with cases pending against them were prevented from returning to their homes. These are the so-called *requisitoriados*, or persons who are being searched for. In many cases, the arbitrary and prolonged detentions of persons suspected of terrorism are due to misunderstandings or error such as the incorrect identification of suspects or confusion in the recording of procedural data.

SUBSISTENCE. The abject poverty of the displaced in Peru was made evident to the representative during brief visits to Huachipa on the outskirts of Lima, to San Felipe in Huamanga, and to San Martín de Pangoa in the province of Satipo. In none of these areas, or for that matter in many of the returnee sites, was there electricity, potable water, or a sewage system. People said that they needed clothes, farming tools and seeds, and materials to rebuild their destroyed homes. In general, long lists of basic needs were recounted at every stop of the representative's mission. The government nutrition program, PRONAA (Programa Nacional de Apoyo Alimentario, or National Program for Food Support), has expanded, but much remains to be done.

In some cases, as many as 80 percent of the displaced indigenous and native communities suffer from malnutrition. Lack of nutritional diversity appears to be one cause. For instance, the Ashaninka displaced communities at San Martín de Pangoa used to hunt, fish, and grow coca and coffee, not only for subsistence purposes but also for trade. However, in San Martín they were able to grow just yucca, in quantities sufficient only to feed themselves. During the first year of displacement, before the first yucca harvest, many of the displaced died of hunger.[55] During the next two years, the yucca cultivation provided some relief; however, the quality of the land gradually deteriorated. One reason why many displaced and migrant families prefer not to return to their home areas is the greater food diversity in the urban centers.

Housing is a serious problem for all of the displaced communities. All are crowded. In San Felipe, Huamanga, the displaced live in mud huts, with roofs made out of plastic or tin sheeting. There was no running water until a week before the representative's visit there, when a water tap was installed. In Huachipa, Lima, the huts are made out of mud bricks or plastic and housed both people and animals. Both areas are arid, with extreme amounts of dust that aggravate the generally unhealthy living conditions. In addition, many settlements are built on land claimed by others. The Huachipa settlement is in an area full of archaeological sites, and the displaced are being threatened with eviction. In San Martín de Pangoa, near Satipo, displaced families lived in wooden huts. Sometimes as many as twelve people occupied one hut. Some members of the family slept on the ground, leaving the space under the mosquito net for the children. Often, widows who could not build their own huts had to sleep outside, where they faced obvious health and security risks.

A lack of basic medication and health care was evident. Respiratory and other infectious diseases, diarrhea and dysentery, chronic deficiency diseases, malaria, and psychological ailments plagued large parts of the rural and *selva* areas.[56] The risk is aggravated when displacement occurs. For instance, following their displacement, the Ashaninka community at San Martín de Pangoa lost access to its traditional medicines found in higher parts of the *selva* and could no longer adequately address the health needs of its members. Similarly, the Andean populations that moved to the coastal cities suffered from respiratory diseases because they were unaccustomed to the humidity and pollution of the towns. Ashaninka women who have babies at a very young age face gynecological problems that were not being addressed. Encouragingly, some family planning programs, which the government supports, were being implemented by NGOs through women's organizations in Ayacucho. The health sector director of Ayacucho also mentioned that health teams had begun visiting marginalized urban areas regularly and providing health kits and some basic health training, through a program supported by UNICEF and the Médicos sin Fronteras.[57]

Children in the rural areas already suffer the highest mortality and malnutrition rates.[58] Displaced children in these areas are at even greater risk, and their flight often puts them beyond the reach of the few government or NGO programs that exist, such as vaccination campaigns and feeding programs.[59] Infant and maternal mortality among the displaced are thought to be much higher, and malnutrition of displaced infants and children is widespread. Moreover, many displaced children witnessed the murder of their parents or the destruction of their homes. As a consequence, they suffer from depression, nightmares, and fear. Psychosocial assistance, however, through which a child can be encouraged to discuss his or her experiences, is severely limited, and parents, caught in the day-to-day struggle for survival, often have little energy for them.[60]

MOVEMENT-RELATED NEEDS. At this writing, freedom of movement in the country appears to be much less restricted than during the war years, when flight was obstructed by military and police checkpoints, return to the "red zones" was impossible, and forced relocation to civil bases was reportedly taking place. An issue of even greater concern that was raised during the representative's mission was the pressure being exerted by the government on some communities to return to their home areas despite precarious security conditions and unsustainable living conditions. Some communities even have been encouraged to return in order to monitor the reaction of the armed opposition groups. At least one returnee community in the *selva* reportedly was returned before the end of the school year, causing children to lose the year (there was no school in the area of return), and after the harvest had finished so that the returnees had no means of supporting themselves. Some died of hunger as a result.

PERSONAL DOCUMENTATION. Many of the displaced do not have personal documentation such as a birth certificate, the *libreta electoral* (the booklet recording participation in elections), which is used as an identity document, or the *libreta militar* (the military registration card). In Huanuco, for example, it was estimated in 1995 that 25 percent of the displaced men and 35 percent of the displaced women over the age of eighteen lacked at least one, and in some cases all, of the documents mentioned above.[61] In the past, soldiers and armed dissidents confiscated identification documents as a form of intimidation. Many displaced persons lost their documents during their flight or destroyed them. Without these papers, official documents cannot be procured, jobs in the formal sector cannot be obtained, and bank transactions cannot be performed. Persons lacking personal documentation are immediately suspect, especially during roundups in the shantytowns. Some schools refuse to register children without birth certificates. Males who do not have a *libreta militar* are subject to conscription.

For years, NGOs have asked the government to address the problem. In 1989 the promulgation of Law 25025 established a special procedure for persons without birth certificates to obtain them, even in areas other than their home areas. However, this special procedure was repealed by

Law 26497, which established a national registry of identification and civil status.

PROPERTY AND LAND ISSUES. The issue of land was raised repeatedly during the representative's mission. According to Article 88 of the Constitution, the state protects the citizen's right to own land. Some, however, believe that land reforms are still necessary. Abandoned lands become state property and can be sold. Lands that are abandoned because of violence also become state property, unless an exemption is granted by the regional agrarian authority.[62] To obtain such an exemption, a certification by the military or police about the violent incident is required, as well as proof of title; frequently, though, those fleeing cannot obtain the documents. In addition, there is no systematized information about the status of many lands since 1980. It is estimated that only 30 percent of those who own land hold title to it. Some of the displaced have moved onto the property of others and are threatened with eviction; some of those who did not flee have taken over the land of those who did. Many of the displaced have no way of proving their property rights. Numerous cases are pending before the courts, but the problems are not being solved promptly or efficiently.

Under the old constitutional regime, lands belonging to communities rather than individual owners were excluded from the registration and ownership regimes. Under the new constitution, this is no longer the case. As a consequence, communal lands can be declared abandoned if not farmed for more than two years. According to the native communities the representative met with, this legal regime does not take into account that the forest agriculture sustainable in the *selva* requires a migratory or shifting type of cultivation. In addition, Law 26505, promulgated on July 18, 1995, allows these lands to be sold. Some fear that the poorest communities will be tempted to sell land for cash and thus lose their most important resource.

Indigenous communities in Peru have preserved to a large extent their traditional living patterns and customs. In the past several decades, however, the war and the displacement have disrupted traditional patterns of land use and have led to greater deterioration of the environment and a significant decrease in agricultural production.[63]

The native communities feel that the authorities do not take into account their ancestral land and property rights and take no interest in the preservation of their cultural heritage. They feel in some cases that road construction and other infrastructure projects have the potential to further erode their communities. Such fears were pervasive in the native communities of the *selva* that have traditionally and for ecological reasons had communitarian ownership of their lands.[64] Paradoxically, the communities the representative met expressed a desire for a stronger government presence. The infrastructure that this requires, however, will bring with it a number of adverse consequences, such as increased in-migration and pressure on land.

One of the most serious problems brought to the representative's attention during his visit to the Río Tambo and Río Ene valleys was the incipient conflict between the Ashaninka communities and the *colonos*, or settlers, who had migrated from the Sierra in search of more fertile lands. Because many of the native lands remain unregistered, settlers were able to take possession of them. This may mean that some of the Ashaninka communities may not be able to return there. Some of the settlers grow coca plants and have become involved with drug trafficking, in some cases forming alliances with the armed opposition groups.[65] Such is the case in particular in the Alto Huallaga valley, and the Ashaninkas fear that drugs and crime might move into the central *selva* as well.[66] It is possible that new conflicts may cause further displacement. Government officials also identified health problems among the *colonos* in the *selva* and noted the disequilibrium they caused in the environment, which in turn created health risks for the native communities.[67] During the representative's visit, the authorities in Satipo acknowledged the enormity of the problem and said that some first steps were being taken to organize a consultation process to find solutions.

FAMILY AND COMMUNITY VALUES. One of the most challenging problems among the displaced is the disintegration of families and communities. Large numbers of widows and orphans lived in every displaced or returnee community the representative visited. For instance, in Puerto Ocopa, a returnee community of 850 persons, most of the adults were women and 50 percent of the population were children; seventy children were orphans. A 1993 study in the marginal urban areas of Ayacucho revealed that of a total of 1,171 families, two hundred were headed by widows and another ninety-five by mothers whose husbands disappeared or were forcibly recruited.[68] Many children had lost one or both parents, either because they had died or because the family had been scattered. Some orphans were taken care of in institutions sponsored by the Catholic Church or in state-sponsored orphanages. However, these institutions existed only in major cities. Practically no state assistance was available in rural areas.

Displaced children frequently develop antisocial and secretive behaviors and learn to be ashamed of their origin and language. The family environment also suffers because of the climate of insecurity and fear and the frequent absence of the father. One study among displaced persons in Ayacucho concluded that 93.1 percent of all families experienced communication breakdown, intolerance, authoritarianism, violence, and aggression.[69]

Conflicts sometimes arise between the returnees and those who did not flee and between the *recuperados* and their families. In group therapy workshops in Lima, displaced women said they experienced indifference and hostility in the urban setting even in their own communities. At the same time, numerous communities have more or less remained together through displacement and have maintained many of their cultural traditions. This helps to alleviate the acute problems of loss of family and community and facilitates the process of return to the areas of origin.

The involvement of the military in rural areas contributed to the erosion of the community authorities in the area of law and justice. Traditional leadership structures have changed and in some cases have become surprisingly more democratic.

SELF-RELIANCE. Unemployment is a major problem affecting the displaced. Because they usually have no access to credit, the displaced have trouble establishing any sort of business to generate income. When they are able to find work, it is in the informal sector, where they are easily exploited. According to one NGO working in Huachipa, many displaced persons, including children, work in mud brick factories, where salaries reach twenty-two to fifty dollars per week for twelve-hour working days. Others work in construction. In fact, those who find such jobs are considered to be fortunate, since they have an income.

Many displaced women complained about having to do everything on their own because their husbands had been killed, had disappeared, or were constantly on patrol (*"están siempre rondeando"*). Women have managed to support each other through mothers' clubs (*clubes de madres*), communal kitchens (*comedores populares*), and other grassroots women's organizations. By buying food in bulk and cooking in large quantities, they have managed to improve the food and health of their families and communities and also to start small businesses that sew and sell blouses, skirts, and other garments. They frequently organize cultural events and have managed to gain the respect of their husbands, who initially objected to these activities. Formidable women leaders have emerged from these organizations. In addition to income-generating projects, women the representative met said that they would like funds to be channeled to their organizations in order to help the most needy among them. They also hope for legal recognition so that they can apply for loans from the government and private banks.

Despite the serious economic problems facing displaced families, many try to enroll their children in the public education system in the cities, which in Peru is an important source of government-sponsored nutrition programs and health care. Public education is officially free; but because many schools are underfunded and others have been destroyed or closed, parents must pay tuition so that the schools can operate. Other displaced children have had to help support their families rather than attend school, and in any event, many do not possess the personal documentation, such as a birth certificate, that is necessary to register. Those who do manage to enroll but do not speak much Spanish cannot communicate well with their teachers. Many have to restart their schooling upon arrival in the cities because the quality of education they received in the rural areas was much lower. The traumatic experiences, isolation, loss of cultural reference points, and psychological fragility of many families, however, lead to problems that account for a very high number of dropouts among the displaced.

Prospects for Return and Alternative Settlement

People's desire to return to their areas of origin has been fully encouraged by the government and the donor community. However, lack of security and sustainable living conditions often inhibit return, impair return projects, and cause new displacements. The lack of schools in the return areas, in particular, is a serious disincentive to return. Such risks are compounded by the traditionally high mobility of the population for farming or other purposes, difficulties gaining access to remote areas, and the institutional weakness of the state, which is not in a position to prevent the militarization of social activities.

Aware of these risks, the government has established a program to support returnees, PAR, and has undertaken a number of infrastructure projects, particularly concerning roads, schools, and health centers, to help improve the living conditions in some rural areas. The government has solicited the assistance of some donor governments and international agencies to strengthen its efforts, including church organizations, domestic NGOs, the International Organization for Migration (IOM), the United Nations Development Programme (UNDP), and others. In particular, in 1995 IOM designed a project to facilitate the return of 25,000 persons over a period of three years. To prevent future displacement, IOM interviewed potential returnees before their move and placed monitoring staff in the area of return for a minimum of three weeks. It also installed a medical post and an electrical cable and constructed a road.

Generally speaking, the IOM studies conducted through 1994 and 1995 showed that any return project should have the following components:[70]

- identification of potential returnees;
- selection of the communities whose return would be promoted, taking into account the level of security in the zone and the minimum conditions of reconstruction of the infrastructure and social fabric;
- implementation of a health program before the return;
- initiation of psycho-emotional assistance before the return;
- human rights promotion;
- organized transfer of communities;
- reintegration in the areas of origin preceded by an evaluation (on the part of communal authorities and executive entities, public and private) of the minimum requirements for self-sustenance and self-protection, as well as of the possibility of detecting imminent conflicts;
- continuation of education;
- medical attention;
- implementation of community works of reconstruction;
- technical assistance for agricultural production;
- reinforcement of social relations through conflict resolution organs;
- integration of mid-term development programs to alleviate poverty.

In addition, the IOM studies recommended that laws be amended to provide for those who lack personal documentation and to provide procedures for the adjudication of land claims, for the demilitarization of the *rondas,* and for the creation of democratic institutions for the resolution of conflicts. Similar suggestions were contained in a study sponsored by the UN High Commissioner for Refugees (UNHCR), which was conducted in 1993 and 1994 by the Andean Commission of Jurists.[71]

One serious problem is the perception by some of those who remained in their areas that those who fled are deserters. Some feel that they defended their lands through the worst of the war and that they should have claim to the property of those who took "the easy way out."[72] The displaced, on the other hand, feel that they fled for legitimate reasons and that their flight should not affect their property rights. It is unclear whether those who have not yet returned to their communities will be able to reclaim their property or whether the lands in question will be redistributed.

Government and agency projects have been able to meet only a small fraction of the enormous needs. For instance, in August 1995 there were 579 PAR community centers in four departments, covering approximately 250,000 persons. This figure covers not only displaced persons but also entire communities. Thus the vast majority of returnees are not reached by government programs, especially those in communities that are difficult to access, such as many remote highland areas and native communities in the *selva*. PAR officials had never been seen in Satipo before the arrival of the representative in August 1995. Returnee communities in the Río Ene valley in particular complained that they had been "dumped" in their home areas and abandoned, without receiving the assistance they had been promised.

Approximately half of the displaced prefer to stay in their urban settlements, despite the harsh, degrading conditions there, because of the availability of services such as schools and nutrition facilities.[73] In addition, many of the younger displaced have little interest in life in the rural areas.

Some of the displaced expressed their reluctance to again become parties to a conflict that is not theirs. Forced to take sides during the years of the war, many of the displaced refuse to join the self-defense committees and do not want to risk being forcibly conscripted by the armed opposition groups. Many also fear arbitrary arrests or reprisals, since for many years those who left were suspected of being Shining Path supporters or members. For these reasons, some of the displaced criticized the government's emphasis on return, which has resulted in implicit and explicit attempts by the authorities to coerce some communities to return. Others criticized the lack of consultation with organizations of the displaced and the emphasis on large infrastructure projects rather than family and community rehabilitation programs.

At this writing, it appears that the government has not given serious thought to the permanent settlement of displaced persons in the areas in which they have sought refuge. The only government agency specifically assisting some displaced persons, PAR, supports only returnee communities. The government mentioned that those who opt for settlement in the areas in which they now live or any other area of the country (hereafter referred to as alternative settlement) would benefit from general social welfare programs. The displaced, however, believe they require qualitatively different attention and support, which is not available through existing government projects, to which they in any case have limited access. In addition, safety net programs in Peru, such as FONCODES, do not appear to be particularly effective.[74]

Measures Taken by the Government

PAR. Until the early 1990s, no action had been taken by the government to address the problems of internally displaced persons. In 1991 the National Technical Commission for the Problem of Displaced Populations was formed by the Council of Ministers.[75] UNDP financed the contracting of consultants and field visits for the first report of the commission, which was presented to the president of the Council of Ministers in April 1992; in September an operational plan was presented. As a follow-up to this process, PAR was created in October 1993 to address the return of displaced persons to their places of origin. PAR is part of the National Institute for Development (Instituto Nacional de Desarrollo, or INADE) and focuses on investing in infrastructure and to a limited extent emergency relief. Its chief defines it as a social development project to support those who were displaced by terrorist violence and who want to return to their areas of origin. Its projects are primarily in four departments: Huancayo, Ayacucho, Apurimac, and Huancavelica. At a later stage, PAR plans to start projects also in Puno, Huanuco, Ucayali, Cajamarca, and Pasco. In April 1994, the PAR Interministerial Committee was established to coordinate the measures taken by the Ministries of Health, Education, Transport, Agriculture, Defense, and Industry and the Office of the President.

Committees with a structure similar to that of the Interministerial Committee of PAR exist in the departments targeted for PAR programs. Their mandate is to respond to all emergency needs in the areas of food, basic health, and education. During the representative's visit, PAR officials mentioned that although PAR had started out as a project to assist returnees, it had become community-based. A constant theme of their presentations was that there were insufficient funds to implement the necessary projects.

Some NGOs mentioned that despite the funds given to PAR and INADE by donor agencies, delivery of services was not substantial and did not reach many communities. Organizations of displaced persons also complained that PAR had not consulted with them despite their better understanding of the basic needs of displaced and returnee communities as well as conditions in their areas of origin.

OTHER EMERGENCY SUPPORT PROGRAMS. A number of other government agencies are mandated to cover emergency and development needs.[76] These include FONCODES, created in 1991, a financial agency charged with administering the state social investment in favor of the poorest sectors of the country; PRONAA, created in February 1992, which has provided some food assistance to the poorest sectors of the population; and the Instituto Nacional de Bienestar Familiar (National Institute for Family Welfare), created in 1981 to evaluate and direct government policy on family welfare matters.[77]

LEGAL STEPS. Before the representative's mission, no concrete steps had been taken to address some of the most critical needs of the displaced. International agencies and NGOs had made a variety of suggestions and submitted draft laws, but no initiatives had been taken. During the mission, the president of the Congressional Commission on Human Rights and Pacification mentioned that a draft law was currently under consideration in the House.

APPROACH TO NGOS. At the time of the representative's visit, the government had no institutional policy of consulting with civil society. In particular, NGOs dealing with human rights issues mentioned that the government's attitude toward them was not only one of exclusion, but also one of hostility. In general there was an impression that the government was reluctant to include in its projects international and local

NGOs, the Church, grass-roots organizations, and even organizations of displaced persons and native and peasant communities.

The Role of the Nongovernmental Community

GRASS-ROOTS ORGANIZATIONS AND ORGANIZATIONS OF THE DIS-PLACED. In Peru, the displaced are organized to a degree not witnessed by the representative in any other country. He spoke to organizations at all levels, including those working for the interests of the displaced, those who have returned, and those who have opted for alternative settlement. These organizations were created during moments of extreme conflict, when both the civilian government and the NGOs had left. Initially, they were very weak and their leaders were always targets of violence. But through local working groups and their federations, the displaced made their voices heard and have contributed to solving their own problems. Among both the indigenous and native communities, formidable leaders impressed the representative with their commitment to their communities and the soundness of their ideas about their future. Women's organizations had managed not only to organize the provision of basic food and medical assistance but also to provide a forum for discussion and social support. In Ayacucho it was estimated that 80,000 women were participating in *clubes de madres*.

RELIEF AND HUMAN RIGHTS ORGANIZATIONS. Church organizations were among the first to provide the displaced with emergency assistance and to encourage them to organize. They have supported both return and settlement projects and have also provided human rights training and legal assistance. In some areas of the country, in particular the *selva*, the church has a stronger presence than the army or the civilian government; during the years of the war, church missions were the only outside presence capable of providing any degree of protection to the victimized native communities. Missionaries paid with their lives for their public opposition to the Shining Path.

Other organizations have provided emergency aid, medical and psychosocial assistance, human rights education, legal defense, and training of community leaders.[78] Many of the NGOs have participated in different coordination initiatives, such as the National Working Group on Displacement.

Nevertheless, the scope of these organizations' activities, even with the support of international NGOs and donor agencies, remains rather limited.

In Ayacucho, for instance, perhaps 20 percent of the population receives some sort of assistance, but not through an integrated assistance program. In the *selva* very few NGOs are present.

Despite the many NGOs in Peru and the high degree of organization in civil society, relationships between the government and the NGOs remain strained and tenuous. The government suspects NGOs of being linked to and supporting the guerrillas. It is skeptical about what it terms the "jungle" of NGOs and is openly hostile to human rights NGOs, which it has publicly declared are suspicious.

An additional cause of concern during the representative's visit was the occasional lack of coordination among local NGOs (including the church organizations) and between local NGOs and the grass-roots organizations of the displaced. Some grass-roots organizations complained that NGOs were patronizing or exploiting them for their own fund-raising purposes or other political objectives.

International Donors and Other Organizations

Until 1991, when the United States Committee for Refugees published its report on the internally displaced in Peru, virtually no international attention had been paid to the problem of internal displacement.[79] Since 1991, UNHCR has undertaken studies of the internally displaced in the context of prevention. It decided not to become directly involved, however, because "the criteria for UNHCR involvement were not met in that, firstly, the situation did not present a link with mandated activities and, secondly, there was no clear indication of humanitarian efforts by other United Nations agencies to which UNHCR's activities could be supplementary."[80] At the same time, it indicated its readiness to become involved if interagency programs were developed dealing with legal documentation, counseling services to prepare displaced persons for return, and public awareness initiatives aimed at mobilizing international funding support.

In 1992, UNDP and the United Nations Development Fund for Women contributed a study on displacement, gender, and development to the government's Technical Commission.[81] Since then, UNDP has provided support to INADE and PAR, and other agencies, such as the World Food Programme, have provided food assistance both to government agencies and to NGOs. UNDP has also undertaken programs for the poor in the amount of $128 million, some of which benefit returnees and internally displaced persons. UNICEF implements a variety of food, health, and education programs for orphaned and displaced children in Ayacucho and the central Amazon region.

IOM's role in Peru has been a significant one. In 1980 the government and IOM concluded an agreement of cooperation that identified internal migration as an important area of cooperation. In 1994, Peru requested technical cooperation from IOM, on the basis of which IOM prepared two reports, published in 1994 and 1995.[82] As mentioned above, IOM has embarked on the implementation of the first phase of a project to assist displaced persons in returning to their home areas.

The International Committee of the Red Cross (ICRC) had a strong presence in Peru throughout the war years. It assisted scores of displaced persons, widows, and orphans in Ayacucho, Apurimac, Huancavelica, San Martín, and Huanuco. The ICRC has provided emergency assistance to displaced persons, when no other resources were available, for periods of two or three months following displacement.

Other donors include Oxfam, which provides funding for local NGOs that promote self-organization among the displaced.[83] The International Council of Voluntary Agencies sponsored a Consultation on Displacement and Refuge in the Andean Region in 1993 that adopted an Andean Declaration on Displacement and Refuge. A Project Counseling Services office, which represents a consortium of Nordic refugee councils (which are NGOs), was subsequently stationed in Lima.

Bilateral cooperation between the government of Peru and other governments also accounts for a number of projects that directly or indirectly benefit the internally displaced.[84] USAID has been the largest donor of food aid to Peru and has provided financial support for a number of human rights projects and return projects of the government.

International organizations have a better dialogue with the central government and with the local military authorities than do local NGOs. However, as many officials in these organizations pointed out during the mission of the representative, coordination among them needs to be improved. A comprehensive approach to implementing the government's policies on internally displaced persons, in particular its emphasis on return, is lacking.

Conclusions

The primary cause for the displacement of as many as a million Peruvians over the past two decades has been the conflict between armed opposition groups and the armed forces of the government. From the brink of nongovernance in the early 1990s, the country at this writing has returned to nearer normal conditions, and hope that life can start up again has been largely restored. As long as the root causes of the violence are not dealt with, however, it is difficult to see how genuine stability will return to the country. Vast areas are still relatively isolated, and economic and social divisions persist among the different ethnic groups.

It is important to recall that the armed opposition gained strength in the most isolated departments that were in states of deepening poverty. Although the Shining Path's elitist ideological policies and the terrorist nature of many of its operations quickly alienated its popular supporters, and although today violence has decreased, it must not be forgotten that the wounds the conflict opened inside many communities will take much longer to heal.

To ensure that the path to peace is irreversible, the government will have to address the structural injustices in rural areas. It will have to include its citizens in such projects, ensure that their human rights are protected and respected, and commit itself to addressing their real needs.

The Participation of Civil Society

Since 1992–93 the government has taken a rigid position, claiming that once terrorism has been defeated development can start, and those displaced because of terrorism can return home. However, as argued forcefully by one displaced leader, the displaced see their displacement and the problems related to it as human rights problems that are caused by the armed dissidents as well as by all the agents of violence and are linked to the underlying causes of the conflict. For this reason they are critical of the government, whose main concern appears to be how to reverse massive migration to the urban centers. The displaced want their organizations to become full interlocutors in decisions affecting them. Where they have managed after years of hard work to adapt to urban life, they want the option to remain there. A dialogue between displaced persons and the government is needed to resolve this issue. Inviting the citizens of Peru to participate in the process toward peace and including them in development projects should become a priority for the government.

Cooperation between the government and the NGOs must be significantly enhanced. NGOs, in collaboration with displaced persons' organizations, are able to extend the reach of assistance into more remote areas. They are also uniquely able to offer community development services aimed at rebuilding the social fabric.

Respect for Human Rights

Legitimacy is the cornerstone of law and order in any country. In the short run, circumvention of the rule of law may appear to be effective in solving structural problems, but in the long term it creates personal insecurity and entrenches unfairness and impunity. Although human rights violations have decreased, there exists a feeling in emergency zones that anything could happen, especially in light of the almost total impunity of the military. This is so because, as some senior government officials admitted to the representative, the parties to the conflict seem likely to maintain the mentality of violence for years to come.

In Peru the leadership distrusts the rule of law and the judiciary, and consequently neither one functions effectively. Ongoing human rights violations must be condemned, and laws that violate international standards (such as the amnesty laws) need to be reconsidered and addressed through more fundamental legal and institutional reforms before they become the source of renewed discontent.

Seeking the cooperation of local human rights organizations that enjoy international respect for their work and expertise (instead of incriminating them) as well as of international specialized institutions should be an element in initiating such reforms.

As for abuses committed by nonstate actors, it must be recalled here that certain of these abuses have been repeatedly denounced by local and international human rights organizations. Enforcement at the international level, however, will remain relatively rare, until states collectively take the necessary steps to ensure international prosecution for such crimes. States have a fundamental responsibility to take all measures possible to protect people who are threatened or victimized by nonstate violence, including measures to prevent the outbreak of such violence.

In general, human rights promotion and protection at the local level are very important. Human rights training in schools, universities, and the armed forces should be improved. The creation of local human rights committees where both state actors and civil society would participate would facilitate both the communication and resolution of cases of human rights violations.

The Impact of Displacement on Indigenous Peoples

The vast majority of the displaced are from indigenous and native communities. Violence and displacement have fundamentally altered their way of life. Even the manner in which they construct their homes and the form in which their communities are physically organized have changed.[85] Psychologists and sociologists working with them have noted that they suffer more than any other social group in the Andean region when they are uprooted, because they lose the links with their lands and traditions. Grief, depression, feelings of guilt, homesickness, and loss of identity are compounded by educational and linguistic barriers, serious health problems, crime, drugs, and insecurity.[86] As a consequence, the displaced have serious difficulties adapting to life in areas of refuge, particularly in the cities.

WOMEN. Women have been affected disproportionately by violence and displacement for many reasons: they belong to marginalized communities; their family units have experienced violence; their subordinate rank in the household subjects them to aggression; their gender makes them vulnerable to gender-based violence; and their participation in organizations triggers persecution. Displacement has given some women new opportunities to organize and play new roles; for most, however, it has entrenched the structures of female subordination. Women who have to sustain their families are often overworked and at high risk of being exploited and abused. The loss of husbands or sons, in addition to the severe effects this has on the emotional well-being and the economic and social position of the women, results in a loss of protection and rights that were previously "accessible" through the husband. In areas of return, where the role of protection is played by the *ronderos*, who are all men, gender inequalities can be acute, and the plight of women is aggravated by the absence or inaccessibility of the official justice system.

CHILDREN. The problems facing displaced children are also grave. The most serious are inadequate opportunities for education, health problems, insufficient family support, difficulties integrating into urban society, and, for returnees, difficulties reintegrating into rural society.

Children who have been conscripted by either side to the conflict and have been traumatized by the violence need specialized attention, especially in the area of psychological rehabilitation and support.

NGOs working with the displaced say that it is necessary for government projects to focus on education, the rehabilitation of families, training and management skills, bilingual education, and psychosocial support. They find small-scale projects to be more beneficial than large infrastructure projects, such as big hospitals and schools. In view of the demonstrated capacity of grass-roots women's organizations such as the *clubes de madres* and the *comedores populares* to address many of these needs, serious consideration should be given to channeling more funds to them. Furthermore, NGOs that have been working for years with the displaced could be relied upon for valuable information and for the implementation of government or agency projects.

Protecting the Internally Displaced

Certain protection problems, while common to many Peruvians, are of particular concern to internally displaced persons. These include issues related to personal documentation, personal liberty, and land.

Lack of personal documentation increases the risk of arbitrary detention, false charges, and forced recruitment by the armed forces. Efforts including the necessary legal reforms must be undertaken to facilitate the registration of displaced persons in their areas of residence and to provide them with the necessary documents. Emphasis should be given to the swift processing and resolution of all cases of *requisitoriados*. The practice of forced recruitment should be abolished and the activities of the self-defense committees should be closely scrutinized.

Efforts to register all lands, to provide property title to those who do not have it, and to enhance the system of adjudication of land disputes, should be accelerated. Equitable policies and sustainable development principles need to be taken into account when making decisions about the ancestral lands of the native communities of the *selva*, and the legal status of these lands should be strengthened and clarified. These communities may have, under emerging international law, restitution, restoration, and compensation rights for the occupation or use of their lands without their free and informed consent, regardless of whether they hold formal property titles.

Devising Preventive Strategies

As areas of the country become more secure and communities begin resuming their lives, it is crucial that they devise their own preventive strategies to defend themselves from new outbreaks of violence. Arming the *rondas* should not be the only way; strengthening community structures and encouraging solidarity and conflict resolution mechanisms might be more effective and constructive. For instance, it appears that the Shining Path was not successful in infiltrating the Aymara-speaking communities because of their strong culture. Displacement in the department of Puno started later than in the Sierra, and the circumstances there have been documented in less detail; it might be useful to explore the reasons for this and suggest possible preventive strategies to be employed by other communities.

Increasing Government Support

Scant support has been provided by the state to the displaced and to its poorest citizens in general. The government was slow and ambivalent in implementing safety net programs when it introduced its austerity measures in the early 1990s; as a result, the welfare of poor communities has deteriorated steadily since then. Although certain programs attempt to reach the most marginalized communities and the president personally has undertaken initiatives in this direction, these efforts are of an ad hoc and almost charitable nature.[87] In addition, deep-rooted centralization means that projects are not targeted enough to the needs of each community and that funds are channeled to them too slowly.

Firmer political will is needed to fund social projects, including those to assist the displaced and returnees. PAR appears to be an underfunded and relatively ineffective agency. However, because it has gained expertise and some recognition, it should be strengthened and supported, and if necessary restructured rather than abolished—especially if it is to attend to the needs of the displaced who opt for settlement in alternative areas, a measure that the representative endorses. Care nevertheless must be taken that such assistance is development oriented and capitalizes on the resources of the communities. Moreover, PAR will have to develop comprehensive strategies that address all human rights concerns.[88] The role of the local administration should also be enhanced, and cooperation with NGOs and grassroots organizations at all levels needs to be strengthened, especially in view of the demonstrated capacity of Peruvian communities to organize themselves.

Despite the continued isolation of many communities, their requests for material support from the government are quite well developed and consistent. The representative was repeatedly asked during his mission to bring their requests for assistance to the attention of the government. Immediate and mid-term needs included food, construction materials, income-generating tools such as sewing machines, clothes, education materials, kerosene stoves and other utensils, and the allocation of space to shelter newly displaced persons.

Return and Alternative Settlement

The authorities stressed that everyone who returned did so voluntarily, and indeed there were few reports that displaced persons had returned against their will, but it must be observed that coercion can take various forms, some more subtle than others. For instance, campaigns that create the impression that there is no other viable option but to return home, or that promise assistance only to returnees, may amount to coercion. Return to unsustainable conditions, however, not only endangers the lives of returnees; it also undermines the return process and can jeopardize the general stability of the country. Equal assistance and protection should, therefore, be provided to those who return to their home areas as well as those who opt for settlement in alternative areas.

In addition, both return and permanent settlement require the gradual integration of organizations of the displaced and returnees into local social organizations, and local organizations need to be informed about the problems of the displaced.

While these processes are going on, it should not be forgotten that emergency assistance will still be required to address the urgent needs of those who are still being displaced by the violence.

In this regard, the frequent coverage of the situation of the displaced and the rural communities in the media, including their needs and their protection concerns, is very productive. Efforts to foster national reconciliation and a greater understanding of the problems of the displaced merit particular praise and should be continued.

It is essential that agencies and donors affirm the principle of voluntary return and the need to assist on equal terms those internally displaced persons who wish to remain where they are now settled. In particular, all agencies involved should make sure that their activities do not endorse wholesale the government's return plans if these plans do not respect the choice of internally displaced persons for alternative areas of settlement.

Adequate safeguards against forcible return should be built into any process preceding return projects.

A Call for International Cooperation

The United Nations should take the lead in encouraging international assistance to the internally displaced in Peru, including both those who are returning to their areas of origin and those who choose to settle in the areas in which they have been living as displaced persons. International aid should address short-term emergency needs but focus primarily on longer-term development needs and on education, which many displaced families see as their main hope for the future.

If the internally displaced were returning home from exile abroad, UNHCR would mobilize international assistance to facilitate the return and reintegration process. In Peru, the UN Office for the Coordination of Humanitarian Affairs (OCHA), in conjunction with the UNDP resident representative, should initiate and coordinate a similar program of international assistance. Initially, a detailed assessment of the needs of the internally displaced should be compiled. The United Nations, in consultation with the government, NGOs, and displaced persons' organizations, could then propose specific projects—both quick-impact projects and longer-term development projects—aimed at addressing those needs. Projects already developed and/or being implemented by the government, IOM, and Peruvian NGOs could serve as models. OCHA could then launch an international appeal for funds to implement the proposed projects. The United Nations should encourage the implementation of such projects through the coordinated efforts of both the government and the private sector. A forum should be established in which the government, NGOs, representatives of displaced persons' organizations, international donors, and other civil institutions would meet regularly to discuss and coordinate their work.

Concluding Comment

The situation in Peru reflects a number of contradictions and paradoxes. On the one hand, the government appears to be concerned about the plight of the marginalized communities, among whom the internally displaced are a particularly vulnerable group. On the other hand, there is a virtual neglect of large communities, including displaced persons and returnees, who remain without state protection and assistance. One reason is that the government lacks the capacity to meet the monumental needs of the people. But existing institutional arrangements and operational strategies for response are also inadequate. Representatives of the United Nations and other donor agencies have indicated that the willingness of the international community to provide assistance will, to a significant degree, depend on the extent to which the government demonstrates a clear political will to respond to the needs of the affected population and sets in place mechanisms for doing so.

Notes

1. Francis M. Deng, *Profiles in Displacement: Peru*, E/CN.4/1996/52/Add.1 (United Nations, Commission on Human Rights, January 4, 1996).

2. Information supplied by the government of Peru to the United Nations. See International Human Rights Instruments, *Core Document Forming Part of the Reports of States Parties: Peru*, HRI/CORE/1/Add.43 (United Nations, 1994), paras. 7ff.

3. Robin Kirk, "The Decade of Chaqwa: Peru's Internal Refugees," U.S. Committee for Refugees, Washington, D.C., May 1991, p. 7.

4. See HRI/CORE/1/Add.43, para. 29.

5. Ibid., para. 31.

6. David Scott Palmer, ed., *The Shining Path of Peru* (New York: St. Martin's, 1992).

7. *Le Monde*, January 1–2, 1995.

8. HRI/CORE/1/Add.43, para. 45.

9. See reports in the Peruvian press, for example, "Senderistas detenidas planeaban recomponer comité regional norte," *El Comercio*, August 26, 1995; and "Mil 800 arrepentidos habrian vuelto a Sendero," *La República*, August 17, 1995.

10. Members of the UN Committee on the Elimination of Racial Discrimination (CERD) expressed serious misgivings at the observations made by the government with regard to these groups and requested more information. See CERD, *Eleventh Periodic Report of Colombia*, CERD/C/225/Add.3 (United Nations, 1994).

11. See also Comisión Inter-Americana de Derechos Humanos (CIDH), "Informe sobre la situación de los derechos humanos en Peru," Costa Rica, 1993.

12. The constitution recognizes two exceptions: in a state of emergency, which is decreed in the event of a disturbance of the peace or internal order, and in a state of siege, imposed in the event of invasion, external war or civil war, or imminent danger that they might arise. See also UN Commission on Human Rights, *Report of the Special Rapporteur on Extrajudicial, Summary or Arbitrary Executions on His Mission to Peru*, E/CN.4/1994/7/Add.2 (United Nations, No-

vember 15, 1993); Amnesty International, "Peru: Human Rights after the Suspension of Constitutional Government," London, May 1993.

13. In these areas the rights connected with personal freedom and security, inviolability of the home, and freedom of movement may be restricted or suspended while the Political-Military Command assumes control of law and order. According to a government report (HRI/CORE/1/Add.43, para. 166), law and order comprises not only pacification strategies, including supervising and facilitating the return of displaced persons, but also civic activities, such as constructing roads and other development projects.

14. Habeas corpus is a constitutionally guaranteed procedure that allows a person to bring a claim against any authority for an action or omission that harms or threatens his or her liberty and related rights prior to such action or omission. *Amparo* is a constitutionally guaranteed procedure that allows a person to bring a claim against any authority for an action or omission that harms or threatens his or her constitutional rights.

15. Judges *sin rostro*. The court sits behind a glass window that allows it to see the defendant, but not vice versa, so as to protect its anonymity and physical security. Critics point out that this measure violates international fair trial standards.

16. See Peruvian legislative decrees, DL 26447 (April 1995) and DL 26537 (October 1995).

17. NGOs note that even civilians who had nothing to do with the armed opposition groups nevertheless "repented" in order to avoid trouble in the future.

18. Urgent appeal by four special rapporteurs of the Commission on Human Rights issued August 1, 1995. The urgent appeal was published in several newspapers in Peru. See for example "ONU expresa su preocupación por la amnistia para asesinos," *La República*, August 18, 1995. See also UN Commission on Human Rights, *Report of the Sub-Commission on Prevention of Discrimination and Protection of Minorities*, E/CN.4/1996/2 (United Nations, October 23, 1995), and E/CN.4/Sub.2/1995/51, para. 338, which expressed "their deepest reservations as to the effects of both the amnesty law and its interpretative law on impunity."

19. Forty-three hundred are considered to be members of the Shining Path, and 700 are considered to be members of the MRTA.

20. These arguments overlook the wide condemnation of the rampant violence inflicted by the armed opposition movement on the civilian population.

21. UN Commission on Human Rights, *Report of the Special Rapporteur on Extrajudicial, Summary or Arbitrary Executions*, E/CN.4/1995/61 (United Nations, December 14, 1994). In cases of counterinsurgency operations, violations of the right to life can be massive. Such was the case in early 1993 when military operations in the Alto Huallaga valley were reported to have caused the death of sixty civilians.

22. See UN Commission on Human Rights, *Report of the Working Group on Arbitrary Detention*, E/CN.4/1995/31 and Add. 1-4 (United Nations, December 21, 1994); UN Commission on Human Rights, *Report of the Special Rapporteur*

on Torture, E/CN.4/1995/34 (United Nations, January 12, 1995), para. 574; UN Committee against Torture, CAT/C/SR.194/Add.1 (United Nations, November 22, 1994); and the various instruments discussed in HRI/CORE/1/Add.43.

23. Committee on the Rights of the Child, Summary Records, October 1993.

24. Television appearance of the president and the general commander of the army, December 8, 1994. See also UN Commission on Human Rights, E/CN.4/1995/61, paras. 250–62.

25. See also World Organization against Torture, Case PER 130795, appeal issued July 13, 1995.

26. One extreme case is Lurigancho prison. According to a newspaper report, in 1995 only 329 of its 4,705 prisoners had actually been sentenced; the rest were awaiting trial. "Las carceles peruanas siguen habitadas por presos sin condena," *El Comercio*, August 27, 1995.

27. Such is the case of one judge who challenged the constitutionality and legality of the amnesty laws. Charges were filed against her by the Office of the Attorney General.

28. In the 1993 constitution, economic and social rights are in a chapter separate from "rights fundamental to the person."

29. Information provided by UNICEF.

30. Statistics provided by the Comisión Episcopal de Acción Social, Lima, August 1995.

31. COTADENA, "Situación del menor y la familia en la ciudad de Ayacucho," Ayacucho, Peru, April 1993.

32. See also HRI/CORE/1/Add.43, para. 66.

33. In the early 1990s, in Apurimac, 69 percent of all women were illiterate, whereas in Lima 6.9 percent were illiterate. See Embajada Real de los Paises Bajos, "La Cooperación Técnica Holandesa en el Perú, 1994–1995," Lima.

34. See HRI/CORE/1/Add.43, para. 45.

35. See APRODEH/CEDAL, "Los derechos económicos y sociales en el Perú," 1994.

36. Shining Path, internal document, "Sobre las dos colinas: la guerra contrasubversiva y sus aliados," cited in Amnesty International, "Peru," p. 37.

37. Kirk, "The Decade of Chaqwa."

38. Interviews during the mission of the representative of the secretary-general on internally displaced persons. See also UN Commission on Human Rights, E/CN.4/1995/61, paras. 250–62.

39. See Coordinadora Nacional de Derechos Humanos, "Los Ashaninkas: Un pueblo que busca renacer," Lima, Peru, June 1995.

40. For example, María Elena Moyano, president of the Women's Popular Federation of Villa El Salvador and an outspoken critic of the Shining Path, was killed by the Shining Path in February 1992. See UN Commission on Human Rights, E/CN.4/1994/7/Add.2.

41. See also HRI/CORE/1/Add.43, para. 38; and CEPRODEP (Centro de Promoción y Desarrollo Poblacional) estimates, cited in Comité de Coordinación

Interministerial del PAR, "Programa de apoyo al desarrollo local, a la consolidación de la paz y al repoblamiento," Lima, March 1995, p. 5.

42. CEPRODEP estimates, cited in Comité de Coordinación Interministerial del PAR, "Programa de apoyo al desarrollo local, a la consolidación de la paz y al repoblamiento." Official and other sources have relied heavily on NGO sources to arrive at these estimates, in particular a study by CEPRODEP. See CEDROPEP, *Propuesta*, no. 1 (Lima, April 1993).

43. See Robin Kirk, "To Build Anew: An Update on Peru's Internally Displaced People," USCR, Washington, D.C., 1993. One study undertaken in Lima showed that out of 180 displaced persons, 118 were women; 13.3 percent of the displaced were widows or widowers.

44. Kirk, "To Build Anew." See also HRI/CORE/1/Add.43, para. 35.

45. In fact, because of the violence, even "traditional" migrants sometimes identify themselves as displaced in order to receive assistance.

46. See Comisión Andina de Juristas y Alto Comisionado de las Naciones Unidas para los Refugiados (ACNUR), "Aproximaciones a la situación de los desplazados en el Perú," Lima, March 1993 (hereafter UNHCR report).

47. For an overview, see Grupo de Trabajo de la Region Central Sobre Desplazamiento, "III encuentro interistitucional sobre desplazamiento en la Region Central," 1995; and "II encuentro de intercambio de experiencias: Alternativas para migrantes de Zonas de Emergencia," 1992, on file with the office of the UN High Commissioner for Human Rights, Geneva.

48. See HRI/CORE/1/Add.43, para. 38.

49. See generally, Asociación Suyasún, "Condiciones de vida de la población desplazada por motivos de violencia política atendida en los programas de Suyasún," on file with the office of the UN High Commissioner for Human Rights, Geneva.

50. For the problems this situation creates, including the disruption of family life, see Isabel Manrique, "Sistematizacion de una experiencia en Terapia Grupal con mujeres desplazadas," 1995, paper on file with the office of the UN High Commissioner for Human Rights, Geneva.

51. See Pompeyo Coronado R. and Marisol Rogríguez V., "La cultura Asháninka: Identidad en conflicto," Centre of Anthropology in Peru, Lima, May 1993.

52. See Americas Watch, "Untold Terror: Violence against Women in Peru's Armed Conflict," Washington, D.C., 1992. See also UNHCR report, p. 61.

53. See, however, Americas Watch, "Untold Terror," p. 4, which says that rape of women by the Shining Path is much less common and that women are targeted because they are activists rather than women.

54. In the case of the Ashaninka traditions, for instance, sexual relations out of wedlock are prohibited, which is why women are married as early as age thirteen or fourteen.

55. See "Ninos Ashaninkas mueren de hambre," *La República*, August 18, 1995.

56. For the specific effects of long-term fear on psychological well-being, see Coordinadora Nacional de Derechos Humanos, "Salud mental y víctimas de la violencia política," Lima, 1994.

57. See Government of Peru, "Programa salud básica para todos," Lima, August 1995.

58. Information provided to the representative on the health situation in Junin by the Health Sector director.

59. Kirk, "The Decade of Chaqwa."

60. One organization that promotes the provision of diagnostic and preliminary psychological assistance for children in schools and hospitals, especially for the displaced, suggests that at all stages of displacement the child should be encouraged to talk about his or her experiences and be told why displacement occurred and what he or she can expect in the near future. See PASMI (Programa de Atención en Salud Mental Infantil) publications, Lima. See also CEDAPP, "La problemática de la niñez desplazada de Zonas de Emergencia," Lima, May 1993.

61. Survey undertaken by the Asociación Jurídica pro Dignidad Humana, Huanuco, Peru, 1995.

62. See Peruvian ministerial decision DS 005-91-AG.

63. A government report notes that communal labor is a very important component of farming, one of the main features and economic activities of the indigenous communities of the Sierra. Communal labor stems from the Inca period and consists of an equal exchange of services and goods. Traditionally it has been used for the construction and maintenance of a complex system of "terracing" that prevents soil erosion and enables farming in the highlands. See HRI/CORE/1/Add.43, para. 10ff.

64. Mineral exploitation remains a prerogative of the state.

65. Illicit coca production and drug trafficking sustain 300,000 peasants with an estimated income of $8 million per year. See also UN Drug Control Program, "UNDCP Activities in Peru, 1984–1993," Lima.

66. One reason the *colonos* are more involved with illegal coca growing may be that they are not familiar with the farming technology suitable for the tropical ecology of the *selva* areas. See ibid.

67. Information provided to the representative on the health situation in Junin by the Health Sector director.

68. COTADENA, "Situación del menor y la familia en la ciudad de Ayacucho."

69. Ibid.

70. International Organization for Migration (IOM), Congreso Constituyente Democrático y Organización Internacional para las Migraciones, "Protección y assistencia a los desplazados internos del Perú," June–August 1994, Lima, p. 32 (hereafter IOM 1994 study); and "Programa de transferencia organizada para desplazados internos en el Perú," December–March 1995, Lima.

71. UNHCR report; and Comisión Andina de Juristas y ACNUR, "Estudio de identificación de pequeños proyectos de generación de ingresos con familias desplazadas por violencia política," Lima, May 1994.

72. See DECAS, "Conclusiones: 1er Congreso Departamental de Comités de Autodefensas Antisubversivas de Ayacucho," Ayacucho, Peru, September 1993.

73. CEPRODEP estimates cited in Comité de Coordinación Interministerial del PAR, "Programa de apoyo al desarrollo local, a la consolidación de la paz y al repoblamiento," p. 5.

74. Carol Graham, *Safety Nets, Politics, and the Poor* (Brookings, 1994), pp. 83ff.

75. CERD, *Eleventh Periodic Report of Colombia*, CERD/C/225/Add.3; the CORE document says the commission was created in 1990. The Comisión Técnica was formed by ministerial resolution no. 229-91-PCM of August 6, 1991.

76. CERD members were concerned that although steps had been taken to promote development in the areas inhabited by indigenous communities, it was unclear what steps had been taken to resolve the problems of disadvantaged districts, such as shantytowns, and for the benefit of children of poor families compelled to work on the streets or in mines, or of especially poor families.

77. IOM 1994 study, p. 20.

78. See publications of the Proyecto Procivismo, Ciudadanos para la Paz, and the Colegio de Abogados de Lima.

79. Kirk, "The Decade of Chaqwa."

80. UNHCR, Division of International Protection, *UNHCR's Operational Experience with Internally Displaced Persons* (Geneva, September 1994), p. 34.

81. The consultancy was undertaken by Giulia Tamayo and José María García Ríos and is on file with the Office of the UN High Commissioner for Human Rights, Geneva.

82. IOM 1994 study.

83. See Oxfam, Tour Report by Ilana Benady and David Huey, "Between Two Fires: Oxfam's Programme in Peru," March 1995.

84. See Embajada Real de Los Paises Bajos, "La cooperación técnica Holandesa en el Perú, 1994–1995."

85. See Marisol Rogríguez Vargas, "Desplazados: Selva Central," 1993, on file with the office of the UN High Commissioner for Human Rights, Geneva.

86. One study in Lima showed that 42.8 percent of the displaced were illiterate, and another that 35 percent had completed only primary education.

87. Problems identified included lack of decentralization, slow administrative procedures, and the overlooking of regional priorities. Information provided to the representative on the health situation in Junin by the Health Sector director.

88. PAR is focused almost exclusively on infrastructure and emergency needs rather than protection of civil rights, even though this component does appear in the report of the Comité de Coordinación Interministerial del PAR. See also "Contenido de la Exposición del Ing. Oscar Galdo Gómez, Jefe del PAR," delivered on August 13, 1995; and compare with PAR, Ayuda Memoria, "Com. Uchuraccay"; and PAR-Oficina Zonal de Ayacucho, Ayuda Memoria. These papers are on file with the Office of the UN High Commissioner for Human Rights, Geneva.

About the Contributors

Roberta Cohen is a guest scholar at the Brookings Institution, serves as co-director of its Project on Internal Displacement, and is co-author with Francis M. Deng of *Masses in Flight: The Global Crisis of Internal Displacement* (Brookings, 1998). She has worked as a consultant to governments, international organizations and NGOs on human rights, humanitarian and refugee issues, and is a former deputy assistant secretary of state for human rights and senior adviser to the U.S. delegation to the UN.

Francis M. Deng is a senior fellow in the Foreign Policy Studies Program at the Brookings Institution. Since 1992, he has been representative of the United Nations secretary-general on internally displaced persons. He previously served as the Sudan's minister of state for foreign affairs and as its ambassador to Canada, the United States, and Scandinavia. His most recent books include *War of Visions: Conflict of Identities in the Sudan* (Brookings, 1996) and *Masses in Flight: The Global Crisis of Internal Displacement*, co-author with Roberta Cohen (Brookings, 1998).

Thomas Greene is a former U.S. Foreign Service officer. He has been involved in refugee-related matters for much of his career and served as counselor for refugee affairs in Islamabad, Pakistan, from 1982 to 1986. He has written on Central Asia and speaks Persian (including Tajik) and Russian. Since 1992, Greene has worked as a consultant for the Refugee Policy Group and other organizations. He received his doctorate from Princeton University in political science.

Randolph C. Kent served as United Nations humanitarian coordinator in Rwanda between October 1994 and November 1995. He also served as special adviser on post-conflict recovery to the under secretary-general for humanitarian affairs, deputy coordinator of the UN Special Emergency Program for the Horn of Africa, and coordinator of the Inter-Agency Support Unit of the Inter-Agency Standing Committee. He received his doctorate from the London School of Economics and Political Science in international economic history. He is the author of *Anatomy of Disaster Relief: The International Network in Action* (Pinter, 1987).

Jennifer McLean is a research assistant at the Brookings Institution and works for the Brookings Institution Project on Internal Displacement. She accompanied the representative of the UN secretary-general on internally displaced persons on his mission to Tajikistan in 1996. She received her M.A. from American University in international development and has written several articles on the subject of internal displacement.

Larry Minear is co-director of the Humanitarianism and War Project at Brown University and is its principal researcher. He has worked on humanitarian and development issues since 1972, serving on the staff of Church World Service and Lutheran World Relief and as a consultant to governments, UN organizations, and nongovernmental organizations. His most recent books include *Soldiers to the Rescue: Humanitarian Lessons from Rwanda* (Organization for Economic Cooperation and Development, 1996, coauthor with Philippe Guillot) and *The News Media, Civil War and Humanitarian Action* (Lynne Rienner, 1996, coauthor with Colin Scott and Thomas G. Weiss).

Liliana Obregón has worked and published on issues of international human rights and humanitarian law, the environment, and international relations in Latin America. She received her J.D. at the Universidad de los Andes, Colombia, and her M.A. at the Johns Hopkins School of Advanced International Studies. Obregón is currently in the doctoral program at Harvard University. She is former publications director for the Center for Justice and International Law (CEJIL) in Washington, D.C., and was research associate at the Center for International Studies of the Universidad de los Andes.

Amir Pasic is deputy director of the Rockefeller Brothers Fund Project on World Security. Before that, he was a postdoctoral fellow at Brown University's Thomas J. Watson Jr. Institute for International Studies. He was a visiting scholar at the Watson Institute for the period 1997–98.

Hiram A. Ruiz is a policy analyst with the U.S. Committee for Refugees (USCR). He has carried out on-site documentation of the situation of refugees, returnees, and internally displaced persons in more than thirty countries in Africa, Asia, and Latin America. He is the author of several USCR Issue Papers and writes for USCR's *Refugee Reports* and *World Refugee Survey*. Ruiz previously worked with the United Nations High Commissioner for Refugees in Somalia and the Sudan.

Colin Scott is a policy and communications consultant based in Washington, D.C. He has worked on conflict and development issues throughout the UN system, for the World Bank, and for independent institutions such as the Humanitarianism and War Project at Brown University's Thomas J. Watson Jr. Institute for International Studies. He served as senior press officer with Save the Children U.K. and managed its programs in Mali, Liberia, and Sierra Leone.

H. L. Seneviratne, a native of Sri Lanka, is on the faculty of the Department of Anthropology at the University of Virginia. He is the author of *Rituals of the Kandyan State* (Cambridge University Press, 1978) and *Identity, Consciousness and the Past* (Oxford University Press, 1997). Seneviratne's undergraduate education was at the Peradeniya University, Sri Lanka. He received his M.A. and doctorate in anthropology from the University of Rochester.

Maria Stavropoulou is a UNHCR protection officer. She has worked on issues of human rights and displacement for several years, first as a legal adviser for refugees in Greece and later as a staff member of the UN Centre for Human Rights, where she was the professional assistant to the representative of the secretary-general on internally displaced persons. She accompanied the representative on his missions to Sri Lanka, Peru, and Colombia. She holds degrees in law from the University of Athens, the University of London, and Harvard University.

U.S. Committee for Refugees is a non-profit organization located in Washington, D.C., that monitors and reports on conditions of refugees and internally displaced persons. USCR publishes the annual *World Refugee Survey*, *Refugee Reports*, and special reports on internally displaced populations.

Thomas G. Weiss is a professor at Brown University and associate director of its Thomas J. Watson Jr. Institute for International Studies. He also serves as executive director of the Academic Council on the United Nations System. He has written or edited some twenty-five books on international organization, conflict management, and humanitarian action. His most recent include *The United Nations and Changing World Politics* (Westview, 1997, 2d edition, coauthor with David P. Forsythe and Roger A. Coate) and *Political Gain and Civilian Pain: Humanitarian Impacts of Economic Sanctions* (Rowman and Littlefield, 1997, co-editor with David Cortright, George A. Lopez, and Larry Minear).

Index

504

508INDEX